"*The Scandal* is an invaluable resource for the thinking and inquisitive reader. Crawford effectively uses the tools of rationalism, logic, and philosophy to dismantle the inappropriate application of these tools to the Scriptures and to Christian and Jewish theology. Kabbalah, often amateurly used by Christian apologists, is described and evaluated. . . . The payoff is at the end, where all that has been learned culminates in a thoughtful and impressive case for the divinity of Yeshua the Messiah."

—**Daniel Nessim**, author of *Torah for Gentiles? What the Jewish Authors of the Didache Had to Say*

"Brian Crawford's chapters on Kabbalah stand out as a meticulously researched and profoundly articulated exploration of Kabbalistic thought. Although, as an Orthodox Jew, I approach his conclusions on Jesus and Christianity from a different perspective, I recognize the strength of his analysis regarding the divergence of certain Kabbalistic doctrines from the classical Maimonidean view of Jewish Monotheism, which is rooted in absolute transcendence, unity, and oneness."

—**Moshe**, an Orthodox Jew from New York City

"Brian Crawford represents the best in the next generation of Messianic apologists, now providing a much-needed, watershed book addressing the philosophical Jewish objections to the deity of the Messiah. Brian offers an in-depth, scholarly analysis, providing practical and reasoned arguments to buttress the faith of believers and to enable them to present the biblical logic of a divine Messiah, even offering a robust philosophical defense of the Incarnation."

—**MICHAEL L. BROWN**, author of *Answering Jewish Objections to Jesus, Vols. 1–5*

"Covering a breadth of scholarship, research, and wealth of discussion of the topic, Crawford models an approach to the subject with graciousness and clarity, explaining complex philosophical and theological ideas with warmth and spiritual wisdom. Thank you, Brian, for this gift to the Messianic movement and all interested in understanding the God of Israel and the Messiah Yeshua!"

—**RICHARD HARVEY**, All Nations Christian College, UK, author of *Mapping Messianic Jewish Theology*

"Combining philosophical analysis with historical study and scriptural concern, this reassessment of Orthodox Judaism and its critique of Christian faith is a key study on how to interact both with the influence of Maimonides and Kabbalah, as well as a look at how the Incarnation fits a biblical perspective. The journey goes deep but is profitable for those curious about how to engage with these major Jewish movements."

—**DARRELL L. BOCK**, executive director of cultural engagement, senior research professor of New Testament studies, Dallas Theological Seminary

"Brian is a senior member of the Chosen People Ministries staff, a ministry I have the privilege of leading. Brian is a bright, curious, and humble person who approaches learning with a passion for serving the Lord and reaching Jewish people with the gospel. This book grew out of his experience of sharing the gospel with religious Jewish people on the streets of Brooklyn, home to more than half a million Jewish people of whom one third are ultra-Orthodox. Brian's grasp of Maimonides, Kabbalah, and the ways in which medieval Neoplatonism influenced them both will intrigue and surprise you."

—**MITCH GLASER**, president, Chosen People Ministries

"As Crawford admits, 'To better grasp the issues at hand, it will be necessary to walk through the Western intellectual tradition and the categories of metaphysics, theology, hermeneutics, ontology, cosmology, epistemology, mystery, paradox, and how God relates to the world.' Add to that the traditions of Maimonides and Kabbalah and you'll begin to understand the expansive objectives of this book. Thankfully, one does not need to be an expert in any of these subjects to enjoy and appreciate what a gift this volume can be."

—**DAVID BRICKNER**, executive chairman, Jews for Jesus

"Brian Crawford thoughtfully examines the development and influence on Judaism of Maimonides's philosophy and Kabbalistic mysticism; persuasive refutations with historical data and biblical support are presented in a respectful, irenic tone.... It should be required reading for anyone seeking to engage the ultra-Orthodox with the life-saving gospel of Messiah Yeshua."

—**LEVI HAZEN**, international executive director, Life in Messiah
—**WES TABER**, global ambassador, Life in Messiah

The Scandal of a Divine Messiah

The Scandal of a Divine Messiah

A Response to Maimonidean and Kabbalistic
Challenges to the Incarnation

BRIAN J. CRAWFORD

Foreword by Garrett J. DeWeese

WIPF & STOCK · Eugene, Oregon

THE SCANDAL OF A DIVINE MESSIAH
A Response to Maimonidean and Kabbalistic Challenges to the Incarnation

Copyright © 2024 Brian J. Crawford. All rights reserved. Except for brief quotations in critical publications or reviews, no part of this book may be reproduced in any manner without prior written permission from the publisher. Write: Permissions, Wipf and Stock Publishers, 199 W. 8th Ave., Suite 3, Eugene, OR 97401.

Wipf & Stock
An Imprint of Wipf and Stock Publishers
199 W. 8th Ave., Suite 3
Eugene, OR 97401

www.wipfandstock.com

PAPERBACK ISBN: 979-8-3852-2534-7
HARDCOVER ISBN: 979-8-3852-2535-4
EBOOK ISBN: 979-8-3852-2536-1

VERSION NUMBER 12/26/24

Unless otherwise indicated, Scripture quotations are from The ESV® Bible (The Holy Bible, English Standard Version®), © 2001 by Crossway, a publishing ministry of Good News Publishers. Used by permission. All rights reserved.

Scripture quotations designated NET are from the NET Bible® copyright ©1996, 2019 by Biblical Studies Press, LLC. https://netbible.com. All rights reserved.

Unless otherwise indicated, all Masoretic Text quotations are from *Biblia Hebraica Stuttgartensia*, @ 2003 by the German Bible Society. All rights reserved.

Publisher acknowledges that the author has an existing agreement with Chosen People Ministries (CPM). CPM shall retain the following Rights to the Work:

A royalty-free, nonexclusive, irrevocable and perpetual license throughout the world to any and all copyright rights and other rights in the Assigned Work, including but not limited to the right to use, reproduce, prepare derivative works, digitize, make adaptations and revisions, distribute, transmit, display, and otherwise make any use of the Assigned Work to serve its mission.

Contents

List of Illustrations | vii
List of Tables | ix
Foreword by Garrett J. DeWeese | xi
Preface | xv
Acknowledgments | xix
Abbreviations | xxiii

Part I: Setting the Stage for the Incarnation

1. Introduction: The Story of a Scandal | 3
2. In Search of the God of the Hebrew Scriptures | 32
3. The Historical-Textual Approach to Contextualizing the Incarnation | 52

Part II: A Critique of Non-Incarnational Maimonidean and Kabbalistic Thought

4. The Greek Philosophical Schools Related to Medieval Judaism | 77
5. Maimonides's System of Absolute Divine Incorporeality | 107
6. An Assessment of Maimonides's System | 133
7. The System of Lurianic Kabbalah | 163
8. An Assessment of Lurianic Kabbalah's Metaphysics | 192
9. An Assessment of Lurianic Kabbalah's History, Predecessors, and Science | 211

Contents

Part III: The Incarnation of the Son of God

10 Foundations of the Incarnation: Cosmology, Revelation, and Theology | 245

11 Implications of the Incarnation: Rationality, Hermeneutics, and Explanatory Scope | 286

12 From Scandal to Shalom: A Defense of the Divine Messiah | 319

Appendices

Appendix A: Glossary | 343

Appendix B: The Philosophical Heritage of Medieval Jewish Theology | 353

Appendix C: Comparisons of Theological Models | 357

Appendix D: Ancient Jewish Sources of Greek Mystical Philosophies? | 363

Appendix E: Kabbalah in the New Testament? | 373

Bibliography | 377
Ancient Document Index | 409
General Index | 429

List of Illustrations

Figure 1. Varieties of Divine Embodiment in Judaism and Christianity | 17

Figure 2. The Ptolemaic Geocentric Model, from *Harmonia Macrocosmica*, by Andreas Cellarius, 1660 | 87

Figure 3. Kabbalistic Cosmology, Part 1 | 176

Figure 4. Kabbalistic Cosmology, Part 2 | 177

Figure 5. Adam Kadmon—Diagram Illustrating the *Sefirot* (Divine Attributes), from L. Ginsburg, "Adam Kadmon" | 181

Figure 6. The Philosophical Heritage of Medieval Jewish Theology | 354

Figure 7. Generic Theological Cosmologies | 358

Figure 8. Neoplatonic and Kabbalistic Cosmologies | 359

Figure 9. Maimonidean and New Testament Cosmologies | 360

List of Tables

Table 1. Spatial Concepts Applied to God | 41

Table 2. Emotions of God | 43

Table 3. Anthropomorphic Divine Actions in the Hebrew Bible | 47

Table 4. Schools of Rabbinic Thought Regarding God's Body | 58

Table 5. The Name of the Lord | 61

Table 6. Neopythagorean Number Metaphysics | 91

Table 7. Ten Pythagorean Opposites (*Metaph.* 1.5) | 91

Table 8. Ten Aristotelian Categories Used by Neopythagoreans (*Cat.* 4) | 92

Table 9. Pythagorean Ten Spheres Cosmology | 92

Table 10. Different Versions of Maimonides's Theological Principles | 109

Table 11. Principles Two and Three of Maimonides's Thirteen Principles | 110

Table 12. Outline of *The Guide to the Perplexed* | 114

Table 13. Kabbalistic Commonalities with Greek Esoteric Philosophies | 188

Table 14. Biblical Counting versus *Gematria* | 221

Table 15. Critiques of Neoplatonic Themes in Kabbalah | 233

Table 16. New Testament Quotations of the Tetragrammaton Applied to Jesus | 260

List of Tables

Table 17. Six Basic New Testament Theological Teachings Relating to the Trinity and Incarnation | 269

Table 18. The Nicene Creed and Chalcedonian Definition | 278

Table 19. Sub-Chalcedonian Heresies | 281

Table 20. Four Theological Worldviews Compared | 361

Foreword

Garrett J. DeWeese

IN THE PAGES AHEAD, Brian J. Crawford offers a tour de force, an impressive achievement of theological dialogue between Christian and Jewish sources, ancient, medieval, and modern. Through a deeply sympathetic reading of those sources, together with careful philosophical analysis, Crawford argues compellingly to the conclusion that the concept of a divine Messiah, of God himself assuming human nature, was previously not and should currently not be a stumbling block for Jewish people.

This conclusion will no doubt be surprising to most Christian theologians as well as those Christians who have tried to share their faith in Jesus (Yeshua) as Messiah with their Jewish friends. And it will no doubt be contentious to most Jewish people who (rightly or wrongly) associate Christianity with irrationality and anti-Semitism.

But Crawford shows that this conclusion should be neither surprising nor contentious. He demonstrates that among some Jewish writers in the lively debates during Second Temple Judaism (roughly 500 BCE–70 CE), the idea of an embodied God was not scandalous. The rejection of this idea became dogmatic in Jewish rabbinic thought primarily through the great Jewish philosopher Maimonides and subsequently through the spread of the mystical teachings of the Kabbalah. Through close reading of both Maimonides and kabbalistic sources, Crawford concludes, "If Maimonides made the Incarnation *impossible*, Kabbalah makes the Incarnation *redundant*."[1]

Crawford challenges both the Maimonidean and kabbalistic dogmas through an impressive process of theological retrieval. In arguing that neither Maimonides nor Kabbalah have sufficient epistemological or

---

1. See this book, 9.

metaphysical resources to sustain a coherent worldview, he skillfully deploys philosophical analysis to compare and evaluate apparently incommensurable positions. Ultimately, he concludes that a robust worldview grounded in New Testament Trinitarianism and Incarnation has the greatest hermeneutical coherence and explanatory scope, and thus that Jesus, the incarnate Son of God, is indeed the promised divine Messiah.

No doubt Crawford's work will be challenging to most readers. Most Jewish readers will likely be unfamiliar with Christian theological developments of Christology following the ecumenical councils of Nicaea (325 CE) and Chalcedon (451 CE). Most Jewish scholars will not have encountered a Christian thinker who engages sympathetically yet critically with Maimonides or the Kabbalah.

Similarly, few Christians know anything more about Maimonides other than that he wrote *A Guide to the Perplexed* (if they even know that), and as for Kabbalah—that's a strange fascination of a few celebrities such as Madonna, Ashton Kutcher, and Ariana Grande (if they even know that).

For both Jewish and Christian readers, then, Crawford will serve as a careful and informed guide through unfamiliar and sometimes difficult territory, but the destination, in the end, will be well worth the journey.

* * *

For surely his concern is not for angels, but he is concerned for Abraham's descendants. Therefore he had to be made like his brothers and sisters in every respect, so that he could become a merciful and faithful high priest in things relating to God, to make atonement for the sins of the people.

—Heb 2:16–17 NET

Brother and sisters, my heart's desire and prayer to God on behalf of my fellow Israelites is for their salvation.

—Rom 10:1 NET

Permit me here a personal reflection that explains why I regard this work so highly. When I was in high school, our family moved to Israel for three years. My parents were Bible-reading, Jesus-loving people, and it was natural for them to care deeply for the young nation of Israel and for the Jewish people. (I remember my father once removing a sign from a nearby property that read "For Sale, No Jews.") So when the opportunity

Foreword

arose for Dad to take a temporary position with his company in Israel, he eagerly accepted.

Tel Aviv in the early 1960s was an exciting city, and travelling around Israel, seeking out sites where biblical events had taken place, was fascinating.

Equally fascinating to me were the discussions I overheard some evenings when Mom or Dad would try to show Jewish friends that Jesus was the Messiah. Mom and Dad believed (and I do too) that Jesus is indeed the promised Messiah, the savior of all who place their faith in him, and we desire the Jewish people's salvation just as eagerly as the apostle Paul. We met a number of missionaries serving in Israel—from the United States, Great Britain, and Denmark, as well as Messianic Jews who accepted Jesus as their Messiah—delightful people from whom we gained an idea of how to share Jesus with Israelis. The method usually went something like this: First, show that Jesus, as described in the gospels and who lived, died, and was resurrected in first-century Israel, was a perfect man and wonderful rabbi. Second, show that Jesus was God incarnate, the divine Messiah who fulfilled so many great Old Testament prophecies.

The results were disappointing.

It seemed that most of our neighbors (and some of my Jewish schoolmates) were somewhat surprised that our family was respectful of Jews, excited to share in events such as Pesach, Sukkot, and the joyous celebration of Israel's fifteenth birthday (Apr. 28, 1963), and delighted to be able to explore the "Holy Land." But any talk of an incarnate God who lived and died as a human was literally inconceivable, far outside their plausibility structure. Claims of fulfilled prophecy could not overcome the scandal of thinking that the eternal God could or would have a physical human body.

We returned to life in the Seattle area, and while memories of our time in Israel were always very special to me (I had met there the girl who would later become my wife!), I was bothered, every once in a while, that the idea of an incarnate God was a stumbling block, a scandal, to Jewish people. But aside from occasional conversations, I never thought through the issue in any depth.

In seminary I studied the Old Testament prophecies in much greater depth and became even more confident that Jesus was indeed the fulfillment of God's manifold promises. But I was increasingly doubtful that fulfilled prophecy would be an effective apologetic in offering Jesus to Jews.

Years later, I became a professor of theology and philosophy at Talbot School of Theology (a graduate school of Biola University, La Mirada,

Foreword

California). Talbot maintains an extension site in Brooklyn, the Charles L. Feinberg Center for Messianic Jewish Studies, and the association offered opportunities to converse with some faculty and students there. Such conversations led me to think that a Christology (doctrine of Christ) that took into account Jewish thought about a divine Messiah was not only possible but would be healthy for the church, for Messianic Jews, and for profitable dialogue with both more secular Jews and with Haredim (ultra-Orthodox Jews). But such theological work was beyond my competence.

Enter Brian Crawford, a member of a doctor of ministry cohort taught by J. P. Moreland and myself. Brian was and is affiliated with Chosen People Ministries, with whom Talbot partnered in the Feinberg Center. Brian himself is a Feinberg graduate. When it came time for him to begin work on his doctoral thesis, I was naturally very interested and agreed to supervise his work.

That thesis, "Pathways for Addressing Jewish Theological and Philosophical Objections to the Incarnation" (available at ProQuest Dissertations and Theses), was not only very well done research but seemed to me to be the heart of just the sort of Christology needed to engage contemporary Jewish thought, influenced largely by Maimonides or the Kabbalah.

Along with staff at Chosen People Ministries, I encouraged Brian to continue research and develop a book-length treatment of his initial work. *The Scandal of a Divine Messiah* is the result.

* * *

So, it is an honor and privilege for me to commend the work that follows to you, the readers. It is academically through (over nine hundred footnotes and a thirty-page bibliography), and in spite of its impressive scholarship, quite reader friendly (many charts, a glossary, and four other appendices of helpful diagrams of the philosophical heritage of medieval Jewish theology, the philosophical and cosmological backgrounds of Orthodox Judaism, and others).

Crawford intends his work to chart a course from scandal to shalom. May it bring you, too, to deeper shalom.

Garrett J. DeWeese
Professor at Large, Philosophy and Theology
Talbot School of Theology
August 12, 2024

Preface

As a young seminary student living in the Holy Land of Brooklyn, New York, I was surrounded by Orthodox Jewish people whom I was tasked to reach with the good news of Yeshua (Jesus) the Messiah through Chosen People Ministries. Despite being a gentile Christian, I occasionally had encounters of real theological substance with them, but they often left me bewildered. I would ask the meaning of a biblical passage, and they would respond with many options, none of which they preferred. I would ask yes or no questions, and they would respond with a story. I would explain what I believe about Jesus, and they would respond that I believe contradictory nonsense. I would describe God as best I knew how, and they would reply that no language can be used to describe God. Despite receiving excellent theological training, including courses in rabbinic theology and Talmud, I had never been exposed to these kinds of responses. I had no map or guide for how to proceed.

Those early experiences propelled me to find a solution, and without intending to, I found profound answers to my questions while studying the Incarnation of the Son of God. *The Scandal of a Divine Messiah* is the book I wish I had years ago. It is an exploration of the nature of God as he has been understood in Greek philosophy, Orthodox Judaism, and Christianity. The book seeks to depict how Orthodox Jewish theology came to be, how it has departed from Scripture and science, and why the Incarnation, as articulated by Chalcedon, is the best solution to the unanswered questions in the Hebrew Scriptures. The discussion in this book builds on recent scholarship on early high Christology but proposes a second, complementary approach that involves theological and philosophical analysis. This book provides a systematic theology of Maimonidean and kabbalistic thought on divine embodiment, a thorough critique of both, and an explanation and defense of the deity of the Messiah while considering significant Jewish philosophical objections. As the book proceeds, readers will learn how I ended up charting my course.

I intend this book to open new vistas of thought for my readers. For several years, I had the privilege of studying under philosophers J. P. Moreland and Garry DeWeese at Talbot School of Theology, who introduced me to the grand Western philosophical tradition. During my studies it was deeply satisfying to realize that philosophical training is what I had been missing on the streets of Brooklyn. This book is designed to gradually introduce readers to philosophical thought and its relevance for Jewish and Christian theological differences. Part philosophical primer, part systematic theology, part apologetics textbook, this book covers a lot of ground and introduces many terms with which readers may be unfamiliar. Readers are encouraged to consult the appendices for definitions of key terms as well as charts and supplementary studies.

Many have struggled with the ideas of the deity of the Messiah and the Trinity, especially those raised in Jewish homes. I intend this book to be a significant contribution to those who face such struggles, to all who yearn with Paul for the fulfillment of Rom 11, and especially to the Messianic Jewish movement, the remnant of Israel chosen by grace (Rom 11:5).

I would like to say a personal word to specific audiences regarding my goals for this book:

Messianic Jews: I intend this book to be a gift to the Messianic Jewish movement. As a gentile observer and participant in your community, I have witnessed the stresses you bear when attempting to hold fast to the teachings of Messiah while experiencing ridicule from both the church and the broader Jewish world. I sympathize with the struggles you have in retaining New Testament orthodoxy while having a strained relationship with the historic gentile theologians of the church. Although there are good studies on messianic prophecies to assist you with Yeshua's deity, I believe there is much more to say. I hope this book will strengthen your faith and articulation when questioned about your faith in Yeshua. I also hope it unlocks a world of theological retrieval that illustrates the benefits of obtaining proficiency in historical "Christian" theology and the Greek philosophical tradition, while also deeply illustrating the excesses of the latter in both Judaism and Christianity.

Gentile Christians: I intend this book to be a model of how sympathetic gentile Christians may deeply integrate truth of Rom 1:16 into their soul and respond with sincere concern and scholarship. I also hope that it will encourage your growth in theological articulation, especially if you worship in a context where historical theology and systematic theology are de-emphasized.

Orthodox Jews: An important goal for this book is to present your revered sages, your *hashkafah*, your concerns, your culture, and your tradition respectfully, accurately, and fairly. Part 2 of this book will analyze Maimonidean and kabbalistic thought in ways that may be a personal challenge for you to read. However, I intend the challenge to be on the academic level of logic, history, biblical interpretation, and metaphysics—hopefully not because I have misrepresented you or argued unfairly. I commend your courage in reading a book such as this, and I hope that you will be richly rewarded.

Scholars of Maimonides and Kabbalah: The fields of Maimonidean and kabbalistic studies have been the domain of Jewish scholars, not by design, but because of a lack of gentile interest in these matters. I intend this book to be a contribution to these fields, not just because of my non-Jewish background, but because of the new insights my perspective affords. Although I write as a devout Christian, I have employed several methods to mitigate my bias. I have endeavored to interact with the best contemporary Jewish scholarship on these matters, and I have found many concurring studies that I affirm and build upon. This book is my first published contribution to these fields, and I hope that it will inspire substantive Jewish and Christian dialogue in the years to come.

Brian J. Crawford
Summer 2024

Acknowledgments

This is a book I did not think I would ever write. I had planned a life of crunching numbers on a graphing calculator in a cubicle while engineering buildings, but the God of Israel had other plans. He used many dear servants to shape my heart, shift my mind, and adjust my path. For my first published book, many acknowledgments are in order.

I thank my parents for providing me with a biblical upbringing, a stable and loving home, and the pursuit of excellence. Of all the things they instilled in me, they could not have predicted what would stick. They taught me to love Israel and the Jewish people from an early age. I thank my mother for her unfailing love. My father introduced me to apologetics in sixth grade, broadening my horizons and inspiring me to never take my faith simplistically. I am blessed to have them near my growing family.

I thank Jon Terrell for continuing what my parents started by inviting me to read Christian classics every week at Denny's and Pipes. My sixteen-year-old head hurt so much while reading Lewis, Moreland, and Willard, and Jon made me a better young man in the process.

Pastor Tonye Holyde's contagious passion for the Jewish people and the teaching of God's word turned my world upside down. Who could forget his Hebrew blessings during communion and quotes from the Talmud in his sermons? The Lord used his enthusiasm to fan the flame that was lit when I visited Israel with him.

Like seemingly everyone in Jewish ministry today, I was recruited for full-time work by Mitch Glaser, president of Chosen People Ministries. How privileged I have been to have Mitch as my mentor for fifteen years. He has invested in me spiritually, intellectually, practically,

Acknowledgments

academically, and professionally. I will be forever grateful for the gift he has been to me. It was terrifying to take him up on the offer to move to Brooklyn, but it was the best decision we could have made. Mitch has made it a thrilling ride ever since.

I thank Gregg Hagg for tirelessly giving himself for the sake of his seminary students, including me. He encouraged me that it is possible for a gentile Christian to find his place in Jewish ministry with high academic pursuits.

Stuart Dauermann took up the task of reading the early work of a young, green, brash, gentile apologist to his people, and he butted heads with me the whole way through. Yet, he provided the voice of conscience I was lacking. I thank Stuart for his patience, and for instilling that conscience into me.

J. P. Moreland and Garry DeWeese provided the missing link in my academic and ministry pursuits. I didn't see it coming, because I didn't know what I didn't know. They provided an intellectual map that enabled me to locate myself across millennia of thought. This book is the direct result.

Although I have never met them, I am thankful for the works of Nancy Pearcey and Charles Thaxton, James Anderson, and Michael McClymond, who provided key early inspiration for how to wrap my mind around Neoplatonism, Maimonides's logical objections, and Kabbalah.

I am deeply appreciative of my many ministry supporters and churches that have prayed for and invested in my ministry. They have been so faithful to Messiah, the Jewish people, and to my family.

So many others have been friends, mentors, role models, and encouragers along the way: Pieter Van den Beukel, Richard Harvey, Rich Robinson, Zhava Glaser, Mitch Forman, Rich Flashman, Bobby Walter, Ari Hauben, Daniel Nessim, Israel Cohen, Jonathan, Erik, Jennifer Miles, Chaim Dauermann, Mike Savage, Jim Melnick, Michael Brown, Wes Taber, Levi Hazen, Kevin Pittle, Darrell Bock, Jimmy Higgins, June Ghrist, Anthony English, Brooks Eckelman, Steve Tomlinson, John McKinley, John Hollenbeck, and my various Orthodox Jewish colleagues.

Through nearly all these relationships, my college sweetheart and wife Liz has been with me along this adventure. She has had a front row seat to see what the Lord has done. She is a woman of excellence, deep faith, and love for our children. She makes our house a home. I thank her for her constant enthusiasm and love.

Acknowledgments

Finally, I am thankful for Messiah, for whom and about whom this book is written. He has been a light for revelation to the gentiles, and for glory to his people Israel (Luke 2:32). Great indeed is the mystery of godliness, that he has been manifested in the flesh (1 Tim 3:16). All this is for him.

Abbreviations

11QMelch	Dead Sea Scroll, Melchizedek
1 Apol.	Justin Martyr, *1 Apology* (ANF 1:163–86)
1 En.	1 Enoch (*OTP* 1:5–91)
1QS	Dead Sea Scroll, the Community Rule
2 Bar.	2 Baruch (*OTP* 1:615–52)
2 Macc	2 Maccabees
3 En.	3 Enoch (*OTP* 1:223–315)
3 Macc	3 Maccabees
ACCS	Ancient Christian Commentary on Scripture
Ag. Ap.	Josephus, *Against Apion*
AJOJ	Brown, Michael L. *Answering Jewish Objections to Jesus.* 4 vols. Grand Rapids: Baker Books, 2000–2007 ———. *Answering Jewish Objections to Jesus: Traditional Jewish Objections.* Vol. 5. San Francisco: Purple Pomegranate, 2009
Alleg. Interp.	Philo, *Allegorical Interpretation* (LCL 1:139–244)
ANF	*The Ante-Nicene Fathers.* Edited by Alexander Roberts and James Donaldson. 10 vols. Buffalo, NY: Christian Literature, 1885–97
An. Post.	Aristotle, *Posterior Analytics*
Ap. Jas.	Nag Hammadi, Secret Book of James
Ap. John	Nag Hammadi, Secret Book of John
Apol. Sec.	Athanasius, *Defense against the Arians* (NPNF² 4:306–447)

Abbreviations

Apos. Con.	Apostolic Constitutions and Canons (*ANF* 7:387–508)
Autol.	Theophilus of Antioch, *To Autolycus* (*ANF* 2:89–121)
b. ʿAbod. Zar.	Babylonian Talmud, Tractate Avodah Zarah
b. Ber.	Babylonian Talmud, Tractate Berakhot
b. Beṣah	Babylonian Talmud, Tractate Betzah
b. B. Meṣ.	Babylonian Talmud, Tractate Baba Metziʾa
BBR	*Bulletin for Biblical Research*
BCE	Before Common Era, equivalent to BC (Before Christ)
BDAG	Danker, Frederick W., et al. *Greek-English Lexicon of the New Testament and Other Early Christian Literature*. 3rd ed. Chicago: University of Chicago Press, 2000 (Danker-Bauer-Arndt-Gingrich)
b. Ḥag.	Babylonian Talmud, Tractate Hagigah
b. Ketub.	Babylonian Talmud, Tractate Ketubbot
b. Mak.	Babylonian Talmud, Tractate Makkot
b. Meg.	Babylonian Talmud, Tractate Megillah
b. Pesaḥ.	Babylonian Talmud, Tractate Pesaḥim
b. Šabb.	Babylonian Talmud, Tractate Shabbat
b. Sanh.	Babylonian Talmud, Tractate Sanhedrin
Cael.	Aristotle, *On the Heavens*
Cat.	Aristotle, *Categories*
CE	Common Era, equivalent to AD (Anno Domini)
Cels.	Origen, *Against Celsus* (*ANF* 4:395–669)
Civ.	Augustine, *The City of God* (*NPNF*[1] 2:ix–511)
ConB	Coniectanea Biblica
Confusion	Philo, *On the Confusion of Tongues* (LCL 4:1–119)
Contempl. Life	Philo, *On the Contemplative Life* (LCL 9:103–69)
Creation	Philo, *On the Creation of the World* (LCL 1:1–137)
CurBR	*Currents in Biblical Research* (formerly *Currents in Research: Biblical Studies*)
De an.	Aristotle, *De anima*
De fide orth.	John of Damascus, *On the Orthodox Faith* (*NPNF*[2] 9:1–101)
Dem. ev.	Eusebius of Caesarea, *Demonstration of the Gospel*

Abbreviations

Dial.	Justin Martyr, *Dialogue with Trypho* (*ANF* 1:194–270)
Did.	*Didache* (*ANF* 7:369–83)
Diogn.	*Epistle of Diognetus* (*ANF* 1:25–30)
Disc. Seth	Nag Hammadi, Second Discourse of Great Seth
Dreams	Philo, *On Dreams* (LCL 5:283–579)
ECL	Early Christianity and Its Literature
Emunot	Saadia Gaon, *Book of Beliefs and Opinions*
Enn.	*The Six Enneads*. Plotinus. In *The Way Things Are; The Discourses Of; The Meditations Of; The Six Enneads*, edited by Mortimer J. Adler et al., translated by Stephen MacKenna and B. S. Page, 295–678. 2nd ed. Vol. 11 of *Great Books of the Western World*. Chicago: Encyclopedia Britannica, 1990
Ep.	Gregory of Nazianzus, *Epistles*
ESV	English Standard Version
Eth. Nic.	Aristotle, *Nicomachean Ethics*
ETS	Evangelical Theological Society
Exeg. Soul	Exegesis of the Soul
Flight	Philo, *On Flight and Finding* (LCL 5:1–125)
Gen. Rab.	Genesis Rabbah
Gos. Phil.	Nag Hammadi, Gospel of Philip
Gos. Thom.	Nag Hammadi, Gospel of Thomas
Guide	*The Guide for the Perplexed*. Moses Maimonides. Translated by Michael Friedländer. 2nd ed. New York: Dutton & Co., 1919
Haer.	Hippolytus, *Refutation of All Heresies* (*ANF* 5:9–162)
Haer.	Irenaeus, *Against Heresies* (*ANF* 1:315–578)
HALOT	*The Hebrew and Aramaic Lexicon of the Old Testament*. Ludwig Koehler et al. Translated and edited under the supervision of Mervyn E. J. Richardson. 4 vols. Leiden: Brill, 1994–99
HAR	*Hebrew Annual Review*
HdO	Handbuch der Orientalistik
Heir	Philo, *Who Is the Heir?* (LCL 4:269–447)
Herm. Mand.	Shepherd of Hermas, Mandate (*ANF* 2:20–30)

Abbreviations

Hist.	Tacitus, *Historiae*
Hist. eccl.	Eusebius of Caesarea, *Ecclesiastical History* (NPNF² 1:vii–403)
Hist. eccl.	Socrates Scholasticus, *Ecclesiastical History* (NPNF² 2:1–178)
HTR	*Harvard Theological Review*
HUCA	*Hebrew Union College Annual*
Ign. *Eph.*	Ignatius, *To the Ephesians* (ANF 1:49–58)
Ign. *Trall.*	Ignatius, *To the Trallians* (ANF 1:66–72)
Inc.	Athanasius, *On the Incarnation* (NPNF² 4:31–67)
Inst.	Lactantius, *The Divine Institutes* (ANF 7:9–223)
Int.	Aristotle, *On Interpretation*
JBL	*Journal of Biblical Literature*
Jdt	Apocrypha, Judith
JETS	*Journal of the Evangelical Theological Society*
JJS	*Journal of Jewish Studies*
JQR	*Jewish Quarterly Review*
JSJ	*Journal for the Study of Judaism in the Persian, Hellenistic, and Roman Periods*
JSJSup	Supplements to the Journal for the Study of Judaism
JSQ	*Jewish Studies Quarterly*
Jub.	Jubilees (*OTP* 2:35–142)
J.W.	Josephus, *Jewish War*
LCL	Loeb Classical Library
Let. Aris.	Letter of Aristeas (*OTP* 2:7–34)
LHBOTS	The Library of Hebrew Bible/Old Testament Studies
LNTS	Library of New Testament Studies
LXX	Septuagint
Macc	Apocrypha, Maccabees
Marc.	Tertullian, *Against Marcion* (ANF 3:269–474)
Metaph.	Aristotle, *Metaphysics*
m. Ḥag.	Mishnah Hagigah
Moses	Philo, *On the Life of Moses* (LCL 6:273–595)
m. Pirke Avot	Mishnah Pirke Avot

Abbreviations

m. Sanh.	Mishnah Sanhedrin
MT	Masoretic Text
NASB	New American Standard Bible
NET	New English Translation
NHL	*The Nag Hammadi Library in English.* Edited by James M. Robinson. 4th rev. ed. Leiden: Brill, 1996
NICNT	New International Commentary on the New Testament
NIGTC	New International Greek Testament Commentary
NJPS	*Tanakh: The Holy Scriptures.* Philadelphia: Jewish Publication Society, 1985
NKJV	New King James Version
NLT	New Living Translation
NovT	*Novum Testamentum*
NPNF[1]	*A Select Library of Nicene and Post-Nicene Fathers of the Christian Church.* Edited by Philip Schaff and Henry Ware. 1st ser. 14 vols. Buffalo, NY: Christian Literature, 1886–89
NPNF[2]	*A Select Library of Nicene and Post-Nicene Fathers of the Christian Church.* Edited by Philip Schaff and Henry Ware. 2nd ser. 14 vols. New York: Christian Literature, 1890–1900
NRSV	New Revised Standard Version
NT	New Testament
NTS	*New Testament Studies*
Odes Sol.	Odes of Solomon (*OTP* 2:725–71)
OTP	*The Old Testament Pseudepigrapha.* Edited by James H. Charlesworth. 2 vols. New York: Doubleday, 1983, 1985
Paed.	Clement of Alexandria, *Christ the Educator* (*ANF* 2:207–98)
Pan.	Epiphanius, *Refutation of All Heresies*
Parm.	Plato, *Parmenides*
Pesiq. Rab Kah.	Pesiqta of Rab Kahana
Phaed.	Plato, *Phaedo*
Planting	Philo, *On Planting* (LCL 3:205–305)
PNTC	Pillar New Testament Commentary

Abbreviations

Pol. *Phil.*	Polycarp, *To the Philippians* (ANF 1:33–36)
Posterity	Philo, *On the Posterity of Cain* (LCL 2:321–439)
Praep. ev.	*Preparation for the Gospel.* Eusebius of Caesarea. Edited by E. H. Gifford. Oxford: Oxford University Press, 1903
Praescr.	Tertullian, *Prescription against Heretics* (ANF 3:243–65)
Prax.	Tertullian, *Against Praxeas* (ANF 3:597–627)
Princ.	Origen, *On First Principles* (ANF 4:239–382)
Pss. Sol.	Psalms of Solomon (*OTP* 2:639–70)
QG	Philo, *Questions and Answers on Genesis* (LCL Suppl. 1:2–551)
RBS	Resources for Biblical Study
Resp.	Plato, *Republic*
RHE	*Revue d'histoire ecclésiastique*
RHR	*Revue de l'histoire des religions*
Sacrifices	Philo, *On the Sacrifices of Cain and Abel* (LCL 2:87–195)
SCG	*Summa Contra Gentiles.* Thomas Aquinas. Translated by Fathers of the English Dominican Province. 5 vols. London: Burns Oates & Washbourne, 1924
SHR	Studies in the History of Religions (supplements to Numen)
Sib. Or.	Sibylline Oracles (*OTP* 1:317–472)
Sir	Apocrypha, Sirach
SJ	Studia Judaica
Spec. Laws	Philo, *On the Special Laws* (LCL 8:1–155)
SPhiloA	Studia Philonica Annual
ST	*Summa Theologica.* Thomas Aquinas. Edited by Mortimer J. Adler et al. 2nd ed. 2 vols. Great Books of the Western World 17–18. Chicago, IL: Encyclopedia Britannica, 1990
Strom.	Clement of Alexandria, *Miscellanies* (ANF 2:299–568)
Symp.	Plato, *Symposium*
Syn.	Athanasius, *On the Councils of Ariminum and Seleucia* (NPNF^2 4:451–80)
t. 'Abod. Zar.	Tosefta, Tractate Avodah Zarah
Tanḥ.	Midrash Tanhuma

T. Ash.	Testament of Asher (*OTP* 1:816–18)
TDOT	*Theological Dictionary of the Old Testament*. Edited by G. Johannes Botterweck et al. Translated by John T. Willis et al. 17 vols. Grand Rapids: Eerdmans, 1974–2018
Test.	Cyprian, *To Quirinius: Testimonies against the Jews*
Tg. Neof.	Targum Neofiti
Tg. Onq.	Targum Onqelos
Theaet.	Plato, *Theaetetus*
Them	*Themelios*
Tim.	Plato, *Timaeus*
TJ	*Trinity Journal*
T. Job	Testament of Job (*OTP* 1:829–68)
T. Naph.	Testament of Naphtali (*OTP* 1:810–14)
Tri. Trac.	Nag Hammadi, Tripartite Tractate
Trin.	Augustine, *On the Trinity* (*NPNF*[1] 3:i–228)
T. Sim.	Testament of Simeon (*OTP* 1:785–88)
Vit. Phil.	Diogenes Laertius, *Lives of Eminent Philosophers*
Wis	Apocrypha, Wisdom of Solomon
WTJ	*Westminster Theological Journal*
y. Mo'ed Qaṭ.	Jerusalem Talmud, Tractate Mo'ed Qatan
y. Ta'an.	Jerusalem Talmud, Tractate Ta'anit
ZAW	*Zeitschrift für die alttestamentliche Wissenschaft*

PART I

Setting the Stage for the Incarnation

1 Introduction
The Story of a Scandal

I will make my dwelling among you,
and my soul shall not abhor you.
And I will walk among you and will be your God,
and you shall be my people.

—Lev 26:11–12

For nothing will be impossible with God.

—Luke 1:37

1.1. A Tale of Two Women

IN THE OPENING PAGES of the Hebrew Scriptures, a woman is confronted with a heaven-sent message that shatters her perception of the possible. Secretly listening from within her tent, Sarah overhears her husband Abraham speaking with three mysterious visitors (Gen 18). One of the visitors—whom Abraham calls Adonai (אֲדֹנָי, Lord)—speaks to Abraham and says, "Sarah your wife shall have a son" (Gen 18:10). Immediately Sarah laughs to herself and scoffs at the idea. "Shall I indeed bear a child, now that I am old?" she replies. Such a response was reasonable, given that it was outside her experience that a woman could give birth at ninety years old (Gen 17:17).

Yet despite the reasonableness of Sarah's skepticism, this was *the Lord* she was scoffing at, and he had relayed something that *would* happen to her.[1] In a subtle rebuke to Sarah's lack of faith, God replies, "Is anything too hard for the LORD?" (Gen 18:14). Soon enough, Sarah would give birth to Isaac, answering the rhetorical question. Thus, the Abrahamic line begins with a miracle that shatters all previous conceptions of what is possible in God's world.

In the opening pages of the New Testament (NT), one of Sarah's descendants faces a similar heaven-sent message. An angel tells a Jewish virgin named Miriam (Mary) that she would be overshadowed by God's Holy Spirit and would miraculously become pregnant with the Son of God (Luke 1:35). How could this be possible? Then, to prevent any temptation toward unbelief, the angel adds, "And behold, your relative Elizabeth in her old age has also conceived a son" (Luke 1:36). In other words, the angel encourages Miriam to verify that God had just repeated the miracle he had done for Sarah. If God had miraculously done the impossible with Sarah and then again with Elizabeth, perhaps it was possible that she, Miriam, would experience the pinnacle of miraculous impossibility by giving birth to the Son of God as the angel had announced.

Miriam thus has a critical choice: Will she scoff as Sarah scoffed? Or, will she humbly submit to the angel's announcement by withholding her skepticism and choosing to trust by faith?

Miriam's crisis at this moment is not unique to her. When considering the identity of Jesus of Nazareth, each person must consider the range of God's power and whether it is possible that God could take on flesh, becoming incarnate as a human being. Each must wrestle with the scandalous question of whether Jesus was merely human or more than human. Some take the way of Sarah, saying that God does not do the unthinkable. Others, however, respond as Miriam did, rejoicing in the hope God set before her. Perhaps the final line of the angel's announcement helped Miriam make her decision: "For nothing will be impossible with God" (Luke 1:37).[2]

---

1. This book employs the small-caps LORD when referring to a biblical text where the Tetragrammaton (יהוה) is written. Genesis 18 includes a curious phenomenon where one of the three men is initially called Adonai (Lord) (Gen 18:3) and then the man is inexplicably described by using the Tetragrammaton (LORD) from v. 10 onward. The physicality of the episode is emphasized by spatial language applied to the LORD's interactions with Abraham (Gen 18:16, 22–23, 33). This kind of language (God talk) is discussed in ch. 2.

2. The Greek of this statement is modeled on Gen 18:14 LXX. What was an open question in Genesis is transformed into a declarative statement of fact in the NT. See Brueggemann, "'Impossibility' and Epistemology."

Introduction

1.2. The Plan and Purpose of This Book

Throughout the Hebrew Bible, the God of Israel comforts his chosen nation by giving them visions of the future. One passage about end-time events includes a distinct prophecy. In Lev 26:12, Moses records God as saying, "I will walk among you and will be your God, and you shall be my people."[3] Here in the Torah of Moses is a prophecy that associates God's relational intimacy with Israel—even her restoration—with God *walking* among them. What does this mean?

Writing in the eleventh century, the revered Jewish commentator Rashi (Rabbi Solomon ben Isaac) considers "I will walk among you" and comments as follows: "I will, as it were, walk with you in the Garden of Eden as though I were one of yourselves and you will not be frightened of Me."[4] Rashi refers here to Adam and Eve's experience of hearing God "walking" in Eden (Gen 3:8), a relational intimacy that had since been lost but would be regained in the eschatological world to come, the restored Eden. Rashi expects a future day when Israel would experience God "as though I were one of yourselves"—that is, *human*.[5] Rashi's interpretation is aligned with an earlier rabbinic tradition (ca. third century CE), which states, "Thus is the Holy One Blessed be He destined to walk with the righteous in the Garden of Eden in time to come. They will see Him and recoil before Him, (and He will say to them) 'I am like you.'"[6] Even further back in Jewish history, there are parallels to the idea that God would one day visit Israel in physical, even human, form. The evidence from the Second Temple period and earlier (pre-70 CE) indicates Jewish people were open to God coming to earth in physical form, as affirmed by Jewish biblical scholar Benjamin Sommer:

> No Jew sensitive to Judaism's own classical sources, however, can fault the theological model Christianity employs when it

---

3. Other passages speak about God "walking" or "going" with Israel during her sojourns in the desert, which did not include an embodied human presence: Exod 29:45; Num 14:14; Deut 23:14–15; 2 Cor 6:16. Thus the "walking" in Lev 26:12 may not necessarily refer to God walking in human form, although I agree with Rashi's interpretation.

4. Rashi, *Pentateuch with Targum Onkelos*, Lev 26:12.

5. There is controversy in contemporary Jewish literature about whether or not Rashi was a corporealist (a believer in God having a physical body). See Slifkin, "Was Rashi a Corporealist?"; Zucker, "No, Rashi Was Not"; Slifkin, "Rashi's Stance on Corporealism" (response to Zucker).

6. Silverstein, *Sifra*, Sifra Behuqqotai 3.

avows belief in a God who has an earthly body as well as a Holy Spirit manifestation, for that model, we have seen, is a perfectly Jewish one.[7]

One might not expect a Jewish scholar to sound so agreeable to what has traditionally been seen as a Christian concept. Why, however, is God walking on earth in the form of a man viewed as a characteristic of *Christian* theology and not also of Judaism? If a Jewish scholar with the stature of Rashi believed God would one day walk in human form, why is that opinion so uncommon in Judaism today? While Rashi remains Orthodox Judaism's most admired commentator on the Hebrew Scriptures, his eleventh-century interpretation of Lev 26:12 represents the end of an era.[8] If Jewish people were supposed to look forward to the coming of God in human form, some came to realize that this afforded intellectual credibility to the Christians—who would spend the Middle Ages increasing their antagonism against Jews and Judaism. In the twelfth century and later, Jewish sages judged that it was too scandalous to believe God would one day appear to Israel as a human with feet that could walk. It was better to deny the idea altogether.

The following contemporary example illustrates the decisive shift that has been in place since the Middle Ages. Modern Orthodox political commentator Ben Shapiro summarizes why he does not believe Jesus is the Messiah, revealing the gap between Rashi and contemporary Orthodox Jewish interpretations of biblical texts. Shapiro responds as follows:

> Judaism never posited that there would be God [coming] to earth in physical form and then acting out in the world in that way. Judaism posits that God is beyond space and time. Occasionally he intervenes in history, but he doesn't take physical form—it's one of the key beliefs of Judaism, actually, an incorporeal God. The idea is actually foreign to Judaism of a merged God-man who is God in physical form who then dies and is resurrected and all this. It's just a different idea than exists in Judaism.[9]

Shapiro quickly identifies the critical issue why he, as an observant Jewish man, does not believe in Jesus. He does not cite unfulfilled messianic prophecies, Jesus's words or actions, or anti-Semitism in church history.

---

7. Sommer, *Bodies of God*, 135.

8. In the subsequent discussions, we will see that Rashi applied a *via positiva* hermeneutic to the idea of God walking. Maimonides was instrumental in making such interpretations out of the question when speaking about God.

9. Shermer, "Michael Shermer," 43:12 (2592 seconds).

Introduction

Instead, he appeals to the fundamental theological divide between gentile Christians (and Messianic Jews)[10] on one side and mainstream Jews on the other: the deity of Jesus of Nazareth.

The claim of God appearing in physical form, Shapiro notes, is considered impossible in Judaism. For most Jews today, God is believed to be absolutely incorporeal, that is, without any physicality or form or body.[11] God is transcendent and never enters into physical spaces in bodily forms. The belief that Jesus is divine is plausible only in a Christian frame of reference.

What accounts for the contrast between Rashi and Shapiro? One aim of this book is to illustrate how Jewish theology was transformed after Rashi's day, providing Jewish people with profound intellectual rebuttals to the Christian claim that Jesus is the incarnate Son of God. Through the incomparable influence of Jewish philosopher Moses Maimonides (twelfth century) on the one hand and the kabbalistic mystical tradition on the other (twelfth century to present), medieval Judaism took a philosophical turn that reverberates to this day—and undermines the NT's claims of Jesus's divine identity. Ben Shapiro's response illustrates the power of Maimonides's theology to stifle the claims of the NT. Yet the medieval sage went further than Shapiro: Maimonides's halakic (legal) ruling deemed Christian doctrine as idolatrous and churches as houses of idolatry.[12] This ruling continues to influence Jewish thought and attitudes toward Christianity today.

The NT presents a different view of the possibility of God indwelling flesh. The author of the NT book of Hebrews states, "[Jesus] is the radiance of the glory of God and the exact imprint of his nature, and he upholds the universe by the word of his power" (Heb 1:3). Paul writes, "For in [Jesus] the whole fullness of deity dwells bodily" (Col 2:9). Indeed, the NT portrays Jesus of Nazareth as both truly God and truly human, at the same time, without devaluation or mixture of his divine nature and his

---

10. Broadly speaking, Messianic Jews are Jews who believe in Jesus and who continue to express their Jewish identity with various forms of Jewish practice, often including observance of the Jewish festivals (Lev 23), corporate worship on Saturday, the practice of circumcision, and continued participation in the wider Jewish world. For a fuller description, see §10.1.

11. Divine incorporeality is the doctrine that God is essentially immaterial and spiritual. This doctrine is held in common by Jews and Christians, with different nuances, as will be discussed in this book.

12. Novak, "Maimonides's View of Christianity."

Part I: Setting the Stage for the Incarnation

human nature. This is what Jesus followers mean by the Incarnation,[13] a teaching that is throughout the NT but was best formulated by the Chalcedonian Definition, a declaration adopted at the Council of Chalcedon in 451 CE. Chalcedon is orthodox theology in Catholicism, Eastern Orthodoxy, Protestantism, and the modern Messianic Jewish movement.[14] In all streams of Judaism, except Messianic Judaism, this understanding of Jesus is seen as idolatrous, impossible, blasphemous, or redundant. For most Jewish people, Jesus is seen simply as a Jewish man who lived in the first century who was crucified by the Romans, but he was not the Messiah nor God in the flesh.

Ben Shapiro exemplifies the belief of many Jewish people today regarding the impossibility of God becoming incarnate as a man. Similar examples abound in Jewish publications. According to Jewish theologian David S. Shapiro, logic illustrates the falsity of the Christian claims:

> Is God capable of dying? Can God commit suicide? Can He create another god? These are questions we should ask of those who maintain that God can do anything. Can He make a circle identical to a square? Can He make one equal two? Can God sin? Can He act unjustly? Can the Creator become a creature? Can the uncreated God become a created God? Such propositions are obviously contradictory and mutually exclusive. God cannot become non-God. He cannot die. He cannot create logical absurdities. God is the unlimited. . . . That God can become man with all human frailties is to maintain that God can become non-God.[15]

Along these same logical lines, medieval Jewish philosopher Hasdai Crescas (1340–1410) asserts that the concept of the Incarnation is self-refuting:

---

13. Throughout this book, the word "Incarnation" is capitalized when referring to the teaching that Jesus of Nazareth is God in the flesh, that is, a single divine person with both a created human nature and an uncreated divine nature. This capitalization will distinguish the word from other uses of the word that denote divine embodiment outside of the dual-natured identity of Jesus of Nazareth.

14. Segments of Protestant Evangelicalism and the Messianic Jewish movement may not be explicit in their acceptance of the Nicene and Chalcedonian formulations, but their doctrinal statements often illustrate their dependence upon them. For example, any doctrinal statement that affirms that Jesus is one person in two natures, divine and human, implicitly agrees with Chalcedon. See §§10.1; 10.8.

15. D. Shapiro, "Possible *Deus Homo*?," 359.

Introduction

> Man's uniting with God is impossible since it would involve a contradiction. This is clear since man is finite and God, may He be blessed, is infinite. Therefore, no other case is so replete with an affirmative and a negative.... God has no power over things from which a contradiction would follow.[16]

Finally, a tenth-century Jewish philosopher and prominent academy leader, Saadia Gaon (882–942), writes, "It is impossible for an infinite force to reside in a finite body, for such a possibility is rejected by all that is known" (*Emunot* 1.1).[17]

In sum, since the Middle Ages, Jewish theologians and philosophers have asserted that divine embodiment is incomprehensible, meaningless, and incompatible with monotheism. In philosophical terms, these Jewish thinkers believe they are on solid ground in rejecting the notion of divine embodiment a priori, similar to rejecting the idea of a married bachelor or evil goodness without further investigation of the idea's plausibility. Since the Incarnation involves divine embodiment, it is disqualified automatically. Logical contradictions merit no further consideration.

Each of these opponents of divine embodiment introduced so far comes from the mainstream rationalist wing of traditional Judaism, which finds its greatest defender in the writings of the twelfth-century rabbi Moses Maimonides. However, there is a second school of thought within Orthodox Judaism: the mystical stream of Kabbalah. Although there have been mystical streams in Judaism for millennia, early Kabbalah emerged in the twelfth century and gained popularity just after Maimonides's death in the thirteenth. Kabbalists protest the rationalists' strong emphasis on the law of noncontradiction, and instead assert a world infused with infinite paradox. An influential eighteenth-century kabbalistic work called the *Tanya* states, "While you see yourself as apart from God, God sees you as a part of God."[18] By claiming such things, Jewish mystics also sideline the incarnate deity of Jesus, but from an alternative philosophical direction, which I will elaborate upon in depth.

If Maimonides made the Incarnation *impossible*, Kabbalah makes the Incarnation *redundant*. If the Incarnation is impossible, then a Christian or Messianic Jew arguing for Jesus's divinity is akin to arguing for

---

16. Crescas, *Refutation of Christian Principles*, 50.

17. Saadia Gaon predated Rashi and was Judaism's greatest philosopher since Philo eight centuries prior (although see Isaac Israeli in appendix B). Saadia was a major precursor to Maimonides in the twelfth century, but it was not until Maimonides that this kind of philosophical thinking took root in Jewish thought.

18. R. Shapiro, *Tanya*, 153.

God's ability to sin, or the possibility that God may cause himself to stop existing. On the other hand, if Jesus is divine just as the rest of the universe is divine, and if Jesus offers a kind of salvation that humanity does not need, then Jesus is redundant.

The Maimonidean and kabbalistic schools of thought encompass the two major poles that drive Orthodox Jewish theology to this day. By Orthodox Jewish theology, I mean the common understandings of God's nature and workings among Modern Orthodox and Haredi (ultra-Orthodox) Jews, including the Haredi subgroups of Hasidic and Yeshivish communities.[19] These groups see themselves as the heirs of the traditional Judaism from before the Enlightenment. Much of Orthodox Jewish religious education is focused on the study of the Talmud and its halakic issues, but theology regarding God's nature is typically driven by post-talmudic thought.[20] Jewish theologian David Novak writes of Orthodox Jewish theology, "Indeed, even today one can see the two main options in Jewish God-talk as being either Maimonidean or Kabbalistic."[21] Maimonides's understanding is reinforced in Orthodox Jewish liturgical practice, particularly in recitations of his Thirteen Principles of Faith and its dogma against divine embodiment.[22] Kabbalistic theology is also widespread in contemporary Orthodox Judaism, particularly among ultra-Orthodox Hasidic communities. Some Orthodox groups emphasize halakic studies and the rational thought of Maimonides, leaving Kabbalah studies for only the deserving few;[23] others teach Kabbalah to

---

19. For profiles of these Orthodox Jewish communities, see Nishma Research, *Nishma Research 2023*.

20. This book clarifies why the medieval opinions tend to steer Jewish theological discussions. Both Maimonides and Kabbalah teach that the study of the Scriptures or Talmud can be misleading without their medieval esoteric insights.

21. Novak, "Mind of Maimonides," 30.

22. Maimonides's Thirteen Principles of Faith are commonly seen as a theological baseline for what is and is not acceptable in Judaism. Maimonides's authority on these matters spans across all Orthodox Jewish groups, with significant but lesser influence on Conservative and Reform Jewish groups. See §5.1.

23. Commonly associated with the Yeshivish/Lithuanian/Mitnagdim position. This is the classic, pre–Shabbatai Tzvi opinion about the danger of mystical thought and the need to protect it from the masses, as found in m. Ḥag. 2:1. The Mitnagdim, the eighteenth-century opponents of the Kabbalah-rich Hasidic movement, did not reject Kabbalah. They were opposed to the emotional excesses of the Hasids and their teaching of Kabbalah to the common people, but they also accepted the truth of Kabbalah. Benjamin Brown studies the controversy and concludes that the two sides had similar beliefs and interpretations, but they differed on their theological emphases ("But Me No Buts").

Introduction

the common people in their community, infuse halakah with kabbalistic meaning, and reinterpret Maimonides kabbalistically.[24] In general, Orthodox Jewish communities in their many manifestations find themselves primarily driven by some combination of the theological doctrines and themes found in Maimonidean and kabbalistic thought.

Yet, both Maimonides and Kabbalah promote theological worldviews that clash with the worldview of the NT writers. Due to cultural and religious unfamiliarity between the Jewish and Christian communities, the worldview clash is often not understood, or rather is misunderstood and presented in caricature. On the one hand, few religious Jewish people study counterarguments against Jesus or Christianity. For most Jewish people, Jesus and Christianity are simply not on their mind, and they let their rabbi handle rebuttals to Christian claims. On the other hand, "objections" to Jesus and Christianity can be latent and implicit within one's worldview even if one is not trained in how to articulate the objections.[25] Educated under Maimonidean and kabbalistic thought, many Jewish people simply have no room in their worldview for a divine Messiah to make any sense. These kinds of deep objections inherent in Jewish worldviews could leave many followers of Jesus unprepared to respond, as they are rarely familiar with Maimonidean or kabbalistic thought. Indeed, there is good reason to believe that the Messianic Jewish and wider Christian communities should be further encouraged to deal with Orthodox Jewish doctrines that make the Incarnation a nonstarter in the Jewish community.[26]

The Jewish apostle Paul earnestly yearned for the salvation of his fellow Jewish people, saying, "Brothers, my heart's desire and prayer to God for [Israel] is that they may be saved" (Rom 10:1). Yet, confession of Jesus as LORD is central to the salvation of Jew and gentile alike (Rom 10:9–12). Paul thus exhorted believers in Jesus to send to the Jewish

---

24. For example, the modern Hasidic movement. There are a wide variety of different Hasidic groups, but all accept the kabbalistic teachings of the Baal Shem Tov and his support of teaching Kabbalah to the masses. See §7.3 for a history of the Hasidic movement. For an example of a Hasidic reformulation of Maimonides, see Gurary, *Thirteen Principles of Faith*.

25. For example, few Christians have spent time considering how to respond to the mystical idea that all things are united as one (see the subsequent Neoplatonism sections). The idea sounds plainly false given their Christian presuppositions, even if they may not know how to articulate a response. Thus, they have a latent objection to Neoplatonism embedded in their Christian worldview.

26. On this, see §10.1 and Crawford, "Pathways."

people those who would preach the good news of the Messiah (Rom 10:14–17), insisting that the gospel is "to the Jew first" (Rom 1:16). However, the Jewish community is undergoing a profound transformation today. Haredim—that is, those ultra-Orthodox Jewish people most committed to Maimonides and Kabbalah—are expected to see a dramatic population increase over the next decades due to high birthrates and religious retention.[27] As the Orthodox Jewish community continues to grow at a rapid pace, religious Jewish objections to the Incarnation will become more prevalent in the global Jewish community and thus a more pressing need for Jesus followers to address if they want to accomplish Paul's exhortations.

Thus, a second aim of this book is to provide a response that affirms Jesus as LORD in light of major Jewish theological objections. Because Jewish and Christian worldviews are complex, accomplishing this goal will not be a simple matter.[28] The intricacies of these challenges to the Incarnation demand a comprehensive study of theology, with an emphasis on the doctrine of God.[29] Who and what is he? How can he be described, how can he be known, and what is he like? Tugging on the thread of the Incarnation reveals an entire tapestry of interdisciplinary complexity on these topics. To better grasp the issues at hand, it will be necessary to walk through the Western intellectual tradition and the categories

---

27. Staetsky, *Haredi Jews Around World*; Alper et al., *Jewish Americans in 2020*; Cooperman et al., "Portrait"; Eliezrie, "US Jewry Is Shifting."

28. Theologian Craig Carter's exhortation is fitting: "No one can be an expert in everything, but statements about God constitute theology, and theology is a single activity. Anyone who wishes to do theology of any sort—from Old Testament exegesis to systematic theology—needs basic competence in all of the following areas: the history of philosophy and theology, biblical languages, biblical hermeneutics, biblical introduction, the history of biblical interpretation, biblical theology, and dogmatic theology. To ask that it be made easier is to ask the impossible; it cannot be less complicated than it is. Asking that theologians without competencies in all these areas be allowed to do theology is like demanding that a person with only high school biology be allowed to perform surgery. It can be done, but the results will not be pretty" (Carter, *Contemplating God*, 296).

29. There are many other branches of theology, such as soteriology, eschatology, halakah, and ethics, but they are not the focus of this book.

Introduction

of metaphysics,[30] theology,[31] hermeneutics,[32] ontology,[33] cosmology,[34] epistemology,[35] mystery,[36] paradox,[37] and how God relates to the world.[38] Each of these subjects contributes to one's understanding of whether the Incarnation of the Son of God is a possibility, and the way one grapples with these categories will have broader implications on one's worldview. In particular, this book interacts with the theological and philosophical positions of:

1. The authors of the Hebrew Scriptures (fifth century BCE and earlier)
2. The Greek Platonists, Pythagoreans, Aristotelians, Gnostics, and Neoplatonists (fourth century BCE and following)
3. The Jewish Hellenists (third century BCE through first century CE)
4. The New Testament (first century CE)
5. The church fathers (second through fifth century CE)
6. The sages of the mishnaic and talmudic era (second through sixth century CE)
7. Maimonides: Jewish rationalism (twelfth century CE)
8. Kabbalah: Jewish mysticism (twelfth century CE to present)

Along the way, this book surveys Greek and Jewish philosophical thought, a discussion of God's attributes (or non-attributes), negative theology, cosmological origins, hermeneutical rules for descriptions of God, and the biblical distinction between the Creator and his creatures. All this is

---

30. The philosophical study of the fundamental nature of reality. Extended definitions for this term and the others in this paragraph are available in appendix A.

31. The nature of God and his relationship with all that exists.

32. Hermeneutics are the principles of biblical interpretation. They include the ways grammar, figures of speech, literary genres, traditional precedent, and extratextual sources lead the reader to determine what a text means.

33. The nature of being, or what it means to exist.

34. The origin of the cosmos and the nature of its order.

35. The nature of knowledge and the validity of that which is claimed to be knowledge.

36. Something that is beyond the discovery of human reason and must be revealed by God.

37. That which appears contradictory but is not, for some unknown reason.

38. For a readable introduction to these philosophical matters, see DeWeese and Moreland, *Philosophy Made Slightly Less Difficult*.

necessary to provide a robust theological response to the medieval and contemporary Jewish claims against Jesus's divinity.

This book is divided into three parts. Part 1 considers introductory matters relating to the Incarnation and one method contemporary scholars have developed to recontextualize the Trinity and Incarnation as Jewish ideas. Parts 2 and 3 introduce a new method for justifying the Incarnation in light of Jewish philosophical objections. These parts are separated epistemologically, with the NT omitted from worldview determinations in part 2 and admitted in part 3. The second part considers the worldviews of Maimonides and Kabbalah on their own terms, focusing on the primary sources that compose contemporary Judaism's theological commitments—especially those that invalidate the Incarnation implicitly or explicitly. Part 2 cites Jewish sages, Jewish scholars, and the classics of Jewish theological thought, such as the *Guide to the Perplexed* and kabbalistic manuals. After providing an exposition of the worldviews of Maimonides and Kabbalah, I offer thorough philosophical and theological critiques of their approaches to divine embodiment. However, I will do so in part 2 largely without drawing upon NT passages or Christian or Messianic Jewish authors nor appealing to the truth of Christian theology. I will argue that the weaknesses of the Maimonidean and kabbalistic worldviews, even without considering the NT, make room for a better solution.

Part 3 introduces the minority Jewish position in the Jewish-authored New Testament, which claims that the God of Israel has visited Israel in Jesus of Nazareth. In this final part, I aim to provide reasons why belief in Jesus as God incarnate, the LORD of Israel, is a coherent position for Jewish people today, just as it was the case for many Jews living in the first century. For roughly eight hundred years, Jewish theology has been primarily driven by the two schools of Maimonidean and kabbalistic thought, but I believe the third and neglected school of the NT deserves a seat at the table. By the end of this book, I hope to establish the incarnational worldview of the NT—in contrast to the theological worldviews of Maimonides, Kabbalah, rabbinic corporealists, Aristotle, and Plotinus—as the most accurate portrayal of the Hebrew Scriptures and reality, a reality that has included historical visitations of the incorporeal God in physical form.

1.3. Jewish Schools of Theology on Divine Embodiment

Before embarking on a journey to understand Jewish challenges to the Incarnation, it is critical to grasp the meaning of the term. Far beyond a mere belief in Jesus's divinity, the Incarnation involves an interconnected web of supporting beliefs in multiple categories, including theology, creation, anthropology, metaphysics, and science. At the most basic level, the Incarnation is a particular understanding of the relationship between God and the universe that is anticipated in the Hebrew Scriptures and fulfilled in Jesus's coming in the NT.

There are many things the Incarnation is *not*, and only one thing that it *is*. Strictly speaking, the Incarnation is the union of the Son of God as a divine person with a created human nature. To be a person is to be an intelligent agent, an interacting conscious self, and a possessor of a nature.[39] In the Incarnation, the Son of God remains one divine person who animates and experiences two natures without mixture or change to his divine nature. He is one *who* in two *whats*. Who is he? He is the Son of God. What is he? He is human, and he is divine. Historically, this has been called the *hypostatic union*, referring to the fourth-century CE Greek word for person, *hypostasis*,[40] and it is best articulated in the Chalcedonian Definition. The Son of God, since his Incarnation, is one person with two natures.

This position depends on a Trinitarian theology, since the NT says that the Son (and not the Father or the Spirit) became incarnate as Jesus of Nazareth, yet all three are equally divine and are one God (see ch. 10). The Trinity can exist without the Incarnation, but the Incarnation (in the NT presentation) cannot happen without the Trinity. Conversely, if the Incarnation is true, then it justifies belief in the Trinity. Thus, while the triunity of three divine persons and the Incarnation are separate doctrines, they mutually support each other.

When defined in this way, the concept of the Incarnation cannot be applied to any historical event before the Holy Spirit overshadowed

---

39. A classic definition of *person* is given by Boethius, *Contra Eutychen* 3: "the individual substance of a rational nature" (*Theological Tractates*, 85). This is employed in Aquinas, *ST* I q.29 a.1. The plural of this technical word is not "people"—implying humans—but rather "persons." For example, a plurality of angels are persons.

40. It is important to distinguish this word as meaning "person" in the fourth century, since it was used in previous centuries (including in Heb 1:3) with other meanings. When the Nicene Creed and Chalcedonian Definition were formulated, the church fathers intended the word to mean "person."

a Jewish virgin to become pregnant with Jesus (Luke 1:35).[41] This book will consider so-called theophanies in the Hebrew Scriptures where God appeared to take physical form.[42] Examples include God appearing as a man in Gen 18 and 32, as fire in Exod 3, and as a messenger in Exod 23:20. If these are examples of God truly appearing in physical form in the Hebrew Scriptures—a position I affirm—they cannot be called instances of Incarnation because God did not "take on" the nature of the physical things he appeared to be. God did not *become* a man or fire in Genesis or Exodus—as if uniting his divine nature with the nature of fire—but instead, he *temporarily* animated a physical body and then left it. In the Incarnation, the Son takes on a human nature that he will never relinquish. Thus, Christian theologians accurately call theophanies in the Hebrew Bible *pre*incarnate visitations of God. However, "preincarnate" implies a future Incarnation and indicates a Christian frame of reference. Instead, I will generally call this phenomenon in the Hebrew Scriptures by the more neutral phrase "divine embodiment."

Thus, there is a distinction between the once-for-all-time Incarnation of Jesus the Messiah and the various divine embodiments found within the Hebrew Scriptures. However, further distinctions and qualifications need to be made. Consider the following chart, which maps out four different schools regarding divine embodiment in Jewish and Christian theology. The schools diverge in their answers to the question "Does God's nature include a body?" and the follow-up question "Can God inhabit a physical body?"

---

41. McFarland, *Word Made Flesh*, 76.

42. *Theophany* is a term referring to "visible appearances of God." The word is derived from Greek *theophania* (θεοφάνια). I have mentioned them as "so-called" particularly because the Maimonidean tradition attempts to distance these events from being actual appearances of God, for God in the Maimonidean mind cannot appear. It is more common for Christian theologians to talk about theophanies in a noncontroversial manner.

Introduction

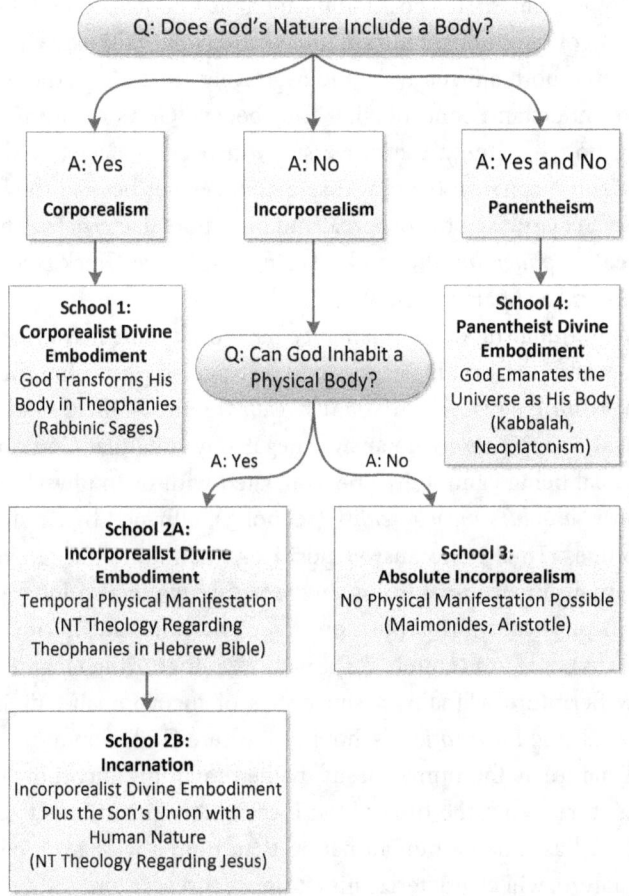

Figure 1. Varieties of Divine Embodiment in Judaism and Christianity

In response to the question "Does God's nature include a body?," there are three classes of answers. Those who respond affirmatively believe that God in his very nature is physical and can exist in bodily form. His body may be of a higher grade of matter than the known universe—perhaps more pure, more ordered, and incorruptible—but God is still a physical being, and he can transform his body at will (thereby accounting for theophanies). This position is called *corporealism*, as corporeal means "to be made of physical parts." This book will illustrate how the rabbinic sages of the talmudic era affirmed a version of corporealism (school 1). Those who answer the question negatively believe that God is incorporeal, that is, a spiritual being who does not have an eternal body and is not made up of physical parts. This position is called *incorporealism*, and it is widespread in contemporary Judaism and Christianity.[43] Those who answer the question both affirmatively *and* negatively are perhaps the most difficult to understand conceptually. They believe God's nature includes a physical body—namely, the universe—which emanates eternally from God, who is a spiritual being whose existence goes beyond the physical universe. So, God is both corporeal and incorporeal, eternally. This position is called *panentheism*,[44] and it is affirmed in the Greek Neoplatonic tradition and Kabbalah (school 4).

While Judaism and Christianity have often affirmed incorporealism, a second question is necessary to distinguish post-talmudic Jewish thought from historical Christianity: *Can* the incorporeal God inhabit a physical body? Those who answer negatively state that God's mode of incorporeal being cannot ever be associated with or in physicality. This position is *absolute incorporeality* (school 3), affirmed by Aristotle and Maimonides. Those who answer positively maintain God can mysteriously remain incorporeal in his divine nature while also interacting in and with physicality. This position is *incorporealist divine embodiment* (school 2A), and it accounts for a plain reading of theophanies in the Hebrew Scriptures. Finally, a subspecies of incorporealist divine embodiment is the *Incarnation* (school 2B), where God's Son took on a full human nature as the human Jesus, while remaining incorporeal in his divine nature. From the time of the Incarnation in Miriam's womb, the Son of God assumed a human nature that, united with his incorporeal divine nature, will characterize his existence forevermore.

There are other answers to these questions, such as pantheism (God is the world) and atheism (there is no God to have a body), but these

---

43. The Jewish position on incorporealism is discussed in pt. 2. Christian affirmations of incorporealism associate the doctrine with God's essential invisibility (John 1:18; Col 1:15; 1 Tim 1:17; 6:16; Heb 11:27; 1 John 4:12) or his simplicity (he is not a compound being made of separable parts). For affirmations of the triune God's essential incorporeality, see Aquinas, *ST* I q.3 a.1; Shedd, *Dogmatic Theology*, 153–64; Bray, *Doctrine of God*, 94–97; Frame, *Systematic Theology*, 383–404; Duby, *Divine Simplicity*; Grudem, *Systematic Theology*, 185–214.

44. *Panentheism* is the belief that "all is in God," meaning the entire universe is an extension of God's being. Everything in the universe is divine, for God animates the universe like the soul animates the body. The universe has emanated from God and is ontologically united with God. This belief is different than pantheism, which states that God is the universe, and the universe is all that God is. For more on panentheism, see Cooper, *Panentheism*.

answers have not been a part of historical Jewish or Christian theology and thus they are outside the purview of this book. The schools of thought given above illustrate what this book aims to make plausible—incorporealist divine embodiment culminating in the Incarnation (2A and 2B)—as well as the points of divergence with various Jewish schools. However, even the position affirmed in this book is a Jewish position that has been forgotten as a credible and faithful option for Jewish people.

1.4. This Book in Comparison to Previous Attempts in History

The field of answering Jewish objections to the Incarnation is nearly two thousand years old. Both the first-century NT writings and the second-century church fathers depict Jewish people who struggled to accept the idea of God in flesh. One of the earliest disputes about the deity of Jesus is found ca. 140 CE in Justin Martyr's *Dialogue with Trypho*,[45] where the Jewish disputant, Trypho, complains: "You [Jesus followers] endeavour to prove an incredible and well-nigh impossible thing; [namely], that God endured to be born and become man."[46]

Other early Christian apologists would follow Justin's lead in the genre of literature now known as *Adversus Judaeos*, but their attempts were usually ill-informed.[47] Relying on assumed Christian presuppositions, Platonic allegorical exegesis, an ignorance of Judaism and Hebrew, a dependency upon the LXX or Vulgate, and the employment of supersessionist triumphalism, many historical Christian attempts at defending Jesus's divinity to Jewish people have been epistemologically, hermeneutically, and ethically deficient. Unfortunately, in this genre, Christian piety was seen as an adequate substitute for persuasive technique.

In the Middle Ages, Christian apologists became increasingly aware of talmudic literature,[48] which was then mined to support Christian

---

45. There is some debate as to whether Trypho was a real Jewish man or just a foil developed by Justin for his apologetics project. I do not intend to enter into that debate here. I quote this opinion from Trypho because Justin intended it to be an authentic Jewish response, and it indeed resonates with many other Jewish objections to the Incarnation of the Son of God.

46. Justin Martyr, *Dial.* 68 (*ANF* 1:232).

47. Williams, *Adversus Judaeos*.

48. There is not much evidence of Christians knowing about the Talmud or interacting with it before Peter Alfonsi in the twelfth century (Alfonsi, *Dialogue Against the Jews*, 29).

claims (often implausibly), or vehemently attacked and burned.[49] Persecution of the Jews who cherished the Talmud frequently followed thereafter. Christian apologetic works written after the Protestant Reformation became more sophisticated and learned but retained a vindictive attitude that sought to shame, scandalize, and insult the Jewish community.[50] Jews typically view Christian apologetics, therefore, as a synonym for Christian anti-Semitism.

On a popular level, many Christian attempts employ simplistic biblical proof-texting of Christian-identified messianic prophecies—a practice of citing Old Testament passages as if they are self-explanatory and obvious evidence for Christianity—while ignoring Jewish hermeneutical practices, historical interpretations, and concerns. Oftentimes, this hermeneutical method of justifying Jesus's deity is the only one with which Jesus followers are familiar. Contrary to popular opinion, Jewish people do not reject Jesus's deity simply because they are unaware of Isa 7:14 or 9:6. They have not ripped Isa 53 out of their Bibles. The religious Jewish community, often aware of these common arguments, has produced voluminous commentaries to rebut Christian citations of messianic prophecies and divine claims for the Messiah.[51]

In contrast to previous attempts, Hebrew Christians, Messianic Jews, and gentile missionaries to the Jewish people have contributed sophisticated explanations and defenses of the deity of Yeshua since the

---

49. Alfonsi, *Dialogue Against the Jews*; Chazan, *Barcelona and Beyond*; Berger, "Christians, Gentiles, and Talmud"; Szpiech, "From *Testimonia* to Testimony"; R. Harvey, "Raymundus Martini"; Hasselhoff and Fidora, *Ramon Martí's "Pugio Fidei"*; Wiersma, "Pearls in a Dunghill"; Sadik, "When Maimonideans and Kabbalists Convert."

50. For example, Anthonius Margaritha (ca. 1500–?), Johannes Buxtorf the Elder (1564–1629), Johann Wagenseil (1633–1705), and Johann Eisenmenger (1654–1704) (Walton, *Anthonius Margaritha*; Buxtorf, *Jewish Synagogue*; Eisenmenger, *Entdecktes Judentum*; Burnett, "Distorted Mirrors"; Burnett, "Luther's Chief Witness"). The Hebrew Christian pioneer Joseph Frey (1771–1850) represented a break from this habit, speaking positively and pastorally to common Jewish people (Frey, *Joseph and Benjamin*). Alexander McCaul (1799–1863) partially followed Frey's attitude, although he continued to speak harshly against rabbis (McCaul, *Old Paths*; Ruderman, *Missionaries, Converts, and Rabbis*; Jocz, *Jewish People*, 194–97).

51. As of this writing, the most accessible place to find such exegetical commentaries is Sefaria (www.sefaria.org). For medieval examples, see Lasker, *Jewish Philosophical Polemics*; Crescas, *Refutation of Christian Principles*. For an enduring early modern example, despite being written by a Karaite, see Troki, *Faith Strengthened*. For a contemporary example, see Singer, *Let's Get Biblical*. The well-trod and conventional apologetic approach is to dig in and debate these messianic prophecies head-on; this book promotes arguments coming from the flanks.

Introduction

nineteenth century.[52] Many have illustrated the compatibility of the Trinity and Incarnation with historical Jewish works, a theme that is explored in chapter 3. Nevertheless, I believe the worldviews of Maimonides and Kabbalah deserve greater engagement than has been previously given in studies on the Jewishness of the Incarnation.[53]

Despite two millennia of Jewish-Christian discussion about the deity of Jesus, I believe this field remains wide open and poised for new and better contributions. Contemporary scholars are spoiled because of the embarrassment of riches at their disposal compared to previous generations. For much of history, many cultural, linguistic, and political factors kept Jews and Christians from understanding each other and reading each other's works. The situation is radically transformed today. The entirety of extant Second Temple Jewish literature is readily available and translated into English, as are the Pseudepigrapha, Mishnah, church fathers, Nag Hammadi literature, two Talmuds, midrashim, medieval Jewish exegetical commentaries, Maimonides's works, kabbalistic primers, Jewish polemics against Christianity, and the works of Greek philosophers such as Plato and Aristotle. Even more, these texts are available digitally in sophisticated software packages that enable rapid study, cross-referencing, deep linguistic analysis, and reverse lookup in the voluminous and ever-growing academic literature, including Jewish and Christian scholars in dialogue. Therefore, cross-disciplinary, cross-linguistic, and cross-religious investigations of the great works of the Jewish world, the church, and the academy are available now like never before. The twenty-first-century scholar has a broad vantage point that previous polemicists and apologists never enjoyed.

The contemporary cultural and ethical atmosphere has changed for the better as well. In the aftermath of the Holocaust, many Christians came to realize that old theological teachings about the Jews—a body of teachings now known as Christian supersessionism—had prepared Europe for the Holocaust and were profoundly unbiblical.[54] Supersessionism drove

---

52. *AJOJ*; Borough Park Symposium, *Symposium II*; Kinzer, "Finding Our Way"; Jocz, "Invisibility of God"; Williams, *Manual of Christian Evidences*; McCaul, *Lectures on the Prophecies*; Frey, *Joseph and Benjamin*. A wider collection of beneficial Messianic Jewish contributions is included in §10.1. For examples of syncretism to avoid, see Crawford, "Pathways," 73–89.

53. See §10.1.

54. On supersessionism, see M. Brown, *Our Hands Are Stained*; Soulen, *God of Israel*; Commission for Religious Relations with the Jews, "Gifts and Calling"; Carroll, *Constantine's Sword*; Crawford, "Christian Antisemitism's Potent Recipe." I should also

Part I: Setting the Stage for the Incarnation

Christians to disassociate their faith from its Jewish foundation while also undermining the dignity, covenantal identity, and prophesied future of the Jewish people. Since becoming aware of the ethical and theological errors of supersessionism, post-Holocaust Christian authors have shifted toward generous and respectful attitudes when discussing Judaism and the Jewish people, which I greatly applaud and attempt to embody myself.

And yet, despite a better climate of scholarship and attitude, disagreements about the divinity of Jesus of Nazareth remain. As a project of theological retrieval,[55] this book seeks to recover the best of past handlings of the Incarnation while avoiding many lamentable pitfalls in historical Jewish-Christian relations. I believe there are good arguments and techniques from the past that may be rehabilitated for a modern age, as well as fallow ground that previous scholars have left untouched. I seek to open new vistas of discussion and debate that have largely gone unnoticed—yet with respect to those who disagree. As we will see, the strongest Jewish objections to Jesus's divinity are anything but unintelligent, simplistic, or ignorant. Christians slander their Jewish cousins when portraying Jewish objections as such. Yet, as philosopher Anthony Kenny notes, "Even the most intelligent people can go wrong if they start from false first principles."[56] This book is an in-depth investigation of those first principles.

1.5. On Intellectual Assimilation and the Definition of Judaism

This book investigates Jewish theological thought across many Jewish communities separated by time, geography, culture, and worldview. Necessarily, such a scope begs multiple questions regarding the constitution of Judaism and Jewish thought.

What is Judaism? This question has generated much controversy throughout history. The rabbinic sages of the Mishnah (ca. 70–200 CE) claimed to have the right to define Judaism due to a continuous chain of

---

note that nineteenth-century premillennial Christians who were supportive of Jewish missions work were strong advocates for the Jewish people and rejected supersessionism. Examples include Alexander McCaul, Horatius Bonar, Charles Spurgeon, and William Blackstone.

55. See §10.2. I have appropriated this phrase, and the goals behind it, from Ortlund, *Theological Retrieval for Evangelicals*.

56. Kenny, *Illustrated Brief History*, 263.

Introduction

tradition from Sinai (m. Pirke Avot 1). While this narrative is popular in classical rabbinic sources and Orthodox Judaism today, a linear and monolithic understanding of Judaism has come under criticism from multiple directions. The idea of a normative Judaism during the Second Temple period is difficult to reconcile with Second Temple Jewish sources.[57] Moreover, scholars now know that post-temple rabbinic Judaism took centuries to gain institutional control over non-rabbinic Judaism[58] and to distinguish itself from early Jewish Christianity.[59]

When describing first-century Jewish society, Josephus famously described three sects with contrasting beliefs: the Pharisees, the Sadducees, and the Essenes (*J.W.* 2.160–66). The thought of Philo of Alexandria could represent a fourth stream, although it is not known how popular it was beyond Philo himself. Philo also mentioned a group called the Theraputae (*Contempl. Life*). Second-century church fathers mentioned various other Jewish sects.[60] Did each of these sects partake in a single religion called "Judaism"? Is there some immutable essential core that distinguishes Judaism from non-Judaism? Or rather, were these sects unique sub-religions that shared a common ancestor?

Scholars and traditional rabbinic authorities are divided. Jacob Neusner famously insisted that the first century was not home to one Judaism but multiple Judaisms.[61] Recently, Steve Mason and Daniel Boyarin have denied there was any one concept of "Judaism" in the first century, garnering criticism from others.[62] In short, while the word "Judaism" was used in the first century—including in the NT (Acts 13:43; Gal 1:13–14)—Jewish academics today have difficulty defining the word

---

57. For more on this theme, see Crawford, "Forgotten Cohanim."

58. Archaeological discoveries of synagogues from the second through seventh centuries show major discrepancies when compared to rabbinic requirements for synagogue architecture. Archaeologist and historian Lee Levine concludes, "It has become clear that the rabbis did not control this institution" (*Ancient Synagogue*, 496). Levine believes the rabbinic sages did not come to rule over a wide range of synagogues until the period of Muslim rule in the Middle Ages.

59. Dunn, *Jews and Christians*; Boyarin, *Border Lines*; Shanks, *Partings*; Zetterholm et al., *Negotiating Identities*.

60. See Justin Martyr, *Dial.* 80; Hegesippus in Eusebius, *Hist. eccl.* 4.22.6. The groups included the Genisae, Meristae, Galileans, Hellenists, Baptists, Hemerobaptists, Masbothaeans, and Samarians. For discussion on these, see Skeb, "'Pharisees' and Early Christian Heresiology."

61. Neusner's use of "Judaisms" is found throughout his work. He gives a definition of what qualifies as "a Judaism" in *Introduction to American Judaism*, 30–31.

62. Mason, "Jews, Judaeans, Judaizing, Judaism"; Boyarin, *Judaism*; Reinhartz, "What's in a Label?"

in relation to the Second Temple period. This skepticism of a normative Judaism in antiquity may be carried through to other eras, such as the contemporary moment, where Haredi[63] and Reconstructionist[64] Jews each lay claim to "Judaism" but vary widely in their beliefs and practices.[65]

What is not Judaism? This may be an easy question to answer when considering gentile worldviews unconnected to the Torah. However, the lack of clarity on what rightly constitutes Judaism and Jewish thought becomes acute when considering the classification of the New Testament. Jewish NT scholar Amy-Jill Levine describes the NT as part of the Jewish literature of the Second Temple period that ranks alongside Philo, Josephus, and deuterocanonical Jewish literature.[66] Commenting on this, Adele Reinhartz writes,

> Levine is reflecting a consensus that the books comprising the New Testament should be situated "within Judaism." Fundamentally, this statement refers to the conviction that the New Testament books were texts that participated in the same thought world, and the same geographical, social, economic, historical, and political contexts—those circumscribed by the Roman Empire—as do books such as the Wisdom of Ben Sira, the Dead Sea Scrolls, and other examples of second Temple and first century Jewish literature.[67]

The notion that the NT can be labeled "Jewish" may be accepted by Jewish academics, but it is not widely embraced in the broader Jewish community. Many Jewish people see the NT as a Christian text with Christian ideas, with "Christian" understood to mean "not Jewish." Thus, just as it is problematic to define what is meant by "Judaism," it is a matter of opinion whether a particular idea or set of works deserves the adjective "Jewish." While Jewish scholars argue that intellectual rigor supports their classification, rabbinic authorities cite traditional and halakic grounds for their judgments, and laypeople often rely on popular

---

63. Haredi Jews (also known as ultra-Orthodox) often regard themselves as the most religiously authentic and observant group of Jews. See 10–11nn19–26.

64. Reconstructionist Judaism was founded in the twentieth century by Mordechai Kaplan and emphasizes the importance of modernity and the evolving nature of Jewish tradition, values, and practices. While it considers Jewish law as a source for illumination, Reconstructionist Judaism does not see traditional halakah as binding.

65. Orthodox Judaism is also difficult to define: Margulies, "What Do We Mean."

66. A. Levine, "Bearing False Witness," 761.

67. Reinhartz, "What's in a Label?," 39.

Introduction

opinion to define Judaism. As a result, the NT's Jewish credentials remain contested.

Is Judaism a moving target? Investigating historical Jewish religious texts uncovers traditions and doctrines that challenge modern conceptions of what is acceptable within Judaism. For example, while the doctrine of original sin is often associated with Christianity, one of the strongest and earliest defenses of the idea may be found in the Jewish pseudepigraphal book of 4 Ezra, dating to the decades after 70 CE.[68] Many rabbinic commentaries assert that the Messiah will suffer and die according to Isa 53, although this position has since fallen out of favor due to its similarity with Christian interpretation.[69] Jewish theological shifts are also apparent outside of controversies with Christianity. Later in this book it will be seen how Maimonides and Kabbalah contributed many innovations to Jewish thought as a whole, yet they differed when compared to each other and the eras preceding their rise. For example, it would be historically incorrect to assume Maimonides's Thirteen Principles of Faith have always been accepted as normative in Judaism.[70] Likewise, the antiquity of kabbalistic doctrine and texts is highly doubtful.[71] Thus, the consensus of the rabbinic elites of one era may differ from the consensus of another era, further complicating what is meant by calling something "Jewish" or "part of Judaism."

When do non-Jewish ideas become Jewish ideas? The biblical text describes God establishing Israelite society with himself as her sole king (Deut 17:14; Judg 8:23). Centuries later, the people become jealous of the benefits the gentile nations enjoyed by having human kings, and they ask to have a human king of their own (1 Sam 8:5–7). God consents to the people's request (cf. Deut 17:15), even though it was not an "Israelite idea" to be ruled by a human king.[72] Soon enough, with the rise of Saul

---

68. For example, 4 Ezra 3:20–22: "Yet you did not take away from them their evil heart, so that your Law might bring forth fruit in them. For the first Adam, burdened with an evil heart, transgressed and was overcome, as were also all who were descended from him" (*OTP* 1:529). A similar idea may be found in the Talmud in b. Šabb. 145b–146a, where the sages state that Eve passed lust on to all people, but Israel had it removed from her through the covenant at Sinai. The version in 4 Ezra does not excuse Jewish people from the effects of Adam and Eve's transmitted sin.

69. A compilation of rabbinic commentaries on Isa 53 that include messianic interpretations may be found in Driver and Neubauer, *Fifty-Third Chapter of Isaiah*.

70. M. Shapiro, *Limits of Orthodox Theology*.

71. This theme is discussed in depth in pt. 2.

72. One could argue that the prophecy of kings coming from Abraham's line (Gen 17:6; cf. Num 24:7) indicates that kingship was an Israelite concept. Perhaps so, *in*

and David to the throne through Samuel's anointing and the associated messianic prophecies of a king from David's line (2 Sam 7), the gentile origin of the kingship idea was no cause for concern; what had originally been a gentile concept now had divine warrant as part of Israelite politico-religious society. In other words, what had not been Jewish became central to Judaism from that point forward according to the will of God as revealed by Israel's prophets.

However, as commonly acknowledged, Israel lacks prophets today. No longer is there a prophetic voice to accept or deny the entrance of non-Jewish ideas into Judaism. Likewise, the Levitical priests, whom Moses assigned as Torah interpreters,[73] are no longer in operation. The Urim and Thummim are also gone (Exod 28:30; 1 Sam 14:41). Thus, the question of what ought to be integrated into Judaism from the outside is a question that must be answered differently today compared to the biblical period.

A significant theme of this book is the integration of many Greek philosophical ideas into the thought patterns that have characterized Judaism since the medieval period. Even though such ideas did not originate in Jewish circles, or from the Hebrew Bible, or given prophetic approval, nevertheless many Greek philosophical concepts would become tightly integrated with Jewish theology, philosophy, and practice. Without biblical systems of divine warrant, their acceptance into Judaism was acquired through some innovative combination of rabbinic majority agreement and popular practice.[74] Many Jewish people forgot the non-Jewish origin of these ideas, a phenomenon sociologists call *stimulus diffusion*.[75]

As a Protestant Evangelical, I bring a Protestant mindset to bear when considering the topics of this book. Admittedly, a Protestant's theological commitments, especially to *sola Scriptura*, the NT, the Trinity, and the Incarnation, differ from contemporary Judaism. As an attempt to lessen my biases, I will not appeal to the NT as a source of divine

---

potentia. However, the people in 1 Samuel did not intend to be faithful to God in their desire for kingship. They had not been directed by God to seek a king. Rather, they desired to pattern their society after gentile politics, and in so doing, God said, "They have rejected me from being king over them" (1 Sam 8:7).

73. See Crawford, "Forgotten Cohanim."

74. Judaism has not always determined its practice by majority rule, but it has been common since talmudic times. The story of the Oven of Akhnai (b. B. Meṣ. 59b; cf. y. Mo'ed Qaṭ. 3:1) states that God cedes authority to the rabbinic sages to determine halakah.

75. Kroeber, "Stimulus Diffusion."

revelation until part 3. Although I believe in the divine inspiration and authority of both the Hebrew Bible and the New Testament, I begin this book with only the assumption that the Hebrew Scriptures have the highest authority concerning what they teach, reflecting their prophetic status and freedom from error. Other sources of knowledge will be accorded less authority as a reflection of their fallibility. Thus, the Hebrew Scriptures serve as the baseline for matters of truth from this point forward until the inclusion of the NT in part 3.

Under these assumptions, it may be healthy to practice a sense of holy skepticism about ideas not originating from the Hebrew Scriptures simply out of a desire to avoid the pitfalls of idolatry, heresy, and doctrinal drift. As a buffer against such influences, I believe ideas from non-Scriptural sources should be reasonably assessed and found innocent of conflict with Scripture before being integrated into a worldview that upholds the Hebrew Scriptures. This, too, is informed by my Protestant mindset, but I hope to demonstrate that this attitude can prove useful in a Jewish sphere as well. Namely, I seek to apply an evenhanded critical method to the doctrines of Maimonides and Kabbalah: keeping what is good and true, and calling for the removal of what is false.

Are there good non-Jewish ideas that belong within Judaism? It is essential to note that the mere derivation of an idea from non-biblical or non-Jewish sources is insufficient for the idea's falsehood. It is an error called the genetic fallacy to deny an idea's truth simply because of the ethnic, religious, or philosophical background of its originator or principal proponent. I may believe that Scripture is the *highest* authority for truth, but it is not the *only* source for truth. Many ideas originating in non-Jewish circles, including Greek sources, pose no conflict with the Bible, Judaism, or Christianity as broadly considered. On the contrary, they ought to be celebrated rather than seen as dangerous examples of syncretism. For example, Aristotle's discussions on logic and habit, Euclid's geometry, Arabic algebra, Vitruvius's architecture, Newton's laws of motion, and the modern scientific method are not found in Scripture nor deduced from any form of Judaism. Yet the fields of knowledge just mentioned have been widely judged as beneficial because they provide accurate intellectual tools to understand and experience the universe God created. These examples of extra-biblical knowledge are uncontroversial because they are widely held to be congruent with God-derived values of truth, goodness, wisdom, and beauty as found in the Scriptures. When integrated into a Jewish worldview, they are examples of intellectual assimilation in a good sense.

However, this book highlights many areas of Greek philosophical thought that were *also* once considered beneficial and were integrated into Jewish thought. Yet, given modern intellectual discoveries, they are highly questionable or definitively disproven. Examples include Aristotelian-Ptolemaic geocentrism, the planets as angelic gatekeepers, astrology, the four Greek elements, reincarnation, *via negativa* theology and interpretation, and more.[76] Unlike the uncontroversial fields of knowledge given above, I find ample reason to question the truth of this second set of ideas. Nevertheless, these *Greek* notions became *Jewish* notions after countless rabbinic sages, mystics, and common people integrated them into their worldview, culture, and practice.

Do disproven extra-biblical ideas deserve to be part of Judaism? While recognizing that Jewish authorities have the right to answer this question on behalf of their communities, this book argues that the answer should usually be no.[77] This question gets to the heart of the chapters ahead of us. My negative answer implies that some expressions of Judaism are better than others because they avoid false extra-biblical ideas. The principle guiding this investigation is as follows: *if an idea originating from non-Jewish sources is based on false science or philosophical assumptions that contradict the Hebrew Bible, then it should be rejected as false and labeled non-Jewish, regardless of its popularity in Jewish thought, philosophy, or Judaism as a whole.*[78] This principle moves away from "Judaism" as a de-

---

76. Although the integration of troublesome false ideas into Christianity is not the focus of this book, similar ideas have been integrated into various Christian expressions in history. Such ideas should also be excised if they compete with biblical or scientific truths. I mention examples and give cautions to Christians along these lines at various places in the book.

77. Some troublesome ideas, through the processes of stimulus diffusion, desacralization, and semantic shift, have been rendered harmless and part of a neutral cultural inheritance. Examples include the names of the seven days after seven pagan gods (associated with the planets) and (in Christian culture) the practice of Christmas trees. Both of these practices have been drained of any idolatrous content or worship and should not be seen as examples of culpable syncretism. These kinds of innocent traditions, in my view, account for why I think that disproven extra-biblical ideas should *usually* (but not always) be removed from Judaism or Christianity. Sometimes I believe we can lighten up.

78. I am aware that this principle, too, is informed by my Protestant attitude and spirit. It could be reformulated as follows: if an idea that originated in non-Christian sources was based on falsified science or assumptions contrary to the Hebrew Scriptures or NT, then the idea ought to be rejected as false and labeled non-Christian,

scriptive sociological title toward a *prescriptive* category that infuses the honorable title of "Jewish" and the teachings of "Judaism" with a sense of divine epistemological warrant.

Under this method, if an idea is proven false, it should be removed from Jewish theology, philosophy, and practice. Doing so would preserve the God of Israel as the ultimate source of truth and would recognize that God does not want his beloved Jewish people to be misled by falsehoods conjured up by pagan minds. If falsehoods are incorporated into Judaism, God does not thereby authorize the falsehoods as Jewish tradition; rather, their incorporation is *syncretism*—the illegitimate blending of incompatible belief systems that ignores the Scriptures' authority to reject false ideas. This is intellectual assimilation at its worst: assimilating aspects of gentile thought and culture that are false.

In sum, this book is concerned about not only the historical origin of ideas within Judaism, but also the ideas' truth value as judged through nonhistorical means. A false idea will be false based on the facts of the matter alone; however, before considering the facts, an idea that originates outside Scripture may be a clue to the idea's falsehood. Yet, this is by no means always the case. An idea that originates within pagan circles may be fully compatible with Scripture. However, if the idea comes from pagan circles and challenges scriptural claims, then the idea ought to be investigated with an elevated level of suspicion.

I recognize it may sound presumptuous for a gentile Christian to advocate a principle whereby he will judge what ought to be accepted as part of Judaism and Jewish thought. Who am I to do so? Some may think it highly ironic that I, a proponent of the Trinity and the Incarnation, would consider myself capable of making such determinations. I admit that such skepticism is fair. My attempts at lessening my bias can go only so far. I accept that Jewish people, not a gentile Christian on the outside, must determine the course of Judaism. To partially mitigate this, the chapters ahead endeavor to cite Jewish scholars—including within Orthodoxy—who have gone before me in calling for a readjustment of the teachings that deserve a place within Judaism today.[79] They, too, have a vision for a Judaism that is free of historically affirmed falsehoods. I seek to amplify these Jewish scholars' voices and complement their work with

---

no matter how popular the idea later became in Christian thought, papal pronouncements, Christian theology, or Christianity as a whole.

79. Some key contributors in this sense include Michael Wyschogrod, David Novak, Daniel Boyarin, Norbert Samuelson, Menachem Kellner, and Marc Shapiro.

additional reasoning. Yet, in contrast to the Jewish Reform movement,[80] I will promote a version of Jewish thought that keeps the integrity and heavenly authority of the Hebrew Scriptures intact. In addition, I will appeal to widely accepted scientific truths and illustrate how they ought to modify common Jewish theological doctrines. This method will enable me to make determinations such as the following:

Aristotelian-Ptolemaic geocentrism:

- Was originally a non-Jewish idea foreign to the Hebrew Scriptures,
- Became a Jewish idea through popularity and rabbinic agreement,
- Formed the basis of Jewish mystical speculations,
- Fortified Maimonides's rejection of divine embodiment (key to this book),
- Has been demonstrably disproven by the telescope, Newtonian physics, and spaceflight,
- And should be removed from Judaism, including the downstream doctrines logically and epistemologically dependent upon it.

Likewise, proto-Trinitarian and proto-incarnational doctrines:

- Were present in various Jewish circles in the Second Temple period,
- Were claimed by such Jewish groups as being deduced from the Hebrew Scriptures,
- Were asserted by the Jewish authors of the NT,
- Were rejected as non-Jewish opinions by the majority of rabbis and Jewish people post-70 CE,
- Retained an underground existence in Jewish mystical streams,
- And may provide better explanations for biblical phenomena than competing Jewish theological models.

Thus, I will be investigating Jewish sources and tracing Jewish ideas over time, considering the origin of the ideas, assessing their truth claims, and advocating for false non-Jewish ideas to be removed from modern Judaism, even if they are popular or have the weight of Jewish tradition.

---

80. Reform Judaism tends to see the Hebrew Scriptures as legendary creations of the Jewish people with little basis in historical fact or divine inspiration (Hirsch and Yosef, *One People, Two Worlds*).

Introduction

I will apply the same methodology to the doctrines of the Trinity and Incarnation, and I will find that they pass the test of Jewish origin, biblical fidelity, no disconfirmations from science, and historical epistemological warrant. My end goal is to demonstrate that the Incarnation—so scandalous in Jewish theology today—deserves a second look.

In particular, this book will employ two approaches to justify the Incarnation in a Jewish frame of reference:

The historical-textual approach. This approach appeals to historical Jewish texts that describe God in modes of being and acting that are similar to incarnational and Trinitarian thought. This field of inquiry has been particularly active since the 1980s due to the publications of both Jewish and Christian scholars such as the late Alan Segal and Larry Hurtado. This is a recommended pathway for framing the Incarnation as a Jewish topic with Jewish precedents. However, I will point out significant drawbacks to this approach, as many Jewish people have alternative objections that this approach does not answer.

The theological-philosophical approach. Most of this book will be devoted to a second and complementary approach to answering objections to the Incarnation. This method recognizes that many of the objections that Jewish people have against Jesus's divinity are grounded in theological and philosophical doctrines that derive from their deeply ingrained worldviews. Given the plausibility structure of their theological and philosophical commitments, the Incarnation falls out of bounds as illogical, impossible, or redundant. In order to build up the plausibility of Jesus's divinity, it will be necessary to investigate and critically examine those aspects of an Orthodox Jewish worldview that make his divinity unbelievable. This will involve a comprehensive theological and philosophical analysis of Maimonidean and kabbalistic thought, as these schools provide the most potent intellectual resources that keep Jewish people from considering the divine claims of the NT. After critically examining these rival worldviews, I will build up the NT teaching of the Incarnation as the pious seeker's best hope for knowing the God of Israel.

2 In Search of the God of the Hebrew Scriptures

[A great Jewish] scholar used to say that inspired Scripture taken as a whole was on account of its obscurity like many locked-up rooms in one house.

—Origen (third century CE)[1]

The secret things belong to the Lord our God.

—Deut 29:29a

2.1. Common Hebrew Scriptures, Different Theological Frameworks

Who is God? This is the loftiest of all questions a human being can ask. Different religious traditions conceptualize God in radically diverse ways even when looking at the same passages in the Hebrew Scriptures. In general, Jews and Christians have come to the Hebrew Scriptures with differing approaches compared to each other and even to those within their own traditions. Orthodox Judaism has emphasized the need for an Oral Torah to explain the Written, whereas historical Christianity has read the Hebrew Scriptures through the lens of the NT. Moreover, the integration of Greek philosophical thought into both Judaism and Christianity has added a further layer to the interpretation of the Scriptures. Although the two faith traditions have often diverged in their answers to

---

1. Origen, *Philocalia* 2.3.

the questions posed by the Hebrew Scriptures, they agree that the Hebrew Bible is a lock that needs a key.

But what about the vantage point of a pious Jewish person in, say, 25 CE, before the Jesus revolution and the rise of the rabbinic movement? Asking contemporary Christians to read the Hebrew Scriptures without thinking of the NT, or Jews without thinking of *Chazal* (the rabbinic sages), can be unfamiliar territory. Nevertheless, this chapter will attempt to portray the Hebrew Scriptures *on their own terms* using a straightforward (*peshat*) approach. I will endeavor to present the foundational theological claims of the Hebrew Scriptures as written, without deciding between later theological grids of any religious or philosophical persuasion.[2] While it is impossible to conduct this exercise without some bias on my part, I believe my attempts will be helpful for seeing how various interpretive frameworks deal with the claims of the Hebrew Scriptures.

To begin, consider a basic question: How do the Hebrew Scriptures describe the nature of God? That may sound like an understandable question, but from the outset, I must point out how such a question is foreign to the Hebrew Scriptures themselves. The question implies that God has a *nature*. Do the Hebrew Scriptures say God has one? No, not exactly. There are no ancient Hebrew words for *nature* or *essence* or *character* or *attributes*.[3] The "nature" of a thing (Greek: φύσις, *physis*) is a concept derived from Greek metaphysics, which was not developed until *after* the writing of most of the Scriptures. All these philosophical concepts originated in the great Greek philosophical quest to describe the phenomena of reality. The closest the Scriptures get to the concept of "God's nature" is the idea that he has a unique name, referred to as the Tetragrammaton (יהוה).[4]

Why do I point this out? It is *not* to invalidate the use of these important Greek metaphysical categories. No, I believe that some metaphysical conceptions that originated in Greek philosophy are essential tools to

---

2. In the Christian world, the method in this chapter is similar to the historical-grammatical interpretation common among Protestant evangelical scholars, yet without integrating the NT into exegetical or theological matters. In the Orthodox Jewish world, the method is closest to the Gush Tanakh method as promoted by Yeshivat Har Etzion. See Kimche, "Assessing Gush Tanakh Method."

3. Postbiblical Hebrew developed equivalent words, such as *elohut* (אֱלֹהוּת) for divine nature and *middot* (מִדּוֹת) for attributes. However, these words are either not found in Scripture (such as *elohut*) or have different meanings in Scripture (i.e., *middot* refers to measurements of length) (*HALOT* s.v. "מִדָּה").

4. See table 5, §3.2.2.

understand the world God created and are *not* examples of syncretism. However, I want to be clear that the question "What is the nature of the God of Israel?" is a question the Scriptures do not directly or explicitly answer. It is still a worthwhile question—actually, it is the central question of this book—but it is vital to be careful and self-aware when responding.

Such self-awareness can come only with practice and reading outside of a person's own religious sphere. Those engaged in particular faith traditions are often comfortable with, and sometimes unaware of, their imposition of philosophical and theological frameworks upon the Hebrew Scriptures. This is especially reinforced if there is a lack of exposure to another religious community's members and literature. It is crucial to be conscious of theological frameworks that are not explicitly derived from the Hebrew Scriptures but are believed by a particular theological community to be implicit within them.[5]

The Hebrew Scriptures' lack of thorough philosophical discussion or common philosophical words indicates the Scriptures are not works of philosophy or metaphysics.[6] It would take centuries before commentators would attempt to understand the Scriptures through Platonic or Aristotelian categories, just as it would take centuries to understand the Scriptures through the lens of the NT and post-temple rabbinic Judaism. Philosopher Charles H. Patterson comments on the relationship between the Hebrew Scriptures and metaphysics:

> Viewed as a complete system of metaphysics, the book which [the biblical authors] produced is lacking in many respects. They left quite untouched most of the problems that come in for discussion in books of philosophy. They were not concerned with the questions of change and identity, the ways of knowing, or the laws that pertain to the structure and operations of the physical universe.[7]

---

5. This is an equal opportunity danger for Jews and Christians. Gericke laments, "Many mainstream Hebrew Bible scholars are Christians who . . . yet remain Platonists at heart" (*Hebrew Bible*, 329).

6. Note Eusebius's reaction after summarizing the views of Aristotle and Plato regarding the mechanics of cosmology, physics, and the "four elements": "Moses and the oracles of the Hebrews trouble themselves about none of these things; and with good reason, because it was thought that those who busied themselves about these matters gained no benefit in regard to the right conduct of life" (*Praep. ev.* 15.8 [*Preparation for Gospel*, 869]). Taken to its furthest extent, Eusebius's comment would disqualify the value of scientific investigation, but for our purposes, it illustrates the limits of the Scriptures' philosophical interest.

7. Patterson, "Philosophy of Old Testament," 65.

Philosopher of religion Jaco Gericke similarly notices the lack of explicit philosophical discussion in the Bible:

> The Hebrew Bible's authors did not spell out [their philosophical] assumptions, as this would have been redundant.... The texts' fundamental presuppositions about the world were assumed to be common knowledge. Since we ourselves are not the implied readers, we cannot assume that we share this knowledge in biblical world views.... The assumptions of the text on such matters are not nonexistent, but are simply unarticulated and implicit.[8]

The incomplete and implicit status of the Hebrew Bible's philosophical and theological system has lent itself to be interpreted using various frameworks, including those of Plato, Aristotle, Maimonides, Kabbalah, and the NT. In light of this, *we must clearly delineate between what the Hebrew Scriptures say and what they have been interpreted as saying when viewed through a later framework.* In my opinion, the Scriptures should be permitted to speak on their own, and any philosophical categories imposed on the Scriptures should be rigorously justified to show that they are entirely in accord with the Scriptures' own truth claims. When this methodology is put into practice, it becomes evident that some philosophical and theological models accord with the Hebrew Scriptures better than others.[9]

2.2. The God Who Is *Echad*

In the quest to know the God of the Scriptures, it is appropriate to begin with the Torah's emphasis on the oneness and the uniqueness of the God of Israel, as found in the daily Jewish prayer, the Shema:

שְׁמַע יִשְׂרָאֵל יְהוָה אֱלֹהֵינוּ יְהוָה אֶחָד׃
Shema Yisrael Adonai Eloheinu Adonai Echad
Hear, O Israel: The LORD our God, the LORD is one. (Deut 6:4)

Scripture is emphatic that Israel shall have no other gods before this God (Exod 20:3). Worship of any other entity is sinful idolatry, for worship is owed to the God of Israel alone. Moreover, the one God does not give his glory to any other (Isa 42:8). He declares, "For I am God, and there is no other; I am God, and there is none like me" (Isa 46:9).

---

8. Gericke, *Hebrew Bible*, 449.
9. For a similar perspective on these matters, see Idel, *Ben*, 602–3.

The key word in the Shema is *echad* (אֶחָד), upon which the meaning of the whole sentence depends. It is usually translated as "one," but there are various uses of *echad* in Scripture. *Echad* can be a cardinal number (Lev 14:10), an ordinal number ("first" [Gen 1:5]), a whole (Exod 36:13), a union of two (Gen 2:24), a union of many (Exod 24:3), a repetition per unit of time (1 Kgs 4:22), and a signifier for "only" (Zech 14:9).[10] How should the word in the Shema be understood? Consulting later Jewish commentators illustrates the difficulty of letting the Scriptures speak for themselves.[11] A variety of options are available, but none have proven decisive. In my opinion, it is not possible to decide the meaning of *echad* based on the text of the Shema alone.[12] Preconceived philosophical and theological worldviews often prove to be the deciding factor on this question. When considering the Hebrew Scriptures on their own, I consider the meaning of *echad* in the Shema as locked, lacking a definitive key. Since I am leaving the potential keys of later frameworks outside the scope of this chapter, for the time being, all that may be said is that the God of Israel is *echad*.

2.3. The Attributes of God

The Hebrew Scriptures portray God through what are best described as *attributes* (or adjectives). While some later philosophers would come to deny that God has attributes, that is not a concern for the current discussion. The classic text that describes the attributes of God is Exod 34:6: "The LORD passed before [Moses] and proclaimed, 'The LORD, the LORD, a God merciful and gracious, slow to anger, and abounding in steadfast love and faithfulness.'" In this passage, the Scriptures assign the following

---

10. *HALOT* s.v. "אֶחָד." Note that the understanding of *echad* as "singularity" does not show up in the word's lexical range in the Hebrew Scriptures.

11. Jewish medieval exegetes Rashi, Rashbam, and Ibn Ezra read the word not as a numerical designation, but rather in the sense of uniqueness or aloneness: the Lord is our God, the Lord *alone*. Thus, the Shema becomes a declaration of Israel's fealty to God, rather than a declaration of monotheism (Carasik, *Deuteronomy*, 46–47). Maimonides understood *echad* as a strict oneness, a *singularity*, in which nothing can be predicated of God except his simple oneness. For more on the complexities of understanding the Shema, see Block, "How Many Is God?"; Wyschogrod, *Abraham's Promise*, 29–42.

12. In his JPS Torah commentary, Tigay says, "For all of its familiarity, the precise meaning of the Shema is uncertain and it permits several possible renderings" (*Deuteronomy*, 76). Also see Messianic Jewish scholar Mark Kinzer's handling of the Shema in "Judaism and Divine-Human Jesus."

attributes to the God of Israel: merciful (רַחוּם, *rachum*), gracious (חַנּוּן, *chanun*), slow to anger (אֶרֶךְ אַפַּיִם, *erech apayim*),[13] abounding in love (רַב־חֶסֶד, *rav-chesed*) and faithfulness (אֱמֶת, *emet*).

Likewise, Deut 32:4 describes him as a God of faithfulness (אֱמוּנָה, *emunah*), and just (צַדִּיק, *tzaddik*) and upright (יָשָׁר, *yashar*). Elsewhere, God is called holy (קָדוֹשׁ, *kadosh*) (Lev 19:2), great (גָּדוֹל, *gadol*) (Ps 145:3), awesome (נוֹרָא, *nora*) (Exod 15:11), mighty (כַּבִּיר, *kabbir*) (Job 36:5), and most high (עֶלְיוֹן, *elyon*) (Gen 14:18). These attributes of God made their way into the daily Jewish prayer called the Amidah, where God is praised as "the great, mighty and awesome God, and most high God."[14] These are positive statements in which attributes are predicated upon God with no hint that they are unintelligible to human minds or inapplicable to God.

2.4. The Unsearchable and Transcendent God

However, while the Scriptures describe God using seemingly understandable attributes, they also present God as being far beyond human rationality and the physical realm. Although human language may capture some truth about who God is, ultimately the human mind and its language cannot comprehend him. Thus, David proclaims, "Great is the Lord, and greatly to be praised, and his greatness is unsearchable" (אֵין חֵקֶר, *ein cheker*) (Ps 145:3). God's understanding is also unsearchable (אֵין חֵקֶר, *ein cheker*) (Isa 40:28). God proclaims, "For as the heavens are higher than the earth, so are my ways higher than your ways and my thoughts than your thoughts" (Isa 55:9). Just as the distance between the heavens and the earth is illustrative of God's transcending thoughts, so too it illustrates his transcendence beyond the physical realm. King Solomon proclaims at the temple's dedication, "Heaven and the highest heaven cannot contain you; how much less this house that I have built!" (1 Kgs 8:27). Job's friend Zophar, while questionable in other areas, concurs when he considers "the limit of the Almighty" and confesses, "It is higher than heaven—what can you do?" (Job 11:7–9).

The Hebrew Scriptures do not use abstract philosophical terminology to describe God as infinite and transcendent. Nevertheless, it is said that humanity's most excellent thoughts about God cannot come close to understanding him. This presents a philosophical problem that the

---

13. Literally, "long of nose," so his "nostrils" take a long time to flare.
14. Adapted from Davis, *Siddur for Weekdays*, 132.

Scriptures do not address: How ought one balance the unsearchability of God with the Scriptures' own use of rational descriptions of God? How can God be both great and unsearchably great at the same time? How can words like "just," "righteous," and "holy"—words that we *think* we have a grasp on at least partially—be used to describe God if he is beyond understanding? Is it foolish to think that these words describe God, or is there something tangible and objective about these words that actually describe him? Later theologians would attempt to answer these questions, for the Hebrew Scriptures do not untangle the knot for the reader.

2.5. The Incomparable and Comparable God

The prophet Isaiah takes the idea of God's transcendence to the highest heights when he records God as saying, "To whom then will you compare me [תְדַמְּיוּנִי, *tedammeyuni*], that I should be like him?" (Isa 40:25) Later on, God says, "To whom will you liken me [תְדַמְּיוּנִי, *tedammeyuni*] and make me equal, and compare me, that we may be alike [נִדְמֶה, *nidmeh*]?" (Isa 46:5). The implied answer to these rhetorical questions is that none can be compared or likened to God.

The root of the key Hebrew words in these verses is *damah* (דמה), used to indicate likeness or resemblance between two things.[15] The word is often used in the Hebrew Scriptures to make analogies and metaphors. For example: "If the LORD of hosts had not left us a few survivors, we should have been like Sodom, and become like [דָּמִינוּ, *daminu*] Gomorrah" (Isa 1:9). When the root Hebrew word is used as a verb in relation to God, in all instances but three it conveys God's incomparability.[16]

Other passages convey the same message as Isaiah using different Hebrew words. Moses and the people of Israel sing, "Who is like you, O LORD, among the gods? Who is like you, majestic in holiness, awesome in glorious deeds, doing wonders?" (Exod 15:11) The psalmist declares, "Your righteousness, O God, reaches the high heavens. You who have done great things, O God, who is like you?" (Ps 71:19)

Yet there is a striking second idea in the Hebrew Scriptures that is in tension with God's incomparability. In the creation account, we read, "Then God said, 'Let us make man in our image, after our likeness'"

---

15. *HALOT* s.v. "דמה I"; *TDOT* s.v. "דָּמָה I."
16. *TDOT* s.v. "דָּמָה I." The exceptions given are Ps 102:7; 144:4; Job 40:9.

(בִּדְמוּתֵנוּ, *kidmutenu*) (Gen 1:26).[17] Here the noun form of *damah* is employed to indicate a similarity or likeness between God and the first man. The idea is repeated in Gen 5:1, where it is said of Adam, "He [God] made him in the likeness [*bidemut*] of God." Immediately thereafter, it is said that Adam "fathered a son in his own likeness [*bidemuto*], after his image, and named him Seth" (Gen 5:3). A parallelism is at play here: just as there is a similarity or likeness between Adam and his son Seth, so too there is a similarity or likeness between God and his implied son, Adam.

Another striking use of *damah* is found in Ezekiel, where the prophet has an intense vision of the heavenly throne. Ezekiel writes, "Seated above the likeness of a throne was a likeness [דְּמוּת, *demut*] with a human appearance" (Ezek 1:26). Theologians Stephen Wellum and Peter Gentry note,

> Ezekiel 1:26 is instructive since, opposite to Genesis 1:26, which speaks of humanity created in the likeness of God, Ezekiel's vision speaks of God appearing in the likeness of humanity. Either way, God and humanity are morphologically similar.[18]

Thus, the Hebrew Scriptures convey two messages in tension: God is incomparable, and humanity retains a likeness with God. This tension rightly generates questions. Can God be compared with humanity or not? If so, which aspects of humanity are likened to God? If those aspects can be identified, what is the extent or the magnitude of the likeness? Is the likeness one of complete overlap, such that aspects of God's nature are perfectly and completely imprinted into humanity? Or, is the likeness lesser in extent, like a fractional amount? Or, given God's transcendence, is the likeness itself unquantifiable? The Hebrew Scriptures do not answer these questions, and later Jewish interpreters and theologians would come to various opinions on the matter.

2.6. The Eternal and Immutable God

God is described as the everlasting God (אֱלֹהֵי עוֹלָם, *elohei olam*) (Isa 40:28), who has no beginning and no end, which is the Scriptures' way of describing his eternality. Genesis describes him as the Creator of physical

---

17. Oftentimes Jewish-Christian discourse is preoccupied with the plural "us" in this verse, with the Trinity in mind. This book's focus is different: the meaning of "likeness" with God is much more important for issues related to the Incarnation.

18. Gentry and Wellum, *God's Kingdom*, 77.

time in the beginning (Gen 1:1) and thus his existence preceded the beginning of time, a concept that finite and time-bound human minds cannot comprehend. A psalm attributed to Moses states, "Before the mountains were brought forth, or ever you had formed the earth and the world, from everlasting to everlasting you are God" (Ps 90:2).

Building on God's eternality, the Scriptures indicate that God is unchangeable or immutable. Speaking about the heavens and the earth, which God created, the psalmist exclaims:

> They will perish, but you will remain;
> they will all wear out like a garment.
> You will change them like a robe, and they will pass away,
> but you are the same, and your years have no end. (Ps 102:26–27)

In this passage, God's immutability is likened to freedom from corruption and decay. God's immutability is also defined by his trustworthy purposes and declarations. He is anything but flippant with his words. Instead, "God is not man, that he should lie, or a son of man, that he should change his mind" (Num 23:19).[19] The prophet Samuel alludes to Numbers, stating that just as God does not lie, so too he does not change his mind (1 Sam 15:29). In Ezekiel, God declares, "I have spoken; it shall come to pass; I will do it. I will not go back" (Ezek 24:14).

The most explicit statement about God's immutability is found in Mal 3:6, which says, "For I the LORD do not change; therefore you, O children of Jacob, are not consumed." The idea is that God is unwavering in his covenant with Abraham—a covenant of blessing and not destruction—such that God will not allow Israel to be destroyed even though she sins against him.[20]

---

19. This verse's initial clause is often used as a proof text against the Incarnation. This is a shallow reading. Numbers affirms that God, in his eternal nature, is not a man, nor is he prone to deceit or flippancy. When followers of Jesus say that Jesus is God, they are saying that the Son of God chose to take onto himself a full human nature while remaining divine in all aspects he was before. The Son of God in his divine nature is still not a man. But in his human nature, he is. So, believers in Jesus's divinity can affirm this verse wholeheartedly, clarifying that God's divine nature did not change in any respect when the Son was born as a Jew for human salvation.

20. Analytic theologians have pointed out that the Scriptures' description of God's relation to time and change is underdetermined and does not necessarily result in a timeless deity. For the theological conversation on these matters, see Ganssle, *God and Time*; Mullins, *The End of the Timeless God*; Craig, *Time and Eternity*; Feinberg, *No One Like Him*, 375–436.

2.7. The Immanent, Omnipresent God

Without using the theological terms "immanence" or "omnipresence," the Hebrew Scriptures describe God as being *present in* and *aware of* all places at all times. Moses declares "that the LORD is God in heaven above and on the earth beneath" (Deut 4:39)—that is, inclusive of all reality spiritual and material. David reflects on the immanence of God when his mind wanders to the furthest and remotest parts of creation and affirms that, even there, God is present (Ps 139:7–10). Solomon warns that "the eyes of the LORD are in every place, keeping watch on the evil and the good" (Prov 15:3). God is not limited to perception from a single location, or from a particular angle: he perceives all from all angles and all places. In fact, as Jeremiah writes, the LORD fills heaven and earth such that there are no secrets for him (Jer 23:23–24). Even in *Sheol*, the abode of the dead, God may manifest his power (Amos 9:2; Ps 139:8). Truly no place is inaccessible to God, for he is everywhere present.

2.8. The Localized God of Spatial Relations

The Scriptures do not untangle the ability or inability of language to describe God. In the same way, they do not untangle the mixture of passages that affirm God's omnipresence with passages that affirm his localization to time and space. The Hebrew Bible speaks forthrightly about God having spatial concepts applied to him.

Table 1. Spatial Concepts Applied to God

Spatial Concept	Scriptural Examples
Up/Down Relations	Gen 11:5–7; 17:22; 18:21; 28:13; 35:13; Exod 19:3, 18–20; 24:1; 2 Sam 22:10; Isa 63:15; Ezek 11:23
Near/Far Relations	Gen 18:22–23; Exod 3:5; 20:21; 24:1–2; Num 16:9; Jer 30:21; Ezek 44:13; Mal 3:5
Left/Right Relations	1 Kgs 22:19; 2 Chr 18:18; Job 23:9
The Place of God	*Makom* (place): Exod 33:21; Ezek 3:12; *Sham* (there): Exod 17:6; 25:22; *Po* (here): Deut 5:31

The Scriptures speak of God moving up and down, or being up or down from a particular location, such as when Moses ascended Sinai to speak with God. The Exodus narrative consistently portrays God as if he is located at the top of the mountain. For example:

- There Israel encamped before the mountain, while Moses *went up to God*. The LORD called to him *out of the mountain*. (Exod 19:2–3)
- Then he said to Moses, "*Come up to the* LORD, you and Aaron, Nadab, and Abihu, and seventy of the elders of Israel, and worship from *afar*." (Exod 24:1)

Likewise, the Scriptures portray God as if one can be spatially near or far from him, or stand to the left or the right of him. Consider the prophet Micaiah, who declares, "I saw the LORD sitting on his throne, and all the host of heaven standing beside him on his right hand and on his left" (1 Kgs 22:19). When God speaks to Moses and tells him that he can see God's back, he tells Moses to go to "a place by me" (מָקוֹם אִתִּי, *makom iti*) (Exod 33:21). Ezekiel speaks of the place (מָקוֹם, *makom*) of the glory of the LORD (Ezek 3:12). Then there is the striking passage of God sending an angel (messenger) who has the name of the LORD "in him" (Exod 23:20–21). How can this be? God gives his holy name and glory to no other (Isa 42:8). Likewise, Exod 3:4 describes God (אֱלֹהִים, *elohim*) calling to Moses from within a fiery bush—a localized created entity.

All this biblical language applies spatial concepts to God, but none of these passages addresses how such language can apply to a divine being who is omnipresent and spiritual. It is unclear how a spiritual being can be described as localized in time and space. How is he any more present *there* rather than *here*? The Scriptures do not explain or give any indication there is a theological problem here whatsoever. Spatial language for God is not controversial in the Scriptures and is not warned against or reinterpreted to mean something other than a localized presence. It portrays God's simultaneous omnipresence and potential localization as two truths without contradiction.

2.9. The Personal, Rational, and Emotive God

The Hebrew Scriptures describe the God of Israel as having a will, a mind, a power, a plan, and rationality. He is unpredictable, patient, and merciful; he judges, chooses, acts, and protects. God is an active force in the world according to his own purposes. He cannot be mastered like one can master the movement of the stars and planets with mathematical equations. God's actions are not deterministic, but rather free, as seen when he expresses his purpose to raise up Pharaoh (Exod 9:15–16). God makes it clear that he could have chosen not to raise up Pharaoh, meaning that God's actions are contingent upon his will. God does not act in the same way toward all beings, or else he would be a constant and impersonal force. Likewise, God can choose to set his love on one people (Israel) while not setting that same love on others (Deut 7:7). He can choose to redeem Israel from slavery after 430 years (Exod 12:40), but not to redeem her at 429 years. He has a secret knowledge that only he retains, but he can choose to reveal his knowledge to Israel for his purposes (Deut 29:29).

The rationality of God is first revealed in the creation account where he employs words to create the universe (Gen 1:3, 6; etc.). For both God and humanity, words have an inherent meaning with rationality, syntax, and purpose. Moreover, the words of God have power (Isa 55:11; Jer 23:29) to make things come into being *ex nihilo* (out of nothing). In the written Scriptures, God has given humanity a different kind of words that do not create material but rather reveal truth to human minds and hearts (Dan 2:22; Ps 86:11). God communicates with humanity because he is a rational God who has created people in his image to think rationally as well (Gen 1:26).

The personal characteristics of God as described in the Scriptures are not limited to categories of rationality or will. The Scriptures also describe God as experiencing *emotions*:

Table 2. Emotions of God

Anger	Regret	Joy
Exod 4:14; Num 11:1, 10; Deut 6:15; 2 Sam 24:1; Ezek 38:18	Gen 6:6–7; 1 Sam 15:11, 35; 2 Sam 24:16	Zeph 3:17; Isa 62:5; Jer 32:41
Jealousy	Hatred and Wrath	Love
Exod 20:5; Deut 4:24; Josh 24:19; Nah 1:2	Prov 6:16; Isa 61:8; Amos 5:21; Exod 15:7; Nah 1:2; Ezek 25:14	Exod 15:13; 34:6; Neh 9:2; 1 Sam 20:14

The ability to experience emotions is an important attribute of human nature. These passages appear to describe emotions as part of the divine experience as well. Even though human emotions can be untrustworthy, unbalanced, and lead to sin, the Scriptures never indicate that a God with emotions is controversial or should be understood in some other way.

In sum, the Hebrew Scriptures portray God as acting in three modes of thought-experience with which human beings are familiar: rationality, will, and emotion. Nowhere do the Scriptures indicate that interpreters should deny God's rationality, will, or capability for emotion. Only subsequent generations of thinkers would begin questioning the passibility of God—that is, his ability to experience passions, or emotions—on grounds outside the Hebrew Scriptures.[21]

2.10. The Omniscient God

The Hebrew Scriptures never use the word "omniscience" for God's relationship with knowledge, nor is God plainly described as "knowing all things" in an abstract sense. Nevertheless, the range and depth of God's knowledge as given in Scripture lead to the reasonable inference that he knows all. The Scriptures say, "The LORD is a God of knowledge" (1 Sam 2:3), even "perfect in knowledge" (Job 37:16). The psalmist writes that God "looks down from heaven; he sees all the children of man ... and observes all their deeds" (Ps 33:13–15). He also knows the hearts, plans, and thoughts of all people (1 Kgs 8:39). Even before individuals come into existence, God knows them (Jer 1:5). God's knowledge extends even to what *would* happen under different circumstances (counterfactuals), not just what *will* happen (1 Sam 23:9–13; Jer 38:17–18). Thus, as an aspect of God's transcendence (Isa 55:8–9), God's knowledge exceeds the capability of the human mind to understand.

2.11. The Unseen God

The Scriptures portray God as both transcendent and immanent. Although these two concepts are different from each other, they both imply that God is a purely spiritual being and has an unseen presence. For example, if God is transcendent, then no faculty of the mind, let alone human vision, can fully comprehend God. If God is omnipresent, when humans see a tree or a mountain, God is present among the objects, even though God is ontologically distinct from them and is not directly seen.

---

21. The definition of impassibility is controversial. In Greek philosophy, *impassibility* is the utter inability to experience "passions," that is, emotions. Both Maimonides and Kabbalah affirm the Greek notion of God's impassibility, although Kabbalah's dual-tiered theology also affirms that God's revealed *Sefirot* manifest emotions. When Christian theologians affirm impassibility, they often define it as "not capable of irrational and unbalanced human emotions." This book does not address how to answer this complex question. For more discussion, see Matz and Thornhill, *Divine Impassibility*.

There is one explicit mention of God's unseen nature in the Hebrew Scriptures.[22] God describes humanity's inability to see him when Moses ascends the mountain and asks to see his glory. The LORD responds to Moses's request:

> And he said, "I will make all my goodness pass before you and will proclaim before you my name 'The LORD.' And I will be gracious to whom I will be gracious, and will show mercy on whom I will show mercy. But," he said, "you cannot see my face, for man shall not see me and live." (Exod 33:19–20)

If a human, even one as holy as Moses, were to see God, that human would die. Because God wanted to preserve Moses's life, he protected Moses from beholding his face. While there are many passages describing people's fear of seeing God (in line with the threat about ceasing to live),[23] Exod 33:20–23 is the only place in the Hebrew Scriptures where human inability to see God is mentioned.

2.12. The Seen God

Considering Moses's inability to see God and live (Exod 33:20), it may seem that God is ontologically unseeable; that is, it is physically and metaphysically impossible for finite human beings to see God. Nevertheless and quite mysteriously, the Hebrew Scriptures report people who *do* actually see God, yet they remain alive.

Many historical narratives in the Hebrew Scriptures can be called theophanies: events where God appears in a visibly perceivable way.[24] There are at least thirty instances in the Hebrew Scriptures where God is spoken of as "being seen" or "appearing."[25] Sometimes the context is in a

---

22. Although Deut 4:15 is commonly cited as an example of God's inability to be seen, I do not believe the verse makes the claim. Moses is merely stating that Israel did not see any form when she was at Sinai. In contrast, Moses himself *did* see God's glory (Num 12:8). Wolfson writes, "One must distinguish between the prohibition of depicting God in images and the claim that God cannot be manifest in a body. One may presume, as indeed the evidence from the Bible seems to suggest, that God is capable of assuming corporeal form, although that form should not be represented pictorially" (Wolfson, "Judaism and Incarnation," 242).

23. See the next section.

24. For an overview of the theophanies in the Hebrew Bible, see Cole, *God Who Became Human*, 49–75.

25. The instances can be found by searching for all uses of the Hebrew word *ra'ah* (ראה) in the Niphal stem with God as the subject of the verb: Gen 12:7; 17:1; 18:1; 26:2,

dream in the night, but in most instances the people doing the seeing are conscious. Sample passages include:

- Then the Lord appeared [וַיֵּרָא, *vayyera*] to Abram. (Gen 12:7)
- God appeared [וַיֵּרָא, *vayyera*] to Jacob again. (Gen 35:9)
- For you, O Lord, are seen [נִרְאָה, *nirah*] face to face. (Num 14:14)
- And the Lord appeared [וַיֵּרָא, *vayyera*] in the tent in a pillar of cloud. (Deut 31:15)

Additionally, the Torah says Moses himself saw God, albeit in a partial and mysterious way. In Exod 24:10–11, Moses, Aaron, Nadab, Abihu, and the seventy elders all "saw the God of Israel" and "beheld God." Furthermore, Moses "beholds the form of the Lord" (Num 12:8). After God kept Moses from seeing his face (Exod 33:20), he still enabled Moses to see his back (Exod 33:23). The text does not explain why it is permissible (and *not* deadly) to see God's back, whereas it *is* deadly to see God's face. It does not elaborate on what the nature of God's back is or whether it should be understood physically or figuratively. The visible quality of God's back remains a mysterious question the Torah does not address.

Another example from the life of Moses is Moses's encounter with the burning bush. In Exod 3:6, Moses hid his face from looking at the bush "for he was afraid to look at God."[26] However, before this in vv. 2–3, Moses did indeed look at the burning bush that somehow contained God. Only *after* God spoke from the bush did Moses hide his face. Thus, in the first episode, Moses saw one part of God (his back) and not another (his face), and in this encounter, Moses briefly looked at God in the bush before turning away out of fear. Later in life, Moses reflected on this and said that he encountered "him who dwells in the bush" (Deut 33:16), which in its context clearly refers to God.

Further examples of theophanies may be found throughout the Scriptures. Isaiah proclaims, "My eyes have seen the King, the Lord of hosts!" (Isa 6:5). After wrestling with a man, Jacob exclaims, "I have seen God face to face, and yet my life has been delivered" (Gen 32:30). Hagar reports seeing God (Gen 16:13). Israel responds to the revelation of the

---

24; 35:9; 48:3; Exod 3:16; 4:1, 5; 16:10; Lev 9:4, 6, 23; Num 14:10, 14; 16:19; 17:7; 20:6; Deut 31:15; 2 Sam 22:11; 1 Kgs 3:5; 9:2; 11:9; 2 Chr 1:7; 7:12; Ps 102:17; Isa 60:2; Jer 31:3; Zech 9:14.

26. Later Jewish tradition interprets *Elohim* (אֱלֹהִים) to mean "angel" instead of "God." For example, Ibn Ezra says: "The messenger—the angel—speaks in the voice of the One who sent him" (Carasik, *Exodus*, 17).

Ten Commandments by saying, "This day we have seen God speak with man, and man still live" (Deut 5:24).

Thus, there are many claims in the Scriptures that people saw God. But how is this possible, if no one may see God and live? (Exod 33:20). Scripture leaves two truths before its readers as a tangled knot: God is unseeable in one passage, and God is seen in many others. Jewish mysticism scholar Elliot Wolfson writes, "The paradox that the hidden God appears to human beings in multiple forms—including, most significantly, that of an anthropos [man]—is the enduring legacy of the prophetic tradition that has informed and challenged Judaism throughout the ages."[27]

2.13. The Anthropomorphic God

One of the most striking features of biblical descriptions of God is the willingness to describe God in humanlike terms. Although God is not human, he is described as having physical human features such as eyes, a nose, feet, and hands. Descriptions of God as humanlike are called anthropomorphisms, from the Greek for "form of man." They fall under a class of language called *God talk*: when humans attempt to speak about who and what God is.[28] Below are some of the anthropomorphic actions the Hebrew Scriptures describe God as taking part in:

Table 3. Anthropomorphic Divine Actions in the Hebrew Bible

Action	Scriptural Examples
Seeing with eyes	Prov 15:3; Ps 34:15; Zech 4:10; 2 Chr 16:9
Hearing with ears	Num 11:1; 1 Sam 8:21; Ps 34:15; Isa 59:1–2
Actions with feet	Walking: Gen 3:8; Standing: Gen 28:13; Ezek 11:23; Amos 7:7; 9:1; Zech 14:4; Having feet: Exod 24:10; 2 Sam 22:10; Zech 14:4
Actions with hands/arms	Planting: Gen 2:8; Holding: Isa 41:10; Lifting up: Ps 145:14; Saving: Isa 59:1
Actions with mouth	Laughing: Ps 2:4; Prov 1:26; Whispering: 1 Kgs 19:12
Actions with nose	Smelling: Gen 8:21; Lev 26:31; Angry with nose: Num 12:9
Actions with body	Sitting on throne: 1 Kgs 22:19; Isa 6:1; Ps 9:7; 47:8; Wearing clothes: Isa 6:1; Dan 7:9; Isa 63:1–6

27. Wolfson, "Judaism and Mysticism," 2:931.

28. On God talk, see Astley, *Exploring God-Talk*; Geisler and Feinberg, *Introduction to Philosophy*, 304–19.

Each of these passages presents God as if he is a human being with a physical body, performing physical actions. However, few passages are as striking as Ezekiel's vision of the heavenly throne room, complete with a physical description of God:

> And above the expanse over their heads there was the likeness of a throne, in appearance like sapphire; and seated above the likeness of a throne was a likeness with a human appearance [דְּמוּת כְּמַרְאֵה אָדָם, *demut kemareh adam*]. And upward from what had the appearance of his waist I saw as it were gleaming metal, like the appearance of fire enclosed all around. And downward from what had the appearance of his waist I saw as it were the appearance of fire, and there was brightness around him. (Ezek 1:26–27)

Although Ezekiel nuances his words with the double abstraction of "likeness of the appearance of" a man, he still intends his readers to believe there is something that looks like a human being sitting on the heavenly throne. Moreover, this appearance of a human being has a waist. This type of physical description of God in his heavenly abode reappears in Dan 7, where the Ancient of Days has white clothing and hair on his head and sits on his throne (Dan 7:9).

In sum, God talk in the Scriptures is often strikingly physical, despite the theological and philosophical challenges presented by a God with a positive relationship with physicality. The meaning of anthropomorphisms is left open, without any philosophical or theological methods present in the Scriptures to solve it.

2.14. Theological and Philosophical Options for Developing a Biblical Doctrine of God

This chapter sought to summarize the foundational assertions of the Hebrew Scriptures regarding the God of Israel without relying on later Greek philosophy or the interpretations of the rabbinic sages or the NT. The method sought to allow the Scriptures to speak for themselves, delineating between what the Scriptures say and what the Scriptures have been interpreted as saying when viewed through a later framework.

Under this methodology, many theological and philosophical questions were left unanswered. The Hebrew Scriptures were indifferent to many controversial topics that would vex later philosophers and theologians. The Scriptures contain many descriptions of God, but they do not present a comprehensive theology or hermeneutical method to bind them all together. Rather, the Scriptures present a series of particulars without a unified universal theology. It appears this omission did not trouble Israel during the biblical period, but since the Second Temple period, Jewish thinkers have been unsatisfied with leaving these questions open. In today's context, the Hebrew Scriptures beg for a theological and philosophical explanation about the nature of God. The trajectory of such an explanation is unclear; one could go multiple ways in attempting to answer the Scriptures' unresolved topics. Thus, in light of the discussions above, various options arise for important theological categories in the Hebrew Scriptures:

The attributes of God: There are three options for dealing with the attributes of God as presented in the Scriptures. They could be *univocal* attributes, meaning that the words used to describe God mean the same thing in describing him as when describing anything else. For instance, when describing God as merciful (as in Exod 34:6) and a human being as merciful (as in 2 Sam 22:26), the authors mean exactly the same thing, with no difference between the human's attribute of mercy and God's attribute of mercy. Second, they could be *equivocal* attributes, meaning that the attribute of mercy signifies something qualitatively different when applied to God compared to when it is applied to anything else. Third, they could be *analogical* attributes, meaning that the attribute of mercy applied to humans is analogous and derived from the attribute of mercy applied to God, but is distinguished by quality and quantity. In theology, these three options are called *via positiva*, *via negativa*, and *via analogia*, respectively. The Hebrew Scriptures do not take sides on this topic. However, later in this book I will affirm the *via analogia* (analogical) view, while having secondary utility for the other two modes in particular situations.

Transcendence and immanence: There are three options in two classes when considering how to resolve the Scriptures' mutual affirmations of God's transcendence and immanence. Option 1: Take an either/or approach, which involves affirming one attribute at the expense of the other, necessitating a hermeneutic that negates the passages of the losing attribute. This approach could affirm the passages that teach transcendence and develop a method of figurative interpretation that denies omnipresence. Option 2: Choose the reverse, resulting in pantheism. This is the first class, an either/or approach. The second class of approach, which is both/and, is to affirm the transcendence *and* the immanence of God *in mystery*, that is, without clear rational explanation how God can exist in both modes simultaneously. This is option 3, and I will affirm this both/and view. The both/and view is compatible with both panentheism and classical NT theism, and I will affirm the latter.

Incomparability and divine likeness: The same options occur here: three options based on either/or and both/and. Option 1: Affirm that God is utterly incomparable and deny the actuality of any likeness or similarity between humanity and God. Option 2: Affirm that humanity shares likeness with God and deny that God is incomparable, because at least he is comparable to humanity. Option 3: Affirm that God is both incomparable and comparable to humanity at the same time, according to a mystery that is not solved in the Hebrew Scriptures. I will affirm this third both/and view with a solution that develops out of Messiah being the image of the invisible God (Col 1:15), the second Adam (Rom 5; 1 Cor 15:47), in conjunction with the principle of *via analogia*.

Immanence and localization. The same options occur here: three options based on either/or and both/and. Option 1: Affirm God's omnipresence (immanence) and deny the possibility of his localization by developing an interpretation that neutralizes all localization. Option 2: Affirm localization and deny omnipresence by developing an interpretation that neutralizes omnipresence. Option 3: Affirm that God can be both immanent and potentially localized at the same time, a position that must be held in mystery. I will affirm this third both/and view.

The unseen and seen God. The same three either/or and both/and options exist here. Option 1: God is fully unable to be seen (usually with the assumption that he is permanently and ontologically incorporeal), and thus passages that describe him as being seen must be reinterpreted. Option 2: God is able to be seen, and thus passages that describe him as unseeable must be reinterpreted. Option 3: God is both seeable and unseeable according to a mystery not revealed in the Hebrew Scriptures. I will adopt the both/and view, principally on the basis of the added clarity afforded to this topic by the NT. I will affirm the Son of God as potentially visible due to his role as mediator, and the Father as invisible, yet both equally divine.

Anthropomorphisms. There are three options for dealing with the anthropomorphisms given in the Scriptures. Two are simple extremes, and the third is a mediating position. Option 1: Interpret *all* anthropomorphisms as literal descriptions of God, leading to a fully corporeal and humanlike understanding of God. Option 2: Interpret *none* of the anthropomorphisms as literal descriptions of God, leading to a fully incorporeal understanding of God, where all anthropomorphisms are mere figures of speech. Option 3: Interpret *some* of the anthropomorphisms as literal descriptions of God, and *some* of them as figures of speech, leading to a limited and nuanced understanding of God as non-essentially corporeal yet humanlike in some situations. I will affirm this third view, which is philosophically more difficult than the other two, as I will need to provide a criterion to determine which descriptions are literal and which ones are not. When I affirm that an anthropomorphism is speaking literally about God, I will assign its referent to the Son of God acting in time and space.

In sum, the ancient Hebrew canon does not give clear definition to the ways, attributes, and nature of God. When considering the wide range of later theological discourse, the Hebrew Scriptures leave some topics unmentioned and implied (divine ontology, causation, and impossibility), some unclear (anthropomorphisms), and others apparently affirmed in paradox without concern (immanence and transcendence). Jewish and Christian philosophers and theologians have provided their own solutions to these unanswered questions, although they have diverged over time. Even so, many aspects of Jewish and Christian thought align with each other. Thus, today's reader has multiple options for answering the unanswered theological questions generated by a plain reading of the Hebrew Scriptures. Although I have been forthright in my own opinions on these matters, I have not yet given argument or reason for my positions. It remains to be seen which solution(s) are the most credible and faithful to the text of the Hebrew Scriptures. I will revisit these issues during subsequent discussions about the differing solutions given by later Jewish and Christian scholars.

3   The Historical-Textual Approach to Contextualizing the Incarnation

The reasons that many Jews came to believe that Jesus was divine was because they were already expecting that the Messiah/Christ would be a god-man. This expectation was part and parcel of Jewish tradition.

—Daniel Boyarin[1]

THE PREVIOUS CHAPTER MAINTAINED that the Hebrew Scriptures' portrayal of the God of Israel is like a lock without a key. How is God's oneness to be understood? How can God be seen and unseen? How are anthropomorphisms to be interpreted? Are descriptions of God's historical appearances to be viewed as examples of God's physical, bodily presence or not? The Hebrew Scriptures never directly answer these questions, and it would be the task of later Jewish interpreters to provide keys to the Scriptures' secrets.

The NT gives a set of answers to these questions that are best expressed in the doctrines of the Trinity and theophanies involving divine embodiment. These answers were borne out of a series of books written by first-century Jewish men, and the answers are also accepted within contemporary Messianic Judaism. However, the wider world recognizes the NT's answers as those promoted by "Christianity." Since this set of answers is not accepted by modern Judaism, some contemporary Jewish and Christian scholars have attempted to illustrate how Judaism *used to*

---

1. Boyarin, *Jewish Gospels*, 56; emphasis in original.

promote doctrines similar to Christian theology. I call this the historical-textual approach.

The historical-textual approach to contextualizing the Incarnation involves highlighting the ancient Jewish interpreters whose solutions share an unmistakable resemblance with Trinitarian and incarnational thought, thereby illustrating the compatibility of the doctrines to a Jewish mindset. Long before Nicaea, Chalcedon, and the influx of gentile thought in Christianity, various Jewish interpreters spoke of God in seemingly "Christian" modes of thought. There is evidence of this phenomenon in multiple eras and segments of Judaism. Modern scholarship draws parallels to the Trinity and the Incarnation from the Hebrew Scriptures themselves,[2] Second Temple Jewish works,[3] rabbinic works,[4] and mystical Jewish works,[5] showing Jewish precedents for the concepts. Scholars have coined the word *binitarianism*, a unity of two divine entities as one, to describe a widespread Jewish belief present in both the Second Temple and post-temple eras.[6] The Jewish interpreters of these periods adhered to God's incorporeality while *also* asserting that God had a divine Son or angel united with him who was uncreated and could manifest himself physically. This enabled Jewish interpreters to handle both incorporeal and corporeal texts in Scripture without the need to appeal to allegory and metaphor. Another solution, illustrated in rabbinic circles, was to postulate divine corporealism, the belief that God in his eternal nature possesses a physical body. This chapter will survey a range of these Jewish precedents and comment on the benefits and limitations of adapting the historical-textual approach to argue for the deity of Jesus.

---

2. Sommer, *Bodies of God*; Wyschogrod, "Jewish Perspective on Incarnation."

3. Hurtado, *One God, One Lord*; Boyarin, *Jewish Gospels*; Boyarin, *Border Lines*, ch. 5; Hengel, *Studies in Early Christology*; Fletcher-Louis, *Christological Origins*; Orlov, *Glory of Invisible God*; Schäfer, *Two Gods in Heaven*; Bauckham, *Son of Man*.

4. Alan Segal, *Two Powers in Heaven*; Boyarin, *Border Lines*, ch. 6; Boyarin, "Two Powers in Heaven"; Boyarin, "Beyond Judaisms"; Boyarin, "Enoch, Ezra"; M. Shapiro, *Limits of Orthodox Theology*, 45–70; Orlov, *Glory of Invisible God*; G. Moore, "Intermediaries in Jewish Theology."

5. See especially Moshe Idel's survey (*Ben*). Shaul Magid argues that Hasidic thought developed in an incarnational direction because it was outside the "gaze" of Christian authorities and influence (*Hasidism Incarnate*, 5). See also Wolfson: "Judaism and Incarnation"; "Metatron and Shi'ur Qomah."

6. Scholars disagree on the precise definition of the term "binitarianism," with some preferring a strict definition that requires worship of the second entity (e.g., Hurtado) and others using the term more loosely (e.g., Boyarin).

Part I: Setting the Stage for the Incarnation

3.1. Divine Intermediaries in Hellenistic Judaism

Hellenistic Jews of the Second Temple period and the rabbinic sages who followed them asserted the existence of divine intermediaries who could bridge the gulf between humanity and God.[7] Among the principal Hellenistic intermediaries were the *Logos* (Word) and the *Sophia* (Wisdom) of God. I will discuss these two intermediaries before moving onto rabbinic examples.

3.1.1. Philo's Logos (Λόγος)

The first Jewish thinker to postulate the absolute incorporeality of God, *via negativa*, and the theory of divine emanations was the Jewish-Hellenistic philosopher Philo of Alexandria (ca. 20 BCE–50 CE). Philo attempted to synthesize Platonic and Stoic philosophy with the teachings of Moses; that is, a fusion of Greek natural theology and Hebrew revealed theology. Philo believed there was no discord between the greatness of Platonic thought and the greatness of divine revelation in Scripture.[8]

Although he understands God as transcendent and unknowable, Philo says that God interacts with the world through his mediating Logos, which is uncreated in one sense, but dependent upon God in another.[9] The Logos is both the rationality that emanates from God and is united with God. Philo writes of the Logos, "He is Himself the Image of God, chiefest of all Beings intellectually perceived, placed nearest, with no intervening distance, to the Alone truly existent One."[10] Philo calls the Logos, "the Name of God," the "First-born" of God, and "the archangel."[11] He even calls the Logos "the second God"[12]—not intending the existence of more than one God, but rather that the Logos is both numerically separate and somehow united with the God of Israel.

---

7. There are far more texts related to early Jewish messianism and intermediaries than will be discussed in this chapter. For a lengthy collation of many relevant passages, see Lanier, *Corpus Christologicum*.

8. For introductions to Philo's thought and influence, see Kamesar, *Cambridge Companion to Philo*; Goodenough, *Introduction to Philo Judæus*; Goodenough, *By Light, Light*.

9. Philo: *Heir* 205–6; *Confusion* 62–63.

10. Philo, *Flight* 101.

11. Philo, *Confusion* 146. Idel says this is the earliest and most influential text exemplifying a "theophoric mediator" who shares resemblance with his father and also shares the divine name (*Ben*, 23).

12. Philo, *QG* 2.62.

The Historical-Textual Approach to Contextualizing the Incarnation

Philo scholar Thomas H. Tobin explains three functions of the Logos in Philo's system.[13] First, the Logos has a cosmological function in that it is the image of God and the pattern upon which the universe is ordered.[14] Second, the Logos serves as the anthropological function of the image according to which humanity's intellect is patterned (cf. Gen 1:27).[15] Third, the Logos is anagogical, serving as a guide for the human soul to detach from physical reality and commune with the divine.[16]

Although Philo indicates that a philosopher should read spatial and anthropomorphic language in the Scriptures figuratively, he does not do so in all places. Instead, Philo maintains that there are times when physical language about God is to be understood as truly (and not figuratively) talking about the Logos taking on the appearance of created things. Philo believes the uneducated masses cannot understand the incorporeality of God, so as an accommodation, God sends his Logos embodied in the form of angels and men so that the people can understand:

> Why, then, do we wonder any longer at His assuming the likeness of angels, seeing that for the succour of those that are in need He assumes that of men? Accordingly, when He says "I am the God who was seen of thee in the place of God" (Gen 31:13), understand that He occupied the place of an angel only so far as appeared, without changing, with a view to the profit of him who was not yet capable of seeing the true God. For just as those who are unable to see the sun itself see the gleam of the parhelion and take it for the sun, and take the halo round the moon for that luminary itself, so some regard the image of God, His angel the Word, as His very self. (*Dreams* 1.238–39; cf. *QG* 3.34)

In this passage, Philo guards the incorporeal God from having any association with corporeal forms, yet he affirms that the Logos of God may assume visible form for the benefit of human understanding.[17] He cites Jacob's experience at Bethel as an example of a time where this took place (Gen 31).

13. Tobin, "Logos," 4:350–51.
14. Philo: *Creation* 16; *Dreams* 2.45.
15. Philo: *Creation* 24–25; *Heir* 231.
16. Philo: *Flight* 91–92; *Heir* 69–74; *Dreams* 2.249.

17. Philo anticipates Maimonides's similar solution by over a millennium. Both postulated an esoteric dimension to the Scriptures that the uninformed masses could not understand. Philo was open to realist interpretations of theophanies, with the Logos as the actor who was seen. Maimonides differed in this respect, preferring nonrealist psychological and visionary solutions instead.

Philo's writings proved to be popular in early Christian circles for several reasons.[18] Philo affirmed the incorporeality of God, with which Christians agreed. However, he also postulated a singular (not multiple) emanation from God, uncreated but subordinate to himself, which was the means by which the universe was created. The NT also identified a singular Logos as the eternal, uncreated, only begotten, divine Son through whom the universe was created, and who is the image of the invisible God (John 1; Col 1:15–17). Moreover, Philo's Logos takes visible form in order to communicate with human beings, and Philo identified the angel of the LORD as the Logos. The NT does the same (John 1:14; Jude 4–5). Jewish scholar of Hellenistic Judaism Samuel Sandmel notes the similarities between Philo's Logos and the Logos of the NT (John 1):

> In many ways Philo spoke of the Logos in ways kindred to the New Testament way of speaking [of] the Logos-Christ. As to the first assertion, my opinion is this, that a Greek Jew would not have denied the possibility of the incarnation, but would have either agreed or disagreed on whether the possible incarnation of the Logos as Jesus had actually taken place.[19]

On the other hand, philosopher Ronald Nash sees Philo's Logos differing from that of the NT:

> Philo's Logos is especially lacking in the personal or messianic or soteriological traits so prominent in the Christian account of Jesus, the soteriological Logos. Philo's Logos is not a person or messiah or savior but a cosmic principle postulated to solve assorted metaphysical and epistemological problems.[20]

Thus, it is best not to make a direct identification of the Logos of Philo with the Logos of the NT. Nash continues, "The idea of the Logos becoming incarnate would have been hard enough for Philo. To compound the foolishness by submitting the Logos to death by crucifixion would have been unthinkable."[21]

---

18. The first uncontested patristic reference to Philo is found in Clement of Alexandria's *Stromateis* ca. 200 CE. Clement extensively interwove Philo's theology and philosophy into his own. Many subsequent church fathers followed suit (Runia, "Philo and Christian Fathers," 211–12).

19. Samuel Sandmel, *We Jews and Jesus*; quoted in Magid, *Hasidism Incarnate*, 33–34.

20. Nash, "Notion of Mediator," 105–6.

21. Nash, "Notion of Mediator," 109.

In sum, Philo promoted the Logos as an intermediary between the created world and the transcendent God. Because of the Logos's unity with God and its differentiation from God, Philo's thought is an example of a Jewish binitarian theology.

3.1.2. Sophia, the Wisdom of God (Σοφία)

The Logos was integral to Philo's philosophical system, but other Hellenistic Jews postulated a similar entity called Wisdom. In Hebrew, the word for wisdom is a feminine noun (*hochmah*, חָכְמָה), and so too is the equivalent Greek word, *Sophia* (Σοφία). In the Hebrew Scriptures in Prov 8, Wisdom is personified as a beautiful woman who was involved in the creation of the world. When Hellenistic Jews read this passage, they provided expanded descriptions of this personified Wisdom who created the world at God's side. In these expanded texts, Sophia is the apex of creation, the preeminent partner through whom God does wonderful things. For example, the author of Sirach (second century BCE) extols Sophia as the one who visits Israel in the pillar of cloud and is seen atop Mount Sinai (Sir 24:3–4). In this text, Wisdom proclaims, "I alone encircled the ring of heaven, and I walked in the depth of the abyss" (Sir 24:5).[22] Sirach even claims Sophia's origin in a kind of atemporal creation or emanation in eternity past: "Before eternity, he created me, from the beginning; and until eternity I will never fail" (Sir 24:9).[23]

In the book Wisdom of Solomon (ca. 1 CE), Wisdom is an "emanation of the pure glory of the Almighty" who "is able to do all things" and who "renews all things" and who makes people to be "friends of God" (Wis 7:25–28). In this text, Wisdom comes from God, is with God, and will always be with God. She is spoken of in personal, even humanlike descriptions, yet she is omniscient and omnipotent. Philo himself was familiar with these teachings on Wisdom and incorporated them into his theology, for he identified Wisdom with the Logos.[24]

Thus, Hellenistic Jews developed creative solutions to the unsolved mysteries of God's omnipresence, immanence, and handiwork in the world. Although God was transcendent and far away, through the Logos and Sophia, the God of Israel was brought near.[25]

---

22. Brannan et al., *Lexham English Septuagint*.
23. Brannan et al., *Lexham English Septuagint*.
24. Philo, *Alleg. Interp.* 1.65.
25. For more discussion on the background of Hellenistic "sonship" texts and their relation to later Jewish mystical traditions, see Idel, *Ben*, 1–107.

Part I: Setting the Stage for the Incarnation

3.2. Divine Embodiment Precedents in Talmudic Judaism

It would be incorrect to conclude that divine intermediaries were a Hellenistic Jewish phenomenon confined to the Second Temple era, since a variety of rabbinic texts promote similar solutions. As illustrated by Maimonidean scholar Marc Shapiro, during the talmudic era, rabbinic thought about God's physicality can be classified into three different schools.[26] Each of these schools of thought provided different solutions for passages in the Hebrew Scriptures where God acts in seemingly physical ways:

Table 4. Schools of Rabbinic Thought Regarding God's Body

	School of Rabbinic Thought	Typical Solution for Physical God Talk
1.	Rabbinic corporealists: God has an eternal body.	God transformed his body into various physical forms perceived by man (fire, smoke, man).
2.	Rabbinic incorporealists: God does not have an eternal body.	God sent an approved representative of himself to act in physical ways and speak for himself.
3.	Rabbinic quasi-corporealists: God has an incomprehensible mystical "body."	Various mystical and psychological interpretations

Below I will elaborate on the first two schools of thought, each of which relates to Jewish versions of divine embodiment. The third school of thought, famously found in texts such as *Shiur Komah*, will not be the focus of this chapter.

3.2.1. Rabbinic Corporealists: God's Body Comes Down

There is considerable evidence across a millennium of texts indicating Jewish belief in a corporeal God. Numerous Jewish scholars have noted that rabbinic sages interpreted anthropomorphisms in Scripture and in the rabbinic corpus as literal descriptions of God's body.[27] Rabbinics scholar José Costa summarizes, "The prevailing trend in current research

---

26. M. Shapiro, *Limits of Orthodox Theology*, 45–70. Also see Sommer, *Bodies of God*. For a popular Orthodox Jewish handling of this subject, and several of the schools involved, see Junik, "Can God Become Man?"

27. Marmorstein, *Old Rabbinic Doctrine*; Goshen-Gottstein, "Body as Image"; M. Shapiro, *Limits of Orthodox Theology*, 45–70; Neusner and Chilton, *God in the World*, 1–94; Costa, "Body of God"; Lorberbaum, *In God's Image*; Kellner, *Science in Bet Midrash*, 157–64.

is to read the texts literally and to accept that the rabbis of antiquity did truly believe in a corporeal God."[28]

Multiple examples illustrate this rabbinic belief. In the Babylonian Talmud (fourth to sixth centuries CE), God wears *tefillin* (phylacteries) on his right hand and his head (b. Ber. 6a). God shows Moses how to tie the *tefillin* by doing it himself (b. Ber. 7a). God physically writes words of Torah while sitting atop Mount Sinai (b. Sanh. 111a). God spends his day studying Torah and riding cherubs (b. 'Abod. Zar. 3b). Rabbi Akiva (second century CE) initially interprets God's throne as a physical throne akin to that which the human Messiah sits upon, implying that God "sits" like the Messiah "sits" (b. Sanh. 38b). Moreover, midrashim portray God as visibly indistinguishable from Adam (Gen. Rab. 8:10) and assert that God sometimes hides himself and sometimes enables himself to be visibly seen (Pesiq. Rab Kah. suppl. 7). Reflecting on God appearing to Israel as a warrior (Exod 15:3) and as an elder teaching Torah (Dan 7:9–10), Rabbi Hiyya bar Abba (third century CE) says, "He appeared to them in a guise appropriate to each and every place and time."[29]

Sources outside the rabbinic writings during late antiquity and the Middle Ages illustrate the widespread Jewish notion that God has a body. Two striking talmudic-era synagogues include artistic representation of both human figures and the body of God. The paintings of two synagogues, Dura Europos (third century CE) and Beit Alfa (sixth century CE), include images of God's corporeal hands.[30] Contemporary Jewish philosopher Joseph Dan comments, "It seems that ancient Judaism was able to accept an image of God that bore resemblance to the image of man without its basic theological monism being threatened."[31] Second- and third-century gentile Christians also criticize Jewish corporealism in their writings against Judaism.[32] Christian criticism of Jewish corporealism continued into the Middle Ages, as depicted by Agobard of Lyons (825 CE)[33] and in Peter the Venerable's twelfth-century diatribe.[34] Jewish historian Moises Orfali cites many polemic works by Spanish Christian authors who charged the Jewish

---

28. Costa, "Body of God," xx.

29. Pesiq. Rab Kah., Piska 12.24.

30. Hachlili, *Ancient Synagogues*, 391–401; M. Shapiro, *Limits of Orthodox Theology*, 53; Finney, "Hand of God," 1:630.

31. Dan, "Imago Dei," 474.

32. Justin Martyr, *Dial.* 114; Arnobius, *Against the Gentiles* 3.12.

33. See Alfonsi, *Dialogue Against the Jews*, 29.

34. Peter the Venerable, *Against the Inveterate Obduracy*, 245–46.

people of their era with believing in a corporeal God.[35] Renowned exegete Rashi (1040–1105) may have been a corporealist,[36] and Ravad (1125–98) says that sages greater than Maimonides had been corporealists.[37]

For the rabbinic sages of the corporealist school of thought, addressing the anthropomorphic texts of Scripture is simple: God's own physical body is the form experienced by Israel. For them, God's body may be made of a different kind of matter than the created world, but it is still directly apprehensible by human beings and is considered part of God's eternal nature. Corporealists have no problem with God appearing in a physical form, even in the form of a human, because they view God as always embodied.

3.2.2. Rabbinic Incorporealists: God's Representative Comes Down

A second school of rabbinic thought regarding God's body is both similar and different to the later medieval consensus. On the one hand, the incorporealist school denied God had a body, and thus God never *directly* interacted with human beings through physical means. This understanding appears in the writings of Roman historian Tacitus in the second century (*Hist.* 5.5; cf. t. ʿAbod. Zar. 5:2) and it approaches the later Maimonidean solution. However, in contrast to Maimonides, the sages also postulated several mysterious intermediaries who could stand in for God and do physical things in his place. These intermediaries included an angel called *Metatron* (מְטַטְרוֹן),[38] the *Memra* (מֵימְרָא, word), the angel of the Lord (מַלְאַךְ יהוה, *malach adonai*), the *Shekhinah* (שְׁכִינָה, dwelling),[39] and the *Kavod* (כָּבוֹד, glory). Scholars disagree whether these rabbinic intermediaries are personal agents, impersonal principles, or merely euphemistic literary devices to thinly veil God's physical actions. However, if these rabbinic concepts are more than euphemisms, then they may be evidence of a quasi-binitarian theology in rabbinic Judaism.[40]

---

35. Orfali, "Anthropomorphism in Christian Reproach."

36. Slifkin, "Was Rashi a Corporealist?"; Zucker, "No, Rashi Was Not"; Slifkin, "Rashi's Stance on Corporealism" (response to Zucker).

37. Ben-Sasson et al., "Maimonidean Controversy." Ravad's note is found in his comment to Hilchos Teshuvah 3:7.

38. The etymology of the word Metatron is unclear, as is its meaning. See Orlov, "Metatron," 943.

39. This word as a theological noun is not found in the Hebrew Scriptures. A parallel verbal idea, from which the noun may be derived, is in Exod 40:35, where the cloud "settled" or "rested" (שָׁכַן, *shakhan*) upon the tabernacle.

40. Alan Segal, *Two Powers in Heaven*.

The Historical-Textual Approach to Contextualizing the Incarnation

Throughout the Hebrew Scriptures, an enigmatic character appears to the patriarchs and to the nation of Israel: the angel of the LORD.[41] In a key passage in Exodus, God tells Israel that the angel of the LORD bears the divine name:

> Behold, I send an angel before you to guard you on the way and to bring you to the place that I have prepared. Pay careful attention to him and obey his voice; do not rebel against him, for he will not pardon your transgression, for my name is in him [כִּי שְׁמִי בְּקִרְבּוֹ, *ki shmi b'kirbo*]. (Exod 23:20-21)

Jewish mysticism scholar Moshe Idel says the final phrase of this passage is central to historical Jewish mystical speculations about God. The passage does not elaborate regarding the identity of this angel, the reason he must be obeyed, the nature of his relationship to forgiveness of transgression, or *how* he can have the name of God within him. Idel writes, "No real separation between the divinity and the emissary is assumed; rather, the divinity is dwelling within the emissary by means of the name."[42]

In Jewish tradition the name of God is set apart, magnificent, and so holy that it is not even spoken. The name of God is the closest thing the Hebrew Scriptures have to the concept of God's *nature*, as may be seen by a variety of attributions to the name of God in Scripture:

Table 5. The Name of the LORD

The Name of the LORD:		
Is never to be blasphemed (Exod 20:7; Lev 24:16)	Is worthy of blessing (Ps 113:2)	Brings salvation (Ps 116:4)
Is worthy of praise (Ps 7:17; 148:5, 13)	Empowers Israel (Ps 118:10–11)	Enables prophecy (Deut 18:22)
Is worthy of proclamation (Deut 32:3)	Brings help to Israel (Ps 124:8)	Is a place of refuge (Zeph 3:12)
Is worthy of trust (Ps 20:7)	Is worthy of fear (Ps 102:15)	Is a strong tower (Prov 18:10)

---

41. Gen 16:7–13; 22:11–18; 31:11–13; Exod 3:2; Num 22:21–35; Judg 2:1–4; 5:23; 6:11–16; 13:3, 13–22; 2 Sam 24:16; 1 Kgs 19:5–7; 2 Kgs 1:3, 15; 19:35; 1 Chr 21:12–18; 2 Chr 32:21; Ps 34:7–8; 35:5–6; Isa 37:36; Zech 1:10–13; 3:1–6; 12:8. I believe that most, if not all, of these appearances of the angel of the LORD were appearances of the Son of God as a messenger. See §11.2.1.

42. Idel, *Ben*, 17.

Part I: Setting the Stage for the Incarnation

Given these magnificent descriptions of the name of the LORD, Exod 23's angel is no regular angel if he has the name *in* him. Early rabbis called this angel *Metatron* (b. Sanh. 38b; 3 En. 12:5), and a segment of the rabbinic movement included *Metatron* within the Godhead as an adopted divinity.[43] This is most pronounced in *Sefer Chanoch* (ספר חנוך), also known as 3 Enoch (ca. fifth century CE), where *Metatron* is called "the Lesser יהוה" (Tetragrammaton). In this text, God makes *Metatron* prince over all created things (3 En. 10), makes *Metatron* omniscient (3 En. 11; 48C:7), bestows his majesty upon him (3 En. 48C:7), and gives him a throne in heaven (3 En. 48C:8). This early rabbinic work describes the angel of the LORD in language remarkably akin to that of the NT about Jesus in his heavenly exaltation,[44] although it differs by saying that Enoch was *adopted* into his identity as the "Lesser יהוה."[45]

Rabbinic authorities of the talmudic era promoted other intermediaries as well. The phenomena of the *Memra* and *Shekhinah* are most pronounced in the Aramaic targums, produced by early rabbinic communities so Aramaic-speaking Jews could understand the Scriptures. In many places where the Hebrew Scriptures speak of God doing something physical, the targums add the words *Memra* or *Shekhinah* to replace God as the subject of the verbs. The following are common examples:

- And they heard the sound of the LORD God walking in the garden in the cool of the day [וַיִּשְׁמְעוּ אֶת־קוֹל יְהוָה אֱלֹהִים מִתְהַלֵּךְ בַּגָּן לְרוּחַ הַיּוֹם]. (Gen 3:8 MT)

- Then they heard the voice of the *Memra* of the Lord God [וּשְׁמַעוּ יָת קָל מֵימְרָא דַיוי אֱלֹהִים] walking in the garden towards the decline of the day. (Gen 3:8 Tg. Onq.)[46]

- The LORD passed before him [וַיַּעֲבֹר יְהוָה עַל־פָּנָיו]. (Exod 34:6 MT)

- And the Glory of the *Shekhinah* of the Lord passed by [ועברת איקר שכינתיה דייי]. (Exod 34:6 Tg. Neof.)[47]

---

43. Abrams, "Boundaries of Divine Ontology."

44. Phil 2:5–11; Eph 1:20–23; Col 1:15–20; Rev 1:4–8.

45. In his study of Jewish mystical texts related to divine sonship, Idel categorizes 3 Enoch as an adoptionist or apotheotic text, which affirms that a being can ascend to unity with God and become a son of God. This is distinguished from the theophanic model, whereby the Son of God comes down to man (*Ben*, 34–35).

46. English translation from Cathcart et al., *Targum Onqelos to Genesis*; Aramaic text from Kaufman, *Targum Onqelos*.

47. English translation from Cathcart et al., *Targum Neofiti 1*; Aramaic text from Kaufman, *Targum Neofiti*.

Here Targums Onkelos and Neofiti shift all physical language away from God himself and onto the *Memra* and *Shekhinah*. These concepts provided ways to discuss God's manifest presence while guarding God's unseen spiritual transcendence. Rabbinics scholar Alan Segal notes,

> Apparently, whenever a second figure, either in the Pentateuch or in Dan[iel], could be identified as a quasi-divine or independent angelic figure, the rabbis would fight vociferously against it. Once it was clear that this divine figure who seemed to be God, who carried His name, and who acted for God, could be called the Shekhina or the Kavod and not an independent deity, the rabbis accepted and expanded the tradition.[48]

Yet the *Memra*, *Shekhinah*, and *Kavod* remain subjects of mystery, fraught with disagreements in contemporary scholarship. Scholars debate the intermediaries' ontology and their relationship with God, including questions of whether they are aspects of God himself, separate beings, literary devices, or visionary and psychological impressions with no independent existence. Scholars take a variety of positions on the matters because the targums and early rabbis did not provide clear answers.

Consequently, the talmudic rabbis did not resolve the problem of God's simultaneous transcendence and immanence, nor did they provide a coherent interpretation of the physical relations attributed to God. Rabbinic divine intermediaries may speak to these problems, but then again, they might not. The corporealist school of rabbinic thought accepted spatial relations applied to God as actual, and the incorporealist school sidestepped the issue through the terms *Memra*, *Shekhinah*, and the like. One might think that the use of these divine intermediaries would be a hint the sages were attempting to protect the incorporeality of God. That may have been the case, but one cannot be certain. Everything is dependent upon the sages' understanding of the intermediaries' relationship with God or their identification as God, which was a metaphysical and theological question the sages left open.

Thus, both Hellenistic and early rabbinic segments of Judaism affirmed the possibility that God or God's appointed agent could appear in physical form and do things on God's behalf, sometimes even with God's name. When God acted in this way, he was conceptually "in two places at once"—both transcendent and physically present at the same time. Because of this theological affirmation, the ancient Jewish sects surveyed

---

48. Alan Segal, *Two Powers in Heaven*, 51–52.

here can be seen as anticipatory and favorable to a high Christology as promoted in Christian theology.

3.3. Contemporary Scholars on the Jewishness of the Trinity and Incarnation

Nineteenth- and twentieth-century scholars attempted to situate the divinity of Jesus as an evolutionary and innovative development that was not present in Jesus's self-consciousness or that of his earliest followers because of a perceived incompatibility between the divinity of Jesus and the Second Temple Judaism within which he lived.[49] It was commonly assumed that the Judaism of Jesus's time was uniformly anti-incarnational, holding to an absolutely incorporealist understanding of God. Consequently, these scholars asserted that belief in Jesus's divinity was likely influenced by non-Jewish and pagan sources, where the divine and the physical mingled without scandal.

This theory has come under significant scholarly criticism from two directions in recent years. First, as illustrated in this chapter, scholars have cited Jewish sources that include concepts similar to Trinitarian and incarnational thought. Second, scholars have come to recognize that Jesus's followers have *always* believed that the human Jesus was fully divine—not merely an exalted human—since the earliest Jewish stage of the movement. New Testament scholar Crispin Fletcher-Louis assessed Larry Hurtado's seminal research on the topic, along with the sympathetic studies of Martin Hengel and Richard Bauckham, and concluded that it has led to an "emerging consensus" in scholarship and a "sea change" that belief in Jesus's divinity originates from the 30s or 40s CE in Jewish circles.[50] High Christology began early, and it grew in the fallow ground of Judaism, which anticipated it.[51]

Whereas the old paradigm—heavily dominated by pre–World War II German scholars—sought to distance Christianity from the Judaism from which it sprung, today the pendulum has swung in the opposite

---

49. Baur, *Christ Party*; Bousset, *Kyrios Christos*; Bauer, *Orthodoxy and Heresy*. The most recognizable proponent of these arguments in the twenty-first century is Bart Ehrman, as seen in Ehrman, *How Jesus Became God*; Köstenberger and Kruger, *Heresy of Orthodoxy*.

50. Fletcher-Louis, *Christological Origins*, 4. For a summary of recent changes in Jewish scholarship on this issue, see Brill, "Jewish View," 307–14.

51. I explore these themes further in §10.5.6.

direction. Many contemporary scholars recognize the significant Trinitarian and incarnational precedents within pre-Christian Judaism, and the debate centers on the *extent* of the overlap. Some, like Hurtado and Bauckham, argue for limited overlap between high Christology and ancient Judaism, whereas others argue for nearly complete continuity.[52] Particularly striking are the views of *Jewish* scholars who argue for various kinds of continuity, such as Alan Segal, Daniel Boyarin, Elliot Wolfson, Benjamin Sommer, Moshe Idel, Esther Hamori, Shaul Magid, and Alan Brill.

Jewish scholarship entered a new stage upon the publication of Alan Segal's 1977 volume *Two Powers in Heaven*. Segal investigated multiple layers of rabbinic tradition, pointing out that the sages of the mishnaic and talmudic periods sought to purge the idea of "two powers in heaven" from within their midst. Although some of the rabbinic argumentation was arrayed against gentile Christians and gnostics outside their circle, Segal held that a considerable amount of rabbinic debate was focused *inward*. The sages were aware of Jews holding views about *Metatron*, Daniel's "son of man," and anthropomorphisms that entailed belief in binitarianism—the union of two divine powers as one. As a project of self-definition and separation, the rabbinic sages sought to purge this theology from their midst.

Talmudist Daniel Boyarin writes, "There is significant evidence (uncovered in large part by [Alan] Segal) that in the first century many—perhaps most—Jews held a binitarian doctrine of God."[53] Although this doctrine was eventually lost in the contest with the rabbinic sages, it once flourished in Jewish soil. Elsewhere, Boyarin claims,

> The road to Nicaea had been well cleared and paved and neither Trinity nor Incarnation can be said to represent a departure from Israelite religion but rather an unfolding of it. Jews came to believe that Jesus was God, because they already believed that the Messiah would be a divine redeemer incarnated in a human being; they just argued about who that human being was.[54]

---

52. In her study on divine embodiment in the Second Temple period, Brittany Wilson places Hurtado and Bauckham in the "exclusive monotheism" camp, and others, such as Boyarin, in the "inclusive monotheism" camp (*Embodied God*, 102–3).

53. Boyarin, "Two Powers in Heaven," 334. Idel disagrees that there was ever such doctrinal homogeneity, while recognizing that binitarianism was part of the stream of tradition (*Ben*, 7).

54. Boyarin, "Enoch, Ezra," 352.

Kabbalah scholar Elliot Wolfson writes, "The idea of incarnation unique to Christianity should be viewed as a 'particular framing' of the conception of incarnation that was idiomatic to a variety of Judaic authors who represented God as a person."[55] Jewish theologian Phillip Sigal writes, "The originators of Christianity were Jews, and they found their notion of a divine Messiah in their own heritage."[56] Biblical scholar Benjamin Sommer concurs:

> We have seen that ancient Near Eastern texts are perfectly comfortable envisioning a deity as possessing a heavenly body as well as several earthly ones; Yhwh could be at home in a heavenly palace and at Zion at one and the same time. That a deity came down did not mean the deity did not also remain up. The presence of God and of God-as-Jesus on earth is nothing more than a particular form of this old idea of multiple embodiment, and hence no more offensive to a monotheistic theology than ... sections of the Pentateuch.[57]

Jewish mysticism scholar Moshe Idel claims divine sonship was common in multiple eras of Jewish mystical thought, long after the emergence of Christianity.[58] Shaul Magid builds on Idel's research with a look at incarnational thought in modern Hasidism. He notes,

> As Christianity became more committed to high Christology and as Judaism defined itself more and more in opposition to Christianity, incarnational thinking faded in Judaism, with the exception of the esoteric traditions, where traces of such doctrine remained but were largely veiled in metaphysical and cosmological jargon. The Maimonidean matrix of a radically transcendent God that stripped any doctrine of incarnational possibilities became the norm in medieval Judaism. Rabbinic incarnational thinking was mostly interpreted out of existence.[59]

In light of this evidence, multiple Jewish scholars have called for an openness toward the Jewishness of the Incarnation idea. Hebrew Bible scholar Esther Hamori writes,

---

55. Wolfson, "Judaism and Incarnation," 240.
56. Sigal, "'Begotten' Messiah," 223.
57. Sommer, *Bodies of God*, 133.
58. Idel argues, however, that while the "sonship" idea was preserved in mystical Judaism, it took a non-incarnational connotation due to a self-conscious reformulation of the concept away from dominant Christianity (*Ben*, 60–63).
59. Magid, *Hasidism Incarnate*, 15–16.

The Historical-Textual Approach to Contextualizing the Incarnation

> It has largely been assumed that the Christian concept of incarnation was a development of Greek ideas.... The type of anthropomorphism evident in the incarnation, however, is not exactly like that in Greek thought. It is in fact more like the anthropomorphic realism from the Hebrew Bible itself. The Christian concept of incarnation has its roots in Israelite thought.[60]

Jewish studies scholar Alan Brill surveys current trends in Jewish scholarship:

> According to many current scholars, Rabbinic Judaism did not have a simple undifferentiated view of God. Historians accept that Judaism in antiquity had a variety of intra-divine structures, logos theories, angelic divine forms, manifestations and bitheism. There were widespread ideas of complex structures of the divine in first-century Judaism, the crucible that formed both religions. These ideas continued in later the Tannaitic and Amoriac era as well as into medieval esotericism and Kabbalah, even if rejected by medieval rational philosophers. Many strands in Judaism did not relinquish the complex views of the Jewish God.[61]

Brill then concludes,

> I do want to move beyond the present view—a widespread Jewish position—that Jewish thought has a pristine monotheism and Christianity has Tri-theism.... Rather than irreconcilable noncomparable differences, we now can explore a variety of relationships, parallel, divergent, and convergent, and we can begin to understand each other, as well as be able to engage in comparative theology.[62]

Speaking about the implications of this recontextualization of "Christian" theology as Jewish, Boyarin writes,

> Jews and Christians will need to begin to tell different stories about each other in the future.... Jews will have to stop vilifying Christian ideas about God as simply a collection of "un-Jewish," perhaps pagan, and in any case bizarre fantasies. God in a human body indeed! Recognizing these ideas as deeply rooted in the ancient complex of Jewish religious ideas may not

---

60. Hamori, "Divine Embodiment," 180.
61. Brill, "Jewish View," 309.
62. Brill, "Jewish View," 325–26.

lead us Jews to accept them but should certainly help us realize that Christian ideas are not alien to us; they are our own offspring and sometimes, perhaps, among the most ancient of all Israelite-Jewish ideas.[63]

These Jewish scholars' studies illustrate how the previous paradigm has fallen. It is demonstratively incorrect to assert that Jews living before Jesus had no conception of proto-Trinitarian and quasi-incarnational theology. Furthermore, such theology continued long after the "parting of the ways"[64] between Christianity and Judaism in late antiquity.

Given these oft-neglected evidences, old misconceptions and prejudices about divine embodiment in Judaism need to be revised.[65] No longer are the Trinity and Incarnation subjects that confine scholars to the texts of the NT or later patristic theological discussions. These subjects are now in the purview of Jewish scholars working from Jewish texts, and they are recontextualizing "Christian" theology as part of the sphere of historic Jewish thought.

The historical-textual approach to defending the Incarnation emphasizes the Jewish precedents for Trinitarian and incarnational thought, arguing that historical Jewish precedents should modify common Jewish theological objections to Christianity. If the Trinity and Incarnation were plausible for Jews two thousand years ago, then perhaps they should be considered acceptable to Jewish people today. For those who are attempting to illustrate the Jewishness of the Trinity and Incarnation, the historical-textual approach is persuasive and is a recommended argument in evangelism and apologetics.[66] However, the historical-textual

---

63. Boyarin, *Jewish Gospels*, 6–7.

64. Scholars use this phrase to denote the messy historical process by which Christianity and Judaism came to be seen as two separate religions: Dunn, *Jews and Christians*; Boyarin, *Border Lines*; Shanks, *Partings*; Commission for Religious Relations with the Jews, "Gifts and Calling," §16.

65. For an example of a recent Christian author who makes this anachronistic mistake, consider Louis Markos: "We must remember that before the age of Christ and the New Testament, no Jew in his wildest imagination could have conceived of an actual incarnation in which deity would allay itself with flesh. . . . They could not have dreamed—as no Muslim today could dream—that God would literally take on flesh, dwell among us, and die a painful death on our behalf" (*From Plato to Christ*, 125–26). Cf. Macleod, *Person of Christ*, 113–14. See also Idel's comments on Géza Vermes and Isaiah Wolfsberg, each of whom totally denied the possibility of Jews accepting a theory of a "Son of God" (Idel, *Ben*, 103n189). Idel notes how Daniel Boyarin was initially taken aback by Jewish acceptance of these ideas (Boyarin, *Border Lines*, 303–4).

66. For examples of Messianic Jewish authors employing this method, see *AJOJ*

approach does not address many questions and objections common in contemporary Judaism, and thus it should be complemented with a secondary strategy.

3.4. Limitations of the Historical-Textual Approach

In my view, the historical-textual approach has at least six significant drawbacks that limit its effectiveness in justifying the Incarnation of the Son of God.

First, sharp-witted Jewish objectors may be quick to reply that ancient Jewish popularity and plausibility does not equate to theological truth. The historical-textual approach highlights opinions of ancient Jewish authors that are at odds with mainstream Jewish thought today. The views espoused in the ancient works (especially the Hellenistic ones) could have been promoted by heretical, schismatic, or naïve Jewish people. Some objectors may argue that the opinions of yesteryear were forgotten for a reason, as "Judaism" is that which is providentially passed on and lived out from generation to generation by the majority. As minority opinions that had negligible impact on later Judaism, proto-Trinitarian and incarnational theories may be seen as having little weight to overturn the careful considerations of generations of Torah scholars.

Second, this approach does not address the philosophical developments in Judaism since the Middle Ages, namely the contributions of Maimonides and the Kabbalists. These medieval thinkers were aware of biblical and rabbinic texts that imply divine embodiment. They countered by embracing philosophical frameworks that reject the idea that God could become embodied in a NT sense. The texts commonly cited in the historical-textual approach usually come from a bygone era of premedieval Judaism, and this limits the approach's use in an age where Maimonides and Kabbalah have changed the status quo and reframed the interpretation of those prior texts.

Third, the historical-textual approach argues on the basis of texts that contemporary Jewish people either do not read (Second Temple literature, Pseudepigrapha[67]) or do not read without medieval and modern commentary (Hebrew Bible, Talmud, midrash). An Orthodox Jewish

---

2:210–20; Klayman, "Jewish History"; Robinson, "Jewish Nature"; Kinzer, "Judaism and Divine-Human Jesus."

67. Such as 3 Enoch, which has previously been considered, as well as 1 Enoch, 4 Ezra, and other texts included in *OTP*.

thinker today finds it naïve to appeal directly to such texts without consulting the sages who commented upon them, a judgment that reflects their epistemological hierarchy.[68] Moreover, if the text in question is an extra-biblical text that the sages do not discuss, such as in the case of Philo's writings or the Wisdom of Solomon, the text is treated as inadmissible and foreign to Judaism.

Fourth, the epistemology of secular, Reform, and liberal Jewish people is incompatible with the intended aim of the historical-textual approach. These Jewish groups tend to see *all* historical works, the Bible and Second Temple Jewish literature included, as human-produced literary works that probably have little relation to ultimate theological reality, if there even is such a reality.[69] At best, the historical-textual approach may convince liberal Jewish people that some Jews *used to believe* in concepts similar to Christianity, not that such concepts are *true*. In other words, secular presuppositions limit discussions to the descriptive realm of historical Jewish sociology, rather than the prescriptive realm of Jewish theology.

Fifth, there is a significant danger when modern-day followers of Jesus place too much emphasis on continuity with Jewish precedents while neglecting theological and philosophical analysis and critique. Related mistakes include practicing unwitting anachronisms and not considering the discontinuities initiated by the new covenant.[70] When rabbinic Judaism, Philo, or Kabbalah are placed higher in one's epistemological hierarchy than the NT, the result can be an unwitting devaluation of Scripture or the promotion of theological heresy and syncretism.[71]

Sixth, the Hebrew Bible's examples of divine embodiment and theophany—and even Second Temple "binitarian" positions—are not

---

68. Epistemological hierarchy refers to which sources of knowledge are believed to be more or less authoritative than others. The sources that are high in a hierarchy are those that have controlling influence on those that are lower. Sources that are low in a hierarchy may be accepted only when judged to be free of conflict with higher sources. This hierarchical structure of knowledge is known as *foundationalism*. For an overview of foundationalism and the competing position *coherentism*, see DeWeese and Moreland, *Philosophy Made Slightly Less Difficult*, 57–64.

69. For a discussion between a Reform rabbi and an Orthodox rabbi on the nature of biblical historicity and authority, see Hirsch and Yosef, *One People, Two Worlds*.

70. Theological and philosophical analysis and discussion about anachronisms are handled throughout the book. On anachronistic misuse of rabbinic literature, see Boskey, "Messianic Use." On discontinuities and the newness of the new covenant, see Feinberg, *Continuity and Discontinuity*.

71. Crawford, "Pathways," 74–90.

exact parallels with the NT's references to Jesus's human nature (Heb 2:17) and divine nature (Heb 1:3).[72] The Incarnation of the Son of God—best formulated by Chalcedon—is a heightened claim that requires more theological justification than the divine embodiments in the Hebrew Scriptures, which did not involve any union of the two natures in one divine person. Additionally, as Hurtado has pointed out, no ancient "binitarian" figure encouraged or accepted worship of himself. In Hurtado's view, the early Christian devotion to Jesus was a "mutation" away from Jewish precedents, and thus the earlier precedents do not deserve to be called "binitarian."[73] Accordingly, it seems unlikely that the pre-Christian-era Jewish community would have affirmed the Nicene *homoousios* (consubstantial clause) regarding the Logos or *Memra*. Because of these factors, I side toward the limited overlap view of Hurtado and Bauckham, rather than the nearly complete overlap view promoted by Boyarin and others.[74] Thus, in my view, the Incarnation does not have exhaustive continuity with ancient Jewish theology, only partial precedents. Nevertheless, I believe those genuine partial precedents should be magnified to overturn erroneous preconceptions of ancient Jewish theology.

Because of these drawbacks, the historical-textual approach cannot be recommended as the only or best way to justify the Trinity and the Incarnation in a Jewish setting. Theologically and philosophically inclined Jewish thinkers may dismiss the opinions of ancient Jewish interpreters because the binitarian and embodiment beliefs they held were a combination of heresy, metaphysical impossibility, and naïveté. Mere proof-texting appeals to biblical texts or ancient Jewish interpretations will not do. Just because a doctrine was plausible to Jewish people millennia ago, it does not follow that it will be plausible today. The question "Can God become incarnate?" deserves more than just historical and textual responses about ancient Jewish opinions; the underlying philosophical and theological issues must be addressed.

---

72. This is a basic distinction familiar to Christian theologians. For an example of a Jewish scholar who recognizes this, see Hamori, "Divine Embodiment," 180.

73. Hurtado, *One God, One Lord*, 97–130.

74. Nevertheless, the question of continuity and overlap between Judaism and Christianity on these matters remains open and the subject of much scholarly discussion. I find it helpful to cite Jewish scholars of the continuity position in order to illustrate the folly of positing that Christian and Jewish theological thought patterns are discontinuous and foreign to one another.

3.5. The Theological-Philosophical Approach

For the remainder of this book, I will defend the Incarnation through a second, complementary approach. The theological-philosophical approach to defending the Trinity and the Incarnation involves reading Scripture along the contours of Western thought and joining the "great conversation"[75] on systematic theology, cosmology, metaphysics, ontology, physics, and ethics, while also making an apologetic case about why some theological models are more faithful to Scripture and reality than others. The historical-textual approach is an appeal to the authority of ancient Jewish opinions; the theological-philosophical approach involves a detailed worldview analysis of the opinions themselves.

The theological-philosophical approach to defending the Trinity and the Incarnation recognizes that the sophisticated theological systems of religious Jewish people often nullify the epistemological power of the Scriptures to deliver truth about God and reality. The historical-textual approach centers on historical texts, exegesis, and appealing to present-day Jewish people based on historical Jewish opinions. However, that approach, as mentioned before, ignores the significant barriers that make previous eras of Jewish thought so implausible in Judaism today. It is unlikely that a Jesus follower's simplistic biblical proof-texting or even *sophisticated* textual reasoning using ancient Jewish sources will have much effect on a Jewish thinker whose mind and heart are unknowingly fortified by Plotinus, Pythagoras, and Plato before they ever allow themselves to understand Moses.[76] Many Orthodox Jewish people consider the Scriptures at the *end* of a long line of philosophical reasoning; in response, a Jesus follower likely needs to learn how to interact with that long line of reasoning, namely, the modes of thought in classical philosophical and theological categories.

This book notes that the talmudic sages, Maimonides, the Kabbalists, and the NT have each proposed competing theological models for the known data of Scripture and the cosmos. The best model will have

---

75. This is a phrase used by Britannica to describe the multilayered and interconnected discourse contained in its *Great Books of the Western World*. The great conversation is "the continuous discussion that runs through the thirty centuries of western civilization" (Adler, *Syntopicon*, 1:xiii). See Adler's two-volume *Syntopicon* within the series for excellent handbooks on the history of great ideas.

76. It is likely that many religious Jewish people are unaware that they are holding to Greek philosophical positions in their ostensibly Jewish theology. This is a major theme of pt. 2.

the greatest explanatory scope and plausibility, the least ad hoc (unevidenced and speculative) doctrines, and the least known falsehoods.[77] In the course of this investigation, I hope to demonstrate that the NT's incarnational model exceeds its rivals in each of these areas. Demonstrating this will require embarking on a significant theological and philosophical journey. Perhaps counterintuitively, to begin addressing Jewish concerns about the Incarnation, we must set sail for Athens and carefully note the contributions of the Greeks.

---

77. For these categories, see Craig, *Reasonable Faith*, 233; McCullagh, *Justifying Historical Descriptions*, 19.

PART II

A Critique of Non-Incarnational Maimonidean and Kabbalistic Thought

4 The Greek Philosophical Schools Related to Medieval Judaism

[Maimonides's] achievement was to synthesize a neo-Platonic Aristotelianism with biblical revelation.

—Jacob Neusner[1]

We may therefore see that the [medieval] Provençal Kabbalah functioned historically to unite old gnostic traditions, which originated in the Orient and maintained a kind of underground existence, with medieval Neoplatonism.

—Gershom Scholem[2]

Every man is born an Aristotelian or a Platonist.

—Samuel Taylor Coleridge[3]

In the seventeenth century, the French Catholic mathematician and philosopher Blaise Pascal proclaimed his allegiance to the "'GOD of Abraham, GOD of Isaac, and GOD of Jacob,' not of the philosophers."[4] Pascal perceived a distinction between these two visions of God. Because of the considerable influence of Greek philosophical thought

---

1. Neusner, *Torah Through the Ages*, 114.
2. Scholem, *Origins of the Kabbalah*, ch. 3.11, loc. 7160.
3. Coleridge, *Specimens*, 95.
4. Pascal, "Memorial," lines 6–7.

Part II: A Critique of Non-Incarnational Maimonidean and Kabbalistic Thought

upon Western understandings of God, Pascal's distinction of divinities can be overlooked.

The need to disentangle Greek theological assumptions from religious thought is present in Judaism, just as it is in Christianity. Under the influence of Maimonides and Kabbalah, the god of the philosophers and the God of the Scriptures become one, and this has held as the status quo of religious Judaism since the Middle Ages. In order to properly understand Judaism of any form after the twelfth century CE, it is critical to become familiar with Plato, Aristotle, Neopythagoreanism, Gnosticism, and Neoplatonism. Only then may it be recognized that common "Jewish" theological and philosophical positions in Judaism today are actually derived from non-Jewish philosophies.[5]

Although many non-academically trained religious Jewish people are unaware that many of their religious ideas stem from the Greeks, some Jewish scholars are involved in the disentangling effort. Distinguishing Greek philosophy–infused medieval Judaism from the talmudic era is half the battle: "The liberation of rabbinic theology from the reins of medieval theology is still underway," writes Jewish studies scholar Alon Goshen-Gottstein.[6] Such a project of liberation will be successful only through understanding how medieval Jewish theology distinguished itself from prior Jewish thought. As long as the various schools of Greek philosophy remain unfamiliar, it will not be possible to grasp the profound transformation Judaism underwent in the Middle Ages.

This chapter provides an overview of several schools of Greek philosophical thought, with an emphasis on their cosmology (nature of the cosmos), theology (nature of God), metaphysics (nature of being), and hermeneutics (method of interpretation). I will focus on a subset of topics that pertain to medieval Jewish thought, but readers desiring a fuller account of the Western philosophical tradition are encouraged to consult one of many available introductory surveys.[7]

---

5. See appendices B and D for a justification of this claim.

6. Goshen-Gottstein, "Body as Image," 171. See also Shatz, "Biblical and Rabbinic Background"; Weiss, "Rabbinic God."

7. For examples, Geisler and Feinberg, *Introduction to Philosophy*; Frame, *History of Western Philosophy*; Kenny, *Illustrated Brief History*; DeWeese and Moreland, *Philosophy Made Slightly Less Difficult*.

4.1. Plato

The philosophy of Plato (427–347 BCE) and his school of thought as developed by his successors is crucial for understanding medieval Judaism. Plato delivered to the world a series of dialogues covering a wide variety of subjects, such as courage, temperance, goodness, friendship, beauty, piety, knowledge, cosmology, politics, and laws. Plato's earlier dialogues include his teacher Socrates (ca. 469–399 BCE) as the primary character, but as Plato matured, he came into his own voice and Socrates's prominence diminished. The twentieth-century philosopher Alfred North Whitehead once famously remarked that Western thought is "a series of footnotes to Plato."[8]

Plato provided foundational modes of metaphysical and theological thought throughout his dialogues. For Plato, the ultimate orientation of the philosopher's soul must be inward, to the inner realities of abstract thought because it is only through this internal move that the divinity of the soul may be comprehended and experienced (*Phaed*. 79). This esoteric movement inward results in sharing the goodness of God in mystical experience. In Plato's view, God may not mingle with humans physically, but he can be apprehended by humans through love and spiritual wisdom (*Symp*. 203a). Moreover, one can become like God through philosophy by becoming enlightened and wise (*Theaet*. 176). This results in better reincarnations after death, eventually entering the company of the gods (*Phaed*. 81–82). This lower world's existence must be transcended; humanity must look above, beyond, and within for its true purpose. This trajectory of escape from the reality below to the higher reality beyond would characterize all subsequent Platonic thought, providing a potent idea to philosophers and mystics alike.

Plato accelerated the Greek philosophical tradition's trajectory toward a "pagan monotheism" or panentheism that approached that of biblical religion but differed from it considerably.[9] For comprehending medieval Judaism, the writings of Plato himself are less important than the writings of his successors such as Plotinus (third century CE). Nevertheless, I will

---

8. The full quote is: "The safest general characterization of the European philosophical tradition is that it consists of a series of footnotes to Plato" (Whitehead, *Process and Reality*, 39).

9. Athanassiadi and Frede, *Pagan Monotheism*; Van Nuffelen and Mitchell, *One God*; Cooper, *Panentheism*.

Part II: A Critique of Non-Incarnational Maimonidean and Kabbalistic Thought

now make mention of various Platonic doctrines that became pivotal ideas for expansion and speculation in later Jewish thought.

4.1.1. Plato's Negative/Apophatic Theology: *Via Negativa*

In *Tim.* 28c, Plato famously writes, "Now that which is created must, as we affirm, of necessity be created by a cause. But the father and maker of all this universe is past finding out; and even if we found him, to tell of him to all men would be impossible."[10] This brief remark would eventually inspire an entire category of theology called negative theology, apophasis, and *via negativa*. Negative theology states that God is so transcendent beyond the universe and human language that he cannot be rationally understood or known. Instead of describing God for who (or what) he *is*, he can only be described for what he is *not*. According to negative theology, asserting, "God is good" is out of bounds, whereas "God is not evil" is appropriate. This idea would go on to inspire later Platonists such as Philo, the gnostics, and especially Plotinus, who is the father of comprehensive negative theology.

4.1.2. Parmenides and the Unity of Being

Plato narrates an important metaphysical and theological idea in his dialogue *Parmenides* without integrating it into other areas of his thought. This dialogue, named after the philosopher Parmenides, includes a metaphysical idea that can be jarring upon first encountering it: only one thing exists. Parmenides argues that nonbeing does not exist,[11] and thus it cannot be used as a principle of differentiation (*Parm.* 141, 166). In other words, he disallows saying that A is not B, because the "not" invokes the principle of nonbeing (which does not exist). On the basis of this reasoning, Parmenides teaches that it is impossible for multiple beings to exist; all things in the universe that appear to be separate are actually united as one: A is B and C and everything else. All multiplicity of being is illusory; the "one" is infinite in multiplicity (*Parm.* 143). According to Parmenides, the nature of this oneness is beyond comprehension, in *via negativa* fashion. The one has no name, cannot be expressed nor perceived, nor can anyone have knowledge of it (*Parm.* 142). This idea leads to a denial of the senses and rational thought in preference

---

10. Plato, *Dialogues*, 447. See Philo's allusion to this statement in *Spec. Laws* 1.32.

11. Being is the principle of existence. Something that does not have being does not have existence: it does not exist.

to a mystical unity between all things that appear to be separate. Under Parmenides, paradox and mystery are infused into everything, and only the unenlightened continue to believe there are multiple things that exist. Plato himself agrees with a similar notion in his *Republic*, where he defines the Good as transcending being itself—without explicitly identifying the Good with Parmenides's "one" (*Resp.* 509b.).

4.1.3. Plato's World Soul: The Universe is Alive

The dialogue *Timaeus* serves as Plato's origin story of the universe, and like its biblical counterpart (Gen 1–2), it has been highly influential in Western thought. Like other Greek philosophers, Plato believed the material universe is eternal. He held that the universe's original state was unformed matter, which was later fashioned into a perfectly designed whole by the highest divine being called the demiurge (*Tim.* 32c). The demiurge took the four elements of fire, water, air, and earth and constructed a beautiful, interconnected sphere that revolved in a circle with Earth at the center.

Among the *Timaeus's* contributions to the Greek understanding of the cosmos is the idea of the world soul. Before fashioning the universe into its final state, the demiurge created a lower divinity called the world soul (*Tim.* 34a–b). The physical universe was fashioned inside the immaterial world soul such that the world soul pervaded the entire universe (*Tim.* 36d–e). The world soul "is herself invisible but partakes in reasoning and harmony" (*Tim.* 36e) and causes the motion and life of the entire universe (*Tim.* 37c–d). Thus, all the pulsating, rotating, invigorating motion of life in all places is due to the life force of the world soul that is embedded in all things. In subsequent centuries, Judaism and Christianity would look to the world soul as an inspiration for the vitality and unity of the world.

4.1.4. Double-Tiered Platonic Metaphysics: The Sensible and Intellectual

One of the most important aspects of Platonic thought is the idea that there are two or more levels of reality, with the higher levels accessible only by the philosophically enlightened. Plato teaches that there is a sensible world that is accessible to the human senses, and an intelligible world accessible only through the mind (*Resp.* 507b–c). For example, there may be a variety of different chairs in the sensible world, such as folding chairs, barstools, and recliners, but they are all instantiations of a single "form" of Chair in the intelligible world. The abstract idea of Chair accounts for all the particular versions of chairs down in the sensible world. This example illustrates how Plato's intelligible world is more basic, more important, and the source of the sensible world's many particulars.

Plato's vision of a two-tiered reality, called extreme realism by philosophers, goes beyond the mundane of everyday objects; it becomes a trajectory for salvation through philosophy. In Plato's famous *Allegory of the Cave* (*Resp.* 514–20), human beings are likened to prisoners chained to a low wall in a darkened cave, forced to look forward at a wall illuminated by fire behind them. Their vision consists only of shadows of figures that walk between themselves and the fire; they are never able to see the figures themselves. "Then in every way," Plato reasons, "such prisoners would deem reality to be nothing else than the shadows of the artificial objects" (*Resp.* 515b–c).[12] If such prisoners were freed from their shackles, they would need to learn how to perceive things other than shadows, such as three-dimensional bodies and the night sky. Moreover, once the freed prisoners learned how to perceive the real world, they would pity any prisoners left shackled in the cave, who perceive only shadows.

Plato uses this analogy to explain the role of philosophy in a human's salvation from the sensible world. Before learning philosophy, each human being can perceive only the sensible world of shadows, never able to perceive the real intelligible world hidden to his eyes. After becoming philosophically enlightened, the philosopher recognizes the illusion of the physical world of shadows and focuses his energy on the true reality behind the sensible world. Plato remarks, "Do not be surprised that those who have attained to this height are not willing to occupy themselves with the affairs of men, but their souls ever feel the upward urge and the yearning for that sojourn above" (*Resp.* 517c–d).[13] This remark encapsulates two trajectories of Platonic thought: a rejection or demotion of the value of the physical world and the melding of philosophy with religious pursuits. Accordingly, Platonic philosophy has little value for what is now called "science"—the investigation of the physical world—because the philosopher is better off studying the unseen world above (*Theaet.* 174).[14] Both Maimonides and Kabbalah integrate this idea into their theological systems, but Kabbalah incorporates it to a far greater extent.

---

12. Plato, *Republic*, 2:123.
13. Plato, *Republic*, 2:131.
14. On the contrast between Aristotelian and Platonic approaches to what we call "science" today, see Tirosh-Samuelson, "Kabbalah and Science," 477–80.

4.1.5. Plato's Allegorical Hermeneutics: Esoteric Versus Exoteric

Plato's understanding of two levels of reality influences his understanding of the meaning of words. Words may have a surface-level or basic meaning corresponding to the shadows on the wall, but the philosopher knows how to decipher the hidden figures *behind* the basic meaning.

For example, when considering the immoral actions of the Greek gods in Homer's works, Plato envisions an ideal republic where such tales would not be taught to little children (*Resp.* 378d–e). The reason, Plato says, was because children have no ability to distinguish between *hyponoia* (ὑπόνοια) and texts that are not *hyponoia*. This Greek word refers to a hidden meaning or the thought underneath the surface of words. In Plato's mind, children do not know whether to understand the gods' actions in Homer's writings metaphorically or straightforwardly, but the philosopher knows how to tell the difference. Other Greek authors use the word allegory (ἀλληγορία, *allegoria*) to describe this phenomenon.

Plato did not invent the allegorical method of interpretation, as it came to be called, but he provided the metaphysical justification for its development. Later followers of Plato paired his double-tiered metaphysical understanding of reality with a double-tiered method of interpretation of words. Although the words on a page may have specific meanings and grammatical constructions, the allegorical method encouraged the interpreter to look for additional meanings of a passage. The first Jewish author to use the allegorical method of interpretation of Scripture was Aristobulus (second century BCE),[15] but it was extended and mastered by Philo (first century CE, *Dreams* 1.234–1.235). Aristobulus writes, "To those who have no share of power and understanding, but who are devoted to the letter alone, [Moses] does not seem to explain anything elevated."[16] This is the first known claim that Moses hid the true meaning of the Torah under allegorical figures which unenlightened readers have no access to. Maimonides would later apply this logic to God talk, and the Kabbalists would apply it to every word in the Hebrew Scriptures.

Modern commentators often distinguish between esoteric and exoteric interpretations of written works, and these words derive from Platonic metaphysics and hermeneutics. The exoteric meaning of a passage is that which is commonly accessible to the wider world through natural

---

15. Fragment 2. For this fragment and a discussion on Aristobulus, see *OTP* 2:831–42.

16. Aristobulus, fragment 2 (*OTP* 2:838). See also Eusebius, *Praep. ev.* 8.10.

language and the tools of grammar, syntax, and dictionaries. In contrast, the esoteric meaning of a passage is inaccessible to the wider world. It is attainable only through special philosophical or religious training from a circle of enlightened adepts—the only ones who have the keys to the deeper meaning hidden behind the exoteric understanding of the masses. The Platonic school exalted the esoteric at the expense of the exoteric.

Each of the Platonic themes discussed in this section would be developed by the medieval Jewish philosophical tradition in their quest to integrate biblical revelation with knowledge of the world.

4.2. Aristotle

Aristotle (384–22 BCE) was Plato's most famous student. Initially studying under Plato at his academy in Athens, Aristotle parted ways with his teacher and founded his own school, the Lyceum. Aristotle taught an encyclopedic range of topics, including logic, grammatical interpretation, physical motion, physical qualities, astronomy, cosmology, causality, metaphysics, theology, botany, zoology, ethics, politics, and rhetoric. Unlike his teacher Plato, Aristotle delivered his writings as monologues, making direct assertions of fact, opinion, and reasoning. He was the founder of several branches of science since his philosophizing included penetrating empirical analyses of the physical world. Aristotle's interest in the physical world derived from his vision of reality, which differed from Plato's double-tiered doctrine. When Maimonides frequently cites "the philosopher," he means one man: Aristotle.

4.2.1. Aristotle's Single-Tiered Metaphysics

According to Aristotle, each thing that exists possesses a single "substance" or "essence" (*Metaph.* 7.1–3). There is something "treeish" about a tree because it has the substance of a tree, and this substance distinguishes it from a dog, which does not have the substance of a tree (*Cat.* 5; *Metaph.* 5.8). Things that exist have essential properties (those attributes each substance has by necessity) and accidental properties (those potential attributes a substance may or may not have [*An. Post.* 1.4]). For example, a tree has essential attributes of photosynthesizing and having a trunk and branches. It cannot *be* a tree (that is, have the substance of a tree) if it does not have those properties. However, some accidental properties of trees include being tall, being green, and having leaves. Some trees have those characteristics, and others do not, such as a variety of short conifer trees in wintertime. Moreover, things that exist have only one substance; they do not have a partial copy of an intellectual form, as with Plato (*Metaph* 1.6; 7.6). Their existence is single tiered, not spread across the sensible and intellectual realms.

Aristotelian metaphysics, called moderate realism, states that each thing that exists possesses its own substance fully. That which makes a tree a tree is within the tree itself. The tree is not a copy of an archetypal "Tree" in Plato's intellectual realm; it is not dependent upon any other realm for its existence as a tree. In Plato's metaphysics, a Tree exists in the intellectual realm even if there are no physical trees in existence; in Aristotle's understanding, if there are no trees in the physical universe, then trees do not exist.

Similarly, Aristotle's understanding of the soul is grounded in the potentiality of each existing thing. The soul is the life principle of living things, possessed individually by each living thing (*De an.* 2.4). In contrast to Plato, Aristotle does not believe that living things are alive because of their participation in a world soul that is spread throughout the cosmos.

This understanding of existence impacts several aspects of Aristotle's philosophy. First, it lays the groundwork for empirical science, since knowledge about what a thing is can be discerned by studying the thing, rather than speculating about an invisible intellectual realm upon which the thing is patterned.[17] Second, Aristotle posits distinct categories for various kinds of things since their classifications are based upon characteristics available to the senses, rather than their participation in another realm. Third, Aristotle's understanding of existence enables him to develop a system of analytical logic whereby he can say, "This is not that," thereby establishing foundational principles like the law of noncontradiction.[18] Thus, Aristotle makes great use of the principle of differentiation, whereas *Parmenides* disallows its use. Fourth, if things have a single substance, so too do words, phrases, and grammatical constructions. Aristotle develops a sophisticated method of rhetoric and interpretation that is grounded on the conventional meaning of words, avoiding the Platonic tendency to look for allegorical meanings behind

---

17. Tirosh-Samuelson, "Kabbalah and Science," 477–78.

18. "The same attribute cannot at the same time belong and not belong to the same subject and in the same respect.... This, then, is the most certain of all principles" (Aristotle, *Metaph.* 4.3 [*Works*, 524]). See also Aristotle, *Int.* 14.

words.[19] Maimonides incorporates each of these Aristotelian ideas into his own system, but they are less compatible with kabbalistic thought.

4.2.2. Aristotelian-Ptolemaic Cosmology

For nearly two millennia, Westerners looked up at the night sky and visualized the cosmos according to the descriptions given by Aristotle and Ptolemy (see fig. 2).[20] In Aristotle's cosmology, the sun, moon, planets, and stars are endowed with life or intelligence, and all move atop ethereal heavenly spheres due to the influence of God, the Prime Mover (*Metaph.* 12.8; *Cael.* 2.12). The Earth is the center of the universe, and the spheres rotate around in concentric layers, like those of an onion. The inner spheres, closer to Earth, have lesser intelligence, and the outermost sphere of fixed stars has the greatest. God is the one who stands eternally outside of the outermost sphere and is the unmoved mover who set the outermost sphere in flight (*Metaph.* 12.7). This outermost motion, in turn, leads to the motion of the lower spheres, each turning within each other. Eventually, the motion of the rolling spheres induces motion on the lowest sphere, that of the Earth, and consequently Aristotle's cosmology explains why there is life and motion on Earth.

Aristotle teaches, with Empedocles (ca. 490–30 BCE), that there are four elements or essences in the sublunary sphere: fire, air, water, and earth. However, he adds a fifth essence (*quinta essentia*), æther, which is eternal and immutable and provides the substance of the heavenly spheres, planets, and stars (*Cael.* 1.2–1.3). Thus, the ancient periodic table had only five elements, four of which were accessible to humans.

---

19. See Aristotle, *Int.*; Seuren, "Aristotle and Linguistics," 26.

20. There were other important Greek philosophers who influenced this cosmology as well. The following account is summarized. For a thorough overview, see Crowe, *Theories of the World*. For a fourth-century survey of cosmological positions in antiquity, see Eusebius, *Praep. ev.* 15.23–58.

Figure 2. The Ptolemaic Geocentric Model, from *Harmonia Macrocosmica*, by Andreas Cellarius, 1660

Aristotle believed there are either fifty-five or forty-seven heavenly spheres (*Metaph.* 12.8), but later Greeks believed in a reduced number. The mathematician Ptolemy (100–170 CE) extends Aristotle's model in his *Almagest* by positing a system of eccentric orbits and epicycles—orbits within orbits—in a complex mathematical system. Aristotle's spheres cosmology, when combined with Ptolemy's astronomical calculations, leads to a remarkably accurate mathematical model by which the motions of the heavenly bodies such as Jupiter and Mars can be predicted. The accuracy of the model explains why the Aristotelian-Ptolemaic cosmology became standard in the West, despite its unproven geocentric assumptions.

The Aristotelian-Ptolemaic cosmology stood at the foundation of Western scientific, philosophical, mystical, and magical thought for millennia—and given modern astrology and occult practices, it continues today. Both Maimonides and the Kabbalists took the

Aristotelian-Ptolemaic model for granted, and each made philosophical and theological determinations based on this cosmology. Nevertheless, this model is no longer accepted as an accurate depiction of the cosmos, since the Renaissance-era mathematical and observational discoveries of Copernicus, Kepler, Brahe, and Galileo invalidated the premises of geocentric cosmology.

4.2.3. Aristotle's Theology

Aristotle's description of God would prove to be influential in later theological thought. He writes, "We say therefore that God is a living being, eternal, most good, so that life and duration continuous and eternal belong to God; for this *is* God" (*Metaph.* 12.7).[21] He continues,

> It is clear then from what has been said that there is a substance which is eternal and unmovable and separate from sensible things. It has been shown also that this substance cannot have any magnitude, but is without parts and indivisible. . . . But it has also been shown that it is impassive and unalterable; for all the other changes are posterior to change of place. (*Metaph.* 12.7)[22]

These Aristotelian descriptions of God, such as unmovable, without magnitude, without parts, indivisible, impassive, and unalterable, continue to impact theological discourse today. Philosopher Bruce Wilshire comments,

> For reasons connected with his astronomy, Aristotle postulated a God. His God, however, had nothing to do with the universe; it was not his creation, and he was, of necessity, indifferent to its vicissitudes (he could not otherwise have been an unmoved mover). It is a mistake to imagine that everything in the Aristotelian universe is trying to fulfill a purpose that God has ordained for it.[23]

In theological terms, Aristotle is on the deistic side of the spectrum, positing a detached God whose primary purpose is to establish the world but little else. Aristotle denies the need for divine providence to sustain existence in the sublunary sphere (*Cael.* 2.1), and he denies that God performs any actions whatsoever besides contemplation (*Eth. Nic.* 10.8). Maimonides summarizes Aristotle's view:

---

21. Aristotle, *Works*, 603; emphasis in original.
22. Aristotle, *Works*, 603.
23. Wilshire, "Metaphysics."

> God ... is in such a relation to the Universe that He cannot change anything; if He wished to make the wing of a fly longer, or to reduce the number of the legs of a worm by one, He could not accomplish it. According to Aristotle, He does not try such a thing, and it is wholly impossible for Him to desire any change in the existing order of things; if He could, it would not increase His perfection; it might, on the contrary, from some point of view, diminish it.[24]

Maimonides was greatly influenced by Aristotle's theology but attempted to align it with Scripture by positing mechanisms by which God can provide creation *ex nihilo*, providence, miracles, revelation, and connection with humanity. The Kabbalists did not think Maimonides's philosophy was successful in retaining God's intimate relationship with creation, and they mostly jettisoned Aristotle's theology in favor of the Platonic tradition.

4.3. Neopythagoreanism

Neopythagoreanism was a first-century BCE to third-century CE school inspired by the sixth-century BCE Greek philosopher Pythagoras, who was also made famous by his Pythagorean Theorem for triangles. Pythagoras did not leave any of his philosophical writings behind, but his many followers (such as Plato) and opponents (such as Aristotle) attested to his teachings.[25] A revival of Pythagorean ideas around the first century, mixed with Platonism and Stoicism, is what scholars now call Neopythagoreanism.

Neopythagoreanism leaves many first-time observers bewildered and confused. It is often difficult to distinguish it from the later movements of Gnosticism (second to fourth centuries CE) or Neoplatonism (third century CE onward). Mystical religions, such as Gnosticism and Neopythagoreanism, are characterized by their fuzzy boundaries and predisposition to adopt doctrines from other schools of thought. However, Neopythagoreanism is sufficiently unique to merit a separate treatment, especially since several of its ideas would one day be adopted by Kabbalah.[26] The four Pythagorean themes most relevant to this book are

---

24. Maimonides, *Guide* 2.22.
25. See also Diogenes Laertius, *Vit. Phil.* 8.25–27.
26. Although our focus will be on how Pythagorean concepts influenced Kabbalah, it is true that Pythagoreanism has been attractive to some Christians as well. For

Part II: A Critique of Non-Incarnational Maimonidean and Kabbalistic Thought

the exalted metaphysical status of numbers, ten as the number of reality, the numerological method of hermeneutics, and the soul's salvation via reincarnation over time.

4.3.1. Pythagorean Number Metaphysics

Neopythagoreanism is notable for a cosmology founded on a unique numerological worldview. Through two separate trains of thought, Neopythagoreans came to believe that numbers are the basis of all reality. The first pathway flowed from Pythagoras's discovery that music is related to mathematics.[27] Pythagorean scholar Richard McKirahan writes that Pythagoras discovered "that the octave is dependent not upon the material of the string that produces it, or its length or thickness or tension, but on the ratio 2:1."[28] This discovery

> was the inspiration for a general theory about the nature of reality. In one way or another, everything depends on number: number is essential or fundamental to all things. This claim was primarily a claim about the nature of things in the world, but it was also an epistemological claim: if we understand the numerical basis of something, then we understand that thing. Number is the key to knowledge.[29]

Pythagoras combined this numerical principle with his geocentric cosmology, positing that each of the heavenly spheres emits a musical tone (number) that harmonizes with all the other spheres' music.[30] For Pythagoras, the "music of the spheres" is inaudible to human ears because of the intense harmony that places it outside human perception.[31] The numerical music that emanates from the higher spheres then condenses into inferior forms in the lower regions, with physical material as the lowest form of the numbers.

Neopythagoreans found a second pathway for asserting the metaphysical importance of numbers by reasoning geometrically from

---

examples of how Pythagorean syncretism worked its way into Christian discourse, see Ephrem the Syrian, *Hymns on the Nativity* 27; *Pseudo-Clementine Homilies* 17.9 (*ANF* 8:320); Wolfson, "Tree That Is All," 37.

27. Aristotle, *Metaph.* 1.5.
28. McKirahan, "Philolaus on Number," 182. See also Thesleff, "Pythagoreanism."
29. McKirahan, "Philolaus on Number," 182.
30. Plato, *Resp.* 617.
31. Plato, *Resp.* 617. Aristotle considers several arguments in favor of the music of the spheres and rejects them all (*Cael.* 2.9).

three-dimensional bodies to points.[32] First, they presupposed that simple things are metaphysically better than complex things. Thus, three dimensions (bodies) are inferior to two dimensions (planes), which are inferior to one dimension (lines), which is inferior to no dimensions (points).[33] Since there is nothing prior to points, and points can be numbered, all human experience can be summed up by numbers. The Neopythagoreans assigned numerical values to these geometrical dimensions and associated the sum of the dimensions (ten, the *tetraktys* pyramid) with ten categories of opposites as well as Aristotle's ten categories,[34] as follows:

Table 6. Neopythagorean Number Metaphysics

Geometrical Pyramid (*Tetraktys*)	Number	Geometrical Feature
•	One	Point
• •	Two	Line
• • •	Three	Plane
• • • •	Four	Solid
	Sum = Ten	

Table 7. Ten Pythagorean Opposites (*Metaph.* 1.5)

Limit	Unlimited
Odd	Even
One	Plurality
Right	Left
Male	Female
Resting	Moving
Straight	Curved
Light	Darkness
Good	Bad
Square	Oblong

32. For the following paragraph and table 6, see Alexander of Aphrodisias (second century CE) in his commentary on Aristotle's *Metaphysics* (Aristotle, *Select Fragments*, 12:117). Also see Hippolytus, *Haer.* 1.2; 4.51; 6.18–23; Diogenes Laertius, *Vit. Phil.* 8.25–26.

33. Aristotle, *Cael.* 1.1.

34. Huffman, "Pythagoreanism." Aristotle's categories may be found in Aristotle, *Cat.* 4, and the ten Pythagorean opposites are found in *Metaph.* 1.5.

Part II: A Critique of Non-Incarnational Maimonidean and Kabbalistic Thought

Table 8. Ten Aristotelian Categories Used by Neopythagoreans (*Cat.* 4)

Substance	Quantity	Place	Time	Action
Quality	Relation	Position	State	Affection

Because the number ten was supposed to have cosmic significance, the Pythagoreans sought to discern patterns of ten in features large and small. In their view, the ten Pythagorean opposites were metaphysically connected to the ten Aristotelian categories, as well as connected to ten rocks, ten people, ten fingers, and ten-ness in general. Ten found in the sensible realm was supposed to be a hint or a consequence of the ten in a higher realm. Accordingly, the Pythagoreans associated the number ten with the number of heavenly spheres, conjecturing a "Counter-Earth" to make their number fit.[35]

Table 9. Pythagorean Ten Spheres Cosmology

First Sphere	Moon
Second Sphere	Mercury
Third Sphere	Venus
Fourth Sphere	Sun
Fifth Sphere	Mars
Sixth Sphere	Jupiter
Seventh Sphere	Saturn
Eighth Sphere	Fixed Stars
Ninth Sphere	Earth
Tenth Sphere	Counter-Earth

Although the Pythagoreans believed that the ten spheres explained all physical reality, they associated a special role with the first seven spheres in their scheme. These seven spheres were the only visible objects in the night sky that moved beneath the furthest sphere of the "fixed stars." The Pythagoreans and the later gnostics referred to these "seven heavens" by the term *Hebdomad*.[36] In the gnostic tradition, each of the spheres was presided over by an angel or deity called an *archon* or *aeon*. The seven spheres were then paired with the seven days of the week,

35. See *Cael.* 2.13 for Aristotle's criticism of the Counter-Earth idea. See also *Metaph.* 1.5 and a fragment by Alexander of Aphrodisias in his commentary on Aristotle's *Metaphysics* (Aristotle, *Select Fragments*, 141–44).

36. Salmon, "Hebdomas." See also Irenaeus, *Haer.* 1.30; Origen, *Cels.* 6.31–32.

with each day overseen by the power of the sphere associated with it (i.e., "Saturn's day" for the seventh day, Saturday). When the Greek mystics referred to the region beyond the control of the seven *archons*, they called it the *Ogdoad*. Thus, while the number ten had an exalted status to explain all known reality, the number seven had a special place, and the ten was partitioned into a seven and a triad.

In summary, in Neopythagoreanism, both the number ten and numbers in general took on cosmic significance. Ten describes the heavens above and the experience of phenomena below. Numbers flow down from the heavenly spheres to the lower regions through the spheres' music, where they coalesce into physical matter. Thus, numbers explain all known reality; indeed, reality is nothing more than numbers. This was fruit for much mystical contemplation in Kabbalah, especially in the interpretations of words.

4.3.2. Pythagorean-Gnostic Isopsephy/Geometrikos

Ancient Greeks were accustomed to using their alphabet for dual purposes: the formation of words, and the counting of numbers. For example, the Greek letters *a* and *e* (alpha and epsilon) could serve as vowels in words, or else as the numbers one and five, respectively. This was originally a "secular" numbering system without metaphysical connotations, but the Neopythagoreans transformed the system into a playground for mystical interpretations. In his book *The Greek Qabalah*, Kieren Barry elaborates:

> The use of the Greek alphabetic system of numerals endowed every word written in the ancient alphabets, such as Greek, Arabic and Hebrew, with a numerical significance, since each of the letters could be added up to form a single number. The Greeks called this phenomenon isopsephos (iso- means "equal"; psephos, "pebble"), since it was common practice among the early Greeks to use patterns of pebbles or stones to learn arithmetic. Another word for pebbles (kalkuli) is the origin of our word "calculate."[37]

The Neopythagoreans did not merely use the Greek letters as numbers, but also assigned cosmic significance to the letters. Since letters are numbers, they are the very substance of reality, flowing down from the seven spheres as they harmonize their music and coalesce into physicality.

---

37. Barry, *Greek Qabalah*, 37.

Letters and words, therefore, are the building blocks of reality, and the adept philosopher could wield the power of words to modify the world as he saw fit.

The key to this power was a secret knowledge of the meaning of the Greek letters and the mathematical computation of new meanings. Barry writes, "The isopsephy used by the Pythagoreans had developed by Gnostic times into several different techniques that were used for a wide range of purposes, including divination, doctrinal allegory, and medical prognosis and treatment."[38] The gnostics, and likely the Neopythagoreans who preceded them, split the twenty-four letters of the Greek alphabet into different classes based upon the sound they make in the mouth and assigned them secret meanings. For example, they assigned letters that make a minor sound to the unspeakable and unutterable Father, whereas they assigned vowels to the lower realm because they are more easily heard.[39] This system of numerical interpretation would eventually find its way into Kabbalah, where it is applied to the Hebrew language and called gematria, perhaps from the Greek phrase *geometrikos arithmos*.[40]

4.3.3. Pythagorean Reincarnation

Just as Pythagorean hermeneutics were tied to Pythagorean cosmology, so too was the Pythagorean notion of transmigration of souls, also known as metempsychosis or reincarnation. The Platonic-Pythagorean philosopher Numenius of Apamea (ca. 150–200 CE) presented a version of reincarnation that would resonate down the centuries. Like gnostic and Neoplatonic philosophers, Numenius believed that the human soul is a spark or fragment of the divinity that pervades and unifies the universe.[41] The divine spark is trapped within a material body, which is a lesser form of existence, and it needs to return to its source in the higher heavenly spheres.

In the ancient scheme, the soul must pass the "seven heavens" of the Hebdomad, which consisted of the spheres (in descending order) of Saturn, Jupiter, Mars, Sun, Venus, Mercury, and Moon. When a soul initially

---

38. Barry, *Greek Qabalah*, 141.
39. Barry, *Greek Qabalah*, 131–33.
40. Bohak, "Gematria." For discussions on how early church fathers variously rejected and accepted numerology in their interpretations, see Ferguson, "Numerology"; Brashear, "Word Magic." Also see appendix E.
41. Cf. Philo, *Dreams* 1.34: "In man the mind is holy, being a sort of fragment of the Deity" (Philo of Alexandria, *Works*, 368).

comes into a body, it descends from the outermost sphere of fixed stars, passing through each of the spheres of the planets, each of which delivers a benefit to the soul such as intelligence and boldness. The soul then lives a full life in a body, during which time the human is supposed to live a good life of philosophical development. At physical death, the soul then repeats its course backwards through the seven heavenly spheres, up to the highest heaven, where it is judged on its performance in the body. The soul is then sent back down into a new body that fits its level of development. Eventually, the soul will cease this cycle once it is purified and can enter the divine realm permanently.[42] Kabbalah deeply integrates similar ideas of divine sparks and reincarnation into its theology.

4.4. Gnosticism

Gnosticism is the general term for a religious and philosophical movement that thrived in the second through fourth centuries CE.[43] The various gnostic schools combined elements of Judaism, Christianity, Persian dualism, and Platonic-Pythagorean esotericism into a secret knowledge tradition. The movement is named after the Greek word for knowledge, *gnosis* (γνῶσις), but it refers to a special, secret, esoteric knowledge accepted by the chosen few. This knowledge consisted of complex metaphysics and theology and resulted in the eternal salvation of all who were fated to accept it.

There were many gnostic groups, or schools of thought, within the movement as a whole (Marcionites, Valentinians, Sethians, Manichees, etc.), and thus any general description of Gnosticism needs to be open to revision when it comes to particular doctrines.[44] The lines between Gnosticism and other movements, such as Hermeticism (a pagan form of magic philosophy), likewise are blurry. The gnostic movement, for many centuries, was primarily understood through the writings of early church fathers (including Irenaeus and Hippolytus), who vehemently opposed gnostic thought.[45] Many of the early gnostics were followers of teachers who had defected from the orthodoxy of the wider Christian

---

42. For this paragraph, see Tripolitis, *Religions of Hellenistic-Roman Age*, 43.

43. Markschies, *Gnosis*; Tripolitis, *Religions of Hellenistic-Roman Age*, 119–42; Versluis, *Magic and Mysticism*, ch. 3; Stroumsa, "Gnosis"; Ramelli, "Gnosis-Gnosticism."

44. Ramelli, "Gnosis-Gnosticism," 2:142; Markschies, *Gnosis*, 16–17.

45. Irenaeus, *Haer.*; Hippolytus, *Haer.*

Part II: A Critique of Non-Incarnational Maimonidean and Kabbalistic Thought

church and had gone on to teach metaphysical systems that were at odds with the NT.[46] With the discovery of the Nag Hammadi texts in 1945, the world received a direct look at the worldview of Gnosticism without dependence on the church fathers.[47]

Gnostics held to cosmological dualism, whereby everything that exists is either part of the divine *pleroma* (fullness) or the evil *kenoma* (emptiness).[48] The pleroma consists of immaterial *aeons* (personal beings) emanating from the highest God through sexual combinations of opposites (*syzygies*).[49] All emanations and combinations in the pleroma above have their companions in the kenoma below, understood under the maxim common to Gnosticism and Hermeticism, "As above, so below."[50] For gnostics, the God from whom everything emanates cannot be known or described, in *via negativa* fashion.[51] He lives in the pleroma, beyond the seven heavens of the Hebdomad. Each of the seven heavens is ruled by one of the aeons, and they each correspond to one of the seven days of the week.[52] The material world is part of the kenoma and needs to rise to the pleroma, its source and pattern. In fact, the material universe is a cosmological mistake, for a rebellious aeon (called the demiurge) left the pleroma and emanated the universe to rule over it.[53] The gnostics often identified this lower, evil god as the God of Israel who delivered the Hebrew Scriptures, which they saw as untrustworthy.[54]

---

46. Gnostic teachers included Valentinus, Marcion, Basilides, Markos, etc.

47. See *NHL*.

48. Ramelli, "Pleroma," 3:227.

49. Irenaeus, *Haer.* 1.1–2; Hippolytus, *Haer.* 6.24.

50. This most famous form of the maxim is from the Emerald Tablet, which has uncertain provenance, but also see Gos. Phil. 67:31–34 (*NHL* 2.3). Arthur Versluis elaborates on the idea: "There is a syzygic relationship between the deity and the cosmos that the deity has created. It is not only that both are said to be good, it is that the cosmos reflects and manifests the spiritual qualities of the deity. The deity is bisexual, and so too are all creatures, who are the outward manifestation of that inner spiritual bisexuality of the deity" (*Magic and Mysticism*, ch. 3, n.p.).

51. See Tri. Trac. 1.2, 1.4 (*NHL* 1.5); Ap. John 2:33—3:30 (*NHL* 2.1).

52. Ap. John 11:4-35 (*NHL* 2.1).

53. Tripolitis, *Religions of Hellenistic-Roman Age*, 122–23; Ap. John 9:25—11:22 (*NHL* 2.1).

54. For example, Disc. Seth 62:27 subverts the biblical narrative by mocking Israel's patriarchs and Moses himself as "laughingstocks" (*NHL* 7.2). Ap. John 22:3–28 says it was good for Adam and Eve to reject the archon who forbid them from eating the fruit, explaining, "It is not the way Moses wrote and you heard" (*NHL* 2.1). On Gnosticism as a form of Jewish revolt, see Dahl, "Arrogant Archon."

In Gnosticism, physicality, which is characterized by multiplicity and diversity, is evil and must be shed.[55] The human body was created in 365 parts by 365 angelic powers, and specific angels have power over specific body parts and senses.[56] Some humans have the divine spark of the pleroma within them, and others do not. The gnostics separated themselves from the unchosen, cloaked their teachings in numerological riddles based on Greek letters (*geometrikos arithmos*), and appropriated biblical texts to subvert their meaning in a gnostic direction.[57] For example, the gnostic text *Pistis Sophia* (ca. third century CE) gives the following *geometrikos* riddle for one of the names of God:

> This is the name of the Deathless One AAA ΩΩΩ [three alphas and three omegas]. . . . [And] these are the interpretations of the names of these Mysteries. The first is AAA [alpha]. Its interpretation is φφφ [phi]. The second is MMM [mu] or ΩΩΩ [omega]. Its interpretation is AAA [alpha]. The third is ΨΨΨ [psi]. Its interpretation is OOO [omicron]. The fourth is φφφ [phi]. Its interpretation is NNN [nu]. The fifth is ΔΔΔ [delta].[58]

No one has the key to these mathematical riddles any longer, so this passage is obscure. Gnostics also taught that human salvation is possible, but only for the elect few who can ascend in mystical soul flight past the seven spheres of the Hebdomad into the unity of the pleroma. The elite few are the "pneumatic" beings with souls made of divine sparks, in contrast to the lower "hylic" and "psychic" beings who have no hope of ascending to the pleroma.[59]

In his study of esoteric knowledge systems, Michael McClymond writes, "Gnostic teachers generally portrayed the story of salvation according to a threefold schema of *unity-diversity-unity*: a primal spiritual unity with God, a lapse into diversity (understood as evil), and a final

---

55. Ap. Jas. 27:1–10 says, "You [must] cast away from yourself blind thought, this bond of flesh which encircles you. And then you will reach Him-who-is. And you will not longer be James; rather you are the One-who-is" (*NHL* 5.3). See also Irenaeus, *Haer.* 1.17.2.

56. Ap. John 15:13—19:15 (*NHL* 2.1). This section explicitly cites "the book of Zoroaster" as the place to find the exhaustive list of names of the aeons (19:10).

57. See especially Disc. Seth and Ap. John for examples of hermeneutical subversion of biblical texts.

58. *Pistis Sophia* bk. 1; quoted in Barry, *Greek Qabalah*, 123.

59. Ramelli, "Psychici."

Part II: A Critique of Non-Incarnational Maimonidean and Kabbalistic Thought

return to unity with God."[60] In this threefold schema and many other ways, Kabbalah shows remarkable similarity with gnostic thought.

4.5. Neoplatonism

Building upon the thought of Plato, Stoicism, and Neopythagoreanism, the Alexandrian-Roman philosopher Plotinus (204–70 CE) took Plato's thought to new heights.[61] Although Platonic-influenced writers such as Basilides, Valentinus, and Numenius anticipated many of Plotinus's teachings, Plotinus would be the most significant influence on subsequent Platonic thought. He founded a syncretistic school of thought now known as Neoplatonism. Plotinus scholar Pauliina Remes summarizes:

> In general, the Neoplatonists were eager to merge Plato's and Aristotle's philosophy into a whole, preserving Plato's metaphysical and spiritual intuitions while combining these with the valuable work on the sensible world by Aristotle, as well as with the latter's laudable clarity and precision.[62]

Plotinus's principal work is *The Six Enneads*, a collection of his lectures compiled by his student Porphyry. Plotinus was succeeded by Porphyry, Iamblichus, and Proclus, each of whom delivered the Western world developments of Plotinus's thought.[63] By the fifth century CE, Neoplatonism became a catchall mystical philosophy that integrated Platonic, Neopythagorean, Aristotelian, and Hermetic (magical) thought into one whole. Plotinian scholar Maria Luisa Gatti writes, "Plotinus has

---

60. McClymond, *Devil's Redemption*, 2:1005; emphasis in original. See also Tri. Trac. 132:16–28 (*NHL* 1.5); Ramelli, "Gnosis-Gnosticism," 2:144.

61. Lilla, "Plotinus"; Lilla, "Neoplatonism"; Gerson, *Cambridge Companion to Plotinus*; Remes, *Neoplatonism*.

62. Remes, *Neoplatonism*, 3–4.

63. Until the Renaissance, these authors' works were not directly influential in the West, but rather indirectly influential through their appropriation by more acceptable Christian authors. For example, Boethius (ca. 480–525 CE) would deliver Porphyry's thought to the West through his commentary on Porphyry's *Isagoge*, and Pseudo-Dionysius (sixth century CE) translated Plotinian and Proclean ideas into Christian thought patterns. In the Middle Ages, Muslims and Jews were led to believe that a selection of Plotinus's *Enneads*, entitled *The Theology of Aristotle*, was attributed to Aristotle. Other Western Christian thinkers associated with Neoplatonic thought include John Scotus Eriugena, Meister Eckhart, Nicholas of Cusa, Jacob Böhme. See Cooper, *Panentheism*.

gathered the legacy of nearly eight centuries of Greek philosophy into a magnificently unified synthesis."[64]

This tradition was mediated to the Christian world in the sixth century through Boethius and spurious Dionysian works,[65] and to the Islamic and Jewish worlds in the ninth century and later. As a result, Plotinus became the authoritative interpreter of Plato for over fifteen hundred years.[66] The story of Western mysticism is largely the story of Plotinus's ideas filtered through the Christian, Jewish, and Islamic traditions.[67] Neoplatonism also shares strong affinities with Eastern mysticism (although the two developed separately), such that modern New Age mysticism tries to synthesize both Western (Neoplatonic) and Eastern (Hindu, Buddhist) traditions into one.[68]

The following brief survey of Neoplatonism will focus on Plotinus's unique theological and cosmological contributions as found in his *Six Enneads*. The teachings of the *Enneads* I consider most relevant to medieval Judaism may be summarized as follows:

1. Divine transcendence: God (the One) is beyond all, even existence itself. (*Enn.* 5.4.1; 6.9)

2. Absolute divine simplicity: Singularity precedes multiplicity. If there are many, there must be a prior One that is free from any kind of multiplicity. (*Enn.* 5.6.3; 6.6.13)

3. *Via negativa*: The One cannot be positively described or known. (*Enn.* 5.3.13–14; 6.7.38)

64. Gatti, "Plotinus," 10.

65. Such as *The Divine Names*, *Mystical Theology*, and *Celestial Hierarchy* (Pseudo-Dionysius, *Complete Works*). To a lesser extent, the Neoplatonic tradition was Christianized by Augustine in the fifth century.

66. Remes writes, "In the course of Western history, it turned out that the Neoplatonic understanding of Platonic philosophy became *the* reading of Plato.... This makes it difficult to disentangle Platonic and Neoplatonic influences" (*Neoplatonism*, 197; emphasis in original). Gatti writes, "Late antiquity and the Middle Ages have known Platonism in the guise of Neoplatonism, making no distinction between the two systems" ("Plotinus," 22). It has been only in the nineteenth century and later that scholars have distinguished the two.

67. McClymond identifies four "lineages" of the Western esoteric traditions: (1) Platonic-Neoplatonic, (2) kabbalistic, (3) alchemical, (4) Böhmist. In my view the first lineage gave birth to the following three (McClymond, *Devil's Redemption*, 2:1068–73). Frame credits the Neoplatonic Pseudo-Dionysius (alongside the gnostics and Clement of Alexandria) for bringing mysticism into Christianity (*History of Western Philosophy*, 126).

68. C. Clark and Geisler, *Apologetics in New Age*, 75–92.

4. An eternal universe of emanations: All that exists emanates from the One eternally. The One emanates mind, which emanates the world soul, which emanates the material cosmos, like the sun emanates light. (*Enn.* 3.2; 5.1.10)

5. Omnipresence as panentheism: Everything is united in God. (*Enn.* 3.2.7; 5.1.2; 6.4.4)

Although Plotinus argued for these notions in the third century, both Maimonides and Kabbalah would construct their theology upon variations of these ideas nearly a millennium later.

4.5.1. The One, Emanations, and Panentheism

As with Pythagoreanism and Gnosticism, Plotinus's philosophy often feels alien and otherworldly to those approaching it for the first time. The key to understanding Plotinus's thought is his notion of the One (or unity), which he derived from Plato's dialogue *Parmenides*. Plotinus believed that logically prior to the *many* existing, there must be the *One*.[69] For Plotinus, singularity precedes multiplicity. The One is the source of all existence—that is, being—but the One itself is so transcendent that it cannot be said to exist. The One is an infinite singularity that cannot be known or described, as it transcends all, including language, but it also mysteriously includes all.

Plotinus applied the idea of emanations to account for the existence of things within the One. The Abrahamic religions have typically defined God as the *Creator* of the universe, entailing a strict separation between the divine and the finite order, which began to exist *ex nihilo* (out of nothing). Neoplatonism has a different vision of the cosmos such that it emerged through emanation *ex Deo* (out of God). In line with much of Greek thought, Plotinus posited the eternality of the universe and employed the idea of divine emanations or overflow to account for the universe's finite existence. Creation *ex nihilo* entails ontological separation from God; emanation *ex Deo* entails ontological unity with God.

Platonic thinkers used the motifs of the sun and fire to justify the idea of cosmological emanations. In their view, light emanates from the sun such that it is always present whenever the sun is present, even though the light is dependent upon the sun for its existence. In this way,

---

69. "If there is to be a manifold there must be a precedent unity" (Plotinus, *Enn.* 6.6.13; cf. 5.4.1). In other words, if many are to come to exist, many must first come from One.

the sun and its light were understood to be one thing despite retaining individual differentiation and cause-effect relationship.[70] In like fashion, to the ancient Platonists, fire and heat were one thing while being causally distinguished as two (*Enn.* 5.1.3; 5.4.2). These kinds of ancient phenomenological analogies are invalid due to modern scientific knowledge,[71] but they provided powerful stimuli for the Greeks to postulate an infinite divine source (similar to the sun) with emanations that could account for finite existence.

Pythagorean conceptions of the nature of numbers contributed a second pathway for thinking about the essential unity of multiple things. Plotinus taught that the number one is "in" all other whole numbers, and that larger whole numbers are potentially contained within smaller whole numbers through addition. However, all whole numbers are dependent upon one for their existence, whereas one is not dependent upon any other number.[72] Jewish theologian David Novak summarizes Plotinus's thought as follows:

> All things are related to the One in the sense that they do not truly exist and cannot be understood outside this relation. But the One is not itself related to all things in that way at all. It does exist apart from them and in no way requires their existence. The relation is wholly nonreciprocal; there is no genuine interaction between the parties: One side is solely absolute and the other solely contingent.[73]

Plotinus applied the concept of nonreciprocal emanations to the cosmological and theological One, the most prior principle of all potential reality. As the sun emanates light by its very nature, so too the One necessarily emanates lower levels of reality that are essentially united with it. The One is the source of a "chain of being," with multiple levels of reality that are logically linked to each other in linear fashion. He explained the chain as follows (also see appendix C, fig. 8):

---

70. Plotinus writes, "Another example would be the sun, central to the light which streams from it and is yet linked to it, or at least is always about it, irremoveably; try all you will to separate the light from the sun, or the sun from its light, for ever the light is in the sun" (*Enn.* 1.7.1).
71. Ancient mystical theology was often based upon faulty empirical analogies. See §§6.3; 9.3.
72. Plotinus, *Enn.* 5.2.1; O'Meara, "Hierarchical Ordering of Reality," 72–73.
73. Novak, "Self-Contraction of Godhead," 313.

Part II: A Critique of Non-Incarnational Maimonidean and Kabbalistic Thought

First, the One emanates mind, the intellectual principle that reflects and thinks about the One. Next, mind emanates the world soul, which is an animating principle from Plato's *Timaeus*. Mind remains "in" the One, and soul remains "in" mind. These three—One, mind, and world soul—form an immaterial triad that is the basis of reality.[74] The world soul then emanates the material world of the universe (*Enn.* 5.2). However, the lower material cosmos is no longer a true unity because it consists of multiple parts that are estranged from one another, unlike the triad's unity. Difference and distance are part of the lower cosmos, which is disorder. Thus, mind communicates its order to the world soul, which then envelops the material world and causes the universe to shed its disorder, resulting in a universe that is alive as a unified dynamic organism (*Enn.* 3.2).

Plotinus's unified vision of reality, where all things emanate from the One and remain united in the One, was highly influential in later theological speculation. Although Plotinus calls the One "God," he also clarifies that understanding it as God is inadequate (*Enn.* 6.9.6). Eventually, many thinkers would merge Plotinus's idea of the One with the Abrahamic religions.[75]

Plotinus's main idea is that all existing things emanate from God and are included in him as aspects of his divinity. This position has been termed panentheism, which means "all is in God."[76] In panentheism, the universe is like God's body, which he animates with his overflowing being, but his existence also goes beyond the limits of the universe. Kabbalah integrates the panentheism of Neoplatonism into its system, with *Ein Sof* taking the place of the One. Maimonides was deeply influenced by Plotinus as well, although he left God outside the One.

4.5.2. Plotinus and Negative Theology (*Via Negativa*)

Previously I highlighted several passages in Plato's writings that point in a negative (apophatic) theology direction, namely the idea that God can be described using only negative language.[77] This idea became central to

---

74. See *Enn.* 5.1.8, where Plotinus calls these "the Primal one, a strictly pure Unity, and a secondary One [Mind] which is a One-Many and a third [Soul] which is a One-and-Many."

75. Christianity: Origen, Augustine, Pseudo-Dionysius, Eriugena, Pico, Bruno, Böhme; Islam: Al-Kindi, Al-Farabi, Avicenna; Judaism: Ibn Gabriol, Maimonides, kabbalistic tradition. See appendix B and McClymond, *Devil's Redemption*, 2:1067–73.

76. Cooper, *Panentheism*.

77. For example, *Tim.* 28c and *Parmenides*, already discussed, as well as Acts 17:23,

Western mysticism, including that of Kabbalah, and is also important in Maimonides's theology and hermeneutics. Plato only partially developed this doctrine despite its comprehensively wide scope and implications for theology and philosophy. In her historical study of apophatic theology, Deirdre Carabine writes,

> Although Plato has sometimes been regarded as the Father of apophasis, and while there are certain unmistakable elements of this method in his writings, along with a rather distinctive mystical outlook, Plato himself cannot be regarded as the founder of the negative way. However, it is true that his ideas provided the spark from which the principles of negative theology were eventually derived.... Very little movement is needed in order to identify the "father" of the *Timaeus* with the "one" of Parmenides, but this remains an identification which Plato himself did not make.[78]

What Plato did not do, Plotinus made explicit. He understood the divine "father" of the *Timaeus* through the lens of emanation and combined it with Parmenides's idea that only one thing exists. Plotinus understood the One to be logically prior to all other things, just as an individual person is logically prior to a crowd, or a cause is logically prior to an effect. Moreover, he inferred that subsequent effects are nonreciprocally related to their causes, such as squares being dependent upon the existence of rectangles, but not vice versa.[79] By understanding the One in this fashion, Plotinus necessarily made the One logically prior to all thought, knowledge, or language, and totally independent of them as well. By definition, the One cannot be thought of, known, or described, for it transcends all, even being. Plotinus writes, "The One is in truth beyond all statement" (*Enn.* 5.3.13). Elsewhere, he describes the One as transcending existence (being), but clarifies,

> Note that the phrase transcending Being assigns no character, makes no assertion, allots no name, carries only the denial of particular being; and in this there is no attempt to circumscribe

---

Philo (*Sacrifices* 101; *Posterity* 15; *Dreams* 1.234–35) and throughout the gnostic corpus. The Greek playwright Aeschylus (fifth century BCE) wrote, "Zeus: whatever he may be, if this name pleases him in invocation, thus I call upon him" (*Agamemnon*, in Aeschylus et al., *Aeschylus*, 4:55–56).

78. Carabine, *Unknown God*, 21.

79. That is, a square cannot exist without rectangles existing, for squares are rectangles with equivalent-length sides. All squares are rectangles, but not all rectangles are squares.

> it: to seek to throw a line about that illimitable Nature would be folly, and anyone thinking to do so cuts himself off from any slightest and most momentary approach to its least vestige. . . . If we are led to think positively of The One, name and thing, there would be more truth in silence. (*Enn.* 5.5.6)

Additionally, he says, "We can and do state what it is not, while we are silent as to what it is: we are, in fact, speaking of it in the light of its sequels; unable to state it, we may still possess it." (*Enn.* 5.3.14) In this passage, Plotinus says that the One cannot be known, but it can be experienced in mystical contemplation.

For Plotinus and the Neoplatonic tradition, the One is ineffable, beyond all comprehension and knowledge, so the enlightened philosopher ought to remain silent and say nothing. Maimonides, familiar with a medieval version of Plotinus's writings, would come to say the same about God.

4.5.3. Plotinus, God, and Infinity

In his book on the philosophical idea of the infinite, A. W. Moore writes, "[Plotinus] supplied one of the first explicit identifications of the infinite with God. In this his thinking marked something of a turning point."[80] Such an idea fit perfectly with Plotinus's negative theology: just as the infinite cannot be described, so too the divine One cannot be described.

In line with Parmenides, Plotinus proposed an understanding of the infinite as an unbounded whole that contains everything that can possibly exist. In *Enn.* 6.5.4, Plotinus writes, "If we think of the divine nature as infinite—and certainly it is confined by no bounds—this must mean that it nowhere fails; its presence must reach to everything; at the point to which it does not reach, there it has failed; something exists in which it is not." Infinity understood in these terms means that there cannot be anything, whether material or abstract, outside the infinite, because that would mean the infinite has limits. For Plotinus, everything that exists is included in God, even concepts, categories, and physical objects, because God is infinite and nothing can exist outside of his infinity. This opinion on the infinite would one day inspire the kabbalistic maxim "Ein od milvado" (nothing exists except God).

---

80. A. Moore, *Infinite*, 45. See also Hart, "Concept of the Infinite," 259.

4.5.4. Divine Sparks Ascending to a Higher Unity

Although Plotinus wrote against the gnostics of his day (*Enn.* 2.9), his system closely resembles theirs.[81] Whereas the gnostics believed that only a few human beings possessed the divine sparks of the pleroma within them—and were thus fated for salvation—Plotinus believed that *everything* that exists has the divine sparks within itself and would one day be returned to the primordial unity of the One. The gnostics prided themselves in being the chosen few, whereas Plotinus universalized the idea and made all things divine through their inclusion in the One. In Plotinus's system, distinctions between things are merely quantitative, depending on the extent of divinity within. Beings higher in the chain of being are more divine than those lower, as if divinity is on a continuum, but eventually all things would ascend to the source of their chain. On the soul's divine nature, Plotinus writes,

> By the power of the soul the manifold and diverse heavenly system is a unit: through soul this universe is a God: and the sun is a God because it is ensouled; so too the stars: and whatsoever we ourselves may be, it is all in virtue of soul. . . . This, by which the gods are divine, must be the oldest God of them all: and our own soul is of that same Ideal nature, so that to consider it, purified, freed from all accruement, is to recognise in ourselves that same value which we have found soul to be, honourable above all that is bodily. (*Enn.* 5.1.2)

In the following passage, Plotinus describes the salvific task of each human being. Humans can choose to ascend upward through philosophy, or remain sunken in the lower existence of the body by forsaking the higher soul in which they participate:

> Cut off as we are by the nature of the body . . . our task, then, is to work for our liberation from this sphere, severing ourselves from all that has gathered about us; the total man is to be something better than a body ensouled. . . . There is another life, emancipated, whose quality is progression towards the higher realm, towards the good and divine, towards that Principle which no one possesses except by deliberate usage but so may appropriate, becoming, each personally, the higher, the beautiful, the Godlike, and living, remote, in and by It—unless one

---

81. For an analysis of Plotinus's familiarity with the Valentinians, a gnostic sect, see Quispel, "Judaism and Gnosis," 561.

> choose to go bereaved of that higher Soul and therefore, to live fate-bound, no longer profiting... but becoming as it were a part sunken in it and dragged along with the whole thus adopted. (*Enn.* 2.3.9)

Humans have two choices: ascend through mystical philosophy to transcend the body and reveal one's inner divinity, or remain sunken in a lower and unprofitable bodily state. Plotinus knew which choice he was making. According to Porphyry, Plotinus's final words were "Now I shall endeavor to make that which is divine in me rise up to that which is divine in the universe."[82]

Neoplatonism, as Plotinus's system is now called, exalts experience over the rational and encourages unity over diversity. As a highly syncretistic worldview that can adapt itself to multiple forms and expressions, Neoplatonism has been diffused across Judaism, Christianity, and Islam, serving as a mystical pathway for seekers wanting more. However, many adherents are unaware of the Neoplatonic background of their theological intuitions, instead thinking that they are inherent to their religion. The remainder of this book will break down these intuitions into their constituent parts, attempting to separate Neoplatonic ingredients from the Jewish and Christian recipes they were baked into.

Thus concludes our tour of Greek philosophical schools. Although many of these Greek notions can seem otherworldly and confusing according to a modern frame of reference, there is a reason part 2 needed to begin with these alien doctrines. Nearly every doctrine discussed in this chapter would find a home in the thought of Maimonides or the proponents of Kabbalah. By integrating Greek thought into their vision of Judaism, the medieval Jewish philosophers and mystics transformed Judaism for generations to come.

---

82. "Biographical Note" (unsigned), in Lucretius et. al., *Way Things Are*, 298.

5 Maimonides's System of Absolute Divine Incorporeality

I believe with perfect faith that the Creator,
blessed be his name, is not physical,
that he is free from all physical properties,
and that there is no comparison with him whatsoever.

—Maimonides's Third Principle from the *Ani Ma'amin* Prayer[1]

While I cannot claim to have made an exhaustive survey of every rabbinic authority who condemns Christianity as idolatry, I have certainly examined quite a few. I have yet to find an exception to the following statement: Maimonides is the halakhic authority upon whom all others base their claim that Christianity is idolatry—and those who deny that Christianity is idolatry are forced to contend with Maimonides.

—Menachem Kellner[2]

With our investigation of the Greek philosophical tradition behind us, we may now transition to medieval Judaism, where the Greek and rabbinic traditions were fused to construct the Maimonidean and kabbalistic worldviews. It is these medieval syntheses that pose the greatest opposition to the doctrine of the Incarnation in the Jewish community

---

1. Adapted from Davis, *Siddur for Weekdays*, 242–43.
2. Kellner, *We Are Not Alone*, 142–43.

Part II: A Critique of Non-Incarnational Maimonidean and Kabbalistic Thought

to this day. As stated in the introduction, Maimonides's synthesis makes the Incarnation impossible, and the kabbalistic tradition makes the Incarnation redundant. In keeping with the design of part 2, the following chapters do not appeal to the NT to speak to the issues at hand. A direct interaction between the Maimonidean, kabbalistic, and NT worldviews is reserved for part 3. Nevertheless, our discussions of Maimonides and Kabbalah in part 2 orbit the Incarnation, so to speak, with issues related to the deity of Jesus never far out of reach.

5.1. From Moses to Moses and the Thirteen Principles of Faith

The Spanish-born Jewish philosopher Moses ben Maimon (1138–1204 CE), also known by Maimonides and the acronym Rambam,[3] is commonly described as the greatest Jewish philosopher. As the popular saying goes, "From Moses to Moses [Maimonides] there was none like Moses." Maimonides's scope of knowledge was vast—a true polymath whose expertise spanned Jewish law (halakah), metaphysics, ethics, medicine, and more. His most well-known works include *Commentary on the Mishnah*, *Mishneh Torah*, and *Guide to the Perplexed*,[4] besides his many responsa that served the Jewish communities seeking his legal expertise. Although he was born in Muslim Spain, he fled with his family due to persecution, eventually residing in Cairo, Egypt, from 1171 until his death in 1204.

Maimonides was not the first influential Jewish philosopher, as Saadia Gaon (882–942) preceded him, as did Philo a millennium before (ca. 20 BCE–50 CE). However, Maimonides was so successful in promoting his philosophical perspective that he can be identified as the most important Jewish philosopher of all time. In his historical survey, David Frank highlights Maimonides's overwhelming influence:

> Without Maimonides, Jewish philosophy would not be. This is a very grand claim, but . . . it is impossible to overlook the impact that the translation of Maimonides' philosophical work into Hebrew had on the intellectual public. From the early thirteen

---

3. RaMBaM: Rabbi Moshe ben Maimon.

4. There are various opinions on how best to translate the title of the *Guide* in English. Friedländer initially chose *Guide of the Perplexed* in 1885, then changed it to *Guide for the Perplexed* in 1904. Pines's translation reverted to "of." A recent English translation of the *Guide* by Goodman and Lieberman opts for *Guide to the Perplexed*. I employ the latter option as well.

Maimonides's System of Absolute Divine Incorporeality

century on Maimonides' views became the starting point for all the relevant theoretical discussions on creation, divine language, prophecy, divine providence, and so on. His positions were agreed upon, disagreed upon, interpreted, and misinterpreted. For some, he was the final word; for others, a singularly dangerous influence. Maimonides' influence is ubiquitous.[5]

Among the most enduring aspects of Maimonides's thought is his codification of the Thirteen Principles of Faith, as found in his commentary on m. Sanh. 10:1.[6] This commentary is studied in Orthodox Jewish yeshivas (religious schools), and some students also study the more advanced *Guide to the Perplexed*, where Maimonides gives extended justification to many of his principles.[7] However, comparatively few Jewish people study Maimonides's works directly. Instead, the Thirteen Principles are best known through popular and liturgical summaries in the siddur, the Jewish prayer book. After Maimonides's death, his Thirteen Principles were summarized into the *Yigdal*, a poetic song, and *Ani Ma'amin*, a prayer that takes the form of a creed.[8] Depending on custom, Orthodox Jewish communities often recite *Yigdal* or *Ani Ma'amin* daily at *Shacharit* prayers and weekly on Shabbat.

Table 10. Different Versions of Maimonides's Theological Principles

Yigdal, Ani Ma'amin	Popular, liturgical, not written by Maimonides	Summarized
Commentary on m. Sanh. 10:1	Maimonides's Thirteen Principles of Faith	Basic reasoning
The Guide to the Perplexed	Maimonides's expanded justification of many aspects of his Thirteen Principles	Expanded reasoning

---

5. Frank, "Medieval Jewish Aristotelianism," loc. 3430.

6. For two English translations of the original form of the Thirteen Principles, see Maimonides, *Maimonides Reader*, ch. Helek; Abelson, "Maimonides on Jewish Creed," 48–49.

7. Kellner argues that Maimonides's *Guide* is structured as an extended exposition of the Thirteen Principles (*Science in Bet Midrash*, 123–31).

8. See the *Yigdal* prayer in the Ashkenazi Siddur in Davis, *Siddur for Weekdays*, 16; and *Ani Ma'amin* on 242. The popular versions of Maimonides's principles have found widespread acceptance as accurate summaries of the larger works.

Part II: A Critique of Non-Incarnational Maimonidean and Kabbalistic Thought

Maimonides's Thirteen Principles find widespread support at the popular level to this day. "If there is one thing Orthodox Jews the world over acknowledge," writes Maimonides scholar Marc B. Shapiro, "it is that Maimonides' Thirteen Principles are the fundamentals of Jewish faith. . . . There is room for debate in matters of faith, as long as one does not contradict any of these Principles."[9] Consequently, Maimonides is no mere twelfth-century Jewish sage; his centuries-old theological determinations command widespread allegiance today. Accordingly, many volumes from across the Jewish theological spectrum are devoted to discussing the importance of the Thirteen Principles in contemporary Judaism.[10]

As this book is primarily concerned with the doctrine of the Incarnation, it is outside the scope of the book to investigate each of the Thirteen Principles. Of the principles, several are unobjectionable from a NT perspective. However, the Second and Third Principles present followers of Jesus with denials of the Trinity and divine embodiment, respectively, and thus they will be our focus from this point forward. These two principles are given below from a translation of the *Ani Ma'amin* version in the Jewish prayer book, the siddur:

Table 11. Second and Third Principles of Maimonides's Thirteen Principles

	Ani Ma'amin (Siddur) Translation[11]	Threatened Doctrines
Second Principle	I believe with perfect faith that the Creator, blessed be His name, is unique [*yachid*], and there is no uniqueness like him in any way, and that he alone is our God, who was, who is, and who always will be.	Trinity, polytheism, multiple divine attributes
Third Principle	I believe with perfect faith that the Creator, blessed be his name, is not physical, that he is free from all physical properties, and that there is no comparison with him whatsoever.	Corporealism, divine embodiment including Incarnation, *via positiva*, *via analogia*

9. M. Shapiro, *Limits of Orthodox Theology*, 17. It should be noted that Shapiro says this ironically, merely describing the predominant state of affairs that he seeks to overturn; the major aim of his book is to argue for flexibility on the principles, as illustrated by respected sages who disagreed with one or more of them.

10. Weinberg and Blumenfeld, *Fundamentals and Faith*; Olitzky and Isaacs, *I Believe*; Maimonides, *Maimonides—Essential Teachings*; Gurary, *Thirteen Principles of Faith*.

11. Adapted from Davis, *Siddur for Weekdays*, 242–43.

As commonly understood, the word *yachid* in the Second Principle refers to God as a singularity that is more "one" than any other kind of oneness, thus rejecting any possibility that the one essence of God consists of three equally divine persons. Under Maimonides's influence, the *echad* of the Shema (Deut 6:4) has been understood to mean *yachid*, a singularity without plurality.[12] Thus, it is common in Jewish circles to assert that the Shema itself is proof against the Trinity.

The Third Principle asserts the essential incorporeality of God—which the NT supports[13]—but goes further in two ways. First, it asserts the impossibility that God has become or could become embodied. Second, it establishes negative theology as the only way to conceive of God ("no comparison with him whatsoever"). Because Maimonides not only holds to God's incorporeality but also to the impossibility that he could ever be associated with corporeality, I call his position *absolute divine incorporeality*.[14]

5.2. Maimonides's Arguments against Christianity

Put together, the Second and Third Principles serve as a summary of Maimonides's rulings against Christianity given elsewhere. In his commentary on Mishnah Avodah Zarah, written early in his life, Maimonides declares,

> Know that the Christian nation, who advocate the messianic claim, in all their various sects, all of them are idolators.... Therefore, one must know that any one of the cities of the Christian nation that has in it a place of worship, namely, a church, which is, without a doubt, a house of idolatry; through that city one must not intentionally pass, let alone dwell there.[15]

---

12. It should be noted that the exposition of the Shema given in §2.2 did not give "singularity" as one of the options for understanding *echad*. This option was omitted because the Maimonidean idea of a singularity does not appear in the Hebrew Scriptures. On the Hebrew Scriptures' own terms, "singularity" falls outside the language used to describe who he is. The first thinker to propose the idea of a singularity was the Greek philosopher Parmenides, who wrote nearly a millennium after the completion of the Torah.

13. John 1:18; 4:24; 1 Tim 1:17.

14. For review, see §1.3.

15. Translation given in Novak, "Maimonides's View of Christianity," 57–58.

Part II: A Critique of Non-Incarnational Maimonidean and Kabbalistic Thought

The young Maimonides merely called Christianity idolatry; the mature Maimonides of the *Guide* gives his reasoning. For Maimonides, ascribing threeness to God violates his oneness:

> Those who believe that God is One, and that He has many attributes, declare the unity with their lips, and assume plurality in their thoughts. This is like the doctrine of the Christians, who say that He is one and He is three, and that the three are one. (*Guide* 1.50; cf. *Enn.* 5.3.13)

Maimonides is consistent elsewhere in his arguments against Jesus.[16] Noting that Christians were more open to see anthropomorphisms as biblical examples of physical divine visitations, theologian David Novak comments, "Christianity is, for [Maimonides] the prime example of the error of such anthropomorphism, both in its original doctrine of the Incarnation and in its related doctrine of the Trinity."[17] Elsewhere, Maimonides criticizes Jesus because he supposedly annulled the Torah.[18] Thus, Maimonides's chief objections to Jesus appear to be theological matters relating to the Trinity and Incarnation, and the continuity of the Torah. This comprises the Second, Third, and Ninth Principles of the Thirteen Principles of Faith.

Whether the Jewish people who pray the siddur regularly know Maimonides's reasoning for his principles or not, these principles have been widely accepted throughout the Jewish world. Under Maimonides's

---

16. In his commentary at the end of *Kings and Wars* 11, Maimonides discusses the effects of Jesus's coming, which in his view led to idolatry: "For has there ever been a greater stumbling than this? All the prophets affirmed that the Messiah would redeem Israel, save them, gather their dispersed, and confirm the commandments. But he caused Israel to be destroyed by the sword, their remnant to be dispersed and humiliated. He was instrumental in changing the Torah and causing the world to err and serve another besides God" (Maimonides, *Maimonides Reader*, loc. 2966).

17. Novak, "Maimonides's View of Christianity," 66.

18. Commentary at the end of *Kings and Wars* 11. Maimonides writes in his "Letter to Yemen," "The first one to have adopted this plan was Jesus the Nazarene, may his bones be ground to dust. He was a Jew because his mother was a Jewess although his father was a Gentile. For in accordance with the principles of our law, a child born of a Jewess and a Gentile, or of a Jewess and a slave, is legitimate (Yevamot 45a). Jesus is only figuratively termed an illegitimate child. He impelled people to believe that he was a prophet sent by God to clarify perplexities in the Torah, and that he was the Messiah that was predicted by each and every seer. He interpreted the Torah and its precepts in such a fashion as to lead to their total annulment, to the abolition of all its commandments and to the violation of its prohibitions. The sages, of blessed memory, having become aware of his plans before his reputation spread among our people, meted out fitting punishment to him" (Maimonides, *Maimonides Reader*, loc. 5866).

influence, the Trinity and Incarnation become idolatrous ideas. This book explores the reasoning undergirding the Third Principle, seeking to show that it is mistaken about God's nature, his actions in the world, and the witness of Scripture. If my argument is correct, the illegitimacy of the Third Principle also makes the Second Principle suspect and calls into question the traditional Jewish rejection of the Trinity and Incarnation.

5.3. Maimonides's *Guide to the Perplexed*

After writing his magisterial *Mishneh Torah* about halakic matters, Maimonides sought to synthesize his philosophy with the teachings of the Hebrew Scriptures. He lamented that his students had difficulty in seeing how philosophical studies could be unified with biblical and rabbinical literature. Thus, to remedy this problem, ca. 1190 he wrote *Dalālāt al-ḥāirin*, known in Hebrew translation as *Moreh Nevuchim* and in English as *Guide to the Perplexed*. After a period of unrest called the Maimonidean Controversy (1180–1306),[19] the Jewish community came to see the *Guide* as "the greatest of all Jewish philosophical works."[20] Maimonides wrote his masterpiece in Arabic, using Hebrew characters, and by 1204, the year of Maimonides's death, it had been translated into Hebrew by Samuel ibn Tibbon. There have been multiple translations of the *Guide* into English, and this book will cite the second edition of Michael Friedländer's translation.[21]

In his introduction to the *Guide*, Maimonides explains the purpose of his work. In his opinion, "ignorant and superficial readers" were reading the anthropomorphisms of Scripture literally, making them perplexed and bewildered. "For this reason I have called this book *Guide to the Perplexed*," he writes. In other words, Maimonides was disappointed that his reasoning for God's absolute incorporeality, as written in his commentary on m. Sanh. 10:1, had not found widespread support. To rectify the situation, he begins part 1 of the *Guide* with a sustained argument

---

19. Ben-Sasson et al., "Maimonidean Controversy."
20. Frank, "Medieval Jewish Aristotelianism," loc. 3110.
21. Most scholarly analyses of the *Guide* employ Pines's translation: Maimonides, *Guide of the Perplexed*. At the time of writing, the Goodman and Lieberman translation was recently released. It is valuable for its introductions and commentary, but I prefer the readability of Friedländer. It remains to be seen if Goodman and Lieberman will become the standard translation used in academia. For a discussion of the differences between Friedländer's and Pines's translations, see Stern et al., *Maimonides' "Guide,"* 209–55.

Part II: A Critique of Non-Incarnational Maimonidean and Kabbalistic Thought

about how to read *all* scriptural language about God as metaphorical, psychological visions, or angelic visits, before moving on to other matters pertaining to metaphysics, prophecy, and the commandments. An outline of the *Guide* is as follows:

Table 12. Outline of *The Guide to the Perplexed*[22]

Pt. 1	Chs. 1–49: Treatment of nouns, verbs, and phrases that refer to God
	50–60: The attributes of God
	61–70: The names of God
	71–76: Criticism of the metaphysics of the Mutakallemim
Pt. 2	1: Proofs for God's existence from Aristotelian cosmology
	2–12: The heavenly spheres and intelligences
	13–29: On the eternity of the universe
	30–31: Exposition of Gen 1–4
	32–48: The nature of prophecy
Pt. 3	1–7: Explanation of the Chariot (*Merkavah*)
	8–12: The nature of evil
	13–15: The purpose of creation
	16–25: Providence and omniscience
	25–50: The purpose of divine commands
	51–54: Concluding remarks

The Guide to the Perplexed serves as Maimonides's fullest defense of his Third Principle in favor of absolute divine incorporeality. As such, the *Guide* presents a formidable challenge to the doctrine of the Incarnation. To draw out his argument, I will focus on part 1 of the *Guide* and the first half of part 2. The third part of the *Guide* is relevant mainly where Maimonides discusses divine providence. Given Maimonides's influence on these matters, anyone seeking to justify belief in Jesus as the incarnate Son of God ought to consider how to handle Maimonides's positions, which are complex, thoroughly argued, and philosophically driven. His determinations in these areas inform his halakic rulings, such that his opinions have significant weight in contemporary Judaism, even for those unaware of Maimonides's reasoning for the Third Principle. Menachem Kellner's quote at the head of this chapter illustrates the power of Maimonides's conclusions. Jewish philosopher Norbert Samuelson concurs:

> Maimonides' *Guide of the Perplexed* is among the most influential works ever written in religious philosophy. It occupies

---

22. I principally follow Friedländer's outline in *Guide*, xliii, xlix, lv.

a unique place in Jewish religious thought. While the majority of subsequent Jewish thinkers have criticized what they understood of Maimonides' text, they have often felt obligated to struggle with his contentions. This obligation constitutes the highest expression of respect in Jewish philosophy.[23]

As one who holds to the truth of the Incarnation of the Son of God as Jesus of Nazareth, I too feel the weight of obligation to respectfully struggle with Maimonides's contentions.

As I survey Maimonides's *Guide*, I draw on a variety of modern scholars' works. The academic literature on Maimonides is vast and consists almost exclusively of Jewish scholars.[24] For a one-volume overview of Maimonides's thought, see *The Cambridge Companion to Maimonides*, edited by Kenneth Seeskin.[25] Daniel Frank and Aaron Segal have provided a recent multiauthored overview of the *Guide*.[26] Many other works relating to this book are available from Maimonidean scholars such as Lenn E. Goodman,[27] Micah Goodman,[28] Menachem Kellner,[29] David Novak,[30] Marc Shapiro,[31] and the Maimonidean Studies series from Yeshiva University.[32]

---

23. Samuelson, "Maimonides' Doctrine of Creation," 249.

24. The *Guide* has received little attention from Christians and Messianic Jews. I am not aware of a major systematic Christian analysis and critique of the *Guide*. The closest I have come across is Bartholomew, *God Who Acts*, 35–60. Messianic Jewish scholar Fischer reviews rabbinic theology and contrasts it with Maimonides's philosophical theology ("Rabbinic View of God"). Craig systemizes Maimonides's cosmological argument for God's existence (*Cosmological Argument from Plato*, 127–52). Another contribution is Downey (*Maimonides's Yahweh*). Downey's work is trailblazing in that it is the first book in decades to critically analyze Maimonides's position on the Incarnation from a Christian perspective. This present study, however, will depart from Downey's method, style, and conclusions. For my review of Downey's book, see Crawford, "Pathways," 94–101.

25. Other relevant works by Seeskin include "No One Can See"; "Maimonides on Creation."

26. Frank and Segal, *Critical Guide*.

27. L. Goodman: *Neoplatonism and Jewish Thought*; "What Is Positive."

28. M. Goodman, *Maimonides and the Book*.

29. Kellner: "On Status of Astronomy"; *Must Jew Believe Anything?*; *Science in Bet Midrash*; *Maimonides' Confrontation with Mysticism*; *We Are Not Alone*.

30. Novak: "Self-Contraction of Godhead"; "Mind of Maimonides"; "Can We Be Maimonideans"; *Athens and Jerusalem*.

31. M. Shapiro: *Limits of Orthodox Theology*; *Studies in Maimonides*.

32. Relevant studies from this series include Manekin, "Belief, Certainty, Divine Attributes"; Davidson, "Maimonides on Metaphysical Knowledge"; Wolfson, "*Via*

As stated previously, although the Thirteen Principles are widespread in Judaism today, few Jewish people, even of Orthodox persuasion, study the *Guide to the Perplexed*. It is often seen as an advanced technical work that is best left to sages and philosophers, less relevant to the common man than halakic study. Instead of understanding Maimonides's philosophical reasoning, many Jewish people merely accept his final dogmas in the principles while remaining unconscious of his theological and philosophical reasoning.[33] In other words, they accept the tip of the iceberg (the Third Principle), while remaining mostly unfamiliar with the colossal theological structure underneath (the justification in the *Guide*). I will not do so here; from this point forward, I will leave the popular version of the Third Principle behind and seek to uncover its complex underpinnings in the *Guide*.

5.4. Maimonides's Philosophical Heritage and Motives

To understand Maimonides's philosophy is to understand Aristotle and Plotinus through the medium of medieval Islamic philosophers, which he then fused with rabbinic Judaism.[34] Maimonides was born in Muslim Spain in the twelfth century and was profoundly influenced by the philosophical currents of his Islamic milieu. Those currents included a resurgent Aristotelianism, a rising Neoplatonic mysticism, and the incorporealist monotheistic fervor of a triumphant Islam. Additionally, Maimonides was exposed to sophisticated Islamic philosophers who chastised Jews for falling behind the times. In the Muslim mind, Muslims were at the forefront of philosophical erudition, whereas Jews were stuck without the benefits of Aristotle and saddled with an unsophisticated corporeal understanding of God.

Negativa in Maimonides."

33. They may outwardly proclaim acceptance of the God of Maimonides but actually envision the God of Heschel. Abraham Heschel's vision of God was far more personal, dynamic, and involved than Maimonides would allow, thus approaching the kabbalistic conception. Thanks to Sam Lebens for pointing out this distinction.

34. See appendix B for a diagram and summary of Maimonides's predecessors and contemporaries. The classic introduction is Pines, "Translator's Introduction." Pines only briefly mentions Maimonides's underlying Neoplatonic influences, instead focusing on Islamic philosophers. See also M. Goodman, *Maimonides and the Book*, 192–93; Pessin, "Influence of Islamic Thought"; Ivry, "Maimonides' Philosophical Sources"; Ivry, "Maimonides and Neoplatonism."

Maimonides sought to address these perceived weaknesses, establishing a sophisticated Judaism that could be admired by the great philosophers of the era. It is widely recognized that one of Maimonides's primary goals was to synthesize Aristotelian metaphysics and cosmology (in *Guide to the Perplexed*) and ethics (*Eight Chapters*) with Judaism. However, he largely followed the same solutions that prior Islamic philosophers had attempted in fusing Aristotle and Neoplatonism with Islam (see appendix B).[35] Thomas Aquinas would follow Maimonides in the thirteenth century by doing the same with Catholicism. Joel Kraemer, a scholar of Islamic and Jewish philosophy, writes,

> The Islamic philosophers were heirs to a late Hellenistic syllabus of Greek learning. They integrated Aristotelian logic, physics, and ethics, Neoplatonic metaphysics, Platonic political philosophy, Ptolemaic astronomy, Euclidian geometry, and Galenic medicine into a cohesive structure, thereby transforming the eclectic diversity of late Hellenistic thought into a coherent system of cumulative knowledge within the broad framework of a Neoplatonic Aristotelianism.[36]

Maimonides was explicit in his dependence upon Aristotle and Muslim Aristotelians; however, he likely did not realize that he was integrating Neoplatonic thought per se.[37] Medieval Islamic and Jewish philosophers erroneously identified Aristotle as the author of an Arabic paraphrase of Plotinus's *Enneads 4–6*, entitled *The Theology of Aristotle*.[38] Maimonidean scholar Sarah Pessin writes,

> Reading this text as Aristotle's own, Maimonides and his Islamic predecessors hold a blend of Aristotelian and Neoplatonic views, including Aristotelian views which are themselves

---

35. His solutions also repeat the theological expositions of Christian Platonists from a millennium prior. For example, Novatian's *On the Trinity* 1–8 (250 CE) is remarkably similar to the *Guide* (Crawford, "Pathways," 117). Maimonides was brilliant, but he was not one of a kind.

36. Kraemer, "Islamic Context," loc. 971.

37. "It seems reasonable to conclude that Maimonides conflated two portraits of God, the Aristotelian and the Neoplatonic, even if it is the case that he was not fully conscious of the discrepancy between the two viewpoints" (Wolfson, "*Via Negativa* in Maimonides," 412).

38. Pessin, "Influence of Islamic Thought"; D'Ancona, "Theology Attributed to Aristotle." It is appropriate to note here that Aquinas the Aristotelian also admitted pseudepigraphal Neoplatonic works into his epistemology, namely those of Pseudo-Dionysius (Hankey, *Aquinas's Neoplatonism*).

often highly Neoplatonized. The blending together of God-as-pure-unity and God-as-intellect is one such example. In these Neoplatonized Aristotelian descriptions of God, we might place Maimonides in clear conversation with his Arabic philosophical predecessors.[39]

Ironically, Plotinus's vision of God and reality opposed that of Aristotle, forcing medieval Islamic and Jewish philosophers to propose unique syntheses to fit the two together.

5.5. Maimonides's Aristotelian-Neoplatonic Cosmology and Theology

Maimonides, like all philosophers of his era, believed the Earth is the center of the universe, and the sun, moon, planets, and stars—rolling on the heavenly spheres of æther—revolve around the Earth in perfect circular orbits and influence physical reality on Earth.[40] As previously discussed (§4.2.2), this understanding of the cosmos is derived from the combination of Aristotelian physics and Ptolemaic mathematics that conjectures eccentric orbits for the heavenly bodies, or else epicycles; that is, orbits within orbits.[41] These assumptions enable the mathematical computation of the heavenly bodies' movement with striking precision: "perfectly correct, within one minute," Maimonides says about Ptolemaic calculations of the moon (*Guide* 2.24). To the medieval world, Ptolemy's astronomical system appeared to be a functional, trustworthy, and mathematically predicted cosmology.[42]

However, the geocentric model was extraordinarily complicated and rested on unproven assumptions, such as the nonexistence of a vacuum, the perfect circularity of orbits, and a dismissal of Aristarchus of Samos's heliocentric model (third century BCE). Maimonides himself points out several contradictions between the cosmologies of Ptolemy

---

39. Pessin, "Influence of Islamic Thought."

40. Maimonides assumes this cosmology throughout the *Guide*, but it is pronounced in pt. 2. His belief in the spheres' influence upon corporeal reality is found in *Guide* 2.10 and 2.12.

41. See Ptolemy, *Almagest* 3.4–9 [Ptolemy et al., *Almagest*, 15:93–108]. For Jewish contributions to geocentric astronomy, see Solomon, "Judaism and Natural Science," 2:965.

42. In his "Letter Concerning Astrology," Maimonides summarized what could be known from scientific calculations at the time (*Maimonides Reader*, locs. 6180–341).

and Aristotle, and he wavers between accepting epicycles or eccentricity or an unspecified system from Abu-Bekr (*Guide* 2.24). Impressed with Maimonides's astuteness in cosmology, philosopher Micah Goodman writes, "Maimonides was one of the earliest figures in the history of science to identify the insoluble problems of medieval astronomy and physics."[43] Indeed, Maimonides was ahead of his time in pointing out observational mysteries of the Aristotelian and Ptolemaic cosmologies, and he admits his inability to settle the controversies decisively because "the heavens are too far from us" (*Guide* 2.24).[44]

Despite these caveats, Maimonides largely accepts the Aristotelian-Ptolemaic spheres cosmology except for the eternality of the universe, which conflicts with creation *ex nihilo* (*Guide* 2.6).[45] In Maimonides's system, the highest sphere is finite, created out of nothing, and only God is eternal. Yet the geocentric spheres cosmology lies at the heart of Maimonides's theological system, for he employs the spheres as the mechanism by which God indirectly delivers creation, providence, prophecy, relational communion, and miracles.

Creation. Maimonides believes God only created one thing, the outermost heavenly sphere, which is pure intelligence (*Guide* 1.72; 2.11). The outermost sphere then emanates another lower sphere, which in turn emanates another, like the sun emanates light (*Guide* 2.11). Maimonides calls the spheres "intelligences" that are equivalent to the biblical angels, and he hints at his acceptance of either four, ten, or eighteen spheres (*Guide* 1.72; 2.4, 2.10).[46] Moreover, the emanated spheres and their multiple compounds are all fundamentally united as one individual being (*Guide* 1.72).

---

43. M. Goodman, *Maimonides and the Book*, 216.

44. Kellner notes that Maimonides makes scattered statements to the effect that humanity cannot know or understand the heavens like they can know the terrestrial world. Yet, as we will see in this section, Maimonides could also be quite dogmatic about the mechanics of the heavens. While Kellner notes Maimonides's agnosticism concerning the cosmos, his essay does not account for why Maimonides could *also* speak about the cosmos with such confidence, even building his theological system upon it (Kellner, *Science in Bet Midrash*, 179–92; M. Goodman, *Maimonides and the Book*, 217).

45. See appendix C for a diagram of Maimonides's cosmology.

46. On Maimonides's different numbering schemes of the spheres, see Kellner, *Science in Bet Midrash*, 187–89.

Part II: A Critique of Non-Incarnational Maimonidean and Kabbalistic Thought

The notion of emanations and the unity of the multiplicity of the cosmos are Neoplatonic ideas;[47] Maimonides modifies the Neoplatonism he inherited by leaving God outside the created unity, in line with creation *ex nihilo* (*Guide* 2.16, 2.29; 3.50). Maimonides's God is not part of his creation, and he created it out of nothing.[48] Thus, in Maimonides's thought, the heavenly spheres explain the mechanism for how humanity and the rest of the universe came to be: they are emanations from the higher realms, united with the higher realms, but infinitely detached from God, who remains transcendent and eternal beyond the highest created realm (*Guide* 3.14). Maimonides is aware the Greeks believed creation *ex nihilo* was irrational and impossible, but he insists "that the theory of *Creatio ex nihilo* includes nothing that is impossible" on the prophetic authority of Moses and Abraham (*Guide* 2.13).

Providence. Maimonides maintains that the movement of the spheres is the mechanism by which God enacts providence on Earth (*Guide* 1.70; 3.17).[49] Like other philosophers of his era, Maimonides believes the motion of the outermost fixed stars filters down to lower realms and enables motion on Earth; providence and motion are seen as related. On this topic, Maimonides follows Aristotle, but he extends individual providence to humanity, which Aristotle did not do. Motivated by scriptural precedent, Maimonides believes human beings, possessing rationality, may be acted upon by higher intelligences in proportion to their intellectual attainment (*Guide* 3.17–3.18). Moreover, the mechanism by which the highest intelligence (God) sends providence to the lowest intelligences (humans) is through the mediatory influence of the heavenly spheres (*Guide* 2.10, 2.12). In the Maimonidean system, God indirectly influences humanity on Earth through power emanating from the stars and planets. He believes "the motion of the uppermost sphere is the greatest proof for the existence of God" (*Guide* 1.70).

Prophecy. Maimonides's cosmology is also the mechanism for delivering prophecy to Moses and the prophets; that is, the origin of Scripture.[50]

---

47. Plotinus, *Enn.* 3.2.

48. However, see the following studies regarding the complexities and controversies concerning Maimonides's views on creation *ex nihilo*: W. Harvey, "Third Approach"; Samuelson, "Maimonides' Doctrine of Creation"; Ivry, "Maimonides on Creation"; Seeskin, "Maimonides on Creation"; Xiuyuan, "Maimonides' Cosmogony-Prophetology Puzzle."

49. See also Maimonides, "Letter Concerning Astrology."

50. Dutmer, "Miracle of Mosaic Prophecy." For a discussion on the various models Maimonides proposed for creation and prophecy, see Xiuyuan, "Maimonides'

In his opinion, only ignorant people believe prophecy occurs when God inspires a person with the spirit of prophecy and gives him a prophetic mission (*Guide* 2.32). Instead, Maimonides insists that prophecy occurs under three conditions. First, an individual prepares his rational faculty through philosophy to be receptive to prophecy (*Guide* 2.32). Second, God chooses to send prophecy to the wise philosopher (*Guide* 2.25, 2.32). Third, God sends prophecy as an emanation from himself through the spheres, down to the active intellect, through which the philosopher's mind and imagination receive the prophecy (*Guide* 2.12, 2.36). In medieval Aristotelian thought, the active intellect is the lowest spiritual being, associated with the sphere of the moon, and thus it is the closest nonhuman intellect that human reason can access.[51] While philosophers such as Aristotle may have received divine influence in their rational faculty, Maimonides says only the prophets of Israel received influence on their imaginative faculty as well (*Guide* 2.36–2.37).

Maimonides distinguishes between either eight or eleven types of prophecy ordered in rank (*Guide* 2.45), such that Moses stands at the top with a unique type of prophecy that produced the Written Torah. Even so, the other prophets still accessed the divine mind through the cosmological mechanisms given above. Other prophets, such as Isaiah, attained lower prophecy than Moses, and any of the authors of the Ketuvim (Writings, e.g., Psalms, Chronicles) attained even lower prophecies, yet were still inspired by the holy spirit. In this way, Maimonides provides a cosmological explanation for why the Torah is more authoritative than the rest of the canon: Moses ascended higher in his ability to understand the active intellect.[52]

Communion with God. Maimonides thinks most Jewish people should not expect to become prophets through their philosophical studies. Nevertheless, in his opinion, connecting with the active intellect

---

Cosmogony-Prophetology Puzzle."

51. For Maimonides's view, see *Guide* 2.11; Herrera, "Episode in Medieval Aristotelianism." Aristotle indicated belief in active and passive intellects without associating the active form with any cosmological entity (*De an.* 3.5). Alexander of Aphrodisias associated the active intellect with a divine mind, and al-Farabi associated it with the lowest sphere accessible to humans, the sphere of the moon (Frede and Martijn, "Alexander of Aphrodisias"; Kraemer, "Farabi," 6:709–10).

52. A case can be made from the Hebrew Scriptures about the greater authority of Moses than the rest of the Hebrew Scriptures (Exod 6:3, Num 12:6–8). However, my point is that Maimonides expanded beyond the biblical precedents through his cosmological mechanisms.

Part II: A Critique of Non-Incarnational Maimonidean and Kabbalistic Thought

through philosophy provides the pathway for intellectual, even mystical, communion with God.[53] Maimonides writes,

> I have shown you that the intellect which emanates from God unto us is the link that joins us to God. You have it in your power to strengthen that bond, if you choose to do so, or to weaken it gradually till it breaks, if you prefer this. It will only become strong when you employ it in the love of God, and seek that love; it will be weakened when you direct your thoughts to other things. (*Guide* 3.51)

Thus, the emanation of God's intellect down through the spheres provides for the relational union between God and individual Jewish people.

Miracles. The *Guide* does not address the concept of miracles as systematically as providence or prophecy, but a coherent picture of the cosmological basis of miracles in Maimonides's system can be pieced together nonetheless.[54] Maimonides's handling of scriptural miracle accounts is multifaceted,[55] and Tzvi Langermann argues that Maimonides's positions late in life include a "sober reassessment" of his earlier views.[56] Early in life, in the cases where he accepted the historical occurrences of miracles, Maimonides attributed them to forces embedded in the initial creation. According to his understanding, when God created the universe, he established its natural laws and included future provisions for "miracles" to happen within those natural laws.[57] Thus, the waters parted before the children of Israel and the lions did not harm Daniel because a series of natural causes, embedded in creation, resulted in the parted sea and the lions' closed mouths at the perfectly designed time. God did not effect a "new creation" in these miracles; he planned for them ahead of

---

53. Kreisel, "*Imitatio Dei*," 185–87.

54. Reines, "Maimonides' Concept of Miracles"; Kasher, "Biblical Miracles."

55. Reines summarizes Maimonides's handling of miracles in four categories: 1) subjectivizing miracle stories, so they occur in a person's psyche and not in objective reality; 2) naturalizing miracle stories by appealing to natural phenomena; 3) optionalizing a miracle story, freeing the reader to prefer a natural explanation for a supposed miracle; 4) temporalizing miracles, limiting a miracle to a short time span so it cannot be said that God did a new creation (Reines, "Maimonides' Concept of Miracles," 272–76). A separate category of indirect miracle may be found in *Guide* 2.4, where God chooses to destroy things with fire by moving the spheres.

56. Langermann, "Maimonides and Miracles," 168. I appreciate Sam Lebens for pointing this out.

57. See *Guide* 2.29, where he cites Gen. Rab. and Midrash Qohelet for this opinion, which he calls "strange." Earlier in life, he gave an equivalent explanation for miracles in *Eight Chapters* (ch. 8) and in his commentary on *Avot* 5:6.

time according to a natural cause-and-effect chain. Langermann points out that later in life, as expressed in the *Guide*, Maimonides believed in miracles that broke with natural cause-and-effect chains, giving several qualifications to that belief.[58] However, Maimonides still cites the naturalistic explanation and holds it to be possible (*Guide* 2.29).

Maimonides's understanding of miracles is related to his cosmology in two respects. First, on the naturalistic explanation, since it is the intelligences of the spheres that emanate the lower worlds into existence, it is through the spheres that the initial conditions for future miracles are baked into the universe. God does not perform miracles directly in Maimonides's system if the naturalistic system of miracles holds; rather, the spheres' influence on the initial creation eventually produces the miraculous result. Second, Maimonides maintains a connection between prophecy and miracles, such that the cosmological mechanism of prophecy applies to both—thus not escaping the naturalistic explanation. For example, on the one hand, Maimonides says Gideon could not do miracles because he was not a prophet (*Guide* 2.46), whereas Moses could do wonders greater than anyone else because of his incomparable prophetic status (*Guide* 2.35). Philosopher Alvin Reines comments, "Miracles are simply anomalies of nature, rationally and scientifically explicable, whose natural causation and future occurrence is known and predictable by the prophet."[59] In Maimonides's understanding, "doing miracles" is redefined as having the prophetic insight to know when the initial conditions baked into the universe will result in an abnormal result. Reines concludes, "Hence Moses whose scientific knowledge was supreme among prophets and all mankind, could predict anomalies as no one else ever could, and consequently, his 'miracles' were greater than those of any other prophet."[60] Because miracle working is tied to prophetic ability, and prophetic ability is tied to cosmological mechanisms, miracle working is thus dependent on cosmological mechanisms.

Therefore, we see that Maimonides's cosmological system is intertwined with his theological understanding of creation, providence, prophecy, relational communion with God, and miracles.[61] He writes,

---

58. Miracles must not effect a permanent change of properties or a new creation (*Guide* 2.29; 3.50). On Maimonides's shift in position, see Langermann.

59. Reines, "Maimonides' Concept of Miracles," 267.

60. Reines, "Maimonides' Concept of Miracles," 269.

61. Goodman repeatedly notes how Maimonides utilized the emanation idea to explain these topics in the *Guide* (L. Goodman, "Object of the *Guide*").

Part II: A Critique of Non-Incarnational Maimonidean and Kabbalistic Thought

> For, on the one hand, it can be proved that God is separate from the universe, and in no contact whatever with it; but, on the other hand, His rule and providence can be proved to exist in all parts of the universe, even in the smallest. Praised be He whose perfection is above our comprehension. (*Guide* 1.72)

Maimonides solves this paradox by employing his spheres cosmology to mediate God's rule and providence down to earth, thus attempting to preserve God's complete separation from the universe. When considering those who doubt his spheres cosmology, Maimonides replies,

> The opposition can only emanate either from an ignorant man ... or from the prejudiced man who deceives himself. Those, however, who wish to study the subject must persevere in their studies until they are convinced that all our observations are true, and until they understand that our account of this universe unquestionably agrees with the existing order of things. (*Guide* 1.72)

Thus, Maimonides appeals to his system as logically and empirically unassailable. By appealing to the spheres as the medium by which God works in the world, Maimonides promotes a system where God works *indirectly* in creation through emanation, *never* directly. This worldview removes any possibility for God to directly enter his creation, such as in the physical form of fire, cloud, or the man Jesus.

5.6. Maimonides's Comprehensive Negative Theology

Maimonides holds to an extreme form of negative theology whereby nothing can be known about God's nature, including the knowledge that he even possesses a nature. Only God's indirect actions in the world can be known (*Guide* 1.52–53, 1.71). This is attributable to Maimonides's Neoplatonic influences. As previously mentioned (§4.5), the significant Neoplatonic teachings of Plotinus's *Six Enneads* may be summarized as follows:

1. Divine transcendence: God (the One) is beyond all, even existence itself. (*Enn.* 5.4.1; 6.9)
2. Absolute divine simplicity: Singularity precedes multiplicity. If there are many, there must be a prior One that is free from any kind of multiplicity. (*Enn.* 5.6.3; 6.6.13)

3. *Via negativa*: The One cannot be positively described or known. (*Enn.* 5.3.13–14; 6.7.38)

4. An eternal universe of emanations: All that exists emanates from the One eternally. The One emanates mind, which emanates the world soul, which emanates the material cosmos, like the sun emanates light. (*Enn.* 3.2; 5.1.10)

5. Omnipresence as panentheism: Everything is united in God. (*Enn.* 3.2.7; 5.1.2; 6.4.4)

Maimonides accepts this Neoplatonist vision partially. He agrees with (1) through (3), but he modifies (4) with the *ex nihilo* temporality of the emanations from the outermost created sphere, and he rejects (5) on the grounds of God's transcendence beyond the *ex nihilo* created order.

Maimonides believes God is in a completely different category from anything else in existence. He denies that there is any relation or similarity between God and humanity. He also denies God can be accurately described as having rationally conceivable attributes such as existence, life, power, wisdom, and will (*Guide* 1.56). He continues, "These attributes, when applied to God, have not the same meaning as when applied to us" (*Guide* 1.56). Every word describing God is equivocal. All descriptions of God "are either attributes of God's actions, or expressions implying the negation of the opposite" (*Guide* 1.59).[62] Moreover, he claims that those who say there is one God with multiple attributes make the same theological mistake as Christians who believe that God is one and three (*Guide* 1.50). As Plotinus wrote, "If we make [the One] knowable, an object of affirmation, we make it a manifold" (*Enn.* 5.3.13). Instead, one must remain silent when speaking about God (*Guide* 1.59). Maimonidean scholar Kenneth Seeskin summarizes, "In the end, Maimonides maintains that all semantic functions, whether attribution, description, or definition, fail when applied to God."[63]

This is a particularly severe version of *via negativa*, or apophatic theology, whereby one may never say anything positive about who God *is*, but only remain silent or state what God is *not*.[64] In her chapter on

---

62. For an introduction to Maimonides's handling of divine attributes, see Rynhold, *Introduction*, 78–103. See also Altmann, "Maimonides on the Intellect," 119–25. For an overview of five schools of pre-Maimonidean rabbinic thought relating to God's attributes, see Idel, *Middot*, 13–43.

63. Seeskin, "No One Can See," 87.

64. Some Christian traditions have strong apophatic themes, but all creedal

Part II: A Critique of Non-Incarnational Maimonidean and Kabbalistic Thought

Jewish negative theology, Sandra Valabregue calls Maimonides's version of *via negativa* "comprehensive negative theology," the first example of such in Jewish history.[65] Previous Jewish authors supported less stringent versions of negative theology (i.e., Saadia Gaon), but Maimonides's version allowed for no exceptions to the rule: *nothing* positive may be known about God.

5.7. Maimonides on the Impossibility of Divine Embodiment

Maimonides does not explicitly address or reject the doctrine of the hypostatic union (Incarnation) in his writings; rather, he rejects its parent concept, the idea that God could ever take on a body whatsoever.[66] Maimonides makes only a passing argument against the Trinity in the *Guide* (*Guide* 1.50; cf. 1.71). As he has already decided Christianity is idolatry in his earlier writings, he does not seem to consider Christianity his primary target in the *Guide*.[67] He likely has Jewish corporealists in mind when defending his vision of an absolutely incorporeal God.[68] Despite his different focus, Maimonides's theology negates any possibility for belief in a Trinitarian God and also negates any type of divine embodiment, including the Incarnation.

Christian theologies must, at a minimum, affirm doctrines such as God being three persons in one essence and the belief that the Son has assumed a human nature. These positive affirmations of God's nature are disallowed in Maimonides's version of apophaticism, which is what makes it particularly severe.

65. Valabregue, "Limits of Negative Theology," 55–62. See also Feldman, "Philosophy and Theology," 2:719.

66. In other words, in reference to the schools mentioned in §1.3, Maimonides explicitly rejects school 2A, which logically implies rejection of school 2B.

67. For an overview of Maimonides's opinions about Christianity, see Novak, "Maimonides's View of Christianity." Christianity is not a major theme in the *Guide*. Kellner writes that Maimonides had a "penchant for attacking objectionable texts and positions from the flanks, rather than frontally" (*Maimonides' Confrontation with Mysticism*, 20).

68. As explained in §3.2.1, many Jewish people throughout the talmudic and medieval eras accepted a corporeal understanding of God. This theology embarrassed Maimonides, as it was out of step with the incorporealism of medieval Islam, which had accepted an Aristotelian-Neoplatonic synthesis. In my view, Maimonides's primary targets in the *Guide* were Jewish corporealists (see *Guide* 1.76), and a secondary effect was a sidelining of Christianity (which Maimonides considered beneficial). On Jewish corporealists as his target, see Aaron Segal, "His Existence Is Essentiality," 105; Kellner, *Maimonides' Confrontation with Mysticism*, 6–7.

Maimonides's System of Absolute Divine Incorporeality

The Third Principle asserts the incorporeality of God and his lack of similarity to anything (*via negativa*). In a limited sense the Jesus follower could agree with the *Ani Ma'amin* version of the Third Principle,[69] as God's eternal nature is indeed incorporeal, and language about God needs to be viewed in a unique way. However, the logic underlying the Third Principle, as given in the *Guide*, implies that temporary divine embodiment and the Incarnation are each disallowed from ever happening. It is not just that God is incorporeal in his eternal nature; it is also impossible that he could ever take on physical form in time.

To have a body is to have specific finite attributes, limitations, and abilities. These categories are distinguishable and multiple (i.e., the attribute of one's age from birth is different from one's ability to be a carpenter). In the *Guide*, Maimonides states that the idea of God taking physical form is a logical impossibility. "It is impossible that God should produce a being like Himself, or annihilate, corporify, or change Himself. The power of God is not assumed to extend to any of these impossibilities" (*Guide* 3.15; cf. 1.75; 2.13). The key word here is "corporify," in Friedländer's translation, or "should become a body," in that of Pines. A narrow reading of this passage would infer that it is logically impossible that God, who transcends all thought, time, and change, could fully transform himself to be finite and limited, shedding all transcendence. In other words, it would be impossible for God to transmute himself from an infinite substance-beyond-substance to a finite substance that has a body.[70] However, the *Guide* does not have this narrow understanding of transformed substance in mind. None of Maimonides's contemporary opponents claimed that God had abandoned heaven and had permanently transmuted into a physical body, shedding his infinitude. Whether referring to Jewish corporealists, the traditional rabbinic opinions on *Shekhinah*, the proto-Kabbalists,[71] or Christians, Maimonides's opponents believed that God could mysteriously remain fully God in heaven while *simultaneously* appearing in physical form.[72]

This is the position that Maimonides finds to be logically impossible. In his view, God cannot remain God if he ever shows up in a physical

---

69. See §5.1.

70. The Christian tradition would agree that such a notion is impossible, as illustrated in the historic rejection of the similar heresy of Monophysitism.

71. Kellner, *Maimonides' Confrontation with Mysticism*.

72. Summarizing the view the Maimonides rejected, Sommer says, "That a deity came down did not mean the deity did not also remain up" (*Bodies of God*, 133).

space, in bodily form, with bodily characteristics. An incorporeal God can never be associated with physicality, or else his incorporeality would be corporeal: a logical contradiction. Just as God cannot "produce a square the diagonal of which be equal to its side" (*Guide* 2.13), so too God cannot appear in physical form. As Tzvi Langermann writes, "Indeed, no distinction is as critical for Maimonides as that holding between the possible and the impossible; his entire religious philosophy can be said to hinge upon that distinction."[73]

In these ways, Maimonidean thought turns the Trinity and Incarnation into absurdities that Jewish people must avoid.[74] In Maimonides's view, any who disagree with him have abandoned basic logic and have embraced irrational impossibilities.

5.8. Maimonides and the God Talk of Scripture

In general, Maimonides sides with Aristotle's view of the natural, everyday nature of words, rhetoric, and logic.[75] As an exegete and halakist, he prides the exoteric (commonly understandable) over the esoteric (mystically hidden). However, he notes that Hebrew sometimes treats subjects with euphemism due to their sensitive nature (*Guide* 3.8).[76] This provides Maimonides an example of esoteric or euphemistic language about earthly things. If some earthly things ought to be hidden by euphemism, then how much more should the ineffable, unknowable, indescribable God?

There are many passages in the Hebrew Scriptures where God is spoken of in exoteric-sounding corporeal terms, such as God walking (Gen 3:8) or smelling (Gen 8:21).[77] The rabbinic sages employed similar depictions of God.[78] Maimonides is very aware of this corporeal language in the Scriptures and the rabbinic tradition. In light of the scriptural and rabbinic

---

73. Langermann, "Maimonides and Miracles," 160.

74. Fully attuned to the Maimonidean spirit, David Shapiro writes, "The very doctrine of the Trinity as applied to the Deity remains for Judaism an irreconcilable absurdity" ("Possible *Deus Homo*?," 361).

75. "Aristotle's philosophy for Maimonides is the model of science and reasoned explanation, the ideal conjoining of logic and nature" (Ivry, "Maimonides and Neoplatonism," 139).

76. Kellner, *Maimonides' Confrontation with Mysticism*, 155–78.

77. As reviewed in ch. 2.

78. As reviewed in ch. 3.

use of corporeal terms for God, it is difficult to avoid the conclusion that they come under Maimonides's condemnation when he declares,

> Therefore bear in mind that by the belief in the corporeality or in anything connected with corporeality, you would provoke God to jealousy and wrath, kindle His fire and anger, become His foe, His enemy, and His adversary in a higher degree than by the worship of idols. (*Guide* 1.36)

This is severe rhetoric. He is surely condemning corporealists as being worse than idolators, but is he also condemning the Scriptures and the rabbinic sages? No, for Maimonides develops a clever method to exonerate them. Maimonides appeals to a time-honored Platonic tool: asserting that corporeal passages about God are esoteric mysteries that may be unlocked through philosophically informed metaphor.[79] His method is to assert the following:

1. The Scriptures and sages speak only to the philosophically unsophisticated.[80]
2. The Scriptures and sages may be correctly interpreted by the philosophically sophisticated.
3. The Scriptures and sages are always esoterically right, even when they appear exoterically wrong.[81]

Maimonides responds in such a way to turn the tables on Judaism's critics. Using his three steps of reasoning, Maimonides cleverly shifts embarrassment from the biblical text and the sages onto the skeptical reader who doubts Maimonides's incorporealist Judaism. Maimonides insists that foes of corporeal language are merely criticizing the *exoteric*

---

79. For the earliest Jewish use of this hermeneutical tool, see Aristobulus, the second-century BCE Jewish philosopher, cited in Eusebius, *Praep. ev.* 8.9–10. Plato encouraged a somewhat similar method for correcting Homer in *Resp.* 377–92. Also see §4.1.5. Maimonides employs the Talmudic dictum "The Torah speaks in the language of man" in a previously unknown sense, using it to justify esoteric interpretations that contradict the exoteric (*Guide* 1.33, 1.53). On the innovative Maimonidean use of this phrase, see Shatz, "Biblical and Rabbinic Background."

80. See *Guide*, introduction, 1.46, 1.54, 1.70. The final citation succinctly reads, "Our Sages spoke of these subjects in metaphors; they are too difficult for the common understanding of the people." See also Ravitzky, "Maimonides' Esotericism."

81. See *Guide* 1.46 for Maimonides's assertion that the sages used physical language for God because no person would be capable of misunderstanding their metaphorical character. For a similar take on Maimonides's methodology, see Klein-Braslavy, "Exoteric and Esoteric," 163.

Part II: A Critique of Non-Incarnational Maimonidean and Kabbalistic Thought

meaning of Scripture and the rabbinic sages, rather than their true *esoteric* meaning. Only the young, and women, and common people are so philosophically ignorant to understand the Scripture and sages so literally.[82] Maimonides thus employs his metaphysics and hermeneutics as arcane gnosis to pull the rug out from under his critics.[83] However, there are two hidden premises to his argument given above:

4. I, Maimonides, am "the sophisticated."

5. I, Maimonides, am right, so trust me about (1) through (3).

Everything in the embarrassment-shifting argument depends on the correctness of the new Greco-Jewish synthesis, namely that of Maimonides himself. One must trust Maimonides that Moses and the rabbinic sages taught the arcane knowledge, even though Moses and the sages did not explicitly include it in their writings.

With this trust in place, Maimonides frees himself to reinterpret Scripture and the sages to agree with Neoplatonic negative theology. This reinterpretation is one of the great triumphs of the *Guide*. For the majority of part 1 of the *Guide*, Maimonides gives a comprehensive lexicon of scriptural words and phrases that must be interpreted as nonliteral metaphors when applied to God. These include verbs like seeing, rising, sitting and nouns of the face, back, heart, and many more.[84] The scope of biblical text that must be reinterpreted under this allegorical hermeneutic is staggering. Maimonidean scholar Alfred Ivry writes, "In as

---

82. *Guide* 1.33–1.35. In this passage, he instructs his readers to teach these "insufficiently intelligent" groups that God is incorporeal, and if they object on the basis of the words of Scripture, then they are to be told that "the wise" understand how to deal with Scripture, whereas they do not.

83. In other words, Maimonides employs secret knowledge, known only to those who agree with him, to criticize those who disagree with him. To those standing outside of agreement with Maimonides, this can hardly be seen as a fair and rational argument. See *Guide* 1.17, 32–35. Moshe Idel classifies Maimonides's hermeneutics about God talk as a form of philosophical "arcanization" that is borne out of crisis (*Absorbing Perfections*, 10–12).

84. See *Guide* 1.1–48 for a comprehensive list of words and phrases that Maimonides said must be viewed as equivocal (metaphorical) language when applied to God: words such as image, form, pattern, verbs of seeing, place, throne, spatial terms, verbs for rising and sitting, verbs of proximity, filling, being high, passing, coming, going, walking, dwelling, eating, nouns of face, back, heart, air, soul, eyes, verbs of hearing and understanding. Reflecting on Maimonides's reinterpretations, nineteenth-century apologist to the Jewish people Alexander McCaul remarks, "To escape from the Christian doctrine, force the most violent must first be done to the text" (*Lectures on the Prophecies*, 47).

thorough a manner as possible, Maimonides removes every human and personal aspect of the Deity, every attribute by which He is conceived and depicted."[85] Maimonidean scholar Moshe Halbertal likens this to an "allegorizing steamroller."[86]

A famous theophany passage from Gen 18 illustrates Maimonides's application of these principles. When the LORD appears to Abraham (Gen 18:1), Maimonides understands "appearing" as "intellectual perception" (*Guide* 1.4). The visitor whom Abraham calls Adonai (אֲדֹנָי) (Gen 18:3) is a majestic angel, not God (*Guide* 1.61). When Abraham "draws near" to God (Gen 18:23), this takes place in a prophetic vision while he is in a trance (*Guide* 1.18; 2.42). When God indicates that he would "go down and see" the situation in Sodom (Gen 18:21), this refers to God's intent to punish, not spatial movement (*Guide* 1.10). For Maimonides, in no case should God be understood as being in a particular place in a particular time, and he certainly could never appear in a physical body.

5.9. Reflections on Maimonides and the Incarnation

Followers of Jesus may be eager to cite scriptural chapter and verse when justifying the divinity of Messiah from the Hebrew Scriptures. For example, when examining Gen 18, they may appeal to the physicality of the episode, which includes a "man" who is called Adonai. Those familiar with Second Temple Jewish and later rabbinic traditions may go even further and cite ancient Jewish interpreters who appeared to interpret the passage in a binitarian way. Unfortunately, this method of justification may be counterproductive in light of the Maimonidean worldview. Maimonides did not build his theology from the Scriptures or the rabbinic sages upward, as if operating in *sola Scriptura* or *sola rabbonim* modes. His approach was not a posteriori reflection on written texts. No, he began with certain a priori philosophical and theological commitments, made plausible from his medieval context, and worked his way *down* to Scripture and Jewish tradition, conforming ancient evidence to his interpretations.

In Maimonides's predetermined philosophical worldview, the Trinity, divine embodiment, and divine attributes are all impossible assertions. Any possible hints of those notions in the Hebrew Scriptures or

---

85. Ivry, "Maimonides' Philosophical Sources," §2.2, loc. 1831.
86. Halbertal, *Maimonides*, 366.

rabbinic traditions must be interpreted otherwise. God is an unknowable, indescribable, remote deity who interacts with humanity only indirectly through the motion of the heavenly spheres. This theological-philosophical worldview must be addressed before any appeals to the Hebrew Scriptures or NT teachings may appear plausible to a Jewish person who has inherited the theological patterns of Maimonidean thought.

6   An Assessment of Maimonides's System

Conventional definitions of reality do not contain or define what God will yet do in Israel.... The trajectory running from Abraham to Jesus challenges both the definitions of the possible and the legitimacy of the definers.

—WALTER BRUEGGEMANN[1]

IN THE PREVIOUS CHAPTER, I considered aspects of Maimonides's worldview related to his Second and Third Principles of Faith, both of which are borne out of a theology of absolute divine incorporeality. In light of his portrayal of God, the world, and biblical interpretation, how accurate is Maimonides's theological understanding? This chapter proceeds with an argument against Maimonides's absolute divine incorporeality, but with appeals to the NT omitted. However, before doing so, I will mention several points of appreciation and agreement I have with Maimonides's worldview.

6.1. Positive Aspects of Maimonides's System

Maimonides was a genius. His towering intellect has justly won admirers for centuries, both within Judaism and in circles outside of it. There is much in his thought that I, as a follower of Jesus, agree with. In my opinion, there is significant congruity between a Maimonidean worldview

1. Brueggemann, "'Impossibility' and Epistemology," 622, 632–33.

Part II: A Critique of Non-Incarnational Maimonidean and Kabbalistic Thought

and the NT, much more than is common between the NT and Kabbalah. Although my exposition of NT doctrine is reserved for part 3, I believe it is proper to convey my areas of appreciation for Maimonides before continuing to a critique.

Creation ex nihilo and the Creator-creation distinction. Maimonides interprets the opening verse of the Bible as God creating the universe out of nothing, distinct from himself. While the Aristotelian and Neoplatonic influences he depends upon asserted an eternal universe, Maimonides parts ways with his Greek influences by insisting that Scripture must trump unproven philosophical intuitions. By teaching that God alone is eternal and the universe is finite and distinct from him, Maimonides portrays the biblical distinction between the Creator and the created. The NT affirms Maimonides's views on these matters.[2]

Anti-divine corporeality. In contrast to many Jewish people of his day, and the rabbinic sages before him, Maimonides asserts that God in his eternal nature does not possess a body. This coincides with Jesus's affirmation, "God is spirit" (John 4:24).

Single-tiered metaphysics and epistemology. Maimonides sides with Aristotle regarding his single-tiered metaphysics. In principle, Maimonides believes that all things in the sublunary sphere are understandable through the senses and reason because their substances are accessible to humanity. He denies that sublunary substances or natures are mere shadows of higher realities.[3] Maimonides's position enables him to agree that the world God created was "very good" (Gen 1:31) and that it operates by natural laws (Jer 31:36; 33:20; Gen 8:22) that can and should reveal God (Rom 1:20). Arguably, the plain sense of the Hebrew Scriptures shares this single-tiered epistemology as well.

The rational nature of words, logic, and rhetoric. Maimonides follows Aristotle's lead in believing that it is humanly possible to find the one "correct" literal or allegorical meaning of a text.[4] Instead of believing that Hebrew is a special mystical pathway for understanding God and reality, Maimonides believes that all language, including Hebrew,

---

2. See §§8.4.1; 10.4.

3. Nevertheless, he still believed that human beings are "exceedingly inferior" compared to the essence and existence is compared to that of the spheres, stars, and intelligences (*Guide* 3.13).

4. Idel calls this the "monosemic" meaning of a text, in contrast to the "polysemic" system of the Kabbalists (*Absorbing Perfections*, 281–96).

is rationally understandable and functionally equivalent.[5] Language is imparted to man in the sublunary sphere, which makes it sensible, not mystical, and not infinite in meaning. He does not have any patience for magical incantations, amulets, or the belief that religious knowledge is better conveyed in Hebrew. Notably, Maimonides writes the *Guide* in Judeo-Arabic.

Acceptance of providence, prophecy, connection with the divine, and miracles. Maimonides's system accounts for the Scriptures' claims that God makes himself accessible to humanity through these categories. Maimonides is no deist; he merely asserts that God connects with humanity indirectly rather than directly.

Practical benefits to negative theology. An apophatic understanding of God avoids the crude anthropomorphism that tends towards corporealism. Negative theology preserves the mystery of God, accepts and emphasizes the limitations of human knowledge, prevents idolatry, and can foster a sense of awe and reverence. However, I believe these benefits may also be found in *via analogia*, yet without the drawbacks of exclusively negative theology.[6]

More could be said to affirm aspects of Maimonides's worldview. Nevertheless, just as I have limited myself to describing those aspects of his worldview that result in his Third Principle, so too my affirmations here are limited. I now turn to my critique of the brilliant medieval sage.

6.2. An Argument against Maimonides's Rejection of Divine Embodiment

Maimonides's worldview disallows the possibility that God can appear in physical form (divine embodiment) or take on human nature (Incarnation). I have called his position absolute divine incorporeality, and the following is an outline of my critique:

1. Maimonides teaches that divine embodiment is impossible.
2. Maimonides supports his belief in the impossibility of divine embodiment from four directions: cosmology, a priori reasoning, comprehensive negative theology, and hermeneutics.
3. Counterpoint: Maimonides's cosmology is false.

---

5. Kellner, *Maimonides' Confrontation with Mysticism*, 155–78.
6. See §11.2.

Part II: A Critique of Non-Incarnational Maimonidean and Kabbalistic Thought

4. Counterpoint: Maimonides's a priori reasoning is false.
5. Counterpoint: Maimonides's comprehensive negative theology is false.
6. Counterpoint: Maimonides's hermeneutics about God talk are false.
7. Therefore, Maimonides's rejection of divine embodiment lacks rational basis.

The previous chapter summarized premises 1 and 2, and this chapter argues in favor of counterpoints 3 through 6. If the first six premises are correct, the conclusion 7 follows. If at least one of counterpoints is correct, but not all four, it still follows that Maimonides's rejection of divine embodiment should be critically reevaluated.

6.3. The Missing Copernican Revolution in Jewish Theology

No rational thinker can accept Maimonides's physics and metaphysics as adequate accounts of the world.
MENACHEM KELLNER[7]

As a man of the medieval era, Maimonides accepted the Aristotelian-Ptolemaic system of the universe. Beyond that, Maimonides grounded many of his theological determinations upon this geocentric model such that they rise and fall together. By this I mean that Maimonides often did not provide support for his theology independent of his cosmological and metaphysical model. If there are non-geocentric methods to support Maimonides's conclusions, Maimonides himself did not provide them.

Long after Maimonides's death came Copernicus, Kepler, the telescope, Galileo, Newton, and Foucault's pendulum, each of which chipped away at the geocentric paradigm, eventually leading to its complete dismissal. At first, Copernicus's heliocentrism was merely theoretical, but the aforementioned natural philosophers provided powerful experimental and mathematical support in its favor. Maimonides's cosmology is long dead in an era where we send astronauts to the moon and probes outside the solar system using heliocentric physical models derived from Newton and Einstein. How does the loss of Maimonides's pre-Copernican

---

7. Kellner, *We Are Not Alone*, 156.

cosmology affect his theology?[8] Is Jewish theology missing its own Copernican revolution?

Few have asked these questions due to religious Jewish acceptance of the geocentric model until recent times. In his book *New Heavens and New Earth*, Jeremy Brown traces the history of Jewish acceptance of Copernican thought. He finds that the Jewish world, with few exceptions,[9] was slow to accept the Copernican model. Jewish authorities continued framing their theological thought in terms of geocentric cosmology long after the Christian world had moved on. Secular Jews of the Enlightenment largely began affirming Copernicus in the nineteenth century, but the religious Jewish world resisted until the twentieth.[10] Moreover, Brown discovered the persistence of some Orthodox Jews proposing geocentrism even into the twenty-first century.[11]

While Christians had access to the latest scientific advances and transitioned between the old and new cosmologies starting in the sixteenth century, Brown argues that the Jewish world was cut off from such advances because "Jewish access to the secular sciences was legally difficult and often religiously perilous."[12] No doubt this refers to the lamentable anti-Semitic policies of Christian kingdoms forcing Jews to live in ghettos and barring them from the academies until the Enlightenment. Yet, even after the gates of the ghettos were opened, many Orthodox Jews continued separating themselves from scientific advancement. The reformers of the nineteenth century accepted scientific pursuits, but the

---

8. Although Christian reactions to Copernicus are outside the scope of this chapter, the Copernican revolution originally befuddled Christian theological authorities as well. Medieval Catholic theologians had so integrated the Aristotelian model into their worldview such that Galileo's heliocentric arguments were rejected out of hand. Catholic authorities appealed to scriptural passages where the sun was described as moving. Luther and Calvin also appealed to Scripture against Copernicus. In contrast to Judaism, however, the Copernican challenge to Christian thought was mainly hermeneutical rather than a threat to the Christian doctrine of God. Core Christian doctrines of the Trinity, Incarnation, and resurrection were not dependent upon a geocentric cosmological system. Thus, the change from Aristotle to Copernicus did not challenge core Christian doctrine; rather, it necessitated the development of hermeneutical principles about phenomenological language in Scripture. On the cosmological and hermeneutical challenges Copernicus posed to Christian thought, see Lennox, *Seven Days*, 15–36.

9. Such as Joseph Delmedigo, Eliakim Hart, and Solomon Maimon.

10. J. Brown, *New Heavens*, 283. See also David Novak's comments in *Athens and Jerusalem*, 156.

11. J. Brown, *New Heavens*, 254–73. See also Kellner's anecdote about a Chabad *physicist* who continues to hold to Maimonides's cosmology (*Science in Bet Midrash*, 197).

12. J. Brown, *New Heavens*, 283.

Part II: A Critique of Non-Incarnational Maimonidean and Kabbalistic Thought

Orthodox often saw such pursuits as a threat to Torah learning.[13] Thus, the Jewish subgroups most committed to geocentric thought were also the ones most cut off from that of Copernicus.

Additionally, many Orthodox Jews have disregarded the study of Maimonides's empirical cosmology, preferring instead to view the universe through the metaphysical system of Kabbalah, which still reflects geocentrism but with less gusto.[14] As unfortunate as this history is, it resulted in few religious Jewish thinkers questioning the Aristotelian-Ptolemaic cosmological paradigm as presented in the *Guide* and the kabbalistic tradition. In sum, even though the *Guide* is over eight hundred years old, few Orthodox Jews were aware of its cosmological problems until relatively recent times.

Now that the Christian and Jewish worlds are united in accepting Copernicus, some Jewish philosophers have called for a major revision of Maimonides's dominance in Jewish thought. Jewish philosopher David Novak writes,

> As for the content of Maimonides's systematic thought, we have seen that it is based on his idea of nature. Like Aristotle, Maimonides grounds his metaphysics in his physics, that is, his view of nature, the inherently intelligible natural world. . . . Again, like Aristotle, Maimonides considered the heavenly bodies to be animated by separate intelligences, whose knowledge of God we humans seek to share in our own embodied existence. Now, after Galileo, can one still use such paradigms of cosmology? Do they still apply in the realms of modern astrophysics?[15]

Not at all, Novak says. He understands that accepting Maimonides's cosmological paradigm would have erroneous theological implications:

> Maimonides did not regard humans as the pinnacle of creation. That was the place of the separate intelligences, entities that no longer command much authority today. Their revival today would raise significant difficulties for theology, the most significant being the implication that the human relationship with God must be mediated by these separate intelligences.[16]

---

13. A notable exception to this tendency is found in the Torah Umaddah movement in modern orthodoxy, as exemplified by Yeshiva University and the Orthodox Union.

14. See §9.3. This lack of engagement with Maimonides's cosmology is an example of how his dogmas were sometimes accepted without explicit acceptance of Maimonides's own rationale for the dogmas.

15. Novak, "Can We Be Maimonideans," 205.

16. Novak, "Can We Be Maimonideans," 205.

An Assessment of Maimonides's System

Because Maimonides cannot be followed on these matters any longer, Novak calls for a new paradigm:

> If we cannot accept Maimonides' metaphysical paradigm, we should try to replace it with a counterpart that is more adequate and fruitful in law and theology. That would be the greatest tribute we could pay to Maimonides: to be mindfully inspired and guided by his own philosophical quest, while not succumbing to any mindless deference to his posthumous authority.[17]

Novak's solution is bold: In order to honor Maimonides in the modern era, we must use our minds thoughtfully like he did, even when we must reject his opinions.[18] In my estimation, Maimonides himself would be in favor of this if he were alive today; his belief in the progress of science shows he is not beholden to a paradigm so strongly that it cannot be questioned.[19] Maimonides boldly writes, "The properties of things cannot adapt themselves to our opinions, but our opinions must be adapted to the existing properties" (*Guide* 1.71).[20] Nevertheless, because we do not have Maimonides alive today to correct himself on the basis of updated properties, Novak is calling on today's Jewish philosophers to do the work for him.

Likewise, Jewish philosopher Norbert Samuelson presses his colleagues to consider the importance of rejecting the medieval cosmological model in modern Jewish thought:

> With very few exceptions, modern Jewish philosophers have little to say about creation. Many affirm that creation is a central doctrine of Judaism, but they either do not discuss it at all or they discuss it in the same terms that the classical Jewish philosophers discussed it. However, by now it should be sufficiently

---

17. Novak, "Can We Be Maimonideans," 206.

18. Novak discusses similar themes in "Maimonides's View of Christianity," 69–70. Novak's solution is an example of what I call for in §1.5. Menachem Kellner comes to this conclusion as well (*We Are Not Alone*, 156–57).

19. *Guide* 3.14: "You must, however, not expect that everything our Sages say respecting astronomical matters should agree with observation, for mathematics were not fully developed in those days; and their statements were not based on the authority of the Prophets, but on the knowledge which they either themselves possessed or derived from contemporary men of science."

20. This remark shows that Maimonides thinks he is subordinating a priori thought to a posteriori evidence. Ironically, in this section, Maimonides believes he is following his maxim about conforming his opinions to existing properties, whereas Christians with their Trinitarian doctrine and Muslims are not. In §§6.5 and 11.1.4, I conclude that Maimonides did not follow this maxim himself.

clear how dependent that discussion is on a clearly obsolete (and untrue) understanding of reality. Hence, the doctrine of creation desperately needs reinterpretation.... To affirm creation or to explain it in terms of an understanding of the cosmos that is obsolete amounts to affirming and explaining nothing at all.[21]

In another publication, Samuelson provides a test case for revising the medieval Jewish doctrine of creation. He notes that the discovery of Newtonian inertia invalidates the Aristotelian physics that Maimonides employs in his proofs for the existence of God.[22] Samuelson calls for Jewish thinkers to provide creative solutions to this problem by engaging modern science and pairing it with sophisticated religious faith.[23]

6.3.1. Maimonidean Theological Categories Needing Revision

As Novak and Samuelson say, the loss of Maimonides's cosmology is not a matter localized to his science alone but also deeply affects his theology. They have sounded the alarm about the need to revise Maimonides, but in their view, few have heeded their calls. In this section, I illustrate how thoroughly Maimonides's false cosmology deconstructs his theology. The invalidation of Aristotelian cosmology adversely affects Maimonides's understanding of creation, providence, prophecy, communion with God, and miracles, as noted below.

Creation. Maimonides believes the universe is shaped like a concentric onion, with layers of heavenly spheres moving by intelligences equivalent to the biblical angels. Moreover, the lower spheres emanate from the higher spheres, with the outermost sphere being the only direct creation God performed *ex nihilo*. The spheres are thus Maimonides's mechanism to explain the cosmos's existence. This mechanism already contains internal inconsistencies. Maimonides says God is "separate from the universe, and in no contact whatever with it" (*Guide* 1.72). If so, how did he create the outermost sphere? If God is infinite, and the outermost sphere is finite, there is an infinite separation between them. If the creation of a finite thing involves God's power metaphorically "crossing" the infinite divide to produce a finite effect, does this undermine Maimonides's vision of God's infinitude? No emanation or cause-and-effect

---

21. Samuelson, *Jewish Faith and Modern Science*, 24.

22. Samuelson, "Challenges of Modern Sciences," 88–91. Maimonides's invalidated premises include premises 17, 18, and 25 as found in the introduction to the *Guide*, pt. 2.

23. Samuelson, "Challenges of Modern Sciences," 94–95.

chain can explain the first finite created intelligence and its associated sphere. It would appear that God's infinitude does not preclude his direct interaction with at least the finite being of the outermost sphere. Yet, with the nullification of the emanating spheres under Copernicus's model, Maimonides cannot today explain how God created anything. For example, Maimonides denies that God directly created Earth; the spheres emanated our planet.

In order to save Maimonides's notion of creation *ex nihilo*, one would have to postulate that God can create Earth *directly* without any intermediaries between his transcendence and the finite realm. Finite intermediaries like angels as agents of creation are insufficient because one must still explain how God "reached down" to create the first finite angel, when that very "reaching down" is what Maimonides rejected.

Finally, Maimonides's model requires that Earth emanates from the power of the spheres above, such as the sun and moon, whereas Gen 1:14 says the heavenly bodies were created after Earth existed. As early as Theophilus of Antioch in the second century, the biblical creation sequence was seen as a rebuttal of Greek emanation theories (*Autol.* 2.15). Another model for creation is necessary, and Maimonides should not be seen as an authority in this area.

Providence. Maimonides teaches that God enacts providence on Earth by moving the outermost sphere, which causes a chain reaction of motion to the lower realms, where it affects humanity.[24] These mechanisms are nullified after Copernicus. Without the celestial spheres to act as transmitters of God's providence, the Maimonidean universe is left vacant of governance. The loss of the spheres turns Maimonides into an unwitting deist; once the spheres are removed, the Maimonidean deity has no mechanism to influence anyone or anything. Additionally, Maimonides does not explain how the first finite transmitter of providence, the outermost sphere, may be moved by a God who does not interact with creation directly. In order to rescue providence, a theologian would need to propose a different set of intermediaries or a solution whereby God can *directly* sustain and lead the universe, bridging the infinite gap between heaven and earth.

Prophecy. Maimonides postulates a system whereby the biblical prophets prepare their intellects and imaginations through philosophy,

---

24. In *Guide* 1.72, Maimonides says that God "sets in motion" the outermost sphere, granting it the power to give motion to all lower entities. This implies an active participation on God's part whereby he directly causes the motion of the highest sphere.

connecting their minds with the active intellect that governs the sphere of the moon. When God chooses to send prophecy to the prophets, he communicates his words from sphere to sphere, ending in the active intellect, to which the prophet has access. With the loss of the spheres due to heliocentrism, no Maimonidean pathway exists for God's words to travel down to human ears. This catastrophic result leaves two options: either one accepts that God does not (or cannot) communicate with human beings—a deist result that disqualifies Scripture as the word of God—or one postulates a different system whereby God can provide prophecy to humanity.

Maimonides denied that God could directly communicate prophecy to man, on the grounds of God's transcendence. Perhaps a post-Maimonidean theology would involve the possibility that God *can* and *has* spoken to humanity *directly* to Moses and the prophets. There should also be a reconsideration of Maimonides's dismissal of the idea that God can choose to send prophecy to anyone at any time according to the wisdom of his own will (*Guide* 2.32). If God bypasses human philosophical ability and speaks directly to prophets, then this would invalidate Maimonides's hierarchy of prophets. While there is scriptural precedent to place Moses at the head of the prophets (Num 12:6–8),[25] other prophets (and their biblical writings) should not be ranked against each other according to the measure of their philosophical ability.

Communion with God. Maimonides teaches that the same cosmological system that enables prophets to hear God's words also allows philosophically inclined Jewish people to commune with God. He writes, "The intellect which emanates from God [through the spheres] unto us is the link that joins us to God" (*Guide* 3.51). Post-Copernicus, there are no spheres to transmit this intellect. The link is severed, and man cannot be joined to God. In order to rescue humanity from abandonment, one must propose a different method for communing with the Almighty. If close relationship with God is not dependent upon philosophical ability, then the groups Maimonides derided as unphilosophical—the young, women, and common people—may yet hope to be near God.

---

25. When comparing Jesus to all previous prophets (1:1–2) and to Moses himself (3:2–6), the NT book of Hebrews places Jesus, as the Son of God, in a category of his own. Quoting from Numbers about Moses "being faithful in all my house," Heb 3:3 notes that Jesus was the *builder* of that house, so Jesus has a greater glory than Moses just as a builder has greater honor than his house. This rejects Maimonides's Seventh Principle, which states that Moses is and forever will be Israel's greatest prophet.

Miracles. Early in his life, Maimonides taught that the miracles recorded in Scripture were embedded in the initial conditions of creation, which emanated from the heavenly spheres. At the end of his life in the *Guide*, it is evident that he is open to this position, although he is also in favor of temporary miracles that go beyond natural processes—yet without any mechanism to explain how they occur. Moreover, he teaches that miracle workers do not actually *perform* miracles; instead, they have prophetic insight through the spheres concerning when an anomaly in nature is destined to occur. The loss of the heavenly spheres in a post-Copernican universe means that the miracles recorded in Scripture never happened, or else God can perform miracles in the universe without the intermediary heavenly spheres. A post-Maimonidean theology is needed to explain how God can perform miracles.

In sum, I see the need for a major revision—even a Copernican revolution—concerning Maimonides's theological positions because of his faulty cosmology. Novak warns that it is "playing with fire" to build one's theology upon wholesale acceptance of an ontological and philosophical paradigm. It risks bringing an entire theological system down when the paradigm is shown to be scientifically false.[26] To the extent that Maimonides justifies his theology on the foundation of disproven cosmology, the theology requires revision.[27] Additionally, any revisions need to be tracked downstream, thoroughly searching for other theological doctrines that Jewish thinkers have built upon the house of cards Maimonides constructed. If Maimonides's doctrines mentioned here (creation, providence, etc.) were used to inform subsequent doctrines, such as hermeneutical methods or the knowability of God, then the subsequent doctrines should be purged of the false premises and revised themselves.

This deconstruction of Maimonides's theology, if pursued thoroughly, may be widespread. Yet I insist, based on the Hebrew Scriptures, that the theological categories Maimonides affirms actually exist, but the mechanisms he employs do not. As opposed to deism and atheism, the plain sense of Scripture affirms creation *ex nihilo*, providence, prophecy, communion with God, and miracles. However, these realities must be explained through a worldview that Maimonides did not affirm.

---

26. Novak, *Athens and Jerusalem*, 156–57.
27. Kellner, *Science in Bet Midrash*, 197n15.

Part II: A Critique of Non-Incarnational Maimonidean and Kabbalistic Thought

The example of scientific paradigm change is illustrative here.[28] It was once observed that metal gains weight when heated, and as late as the eighteenth century, this was attributed to the object's loss of phlogiston, an impurity with negative weight. Moreover, it was believed that heated objects gain an invisible fluid called caloric. Today, we know that heated objects still exist, but that their properties are not determined by phlogiston and caloric, for those things do not exist. Instead, the weight gain of heated metals is due to oxygen attaching itself to the metal, and heat gain is due to the vibration of the object's molecules. The phenomena that were once attributed to phlogiston and caloric are now attributed to other mechanisms.[29] So too, we should retain the theological categories that Maimonides affirms from Scripture, but we need to attribute their existence to different mechanisms than Maimonides provides. As with the history of chemical science and cosmology, this will require a revolution for anyone justifying their theology using the Maimonidean system.

In each of the theological categories, Maimonides employs his cosmology to keep God far away from the physical universe, safely hidden away in his transcendence. Maimonides's deity could never affect anything directly in the finite creation. Under his worldview, both divine embodiment and the Incarnation are implausible to the point of impossibility; they break the rule of God's transcendence by making him incredibly *near*. Yet, the scientific justifications he provides for his worldview are no longer tenable. The universe upon which he builds his theology does not exist; it is not science but science fiction. In response, a contemporary admirer of Maimonides should reconsider the impossible gulf Maimonides establishes between God and man. If his universe does not exist, then perhaps the theological gulf he posits does not exist either.

However, once that gulf is questioned, the road is significantly cleared for the possibility that God can do things *directly* in creation.[30] Is

28. For more on scientific paradigm change, see Kuhn, *Structure of Scientific Revolutions*; Psillos, "Realism and Theory Change."

29. Moreland and Craig, *Philosophical Foundations*, 183; Kuhn, *Structure of Scientific Revolutions*, 52–57.

30. On the *Judaism Demystified* podcast, the hosts submitted a question from me to Maimonidean scholar Lenn Goodman. The question involved the predicament posed in this section regarding the effect of Copernicus on Maimonides's theological model. Goodman suggested that the solution in each category was easy: all one must do is postulate that God can do these things directly in the universe. That is my solution as well. However, this response turns Maimonides's theology on its head. It opens the possibility that God could have a direct, positive relationship with the physical world, even taking physical form. See L. Goodman, "Depopulating the Heavens," loc. 49:03.

the Incarnation one of the things that God can do in a post-Maimonidean cosmology? Philosopher Katherin Rogers writes, "The question of the reasonableness of believing in the Incarnation can properly arise if you take it that there exists a God who acts as an agent in the world. On the assumption that there is no such God, the epistemic probability of the Incarnation is nil."[31] This investigation has shown that Maimonides's assumption that there is no such God is untenable. Thus, the probability for the Incarnation goes from nil to something higher. What was once unthinkable now deserves a place at the table.

6.4. The Conflict between Negative Theology and Revelation

As catastrophic as the Copernican worldview is to Maimonides's theological system, there are additional reasons for questioning his anti-incarnational worldview. To begin with, his insistence that God cannot be rationally known or described has justly generated much criticism from medieval and contemporary philosophers.[32]

Plato and Aristotle each reasoned toward a single highest deity who was the source of all lower reality. They conjectured the "God of the philosophers" through natural theology, starting with the existing cosmos and reasoning up to God (cf. Rom 1:20; Ps 19; Wis 13:3–9). In their theologizing, they largely avoided the written theology of Homer, charting a course in which philosophers do not need propositional revelation from above. The Hebrew tradition began from the opposite direction. Instead of reasoning up to God, the Hebrew Scriptures emphasize God revealing propositional truth downward to man through prophets. While the Greek tradition says that man cannot speak of God, the Hebrew tradition says that God can speak of himself.[33] In the course of that revelation, the Hebrew Scriptures use words to describe God's attributes, his face, form, back, image, feet, voice, sound, and location. The Torah, written by Moses, includes such language, and God insists that he spoke to Moses clearly and "not in riddles" (Num 12:8). The Scriptures never instruct

---

31. Rogers, "Anselmian Defense of Incarnation," 394.

32. Gersonides, *Wars of the Lord* 3.3; Crescas, *Or Hashem* 1:3:3; Spinoza, *Theologico-Political Treatise* 7; Wyschogrod, *Body of Faith*, 84–85; Wyschogrod, "Jewish Perspective on Incarnation"; Sommer, *Bodies of God*, 136; Rynhold, *Introduction*, 78–103.

33. Wyschogrod, *Body of Faith*, 171.

readers to interpret all such language metaphorically, esoterically, or as subjective psychological visions.

Via negativa interpretations of such language entered the Jewish-Christian sphere through Aristobulus, Philo, and Platonizing[34] church fathers (Justin, Clement of Alexandria, Origen, Novatian). Philosopher John Frame notes, "But [the] principles [of *via negativa*] are not biblical. Scripture itself does not hesitate to ascribe names and positive descriptions to God. The denial of meaningful speech about God is more characteristic of Gnosticism and Neoplatonism than of the Bible."[35] Nevertheless, Christian interpreters began syncretizing with negative theology in their project of making Christianity palatable to Greek thought. Even so, its total dominance over Christian hermeneutics was prevented through positive concepts like the Logos, the historicity of theophanies, and the Incarnation.

Centuries later, the idea of *via negativa* was delivered to medieval Islam, and Muslims developed strong anti-Trinitarian motives to remove the previous positive safeguards.[36] Maimonides inherited this tradition from Islam and employed *via negativa* as if he was Plotinus reborn. The third-century pagan Neoplatonist had no desire or rational need to integrate, modify, or dampen his negative theology because of biblical revelation, for he rejected the Bible. Similarly, Maimonides saw no need to integrate, modify, or dampen his negative theology on account of the revelation of Scripture, because he placed negative theology higher in his epistemological hierarchy than Moses and the prophets.[37] It is *via negativa* that provides Maimonides the weapon to combat Jewish corporealists and Trinitarians.[38] In other words, given the collision between negative theology and Scripture's literal truth claims, Maimonides uses the former to overrule the latter for polemic reasons. Ivry notes that

---

34. This is similar to Hellenization, but focused on the acceptance of Platonism. Platonizing is when a philosopher or theologian syncretizes one belief system with Plato's thought, obscuring the original belief system and making Plato's determinations the controlling ones.

35. Frame, *History of Western Philosophy*, 91.

36. L. Goodman, "What Is Positive," 104–5.

37. For example, in *Guide* 2.2, Maimonides mentions three categories that he believes can be demonstrated with proofs: natural philosophy, metaphysics, and mathematics. *Via negativa* is embedded in Maimonides's understanding of the first two categories. He then notes that these demonstrable proofs provide the key for understanding esoteric passages in Scripture. See also Davies, *Method and Metaphysics*, 39.

38. *Guide* 1.50; Kavka, "Politics of Negative Theology," 533–36.

An Assessment of Maimonides's System

Maimonides was preceded by Saadia Gaon (882–942)[39] in his allegorization of anthropomorphisms, but "neither Sa'adia nor those who followed him in the rabbinic tradition were prepared for the thoroughgoing deconstruction of the biblical text that Maimonides undertook."[40]

Maimonides's methodology results in the propositional truth of the following parody:[41]

> Give thanks to the LORD, for he is not good, for his steadfast non-love endures forever. Do not ascribe to the LORD the glory not due to his name. The LORD is not my shepherd, I shall not want. Worship the LORD in the splendor of his non-holiness. The LORD, the LORD, a God not merciful or gracious, never having anger, abounding in steadfast non-love and non-faithfulness. The not great, not mighty, not awesome God, who is not righteous in all of his works. Not great is our LORD, and lacking in power; his vacuity of understanding is beyond measure. Let us press on to not know the LORD, for we say, "How can God know? Is there knowledge in the Not Most High?" There is no knowledge of God in the land.

As irreverent and subversive of actual Scripture this sounds, it is not subversive enough. Plotinus declares, "If we are led to think positively of The One, name and thing, there would be more truth in silence" (*Enn.* 5.5.6). Likewise, Maimonides writes,

> For whatever we utter with the intention of extolling and of praising Him, contains something that cannot be applied to God, and includes derogatory expressions; it is therefore more becoming to be silent, and to be content with intellectual

---

39. Saadia Gaon was Maimonides's closest Jewish philosophical predecessor, but even Saadia believed that God possessed the attributes of life, omnipotence, and omniscience (*Emunot* 2.1). He clarified that the three attributes were not three, but one, although human language had no capability to describe that one attribute (*Emunot* 2.4). This is essentially the same formulation that Augustine (*Trin.* 6.7) and Aquinas (*ST* I q.3 a.3 ad 1) give to the simplicity and equality of God's attributes. Saadia's polemical chapter against Christianity argues against only some versions of Trinitarian thought (*Emunot* 2.5).

40. Ivry, "Maimonides' Philosophical Sources," §2.2, loc. 1841. Ivry here even says Maimonides "for the most part turns the historic God of Israel into an ahistoric Deity." For Saadia as a predecessor of Maimonides in his reappropriation of Jewish mystical sources, see Wolfson, *Through Speculum That Shines*, 192–93.

41. This parody is written in the spirit of Gersonides.

reflection, as has been recommended by men of the highest culture. (*Guide* 1.59)⁴²

Rather than understanding Scripture on its own terms, or subverting Scripture through negations, for Maimonides it is better to not say *anything* about God. Commenting on Maimonides's and Saadia's handling of Scripture, Jewish philosopher Daniel Rynhold notes, "The first obstacle to a correct philosophic understanding of God is the language of Scripture itself."⁴³

Comprehensive *via negativa* and the revealed words of Scripture are in deep conflict with each other. One must subordinate the other because they make competing claims. One must either allow *via negativa* to modify or overrule Scripture, or allow Scripture to modify or overrule *via negativa*.⁴⁴ Maimonides's radical choice is to side with *via negativa* always, without exception, never allowing Scripture's positive claims to shine through. In sum, Maimonides's hermeneutics and his negative theology are two sides of the same coin. In the following sections, I provide reasons to doubt both.

6.5. Maimonides's Erroneous Deduction of Divine Impossibilities

In his major theological exposition of Trinitarian doctrine, Vern Poythress writes, "The most basic problem in philosophy is the dominance of

---

42. Maimonides justifies this position by citing Ps 65:1(2) as saying, "Silence is praise to you." Unfortunately, as many commentators have noted, the Masoretic manuscripts at this location suffer from two problems. First is the meaning problem: the Psalms exist as verbal proclamations of praise toward God, so it is prima facie odd to see silence described as praise. This oddity could be lessened with apophaticism, but the apophatic impulse is nowhere present in the rest of the Hebrew Scriptures, so it is out of place here. Second, there is a text-critical problem with the MT word for "silence" (דֻּמִיָּה, *dumiyah*). The LXX and Syriac read the vowels differently. Thus some translations emend the word to דֹּמִיָּה, *domiyah*, and translate as "Praise is due to you" (ESV), "Praise awaits you" (NET), or "Praise befits You" (NJPS). These renderings remove the idea of silence. Aquila's Greek reads, "To you I have given silent praise, God, in Zion." This verbal reading avoids making the metaphysical equation of silence and praise (Origen, *Origenis Hexalporum*, 2:195).

43. Rynhold, *Introduction*, 82.

44. As I explain in §11.2, along with Aquinas I hold that *via negativa* has a limited preparatory role in cleaning the intellectual palate for *via analogia*. See Aquinas, *SCG* 1.14, 1.29–34. Fagenblat distinguishes Maimonides's skeptical form of *via negativa* from his contemporaries, who employed *via negativa* in more limited fashion, thereby allowing some positive God talk to survive ("Introduction," 12–14).

autonomous reason. Autonomous reason cannot stand the mystery of God's revelation, and refuses to submit to it."[45] In other words, man's self-derived a priori reasoning can be the greatest enemy of a posteriori evidence provided by God. Instead, the proper posture is to submit one's human reasoning to correction by the divine revelation of Scripture.[46]

Maimonides turns this relationship around, as do many who are overly subservient to Greek modes of thought. For Maimonides, if he can reason on philosophical grounds toward a necessary logical impossibility (in his opinion), he considers the matter settled, and he reinterprets the Scriptures to fit his philosophical proof. For example, *via negativa* is one of Maimonides's foundational dogmas, as is the impossibility of God to "corporify" himself (*Guide* 3.15). For him, Scripture cannot not be taken on its own terms because doing so is impossible according to his a priori reasoning. Thus, his reasoning begins a priori with dogmatic assertions of necessary proofs that God has to abide by; thereafter, he conforms the a posteriori evidence of Scripture to fit his proofs through allegory and metaphor.

I have more to say on the topic of divine impossibility when I discuss the rationality of the Incarnation in chapter 11. For the present discussion, I will respond to Maimonides's subversion of a posteriori evidence through four counterarguments that are independent of NT revelation and later Christian theology.

The rationality of miracles. It could be argued that all miracles have been considered impossible in human minds until God actually performs them in history. The Torah is full of miracle reports: serpents and donkeys talk, elderly women become pregnant, the Nile turns to blood, fire descends on the mountain, and water gushes from a rock. In each case, nothing of the sort had ever been done in previous human experience. Before God performed those miracles, it may have been reasonable (by human standards) to develop philosophical and theological principles and conclude a priori, "Such things are impossible for God to do." This is the reason for Sarah's laughter when she is told she will have a child in her old age. The Lord rebukes her, saying, "Is anything too hard for the Lord?" (Gen 18:14). The Orthodox Jewish Stone Edition commentary says, "God was angered at her reaction, for a person of her great stature

---

45. Poythress, *Mystery of the Trinity*, 586.

46. Henry, *God, Revelation, and Authority*, 1:181–201; Anderson, *Paradox in Christian Theology*, 293–97.

Part II: A Critique of Non-Incarnational Maimonidean and Kabbalistic Thought

should have had faith that the miracle of birth *could* happen."[47] Thus, according to the Jewish writers of this commentary, *those who believe that God cannot do certain actions may be disbelieving the true God of Israel.*[48] God proved through his rebuke and the subsequent birth of Isaac that Sarah's a priori assumptions were wrong. In this sense, all human reasoning processes about divine impossibilities need to be provisional and open to revision in case God does, in fact and in history, perform what was previously considered impossible.

Maimonides's questionable philosophical sources. No one philosophizes in a vacuum. Human language and reasoning operate out of one's worldview. Although it is a laudable goal to seek out the first principles of rationality and deduce a philosophical worldview on top of those first principles,[49] it is all too easy to think that one's skill in deducing answers approaches the infallibility of the divine mind. Maimonides deduces his first principles under the Neoplatonized Aristotelianism he inherited from medieval Islamic philosophers. All his determinations of divine impossibilities filter through concepts as follows: Aristotelian matter, form, and physics, Aristotelian-Ptolemaic cosmology, Parmenides's unity of Being, Plotinus's divine simplicity and emanations, Proclus's formulations of Neoplatonic principles, Plato's exoteric and esoteric hermeneutics, and more. Maimonides tends to treat these as givens,[50] which may have been in vogue in his era, but not so today. Because his mental calculations about divine impossibilities are worked out in the context of questionable first principles, his dogmatic assertions about logical impossibilities are highly problematic.[51]

Alternative philosophical frameworks may redefine what is possible. Maimonides appears to conflate logical impossibility with metaphysical and epistemic impossibilities. Logical impossibilities are a priori violations

---

47. Scherman, *Chumash*, 81; emphasis in original.

48. See §11.1.4.

49. Maimonides's first principles can be found in *Guide*, introduction to pt. 2. For a contemporary Christian formulation, see Geisler, "First Principles." A pagan Neoplatonist version of first principles, which had indirect influence on Maimonides's thought, may be found in Proclus, *Elements of Theology*.

50. With some modifications, of course, such as seeing Parmenides's One as separate from God himself. When discussing the substances and forms of the heavenly spheres and their relationship with bodies in the sublunary sphere, Maimonides remarks, "All this has been demonstrated by proof" (*Guide* 2.19). I believe Maimonides would change his opinions if he were alive today.

51. Wyschogrod, *Abraham's Promise*, 34.

of the laws of logic and are not derived from empirical observations (i.e., a equals not-a). Metaphysical impossibilities contradict the way reality is in an a posteriori sense (i.e., a perpetual motion machine), and epistemic impossibilities contradict what one knows (i.e., one's worldview) or can know (i.e., conceiving infinity).[52] In *Guide* 3.15, Maimonides asserts the impossibility of God "annihilating" himself. Since God, as a necessary being, cannot cease existing, this is an example of a logical impossibility.[53] But then Maimonides lists God "corporifying" himself as another impossibility. If Maimonides intended this to mean God fully transmuting himself into a finite embodied being—which he did not—then this would indeed be a logical impossibility. But Maimonides's dogma is even against those who would say God is essentially incorporeal but can simultaneously inhabit physical spaces.[54] This is not a logical impossibility akin to a equals not-a, but rather an impossibility according to Maimonides's metaphysics, derived from his epistemic sources.

When working under a different metaphysical system, the impossibility may evaporate. For example, non-Euclidean geometry and Einsteinian space-time were once considered metaphysical impossibilities (disproven by reality) and epistemic impossibilities (contradicted Euclid and Newton). Yet, the strength of a posteriori evidence in their favor forced a change upon the prevailing metaphysics and epistemology, and what was previously inconceivable is now accepted as true. Likewise, an exchange of the Maimonidean framework for an alternative could make divine embodiment possible rather than impossible.

Maimonides's handling of creation ex nihilo. When he summarizes three theories about the origin of the universe, Maimonides notes that the Greeks considered the idea of creation *ex nihilo* to be nonsense, an impossibility for God (*Guide* 2.13). Moreover, he notes that Aristotle "considers it impossible for God to change His will or conceive a new desire." These Greek conceptions of divine impossibility were based upon a series of logical deductions that Maimonides concedes are consistent with the principles of the already-existing and developed world (*Guide* 2.17). What is Maimonides, the admirer of Aristotle, to do? Accept the Greek paradigm and reinterpret Genesis in terms of an eternal universe and a static God? Maimonides cautiously chooses a different path. He provides a critique of Aristotelian presuppositions against creation *ex*

---

52. On different kinds of impossibility, see Swinburne, *Coherence of Theism*, 1–54.

53. That is, God cannot be necessary and non-necessary at the same time.

54. See §5.7.

nihilo, but also concedes that his critiques are not definitive proof that Aristotle was wrong (*Guide* 2.17–2.22). Using reason alone, Maimonides argues himself into a draw.

Since Aristotle did not have the strength of demonstrable proof, and neither did creation *ex nihilo*, Maimonides allows Scripture to be the tiebreaker. He writes that creation *ex nihilo* is "a fundamental principle of the Law of our teacher Moses" (*Guide* 2.13). He continues, "All who follow the Law of Moses, our Teacher, and Abraham, our Father, and all who adopt similar theories, assume that nothing is eternal except God, and that the theory of *Creatio ex nihilo* includes nothing that is impossible." Thus, Maimonides makes three moves: (1) he investigates the logical basis of those who claimed that some things were impossible for God, (2) he critiques the presuppositions of pagan authors who reasoned against Scripture's exoteric claims, and (3) he sides with the exoteric meaning of Scripture when faced with philosophical challenge, rather than allegorize Scripture into esoteric contortions. I applaud Maimonides for this methodology. However, I contend that Maimonides neglects to apply this strategy to his assertion that God cannot take physical form. He should have been open to a posteriori evidence in Scripture regarding God's ability to localize himself physically, but he chose to side with the Greeks instead.

Due to Maimonides's reliance on a priori logic derived from his Neoplatonic-Aristotelian worldview, he does not allow himself to see counterevidence that disagrees with his thesis of God's absolute incorporeality. Every time Scripture communicates something other than his thesis, he employs philosophical equivocation to change the meaning of the text. This makes his assertions needlessly and haughtily uncorrectable by God's self-revelation.[55]

On the contrary, the Hebrew Scriptures *do* have something to say about God being localized in time, space, and body, but Maimonides represses it. He delegitimizes the Scriptures' ability to speak using plain language. He gives Aristotle and Plotinus the power to deliver an unassailable metaphysical theology, overruling even Moses. Instead, the Scriptures should be allowed to modify and correct a priori assumptions

---

55. If someone were to say to Maimonides, "I have biblical evidence against your position," Maimonides would reply, "That's not evidence, because my position makes that evidence inadmissible." In this reply, Maimonides treats his position as infallible and Scripture as inadmissible, rather than Scripture's evidence as admissible and his own position as fallible.

that are asserted without any basis in the holy text, such as assumptions from the Greeks or any other source. Maimonides grants Moses that authority regarding creation *ex nihilo*, and he should do the same with the question of divine embodiment.

6.6. The Invalidity of Maimonides's Negative Theology

The topic of negative theology is vast and bewildering, attracting the minds of adherents and detractors across various disciplines and across the religious spectrum. *Via negativa* has a classic heritage in all three Abrahamic religions, as each adopted Neoplatonic metaphysics to varying degrees across the centuries.[56] The resulting diversity on the subject means that one person's *via negativa* is likely not the same as another's, so it would be rash to argue against the notion with a broad brush. Indeed, grounded in the biblical doctrine of divine incomprehensibility, I hold to a limited version of negative theology that prepares the mind for analogy (*via analogia*) while leaving room for limited application of univocal language (*via positiva*).[57]

However, the Maimonidean form of the doctrine, which I have called comprehensive negative theology, is in a separate class and is an easier target, just as the claim of dogmatic atheism is more straightforward to rebut than agnosticism.[58] Maimonides leaves no room for any positive knowledge of God, or similarity, or description, or any bridge concept that would mitigate the distance between the finite and the infinite. Except, that is, when he famously contradicts himself. Below are reasons why Maimonides's *via negativa* ought to be reevaluated:

Only one justified and true example of similarity between God and creation breaks Maimonides's Third Principle. Since Maimonides is insistent in his Third Principle that there is precisely zero similarity between God and the created order—and that all scriptural and intuitive

---

56. Carabine, *Unknown God*; L. Goodman, *Neoplatonism and Jewish Thought*; Rist, "Plotinus and Christian Philosophy"; Kraemer, "Islamic Context"; Pessin, "Influence of Islamic Thought"; McClymond, *Devil's Redemption*.

57. Discussion on this position will be reserved for §11.2.

58. Dogmatic forms of atheism make the claim that it is impossible that God exists. If so, every theistic argument must be shown to be impossible—a very high bar. To rebut this position, all one must do is demonstrate that it is *possible* that God exists. In contrast, an agnostic accepts that it is possible that God exists, but that it is not possible to *know* he exists. Thus, an agnostic may accept evidence in God's favor but assess it to be inconclusive.

Part II: A Critique of Non-Incarnational Maimonidean and Kabbalistic Thought

similarity is equivocal and not real—finding a *single* justified, reasonable example of univocal or analogical similarity between God and creation causes the "no comparison" clause of Maimonides's Third Principle to fail. Maimonides himself provides several examples where he breaks his own rule.

Maimonides's handling of the human and divine intellects is the blind spot in his system. Maimonides makes this error in (1) identifying God as an intellect, (2) asserting positive similarities between God's intellect and man's intellect, and (3) being unaware that his solution is *via analogia* rather than *via negativa*.

(1) *Maimonides positively affirms that God is an intellect.* In Guide 1.68, Maimonides asserts, "Now, it has been proved, that God is an intellect which is always in action." In further Aristotelian fashion, he says that God "is always the intellect as well as the intellectually cognizing subject and the intellectually cognized object."[59] By making these positive assertions, Maimonides undermines his claims that God cannot be positively known or described, for at least we know that he is an intellect.

(2) *Maimonides asserts similarity between the divine and human intellects.* Maimonides was aware that the key verse corporealists cited in favor of God's body was Gen 1:26: "Let us make man in our image [צֶלֶם, *tzelem*], in our likeness [דְּמוּת, *demut*]." Maimonides handles this verse at the very beginning of the *Guide* (1.1), where he identifies "image" as "intellectual perception" and "likeness" as "agreement with regard to some abstract relation." If so, how can humans be "made in God's intellectual perception and agreement with some abstract relation with God" and yet have no similarity whatsoever with him?

In *Guide* 1.72, Maimonides draws a parallel between how God relates to the world and how man relates to his body: both interact with the physical through the intellect, implying a similarity between the function of the divine and human intellects.[60] In *Guide* 3.51, Maimonides writes, "The intellect which emanates from God unto us is the link that joins us to God," and the link is accessed via human intellect. Thus, the human intellect can connect and relate with the divine intellect. This implies that they are in the same category, with similar functions, rather than separated by an infinite gulf of dissimilarity.

---

59. Maimonides, *Guide* (Pines), 1:165.
60. Kreisel, "*Imitatio Dei*," 187.

An Assessment of Maimonides's System

Maimonidean scholar Shlomo Pines writes, "The parallel drawn by Maimonides between the human and the divine intellect quite evidently implies a certain similarity between the two; in other words, it is incompatible with the negative theology of other passages of the *Guide*."[61] Howard Kreisel joins in this identification of a basic Maimonidean contradiction:

> God is said to possess apprehension,[62] though totally unlike human apprehension. Hence by means of intellectual apprehension man in some way resembles God, though he can never in fact resemble God at all. I do not think that Maimonides ever fully resolved this tension. Yet he leaves no doubt in this passage that the intellect is in some significant sense "divine."[63]

Because there is a similarity between God's infinite intellect and the intellect given to man—by virtue of being made in God's "image" and "likeness"—Maimonides's logic on this issue undermines the Third Principle's declaration that "there is no comparison with him whatsoever."

(3) *If there is similarity (in kind, not degree) between God and man in their respective intellects, then Maimonides unwittingly supports* via analogia *for the intellect.* In *Guide* 1.1, after asserting a similarity between the divine and human intellects, Maimonides writes, "This [human] perception has been compared—though only apparently, not in truth—to the Divine perception." Thus, Maimonides asserts similarity in one sense, but dissimilarity in another. This is the method of *via analogia*, whereby it is asserted that human faculties and concepts are finite analogies to the divine faculties, which infinitely exceed the human faculties in perfection and magnitude.[64] This method, classically defended by Thomas Aquinas, allows for simultaneous similarity and dissimilarity, just as Maimonides achieves here. However, to be consistent with his comprehensive negative theology, Maimonides should not have accepted any similarity whatsoever.

A functionalist language model enables positive knowledge of God while acknowledging the categorical difference between God and man. Analytic philosopher William Alston proposes a functionalist language

---

61. Pines, "Judaism, Jewish Tradition."

62. Shlomo Pines translates "intellectual perception" as "intellectual apprehension," whose translation Kreisel cites.

63. Kreisel, "*Imitatio Dei*," 180.

64. For more on *via analogia*, see §11.2.3.

Part II: A Critique of Non-Incarnational Maimonidean and Kabbalistic Thought

model that allows for the accurate expression of positive language about God due to the common functions between the human and divine psyches (which Maimonides would have called intellect).[65] Alston acknowledges God is incorporeal, infinite, and timeless, which makes God's psyche a black box, inaccessible to human comprehension. However, given the radical difference between intellects, the divine psyche and the human psyche *still produce equivalent end results*: they bring about "a change in the world—directly or indirectly—by an act of will, decision, or intention."[66] Alston calls these end results *functions*, such as when a variety of loudspeakers made by different manufacturers with different internal components each function equivalently as loudspeakers.[67] With a functional understanding of language about God, it is irrelevant that human intelligence's internal structure is radically different from divine intelligence, for the same language of functions can still literally apply to both. Theologian John Feinberg expands on Alston's point: "It makes a certain amount of literal sense to say that a computer, a robot, and a human being 'made a decision' even though the internal structure of each is quite different."[68] So too, one can accurately use univocal language to say that God and a human being *know*, *decide*, and *act*. Furthermore, God is the kind of being whose intrinsic essence enables him to *know*, *decide*, and *act*, as opposed to the essence of a rock, which does not allow such functions. It may be unclear *how* God knows, decides, or acts, but it is certain *that* he does them—and his knowledge, decisions, and actions function like our own. Thus, this is an example of the possibility of humans having positive knowledge of God and intellectual similarity with him.

Maimonides's methods for knowing God are flawed. In *Guide* 1.60, Maimonides explains his preferred method of knowing God through the analogy of a ship. He gives the hypothetical example of a person who knows that a "ship" exists without knowing *what* it is (perhaps this person is a hermit in Plato's cave). Through the process of negation, this person could come closer and closer to understanding what a ship actually is (i.e., a "ship" is not a property, not a mineral, not a plant, not joined

---

65. Alston's essay "Functionalism and Theological Language" was first published in 1985 but has been republished multiple times. References here are to Alston, *Divine Nature*, 64–80. See also Alston, "Religious Language," 235–42.

66. Alston, *Divine Nature*, 72.

67. Alston, *Divine Nature*, 68.

68. Feinberg, *No One Like Him*, 79.

together by nature, etc.). Given enough negations, Maimonides claims the person would arrive at accurate knowledge and would have a rational positive notion and image of what a ship is. However, this analogy is fundamentally flawed because it works only with finite things that exist in sensible reality—that is, things that exist within the set of all finite things. Philosopher Daniel Rynhold comments on Maimonides's ship analogy, "It seems, however, that Maimonides is being a little disingenuous here."[69] Rynhold notes that one could negate a universe worth of finite nouns and adjectives and still not arrive at knowledge of the Maimonidean God, because he is not a thing in the universe nor can be described by anything in the universe. Negating the universe leaves one no closer than when he started, as Maimonides's medieval critic Hasdai Crescas argued.[70] The second way Maimonides asserts an individual can know God is through a philosophical connection with the active intellect associated with the lunar sphere, which I have already criticized above.

Making truthful negative statements requires some positive knowledge. How can there be certainty that negative descriptions of the "ship" are accurate? Maimonides's model implies there is a test by which negative statements about God can be judged to be truthful. The test is as follows: *all* negative statements about God's essence are truthful, for no positive statements apply. However, this test collapses into self-contradiction. To accurately know that positive descriptions cannot describe God, it must be positively known that God is not the kind of being who can be described. How does one come to know that principle? Maimonides's comprehensive *via negativa* argues in a circle by asserting at the outset what it intends to prove.[71] Moreover, Maimonides does not hold to his central principle when he describes God as the kind of being who engages in actions like living and knowing (*Guide* 1.57), who is an intellect (*Guide* 1.68), who mysteriously moves the outermost sphere

---

69. Rynhold, *Introduction*, 92.

70. Crescas writes, "If this were truly the case—that positive attributes are ruled out in relation to God, because they imply a compound essence, which is not the reality of Him—then one who has achieved great knowledge has no advantage over someone who has just begun his studies.... Thus, study of the detailed list of attributes which are ruled out in relation to God does not add in any way to the general knowledge which was already possessed by one who had just commenced his study" (*Or Hashem* 1.3.3; quoted in Navon, "Negative Attributes," under "How Can We Know God," para. 8).

71. On the circular reasoning of *via negativa*, see Feinberg, *No One Like Him*, 75–80. For further criticism, see Mullins, *End of Timeless God*, 6–10.

(*Guide* 1.72), who is the First Cause (*Guide* 2.48), and the like.[72] Philosopher Samuel Lebens notes, "Maimonides' argument for God's existence describes God as falling under the genus 'cause.' Thus, Maimonides' argument for God's existence violates the linguistic constraints that it is supposed to introduce."[73] Furthermore, calling God a "he" rather than an "it" is problematic in that it implies knowledge of God's personhood or gender. To be consistent, Maimonides should not speak of God using nouns, pronouns, verbs, participles, or adjectives at all (cf. the "silence" of *Guide* 1.59),[74] because doing so implies positive knowledge of God or his doings. This would have made the *Guide* much shorter. Plotinus the Neoplatonist also falls prey to this self-contradiction when he writes, "It is impossible to say 'Not that' if one is utterly without experience or conception of the 'That'" (*Enn.* 6.7.29).

Comprehensive via negativa *makes God indistinguishable from nothing.* Many have charged Maimonides with advocating a deity that is indistinguishable from atheism.[75] Atheism states that nothing can be predicated of God because the subject does not exist; Maimonides states that God is not the kind of thing that can have any predications, including existence (*Guide* 1.35). Granted, Maimonides attempts to mitigate this comparison by asserting that God can perform actions through the heavenly spheres, but on an ontological and epistemological level, the word "God" has similar propositional content in atheism and Maimonideanism. Orthodox theologian Michael Wyschogrod writes that Maimonides's position results in "an overly rarefied God who is so beyond all conception that he cannot be distinguished from no god at all."[76]

Comprehensive via negativa *leads to impiety.* If all positive language about God is inadmissible, with only negative descriptors permitted, then

---

72. Commenting on Maimonides's self-contradictions, Rynhold writes, "This is a recurrent problem for Maimonides, who does speak about God throughout the *Guide*. Either we have to say that he intended us to use his theory of negation to interpret his own [positive] references to God, which is entirely possible given the esoteric manner in which he wrote the *Guide*, or we have to concede that it is simply not possible to remain within these strictures" (*Introduction*, 95).

73. Lebens, *Principles of Judaism*, 10. Lebens contends that apophaticism may be false, but it promotes "falsehoods with power . . . to *show* us things that can't be *said* and/or to cure us of intellectual hubris" (28).

74. See 148n42.

75. Fagenblat, "Introduction," 13–14; Wolfson, "*Via Negativa* and Imaginal Configuring," 33.

76. Wyschogrod, *Abraham's Promise*, 168; Swinburne, *Coherence of Theism*, 8.

An Assessment of Maimonides's System

this results in faith-threatening assertions. Medieval critic Gersonides (1288–1344) notes that, if no language applies to God, then one could accurately say, "God does not have knowledge."[77] This argument could be extended to other notions about God: God is not wise, not intelligent, not careful, not truthful, not great, and not mighty.[78] It might be reasonable to ask whether such a god is worthy of worship and obedience.[79] Furthermore, since comprehensive negative theology would not permit saying, "God is identical to himself," instead one would be required to say, "God is not identical to himself." This negation would appear to shake the very foundation of theism.

Beyond these critiques, I will briefly reiterate others that have already been discussed:

- *Comprehensive* via negativa *places God's self-revelation outside of his omnipotence.*
- *There is no explicit support in the Hebrew Scriptures for comprehensive negative theology.*
- *Many scriptural passages imply the falsehood of comprehensive* via negativa.
- *Via negativa entered theological discourse through Platonic, not scriptural, vectors.*

---

77. Gersonides, *Wars of the Lord* 3.3. See Rynhold, *Introduction*, 94–98.
78. Cf. the parody in §6.4.
79. In their handling of this subject, Rynhold and Lebens propose anthropocentric solutions. Rynhold suggests that Maimonides could appeal to the pragmatic effect that certain language has on human piety, such that language with damaging effects should be avoided, even though the damaging language is truth equivalent to non-damaging statements. This solution subordinates theological discourse to subjective human emotions and culture-laden taboos rather than anything objective or real. Why is such language damaging in the first place? Perhaps it is due to the lingering memory of exoteric counterclaims in Scripture? Likewise, Lebens invokes the category of "illuminating falsehoods" that serve as a kind of therapy under a Wittgensteinian language game. While many truth claims about God may be false, some falsehoods are more illuminating than others, pointing the mind to unknowable truths that lay beyond reason. This leads to the question of *how* one should determine which falsehoods are illuminating and which are not. Unmoored from any restraints provided by Scriptural language, it is hard to see how this position can escape the result of individualizing all religious language or promoting language-game communities (synagogues?) where all agree to promote theological falsehoods for their own epistemic benefit (Rynhold, *Introduction*, 97–98; Lebens, *Principles of Judaism*, 10–28).

Part II: A Critique of Non-Incarnational Maimonidean and Kabbalistic Thought

In light of the multiple problems in Maimonides's negative theology, I find no reasonable basis for its acceptance. Thus, when his Third Principle of Faith states, "There is no comparison with him whatsoever," I reject this as a failure.

6.7. No Ground Left under Maimonides's Hermeneutics

I contend that Maimonides begins his theological knowledge with a priori considerations derived from Neoplatonized Aristotelianism, which then in turn requires him to reinterpret a posteriori scriptural God talk with metaphorical, esoteric, or angelic modifications. For example, he claims, "You must know that whenever Scripture relates that the Lord or an angel spoke to a person, this took place in a dream or in a prophetic vision" (*Guide* 2.41). Maimonides attempts to justify this maxim through Num 12:6–8, where a distinction is made between Moses and other prophets, who see only in dreams and visions. However, this position neglects the many events in Scripture—*even those experienced by Moses or written down by him in the Torah*—that appear to happen in real space and history with the LORD himself as actor (see §2.12). Thus, the plain sense of the Torah does not lead to Maimonides's conclusions; they are grounded, rather, in Maimonides's a priori reasoning as informed by his philosophical worldview.

If Maimonides's hermeneutics are accurate for every biblical occurrence, his position appears to criticize the plain sense (*peshat*) of God talk by the Scriptures and the sages of the Talmud. In the previous exposition of Maimonides's hermeneutics, I summarized his method of exonerating the Scriptures and the sages from such criticism:

1. The Scriptures and sages speak only to the philosophically unsophisticated.
2. The Scriptures and sages may be correctly interpreted by the philosophically sophisticated.
3. The Scriptures and sages are always esoterically right, even when they appear exoterically wrong.
4. I, Maimonides, am "the sophisticated."
5. I, Maimonides, am right, so trust me about (1) through (3).

An Assessment of Maimonides's System

By now, it should be clear that Maimonides's sophistication (4) is not grounded in truth or reality; he intelligently and brilliantly constructs a universe of interconnected logic that is founded on falsehoods he inherits from the Greeks. He may have been "sophisticated" according to the standards of his age, and he may well deserve admiration for his brilliance and piety today, but in the final analysis, his sophisticated system is based on false cosmology and metaphysics. He was sophisticated and brilliant, like George Lucas, in creating a coherent universe, but Lucas neither believed his galaxy far, far away was true in reality, nor did he attempt to show it was built upon real-world physics.

If (5) is false for Maimonides, then there is no ground for trusting Maimonides about the hidden meanings of Scripture and the sages in premises (1) through (3). If the first three premises are false, then the Platonic exoteric-esoteric matrix Maimonides imposes on Scripture ought to be seen as alien and subversive of the Scriptures themselves. His handling of physical God talk should be discarded and replaced with a better solution. Wolfson comments, "There is no reason to suppose, as have apologists of Judaism in both medieval and modern times, that the anthropomorphic characterizations of God in Scripture are to be treated figuratively or allegorically."[80] The *Guide's* esoteric reinterpretation of God talk has been widely influential in Jewish theology for centuries, but it is never too late to undo a bad idea.

6.8. Conclusion on Maimonides and Incarnation

Maimonides is a big deal. He is the towering central figure of medieval Jewish philosophy whose influence reverberates today in Jewish academic circles and in popular-level religious devotion. He is also the most influential Jewish thinker when Jewish people consider the claim that Jesus is the Son of God incarnate. As cited previously, Maimonidean scholar Menachem Kellner writes, "Maimonides is the halakhic authority upon whom all others base their claim that Christianity is idolatry—and those who deny that Christianity is idolatry are forced to contend with Maimonides."[81]

So contend with Maimonides I have. His Second and Third Principles of Faith are incompatible with Christianity's central theological

---

80. Wolfson, "Judaism and Incarnation," 242.
81. Kellner, *We Are Not Alone*, 142–43.

Part II: A Critique of Non-Incarnational Maimonidean and Kabbalistic Thought

doctrines of the Trinity and the Incarnation, respectively. I have investigated the Third Principle's assertions of absolute divine incorporeality and divine incomparability and found them wanting. My conclusion is that the premises of his Third Principle are built upon a false cosmology, false a priori reasoning, false comprehensive negative theology, and false hermeneutics about God talk. Nothing remains in its favor. If contemporary Jewish people are going to criticize the Incarnation as an idolatrous and scandalous idea, then they must do so without recourse to Maimonides's false assumptions, methodology, or dogmas.[82]

If the Third Principle is based on a false foundation, then room is made for God to localize himself in time and space, in physical form or even the body of a man. If such be the case, then God could be conceptually in two "places" simultaneously: transcendent beyond the universe *and* localized in the physical form. The idea of God's irreducible singularity (*yachid*), as found in the Second Principle, comes under suspicion by introducing the concept of twoness into God's mode of being if he takes on physical form.[83] In this way, if God were to violate Maimonides's Third Principle by appearing in physical form, this may be grounds for questioning the accuracy of the Second Principle—such that contemporary Jews could consider returning to the proto-Trinitarianism (or binitarianism) of Second Temple Judaism, or the Trinitarianism of the Jewish apostles. I will explore the plausibility of this latter option in part 3.

Granted, a dilution of Maimonides's authority on these matters might also encourage Jewish people today to move in a kabbalistic direction. It might be thought, "Maimonides may be wrong on these matters, but that is why Judaism needs the kabbalistic tradition." In the next three chapters, I hope to demonstrate that Kabbalah is not a reasonable solution.

---

82. Kellner also comes to this conclusion. He notes that Maimonidean dogma, strictly interpreted, would "reject as idolatry much of the Judaism of the last 1,000 years," including that of Orthodox Jews in Chabad. Finding this to be overly demanding, he advocates demoting Maimonides as the provider of the criteria for what is and is not idolatry. He says that contemporary Jews should "say that the whole issue is irrelevant today and look for new ways to disagree with fellow Jews and with fellow monotheists [Christians]" (*We Are Not Alone*, 155).

83. This insight on its own does not necessarily lead to binitarianism or Trinitarianism, because a hypothetical uni-personal deity could unite himself with a human nature in a hypostatic-union sort of way such that there is a unity between his divine and human natures. This would be twoness without a triunity of persons. Thus, a rebuttal of the Third Principle may rebut the singularity (*yachid*) assertion of the Second Principle, but more argument is necessary to justify God as tripersonal.

7   The System of Lurianic Kabbalah

While you see yourself as apart from God,
God sees you as a part of God.

—Rabbi Zalman of Liadi[1]

Ein Sof does not abide being known,
does not produce end or beginning.
Primordial Nothingness engendered beginning and end. . . .
No desires, no lights, no sparks in that Infinity.
All these lights and sparks are dependent on It
but cannot comprehend.

—The Zohar[2]

7.1. Introduction: God and the Infinite

Reflections on the infinite are the gateway to mysticism. The infinite beckons the mind to ponder its limitless nature, but the mind's finite thoughts cannot reach the unreachable shore. The further thoughts wander into the horizon, the deeper they search into the depths, no closer has the infinite become. The mind attempts to pierce the darkness to find the primordial, endless light, but eventually it recognizes that it cannot get there. The gulf between the infinite and the finite is indeed infinite itself.

1. R. Shapiro, *Tanya*, 153.
2. Matt, *Zohar*, 87.

Part II: A Critique of Non-Incarnational Maimonidean and Kabbalistic Thought

The intellectual wayfarer has few options upon understanding God as the infinite.

The pessimistic option, taken by Maimonides in the twelfth century, is to declare the search for God a vain endeavor. In line with his Neoplatonic influences, Maimonides declared that the infinite God cannot be known, described, or comprehended in any way. Words and rationality fail to give any semblance of knowledge of God. Thus, one must remain silent and refrain from the quest to understand the infinite.

"Not so!" the Kabbalists respond in the thirteenth century. The mystical tradition known as Kabbalah (קַבָּלָה, received tradition) would not stand for such a cold and lifeless conclusion.[3] While recognizing the infinite distance of God from the human mind, the Kabbalists consider a second Neoplatonic idea: the finite has emanated from the infinite, and indeed is contained *within* the infinite. *The finite is actually infinite; thus, infinity can be known by mystical experience.*

As the Kabbalist's mind travels toward the infinite, he[4] realizes that the rush of wind against his skin is part of the divine. Although the mind dives into the infinite depths with no hope for reaching the destination, the Kabbalist trains himself to recognize that the coolness of the depths is itself a manifestation of the ineffable. Then, to complete the circle, the Kabbalist recognizes that he, too, is part of the infinite that he cannot reach. This intensely personal experience brings deep satisfaction that words cannot express. Unification with infinity has been achieved. Jewish mysticism scholar Elliot Wolfson writes of this phenomenon, the *unio mystica*:

> Mysticism is defined, therefore, as the immediate and direct encounter with the one true source of all being. Through the contemplative experience of this oneness, all things are unified. The splintering of consciousness into subject and object is thus overcome in the *unio mystica*. For that reason the contemplative state often is marked as that which cannot be expressed.

---

3. Valabregue-Perry, "Philosophy, Heresy."

4. Kabbalistic study and practice have historically been limited to men. It is only in a few modern circles (e.g., the Kabbalah Centre) that women have been invited to study the mysteries of Kabbalah. Gershom Scholem writes, "Both historically and metaphysically it is a masculine doctrine, made for men and by men. The long history of Jewish mysticism shows no trace of feminine influence. There have been no women Kabbalists" (*Major Trends*, 78).

The conventional dichotomies of linguistic expression yield the silence of mystical enlightenment.[5]

With its focus on religious experience and unification with the infinite, Kabbalah is one manifestation of the Western mystical tradition.[6] This chapter summarizes contemporary kabbalistic thought and the barriers it places between its adherents and the teaching of the NT, especially that of the Incarnation. As explained in §1.3, Kabbalah holds to a different school of thought on divine embodiment compared to the NT. In this chapter, I give an uncritical overview of kabbalistic thought, and in the following two chapters, I provide a critical assessment.

7.2. Recommended Studies on Kabbalah

Only a profound Jewish scholar can speak of the Kabbalah without the greatest hesitation.

—EDWIN GOODENOUGH[7]

As a fluid system of thought and practice that has similarities with other mysticisms, Kabbalah can be difficult to study on its own terms and in its Jewish context. Many popular-level introductions to Kabbalah are interwoven with non-Jewish ideologies like modern occultism, New Age, or anti-Semitism, but I will not include those here. Instead, I will investigate Kabbalah through the works of Jewish practitioners and scholars of Jewish mysticism.

Due to the barriers of the Hebrew and Aramaic languages and arcane terminology, many primary kabbalistic works (such as the *Zohar* or *Tanya*) were inaccessible to non-Kabbalists for centuries. The contemporary situation is much improved, as there are both popular-level and academic treatments of Kabbalah available in English today, as well as translations of primary works. Even so, the learning curve for non-Kabbalists is quite steep. In keeping with Goodenough's caution, I do not consider myself a scholar of Kabbalah, and my analysis is highly

---

5. Wolfson, "Judaism and Mysticism," 2:927.

6. For overviews of Western mysticism in general, see Jones and Gellman, "Mysticism"; Versluis, *Magic and Mysticism*; Faivre, *Western Esotericism*; McClymond, *Devil's Redemption*, 2:1067–73.

7. Goodenough, *By Light, Light*, 359.

dependent upon secondary sources of Jewish scholars in English. Some of those sources are as follows.

On the popular level, at least three introductions to Kabbalah, written in English by Chabad[8] practitioners, may be recommended: Immanuel Schochet's "Mystical Concepts in Chasidism," Chaim Dalfin's *Demystifying the Mystical*, and Nissan Dovid Dubov's *Discovering Jewish Mysticism*.[9] Schochet focuses on the metaphysical and cosmological aspects of Kabbalah; Dalfin emphasizes the psychological and moral aspects; and Dubov discusses history, theology, and practice. These works, while popular, are each exemplary in providing an insider's take on kabbalistic thought and practice.

In the academic literature, the most important scholar of Kabbalah continues to be Gershom Scholem (1897–1982), who first established a comprehensive academic study of Jewish mysticism. Scholem provides a broad overview in his groundbreaking *Major Trends in Jewish Mysticism* (1946), and his *Origins of the Kabbalah* (1962) provides an intellectual history of the movement.[10] Scholem's nearly 100-page article on Kabbalah in *Encyclopaedia Judaica* is also a good starting point for a historical and theological overview.[11]

Subsequent Jewish scholars both follow and diverge from Scholem's trailblazing path. Advanced academic studies may be found in the works of Moshe Idel,[12] Elliot Wolfson,[13] Shaul Magid,[14] Rachel Elior,[15] Joseph Dan,[16] and Moshe Halbertal.[17] Idel's contribution to *Encyclopaedia Judaica* includes an extensive bibliography through 2007.[18] For a recent one-volume introduction, Marvin Sweeney reviews Kabbalah's intellectual

---

8. Chabad is an influential Hasidic movement, derived from the Baal Shem Tov in the eighteenth century. See the section on history below.

9. A shorter summary of Kabbalah by a Chabad author is available in Shyfrin, *From Infinity to Man*, 7–21.

10. Scholem: *Major Trends*; *Origins of the Kabbalah*.

11. Scholem, "Kabbalah."

12. Idel: *Kabbalah*; *Absorbing Perfections*; *Ben*; *Primeval Evil in Kabbalah*; *Middot*.

13. Wolfson: *Through Speculum That Shines*; "Metatron and Shi'ur Qomah"; "Jewish Mysticism"; "Judaism and Mysticism"; "Imaginal Configuring."

14. Magid: *From Metaphysics to Midrash*; *Hasidism Incarnate*; *Piety and Rebellion*.

15. Elior and Louvish, *Three Temples*; Elior, *Jewish Mysticism*; Elior and Green, *Paradoxical Ascent to God*.

16. Dan: *Jewish Mysticism*; *Early Kabbalah*; "Jewish Gnosticism?"

17. Halbertal, *Concealment and Revelation*.

18. Idel, "Kabbalah," 11:686–92.

history in *Jewish Mysticism: From Ancient Times through Today*. Modern Orthodox philosopher Samuel Lebens provides a defense of aspects of kabbalistic thought in his *Principles of Judaism*. In contrast, relatively few scholarly interactions with Kabbalah by Jesus followers have been published in the last 150 years, but three recommended works are Christian Ginsburg's *The Kabbalah* (1869), Bernhard Pick's *The Cabala* (1913), and Michael McClymond's 105-page chapter in *The Devil's Redemption* (2018).[19] These are but a few recommendations, for the scholarship on Kabbalah is vast.

7.3. A Brief History of Kabbalah

The history of Kabbalah is a fascinating tale of intrigue with many mysteries along the way. In my theological overview of Kabbalah later in this chapter, I will primarily focus on the dominant school of Lurianic Kabbalah rather than its ancestors or other schools.[20] Nevertheless, knowledge of prior stages in Kabbalah's development is vital for understanding how Kabbalah came to be. This section briefly surveys some of the key texts and turning points in the history of Jewish mysticism, but readers are recommended to continue elsewhere for more comprehensive historical overviews.[21] Additionally, the controversial question of Kabbalah's prehistory, not handled here, is discussed in appendix D.

Broadly speaking, the history of Jewish mysticism can be segmented into several eras:

Second Temple apocalypticism (first century BCE to first century CE). The earliest form of Jewish mysticism can be traced to the visionary

---

19. McClymond, *Devil's Redemption*, 1:125–230.

20. Kabbalah is not monolithic. Lurianic Kabbalah derives from Rabbi Isaac Luria (*HaAri* or *Arizal*), who lived from 1534–72. Lurianic Kabbalah focuses on theosophical speculations about the divine and how to integrate one's halakic duties with the repair of the world. In contrast, ecstatic Kabbalah (*Kabbalah Nevu'it*) emphasizes mystical experience that results in oneness with God, and practical Kabbalah (*Kabbalah Ma'asit*) focuses on magical practices to bring about desired effects. There are also kabbalistic schools of thought stemming from different traditions (Abulafia, Ashlag, Mitnagdim, differing Hasidic rebbes, and earlier forms represented by *Sefer Yezirah*, *Sefer Bahir*, and the *Zohar*). It is beyond the scope of this chapter to address these nuances. Given the accessibility of kabbalistic manuals written by Chabad practitioners, my portrayal may be most attuned to Chabad's theology.

21. Scholem, *Major Trends*; Scholem, *Origins of the Kabbalah*; Idel, *Kabbalah*; Idel, "Mysticism"; Wolfson, "Jewish Mysticism"; Sweeney, *Jewish Mysticism*; Alexander, "Mysticism"; Horwitz, *Kabbalah and Jewish Mysticism*.

apocalyptic works of this period, including 1 Enoch, 2 Enoch, 2 Baruch, 4 Ezra, and the NT book of Revelation. Each of these draws inspiration from the visions in the book of Daniel. These works emphasize visions of the heavenly realm, angelic messengers, and revealed knowledge about cataclysmic events on earth.[22]

Merkavah mysticism (second to tenth centuries CE). Mystics in this period meditate on the works of creation (*Ma'ase Bereshit*, Gen 1) for the secrets of creation and the works of the chariot (*Ma'ase Merkavah*, Ezek 1),[23] hoping to ascend into the heavenly realms in an out-of-body experience. Elements of these practices are found in talmudic literature (m. Ḥag. 2:1; b. Ḥag. 13a; b. Sanh. 65b), most famously in the tale of the four sages who entered paradise (b. Ḥag. 14b). In this story, only Rabbi Akiva returns from paradise unharmed, illustrating the sages' warning of the danger of mystical practice without proper learning and piety.

The *hekhalot* (divine palaces) literature produced during this period develops a method for mystical ascent past the seven palaces (associated with the seven planetary spheres) through reciting a series of divine names that act as passwords. Scholem calls this soul-flight practice a "Judaized and monotheistic Gnosticism."[24] Key texts from this period are 3 Enoch, *Hekhalot Rabbati*, *Hekhalot Zutarti*, *Ma'aseh Merkavah*, and *Merkavah Rabbah*. A prime example of *Ma'ase Bereshit*, *Sefer Yetzirah*, was also written during this period. *Sefer Yetzirah* is a gnostic and Pythagorean text about the power of Hebrew letters in the creation of the world.[25] It states that the world was created through combinations of the

22. For an overview of Jewish apocalypticism and its relation to later rabbinic (Merkavah) mysticism, see Rowland, "Apocalypticism." See also Sweeney, *Jewish Mysticism*, 167–206.

23. The interpretation of Ezek 1 as a heavenly "chariot" is a post-Ezekiel development. Scholem notes the word for chariot, *merkavah*, does not appear in Ezekiel. In 1 Chr 28:18, the cover of the temple's ark is described as having a "golden chariot of the cherubim." Scholem suggests that this became the source for the idea of heavenly cherubim riding on a chariot, due to conjectured parallels between the two realms. The first source to describe Ezekiel's vision as a chariot is Sir 49:8 (second century BCE) (Scholem, "Merkabah Mysticism," 14:66). By the time of the Mishnah, the chariot is shorthand for Ezek 1, and it is forbidden knowledge to all but the most adept in the mysteries. Christian exegesis of Ezek 1 does not follow the Jewish tradition of seeing the "chariot" as the gateway to a mystical connection with God.

24. Scholem, *Major Trends*, 94. Also relevant to this discussion is the prevalence of zodiac signs in many synagogues dated to the fourth through seventh centuries, such as in the Hammat Tiberias synagogue (L. Levine, "Jewish Art," 1:750).

25. Barry notes, "This early work was essentially a product of the impact of Greek Gnosticism on Jewish mysticism, and shows the influence of numerous concepts, such

The System of Lurianic Kabbalah

twenty-two Hebrew letters and the ten *Sefirot*, which are defined as spirit, air, water, fire, and the six dimensions of height, depth, east, west, south, and north.[26] Additionally, *Shiur Qomah* is a mystical work from this period that explores the measurement of God's "body," including individual divine body parts. Sweeney writes, "The *Shiur Qomah* is easily one of the most problematic, controversial, and misunderstood writings in all of Jewish tradition."[27] Its bewildering symbolism prepared the way for a new period of Jewish mysticism.[28]

Early Kabbalah (twelfth to thirteenth centuries CE). During this period, various new mystical ideas emerge that anticipate more mature forms of Kabbalah. The German Jewish pietists (or Hasidei Ashkenaz) developed an understanding of the glory (*Kavod*) of God to account for the infinite God's relationship with the finite world.[29] Menachem Kellner uncovers strands of proto-Kabbalah that Maimonides stealthily writes against in the *Guide* at the end of the twelfth century.[30] Various others integrated Neoplatonic and gnostic ideas into their poetry and theological speculations.[31] Isaac the Blind (ca. 1160–1235) developed the concept of the ten *Sefirot* (divine potencies or attributes) that would eventually take root in Kabbalah. Azriel ben Menachem (1160–1238) coined the term *Ein Sof* (without end) for God's highest unknowable essence, and his student Nachmanides (or Ramban, 1194–1270) became renowned for his mystical insights in his biblical commentaries. Works in the twelfth through thirteenth centuries are distinctive for their variety of conceptual schemes. Some mystics focus on the ten *Sefirot*, others detail the older "thirty-two paths of wisdom" from *Sefer Yetzirah*, or on the

---

as the Gnostic theory of creation by emanations, the Pythagorean decade, Platonic philosophy, Ptolemaic astrology, and the four elements of Empedocles, all of which were already part of existing Greek alphabetical symbolism" (*Greek Qabalah*, 10). For an analysis of *Sefer Yezirah* and its influence on the scientific perspective of the Kabbalists, see Tirosh-Samuelson, "Kabbalah and Science."

26. For a similar theosophical passage about God extending the universe in six directions, and one that likely predates *Sefer Yetzirah*, see *Pseudo-Clementine Homilies* 17.9.

27. Sweeney, *Jewish Mysticism*, 255.

28. For more on this period of Jewish mysticism, see Scholem, *Major Trends*, ch. 2; Alan Segal, "Mysticism"; Boustan, "Hekhalot Literature"; Sweeney, *Jewish Mysticism*, 207–45; Scholem, *Origins of the Kabbalah*, ch. 1.

29. For more on the Hasidei Ashkenaz, see Wolfson, *Through Speculum That Shines*, 188–269.

30. Kellner, *Maimonides' Confrontation with Mysticism*.

31. Idel, *Middot*, 249–51.

Part II: A Critique of Non-Incarnational Maimonidean and Kabbalistic Thought

forty-two-lettered name of God. Some speak of a chain of emanations from God but differ from others' descriptions of what effect emanated from what source. Some attempt to interpret the Thirteen Attributes of Mercy (cf. Exod 34:6–7) as within the *Sefirot*, and others add the three extra attributes ("lights") to the top of the ten *Sefirot*. Scholem remarks, "There were considerable differences of opinion within this circle, and each individual author seems to have been trying to define the content of the world of emanation as it was disclosed to his vision or contemplation."[32] This period of diverse mystical speculation fades as the *Zohar* gains ascendancy.[33]

Zoharic Kabbalah (twelfth to fifteenth centuries CE). The distinctive Jewish mysticism known as Kabbalah is best traced to its minor origin in the twelfth-century *Sefer haBahir* (The book of brightness), and its major origin in *Sefer haZohar* (The book of splendor), which emerges in 1290 in Spain. The *Zohar* eventually becomes a key text of the Jewish mystical canon. Purportedly written by Shimon bar Yochai of the second century, the *Zohar* is in fact a pseudepigraphal work authored by Moses de León (1240–1305).[34] The work is non-systematic and mostly midrashic in character, but it intersperses its kabbalistic thought throughout. Foundational concepts include *Ein Sof*, the *Sefirot*, the *Shekhinah*, and the PaRDeS interpretational scheme.[35] The *Sefirot* are depicted as three triads of divine attributes consisting of dialectical opposites that are balanced by the third. A seminal idea in the *Zohar* is a sexualized godhead where the upper *Sefirot* channel their power through the lower *Sefirah Yesod*, analogous to the human penis, which then unites with the *Sefirah* known as *Shekhinah* or *Malchut*, analogous to the human vagina, a bond which then gives existence to the finite world.[36] The goal of the individual Jew-

32. Scholem, "Kabbalah," 11:604.

33. For more on this transition period between earlier *hekhalot* mysticism and Kabbalah, see Sweeney, *Jewish Mysticism*, 246–84; Dan, *Early Kabbalah*, 1–37; Scholem, *Major Trends*, ch. 3; Scholem, *Origins of the Kabbalah*.

34. Scholem, *Major Trends*, ch. 5; Dweck, *Scandal of Kabbalah*; Huss, *Zohar*. For an overview of reasons why the *Zohar* should not be dated to the second century but rather to the thirteenth, see Scholem, "Zohar," 21:652–58. Also see the summary of Huss's work in §9.1.

35. Each of these concepts is described later in this chapter.

36. Sweeney, *Jewish Mysticism*, 292. For example, *Zohar* 1:29b: "When the upper world was filled and became pregnant, it brought forth two children together, a male and a female, these being heaven and earth after the supernal pattern. The earth is fed from the waters of the heaven which are poured into it. These upper waters, however, are male, whereas the lower are female, and the lower are fed from the male and the

ish person is to unite the masculine and feminine potencies inherent in the human self, consciousness, and matter, thus repeating the unification process operative in the heavens. Human efforts to reunify the universe bring about God's will in the world. *Zohar* translator Daniel Matt remarks, "Tradition has always taught us that we need God; the innovative message of the *Zohar* is that in order to manifest in the world, God needs us."[37] All subsequent versions of Jewish mysticism would cite the *Zohar* as a primary inspiration.[38]

Lurianic Kabbalah (sixteenth century CE to present). After the traumatic exile of the Jewish people from Spain in 1492, Safed (Tzfat) in northern Israel (then Ottoman Syria) became a center of kabbalistic thought under the leadership of Moses ben Jacob Cordovero (1522–70) and his disciple Isaac Luria (1534–72). Cordovero systematized the doctrine of the Zohar through his works *Pardes Rimmonim* and *Elimah Rabbati*. He claimed to receive revelation from a *maggid*, an angelic visitor. Building on Cordovero's work, Luria gathered a collection of disciples and began orally revealing his new formulations of kabbalistic doctrine. His innovations included the doctrine of *tzimtzum* (divine contraction), the *shevirat ha-kelim* (shattering of the vessels), and the infusion of eschatological *tikkun* (cosmic repair) into kabbalistic practice. Although *gilgul* (reincarnation) was a minor aspect of earlier kabbalistic works (beginning with *Sefer Bahir*), Luria's system integrated the transmigration of souls into its core doctrines.[39] Luria did not write down his systematization; rather, his system was published through his various disciples after his death. A key publication is Chaim Vital's *Etz Chaim*, the most elaborate of his disciples' systematizations. Luria's disciples succeeded in transforming Kabbalah from an underground movement into a popular one with messianic implications. His teachings prepared the Jewish world for the rise of Shabbetai Tzvi as a kabbalistic false messiah in 1665.

---

lower waters call to the upper, like a female that receives the male, and pour out water to meet the water of the male to produce seed. Thus the female is fed from the male" (Sperling et al., *Zohar*). See Gen. Rab. 13:13 for an early pre-kabbalistic example of this motif: "R. Levi said: 'The upper waters are male while the lower are female.'" For more on the sexual metaphors inherent in Kabbalah, see the various works of Elliot Wolfson, who writes, "The mystic vision expressed in Jewish sources is fundamentally a phallic gaze" (*Through Speculum That Shines*, 5).

37. Matt, *Zohar*, xxix.

38. For further overviews of the *Zohar*, see Scholem, *Major Trends*, chs. 5–6; Sweeney, *Jewish Mysticism*, 285–324; Matt, *Zohar*; Dweck, *Scandal of Kabbalah*.

39. Scholem, "Gilgul."

Part II: A Critique of Non-Incarnational Maimonidean and Kabbalistic Thought

To this day, Lurianic Kabbalah is the dominant school of thought in Jewish mysticism.[40]

Hasidic mysticism (eighteenth century CE to present). After the failure of Shabbetai Tzvi, a new popular-level kabbalistic movement arose in what is now Ukraine under the leadership of Israel ben Eliezer (1700–60), also known as the Baal Shem Tov, or the Besht. This charismatic healer and mystic did not leave any writings behind, and after his death, legendary tales of his life proliferated. A distinctive feature of Hasidic teaching is the role of the *tzaddik* or *rebbe* whose role is to model holiness to his followers and transmit holiness to them to repair the world (*tikkun olam*). The Baal Shem Tov, the original *tzaddik*, died without a clear successor, leading to a succession crisis. An early claimant was Dov Ber (ca. 1710–84), known as the Maggid, who popularized the Baal Shem Tov's teachings. After Dov Ber's death, the movement splintered into different dynasties, each led by a separate *tzaddik*. Beginning in 1772, the Vilna Gaon led a countermovement of *Mitnagdim* (opponents) to excommunicate and oppose Hasidic groups, but they continued to grow. Today's surviving Hasidic dynasties include Chabad (known for its missionary fervor to Jews and its systematized philosophical text called *The Tanya*), Satmar, Breslov, Bobov, Belz, and many others. Hasidic mystics were not initially known for their mastery of traditional talmudic study and halakic determinations but for their pious prayers, ecstatic emotionalism, and popular fervency. Today Hasidic groups are among the most populous of those called "ultra-Orthodox" or "Haredi Jews," and they have major population centers in Israel, the greater New York area, London, and Montreal.[41]

Thus concludes our brief survey of the history of Jewish mystical thought, culminating in the Lurianic kabbalistic thought as taught in contemporary Hasidism. The remainder of this chapter will seek to portray some of the most common features of mainstream Lurianic Kabbalah (hereafter referred to as Kabbalah) while acknowledging that multiple Kabbalist streams articulate their teachings differently.[42]

---

40. For more about Lurianic Kabbalah, see Scholem, *Major Trends*, ch. 7; Scholem and Idel, "Isaac Ben Solomon Luria"; Scholem, "Shabbetai Zevi"; Sweeney, *Jewish Mysticism*, 325–62.

41. For more about the Hasidic movement, see Scholem, *Major Trends*, ch. 9; Sweeney, *Jewish Mysticism*, 363–401; D. Ariel, *Kabbalah*, ch. 9.

42. As explained in 167n20, this chapter is deliberately limited in scope.

7.4. The Kabbalistic Story of Panentheism

Cosmology is the study of the origin of the universe and its current composition.[43] In Kabbalah, cosmology is theology, and theology is cosmology. These two are identical in Kabbalah due to its teaching of panentheism, which means "all is in God."[44] This is to be distinguished from the Maimonidean model. For Maimonides, the universe is not part of God, but rather is in a separate category. Maimonides's theology is intertwined with his understanding of cosmology, namely in the mechanisms by which God works in the world, but his cosmology is not synonymous with the being of God.

According to panentheism, all that exists in the universe is a continuous emanation of God's own being.[45] Panentheism was classically affirmed by Parmenides (fourth century BCE) and the Neoplatonist Plotinus (third century CE), but Kabbalah contains its own interpretation of the idea.[46] Scholem writes that Kabbalah "is driven to something very much like a mythos of God giving birth to himself."[47] Idel calls it "divine autogenesis."[48] Kabbalistic theology can be summarized as follows.

Kabbalah begins at the same place as Maimonides and other apophatic theological systems: the unknowable, infinite, indescribable, wholly other *Ein Sof* (אֵין סוֹף), which means "that which has no end."[49]

43. This definition employs the broad form of the term. A narrow definition would relegate cosmology only to the composition of the universe, with cosmogony defined as the study of its origin.

44. On the panentheism of kabbalistic thought, see L. Jacobs, "God," 294–95; Artson, "Holy, Holy, Holy!"; Ciucu, "Kabbalistic Pan(En)Theism"; Ross, "Traditional Concepts of God." A classic rabbinic statement appearing to endorse panentheism may be found in Gen. Rab. 68:9. Lebens believes that the kabbalistic worldview is distinguished from panentheism, but he comes to this conclusion by denying that physical or material objects exist, in line with his metaphysical idealism. His model promotes *ideas* as emanating from God continuously and included within his mind but not as constituents thereof. I see this as merely idealist panentheism, which presents similar problems as non-idealist panentheism. Mullins agrees ("Theism," 40–43). Whether the universe is God's body (with actual physicality) or imaginations within God's mind (idealism), the inclusion of the universe "within" God has similar detrimental side effects (Lebens, *Principles of Judaism*, 86, 113–18).

45. For a discussion of various historical panentheistic models, see Cooper, *Panentheism*. For parsing the differences between emanationism, continuous creation, and creation *ex nihilo*, see Mullins, "Theism," 30–35.

46. For a review of these Greek philosophical schools, see §§4.1.2; 4.5.1.

47. Scholem, *Major Trends*, 375.

48. Idel, *Primeval Evil in Kabbalah*, xiv.

49. Scholem, "Kabbalah," 11:623. Other transliterations include *En Sof, Ain Sof,*

Part II: A Critique of Non-Incarnational Maimonidean and Kabbalistic Thought

An early Kabbalist, Azriel of Gerona (1160–1238), describes *Ein Sof* in the following way: "*En-sof* is the absolute indistinctness in the perfect unity, in which there is no change. And since it is without limits, nothing exists outside of it."[50] The kabbalistic understanding of infinity states that the truly infinite cannot have any limits or boundaries, whether physical, spiritual, conceptual, or ontological.[51] The kabbalistic infinite is the set of all possible sets, the infinity of infinities, exhaustively and truly unbounded. Although some Kabbalists, such as Schochet, describe *Ein Sof* as "he," many others are consistent with negative theology and refer to *Ein Sof* as "it."[52] A common kabbalistic maxim reflecting this (supposedly derived from Deut 4:35) is "Ein od milvado," which means "There is nothing besides him [*Ein Sof*]." Samuel Lebens calls it "Jewish Nothing-Elsism."[53]

If nothing exists outside of *Ein Sof*, but *Ein Sof* has no change, and it cannot have anything predicated about itself, then the existence of external reality becomes an immediate philosophical problem. How can finite things with names, limits, and definitions exist, if only the infinite exists, and the infinite cannot be known, described, or delimited? How can physical material, the idea of a tree, the set of even numbers, the category of evil, or individual beings exist, if *Ein Sof* fills up all the "space" for them to exist? The kabbalistic answer to this predicament is the doctrine of *tzimtzum*. Immanuel Schochet, a Chabad-Lubavitch Kabbalist scholar, describes *tzimtzum* as the process by which the infinite *Ein Sof* contracts itself and conceals its infinity in order to bring about an "empty place" or "void" that evolves within the primordial space of *Ein Sof*'s infinity. As Schochet writes, it is "an act of Divine Self-limitation."[54] Nevertheless, some Kabbalists insist that *tzimtzum* is only a metaphor, for *Ein Sof* is still fully present in its concealment, and there is no "space" within an

---

and *Eyn Sof*.

50. Azriel of Gerona, *Sha'ar ha-Sho'el*, §2, quoted in Scholem, *Origins of the Kabbalah*, loc. 9542.

51. One of the first affirmations of this idea is found in Plotinus, who asserts that the One "is under no limit either in regard to any external or within itself" (*Enn.* 5.5.11). See also A. Moore, *Infinite*, 45; McClymond, *Devil's Redemption*, 1:161; D. Ariel, *Kabbalah*, 174–75.

52. I will follow the impersonal "it" pronoun tradition, as it is more consistent with Kabbalah's stated negative theology.

53. Lebens, *Principles of Judaism*, 107–8.

54. Schochet, "Mystical Concepts in Chasidism," a53.

incorporeal being.⁵⁵ Thus Kabbalah teaches that *Ein Sof* is unbounded from its infinite perspective, but bounded and delimited according to its partial concealment.

With this metaphysical "void" in place within the infinity of *Ein Sof*, the stage is set for Kabbalah's solution for finite reality: emanations from the divine, an idea deriving from Neoplatonism. Schochet's introductory Chabad manual to kabbalistic cosmology, *Mystical Concepts in Chasidism*, narrates the process, which I have summarized below. Although Schochet provides a linear, rational process by which the emanations proceed, it must be emphasized that he believes the following sequence must be seen as a mere metaphor. The sequence is nonsequential, the contraction is not physical, the process is only apparent, and from the perspective of *Ein Sof*, none of the following actually happens.⁵⁶ I have produced two diagrams adapted from Schochet's narrative to accompany the summary, which may assist in comprehending this unique Jewish mystical vision of reality.

---

55. Ross gives an overview of the rise of allegorical (nonliteral) interpretations of *tzimtzum* ("Doctrine"). According to Lebens, in general, the Hasidic world today accepts a nonliteral *tzimtzum*, whereas the Mitnagdim tend to accept a literal *tzimtzum*. He provides several arguments against seeing the contraction as literal or physical. Instead, *tzimtzum*, in his view, ought to be seen as metaphorical (Lebens, *Principles of Judaism*, 81–86). A second Chabad handling of *tzimtzum*, in addition to Schochet's, may be found in Dubov, "Tzimtzum."

56. I will expand on these paradoxical themes in §8.4.3.

Part II: A Critique of Non-Incarnational Maimonidean and Kabbalistic Thought

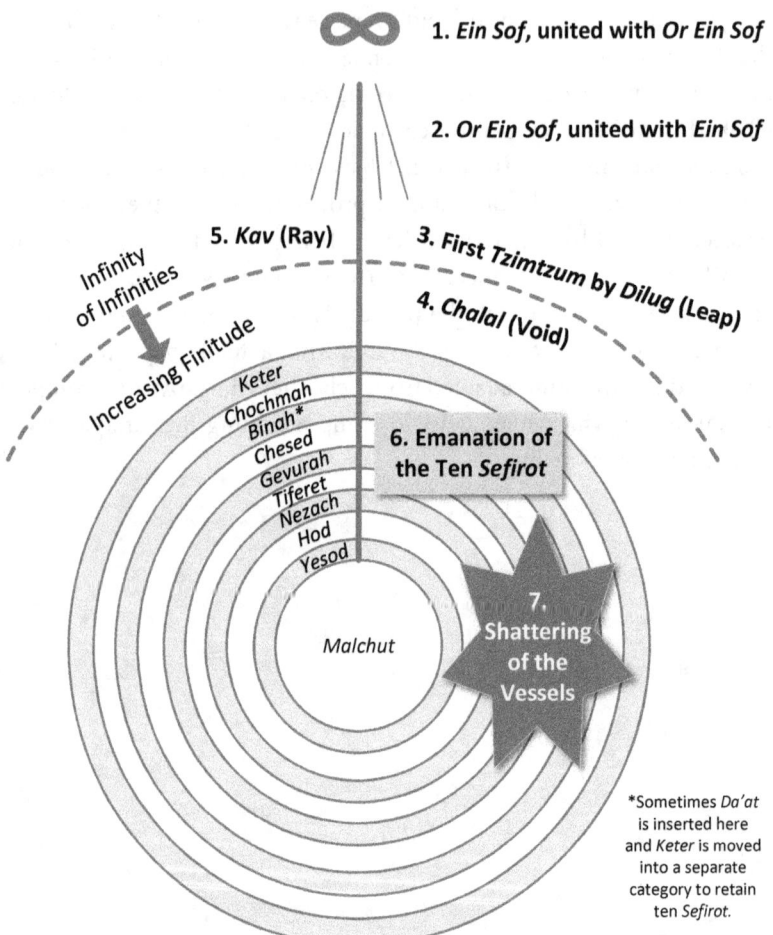

Figure 3. Kabbalistic Cosmology, Pt. 1. Adapted from descriptions by Schochet, "Mystical Concepts in Chasidism."

The System of Lurianic Kabbalah

Kabbalistic Cosmology
Part 2: Adam Kadmon and the Emergence of Multiple Worlds

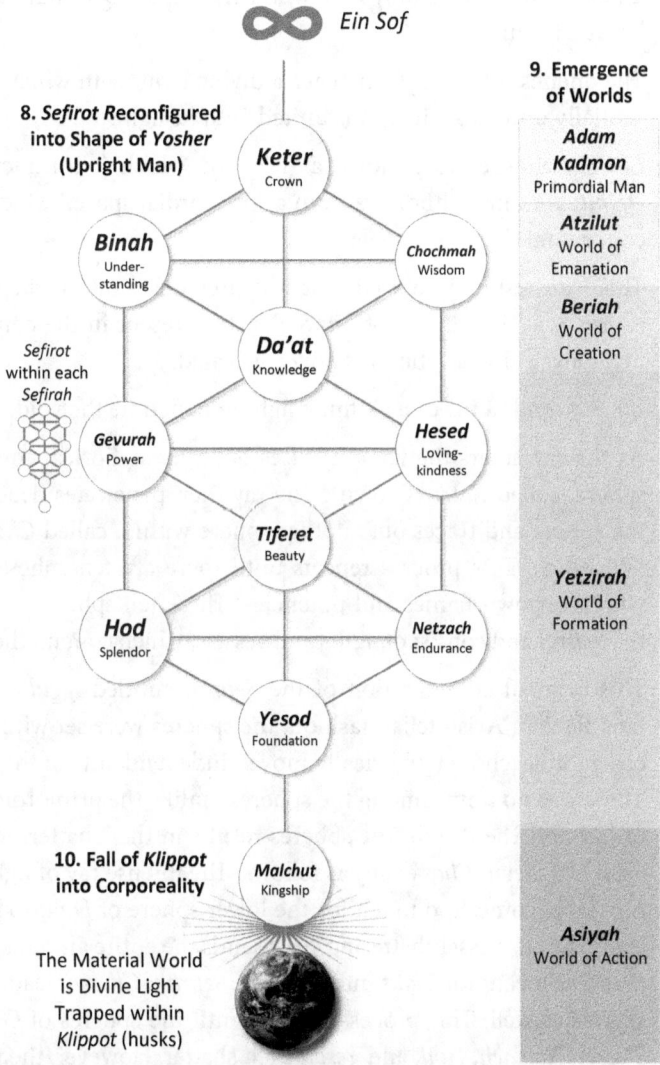

Figure 4. Kabbalistic Cosmology, Pt. 2

Part II: A Critique of Non-Incarnational Maimonidean and Kabbalistic Thought

The ten-step process of the emergence of the physical world in Lurianic Kabbalah as presented by Schochet may be summarized as follows:

1. There is *Ein Sof*, the only One who exists, existing as pure and unlimited infinity.
2. The oneness of *Ein Sof* emanates a divine light, with which it is essentially united, as the sun is united with its light.
3. *Ein Sof* chooses to perform a "leap" by which it contracts itself (*tzimtzum*) and withdraws from a "primordial space," which is the conceptual shape of a sphere.
4. This leap results in a void that was previously full of the infinity of *Ein Sof*. The infinity of *Ein Sof* is still present in the contracted metaphysical space, but it is now concealed.
5. *Ein Sof* sends a ray of its infinite light to penetrate the void.
6. As the ray enters the void, it traces out a metaphorical concentric sphere, called *Keter* (Crown). The ray then penetrates deeper into the sphere and traces out another sphere within, called *Chochmah* (Wisdom). This process repeats until there are ten spheres, each with their own names and potencies. These ten spheres are called the *Sefirot* and consist of lights and vessels, which contain the lights.
7. This original configuration of the *Sefirot*, entitled *Iggulim*, had a fatal flaw. In Aristotelian fashion, the spheres were set within each other, but each metaphorically moved independently of the others. There was no unity among the spheres, unlike the primordial unity of *Ein Sof*. The flaw in the spheres results in the "shattering of the vessels" (*shevirat ha-kelim*) as follows. The intense ray of light from *Ein Sof* becomes too much for the lower sphere of *Da'at* to handle, leading to its vessel shattering. This sends the entire amount of light that was meant for *Da'at* into the next *Sefirah*, *Chesed*, leading it to shatter as well. This process repeats until the spheres of *Gevurah*, *Tiferet*, *Netzach*, *Hod*, and *Yesod* each shatter. However, the process is halted when a partial amount of light is absorbed by the lowest sphere, *Malchut*, resulting in only a partial shattering.
8. This catastrophic event results in a total reconfiguration of all the *Sefirot*. The *Sefirot* that were previously concentric spheres are reconfigured into an interdependent and dynamic arrangement with a human shape called *Yosher*, or *Adam Kadmon* (primordial man).

This new arrangement of the *Sefirot* now includes interpenetrating relationships among the *Sefirot*: each *Sefirah* has within it all the other *Sefirot*. What had been multiple now becomes unified.

9. As the spheres rearrange themselves into primordial man, from them emerge a tiered system of "worlds," each associated with specific *Sefirot*.

10. The shattering of the higher vessels results in them falling down into lower and lower worlds. Some of them are absorbed by lower *Sefirot*, and some are not. Only the cruder vessels pass through to the lowest level. At this point, the tradition calls these vessels *klippot*, the waste parts of the broken vessels. These *klippot* are called evil, and they come to rest in the lowest world, *Asiyah*, where people live—a world infused with evil physicality. This world comes into being through the final *Sefirah*, *Malchut*, speaking words. It is only now, at this late stage in the cosmological process, that a clear parallel with the biblical creation account presents itself. The words by which *Malchut* creates the known world are a reference to God's speech in Gen 1:3–26: "And God said, 'Let there be light,'" and an "expanse" and "vegetation" and so on, up until the creation of Adam on the sixth day.

With the provision for materiality and life on earth, the kabbalistic cosmological story is complete. *Ein Sof* was originally pure unity, and it unraveled into multiplicity through the process of *tzimtzum* and the shattering of the vessels. The shattering is a cosmic problem that occurs within God himself. The unfurling of *Ein Sof* into multiplicity is portrayed as a catastrophe. Sparks of God's being are trapped in evil *klippot* in the physical realm, and they need to find freedom above. Thus, the eschatological goal of Kabbalah is to restore all of existence into the simple unity from which it once came.

The kabbalistic meaning of *tikkun olam* (repair of the world) refers to restoring the world by releasing the infinite sparks of divinity that are hidden in all existing things. To put it in theological terms, soteriology and eschatology are very closely related in Kabbalah, because to "save" the universe is to reduce the multiplicity until there is nothing but unity, which will eventually happen in the future. All will be saved, and Israel is the central actor tasked with repairing the shattering within *Ein Sof*. *In Kabbalah, the world's problem is not sin but metaphysical multiplicity.* As long as there are multiple things in existence and as long as people perceive things as multiple, the world remains broken. Moreover, it is not *people* who need a savior; rather, *God himself*, who is shattered into pieces across the cosmos, needs the salvation Israel provides.

The kabbalistic vision is comprehensive in scope. Panentheism quite literally means *all* is in God, which includes even the unsavory parts of existence. In the biblical presentation, it would be unthinkable to consider whether God's essence includes evil (Ps 136:1).[57] But in Kabbalah, the presence of evil within God is a stubborn problem demanded by the system as a whole.[58]

7.5. Symbols, Patterns, and Correspondences

Kabbalah shares a feature with many other mystical schools of thought: the doctrine of correspondences. This view is based upon the Platonic understanding of a two-tiered reality, with each tier related to the other through patterns. Nowadays, this concept is often summarized using the maxim "As above, so below."[59] The basic idea is that lower realms of reality (microcosm) are patterned upon higher realms (macrocosm). Discerning the nature of the divine essence and its dynamics above results in mystical insight into how things work below.[60] In practice, the relationship often works in reverse as well: the ability to discern reality below results in more insight into the divine essence above. Schochet words it this way: "All terrestrial concepts are allusions to supernal ones!"[61] Consequently, in Kabbalah, understanding the nature and interrelationships of the ten *Sefirot* above is crucial for knowing how to live everyday life below, and vice versa.

---

57. On Isa 45:7, see this book, 206n50.

58. Idel, *Primeval Evil in Kabbalah*; McClymond, *Devil's Redemption*, 1:165–66.

59. *Zohar*, 2:20a: "And He made this world corresponding to the world above, and everything which is above has its counterpart here below, and everything here below has its counterpart in the sea; and yet all constitute a unity" (Sperling et al., *Zohar*). The maxim "as above, so below" is a modern paraphrase of this concept, often said to derive from the *Emerald Tablet* (Versluis, *Magic and Mysticism*, ch. 3; McClymond, *Devil's Redemption*, 2:1072).

60. This is a concept separate from astrology, but it shares similar metaphysical logic. Astrology focuses on observable phenomena, whereas the doctrine of correspondences also relates to non-observable spiritual entities. Nevertheless, Kabbalah encourages astrological speculations. For a list of many medieval Jewish sages who practiced astrology, see Dennis, "Astrology."

61. Schochet, "Mystical Concepts in Chasidism," a45.

The doctrine of correspondences informs Kabbalist practitioners' psychological teachings and mystical experiences. The famous "tree of life" depiction of the *Sefirot* often includes the image of a man (*Adam Kadmon*) as the "shape" of the *Sefirot* after the shattering of the spheres. This image conveys how the human body and soul are thought to correspond with divine inner workings.[62] Various authors trace the idea of *Adam Kadmon* through Jewish, Jewish-Christian, and gnostic traditions until it emerges in Kabbalah.[63] One can unify with, strengthen, or harm the corresponding potencies in the higher realms by uniting various aspects of the human psyche through mitzvot (commandments) and mystical practices. Thus, Kabbalah can be aptly summarized as a psychologized theology that is worked out in mystical practice, Jewish religious observance, and study.

The psychological teachings of Kabbalah are multifaceted and profoundly complicated, full of arcane correspondences with metaphysical concepts and layers of experience.[64] Descriptions

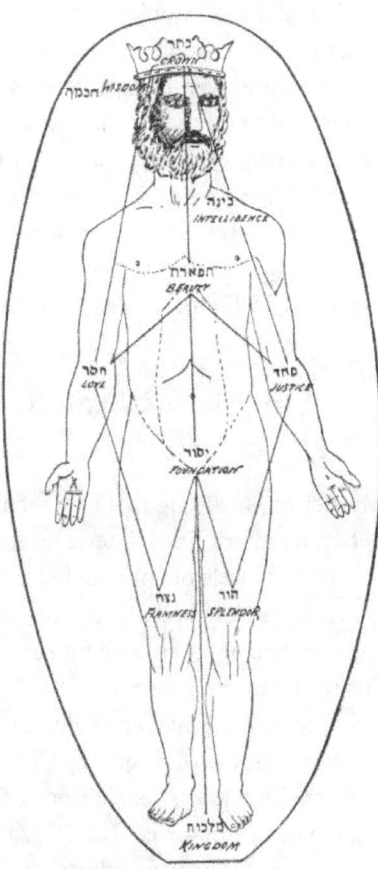

Figure 5. Adam Kadmon—Diagram Illustrating the *Sefirot* (Divine Attributes), from L. Ginsburg, "Adam Kadmon"

---

62. See *Zohar* 1:19b–20a.

63. There are important precedents in Philo, the *Pseudo-Clementine Homilies*, and gnostic works. See L. Ginsburg, "Adam Kadmon"; Wolfson, "Tree That Is All."

64. Shahar Arzy and Moshe Idel write, "Major trends in Jewish Kabbalah managed to alter distinct neurocognitive mechanisms through the use of specific techniques. These excitations caused a change in the mystic's processing of functions related to his own self, such as the sense of embodiment or visuo-spatial perspective taking, leading to different variants of autoscopic and trance experiences and accompanied by prominent prophetic-like experiences of a 'speaking double' or internal 'maggidic' voice, thus facilitating further expansion of the borders of the mind and consciousness. We

of the divine unification process often take on erotic connotations in kabbalistic discourse, as the male-female relationship on earth is thought to exist in the divine realm as well. From this idea comes some of Kabbalah's most alien teachings for those accustomed to scriptural descriptions of God.[65]

Because everything that exists is patterned upon something else, and joined to others in a divine hierarchy, kabbalistic thought encourages the pursuit of patterns and correspondences in everything. Numbers relate to letters, which relate to words, which relate to rituals and psychological processes, and all can be seen as equivalent to each other through symbolic speech and action. The symbolic nature of kabbalistic thought expresses itself most clearly in its methods for interpreting Scripture.

7.6. Esoteric and Exoteric Meanings of Words and Scripture

Mysticism, including that of Kabbalah, often makes a strong distinction between esoteric and exoteric teachings. Esoteric teachings are restricted to an inner circle of enlightened initiates, whereas exoteric teachings are generally understandable by the masses without special enlightenment. Exoteric teachings are safe for the masses; esoteric teachings are dangerous to all but the deserving.

Judaism has had an esoteric undercurrent since at least the time of the Mishnah (second century CE), which famously declares that knowledge of the mysterious chariot of Ezekiel is not permissible for anyone but the most adept sages (m. Ḥag. 2:1). In the same mishnaic passage, the sages warn, "Whoever reflects upon four things would have been better off had he not been born: what is above, what is below, what is before, and what is beyond."[66] Jewish mysticism portrays itself as the vehicle for delivering these dangerous mysteries, and Hasidism in particular chooses to ignore (or reinterpret away) the mishnaic warnings. Today

---

therefore propose that it is the mystical technique that leads the mystic to experience autoscopy, heautoscopy, out-of-body experience, or trance. The mystic might interpret these as sacred or prophetic experiences that reveal mystical secrets about human or divine nature" (Arzy and Idel, *Kabbalah*, 116–17).

65. As quoted previously, Elliot Wolfson writes, "The mystic vision expressed in Jewish sources is fundamentally a phallic gaze" (*Through Speculum That Shines*, 5).

66. Neusner, *Mishnah*, 330.

it is said in Hasidic circles that all Jews are obligated to learn Kabbalah.[67] To Kabbalists, anyone on the outside of the mystic circle is trapped with a surface-level understanding of Judaism and the Torah. Moreover, it is claimed that the esoteric teachings of Kabbalah must be learned experientially within a kabbalistic community. That is, one cannot know the secrets of Kabbalah by reading books as an outsider (as I have done in preparation for this book), but only as an insider who adopts the tradition and practice fully alongside an adept teacher.

Because of this esoteric dimension of Kabbalah, the written words of Torah (and its plain sense) are portrayed as the mere garment of the Torah that must be peeked behind through mystical means. Exoteric knowledge, accessible to the masses, is only a prelude to mystical illumination. Yet, mystical illumination is by definition unavailable to non-Kabbalists, so the multifaceted true meaning of a biblical passage is thereby irrevocably shielded from outsiders' eyes. Furthermore, the unique aspects of kabbalistic interpretation are hard to fathom without understanding the metaphysical worldview standing behind the Kabbalists' vision, again shielding themselves from outside criticism.[68] Kabbalah scholar Joseph Dan explains the kabbalistic approach to biblical interpretation:

> The Kabbalists saw in Scripture an enormous library of mystical symbols that express the true function and interrelationship of the ten *sefirot*. Every biblical noun became a symbol for one of the *sefirot* and every verb helped to describe the dynamic interplay of the sefirotic organism. Thus Kabbalah acquired an extensive symbolic vocabulary thought to be of divine origin, derived from the fount of Torah. This attitude toward Scripture necessitated a revolutionary reinterpretation of Torah, uncovering new, esoteric, and mystical strata in every verse. Therefore, much of Kabbalistic literature throughout the ages is nothing more than extended commentaries and exegetical homilies on the Bible. By extension, the great rabbinic continuations of Scripture—the Talmud and Midrash—were also regarded as repositories of profound symbols.[69]

In order to find the secret meaning of the symbols, the kabbalistic interpreter must climb the ladder of interpretation to the mystical level,

---

67. Dubov, "Key FAQs," under q. 3, "Who may study Kabbalah?"
68. Idel, *Absorbing Perfections*, 16.
69. Dan, *Early Kabbalah*, 11.

called *sod*. Since the time of the *Zohar* (thirteenth century), kabbalistic hermeneutics have consisted of four levels[70] of interpretation, summarized with the acronym PaRDeS:

- *Peshat*: The literal or "simple" meaning. This is the exoteric meaning of Scripture, generally mapping to a grammatical-historical interpretation of literature.
- *Remez*: The allegorical meaning due to a "hint" in the text.
- *Derash*: The homiletical or halakic (legal) interpretation.
- *Sod*: The "secret" meaning according to esoteric, mystical methods of interpretation.[71]

Judaism and Christianity employed the first three "levels of meaning" prior to the emergence of the *Zohar* in the thirteenth century, but *sod* provided the medieval kabbalistic exegete with a new mystical interpretation of the text.[72] The *sod* method includes the use of gematria, a mathematical system for deducing the secret meaning of words and phrases by assigning numerical values to each Hebrew letter—values and methods only known to the Kabbalists. While talmudic sages had used gematria before, with the *Zohar* it gained considerable importance. *The Jewish Study Bible* explains,

> By introducing a fourth level and presenting it as the culmination of the exegetical process, the most profound understanding of the biblical text attainable, the kabbalists were validating the work of their predecessors while at the same time claiming pride of place for their own innovative approach to the text.[73]

It should also be noted that Kabbalists anthropomorphize the process of interpretation with an "as above, so below" motif, whereby the *peshat*

---

70. The PaRDeS scheme is the most common in Kabbalah, but in one passage of the *Zohar* (3.202a), a list of seven kinds of interpretation are given: (1) literal, (2) homiletical or midrashic, (3) allegorical or "mystery of wisdom," (4) numerical interpretation, (5) hidden mysteries, (6) deeper mysteries, and (7) legal interpretation. Michael Fishbane also explains there were other interpretational schemes used during the medieval period ("Biblical Interpretation," 698).

71. Van der Heide, "Pardes."

72. This fourfold system was new and was not part of Judaism before the thirteenth century. Idel writes, "The emergence of the fourfold exegetical method, as well as Abulafia's sevenfold exegetical system, coincides with the nascent innovative Kabbalah" (*Absorbing Perfections*, 435). Also see Fishbane, "Biblical Interpretation," 698.

73. Berlin et al., *Jewish Study Bible*, 1893.

(exoteric) interpretation is likened to the "body of Torah," the *remez* is likened to the "soul of Torah," and the *sod* is likened to the "super-soul of Torah."[74] The kabbalistic pattern finders also apply the fourfold system of interpretation to the four emanated worlds, with the *peshat* likened to the lowest world of *Asiya*, and *sod* as the key to the highest world, *Atzilut*.[75]

Moshe Idel calls the process by which non-esoteric texts are interpreted through mystical means "arcanization."[76] By making previously non-arcane texts into esoteric mysteries through *sod*, Kabbalah positions itself as the only method by which all previous Jewish religious works can be truly understood. For the Kabbalist, reading Scripture, the Mishnah, the Talmud, or any other Jewish text without the insight of *sod* yields only lesser results.[77] In this way, Kabbalah rejects as insufficient the down-to-earth textual exegesis of Maimonides[78] and grammatical-historical interpretation in general.[79]

In Kabbalah, the grammatical-historical interpretation of a text is not *the* meaning of a text, but only the first and lowest meaning. Those who stop at the literal meaning are merely analyzing the husk, shell, or cloak of the Torah, rather than the hidden beauty beneath.[80] Literal interpretation on its own is foreign to the Kabbalist mode of thought and is viewed as foolish and limiting.[81] If one takes solely a grammatical-historical interpretive approach to the Torah, or even reads the talmudic sages literally, a Kabbalist will likely view that person as unsophisticated, unenlightened, and focused on the mere garment while ignoring the esoteric reality of Torah hidden in the *remez* (allegorical) and *sod* (mystical).[82]

74. Fishbane, "Biblical Interpretation," 697.

75. Idel, *Absorbing Perfections*, 433.

76. Idel, *Absorbing Perfections*, 1–12.

77. Idel, *Absorbing Perfections*, 7, 431.

78. Except, of course, in the case of God talk. Maimonides prizes literal interpretation until the passage describes anything about God, at which point he switches to allegorical and psychological interpretations. See §5.8.

79. D. Ariel, *Kabbalah*, ch. 2; Kellner, *Maimonides' Confrontation with Mysticism*, 155–78.

80. Wolfson, "Bible in Mystical Tradition," 1989.

81. Moshe Idel notes that Rabbi Hayyim Yoseph David Azulai (1724–1806) uses a pun to describe such "fools": "Whoever believes only in the plain sense of the Bible, *peshat*, is indeed a fool, as a permutation of the consonants of *peshat* 'demonstrates': *tipesh*." This Hebrew word (שטיפ) means stupid or foolish (quoted in Idel, *Absorbing Perfections*, 432).

82. Kabbalah and Maimonides employ similar hermeneutical methods, but with different scopes. See §§5.8; 6.7. Kabbalah employs its secret hermeneutics

Part II: A Critique of Non-Incarnational Maimonidean and Kabbalistic Thought

7.7. Theurgical-Magical Uses of Scripture and Gematria

The kabbalistic understanding of words as symbols leads in a theurgical or magical direction. *Theurgy* refers to the use of practices and incantations to influence the divine sphere and produce desired results. Moshe Idel writes of kabbalistic theurgy, "[The Hebrew language] was conceived also as a powerful tool which, used by God in order to create the world, could also be used by the Kabbalist masters in imitation of God to achieve their own marvelous creations or attain mystical experiences or sometimes even *unio mystica*."[83]

The thought process behind this notion is that God gives being to the world through a continuous emanation of Hebrew words.[84] The Kabbalist, awakened to the divine spark within, can learn the same words that God uses to create the world, and thus can create as God creates, modify the world as God modifies the world, and can generally produce whatever effects the Kabbalist wants.[85] If the Kabbalist intends to create a man using arcane Hebrew incantations, he can do so (as with the *golem* of Prague),[86] just as the sages of the Talmud used *Sefer Yetzirah* to create a man and a calf (b. Sanh. 65b). Words constitute reality and can be used by adept mystics to create new realities.

The kabbalistic practice of gematria is intimately connected with the theurgical impulse because mathematical permutations of letters and words enable the Kabbalist to produce more advanced effects in the world.[87] Gershom Scholem notes that one kabbalistic manuscript lists

---

comprehensively, whereas Maimonides limits it to God talk. Just as Maimonides chides those who read anthropomorphisms literally and not according to sophisticated and unwritten philosophical wisdom, so too the Kabbalists chide those who read any text of the Jewish tradition literally and not according to its esoteric *sod* interpretation.

83. Idel, *Absorbing Perfections*, 81.

84. Chabad writer Shifra Hendrie (a rare female writer on Kabbalah) claims, "According to Kabbalah, the words of creation are being 'spoken' by G-d continuously. Therefore, the world is being brought into being anew out of the Divine 'nothingness' at every moment. In fact, the natural state of the universe is nonexistence. If G-d were to stop 'speaking' the words of creation for even an instant, the whole universe would disappear as if it had never been!" (Hendrie, "Kabbalah of Speech," para. 12).

85. Hendrie: "As a human being, you have been invested with the power and the purpose to act as a partner in creation. And as such, you are invested with the same extraordinary Divine power to speak your world into existence! You have the ability to create with your words; to start to bring into being what you truly want out of the infinite potential of your own soul" (Hendrie, "Kabbalah of Speech," para. 13).

86. J. Jacobs and Eisenstein, "Golem."

87. On the emergence of kabbalistic gematria, see Idel, *Absorbing Perfections*,

The System of Lurianic Kabbalah

seventy-five different forms of mathematical calculations of letters and words.[88] The most basic numbering system, *mispar hekhrehi*, assigns the first ten Hebrew letters ordinal values (one to ten), and then assigns numbers by tens and hundreds.[89] Once the numerical calculation of the word is determined, the interpreter can rearrange and substitute words according to a second set of rules. In this way, kabbalistic hermeneutics is truly infinite, with no final or conclusive "meaning." No question about Scripture can be answered with a simple yes or no. While the early Kabbalists did not invent gematria, they used it so comprehensively that it became integrally attached to their system.

7.8. Kabbalah's Correlations with Greek Esoteric Philosophies

Although Kabbalah may appear to be distinctly Jewish, when viewing it from a historical and philosophical perspective—thereby considering parallels outside of Judaism—scholars have noticed striking correlations between kabbalistic thought and Greek esoteric philosophies such as Neopythagoreanism, Gnosticism, Hermeticism, and Neoplatonism.

The works of the Greek esoteric philosophies predate the medieval kabbalistic movement by a millennium or more.[90] I previously surveyed some of these philosophical schools in chapter 4. As a review, consider the following. Neopythagoreanism arose in the first century BCE as a revival of the mystical teachings of Pythagoras from the fifth century BCE. Gnosticism's heyday was the second and third centuries CE, as evidenced by the Nag Hammadi Codices and Irenaeus's *Against Heresies*. Hermeticism was a Greco-Egyptian magical philosophy dated to the second and third centuries CE, also evidenced by Nag Hammadi.[91] Neoplatonism was developed in the third through fifth centuries CE by Plotinus, Porphyry, Iamblichus, and Proclus, serving as a syncretistic catchall philosophy that integrated many elements of the previously mentioned schools. This

---

256–65.

88. Scholem, "Gematria," 7:426.

89. Derovan, "Gematria," 7:424.

90. This takes into account that Kabbalah's core doctrines, as given in the *Zohar*, are dated to the thirteenth century, rather than attributable to Shimon bar Yochai in the second century CE.

91. Pearson, "Hermeticism"; Tripolitis, *Religions of Hellenistic-Roman Age*, 135–40.

Part II: A Critique of Non-Incarnational Maimonidean and Kabbalistic Thought

Neoplatonic tradition continued as an underground Western mystical philosophy throughout the medieval period.

See the following table for the correlations between Lurianic Kabbalah and its Greek predecessors:

Table 13. Kabbalistic Commonalities with Greek Esoteric Philosophies

Kabbalistic Theme	Summary	Similar Proponents
Emanationism	The universe continually emanates from God as light from the sun.	Plotinus
Panentheism	The universe is metaphysically and physically "in" God.	Parmenides, Plotinus, Proclus
Via Negativa	It is impossible to have any positive knowledge of God.	Plotinus
Sefirot	Divine potencies or attributes that emanate from God and perform his will.	Gnosticism
The Number Ten	Ten explains all reality in heaven and earth.	Neopythagoreanism
Dialectical Ontology of Triads	One aspect of reality unites with another aspect to produce a third aspect, repeating forever.	Gnosticism, Plotinus, Proclus
Divine Catastrophe	God has had a crisis within himself that has led to the emergence of the physical universe.	Gnosticism
Multiplicity as Evil	All things that appear multiple (such as bodies) have a lower value than simpler things.	Gnosticism, Plotinus, Proclus
Metaphysical Numerology	The physical universe is composed of letters and numbers that have descended from God.	Neopythagoreanism, Gnosticism, Iamblichus
Interpretational Numerology (Gematria)	All words and sentences have secret layers of meaning dependent upon mathematical formulas.	Neopythagoreanism, Gnosticism, Iamblichus
Cosmic Patterning	"As above, so below." Lower physical and psychological realities are patterned upon heavenly ones.	Plato, Gnosticism, Hermeticism
Metaphysical Dualism	Higher and lower realities are separated into male/female, light/dark, and left/right categories that must be reunited by man's efforts.	Gnosticism

The System of Lurianic Kabbalah

Kabbalistic Theme	Summary	Similar Proponents
Sexualized Ontology	All concepts are either male or female and must be united according to prescribed practices analogous to human sexuality.	Gnosticism
Theurgy/Magic/Incantations	One may affect higher realities through ritual, producing desired results in the lower realities.	Hermeticism, Gnosticism, Iamblichus
Reincarnation	People are repeatedly given new bodies after death, the form of which depends upon one's moral and spiritual performance.	Pythagoras, Plato, Gnosticism, Plotinus
Salvation through Philosophy	Meditation on the truths of philosophy, its symbolism, and mystical practice results in transcending the body and uniting with God.	Plato, Gnosticism, Plotinus
Dangerous Esoteric Knowledge	Knowledge about God must be kept hidden from unworthy people for their protection.	Plato, Gnosticism
Divine Sparks	Physical things contain sparks of the divine, and Jews have more than gentiles.	Gnosticism, Plotinus (without a focus on Jews)
People Have Multiple Souls	The human being has a vegetative soul, an animal soul, a rational soul, and according to some, in the case of Jews, a divine soul.	Aristotle (without a focus on Jews)
Extra Jewish Soul	Jews, as the chosen people, have an extra divine soul that gentiles do not have.[92]	Gnosticism (without a focus on Jews)
Fourfold Biblical Interpretation	Scripture must be interpreted in the fourfold PaRDeS scheme.	Philo, Christian Platonists
Geocentrism	The Earth is the lowest part of the universe, with planets and stars seen as progressively higher and more spiritual.	Aristotle, Ptolemy
Four Elements	Belief that the physical world is composed of fire, air, water, and earth.	Empedocles, Plato, Aristotle

92. This doctrine, as summarized, is characteristic of Chabad and is found in the *Tanya*. The earliest mention of Jews having an extra soul is found in b. Beṣah 16a, where R. Simeon b. Laqish says that Jews receive an extra soul temporarily on Shabbat. Thus, the talmudic version of the doctrine does not imply Jews have an ontological advantage compared to gentiles.

Part II: A Critique of Non-Incarnational Maimonidean and Kabbalistic Thought

These correlations between Lurianic Kabbalah and Greek esoteric philosophies are specific, profound, and wide ranging. The following chapters discuss these correlations in depth, and appendix D investigates how to account for the correlations in the first place.

7.9. Kabbalistic Challenges to the Incarnation

Kabbalah's vision of the world is incompatible with a particular man having a divine identity that is permanently and qualitatively distinguished from all other human beings and all other created beings. In the NT, Jesus alone is divine, unlike any other corporeal being, and divinity is a binary property, rather than plotted on a continuum. A categorical ontological divide separates God's divine essence from the created order, which came into being by his unique and sovereign power *ex nihilo*. Kabbalah does not maintain a division between God and the created order; the created order is divine already, that is, divinized by the sparks of *Ein Sof* that need release from evil *klippot*. The complex and detailed process of *tzimtzum* provides the basis for why humans can know they have the infinite within. The only reason the created order *appears* to be finite is because of the emergence of the evil *klippot*. Yet, Jewish philosopher Jacob Bernard Agus states, "Those shells are also incarnations of the divine Being, save that they are more removed from Him in the chain of being."[93]

Therefore, the idea of Jesus being qualitatively different than anything else is foreign to Kabbalah; at best, Jesus could only be *quantitatively* more holy than others through performing mitzvot (commandments). Even if this were granted (which of course it is not in Judaism), Jesus could only have been included among Israel's holy *tzaddikim* (righteous men), not ascribed the exalted ontological status of deserving worship as God, as the NT teaches (Phil 2:5–11; Rom 10:9; John 20:28).

Moreover, in a kabbalistic understanding, the idea of God becoming specially incarnate in a human being is a backward, counterproductive concept, even outside of a panentheistic framework. In Kabbalah, the greater the multiplicity, the more evil; and the lesser the multiplicity, the less evil. For God to enter into time and space in a corporeal body, which consists of evil *klippot*, would be to add to the multiplicity of the universe and contribute to its evil. God would be committing the same

---

93. Jacob Bernard Agus, in Rabinowicz, *Encyclopedia of Hasidism*, s.v. "God." Note the use of the word "incarnation" here, which is not aligned with the Chalcedonian sense of the word.

disunity Kabbalah says humanity must free itself from, all in the name of "saving" humanity.

Finally, human sin is not the fundamental problem of the universe in Kabbalah. The problem of the universe is not moral, but ontological. The moral fall of Adam (Gen 3) was a lesser fall that took place in a cosmos that had already catastrophically descended into physicality and multiplicity. Theoretically speaking, a human being could live a sinless life and still need redemption in the kabbalistic worldview, because that person is still encumbered by a body, a distinct consciousness, and a sense of self. Consequently, those invested in kabbalistic thought see no need for the Son of God to become incarnate as a human being (hypothetically, if such a Son exists), for indeed the entire universe is *already* God's body and *already* has the seed of its own redemption within. Humans need no atonement to be spiritually restored to God, for they are already ontologically united with God, but trapped in an illusion of finitude. All Jewish people need to do is become mystically enlightened about their divinity within, freeing themselves from the garments of physicality by practicing mitzvot to release the waste parts (*klippot*) of the universe into the higher realms, reuniting God in the process. Israel already has all she needs to save herself and God.

In sum, none of Jesus's salvific or ontological attractiveness is comprehensible in Kabbalah. The gospel as commonly preached makes little sense in kabbalistic thought. The salvation from sin that Jesus offers is simply not required in Jewish mysticism. The divinity he mediates to humanity through his Incarnation is also unnecessary, for everything is already a conduit for the divine. In short, Kabbalah makes Jesus redundant.

8 An Assessment of Lurianic Kabbalah's Metaphysics

Whoever reflects upon four things
would have been better off had he not been born:
What is above,
What is below,
What is before,
And what is beyond.

—M. Ḥag. 2:1

IN THE PREVIOUS CHAPTER, I surveyed kabbalistic theology, cosmology, and metaphysics, depicting its unique mystical vision of the world according to kabbalistic practitioners and scholars. In this chapter and the one following, I critically assess the metaphysics, history, intellectual predecessors, and scientific claims of Kabbalah. Admittedly, I conduct this assessment as a non-kabbalistic outsider and as a Christian, but the following two chapters will not consider the NT or Christian theology as a source for argumentation. Direct comparison and critique of Kabbalah with the NT in mind is reserved for part 3.

8.1. Positive Aspects of Kabbalah

Although my exposition of NT doctrine is reserved for part 3, I believe it is proper to begin my assessment of Kabbalah with themes that I

An Assessment of Lurianic Kabbalah's Metaphysics

appreciate as a follower of Jesus. However, I must emphasize that this list is *limited*, as I have fewer positive things to say about Kabbalah than I did about Maimonides's more grounded Aristotelian worldview.

Allowance for divine complexity. Kabbalah's understanding of God is multifaceted and involves a dynamic, pulsating system of divine potencies that interpenetrate and interact with each other in a mysterious unity (cf. perichoresis). *The Encyclopedia of Hasidism* states, "The Kabbalists never tire of affirming the essential unit of *Ein Sof* and the *Sefirot*."[1] While I do not believe the kabbalistic vision of the ten *Sefirot* reflects divine truth in a biblical sense, the kabbalistic system is helpful because it undermines the Maimonidean tendency to shrink God into an unknowable singularity with no complexity whatsoever. The NT's vision of God's oneness includes the limited complexity of three persons with unified divine attributes—not Kabbalah's infinite complexity of the ten *Sefirot* and all existing things—but both the NT and Kabbalah are strictly forbidden in a Maimonidean understanding. If Kabbalah, with its complex godhead, is allowed to be a "Jewish" option given the Shema (Deut 6:4), then the NT's Trinitarian theology should be seen as a Jewish option as well.[2]

Allowance for divine nearness. Kabbalah instructs its followers to consider the divine in all things, including within their own bodies and psyches. Kabbalists have a heightened sense of God's nearness and immanence in everyday life. God speaks at all times and infuses his providence directly into all aspects of life. In contrast with Maimonides, Kabbalists do not see God as some unknowable, distant deity who interacts with the world only in indirect ways. Instead, they recognize God's nearness and yearn to increase their union with him in everyday life. Similarly, the Hebrew Scriptures speak about God indwelling his people by his Spirit (Exod 31:1–5; Num 11:24–30), and the NT speaks about the Holy Spirit living in believers' hearts after being born again (John 3; 2 Cor 1:22). Thus, by positing that God is near to Israel, Kabbalah approaches NT theology, yet opposes it through its panentheistic reasoning for God's closeness.

Emphasis on experience in conjunction with knowledge. Kabbalah teaches that religious truth must be experienced rather than simply assented to. It encourages Jewish people to immerse themselves into mystical practice and experience prior to having all their questions answered. This is similar to the classic Christian position of "faith seeking

---

1. Rabinowicz, *Encyclopedia of Hasidism*, s.v. "Ein Sof."
2. Kellner, *We Are Not Alone*, 155.

understanding," associated with Augustine and Anselm.[3] This maxim states that knowledge of the truth (and ultimately personal salvation) cannot come through rational processes alone, but must begin from an orientation of faith in God. As Jesus taught, "You must be born again" (John 3:7). Both the kabbalistic and Christian traditions recognize that faith, experience, and knowledge depend on each other, and that rationality is not supreme.

Acknowledgment of the brokenness of the world and the purity of the spiritual realm. Kabbalah has a deep sense that the world is not how it is supposed to be and that human beings and the entire cosmos need spiritual restoration. These attitudes discourage placing possessions, wealth, and worldly accomplishments in the center of human pursuits. Likewise, Jesus asks what good it is if a man gains the whole world, but forfeits his soul (Matt 16:26). A person's spiritual life and connection with God is of utmost importance. The NT also teaches that the creation groans for redemption from the effects of sin (Rom 8:20–23), and that God will restore the universe in the world to come (Rev 21–22).

Thus ends my affirmation of kabbalistic thought. In my opinion, when considering Kabbalah, Jesus followers should practice a biblically grounded epistemic distance. In most cases, a Jesus follower should not approach kabbalistic thought to learn *from* it but rather to learn *about* it. At times there may be room for a fruitful application of "comparative theology" and "redemptive analogies" where one remains grounded in biblical orthodoxy while seeking instances where kabbalistic thought may be compatible.[4] However, kabbalistic teaching is largely incompatible with Scripture and sound philosophy, and it does not have the historical Jewish pedigree it claims for itself. There are both recent[5] and historical[6] examples of how easily syncretism takes root when Jesus followers are attracted to Kabbalah with an uncritical eye. If these warnings are not heeded, then a dilution of biblical authority and the loss of theological orthodoxy will likely result.[7]

---

3 Augustine, *NPNF*[1] 7:184; Anselm, *Prosologion*.

4. Kärkkäinen, *Work of Comparative Theology*, 3–4.

5. Shapira, *Return of Kosher Pig*; Levertoff, *Love and Messianic Age*; Janicki et al., *Study Guide and Commentary*; Wolfson, "Paul Philip Levertoff."

6. For Renaissance and early modern Christian Kabbalists who syncretized with Kabbalah, see Pico della Mirandola, Nicholas of Cusa, Jacob Böhme, and Johannes Reuchlin. Also consult Pauli, *Great Mystery*; Oxlee, *Christian Doctrines of Trinity*; Varner, "Jewish Numerology"; R. Harvey, "Worship and Witness," 133–40.

7. For more on this theme, see Crawford, "Pathways," 73–89.

8.2. The Challenge of Kabbalah's Two-Tiered Epistemology

As I lay out my case against the kabbalistic worldview, I should be clear about my starting point. I am like an Aristotelian venturing into a strange Pythagorean land—a rationalist and realist attempting to make analytic arguments about the worldview of citizens living in a mystical world of experience and ineffable splendor.

Philosophically speaking, Kabbalah promotes an *idealist* view of the world rather than a *realist* one.[8] In contrast to the realism of Aristotle, Kabbalah sides with the minority philosophical position of idealism, which states that the only reality that exists is intellectual, namely the mental emanations and processes of *Ein Sof*.[9] In this view, truth is a graded spectrum, and the physical world is so low in the kabbalistic scheme that it does not factor into determinations of ultimate truth or falsehood. The idealist does not need to make arguments about what truly *is*—since he has no access to *Ein Sof*—but only about what *appears to be* down in our less-than-real and less-than-fully-true world.[10] If there is some logical contradiction between what *appears* to be *here* and what *appears* to be *there*, this is no matter for the Kabbalist, because all he is doing is describing the lower tier of appearances, not the hidden higher reality. In this way, the Kabbalist can squeeze his way out of contradictions in his system and shield his worldview from rational critique. All is symbolic, metaphorical, and merely apparent, and thus it escapes rational criticism.[11]

---

8. These terms are often used when considering ontology—that which exists. For overviews of these ontological schools, see Guyer and Horstmann, "Idealism"; Miller, "Realism"; Gordon, "Idealism." In epistemology, idealism is associated with internalism (all beliefs are justified through internal reflection in a subject), and realism is associated with externalism (beliefs are justified through causal processes that are often external to the subject) (Moreland and Craig, *Philosophical Foundations*, 66–67).

9. For example, Chabad proponent Eduard Shyfrin says, "All individual mental spaces are subsystems of a worldwide mental space encompassing all spiritual worlds and *sefirot*, and, under certain conditions, those individual mental spaces can correlate and establish interaction among themselves" (Shyfrin, *From Infinity to Man*, 48).

10. Lebens writes, "One of the key features of Hassidic Idealism [Kabbalah] is the way in which it stratifies reality into two. A consequence of this stratification is that any sentence that we utter, before we can evaluate its truth-conditions, has to be indexed to one of these two levels or strata" ("Creation and Modality," 50).

11. Dan, *Early Kabbalah*, 8–9.

As an analogy, consider a magical kaleidoscope. When looking through one end of the kaleidoscope, the eye is filled with a brilliant light show of dynamic colors and shapes folding in on each other. When looking through the other end, nothing but a clear view is perceived, such as with a telescope. In Kabbalah, humanity is confined to the kaleidoscopic view, whereas God (*Ein Sof*) has the clear view. Although Kabbalists can become engrossed with the kaleidoscope of dynamic *Sefirot*, they believe from God's perspective, there are no *Sefirot*. Actually, from *Ein Sof*'s perspective, nothing but *Ein Sof* exists, and there is no magical kaleidoscope at all.

Accordingly, Kabbalah tends to side more with the coherence theory of truth, rather than with the mainstream correspondence theory of truth.[12] The correspondence theory asserts that a statement is true if and only if it corresponds with external reality. Truth is univocal, objective, and is not a graded spectrum. This view assumes there is only one external reality, and humanity has true access to that external reality through the senses and the mind. This is the historical and mainstream view of truth, arguably serving as the theory of truth that undergirds the Hebrew Scriptures. In contrast, the coherence theory of truth states that humanity does not have adequate access to "reality"—whatever it is—and thus statements can be called "true" in a subjective sense if they cohere with other statements that are held to be true in a particular sphere of reference. Truth is equivocal, subjective, and has more or less value depending on the sphere of reference being discussed.[13] Therefore, this view is about constructing an interconnected web of truth claims within a specific sphere of perception without needing to tie it to a singular external reality.[14]

Kabbalah sees no need to tie its teachings with external reality, because humanity has no access to the only reality that exists: *Ein Sof*. People have no access to truth as it really is, but only to the truth as it

---

12. Young, "Coherence Theory of Truth"; David, "Correspondence Theory of Truth." The coherence theory of truth follows from metaphysical idealism because it assumes that reality is essentially mental or spiritual, and that propositions are expressions of ideas or thoughts. Therefore, propositions cannot be compared to anything outside the mind, but only to other propositions within the mind. The coherence theory of truth also supports metaphysical idealism because it implies that reality is a coherent system of ideas or thoughts, which can be understood as a manifestation of a single mind or spirit. Kant's transcendental idealism, which I do not hold, also supports the coherence theory.

13. Modern subjective maxims such as "Live your truth," "Be true to yourself," and "This is my truth" are examples of the coherence view of truth.

14. For example, Lebens constructs a theory of truth that is indexed to a particular realm, rather than to a single external reality (*Principles of Judaism*, 121–31).

appears in human perceptions of the world.[15] We are prisoners chained in Plato's cave, yearning for understanding of the world outside. We are captivated by the lights of the kaleidoscope that both exists (in a lower sense) and does not exist (in the ultimate sense).

This view opens Kabbalah to various criticisms, such as not being able to distinguish ontologically between horses and unicorns (which one[s] are real?), and struggling to have an adequate basis to differentiate between the coherent, interconnected, complex system of Kabbalist thought and the coherent, interconnected, complex systems of fictional universes like that of *Star Wars*, *Star Trek*, and *The Lord of the Rings*.[16]

Like other mysticisms, Kabbalah has difficulty with the law of noncontradiction. Kabbalah cannot agree with making fully true distinctions between *a* and not-*a* because such distinctions are *apparent only from human perspectives*, to those encased in evil *klippot*, whereas from the divine perspective of *Ein Sof*, all is one. Kabbalah therefore recontextualizes contradictions within its hierarchical, dialectical understanding of reality where apparent distinctions yield to ultimate unity. The loss of common ground in the law of noncontradiction is one of the most vexing barriers for non-mystics when considering mystical modes of thought.

Modern Orthodox philosopher Samuel Lebens defends a version of what he calls "extreme Hassidic idealism" that attempts to address these concerns directly.[17] With philosophical sophistication, he handles accusations that the kabbalistic worldview entails a loss of human freedom, a loss of significance, a poor account of the problem of evil, and a playground for contradictions. Lebens believes that classical theism,

---

15. Lebens calls these, respectively, "truth *simpliciter*" and truth relative to the fiction of our world in God's story. Using insights from the philosophy of fiction, Lebens states that it is false *simpliciter* that "Hamlet is the prince of Denmark," but *relative to the story Shakespeare tells*, the statement is true. Lebens employs this phenomenon to support the idea that all truths we have access to are still truths *relative to our story*, even though they are fiction dreamt up in God's mind (*Principles of Judaism*, 77, 94–98).

16. Recall that, in Platonic thought, a chair exists even if there are no chairs in the sensible world, since the idea of a chair exists in the intellectual world. Aristotle protested, saying that chairs do not exist unless they are present in the sensible world. Aristotle separated potentiality from actuality, saying that only things that are actual exist. Thus, a Platonist of the idealist or panpsychist variety could say that Captain Jean Luc Picard and Frodo Baggins truly do exist, since they are in the intellectual world, whereas an Aristotelian would say that fictional characters do not exist since they are not in the sensible world. For a Platonist idealist, reality conforms to thoughts; for an Aristotelian, thoughts must conform to reality, or else be false thoughts. See §§4.1.4–4.1.5; 4.2.1.

17. Lebens, *Principles of Judaism*, 1–142.

Part II: A Critique of Non-Incarnational Maimonidean and Kabbalistic Thought

when understood consistently, must lead to metaphysical idealism of the kabbalistic sort. His argument is a rare coupling of apologetics with intellectual humility. Lebens's proposal represents a high watermark in bringing analytical philosophical justification to the kabbalistic worldview in the twenty-first century.[18]

Nevertheless, Lebens's argument is a linear train of thought from which I depart at multiple points along the journey.[19] Consequently, I do not believe the kabbalistic worldview ultimately escapes the critiques that may be brought against it metaphysically, scripturally, scientifically, and historically. This book will therefore proceed under the assumptions of metaphysical realism and the correspondence theory of truth, with the corollary that Scripture speaks capital-*t* objective Truth, not merely subjective fiction-as-truth in our perceived experience.

8.3. An Argument against Lurianic Kabbalah's Pan-Incarnational Panentheism

As with the chapter assessing Maimonides, this chapter presents an argument against multiple facets of kabbalistic thought, especially those that combine to make the Incarnation irrelevant and redundant. Since subjective and mystical personal experience is not open to study by others, the range of my critique is necessarily limited to that to which I have access, but I believe that is sufficient. The outline of my argument is as follows:

---

18. As may be seen in footnotes throughout the book, I find many of Lebens's insights and analytical methods to be helpful in a variety of areas. Lebens is a trailblazer in attempting to fuse the modern analytical philosophical tradition (which is often the domain of Aristotelian logic and precision) with the kabbalistic tradition (which is the domain of mysticism of the Neoplatonic variety).

19. For example, I find Lebens's use of fiction to justify idealism unconvincing. He believes that the world is merely a story dreamt up in God's mind, where we are his characters he imagines, like how Shakespeare created Hamlet. Yet Lebens's exposition does not ask or answer the question "Can Hamlet disobey Shakespeare?" Thus, while the fiction model handles abstract *evil* as a plot device which serves the author's story, it does not handle the reality of *sin* (Lebens, *Principles of Judaism*, 94–97). I also see his handling of the problem of evil as a neo-gnostic model where the God with whom we interact is a demiurge-like lesser manifestation who "is at least immoral *enough*, or irrational *enough*, or both, to have created this world" (80; emphasis in original). Thus, critiques found in this book and in the classic Christian apologists against Gnosticism may have relevance to Lebens's two-tiered God. For responses to Lebens, see Association for the Philosophy of Judaism, "Symposium"; Mullins, "Theism." In reviewing this footnote, Lebens humorously quipped that his book's linear train of thought is "eminently get-offable."

An Assessment of Lurianic Kabbalah's Metaphysics

1. Kabbalah affirms panentheism, such that the universe is God incarnate.[20]
2. Kabbalah grounds its panentheism in its doctrines of cosmology, metaphysics, and hermeneutics.
3. Counterpoint: key aspects of Kabbalah's cosmology are false.
4. Counterpoint: key aspects of Kabbalah's metaphysics are false.
5. Counterpoint: key aspects of Kabbalah's hermeneutics are false.
6. Counterpoint: Kabbalah's epistemic authority is historically dubious.
7. Therefore, Kabbalah's panentheism is false.

Premises 1 and 2 were summarized in the previous chapter. This chapter and the following will provide counterpoints 3 through 6, with the conclusion that the panentheism that drives Kabbalah is a mistaken way to view the world. The result of challenging Kabbalah's conclusions allows for the NT's approach to the Incarnation to become a possibility. If the universe is *not* God's body, and if humans are *not* ontologically one with God already, then this makes room for God to take up residence in our world as the *unique* incarnate Son of God, an idea explored in part 3.

8.4. Metaphysical, Theological, and Cosmological Critiques of Kabbalah

For the remainder of this chapter, I will employ tools from a realist's intellectual toolbox to highlight inconsistencies and objective falsehoods present in the kabbalistic worldview. To begin, I will investigate Kabbalah's notion of the cosmos.

8.4.1. Evidence in Favor of Creation *ex Nihilo*

Few theological concepts are as foundational to the Bible as the notion of creation *ex nihilo*, for it establishes a categorical Creator-creation distinction—the very distinction that is uniquely bridged in the Incarnation. Creation *ex nihilo*[21] is the doctrine that God created the universe out

---

20. Alternatively, under a nonliteral and idealist understanding of *tzimtzum*, the universe as a physical object does not exist and, as such, cannot be called a "body." Thus, this point could be restated as "Kabbalah affirms panentheism, such that the universe is an imagination in God's mind."

21. *Ex nihilo* is Latin for "from nothing." In Hebrew, the concept is often called *Yesh*

of nothing, through the power of his spoken word (Gen 1:3; Ps 33:6),[22] rather than a rearrangement of preexistent matter (creation *ex matria*) or as an extension of his own eternal being (emanation *ex Deo*).

The foundation of creation *ex nihilo* comes from the opening words of the Bible: "In the beginning, God created the heavens and the earth" (Gen 1:1). Most current and historical Hebrew scholars believe the textual evidence indicates that this should be read as an absolute introductory statement, rather than a relative clause that merely summarizes the second verse.[23] When read in an absolute way, the phrase "In the beginning" (בְּרֵאשִׁית, *bereshit*) indicates the first moment of physical time, situating the action verb, "created" (בָּרָא, *bara*), within finite time and not in an eternal past. This results in "the heavens and the earth" coming into existence after the completion of the process described by the verb *bara*. The phrase "heavens and the earth" is a merism (mentioning two extremes to suggest all in between) that means "the universe" or "cosmos," for the ancient Hebrew language had no word to denote all of reality.[24] Thus the biblical cosmological sequence is (1) God by himself, (2) God initiates physical time, (3) God creates the universe (it begins to exist), (4) the universe continues to exist by God's providence.[25]

Additionally, creation *ex nihilo* entails that God chose to begin creating through his own volition, such that there was a state of affairs in which only God existed, and then a post-creation state of affairs where God and his creation coexist as two separate existences. Creation *ex nihilo* posits an ontological dividing line with a binary view of reality, whereby there are only two classes of existence: (1) God, the necessary being, and (2) the contingent beings he created separate from himself.

---

me-Ayin (יש מאין), meaning "existence from nothingness."

22. The biblical doctrine of creation could also be called creation *ex verbo* (out of the word), signifying the transcendent instrumentality through which the universe was made. Thus, God created *ex nihilo*, signifying his unique ability to bring being out of nonbeing, but *also* created *ex verbo*, signifying the method by which he did so.

23. Tal, *Genesis*, Gen 1:1; Copan and Craig, *Creation Out of Nothing*, 36–60; Feinberg, *No One Like Him*, 551–57. Also see Gen 1:1 LXX.

24. Copan and Craig, *Creation Out of Nothing*, 43.

25. It is likely that steps (2) and (3) were performed simultaneously, as time is a constituent dimension of the universe. The steps have been separated in this sequence only because of the grammatical form of Gen 1:1. This is a limitation of human language. Without tying grammatical form to temporal or logical sequence, the sequence could be restated as (1) God by himself; (2) God initiates physical time through the creation of the universe; (3) the universe continues to exist by God's providence.

There is nothing else in between.[26] These two categories are distinguished respectively as Creator and created, maximally-great and finite, incorporeal and corporeal, and the like. God is the former in each case, and all created things are the latter, with the exception that some created things are incorporeal (e.g., souls). Under creation *ex nihilo*, divinity is not a fluid property that a thing can have more or less of; it is a binary property that a subject either has fully (God) or does not have at all (all else).

The Hebrew Scriptures reflect this binary view of reality, rather than a continuous spectrum or chain of being that would blur the distinctions. In Scripture, human beings speak of God as unique, not as ontologically united to humanity.[27] Isaiah declares that men are not God, with a corresponding contrast between flesh and spirit (Isa 31:3; cf. 2 Chr 32:8). Likewise, God himself asserts his uniqueness and distinction from all others (Isa 43:11; 45:21). In the Hebrew Scriptures, perhaps Ecclesiastes says it best: "God is in heaven and you are on earth. Therefore let your words be few" (Eccl 5:2). He is God, and his creation is not.

Creation *ex nihilo* is affirmed throughout the Hebrew Scriptures,[28] the NT,[29] and in ancient Jewish sources.[30] The doctrine has been the traditional position within Judaism, appearing in the Talmud[31] and garnering the support of Saadia Gaon and Maimonides.[32] In opposition to the

26. W. Wright and Martin, *Encountering the Living God*, 109–26.

27. Ps 8; 72:18; 86:10; Isa 37:16.

28. Proverbs 8:22–31 indicates the preexistence of wisdom "before the beginning of the earth" and before there were depths, or springs, or mountains, or fields. Psalm 102:25–28 speaks of the finite nature of the universe, in contrast to God whose "years have no end." Psalm 33:6–9 goes beyond the Genesis account to explain that even the heavens were created by God's word. Jeremiah 10:12 attributes the existence of the earth and the heavens to God's power and understanding.

29. Romans 4:17 says that God gives being to nonbeing through his speech. Hebrews 11:3 directly denies creation *ex matria* in favor of creation *ex nihilo*. John 1:3 asserts that all things were made by the Word of God. The same is taught in Rom 11:36; 1 Cor 8:6; and Col 1:16. The final verse includes both visible and invisible things, just in case one might think that nonmaterial things may be excluded in biblical cosmology.

30. Gen 1:1 LXX; 4 Ezra 6:38; Sib. Or. 1.7–21; 2 Bar. 14:17; Jdt 16:14; Wis 9:1 (although 11:17 speaks of creation out of "formless matter," which is acceptable if God first creates the formless matter); 2 Macc. 7:28; 3 Macc. 2:3; Jub. 12:4; Philo, *Planting* 50; 1QS 3.15. For more, see Oegema, "Creation."

31. b. Meg. 13b: "It was clearly known to the one who spoke and made the world come into being." b. Sanh. 19a: "Him who spoke and brought the world into being" (Neusner, *Babylonian Talmud*). This affirmation of God's creation of everything from nothing forms the beginning of the traditional prayer *Baruch She'amar*.

32. For Saadia, see Feldman, "Philosophy and Theology," 2:711–12; for Maimonides, see 2:720–21. Gersonides holds to a version of creation *ex matria*, but it does not hold

Platonic *ex matria* and Neoplatonic *ex Deo* cosmologies around them, the church fathers also asserted creation *ex nihilo*.[33] It has continued to be upheld in the Christian tradition ever since.[34] Thus, creation *ex nihilo* is a foundational doctrine of classical theism in both Judaism and Christianity.

Outside of religious sources of knowledge, the idea of the universe having a temporal and spatial beginning is corroborated both scientifically and philosophically. The standard big bang model of cosmology is based on extrapolations of observable data, and it implies a temporal and spatial beginning.[35] Philosophically, the impossibility of the existence of an actual infinite, among other arguments, indicates that the universe is finite, and not infinite in age.[36] Thus, the doctrine of creation *ex nihilo* has scriptural, traditional, scientific, and philosophical arguments in its favor.

I believe this range of support justifies its acceptance as a fundamental truth of reality.[37] Cosmological theories that do not coincide with creation *ex nihilo* should be rejected as false. For example, the modern cosmological models of the oscillating, steady-state, and multiverse theories are incompatible and should be rejected.[38] How does the kabbalistic cosmology fare?

8.4.2. Implications of Creation *ex Nihilo* on the Kabbalistic Worldview

Kabbalah teaches that the universe is a continuous emanation of the divine being, classifying Kabbalah as a version of emanation *ex Deo*. This calls into question a beginning of time and a distinction between God and finite creation.[39] Systems of continuous divine emanation, such as

---

up to philosophical scrutiny. On Gersonides, see Lebens, *Principles of Judaism*, 63–69.

33. Irenaeus, *Haer.* 2.34.2, 3.8.3; Herm. Mand. 1.1; Diogn. 7.2; Aristedes, *Apology* 2 (Syriac); Justin Martyr, *Dial.* 5; Odes Sol. 16:18–19.

34. Carter, *Contemplating God*, 243–56.

35. Copan and Craig, *Creation Out of Nothing*, 222–24; Craig, *Reasonable Faith*, 126–28.

36. Copan and Craig, *Creation Out of Nothing*, 197–218; Craig, *Kalām Cosmological Argument*; Moreland, *Scaling the Secular City*, 15–42; Pruss, *Infinity, Causation, and Paradox*.

37. For Christian defenses of creation *ex nihilo*, see Copan and Craig, *Creation Out of Nothing*; Henry, *God, Revelation, and Authority*, 6:120–32; Grudem, *Systematic Theology*, 338–43; Shedd, *Dogmatic Theology*, 366–71; Carter, *Contemplating God*, 237–68. Also see Aquinas, *ST* I q.45 a.1; *SCG* 2.16.

38. Copan and Craig, *Creation Out of Nothing*, 219–66.

39. Mullins, "Theism."

with Plotinus and Kabbalah, have difficulty accounting for radical discontinuities such as these. The chain of being must be eternally gradual and continuous, as God is eternally unchanging. In contrast, creation *ex nihilo* rejects a single chain of being and posits categorical distinctions between God and his creation, and among created things themselves.

Nevertheless, kabbalistic sources still claim to affirm creation *ex nihilo*, but only because they change the meaning of "nothing"[40] and attempt to situate the emergence of time within a larger eternally emanating system.[41] They equate God with nothing because there is "nothing" to hold onto in the mind when considering *Ein Sof* (negative theology).[42] If *Ein Sof* is nothing, then Kabbalists feel justified saying that they hold to creation out of "nothing." However, Kabbalah's supposed alignment with creation *ex nihilo* is due to a subversive use of language. This equivocation of terms should be seen for what it is: a rejection of actual creation *ex nihilo*.

Kabbalah is fully incompatible with the doctrine of creation *ex nihilo* as it denies both the cosmological and the ontological features of the doctrine. By collapsing the categories of Creator and created into each other, and calling into question a beginning of the universe, Kabbalah undermines the claims of the Hebrew Scriptures and sets itself at odds with Jewish tradition and scientific and philosophical truths. Thus, creation *ex nihilo* is a crucial doctrine that provides significant opposition to the enchanted universe promoted by Kabbalah. If there was a beginning of the universe, created out of nothing, not an emanated extension of God's being but rather distinguished from him, then Kabbalah's elaborate emanative theology-cosmology gets cut off right from the start.

8.4.3. Various Problems with *Ein Sof* and *Tzimtzum*

Although the kabbalistic mode of creation starts off in the wrong direction, I will continue to follow its path and point out further inconsistencies. The kabbalistic doctrine of *tzimtzum* attempts to explain how the

---

40. McClymond, *Devil's Redemption*, 1:162–63. See also Biale, *Gershom Scholem*, 59. Properly defined, *nothing* is not a thing, but rather metaphysical nonbeing that lacks all conceivable and inconceivable concepts, definitions, properties, and potential, such that the word "is" used previously in this sentence becomes null by necessity, since nonbeing cannot have anything predicated about it. Nothing cannot develop, cannot emanate, cannot undergo processes, and cannot have any verbs or adjectives attached to it.

41. Valabregue-Perry, "Philosophy, Heresy," 249–51.

42. A preferred way of speaking about *Ein Sof* is to liken it to the Hebrew letter *ayin*, which has no audible sound (Matt, "Ayin").

finite could emanate from the infinite: *Ein Sof* "conceals" or "contracts" within itself a primordial "space"—yet according to some, only metaphorically—in order to emanate his light into lower and lower gradations, which eventually get encased in *klippot*, resulting in the emergence of the physical, finite universe. Metaphor or not, this system is asserted as accurate and true, as far as human rationality is concerned. Thus, I will apply rational criteria to judge its claims. Is Kabbalah's acceptance of *Ein Sof* as the infinitely dimensional being-beyond-being who performs *tzimtzum* justified? For several reasons, I believe it is not.

Kabbalah's understanding of God's infinity is Greek syncretism, not taught in the Hebrew Scriptures. The doctrine of *tzimtzum* becomes necessary because of Kabbalah's unjustified assumption regarding what it means for God to be infinite. Kabbalah holds that *Ein Sof* is unbounded and delimited by nothing. There is no metaphorical "space" for anything to exist besides *Ein Sof* because it takes up all possible "space" in every possible "dimension" and abstract concept. In the mathematical terms of set theory pioneered by Georg Cantor (1845–1918), *Ein Sof* could be conceptualized as the set of all infinite sets, the infinitely dimensional "transfinite" number. As was recognized when Cantor put forward his theory of a concrete transfinite number, this idea results in pantheism or panentheism.[43]

The understanding of God as an infinitely dimensional being-beyond-being is foreign to the Hebrew Scriptures and derives from Greek metaphysical speculations.[44] Strictly speaking, "infinity" is not a concept defined or discussed in the Hebrew Scriptures. Its first emergence in extant literature was with the Greek philosopher Anaximander of Miletus in the sixth century BCE (long after the Torah was written), who developed a concept called *apeiron* (ἄπειρον), the unlimited or unbounded.[45] About a century later, Parmenides's understanding of the unbounded oneness of existence provided the seminal idea that there are no fundamental distinctions between any two things, and Kabbalah stands squarely in the Parmenidean tradition. It is an imposition on the Torah

---

43. Dauben, "Georg Cantor," 102–3. For a readable introduction to set theory, see Cheng, *Beyond Infinity*. For advanced surveys of the infinite, see A. Moore, *Infinite*; Easwaran et al., "Infinity." For an advanced article on one of the unsolved mysteries about transfinite numbers (and thus the shaky ground under positing an infinity of infinities), see Koellner, "Continuum Hypothesis."

44. Cf. Irenaeus, *Haer.* 2.4.2 and 2.8.2, arguing against a gnostic form of *tzimtzum*.

45. A. Moore, *Infinite*, 15.

An Assessment of Lurianic Kabbalah's Metaphysics

to view it through later Greek metaphysical speculations that counter biblical teachings regarding the Creator-creation distinction.

There are other, better understandings of God's infinitude. Philosopher Christian Tapp explains that philosophers generally apply "infinity" to God in terms of a quantitative sense (God's properties are extended infinitely), an eminent sense (God's properties are attributed to him in a way differently than to creatures), or a metaphysical/pre-categorical sense (God's essence is beyond natural reality and bounded by finite reality).[46] Each of these options for God's infinitude preserves the biblical Creator-creature distinction. Tapp also clarifies,

> Taking "having no limits" as the most general concept of infinity, one has to note, however, that infinity is seldom used to describe something as having no limits whatsoever (*infinitum simpliciter*), but rather is used to mean having no limits in a certain respect or of a certain kind (*infinitum secundum quid*).[47]

Kabbalah thus represents the path "seldom" taken, and other options are better.[48]

An infinitely dimensional panentheistic God includes evil within him, which is unbiblical. The psalmists repeatedly proclaim, "O give thanks to the LORD, for he is good!" (Ps 106:1; 107:1; 118:1). The Scriptures repeatedly call God "the Holy One of Israel" as a reflection of his transcendent otherness and his moral perfection (Ps 78:41; Isa 1:4; Jer 51:5; cf. Isa 6:3–5).[49] Deuteronomy 32:4 describes God as a God of faithfulness (אֱמוּנָה, *emunah*), and just (צַדִּיק, *tzaddik*) and upright (יָשָׁר, *yashar*). Crucially, the same verse says that God is "without iniquity" (אֵין עָוֶל, *ein avel*). All these biblical affirmations of God's innate goodness are problematic under Kabbalah's understanding of God. If God is truly infinitely dimensional, such that nothing exists outside of him, then evil is not outside of him either; rather, evil is metaphysically in him as a part of him. Moreover, as the only being truly in existence, and as the one who is responsible for everything that emanates from him, God becomes the

---

46. Tapp, "Infinity in Mathematics," 95.

47. Tapp, "Infinity in Mathematics," 99.

48. Also see Christian philosopher Alvin Plantinga on the ways God is and is not unlimited (*Warranted Christian Belief*, 55).

49. The predominant view of holiness or sanctification in rabbinic theology is that of separation. However, the moral quality of holiness—whether in God or as reflected in man's actions—is present in Judaism as well. See Friedman et al., "Kedushah."

actor of acts called "evil" by Scripture.[50] This can force Kabbalists to take a non-realist view of evil, such that evil is merely a concealed good.[51]

Others accept that evil is within *Ein Sof* but differ on how to account for it. Moshe Idel classifies three schools of thought among Kabbalists on the topic of evil emerging from God: (1) evil came first, and good emerged from it; (2) evil and its roots within God are a part of God's perfection; (3) evil and good are mixed together at the highest level of the divine sphere, but through the emanation process they separate from each other.[52] When coming from the biblical depiction of God's moral goodness, all these solutions are unsatisfying because evil should never be seen as emanating from God in the first place. Comparative religion scholar R. J. Zwi Werblowsky writes, "More than anything else, it is this awareness of the reality of evil, coupled with an essentially monotheistic rather than dualistic theology of the Zoroastrian type, which gives kabbalistic speculation such an audacious and indeed all but 'heretical' quality."[53]

Under consistent kabbalistic metaphysics, there is no such thing as idolatry. God commands Israel to have no other gods before him (Exod 20:3). This entails making a distinction between God and not-God,

---

50. Since the time of Tertullian in the second century, gnostic-thinking theologians have appealed to Isa 45:7 as evidence that God is the Creator of metaphysical evil. The crucial word in the verse is רָע (*ra*), which has given rise to gnostic interpretations. However, as pointed out by many non-gnostic exegetes in history, the Hebrew word *ra* has a range of meanings, including calamities, misfortunes, and general disorder, besides metaphysical evil. The use of the word in Isa 45:7 aligns with its use in Amos 3:6, Mic 1:12, and Jer 18:11, referring to the idea that God "brings calamity" upon sinners as judgment. Thus, there is no need to posit that God creates or does metaphysical evil. The ESV translates the phrase correctly as "I make well-being and create calamity." Concurring translations are found in NJPS, NASB, NKJV, NET, NRSV, NIV, NLT. For historical rebuttals of the idea that God created metaphysical evil in this verse, see Rashi; Ibn Ezra; Tertullian, *Marc.* 2.13; Chrysostom, *Of Demons* 1.5; John of Damascus, *De fide orth.* 4.19; Theodoret of Cyr, *Commentary on Isaiah* 14.45.7; John Cassian, *Conferences* 1.6.6; Aquinas, *ST* I q.49 a.2.

51. In two independent encounters, Chabad members have given this answer to me. I agree that evil, in and of itself, has no independent existence, but I disagree that it is a "concealed good." There is nothing purely evil, for to exist is better than to not exist, so anything that exists participates in at least some goodness, namely existence. Norman Geisler writes, "Evil is not a substance but a corruption of the good substances God made. Evil is like rust on a car or rot on a tree. Evil is like a wound in an arm or moth-holes in a garment. It is a lack in good things, not a thing in itself. It exists only in another but not in itself" (Geisler, *Thomas Aquinas*, 154). As a *corruption* of good, rather than a *concealed* good, evil is real. On responding to the idea that evil is an illusion, see C. Clark and Geisler, *Apologetics in New Age*, 203–21.

52. Idel, *Primeval Evil in Kabbalah*, xlviii–li.

53. Werblowsky, "Dualism," 6:30.

An Assessment of Lurianic Kabbalah's Metaphysics

which is problematic in a panentheistic system where *everything* is God. God also commands prohibits the creation and worship of idols (Exod 20:4–6). This is problematic in a panentheistic system where every created thing, including an idol, is inhabited by the infinite divine light. Thus in Kabbalah there is no ontological reason why Israel should not worship created things, for "Ein od milvado" (there is nothing but him). In order to rescue themselves from this pro-idolatry position, Kabbalists posit that Israel is prohibited from doing so simply because God commanded the prohibition—without there being a rational or ontological basis behind the prohibition. This irrational solution is arbitrary, and Scripture never hints that an evil as serious as idolatry has a non-ontological basis.

As a rational solution to the emergence of the finite from the infinite, tzimtzum *fails*. There are no gradations between infinity and finite numbers or concepts. Cantor's mathematical set theory illustrates that there are larger and smaller infinities, but there is no such thing as partial or half infinity. Mathematical intuitions for nonfinite numbers do not translate to the math of infinity. Infinity divided an infinite number of times is undefined (no answer), not a finite number. Infinity subtracted from infinity is not zero, but rather still infinity.[54] There are no humanly accessible rational ways that the infinite may be "brought down" into finitude without losing its infinity.[55]

In his exposition of *tzimtzum*, Immanuel Schochet appears to understand this predicament, postulating that a radical "leap" or "jump" is necessary to account for the transition.[56] He writes, "This first act of *tzimtzum* is a radical 'leap' (*dilug*) that creates the possibility for a gradual process and evolution of emanations to take place and to culminate in the creation of finite and corporeal entities."[57] However, this solution is inadequate as a rational solution. Note how Schochet says that *after* the *tzimtzum* has taken place, there is "a gradual process and evolution of emanations" before the culminating emergence of the finite. Hence, *tzimtzum* does not signify the point at which the infinite miraculously divides into the finite, for that takes place later, *after* the emergence of

---

54. For a readable introduction to the paradoxes of infinite mathematics, see Cheng, *Beyond Infinity*.

55. This insight, coincidentally, is the intuition behind Maimonides denying that the infinite God can have any positive relationship with physicality; in his view, "coming down" entails losing his infinity. This predicament is solved for Messiah through the hypostatic union, which I discuss in ch. 10.

56. Schochet, "Mystical Concepts in Chasidism," a50–51.

57. Schochet, "Mystical Concepts in Chasidism," a54–55.

Part II: A Critique of Non-Incarnational Maimonidean and Kabbalistic Thought

the *Sefirot* (which are presumably still infinite, but lesser in some sense) and *after* the emergence of lesser worlds. Thus, *tzimtzum* does not solve the problem of the infinite evolving downwards into the finite. The inability of the infinite to diminish its infinity down into finitude means that *tzimtzum* does not provide a rational explanation for finite things. Given the kabbalistic understanding of *Ein Sof*, either *tzimtzum* happens and we remain infinite (contradicting our experience), or *tzimtzum* does not happen and we cannot exist. We cannot be both finite and generated through *tzimtzum*.

As a metaphor intended only for human understanding, tzimtzum *is irrational*. Immanuel Schochet takes pains to clarify that the Hasidic understanding of *tzimtzum* and its concepts of a "void," a "leap," and the divine light tracing out the *Sefirot* are all metaphors. This teaching has an early root in the *Zohar*, where it says, "He is the mighty ruler ... before whom all existing things are as naught" (1:11b).[58] *Likkutei Amarim (Tanya)* 2.6 elaborates:

> These are his restraining powers ... so that heaven and earth and all their hosts should appear as if they were independently existing entities. However, the *tzimtzum* and concealment is only for the lower [worlds], but in relation to the Holy One, blessed is He, "everything before Him is considered as actually naught."[59]

In other words, *tzimtzum* is an illusion for humans to accept as a true metaphor, but God knows there is no *tzimtzum*. This application of Platonic dual-tiered epistemology is irrational. If there is no *tzimtzum* according to God's perspective, then on what basis may it be called concealment, if there is nothing to conceal? Does not God's opinion on the matter end the discussion?[60] Moreover, at the early stage of the

---

58. The *Zohar* takes this quote from Dan 4:35 but twists it in a metaphysical and cosmological direction that is not the context of Daniel. See also Isa 40:17.

59. Zalman of Liadi, *Tanya*, 310–12.

60. Lebens argues no. In his view, while it may be true in *my* perception (in the lower tier of reality) that "I am free" and "I am real," these statements are false according to *God's* perspective (in the higher tier of reality). People should still believe they are free and real, even though God knows these beliefs are false. Appealing to the practicality and relevance of these statements, he opines that their ultimate falsehood should not bother us. Why should we be concerned by the falsehood of the claims, if for all practical purposes, they are true in our everyday experience? (Lebens, *Principles of Judaism*, 98). However, I would argue that concern is justified. When learning that their practical everyday experience is ultimately false, Neo seeks to escape the Matrix, Truman seeks to escape Seahaven Island, and Plato's prisoners seek to escape the cave. There is something intuitively magnetic about ultimate truth claims that make practical

process before *tzimtzum* occurs, no observers besides *Ein Sof* could interpret *tzimtzum* as concealment. The *Sefirot* and humanity have not yet emanated. From whom is *tzimtzum* concealed, if not God himself—thus challenging his omniscience? How can the process of the nonexistent concealment continue if it has not begun? This is an example of an irrational nonsequential causation chain being hidden under metaphor and the limits of human epistemology.

Creation is very good. According to the Hebrew Scriptures, on the sixth day of creation, when the Creator completed his work, the God of Israel "saw everything that he had made, and behold, it was very good" (Gen 1:31).[61] According to this passage, it is not metaphysically evil for the material world to exist. Multiplicity is not a cosmic catastrophe. Rather, the Creator saw all the world's diversity, complexity, and multiplicity, and declared it to be *very good* (טוֹב מְאֹד, *tov me'od*).[62] In contrast, the Scriptures spend very little time talking about the metaphysical categories Kabbalah cares so much about—they are not even "on the radar," so to speak. The Scriptures do not define the problem with the cosmos as materiality or multiplicity, but rather as fallen morality (Gen 3; 6:5–6). Human beings have ruptured a good creation not by virtue of their existence as complex beings, but rather through the evil actions they choose to perform, from Adam and Eve on forward. By neglecting the moral problem and shifting the drama of the universe to metaphysics, Kabbalah misidentifies the human predicament.

It is unbiblical to believe that the cosmos needs release from its multiplicity. As a corollary to the goodness of creation (Gen 1:31), it is unbiblical to assert that the creation that existed in the first chapter of Genesis was fundamentally flawed. In Kabbalah, as with Gnosticism and Neoplatonism, multiplicity is evil, and physical things are the lowest of all evils. Salvation in these mystical systems involves shedding the multiplicity of

---

falsehoods unlivable.

61. Note that Gen 1:31 calls creation "very good," not "maximally optimal." This removes the burden of proving that a maximally good God would only create a maximally good or optimal world. Also, Genesis does not say, "Creation is very good *for the purpose of x*," as if the goodness of creation is not inherent within it but is based on some outside relation or telos. Creation as God created it was *ontologically* very good.

62. This point is best explained by the Trinitarian doctrine that God is both One and Many in a mysterious unity. If God is not Many, then multiplicity cannot be good. But if, as Genesis relates, multiplicity is good, then there is likely multiplicity within the unity of God. It is the analogy of the world's harmonious multiplicity compared to God's triune multiplicity that makes the world good.

Part II: A Critique of Non-Incarnational Maimonidean and Kabbalistic Thought

the body and reuniting with the oneness beyond the heavens. This idea is both foreign and antithetical to the Scriptures.

To conclude this series of arguments against Kabbalah's cosmological teachings, I quote from Jewish philosopher David Novak, who asks Kabbalah a series of similar questions and concludes that its solution for the human predicament is "a failed experiment."

> For Rabbi Hayyim Vital, Luria's chief disciple, the ultimate purpose of all human striving, through the commandments properly intended, is the return of human souls to their pre-*zimzum* union with God. But acceptance of this teleology poses a severe problem for Jewish theologians. For if God created finite multiplicity, why is it His and our goal to overcome it? Did God make a cosmic mistake? Is creation not really good after all, as the Gnostics maintained? Why should God have created it in the first place? Subordinating present relationality to future unification seems to negate the original goodness of God's act of creation and to cancel the worth of created beings. If creation is good, why should it be returned to its source? If creation is to be overcome, why create at all? Why should God have not left everything in its primordial unity? The challenge of Gnosticism is particularly telling for the Neoplatonism of Jews, Christians or Muslims, since their traditional theologies affirm *creatio ex nihilo*. When Kabbalah comes to share the same teleology, which animates so much of medieval theology, more theological problems arise than are solved. It is the demand for a return to pristine unity, I would argue, whether in Kabbalah or in the rationalist theology it attempted to surpass, that must now be set aside or bracketed as a failed experiment.[63]

In conclusion, in this chapter I have highlighted many theological, metaphysical, and scriptural problems related to Kabbalah's intertwined theology and cosmology. When understood correctly, creation *ex nihilo* prevents the kabbalistic story from beginning. The unfolding of *Ein Sof* through *tzimtzum* and the emergence of the physical world cannot be sustained when compared to the teachings of the Hebrew Scriptures. Instead, the Kabbalists received their vision of the cosmos through non-biblical historical processes and philosophical influences, which the next chapter critiques.

---

63. Novak, "Self-Contraction of Godhead," 314.

9   An Assessment of Lurianic Kabbalah's History, Predecessors, and Science

The Cabala is as completely dominated by Pythagoras—or rather by the Neopythagorean school.... [Kabbalah's] vital elements are always the Pythagorean number-symbolism on the one hand, and the Neoplatonic emanation-theory on the other.

—Ludwig Stein[1]

The fundamental ideas of the Cabala are un-Jewish, derived from Philo, the neo-Platonists and the neo-Pythagoreans; we sometimes even notice Gnostic influences. But the close amalgamation of these different elements with Biblical and Midrashic ideas has given to these foreign parts such a Jewish coloring, that at the first glance they appear as an emanation of the Jewish mental life.

—Bernhard Pick[2]

The Kabbalists were immensely successful in concealing whatever philosophical sources they used in the construction of their own theology.

—David Novak[3]

---

1. Stein, "Arabic-Jewish Philosophy," 2:47.
2. Pick, *Cabala*, 15.
3. Novak, "Self-Contraction of Godhead," 304.

Part II: A Critique of Non-Incarnational Maimonidean and Kabbalistic Thought

THE PREVIOUS CHAPTER ASSESSED the metaphysical teachings of Kabbalah with respect to their lack of internal logical consistency and their incompatibility with biblical revelation. In this chapter, I will assess Kabbalah primarily through the lens of history, specifically regarding its historical relationship with other philosophical systems and scientific schools.

9.1. History Argues against Kabbalah's Authority and Truthfulness

The ideas of historical cause and effect and progression are ingrained in the Western mind due to the influence of the Hebrew Scriptures. The biblical worldview includes a beginning, an end, and a linear series of events, prophecies, fulfillments, and accomplishments in between. The importance of history is most evident in the books called "historical books" by Christians and "Writings" (Ketuvim) in Judaism, but the Torah and the Prophets include a robust historical orientation as well.

Unfortunately, the cause-and-effect process of historical thinking is not encouraged in kabbalistic circles. Gershom Scholem writes, "Kabbalists themselves rarely attempt to attain a historical orientation."[4] Instead, they tend to make three moves. First, they flatten the various historical layers of their worldview into a simpler story of revelation given by God. At its most extreme, this tendency results in claiming that their teachings originate from the oral tradition given to Moses on Sinai. This notion encourages Kabbalists to ignore the historical progress and differentiation within Judaism throughout a three-thousand-year period. A second, less extreme anti-historical tendency is to accept as authoritative pseudepigraphal works that date from a much later period than the works themselves claim, thereby ignoring the historical developments between the two dates.

Modern Orthodox scholar Marc Shapiro explains a third move that keeps Orthodox Jewish people from "attaining a historical orientation." Shapiro writes that large segments of the Orthodox Jewish community, including many who accept Kabbalah, remain within a medieval mindset that mixes up history with heritage.[5] He cites David Lowenthal's distinction, as Lowenthal writes:

---

4. Scholem, "Kabbalah," 11:587–88.
5. M. Shapiro, *Changing the Immutable*, 1–7.

An Assessment of Lurianic Kabbalah's History, Predecessors, and Science

> Heritage should not be confused with history. History seeks to convince by truth, and succumbs to falsehood.... Heritage is immune to criticism because it is not erudition but catechism—not checkable fact but credulous allegiance. Heritage is not a testable or even plausible version of our past; it is a declaration of faith in the past. Loyalty and bonding demand uncritical endorsement and preclude dissent.[6]

It is not that Orthodox Jewish people do not care about the past or ignore the past. Absolutely not. Instead, many accept the account of the past handed to them by their communal authorities. For example, the modern Haredi educational system institutionalizes this method of "heritage, not history" by neglecting to teach general history courses in its schools.[7] What ought to happen, however, when the heritage passed on by the authorities conflicts with historical fact? Shapiro writes of Orthodox Judaism,

> There is often a tension between the quest for historical truth and the desire of communities of faith to pass on their religious message.... Before the rise of modern historical scholarship, this was an issue that rarely if ever came to the fore. Yet now, when we are so much more attuned to the past, and the study of history is an important part of our lives, there is no escaping the fact that "tradition" and history are often at odds with each other.[8]

As an outsider to the kabbalistic school of thought, and as one who has no allegiance to the "heritage" or catechized past as given in Orthodox circles, I find that turning toward a historical orientation can provide many avenues through which Kabbalah can be criticized. When one's head is "in the system," so to speak, and unaware of historical events outside the Kabbalist sphere of knowledge, Kabbalah's understanding of the past appears internally consistent. For those Kabbalists committed to the coherence view of truth, this internal consistency is all that is necessary to convince them of the truth of their worldview. However, once one steps out of the cave of kabbalistic shadows on the wall, it is no longer reasonable to accept the system. I find the following historical critiques to be problematic to the kabbalistic worldview:

---

6. Lowenthal, "Fabricating Heritage," 7–8.

7. Barron, "Closer Look"; K. Moore, "Ultra-Orthodox Rabbis." Also see the activist nonprofit group Yaffed, which is attempting to get Haredi yeshivas to include more "secular education" (https://yaffed.org/).

8. M. Shapiro, *Changing the Immutable*, 1.

Part II: A Critique of Non-Incarnational Maimonidean and Kabbalistic Thought

The late historical emergence of kabbalistic doctrines. Although there has been a continuous stream of mystical teachings in Judaism since at least the Mishnah, the distinctive teachings of Kabbalah did not emerge until the medieval period. Ideas such as *Ein Sof*, emanationism, *tzimtzum*, *Sefirot* as divine potencies, *klippot*, *gilgul*, and the *sod* interpretive method (along with PaRDeS) each have their historical emergence located on the medieval timeline of Jewish history. Before their emergence, they were unknown in Judaism and show up in no written documents; after their emergence, they are written down and discussed with increasing frequency. Some Kabbalists attempt to respond to this charge of anachronism by saying that these doctrines were merely *secret* oral traditions never revealed in writing before the medieval period. The plausibility of this arbitrary and non-evidenced response is low due to other factors that point to late dates, as will be discussed below.

Kabbalah's key mystical works gained acceptance before the rise of historical criticism, when people were more naïve about claims of antiquity. During the medieval period, many pseudepigraphal books and manuscripts circulated in the Christian, Islamic, and Jewish worlds. "Pseudepigraphal" means they were ascribed to an ancient respected author but in fact had been written much later by others. I previously described one work that had fooled Maimonides's generation: *The Theology of Aristotle* had not in fact been written by Aristotle, but rather by the Neoplatonist Plotinus. Many other books confused medieval writers in each of the major religions. A key Christian forgery, the Pseudo-Dionysian works, had been ascribed to one of the apostle Paul's associates, when in fact it had been produced by a sixth-century Christian Neoplatonist. It was not until the fifteenth-century rise of the Renaissance humanists (especially Lorenzo Valla's criticism of *The Donation of Constantine*) that scholars critically examined Western libraries for the purpose of rooting out forgeries.

Each of the three major kabbalistic books emerged before this development of historical criticism: *Sefer Yetzirah*, *Sefer Bahir*, and the *Zohar*. Two of the three grew in popularity in the twelfth and thirteenth centuries: *Sefer Bahir*, from the twelfth, claimed to be authored by Rabbi Nehunya ben Haqqanah, a first-century sage. *The Zohar*, from the late thirteenth century, claimed to be authored by Rabbi Shimon bar Yochai, a second-century sage. *Sefer Yetzirah*, which was known during the talmudic period, was ascribed to Abraham. Given the prevalence of pseudepigraphal religious works and many examples of how people could be fooled into accepting forgeries, the three major kabbalistic books should not be accepted as authentic solely on the basis of popular Jewish tradition. Indeed, on the basis of historical-critical principles, none of the three should be accepted as having been written by their purported authors.

The pseudepigraphal medieval authorship of the Zohar. When the *Zohar* emerged in Spanish circles in the late thirteenth century, it changed Kabbalah forever. One of the key factors that led to its acceptance was its attribution to Rabbi Shimon bar Yochai (Rashbi) of the second century. This attribution is almost universally rejected by Jewish scholarship today. Instead, its authorship is assigned to Spanish rabbi Moses de León (ca. 1240–1305). Scholar of Kabbalah Boaz Huss traces the history of criticism of the *Zohar*, and I will summarize his findings here.[9]

Rabbi Isaac of Acre, a contemporary of Moses de León, mockingly claimed that León fabricated the *Zohar* for gold while hanging from a tree as famously associated with Rashbi in the Talmud (b. Pesaḥ. 112a). After Moses de León's death, his wife was quoted as saying that her husband composed the book out of his own head, and that when she questioned him why he was writing in the name of Rashbi, he replied that no one would pay for his book otherwise. In the 1340s, Rabbi Joseph ibn Wakar gave a list of authoritative mystical books and left out the *Zohar*, claiming that it contained many mistakes and was misleading. Rabbi Elijah Del-Medigo in 1491 was the first to note that the *Zohar* was never referenced in the Talmud and includes anachronistic references to rabbis who lived after Rashbi. Del-Medigo gave instances where the *Zohar* disagreed with widely accepted halakah, which one would not expect of Rashbi. He also criticized the *Zohar* for its Platonism, which he knew had become influential in Jewish circles only within the previous three hundred years. Rabbi Elijah Bahur (1469–1549) criticized the *Zohar* for referring to cantillation and vocalization marks in biblical texts, which were not developed until much later than the second century. In 1639, Leon Modena wrote the first-ever monograph against the *Zohar*, entitled *Ari Nohem*.[10] Modena subjected the *Zohar* to philological analysis, highlighting phrases and puns common among Spanish rabbis of Moses de León's era. He placed the origin of Kabbalah after Maimonides's death and attributed it to "the vain ideas of Greek philosophy that entered the ears of some of our more recent sages, who renamed and arranged them according to their ideas, and referred to them as supreme holiness and

---

9. For the following paragraph, see Huss, *Zohar*, 239–93.
10. On Leon of Modena's work and reception, see Dweck, *Scandal of Kabbalah*.

the secrets of divinity."[11] In 1768, Rabbi Jacob Emden pointed out that the odd Zoharic phrase *ash noga* (synagogue) was derived from the Iberian word *esnoga*, that the *Zohar* included further anachronisms like references to Islam, and that the *Zohar's* description of the Holy Land was inaccurate. In the nineteenth century, many *Maskilim* (reformers) sought to discredit the authority of the *Zohar*. When Gershom Scholem began his scholarly career in Jewish mysticism, he initially accepted the *Zohar's* authorship by Rashbi. However, he soon came to repudiate that position, and in his *Major Trends in Jewish Mysticism*, he delivered an extended analysis for why Moses de León must be regarded as the author.[12] Few scholars question that conclusion today.

Kabbalah's key doctrines always postdate their emergence in pagan mysticisms. When key kabbalistic doctrines first emerged within Judaism, they could usually be found during a prior time in a similar or identical form in some pagan mysticism.[13] This point does not necessarily provide direct evidence that the doctrines are false. However, given what I discussed in §1.5, the initial emergence of these doctrines in pagan mysticisms should engender suspicion. In §7.8, I illustrated a variety of doctrines that are traceable to non-Jewish pagan sources in antiquity, and later in this chapter I will challenge their accuracy.

Contradictions between historical sources regarding Jewish mysticism. Jewish mysticism is not one thing, but rather a dynamic movement with various schools and a historical development discerned by scholars. Kabbalistic texts claim to have divine authority, either from Sinai, revered sages, angelic inspiration, or some combination of these divine origins. If so, one would expect that the mystical themes of the various eras of Jewish history would be coherent and noncontradictory. However, this is not the case. Before the doctrinal consolidation brought about by the *Zohar* after the thirteenth century, Jewish mysticism included a cacophony of voices that did not harmonize with each other. Scholem notes that the early kabbalistic period was distinctive for its variety of conceptual schemes.[14] I will highlight two contradictions here, beginning with the identification of the ten *Sefirot*.

11. Huss, *Zohar*, 253.
12. Huss, *Zohar*, 312–13.
13. Given the evidence of Philo, the possible Jewish sources of Gnosticism, and ancient claims of Platonic dependence upon Moses, this position requires some nuancing, which I handle in appendix D.
14. Scholem, "Kabbalah," 11:604.

Sefer Yetzirah was the first mystical text to teach that there are ten *Sefirot* and that they are responsible for the creation of the world. Here is how the ten *Sefirot* are described in that text: (1) spirit, (2) air, (3) water, (4) fire, and the six dimensions of (5) height, (6) depth, (7) east, (8) west, (9) south, and (10) north.[15] Clearly, in this text the *Sefirot* refer to physical properties and dimensions that are accessible to human senses. *Sefer Yetzirah* also appears to be dependent upon the scientifically invalid four elements theory of Greek physics (with "spirit" in the place of "earth"). In contrast, the *Zohar* and later Kabbalists take the concept of ten *Sefirot* but de-physicalize them, turning them into non-sensible higher realities that represent divine attributes. While both texts talk about the ten *Sefirot* responsible for the creation of the world, their definitions of the *Sefirot* are incompatible. This is a sign that one (or both) of these texts is wrong.

A second contradiction may be found with the kabbalistic PaRDeS scheme. Perhaps the greatest sage of the tenth century was Saadia Gaon (882–942), and in his *Book of Beliefs and Opinions* (*Emunot*), he gives his hermeneutical rules. Saadia favors the literal (*peshat*) interpretation at all times except when it contradicts known reality, reason, another text, or rabbinic tradition (*Emunot* 7.2). He states that no other exception but these four can justify nonliteral interpretations. He cleverly illustrates how the allegorical method can be used to twist a text into meaning anything, undermining both halakah and history (*Emunot* 7.4).[16] Thus, the greatest rabbinic sage of the tenth century had no place for the *sod* (mystical) interpretation, and he severely criticized the *remez* (allegorical) method, both of which are essential for Kabbalah. If kabbalistic interpretation existed during Saadia's time, originally given by Moses but remaining unwritten and known only by the greatest sages, why did this great sage reject its methods?

In sum, the kabbalistic tradition, when assessed from a historical angle, appears to be a novel medieval invention of broadly Platonic Jewish mystics who departed from the Jewish mysticism of previous generations. Contemporary Kabbalists have an ahistorical worldview that prioritizes heritage (folk myth) over the cause and effect of historical evidence. They mistakenly assume their mystical tradition goes back to Sinai, and they accept pseudepigraphal texts as authoritative. This obscures the many problems with the origin story of key kabbalistic ideas,

---

15. For other Jewish solutions to the fundamental constituents of the created universe, see Kohler, "Cosmogony."

16. L. Ginsburg, "Allegorical Interpretation," 1:407.

Part II: A Critique of Non-Incarnational Maimonidean and Kabbalistic Thought

which typically postdate the Greek philosophical themes upon which the Kabbalists drew. Thus, Kabbalah does not have the ancient ancestry it claims for itself, which undermines its grasp on truth.

9.2. Kabbalah's Troubling Philosophical Predecessors

Kabbalah can be understood as a cholent-like mixture of many streams of ancient Greek esoteric philosophies according to a Hebrew recipe, served from a halakically authorized hot plate.[17] The Greek background of Jewish mysticism often goes unnoticed because Kabbalah claims its origin from rabbinic sages, such as Shimon bar Yochai, or as far back as Adam himself.[18] On the contrary, much of Kabbalah's view of the world is drawn primarily from Neopythagoreanism (first century CE), Gnosticism (second to fourth centuries CE), and Neoplatonism (third century CE and later), rather than from the Hebrew Scriptures or early rabbis.[19] In other words, Kabbalah first trains Jewish people to be metaphysical disciples of Greeks such as Plato, Aristotle, Pythagoras, and Plotinus—as transmitted through Jewish authorities—and only when this is achieved may an adherent become a disciple of Moses and the sages.

Kabbalah represents a movement that often accepts minority positions on major philosophical and scientific questions, thereby keeping alive old ideas that mainstream philosophers have long discarded. In order to reasonably critique Kabbalah, it is not enough to merely point out Kabbalah's dependence upon prior philosophies I deem unfavorable—a "guilt by association" approach called the genetic fallacy. Rather, the particular doctrines of the systems must be critiqued as well. In this section,

---

17. Cholent is a traditional Ashkenazi stew prepared on Friday afternoons for a Shabbat meal. In modern Orthodox homes, the cholent is kept in a pot on a hot plate, which is left on throughout Shabbat. The use of the hot plate enables observant families to have hot food while not changing the state of electricity during the Sabbath. The cholent analogy encourages an investigation of the ingredients themselves, rather than just the resulting taste. No Orthodox family considers the experience of the food above all else, because there may be *treif* (nonkosher food) inside. In the same way, mystical experience should be investigated for counter-biblical ideas.

18. Dubov, "Adam."

19. "The Kabbalah, in its historical significance, can be defined as the product of the interpenetration of Jewish Gnosticism and neoplatonism" (Scholem, "Kabbalah," 11:603). In this remark, Scholem includes Neopythagoreanism as well, as he indicates elsewhere (*Origins of the Kabbalah*, ch. 1.4, loc. 687), since Neopythagoreanism was incorporated into Neoplatonism by the Middle Ages. For more on this theme, see §7.8 and Crawford, "Pathways," 179–84.

An Assessment of Lurianic Kabbalah's History, Predecessors, and Science

I will illustrate why individual ideas of Kabbalah—derived from pagan philosophical sources—should be rejected for the purpose of fidelity to the teachings of the Hebrew Scriptures.

9.2.1. Errors in Kabbalah's Neopythagoreanism

I find both Neopythagoreanism and Kabbalah erroneous in their numerology, *geometrikos*/gematria, the metaphysical importance of ten, their acceptance of ten spheres, and reincarnation.[20]

Pythagoras's erroneous metaphysical numerology. It is significant that Pythagoras discovered that musical octaves are dependent upon the mathematical ratio of two to one, as this anticipated the findings of Newton and Einstein that aspects of the universe are governed by mathematical laws. However, while the motion of Jupiter may be governed by mathematics, the love a father has for his daughter is not. Moreover, when physicists observe reality at the quantum level, the regularity of mathematics appears to give way to chaotic randomness. Numbers as a governing principle for all of reality does not hold, so it was illegitimate for Pythagoras to apply his musical discovery to all that exists. Philosopher Richard McKirahan writes, "This kind of generalization is typical of the early Presocratic period, where large theories about fundamental entities and mechanisms were typically grounded in a small number of examples."[21] Adding to the errors, the Pythagoreans conjectured that the planets emit numbers downward—the music of the spheres—which coalesce into physical stuff once they reach the low level of the earth. We now know that this notion is nonsense, both in its supposition of planetary music and its geocentric standpoint.

> *Related kabbalistic motifs:* Kabbalah teaches that the physical universe came into being through descending Hebrew letters (numbers) that continuously fall from the heavens. Every existing thing, at its core, is a series of Hebrew letters continuously spoken by God as with the music of the spheres. If the cosmological and inferential basis of the Pythagorean system is incorrect, so too is that of Kabbalah, which postdates the Pythagoreans and was derived from them. Additionally, the kabbalistic system results in cosmos-wide numerical determinism (as with a computer), for things cannot be or do anything except through the letters that God speaks. This removes human choice and any basis for morality, rewards, or punishments. A reductionist

---

20. Refer to §4.3 for the exposition of Neopythagoreanism.
21. McKirahan, "Philolaus on Number," 182.

Part II: A Critique of Non-Incarnational Maimonidean and Kabbalistic Thought

worldview is one that attempts to explain the phenomena of reality using a simple governing principle, and then resorts to ignoring parts of reality that do not fit the principle, or forces reality to conform to the principle rather than the other way around. It thereby reduces the sphere of reality from what actually exists to something lesser, making reality its enemy. Both Pythagorean thought and Kabbalah are reductionist worldviews in that they conform everything to numbers. Mathematics may be an important factor governing a portion of reality, but math does not govern all of reality.

Neopythagorean geometrikos *is false.* The Neopythagoreans mystified their cosmological system by using the Greek alphabet for mystical correspondences, incantations, and secret interpretations to understand and manipulate the numbers (letters) falling from the sky: *geometrikos arithmos*.[22] Without the mystical cosmology upon which *geometrikos* was based, the mathematical formulas applied to Greek words are meaningless, just random noise data with no correspondence to reality.

Related kabbalistic motifs: Kabbalah (and to a lesser extent, the earlier talmudic tradition) took the Neopythagorean *geometrikos* method and translated it into the Hebrew gematria.[23] The Hebrew Scriptures do not employ gematria for counting, but rather use discrete words to indicate numbers (see table 14). Thus, the practice of gematria for counting and interpretation is a postbiblical innovation. Without a numbers-infused metaphysical world, as with Pythagorean thought, gematria is meaningless—just random mathematical formulas without connection to reality, magical influence over the world, or prophetic insight into it. Furthermore, a *geometrikos* system with twenty-four Greek letters cannot be the accurate source of gematria with only twenty-two Hebrew letters, as the math does not line up. The same goes for *Sefer Yetzirah's* classification of Hebrew letters (and their mystical meanings) by their audible sounds, for these secret meanings do not line up with the Greek letters from which *Yetzirah* derived its linguistic ideas.[24]

---

22. The later gnostics took this concept and fused it to biblical interpretation. See Irenaeus *Haer.* 1.18 for an example of how the gnostics drew parallels between all the instances of "ten" in the Scriptures, supposedly as evidence for the metaphysical importance of ten.

23. Barry, *Greek Qabalah*.

24. For a gnostic example, see Irenaeus *Haer.* 1.14. See also L. Ginsburg, "Sefer Yezirah."

An Assessment of Lurianic Kabbalah's History, Predecessors, and Science

Moreover, gematria calculations on biblical passages require an inerrant Hebrew manuscript tradition where not one letter in the tradition is out of place (or else the math is altered). The sages of the Talmud knew that there was no such inerrant manuscript tradition (y. Ta'an. 4:2).[25] Modern textual criticism illustrates that the Masoretic text tradition—from which Kabbalists conduct their gematria calculations—has errors and must be corrected through consulting minority Masoretic manuscripts, the Dead Sea Scrolls, LXX, and other sources.[26] Finally, given the infinite potentialities of mathematical formulas that can be applied to the biblical text, a mathematician can come up with a formula to make any text mean whatever he wants, whether that text is the Bible or something more mundane.[27] In gematria, the meaning is generated by the mathematician's finite, biased manipulations, not given from the heavens.[28]

Table 14. Biblical Counting versus Gematria

	Biblical Counting Words[29]	Gematria (*Mispar Hekhrehi*)
One	אֶחָד—echad	א
Two	שְׁנַיִם—shenaim	ב
Three	שָׁלֹשׁ—shalosh	ג
Four	אַרְבַּע—arba	ד
...	Discrete words, not letters	Letters, not discrete words

25. Further examples: R. Akiva (b. Pesaḥ. 112a) and R. Ammi (b. Ketub. 19b) acknowledged the existence of scrolls that had not been proofread for accuracy. R. Meir kept a scroll that differed from the other sages (Gen. Rab. 9:5). The men of the Great Assembly altered some of the words of the Torah (Tanḥ., Yalkut Hamakhiri). For these and more examples of textual criticism in rabbinic Judaism, see M. Shapiro, *Limits of Orthodox Theology*, 91–121; Yuter, "Biblical Criticism."

26. See Tov, *Textual Criticism*.

27. Jewish scholar Jay Michelson considers the proliferation of "Bible codes" in the late 1990s due to Michael Drosnin's use of computer algorithms to find secret meanings in the Bible. This was a tech-infused update to kabbalistic hermeneutics. Michelson writes, "One reason that Bible Codes have gone out of fashion is that mathematicians and statisticians have thoroughly, completely and convincingly disproved them" ("Bible Codes," para. 3).

28. For discussion about supposed gematria in the NT, see appendix E.

29. The biblical Hebrew numbering system is a bit more complex than this column's simplification, as there are masculine, feminine, and construct forms of the numbers in Scripture. Nevertheless, each of the Scriptures' numerical forms are discrete words that are variations of the Hebrew spellings given in this column.

Part II: A Critique of Non-Incarnational Maimonidean and Kabbalistic Thought

The Neopythagorean "ten" in the tetraktys *is contrived.* The Neopythagoreans identified the number ten as the basis of all reality due to their idea of a pyramidal four-three-two-one *tetraktys*. This is a superficially interesting theory that collapses under its own arbitrariness. The four steps of the pyramid may describe all possible *geometrical* reality (solid, plane, line, point), but it is arbitrary to stop at geometry, and also arbitrary to associate each geometric dimension with a number that has any metaphysical meaning. Why not include a fifth step to the pyramid, symbolized by the number five, which represents temperature? Or electric charge? Or velocity, or acceleration? Why not have fifteen levels?[30] Or, why not assign each of the four levels to the number one, leading to a sum of four instead of ten? If the number ten is an arbitrary and unjustified principle for the governance of reality, then certainly any correspondences with it are devoid of metaphysical importance. It is a nice coincidence that Aristotle offered ten categories for analyzing the qualitative and quantitative states of reality, but he could have come up with a different number of categories, and in any case, there is no justification for pairing Aristotle's categories with cosmic ten-ness.

The ten Neopythagorean spheres are false. Aristotle points out that the Pythagoreans' obsession with ten led them to conform reality to their theory, rather than the other way around (*Cael.* 2.13). He notes that only nine celestial spheres were visible,[31] so the Pythagoreans needed to conjecture an invisible tenth sphere to make their ten have cosmological correspondence. Aristotle rejected this as spurious. Of course, he was right in his judgment, but given his geocentrism and belief in the other nine "spheres," Aristotle did not recognize the depth to which the Pythagorean cosmology was incorrect.

> *Related kabbalistic motifs*: The number ten in the Greek mystical tradition allured the kabbalistic mystics as well. No one has certainty about the origin of the word *Sefirot* (sg., *Sefirah*), but the Greek σφαίρα (*sphaira*, sphere, with the *ph* phonetically changed to *f*) is a reasonable candidate along with other similar-sounding words.[32] The first Jewish text to show Neopythagorean

---

30. Aristotle also criticized the Pythagoreans for the arbitrariness of assigning the concepts of "right" and "left" with meaning, while leaving other concepts unassigned any meaning (*Cael.* 2.2).

31. Moon, Mercury, Venus, Sun, Mars, Jupiter, Saturn, fixed stars, Earth. The Pythagoreans added "Counter-Earth" as the tenth.

32. The etymology of *Sefirah* (ספירה) is contested. Scholars have suggested ספר (*safor*), which means "to count," and ספיר (*sappir*), which means "sapphire." However,

motifs, *Sefer Yetzirah*, identifies ten *Sefirot* as the constitution of physical reality, just as the Neopythagoreans identified ten spheres as the constitution of physical reality. In the later Kabbalah and the *Zohar*, the ten *Sefirot* were de-physicalized and turned into the metaphysical source of multiple layers of reality. They still retained hints of their Greek origin: (1) In the initial *sefirotic* scheme of the *Iggulim*, the *Sefirot* were set within themselves like spherical layers of an onion. This initial configuration of the *Sefirot* was essentially a metaphysical rendering of the Aristotelian-Ptolemaic geocentric universe, which was eventually proven false.[33] (2) The false Pythagorean concept of the "music of the spheres" was retained in two ways. First, the *Sefirot*, commonly depicted as spheres, are said to interpenetrate each other and balance each other with a perfect harmony among them, just as with the inaudible harmony of the music emanating from the planets in Pythagorean thought. Second, Kabbalah retained the idea that the universe owes its existence to Hebrew letters (numbers) continuously falling from the highest heavens, down to the lowest region, Earth. This is an erroneous geocentric model of the cosmos that imports Pythagoras's conjectural overreach about numbers constituting reality. Kabbalah's dependence upon Neopythagoreanism's spurious metaphysical ten-ness, the music of the spheres, and its geocentric-influenced model of the *Sefirot* are examples of its false metaphysical foundations.

Reincarnation is based on false cosmology and is opposed by the Hebrew Scriptures. The Pythagoreans taught that the divine sparks constituting the human soul ascend after death past the planets to be judged. Afterward, they return downward past the planets to be placed in a new body that matches the soul's philosophical attainment. The Pythagoreans added a mystical cosmological element to this scheme, whereby the

---

in mysticism, where patterns and correspondences are important, it is unlikely that the etymology should stop at a single answer. The audible similarity between the Hebrew roots with the Greek *sphaira* could have merged the multiple meanings. Namely, the *Sefirot* are sapphire-like spheres that are counted to ten. Gershom Scholem opposed accepting the Greek *sphaira* as etymologically related to the *Sefirot*. However, on the basis of the astronomical descriptions and depictions of Kabbalist authors, J. H. Chajes demonstrates that the relationship between Greek astronomical science and kabbalistic *Sefirot* should not be ignored (Scholem, "Sefirot"; Broydé, "Ten Sefirot"; Chajes, "Spheres, Sefirot").

33. See Chajes for many more examples of descriptions and depictions in kabbalistic literature that reflect the Aristotelian-Ptolemaic cosmological paradigm ("Spheres, Sefirot").

"seven heavens" of the planetary spheres (the Hebdomad) confer benefits to the souls that pass through. All of this is based on an inaccurate geocentric cosmological vision. We now know there are no planetary spheres of spiritual material, and the myth of the seven heavens is false.

Outside of cosmological critiques, the idea of reincarnation also contradicts the biblical account. The Hebrew Scriptures are not silent about the afterlife, and they do not support the idea of reincarnation in the metaphysical sense employed in Pythagorean and kabbalistic thought. The Hebrew vision for the future is resurrection at the end of the age (Dan 12:2; Ezek 37), which is a one-time-only reunification of human souls with new physical bodies. The unitary nature of Hebrew resurrection speaks against the repeated reincarnations of the Greek mystics.[34] Moreover, the Hebrew Scriptures (and the NT[35]) portray the afterlife in ways that leave no room for any cosmic machinery that produces reincarnations.

For example, King Saul sins by consulting a necromancer to "bring up" the prophet Samuel from the dead to speak with him (1 Sam 28:8). Samuel had not yet received a new body, but remained in the realm of the dead. Why would a prophet of the stature of Samuel have not already ascended into the pleroma (unification with God), outside of the necromancer's reach, or immediately been given a new body on account of his stature? After the necromancer summons Samuel through her magic arts, Samuel chastises Saul for having her do so (1 Sam 28:15). His disapproval for being "brought up" is inconsistent with reincarnation, for Samuel being brought back to the physical world should have been seen as a good thing: it would have enabled him to have a new life on Earth and thus take one step closer to ascending to the pleroma. This is an example of the incompatibility between the repetitive here-and-back-again cosmic machinery of reincarnation and the biblical account.

> *Related kabbalistic motifs*: The kabbalistic doctrine of *gilgul* is a version of Pythagorean reincarnation with strong gnostic elements. Gershom Scholem writes, "There is no definite proof of the existence of the doctrine of *gilgul* in Judaism during the

---

34. Orthodox Judaism has a parallel debate between resurrection over reincarnation. The pro-resurrection position, which Segal and Lebens call "devotionalism," is the one promoted by the NT, especially in 1 Cor 15. The contrasting position, "intellectualism," is the Greek-influenced position that makes the resurrection a "sideshow" (Lebens's terminology) (Aaron Segal, "Immortality," 152–53; Lebens, *Principles of Judaism*, 235–36).

35. Luke 16:19–31; 2 Cor 5:8; 12:1–6; Phil 1:23; Heb 9:27; Rev 6:9; 19:20.

Second Temple Period. In the Talmud there is no reference to it.... The major Jewish philosophers rejected this doctrine.... In contrast with the conspicuous opposition of Jewish philosophy, metempsychosis [*gilgul*] is taken for granted in the Kabbalah."[36] For example, Saadia Gaon made an impassioned attack against reincarnation centuries before the rise of Kabbalah, calling it nonsense and stupidity (*Emunot* 6.8). Thus, the medieval Kabbalists resurrected the idea of reincarnation from the ancient Greek mystery philosophies, in opposition to all prior Jewish tradition. The new acceptance of *gilgul* may have been prepared by the earlier Merkavah mysticism, which encouraged Jewish mystics to participate in soul flight past the seven spheres using secret codes to get past the archons associated with each planet.[37] In order to result in *gilgul*, the Merkavah tradition simply needed to be extended beyond the one life of the mystic into planetary trips after death.

9.2.2. Errors in Kabbalah's Gnosticism

Gnosticism is a kind of rebellion against the cosmos, and the church fathers contended that it was a parasite on top of the Jewish, Christian, and Platonic ideologies it drew from. The second-century Christian apologist Irenaeus wrote of the gnostics, "Each one of them, as far as he is able, thinks up every day something more novel. None of them is perfect if he does not produce among them the greatest lies."[38] As I have written previously, the Greek mystical philosophies tend to blend into one another. I have already criticized aspects of Gnosticism that first originated in Pythagorean thought. In this section, I will focus on teachings that are most closely associated with Gnosticism, such as the weakness of the gnostic deity, creation as a catastrophe, sexualized emanationism, the practice of theurgy, the ideas of divine sparks and esotericism, and unsourced syncretism.[39]

The god of Gnosticism is weak, not like the God of the Bible. Gnosticism teaches that a rebellious or ignorant aeon (divine angel) escaped from the divine pleroma and created the physical universe against the highest god's wishes. This highest god is incomplete without emanating

---

36. Scholem, "Gilgul," 7:602.

37. While there is a superficial resemblance between this soul-flight motif and Paul's experience in 2 Cor 12:2–4, the metaphysics, cosmology, and purpose of Paul's experience differ. See appendix E.

38. Irenaeus, *Haer.* 1.18; Irenaeus of Lyons, *Against the Heresies* (ed. Dillon), 1:72.

39. Refer to §4.4 for the exposition of Gnosticism.

its pleroma of aeons and indeed is dependent upon them. This god is impersonal (not a "he") and is aloof from the material world. The gnostic god is not sovereign or all-powerful over the universe, or else it would not have allowed a rupture of the perfect pleroma or the creation of the material world in rebellion against its wishes.[40] Consequently, the god of Gnosticism is a weak, unknowable, distant deity that loses control of the cosmos, has no purpose for its creation, and is indifferent to the plight of physical beings.

> *Related kabbalistic motifs*: When viewed from a lower, human angle, Kabbalah teaches that *Ein Sof* concealed and contracted itself in *tzimtzum* (a lessening of itself), and that the *Sefirot* were not complete until there were ten within itself (*Ein Sof* is dependent on the ten), and that it lost control of its light within the *Sefirot* (a catastrophe), leading to the emergence of physicality (which is evil). All of these, when viewed from a human angle, make *Ein Sof* appear to be weak, non-sovereign, dependent, and contaminated with evil *klippot*. According to some kabbalistic authorities, God's power may be weakened, even separating him from his attributes, when Israel sins.[41] Some Kabbalists respond by saying all this is metaphor, and none of these things have *really* happened to *Ein Sof*. However, this response is irrational, as explained in §8.4.3. In addition, since the human angle is the only angle we have, the god of Kabbalah appears to be a lesser god, less worthy of worship and obedience, when compared to the God of the Hebrew Scriptures, who is the cosmic King and LORD and sovereign over all (Ps 103:19; 1 Chr 29:11), whose angelic ministers never act outside his knowledge and jurisdiction (Job 1:6–12), and who is so nondependent upon the created order that he can say, "I the Lord do not change" (Mal 3:6; cf. Ps 102:27).

---

40. A biblical worldview must struggle with the problem of evil, how the first being sinned against God (Satan/the serpent), and how God's sovereignty relates to human sin and catastrophes. However, these struggles assume that creation is a good creation by a good God and that God will repair what has gone wrong. Gnosticism, in contrast, defines the entire universe as a cosmic mistake and evil in its own existence. Whereas the sovereign God of the Hebrew Scriptures has a plan to restore and redeem his corrupted creation, the god of Gnosticism has no such power, plan, or interest.

41. Eduard Shyfrin writes, "By committing evil and not obeying the laws and statutes of the Almighty, a person weakens the power of God. The sages suggested that the power of Divine attributes depends on the actions of man. According to the view of Rabbi Bahya ben Asher, man's failure to carry out the will of Heaven leads to the Almighty being distanced from His attributes (the system of *sefirot*)" (*From Infinity to Man*, 49).

An Assessment of Lurianic Kabbalah's History, Predecessors, and Science

Creation as a divine catastrophe conflicts with the biblical accounts. The gnostics hated the physical world because they saw it as the production of an evil, ignorant demiurge that distracted people from the delights of the pleroma above. The gnostics held to a philosophy of distrust and cosmic conspiracy theories. They refused to trust their eyes, because they saw the physical world as evil. They did not trust their ears, because everything was trying to deceive them. They did not trust human institutions, because they were corrupt. They did not trust anyone except the one divine teacher they chose to follow as the conduit to the pleroma above. All these ideas are contradicted by two Hebrew words: *tov me'od*. Genesis 1:31 says, "God saw everything that he had made, and behold, it was *very good* [טוֹב מְאֹד, *tov me'od*]." God made the created order directly himself and it was originally ontologically very good according to God's own design (Jer 31:35; Ps 8).[42] It was not a creation wrought by deceit and corruption, as if creation deceives the created beings who perceive it. No, in the biblical account, the original state of creation was beautiful and holy, for it was lovingly created by a beautiful and holy God.

> *Related kabbalistic motifs*: The shattering of the vessels that resulted in the reconfiguration of the *Sefirot* and the descent of the *klippot* into the lower regions was a catastrophe that happened within *Ein Sof*. It is a situation that must be remedied, according to Kabbalah, through Israel's partnership in releasing the *klippot* through Torah observance. God is shattered into pieces of brilliant light and needs Israel's help to reunify him in a process called *tikkun olam*. Such a catastrophe is never hinted at in the Hebrew Scriptures, nor is the belief that humans need to escape the physical universe because its very nature is evil. On the contrary, the Scriptures present the physical universe initially as very good, created according to design (not catastrophically) by a good God, who will redeem and restore the brokenness of the world that was eventually brought about by human sin (Gen 3; 6:5–6; 12:1–3; Isa 65:17).

The sexualized emanationism of Gnosticism and Kabbalah is fantasy. The gnostics tended to classify everything in polarities (dualism) such as light/dark, good/evil, male/female. The gnostic aeons in the world above (the pleroma) are examples of "syzygies" (pairs) that combine in perfect

---

42. Ancient Jewish affirmations of the good order of creation include: Sir 16:26–29; 1 En. 2:1—5:3; 69:20–21; Pss. Sol. 18:11–14; Odes Sol. 16:13–19; 2 Bar. 48:9.

fashion to produce further effects.[43] Using the concept of "as above, so below," they taught that this dualism exists down on Earth as well.[44] The goal of the gnostics was to reunify the polarities in the world below (kenoma) into their original non-dual state. Human sexuality was seen as a pattern of the world above and a means through which the world could be restored (i.e., when male and female unite [Irenaeus, *Haer.* 1.21.3]). The gnostic texts of Nag Hammadi said that the world would not be restored until all twos are made one, including all distinctions of male and female transcending into a higher oneness.[45]

This sexualization of heaven above and the metaphysical meaning of sexuality below were fabrications on the part of the gnostics. Although there are indeed pairings and opposites in the universe God created,[46] there is no empirical evidence that the world ought to be structured in polarities from top to bottom. As Saadia Gaon argued, there are many things in the world that escape classification in pairs (*Emunot* 2.2). What is the counterpart of the number pi (π), the pair of the gravitational constant, the opposite of the scent of lavender, and the match for time? As none of these concepts fits into a binary system, cosmic dualism is a forced view of reality. In addition, the Scriptures give no indication that the creation of Eve from Adam's rib (Gen 2:21–22) was a bad thing (the gnostics attributed this to an evil deity),[47] nor that the sexual union has some kind of metaphysical purpose or effect on the cosmos or the reunification of the human soul.

---

43. Irenaeus, *Haer.* 1.11.1. For example, Thunder: Perfect Mind states the following dualistic paradoxes from the divine: "I am the first and the last. . . . I am the whore and the holy one. I am the wife and the virgin. . . . I am the barren one and many are her sons. I am she whose wedding is great, and I have not taken a husband. . . . I am the mother of my father and the sister of my husband and he is my offspring" (*NHL* 6.2).

44. For a Christian gnostic example of this unbiblical idea, see *Pseudo-Clementine Homilies* 3.33.

45. Gos. Thom. 22: "When you make the two one, and when you make the inside like the outside and the outside like the inside, and the above like the below, and when you make the male and the female one and the same, so that the male not be male nor the female female . . . then will you enter [the kingdom]" (*NHL* 2.2). See also Gos. Phil. 68:22–26; 70:9–22 (*NHL* 2.3); Exeg. Soul 133:4–9 (*NHL* 2.6).

46. The Hebrew Scriptures describe polarities like man and woman, light and darkness, good and evil, clean and unclean, and many others. However, just because polarities can accurately describe *some* aspects of creation, it does not follow that polarities describe *all* aspects of creation.

47. Ap. John 22:3—23:4 (*NHL* 2.1).

Related kabbalistic motifs: Kabbalah takes the sexualized theological vision of Gnosticism and deepens it even further. In his forward to a book on the *Zohar*, Andrew Harvey writes, "Kabbalists believe that no human being can be completely divine, unless, like the original Adam, he or she fuses within himself masculine power and feminine sensitivity on every level of being and in every activity."[48] Thus, sexual combinations become a pathway to divinity and salvation. For example, references to "the divine phallus" abound in the works of Kabbalah according to Jewish mysticism scholar Elliot Wolfson.[49] These unbiblical motifs applied to God originate from Kabbalah's false notion of "as above, so below," specifically in its depiction of the *Sefirot* in a man-shaped tree of life (*Adam Kadmon*). If man is in the shape of the *Sefirot*, which are aspects of God, then necessarily each human body part—including genitalia—has its correlation in heaven. Religious readers of the Bible should reject the kabbalistic version of sexualized theology for the same reasons they reject the gnostic forerunner.

Theurgy is denounced as sorcery in the Scriptures. Through their maxim "as above, so below," the gnostics and practitioners of the Hermetic literature brought the divine realm down to Earth so they could manipulate the divine to obtain their desired effects (theurgy). By viewing the universe as an interconnected whole with patterns and correspondences in the divine realms, every action on Earth or in the heavens has its counterpart in the divine realm, as well as the angelic and demonic realms. This worldview motivates the practice of astrology (for determining prophecies, omens, and personalities) and the practice of magical arts such as incantations, amulets, and more.

The Hebrew Scriptures explicitly deny the cosmological basis of theurgy and reject its practice. There is no biblical support for an exhaustive metaphysical mirroring between heaven and earth, nor the idea that the divine nature may be influenced by combinations and manipulations of physical objects. God is not dependent upon physical things nor actualized by the working of physical things. Instead, the divine and the created are radically distinct due to creation *ex nihilo*. Thus, the worldview behind gnostic theurgy is removed from the biblical vision. The impulse to practice theurgy is explicitly negated in the Scriptures (Exod 22:18; Deut 18:10–12; 2 Chr 33:6) and implicitly negated through the biblical

---

48. Matt, *Zohar*, xiii.
49. Wolfson, *Through Speculum That Shines*, 274.

Part II: A Critique of Non-Incarnational Maimonidean and Kabbalistic Thought

admonitions and examples to *pray* and *petition* the sovereign LORD of the universe, rather than cajole and manipulate him (or angels and demons) through mystical and magical means.

> *Related kabbalistic motifs*: The main aspect of Kabbalah I have responded to up to this point has been its theosophy, that is, its mystical understanding of the divine nature and its emanations into the physical world. However, I have said little about the theurgical, magical, and superstitious aspects of what is called the "practical Kabbalah" or *Kabbalah Ma'asit*. In the more Reform-minded (Enlightenment-driven) *Jewish Encyclopedia*, Joseph Jacobs highlights many examples of common Jewish superstitions, primarily drawn from the times of the Talmud and Jacobs' contemporaries in the early twentieth century.[50] Other more or less academic descriptions of Jewish and kabbalistic magical practices are available in the literature.[51] Historically, the Christian moral and theological aversion to kabbalistic magic and superstition has been used as an anti-Semitic theme to attack Jews as a whole. Out of respect for the dignity of Jewish people I will decline to discuss or criticize kabbalistic theurgy any further than saying that it is prohibited by the Torah and, in my opinion, should be opposed by all forms of Judaism.

Fallen divine sparks—elitist or otherwise—are unbiblical. A central idea of pagan mysticisms is that human beings are sparks of divinity that have fallen from the higher realms into the physical prison of the body. Gnosticism accepted this idea but turned it inward to an esoteric, elitist doctrine: not all people have the divine sparks, but only the chosen few, called the "pneumatics." Only they, the few who have accepted the secret *gnosis*, will ascend into the pleroma.[52] All others are condemned to a meaningless existence, trapped in the physical world with no chance of escape. Because the non-pneumatics had a sealed fate, the gnostics actively cloaked their teachings in riddles to confuse outsiders and shield their true teachings from opponents.

There are two aspects to be argued against here: the idea of divine sparks, and the idea of religious truth needing to be hidden using esoteric mysteries. The concept of divine sparks depends upon a panentheistic or pantheistic vision of the world and the concepts of emanations and

---

50. J. Jacobs, "Superstition."
51. Harari et al., "Magic"; Dennis, *Encyclopedia of Jewish Myth*.
52. Irenaeus *Haer.* 1.24.2.

gradations of the divine being descending to the physical world. Neither of these is taught in Scripture, and both actively contradict creation *ex nihilo* (see §8.4.1). The idea of the need to hide religious knowledge from other human beings is present in Scripture in limited instances (Isa 6:9–10; Dan 8:26; 12:4–10),[53] but the overriding thrust of Scripture is that all people should be told plainly about who God is and what he expects of them. Moreover, the Scriptures present God as the sovereign LORD of Israel who, in his transcendent wisdom, decides when someone should not hear the truth about himself (i.e., he hardens people's hearts).[54] It is not the prerogative of mere human beings to dictate who may hear and who may not and to cloak truths of salvation in riddles.

> *Related kabbalistic motifs*: Kabbalah accepts the "divine sparks" idea and also its elitist gnostic twist. The unique feature of some kabbalistic ideology (particularly in Chabad) is that the Jewish people have a unique *neshama* (soul) that gentiles do not, and this *neshama* is a spark of the divine and ensures Israel's perpetuity and spiritual blessedness.[55] Whether or not a Kabbalist believes that he has an extra soul that gentiles do not have, Kabbalah does teach that one may uncover one's own divinity through performance of the mitzvot, which Jewish people perform more than gentiles. Thus, through their Torah observance, Jewish people actualize their divinity, whereas gentiles have little opportunity to do so. This idea takes the true biblical concept of the "chosen people" based on God's covenants with Abraham, Isaac, Jacob, Moses, and David, and corrupts it in a panentheistic and metaphysical direction. A counter to these ideas is the Hebrew Scriptures' repeated affirmation of the value of the gentiles' praise and worship of the God of Israel.[56]

---

53. Also see Matt 7:6 and related commentaries on the wisdom of withholding information temporarily.

54. Exod 4:21; Deut 2:30; Josh 11:20; Isa 6:9–10; 63:17.

55. For example, from a contemporary Chabad rabbi: "Every Jew shares the same experience of G-d and his essence is a literal part of G-d" (Gurary, *Thirteen Principles of Faith*, 3). The ontological status of gentiles is not mentioned in Gurary's book.

56. Gen 12:3; 1 Kgs 8:60; Ps 47:8–9; 68:32; 96:1–9; 98:2–3; 102:15, 22; 117:1; Is 12:4–5; 14:1; 25:6; 51:5; 52:10; 56:6–8; 60:3; Ezek 3:6; Zeph 3:9–10; Zech 2:11; 9:7; 14:16–19; Mal 1:11. Paul makes an exegetical argument that the sequence of Genesis indicates that Abraham is the father of all Jews by the covenant of circumcision (not by metaphysical ontology) and also the father of all gentiles who have faith like Abraham, who was a gentile before the circumcision (Rom 4:9–12). Paul's view affirms ontological equality of humans (Gen 1:26) while grounding difference in contingent covenantal promises.

Part II: A Critique of Non-Incarnational Maimonidean and Kabbalistic Thought

Unsourced syncretism used as "divine revelation" to deceive the gullible. Ancient Gnosticism styled itself as new divine revelation from chosen teachers such as Basilides, Valentinus, and Markos. Their impressive, complicated, intricate metaphysical and moral systems had a degree of success among the Christians and Jews of the second and third centuries CE. In vehement response, the early Christian apologists argued that the impressive nature of the gnostics' teachings was not due to its novelty, but rather due to the gnostics' ability to sell their system as new ideas to gullible people who did not know otherwise. Irenaeus complains, "They boast of being originators and authors of this sort of imagined fabrication by changing the name."[57] The gnostics syncretized with previous worldview systems, covered up their intellectual sources, and claimed divine revelation for their ideas. This was intellectual theft posing as secret religion. The Christian apologists therefore relished in the opportunity to point out the source of gnostic ideas on behalf of the gnostic leaders, thereby pulling the rug out from their claims to new divine revelation.[58]

> *Related kabbalistic motifs*: Kabbalah is averse to the concept of an accurate footnote. It is a patchwork of pagan mysticisms cloaked in the Hebrew language, convincing many who lack a historical orientation in their Judaism. When there was not an actual verifiable Jewish source for their teachings, the Jewish mystics fabricated pseudepigraphal writings to provide the "historical source." These fabricated writings—such as *Sefer Yetzirah*, *Sefer Bahir*, and the *Zohar*—deeply integrate gnostic, Pythagorean, and Neopythagorean metaphysical concepts, but none of the works credit the various Greek mysticisms for their ideas. To do so would have been to admit that the ideas were pagan and did not originate from the Written Torah, or from the oral tradition from Sinai, or from the Hebrew prophets. By way of contrast, Maimonides often cites the sources of his ideas, and he may be excused for falling prey to the pseudepigraphal *Theology of Aristotle*, as all in his generation fell for it.

---

57. Irenaeus, *Haer*. 2.14.3; Irenaeus of Lyons, *Against the Heresies* (ed. Dillon), 2:49. Also see Irenaeus's analogy of the "fictitious cloak" in 2.14.2.

58. In *Haer*. 2.14, Irenaeus traces the gnostic doctrines back to Democritus, Epicurus, Anaxagoras, Empedocles, Plato, the Stoics, Hesiod, and the Pythagoreans. This is criticism of mystical thought through historical investigation of the source of ideas. The argument against Kabbalah throughout this book stands in the same Irenaean tradition.

An Assessment of Lurianic Kabbalah's History, Predecessors, and Science

9.2.3. Errors in Kabbalah's Neoplatonism

Kabbalah deeply integrates the ideas of Neoplatonism into its metaphysical system. Concepts such as *Ein Sof*, emanations, *via negativa*, divine sparks, philosophy as salvation, and cosmic return to singularity are all typical of Neoplatonism (see §4.5). However, the Neoplatonism that Plotinus delivered to the West was strongly related to the broadly Platonic metaphysics of the Pythagorean and gnostic systems before him. Additionally, as Plotinus's successors expanded his system (such as Porphyry, Iamblicus, and Proclus), they continued integrating previous mysticisms into the Neoplatonic tradition. Consequently, there are few aspects of Neoplatonism remaining to critique that have not already been addressed above. I refer the reader to the following table for the sections that respond to the kabbalistic positions that relate to Neoplatonism:

Table 15. Critiques of Neoplatonic Themes in Kabbalah

Neoplatonic Theme	Refer to Section:
The One and *Ein Sof*	8.4 and especially 8.4.3
Emanations from the One/*Ein Sof*	8.4 and especially 8.4.3
Panentheism and creation *ex nihilo*	8.4.1 and 8.4.2
Multiplicity as evil	8.4.3
Cosmos has divine sparks within it	8.4 and 9.2.2
Comprehensive *via negativa*	6.6
No idolatry in panentheism	8.4.3

9.3. Scientific Critiques of Kabbalah

For my concluding critique, I will investigate various challenges modern science poses to Kabbalah's worldview. However, before continuing, I must do my best to avoid anachronism and stacking the deck in my favor by using the term "science." While this term is ubiquitous in modern discourse, it gained widespread use only in the nineteenth century, when it replaced the phrase "natural philosophy." Today, science usually refers to the pursuit of knowledge of the physical world through the "scientific method" of hypotheses tested through experimentation. In previous eras, this was the domain of philosophers.[59] Moreover, there were differ-

---

59. The Christian philosopher Francis Bacon (1561–1626) was the first to set forth

ent schools of "natural philosophy," such that it was controversial as to what constituted natural philosophy and what did not.

For example, the study of physical movement was first carried out by Aristotle in his *Physics*. This subject forms a key pillar of the contemporary scientific pursuit, now dominated by the reformulations of Newton, Einstein, and Schrödinger. However, other "natural philosophers" studied different physical phenomena under the guise of magic, alchemy, and astrology. Do those count as science? The extent to which a twenty-first-century reader answers, "No, obviously," is the extent to which Aristotelian science has arisen to contemporary dominance over the science of Plato.[60] It is important to distinguish these two types of investigation of the world.

9.3.1. Distinguishing Two Types of "Science" in Judaism

In her chapter "Kabbalah and Science in the Middle Ages," Hava Tirosh-Samuelson contrasts the Aristotelian and Platonic methods of science and comments on their relationship with Maimonides and Kabbalah. I agree with her view that Maimonides supports the Aristotelian scientific method, derived from his single-tiered metaphysics, and that Kabbalah supports the Platonic scientific method, derived from his double-tiered metaphysics.[61] Tirosh-Samuelson writes,

> The difference between the two programs boiled down to the differences between Aristotle and Plato with regard to the definition of scientific knowledge. For the Jewish Aristotelians, science (i.e., natural philosophy) meant a causal explanation of the physical world on the basis of sensory perception and observation; for the kabbalists, in accord with the Platonic view, the physical world was only a metaphor of reality, a reflection of intelligible forms that cannot be perceived by the senses.[62]

Thus, the Kabbalists followed the broad Platonic pattern of rejecting the physical shadows on the cave wall in preference for the unseen world

---

the modern theory of the scientific method in his *New Organon*, which cast itself as a new method for study of the world, replacing Aristotle's *Organon* (Bartholomew and Goheen, *Christian Philosophy*, 115–17).

60. For an account of the history of science and its interrelationship with various philosophical movements, see Pearcey and Thaxton, *Soul of Science*.

61. On the definitions of these two metaphysical understandings, see §4.1.4 for Plato and §4.2.1 for Aristotle.

62. Tirosh-Samuelson, "Kabbalah and Science," 497.

outside. Why study the misleading metaphors of shadowy physical things when one can instead study the higher truths of immaterial things?[63] In their view, only the study of the emanated *Sefirot* of *Ein Sof* constituted science, and the study of the physical world was of much lesser value. Tirosh-Samuelson continues, speaking of Kabbalah:

> The corporeal world of nature only mirrors the divine; given the low status of empirical knowledge in the ontological order, empirical knowledge of the sensible world is not scientific. So even though the kabbalists were attentive to a whole array of physical phenomena, they did not value the physical world for its own sake and did not consider knowledge of physical things to have moral and religious value in the pursuit of perfection. Furthermore, the very materiality of the sensible world is a source of error and even evil. At best, the material world should be spiritualized through observance of the commandments, thereby transcending its material limitation. Such a negative attitude toward the physical world is not conducive to interest in natural phenomena.[64]

On the one hand, it is technically incorrect to state that Kabbalah is "anti-science," but rather an opponent of *Aristotelian* natural science, and a proponent of *Platonic* science, which focuses on the unseen realm while demoting the seen. On the other hand, there are three significant ways in which Kabbalah deserves to be called "anti-science." First, to the extent that kabbalistic descriptions of the unseen realm are false, Kabbalah is "anti-science" even under the Platonic definition (see below). Second, to the extent that the Platonic paradigm for science is invalid (which I believe it is), Kabbalah's approach to science is unworthy of the name. Third, to the extent that Kabbalah's understanding of natural phenomena conflicts with modern observation, experimentation, and physical laws, Kabbalah is "anti-science."

---

63. Once one has been clued into the existence of another realm that turns all previously believed truth claims into lies, it makes sense that one would focus attention to that more fundamental realm. Thus, Neo takes the red pill to escape the Matrix, and Truman sacrifices his safety to escape from Seahaven Island. As Plato predicted, "Do not be surprised that those who have attained to this height are not willing to occupy themselves with the affairs of men, but their souls ever feel the upward urge and the yearning for that sojourn above" (*Resp.* 517c–d [*Republic*, 2:131]). Socrates said of Thales, "He was so eager to know what was going on in heaven, that he could not see what was before his feet" (*Theaet.* 174 [*Dialogues*, 529]).

64. Tirosh-Samuelson, "Kabbalah and Science," 509.

Part II: A Critique of Non-Incarnational Maimonidean and Kabbalistic Thought

This fundamental opposition to Aristotelian science explains the predominant attitude of contemporary Hasidic groups against this-worldly scientific education in their schools.[65] It also explains why kabbalistic works, such as the *Tanya*, repudiate the study of the physical world. *Tanya* 1.8 says, "He who occupies himself with the sciences of the nations of the world is included among those who waste their time in profane matters.... Moreover, the uncleanness of the science of the nations is greater than that of profane speech."[66] Such attitudes keep ultra-Orthodox Jewish people from seeing the conflict between their kabbalistic worldview and that of the observed world.

9.3.2. Modern "Aristotelian Science" Objections to Kabbalah

For the remainder of this chapter, I will highlight several aspects of modern scientific knowledge that challenge important concepts in kabbalistic thought. This includes Kabbalah's geocentrism, its rejection of creation *ex nihilo*, its lack of empirical evidence, and its mistakes in employing "as below, so above."

Kabbalah's mechanics and metaphors are dependent on a geocentric universe. Although the predominant focus of kabbalistic theological speculation relates to metaphysical and psychological ideas, the Kabbalists paired their metaphysics with their understanding of physics, namely a geocentric universe. As shown by Chajes, the Aristotelian-Ptolemaic model of the medieval period inspires the pattern of kabbalistic metaphysical thought.[67] Also, as Brown has shown, Kabbalah-affirming ultra-Orthodoxy has difficulty rejecting geocentric thought even in the twenty-first century.[68] To reject it outright would require accepting the authority of modern scientific progress (from Copernicus to Newton to NASA) over the pronouncements of earlier kabbalistic luminaries. It would mean rejecting the pairing of the seven planets to the seven days of the week, the rejection of esoteric soul flight past the seven planets, and the rejection of all forms of astrology and astral magic, as they are dependent on geocentrism. This would involve a rejection of the epistemic value of a wide variety of historic sages and traditional Jewish works that

---

65. Barron, "Closer Look"; K. Moore, "Ultra-Orthodox Rabbis."

66. Zalman of Liadi, *Tanya*, 34.

67. Chajes, "Spheres, Sefirot." Also see Tirosh-Samuelson, "Philosophy and Kabbalah," loc. 4972.

68. J. Brown, *New Heavens*, 254–73.

affirmed such notions. For example, Gen. Rab. 10.6 says, "There is no single herb below without its corresponding star above."[69] A rejection of astrology requires the rejection of the authority of this saying, as well as many sages who taught astrology: Saadia Gaon, Abraham ibn Ezra, Nachmanides, Gersonides, and Abarbanel, among many others.[70]

Kabbalah rejects creation ex nihilo, *thereby rejecting the contemporary model of the big bang.* The current scientific paradigm for the physical origin of the universe is the big bang model, which calculates the rate of the universe's expansion (observed by redshift) and extrapolates to a beginning point in the finite past. This implies a temporal and spatial beginning, rather than an eternal past continuously emanating from a nonphysical realm.[71] Although the big bang model continues to be updated (as seen recently with the launch of the James Webb Space Telescope),[72] and the time span needed for the expansion is contested (i.e., the "age of the universe"),[73] the big bang is currently the best model to explain observable cosmic phenomena. Because Kabbalah rejects actual creation *ex nihilo* with equivocal word games, it cannot accept the big bang's spatiotemporal origin point, whereas the historical Jewish and Christian understanding of creation *ex nihilo* aligns nicely with the model.

No empirical verification is possible for many kabbalistic ideas. As an example of the difference between Platonic and Aristotelian sciences, Kabbalah sides with Plato in needing no empirical evidence in favor of its highest epistemological theories. No one has access to the *Sefirot* for observation or testing, not even for the verification that they exist. All is to be taken on faith that the kabbalistic system is true, and this book has shown the folly of making such an assumption. The demotion of scientific knowledge also opens Kabbalah to criticism like that of Aristocles of Messene (first century CE): "But now this is the very greatest absurdity;

---

69. Gen. Rab. 10.6; cf. Maimonides, *Guide* 2.10. As Maimonides holds to this principle (and quotes it), his authority in this area is compromised as well.

70. Altmann, "Astrology"; Sela, "Astrology."

71. Copan and Craig, *Creation Out of Nothing*, 222–24; Craig, *Reasonable Faith*, 126–28.

72. Sutter, "'Breaking' Cosmology?"

73. The harmonization of Gen 1–2 with cosmological models continues to be a lively debate among biblical scholars and cosmologists. While a believer in the Hebrew Bible must believe in some form of creationism out of nothing (see §8.4), contemporary creationists are divided between "old earth" and "young earth" camps. Given the myriad assumptions involved in the matter, I prefer not to worry much about the age of the universe. In any case, I do not believe Rom 5 and inferences from Isa 11 and Rev 22 allow for the possibility of death or decay before Gen 3.

Part II: A Critique of Non-Incarnational Maimonidean and Kabbalistic Thought

for though in their words they declare their senses to be useless, in their deeds they continue to make the fullest use of them."[74]

"As above, so below" backfires when false ideas of "below" are thrust into the heavens. Kabbalah uses invalidated physical metaphors to describe metaphysical processes; when the physical metaphor is proven scientifically false, the patterned metaphysical metaphor should be discarded as well. In this way, kabbalistic ideas about the unseen realm, which is otherwise inaccessible to observation and testing, may be disproven. The following three examples illustrate how to accomplish this.

First, Kabbalists may say, "The unseen world above consists of pairs of opposites that are perfectly balanced within the *Sefirot*." This may be untestable in a *scientific* way, but it *is* testable *epistemologically*. Kabbalists claim to know there are pairs in the heavenly realm because of the pairings of all things in the sensible realm. Because the lower realm is patterned on the higher one (in their mind), they conjecture that pairings down below are present above. This grand inference is thus dependent upon the truth of the statement "The sensible world consists of pairs." This statement is falsifiable both scientifically and philosophically. Once that statement about the lower realm is discarded, its influence on the upper realm is discarded as well, leading to the collapse of the idea of pairs in the unseen realm.

As a second example, kabbalistic discourse commonly references the "four elements" of fire, air, water, and earth—an outdated idea from Greek natural philosophy that has been disproven for centuries under the power of the microscope, as reflected in the modern periodic table. Kabbalah uses these four elements for metaphysical patterning, such as when the *Tanya* says that anger and pride emanate from fire, appetites for pleasures emanate from water, idle talk emanates from air, and melancholy emanates from earth (*Tanya* 1.1).[75] Continuing on, *Tanya* 1.6 says that seven evil attributes originate from the four elements and three parts of the intellect that beget them. All these attributes and descriptions are

---

74. Eusebius, *Praep. ev.* 14.17.

75. There are many examples of this mistake before the *Tanya*. Maimonides constructed a fanciful system based on the four elements, four spheres, and four angels in *Guide* 2.10. *Zohar* 2:23b says, "Therefore man was created from the dust of the lower Sanctuary; and the four winds of the world united at that place which afterwards was named the House of Holiness, and these four were then joined to the four elements of the lower world: fire, air, earth, and water. And when these winds and these elements were thus mingled, the Holy One, blessed be He, formed one body of wondrous perfection" (Simon et al., *Soncino Zohar*).

based on mental constructs that do not reflect the structure of reality, and thus they should be rejected.

A final example of this kind of backfiring may be found in the principal analogy used by Kabbalists to explain the emanation process: the relationship between the sun and light. The emanative process of one eternal thing from another eternal thing is likened to the sun emanating light, which was historically seen as a mysterious unity of source and effect. This analogy is a long-standing tradition, used in Plotinus[76] and premodern Christian works as well,[77] but modern science shows it to be misleading.

In his explanation of kabbalistic metaphysics using the light analogy, Immanual Schochet quotes Rabbi Joseph Ergas (1685–1730) as saying, "Light has numerous qualities characteristic of the Divine emanations, as, for example: (i) Light is emitted from the luminary without ever becoming separated from it. . . . (ii) Light spreads itself instantaneously. . . . (iv) Light does not mix and mingle with another substance. (v) Light per se never changes."[78] Schochet intends this to mean that *Ein Sof* may be seen as simultaneously united with and distinguished from the light it emits, a light that is embedded in all things.

These claims about light may have been plausible before modern scientific advances, but they are incorrect as follows: (i) Light is a physical particle-wave duality that spatially departs from the emitting source and is thus disconnected from it. (ii) Light has a fast but not instantaneous speed of approximately three hundred million meters per second in a vacuum. It is finite, not infinite, in speed. (iv) Light can encode and transmit data, such as in fiber optics, illustrating how light may mingle with information. (v) Visible light may be converted up and down the electromagnetic spectrum (such as into invisible ultraviolet light and microwaves), such that light changes and can acquire different properties. Light also undergoes absorption when it strikes an object, converting its luminescence into heat, such that the light ceases to exist. Nuclear scientists have also successfully employed particle accelerators to convert

---

76. Plotinus, *Enn.* 1.7.1; 1.7.6.

77. Tertullian, *Prax.* 13; Origen, *Princ.* 1.2.7; Athanasius, *Apol. Sec.* 2.33; Novatian, *On the Trinity* 18.4–5. On the analogical Nicene phrase "light of light," see Swinburne, *Coherence of Theism*, 76–77.

78. Schochet, "Mystical Concepts in Chasidism," a47–48. The falsehood of these statements was readily available during Schochet's lifetime (d. 2013), and despite having a PhD, in his exposition Schochet shows no sign that there are any scientific errors in these descriptions of light.

light into matter.[79] Each of these truths about light illustrates how light is a separate, changeable thing in our finite universe, and not an infinite thing that should be used to conjecture truths about the unchangeable divine essence emanating the universe. This is an example of the doctrine of correspondences backfiring: bad science leads to bad theology.

9.4. Final Reflections on Kabbalah and Incarnation

Our journey through Lurianic Kabbalah is now complete. I have investigated its broad worldview claims and have found ample reason to discard them as inaccurate. I have investigated Kabbalah's cosmology, metaphysics, hermeneutics, historical ancestry, philosophical sources, and scientific claims, each leading to the conclusion that Kabbalah should be rejected as a source of theological truth. I believe these investigations have led to the conclusion of my argument in §8.3, namely establishing the falsehood of Kabbalah's pan-incarnational panentheism. Because I conclude that the universe is *not* God's body, and because humans are *not* ontologically one with God already, this makes room for God to take up residence in our world as the *unique* incarnate Son of God, an idea that will be explored in part 3. Thus, Kabbalah's adverse effects on incarnational theology may be set aside.

In my exposition of kabbalistic doctrine, I made the claim that Kabbalah makes Jesus redundant. Under Kabbalah's teaching that the entire cosmos is ontologically permeated by God and united with him, there is nothing special about saying that Jesus is God in the flesh. *Everything* is God in the flesh. By teaching that the real problem in the cosmos is physicality and multiplicity, for Kabbalists there is little attractive about the gospel's offer of redemption from sin through Jesus's vicarious sacrifice. The message of Jesus and the NT does not make sense to a Kabbalist because he operates on a different wavelength with different values and presuppositions.

Unfortunately, the worldview of Kabbalah on the one side, and those of the Hebrew Scriptures and NT on the other, are fundamentally incompatible with one another in multiple categories, as explored in part 3. In order for Jesus to be the unique incarnate Son of God, categorically distinguished from all others, the panentheism of Kabbalah cannot stand. There is no middle ground between the two worldviews. Kabbalah

---

79. Brookhaven National Laboratory, "Collisions of Light."

is a cosmos-wide system of panentheistic claims that comes as a whole package; mystical doctrines based on panentheism cannot be accepted piecemeal without accepting panentheism itself. The Parmenidean One repackaged as *Ein Sof* admits no compromise with anything second. Either only one thing exists, or Parmenides, Plotinus, and Kabbalah are irreparably mistaken.

Accordingly, during my assessment I did not stress commonalities between Kabbalah and NT thought. In my view, there should be little attractive in the kabbalistic worldview to a Jesus follower, whether one is Jewish or gentile. At best, a Jesus follower can cite Kabbalah's rejection of Maimonides's singularity dogma as a reason to reconsider the Jewishness of a triune God—but not much else. I am open to finding further redemptive analogies and commonalities, but to the extent that they are grounded upon Kabbalah's misleading cosmology, metaphysics, and hermeneutics, I will remain skeptical.

This is even true about the supposed correlation between the triadic system of the *Sefirot* and the Trinity, something that I have not explored here. Because of its allowance for divine complexity, some have seen Kabbalah as a model for justifying Trinitarian and incarnational theology in the context of Judaism. Examples include Christian Kabbalists from the fifteenth through seventeenth centuries such as Pico di Mirandola, Johannes Reuchlin, and Jacob Böhme.[80] Each of these men syncretized with Kabbalah to such an extent that their Christian orthodoxy was obscured. I believe the same is often true of more recent believers in Jesus who attempt to adopt kabbalistic ideas.[81] In my judgment, no one should use Kabbalah to justify the Trinity or the Incarnation, or to interpret NT passages, or to explain a "hidden Jewish tradition." Those who do such things are not only making inaccurate claims, but are also guilty of syncretism and intellectual assimilation that devalue the NT in favor of a foreign and misleading system.[82] The triunity of God does not need Kabbalah's help in order to sound Jewish, nor does the Incarnation, since its inception is found in the Jewish texts of the NT and is supported by the Jewish texts surveyed in chapter 3. There is too little to be gained through accepting kabbalistic thought, and much to be lost through its

---

80. McClymond, *Devil's Redemption*, 1:397–98, 441–82.

81. Oxlee, *Christian Doctrines of Trinity*; Pauli, *Great Mystery*; Shapira, *Return of Kosher Pig*. For critical reviews, see Crawford, "Pathways," 85–90.

82. For more on this theme, see Crawford, "Pathways," 73–89. Also see appendices D and E.

totalizing panentheist vision.[83] In my opinion, it would be best to leave the kabbalistic tradition behind.

---

83. McClymond, *Devil's Redemption*; Cooper, *Panentheism*.

PART III

The Incarnation of the Son of God

10 Foundations of the Incarnation
Cosmology, Revelation, and Theology

He helps the offspring of Abraham. Therefore he had to be made like his brothers in every respect.

—Heb 2:16b–17a

He remained what he was, and he became what he was not.

—Patristic maxim

So far, this book has spanned millennia of Jewish thought, beginning with the unsolved theological mysteries of the Hebrew Scriptures. I then examined the various Jewish theological solutions given by Philo (first century), the talmudic sages (second through sixth centuries), Maimonides (twelfth century), and Kabbalah (medieval period to present). Now I will return to the first century to present an often-neglected Jewish theological solution to the Hebrew Scriptures' theological mysteries: the embodied Son of God. As a set of Jewish religious documents written by Jews, about a Jewish rabbi, taking place in Judea and the Jewish diaspora, the books of the New Testament (*Brit Hadashah*) seek to explain the unanswered questions of the Hebrew Scriptures. The NT presents the answer in Yeshua (Jesus), the Son of God, whose various divine embodiments in the Hebrew Scriptures culminated in his epoch-changing Incarnation in a Jewish virgin's womb.

Part 3 of this book investigates the theological model presented by the NT, treating it as divine revelation (which I hold it to be).

Nevertheless, I will assess whether its theology presents a coherent and justifiable worldview. Specific treatment will be given to the cosmological, revelatory, philosophical, rational, and hermeneutical aspects of the Incarnation. After investigating the Trinitarian and incarnational model proposed by the NT, I will compare its doctrine of God with the Maimonidean and kabbalistic models. The best theological model will have the greatest explanatory scope and plausibility, the least ad hoc doctrines, and the least known falsehoods.[1] In the course of this investigation, I hope to demonstrate that the NT's incarnational model exceeds its rivals in each of these areas.

10.1. In Search of a Jewish Incarnational Theology

This book is an investigation of Jewish doctrines of God, and as we transition to the NT, we remain within that Jewish context.[2] Contemporary Jewish scholars see the NT as a thoroughly Jewish set of works composed within a richly varied Second Temple Jewish environment.[3] However, in order to deal with the full range of issues related to the NT's incarnational theology, I will consider theological and philosophical contributions outside the canon of the NT. As explained below, the NT presents the essential ingredients of its incarnational theology, but post-NT authors articulate the theology with precision and holistic consistency.

Ideally, in my search for a coherent articulation of the NT's doctrine of the Incarnation, I would cite Jewish proponents throughout the last two millennia. Such a search would not be fruitless, as there have been Jewish believers in Jesus's divinity throughout the lifetime of the church.[4] Several such believers will be quoted below. However, with the exception of the Jewish authors of the NT, Jewish believers in Jesus have rarely been at the forefront of explaining and defending the deity of Jesus. For the past two thousand years, the most sophisticated and thorough incarnational theologians have been found among gentile Christians. From

---

1. For these categories, see Craig, *Reasonable Faith*, 233; McCullagh, *Justifying Historical Descriptions*, 19.

2. I appreciate the aid of David Rudolph and Mitch Glaser as I crafted this section.

3. Zetterholm and Runesson, *Within Judaism?*; A. Levine and Brettler, *Jewish Annotated New Testament*. Also see §1.5.

4. Skarsaune and Hvalvik, *Early Centuries*; Skarsaune, *Spain 300–1300 C.E.*; Schonfield, *History of Jewish Christianity*. Also see Paul's principle in Rom 11:5, which implies that every generation will have a remnant of Jewish believers in Jesus.

Foundations of the Incarnation

Justin Martyr (second century CE), to the Nicene Council and Athanasius (325 CE), to Augustine (354-430 CE), to Aquinas (1225-74 CE), and to gentile theologians today, the Christian theological tradition has produced a thorough body of literature on the NT's theological claims.

Upon mentioning this fact, it might appear that we have left the Jewish sphere and have crossed into exclusively Christian territory. Despite my disagreement that this is a Christian-only subject matter, I sympathize with the sentiment. Justin Martyr was the first to assert that the church is the New Israel, hardly attractive to the "old" Israel to whom a myriad of promises were given.[5] The Nicene Council promulgated anti-Jewish canons in addition to its creed.[6] Augustine was the father of the medieval subjugation of Jews in Christian societies.[7] Consequently, these names do not generate warm affection in the Jewish heart. It can rightly be asked whether acceptance of the Incarnation should have anything to do with gentile theologians who presented such offensive attitudes toward Jews.

One might think the modern Messianic Jewish movement could provide a way forward without the baggage of anti-Jewish rhetoric. Messianic Judaism consists of Jewish believers in Jesus who are committed to a pro-Judaic expression of their faith. The movement traces its roots to nineteenth-century Protestant Jewish missions, the subsequent Hebrew Christian movement, and various developments in the 1970s onward.[8]

---

5. Justin says Christians "are the true Israelitic race" (*Dial.* 135 [*ANF* 1:267]; cf. *Dial.* 123).

6. This council is notorious in the Messianic Jewish movement for outlawing the practice of Jewish customs, even when there is evidence of the apostles themselves practicing them (see the Quartodeciman controversy and laws against Saturday sabbath observance). This kind of thing makes it difficult for Jewish believers in Jesus to speak highly of Nicaea. See canon 52 and Constantine's post-council letter (*NPNF*² 14:54; Bauckham, "Sabbath and Sunday").

7. Crawford, "Christian Antisemitism's Potent Recipe," 74-78; Fredriksen, *Augustine and the Jews*; Utterback and Price, *Jews in Medieval Christendom*.

8. For an overview of the movement as a whole, including the various subgroups within it, see Glaser, "Messianic Jewish National Organizations." Today, there is a wide spectrum of Messianic Jewish self-definition, theology, and practice, especially diverging on the role of Torah observance and rabbinic tradition in Messianic Jewish life, as shown in R. Harvey, *Mapping Messianic Jewish Theology*. Broadly speaking, the movement has two wings: the congregational movement, represented principally by the IAMCS (International Association of Messianic Congregations and Synagogues) and UMJC (Union of Messianic Jewish Congregations), and Jewish missions organizations, such as Chosen People Ministries and Jews for Jesus. The two wings have porous boundaries and often overlap. For example, Chosen People Ministries plants Messianic congregations that can affiliate with the IAMCS or UMJC. For more detail on the

Part III: The Incarnation of the Son of God

As a means of self-definition, Messianic Jewish scholars have focused their attention on carving out a middle space for Jews who believe in Yeshua to remain culturally and covenantally identifiable as Jews. When their audience is the wider church, Messianic Jewish scholarship tends to emphasize supersessionism, hermeneutics, ecclesiology, eschatology, Zionism, and anti-Semitism. When the audience is the wider Jewish world, Messianic Jewish scholarship tends to emphasize covenantal identity, Torah observance, Jewish communal traditions, continuity with historic Judaism, evangelistic concerns, and a variety of biblical subjects. These topics are addressed in countless publications by Messianic Jewish leaders as they identify themselves in their middle space and break away from centuries of suppression of their Jewish identity.[9]

Is Christology—the doctrine of Christ (Messiah)—one of the areas where Messianic Jewish theologians provide assistance? Years ago, as a new gentile Christian participant in the Messianic Jewish movement, I asked my seasoned colleagues to recommend works about the Incarnation written from a Messianic Jewish perspective. In so doing, I learned that the topic of Christology has been a lesser focus among Messianic Jewish scholars.[10] Messianic Jews have largely inherited the Nicene theological tradition of the wider church without major controversy. The largest Messianic organizations retain broadly orthodox statements of faith in the Protestant tradition, including affirmations of the Trinity and Incarnation, even if they employ different words.[11] Because the

---

history of the Messianic Jewish movement, see Thompson, *Century of Jewish Missions*; Schonfield, *History of Jewish Christianity*; Glaser, "Missions to the Jews"; Y. Ariel, *Evangelizing the Chosen People*; Reason, "Competing Trends"; Rudolph, "Messianic Judaism in Antiquity"; Ruderman, *Missionaries, Converts, and Rabbis*.

9. Each of these topics is addressed by Messianic Jewish journals like *Kesher* and *Mishkan*, as well as the numerous contributors to the chapters in Rudolph and Willitts, *Introduction to Messianic Judaism*. The latter volume is excellent in its scope and handling of its topics. However, it should also be noted that no chapter in *Introduction* is given to theology proper, such as the Trinity, Incarnation, or creeds. Scattered and short affirmations are made in various chapters to Yeshua's deity or divinity or the Trinity—illustrating the authors' christological orthodoxy—but theology proper is excluded from extended discussion.

10. The most common recommendation I received was Michael Brown's *Answering Jewish Objections* series. One leader recommended that I read Pauli's *Can Three Be One?*, and others suggested I read Shapira's *Return of Kosher Pig*. For my review of these books and a presentation of the three paradigms they represent, see Crawford, "Pathways," 79–90.

11. Messianic Jewish Alliance of America, "Statement of Faith"; Union of Messianic Jewish Congregations, "Statement of Faith"; Chosen People Ministries, "Doctrinal

Messianic Jewish movement holds no discernible difference on Yeshua's deity compared to the wider church, the deity of Yeshua has been a less pressing matter for Messianic Jewish theologians than the self-definition of their movement.

Nevertheless, in the past twenty years, several Jewish believers in Jesus have written systematic theologies for the benefit of the wider movement.[12] Various articles on the Incarnation and related issues may be found in the Messianic Jewish movement's academic journals and forums.[13] During the same period, several monographs on the deity of Yeshua have been written by those involved with the Messianic Jewish movement.[14] Michael Brown has written an influential series of apologetic works with Orthodox Jewish theological concerns in mind, including the handling of Yeshua's deity.[15] Richard Harvey has surveyed a variety of Messianic Jewish leaders' positions on Yeshua's deity (as of 2009) and proposed a taxonomy of positions.[16] In the past twenty years, perhaps the best essays from a Messianic Jewish perspective on Yeshua's deity are by Mark Kinzer,[17] and the most sophisticated and comprehensive Messianic

---

Statement"; Jews for Jesus, "Statement of Faith"; One for Israel, "Statement of Faith." On the relationship between the Messianic Jewish movement and Protestant Evangelicalism, see Reason, "Competing Trends."

12. Jews for Jesus published a posthumous systematic theology by Louis Goldberg, *God, Torah, Messiah*. Arnold Fruchtenbaum has a series of systematic theology lectures, some of which have been turned into books: *What We Know About God*; *Messiah Yeshua, Divine Redeemer*. See also Midgley et al., *Be Mature in Understanding*.

13. Besides the Borough Park Symposium, mentioned below, I have in mind the *Kesher* journal, *Mishkan* journal, the Hashivenu Forum, Yachad BeYeshua, and the Helsinki Consultation. In the past twenty years, among these four associations the following articles have been devoted to the Incarnation, in chronological order: Harrington, "Wisdom Christology"; Nerel, "Christological Observations"; Bock, "Is It Kosher"; Brumbach, Review of *Border Lines*; Silverman, Review of *Incarnation*; Kinzer, "Finding Our Way"; Bock, "Response to Mark Kinzer"; Postell, "Messiah as Wisdom"; Kinbar, "I Will Dwell"; Kinzer, "Is Jesus of Nazareth"; Downey, "What Hath Maimonides Wrought?"; Westerman, "Presence and Involvement." Among these papers mentioned, only Downey attempts to address Maimonides's worldview, and none grapple with the challenges posed by Kabbalah.

14. Shapira, *Return of Kosher Pig*; Downey, *Maimonides's Yahweh*; Sobel, *Mysteries of the Messiah*. For reviews of Shapira and Downey, see Crawford, "Pathways," 79–101.

15. *AJOJ*. Brown's five volumes set the standard for contemporary Messianic Jewish apologetics.

16. R. Harvey, *Mapping Messianic Jewish Theology*, 96–139.

17. Kinzer: "Finding Our Way"; "Judaism and Divine-Human Jesus." The latter essay handles Maimonidean "absolute monotheism" and argues against it using the historical-textual approach from ch. 3. Both essays are reprinted in Kinzer, *Stones the*

Part III: The Incarnation of the Son of God

Jewish work on the deity of Yeshua is a collection of papers by a cross-section of the movement's scholars.[18] These papers, originally delivered in 2010, often remark about the need for more work to explain orthodox Christology in a Jewish context. This remains true fourteen years later.

It was in this context that I began my research into a Jewish understanding of the Incarnation. Since I was serving in an Orthodox Jewish neighborhood in Brooklyn, my interests were attuned to the thought patterns and objections that come from an Orthodox Jewish mindset. Early on, I discovered that the major Orthodox Jewish objections to the Incarnation were grounded in Maimonidean and kabbalistic thought, but the available Messianic Jewish literature did not help me much with these subjects. The works mentioned above sometimes deal with the Incarnation in relation to Second Temple Judaism or the Talmud, but very rarely do they venture into medieval Judaism's philosophical transformation.

In this respect, I found some assistance from Hebrew Christian and missionary publications over a century old.[19] In the nineteenth century, Jewish mission organizations had been more adept at understanding Orthodox Jewish concerns, especially with so many Jewish believers coming from Orthodox Jewish backgrounds.[20] However, various factors in the twentieth century—especially the murder of so many Orthodox Jews and Orthodox-background Jesus followers in the Holocaust[21]—shifted the Messianic Jewish movement's context to non-Orthodox Judaism. The result of this shift has been a lessening of proficiency in Orthodox Jewish theology, literature, language,[22] and objections since World War II. Out

---

Builders Rejected.

18. Borough Park Symposium, *Symposium II*. This symposium includes papers by Bock, Rudolph, Rosenberg, Kinzer, Glaser, Klayman, Shulam, Nessim, R. Harvey, Moskowitz, and Cohen. Two *Mishkan* journals older than twenty years are also helpful: vol. 39 (2003), on Jesus's deity, and vol. 34 (2001) on the creeds.

19. McCaul, *Lectures on the Prophecies*, 28–57; C. Ginsburg, *Kabbalah*; Pick, *Cabala*. Also see the serialized Kabbalah analysis starting in Herschell, *Voice of Israel*, 155.

20. Ruderman, *Missionaries, Converts, and Rabbis*; Thompson, *Century of Jewish Missions*.

21. One of the lesser-known stories of the Holocaust is how many Jewish believers in Jesus were killed by the Nazis. In 1936, Schonfeld reported that 97,000 Jews had joined the Hungarian church alone. There were hundreds of thousands elsewhere in Europe. These Jewish believers in Jesus suffered the same fate as the rest of their people (Schonfield, *History of Jewish Christianity*, 166; Glaser, "Missions to the Jews").

22. For example, many prewar missionary tracts and books were written in Yiddish, the language of European Jews and especially the Orthodox. Today, although there are still many Orthodox Jewish communities with Yiddish as their mother tongue, missions organizations are hard pressed to create Yiddish materials.

on the streets of Brooklyn, I came to recognize that the waning proficiencies needed to be regained if there was to be ongoing evangelistic dialogue with the Orthodox Jewish world.

Thus, I immersed myself in the publications of non–Messianic Jewish scholars focused on Maimonidean and kabbalistic thought. I came to recognize that their worldviews had many similarities with Greek thought, so I found great inspiration from Christian theologians who dealt with philosophical objections to Christianity.[23] I became convinced that philosophical proficiency was the missing ingredient for Jesus followers to understand Orthodox Jewish theology and to present an evangelistic message sensitive to their concerns. This eventually led to a doctor of ministry project on the Incarnation, Maimonides, and Kabbalah at Talbot School of Theology.[24] As part of the doctoral project, I surveyed fifty-three people in the Jewish missions arm of the Messianic Jewish movement,[25] focusing on their familiarity with Greek philosophy, Maimonides, and Kabbalah. The average length of full-time ministry among the participants was 21.2 years. Twenty-six participants had master's degrees in biblical studies or related fields, sixteen had bachelor's degrees, and seven had doctorates. None had degrees in philosophy. Crucially, each participant indicated interest and experience in relating to Haredim (ultra-Orthodox Jewish people). Despite these factors, I predicted the surveys would illustrate a low level of proficiency in the subjects involved. This prediction was proven correct.[26]

Since World War II, Jewish believers in Jesus have had limited need to respond to arguments against the Incarnation deriving from

---

23. Four books were key in my exploration. Pearcey and Thaxton introduced me to the influence of Neoplatonism and its relationship with science; Anderson inspired me with ways to rebut Maimonides, as did Shapiro, an Orthodox Jew; McClymond helped get my mind around Kabbalah (Pearcey and Thaxton, *Soul of Science*; Anderson, *Paradox in Christian Theology*; M. Shapiro, *Limits of Orthodox Theology*; McClymond, *Devil's Redemption*). Once I had these four under my belt, acquiring the *Great Books of the Western World* anthology launched me into a trek through Western thought.

24. Crawford, "Pathways."

25. Unfortunately, since most of the participants in my surveys came from the missions arm of the Messianic Jewish movement, this leads to a statistical lacuna in my research. Nevertheless, members of the congregational arm of the Messianic Jewish movement have not produced any major christological works or extensively dealt with the theology and philosophy of Maimonides and Kabbalah, so it likely has a gap of understanding as well.

26. Among the most proficient participants were those who had taken part in Borough Park Symposium II. For the results of the surveys, see Crawford, "Pathways," 119–60.

Maimonidean impossibility and kabbalistic redundancy. This is reflected in the lack of publications on the subjects after the war. However, in the twenty-first century, I believe the Jewish community is experiencing a change of tide, and Jesus followers sympathetic to the Jewish people need to likewise adjust course. Recent trends show the Jewish community is becoming more Orthodox again, with projections that up to 23 percent of the worldwide Jewish population will be Haredim by 2040.[27] This percentage does not include the additional Orthodox Jewish people, such as the Modern Orthodox, who also hold to Maimonidean and kabbalistic worldviews. Because the Jewish community is becoming more Orthodox, I believe there is a pressing evangelistic need for the Messianic Jewish movement and sympathetic Christians to regain proficiency in Orthodox Jewish theology and philosophy. This need is especially urgent for providing reasoned responses to the challenges Maimonides and Kabbalah pose to the Incarnation (1 Pet 3:15).

10.2. Retrieving a Jewish Understanding of the Incarnation

In recent years, evangelical Christian theologians have increasingly published on the need for "theological retrieval" within their circles.[28] This term describes the process of reexamining and reaffirming traditional Christian doctrines, particularly those that have been neglected or marginalized over time. This endeavor draws upon the wisdom of great theologians from church history, such as the early church fathers, the Reformers, and other influential thinkers. The goal of theological retrieval is not to develop new doctrine or undermine the old, but rather to shore up important already-held beliefs that have receded into the background through contemporary neglect and unfamiliarity. Without retrieval, an important neglected (but still believed) belief may no longer be believed by subsequent generations, especially if the belief comes under strong criticism.

As a gentile participant in the Messianic Jewish movement, I have observed that the movement holds to Yeshua's deity and confesses him

---

27. Staetsky, *Haredi Jews Around World*, 4; Alper et al., *Jewish Americans in 2020*; Eliezrie, "US Jewry Is Shifting"; Cooperman and Smith, "Eight Facts"; Lugo et al., *Portrait of Jewish Americans*.

28. Ortlund, *Theological Retrieval for Evangelicals*; Crisp, *Retrieving Doctrine*; Barrett, *On Classical Trinitarianism*; Wilkinson, *Crowned with Glory*, 105–17; Sanders and Swain, *Retrieving Eternal Generation*.

as LORD in the fullest sense. There is no christological controversy raging among the leaders of the movement.[29] Doubts about his divinity are limited to the popular level and the periphery.[30] However, Messianic Jews need a robust exposition and defense of the deity of Yeshua if they are going to transmit their theological consensus to subsequent generations. Additionally, Jewish believers in Jesus increasingly need to respond to the objections posed by Maimonidean and kabbalistic thought. As a contribution to these ends by a gentile participant in the Messianic Jewish movement, I intend the remainder of this book to be a project of theological retrieval for the deity of Yeshua among Jewish believers in Jesus and sympathetic gentile Christians in their midst.[31]

I believe an increase in philosophical proficiency will be necessary to accomplish these goals. In my experience, attempts to rebut Maimonidean and kabbalistic roadblocks are hindered without such philosophical training. However, something more is needed as well: deep interaction with the theological classics of the Christian faith. This brings us back full circle to the beginning of this chapter. An essential part of this project of theological retrieval is citing and interacting with the great Christian theologians of the church who have provided the theological articulation and sophistication necessary to adequately explain and defend the doctrine of the Incarnation. I believe this dependence is a proper reflection of the one universal congregation of Messiah, Jew and gentile united as one (Eph 2). Gentile Christian theologians have provided the most comprehensive, cogent, and sophisticated defenses of the deity of Jesus. Therefore, I believe any attempt to defend Jesus's deity to a

---

29. Emphasizing his forty-five years in the Messianic Jewish movement, in 2020 Messianic Jewish scholar David Rudolph said, "I am not aware of any theological crisis in our movement over this issue, though we are still working out the best way to communicate Jesus's divinity in a way that is informed by traditional Jewish and Christian theologies" (Two Messianic Jews, "Did Jesus Claim," 27:08).

30. R. Harvey, *Mapping Messianic Jewish Theology*, 131–36.

31. This book is intended to be a new contribution, even though aspects of it may be found in others' works. Other Jesus-following authors have employed the historical textual approach of ch. 3 (Kinzer, Klayman, Kinbar, Brown, Brumbach), critically analyzed Maimonides as in chs. 5–6 (Downey, Fischer, Kinzer), critically analyzed Kabbalah as in chs. 7–9 (Ginsburg, Pick, McClymond), surveyed the NT's presentation of Yeshua's deity as in ch. 10 (Bock, M. Brown, Goldberg, Fruchtenbaum), and given a Messianic analysis of the church's creeds as in ch. 10 (Kinzer, Skarsaune, Juster, Nerel, R. Harvey, Nessim). None have included each of these topics in one monograph. Furthermore, this book adds to the conversation by introducing the theological-philosophical approach to the topics at hand.

skeptical Jewish audience will be hindered if the great Christian theological tradition is avoided.

Yet, I also believe the Christian theological tradition includes supersessionist teachings from which Messianic Jews are right to distance themselves.[32] Thus, the integration of Christian theologians into my investigation compels me to separate the wheat (Trinitarian orthodoxy) from the chaff (supersessionism) in the Christian tradition. Because there is true wheat to be gleaned, historical Christian theologians should not be ignored or rejected outright. In agreement with many Messianic Jewish publications, I believe in the need to accept historical Christians' theological brilliance along with a rejection of their errors.[33] As uncomfortable as this situation is for some Jewish followers of Jesus, it is important to recognize the contributions of the Christian tradition to Messianic Jewish doctrine, including the Trinity and Incarnation. On the other hand, a Jewish incarnational theology should not reason within the sphere of the NT and Christian tradition alone; any portrayal of the Incarnation in a Jewish context should also consider Jewish theological tradition, with all the benefits and challenges it provides. Thus, the following chapters will keep an eye on Jewish concerns while appropriating the classic Christian theological tradition, thereby attempting to provide the best of both worlds.

---

32. Soulen, *God of Israel*; Soulen, "Standard Canonical Narrative"; M. Brown, *Our Hands Are Stained*; Crawford, "Christian Antisemitism's Potent Recipe"; Cantor, "Reconciling the Antisemitism."

33. Messianic Jewish leader Ron Cantor writes, "We, too, must not judge the Church Fathers too harshly, but show kindness and mercy while unashamedly and zealously correcting the deadly theology" ("Reconciling the Antisemitism," under "Conclusion"). The Messianic Jewish Theological Institute, affiliated with the UMJC, says, "While Christian history (like Jewish history) has many problematic elements, it also has produced a wide-ranging tradition of scholarship and theological interpretation filled with spiritual insight. We cannot adequately understand devotion to God through Yeshua in the Spirit without drawing upon that tradition. Therefore, in its learning and teaching MJTI seeks a serious and fruitful engagement with the breadth and depth of Christian tradition and scholarship" ("Core Values," under "3. Sources of Guidance: Christian Tradition"). Also see Helsinki Consultation, "Statement." A practical application of this may be seen in how I include several approving quotations of Origen in this book. I quote him when I agree with him, while simultaneously being opposed to his overall posture of syncretizing with Platonism.

10.3. A Brief Review of the Hebrew Scriptures' Unanswered Theological Questions

This book has taken a long philosophical detour since part 1, so I will review what the Hebrew Scriptures say about God, his attributes, and his relationship with the physical world. In chapter 2, I surveyed a range of biblical passages about these matters, including:

The attributes of God: When the Hebrew Scriptures say that God is faithful, just, upright, merciful, and gracious (Exod 34:6; Deut 32:4), how are those words to be understood? Do they have the same meaning (univocal) as when those words describe people? Do they have completely different meanings (equivocal)? Or are they analogies (analogical), both similar and dissimilar from ordinary language?

Transcendence and immanence: When the Hebrew Scriptures say that God fills heaven and earth (Jer 23:24) but that he is also beyond the farthest heavens (1 Kgs 8:27), how should these two ideas be balanced?

Incomparability and comparability: Is God absolutely incomparable, such that nothing can ever have any similarity with God (Ps 71:19; Isa 40:25; 46:5)? If so, how should interpreters handle passages stating humans are made in the image and likeness of God (Gen 1:26; 5:1) and the enigmatic passage where Ezekiel sees God in human likeness in heaven (Ezek 1:26)?

Immanence and localization: When the Hebrew Scriptures say that God is present in all places and aware of all places and fills heaven and earth, what does it mean when other Scriptures say that Moses goes *up* to God (Exod 19:20), that God speaks to Moses *from within* Mount Sinai (Exod 19:3), that humans can be spatially *near* or *far* from God (Gen 18:23), and that God has a *place* (Exod 33:21)? If God is everywhere, how can he accurately be described as being *here* or *there* in a particular way?

The unseen and seen God: God tells Moses, "Man shall not see me and live" (Exod 33:20). If so, how does God speak to Moses *face-to-face* so that Moses sees God's *form* (Num 12:8)?

Anthropomorphism: The Hebrew Scriptures include many passages that speak about God using human bodily features, such as *seeing with eyes* (Ps 34:15) and doing *actions with his feet* (Gen 3:8). How should these passages be understood?

The previous chapters have given various answers to these questions derived from post-NT Jewish tradition. For example, if a theologian fully emphasizes God's immanence, then all spatial and corporeal passages must be allegorized or turned into metaphor, for God is ontologically in *all* things. This is Kabbalah's panentheistic position (ch. 7). The same allegorization is necessary if God's transcendence is given exclusive importance, for God is *nowhere*. This is Maimonides's position (ch. 5). Otherwise, if a theologian gives exclusive emphasis to literalist readings, then he would conclude that God possesses a humanlike body. This was the position of talmudic and medieval Jewish corporealists (§3.2.1).

The NT indicates that the accurate solution resides in the middle of these hermeneutical extremes. Rather than reading *all* divine attributes, anthropomorphisms, and localized language as metaphor, or *all* physical God talk as simple depictions of God's body, I propose a more balanced solution: *some* of these passages are to be read metaphorically, and *some* are to be read as depictions of God in physical form.[34] This solution requires criteria to determine when metaphor is preferable to literal interpretation, and vice versa. My answer to the question of corporeal God talk will be given in the next chapter after discussing reasons to accept a God who can become incarnate. With my preferred hermeneutical solution—which has a historical Christian pedigree—an interpreter can properly affirm the incorporeality of God (John 1:18; 4:24; 1 Tim 1:17), while also recognizing that God has the freedom to personally interact in and through his creation in a way compatible with theophany and Incarnation. Before handling hermeneutics, however, I need to lay some other groundwork for belief in the incarnate Son of God.

10.4. The Cosmological Foundation: Creation *ex Nihilo*

God's creation of the finite universe from a prior state of absolute nothingness is essential for answering the Hebrew Scriptures' theological questions. In §8.4.1, I surveyed a range of biblical, philosophical, traditional, and scientific arguments in support of creation *ex nihilo* as opposed to creation *ex matria* or emanation *ex Deo*. The accuracy of the doctrine of creation *ex nihilo* results in the following:

- God and his creation are not the same being, but rather separate beings. There is more than one thing that exists, contra Parmenides, Plotinus, and panentheism (emanation *ex Deo*).

---

34. McCaul, *Lectures on the Prophecies*, 36–40.

- Creation depends on God's providence for its continued existence and does not depend on a shared ontology with God.
- Only God is uncreated, necessary, and infinite in the sense of having limitless perfections;[35] all other things are finite (limited), contra emanation *ex Deo* and creation *ex matria*.
- Finite things are finite, period—not hiding infinity within them, or only finite as an illusion, but truly limited and finite.
- Finite things may last forever into the future, but since they have an origination point in time, they cannot be called eternal like God is eternal. Only God is without beginning and without end.
- To be finite is to be distinguished from God's being; God's being is delimited by finite things.

Thus, creation *ex nihilo* illustrates the vast gulf between what it means to be human and what it means to be God. When presented in these terms, the difficulties presented by the doctrine of the Incarnation come into sharp relief: if God and humanity are separated by such a gulf, then how can a human be God?

Despite the initial difficulty in conceiving how to answer that question, I contend that creation *ex nihilo* is a crucial precondition for what is meant by the Incarnation.[36] When the Son of God became human, he took on attributes and qualities that are radically distinct from his divine nature. After the Incarnation, the same Son remained divine yet also became finite, was eternal yet born, omnipresent yet local, and all-powerful yet capable of tiredness, hunger, and thirst. Before venturing into the question of *how* this can be possible, I will first provide a survey of the NT evidence indicating *that* a man is the incarnate Son of God.

---

35. Describing God as infinite risks importing unbiblical Parmenidean notions of God lacking all limits, resulting in pantheism or panentheism. I do not intend to predicate this type of infinity to God, but rather something approaching Anselm's perfect being theology: God possesses all great-making properties with maximal perfection and quality. See my argument against Parmenidean infinity in §8.4.3. As John Feinberg writes, "To say that God is infinite or unlimited in love, justice, power, wisdom, or knowledge is not to say that he has an infinite amount of these qualities. Instead, it means that his attributes are qualitatively unlimited and thus make him a qualitatively different kind of being than anything else in the universe, a being who is unlimited in respect to those attributes." Feinberg, *No One Like Him*, 213.

36. Carter, *Contemplating God*, 238.

10.5. The Revelatory Foundation: Jesus's Divinity and Humanity in the New Testament

The books of the NT present a multifaceted and comprehensive case for Jesus's divinity while also affirming his humanity. The texts speak of Messiah in cosmological and ontological terms that apply to no mere human being created in an *ex nihilo* universe. These claims about Jesus are either false or they classify Jesus as the unique God-Man who requires humanity to rethink categories and the conception of what is possible for God to do.

10.5.1. Jesus as the Divine *Adonai Tzevaot* (the Lord Almighty)

The NT presents Jesus as the Lord Almighty through its cosmology, its use of divine names, and its descriptions of Jesus's actions.

Cosmology. The NT emphasizes that the crucial background for understanding Jesus is not only his historical circumstances as a first-century Jewish man. He is not only a special anointed man from King David's prophesied line. The NT's vision is far wider; as the Son of God, he has always existed.[37] When John speaks about the Son of God, he begins with divine ontology: "In the beginning was the Word [Logos], and the Word was with God, and the Word was God" (John 1:1). John continues with cosmology that includes all other ontological categories: "All things were made through him, and without him was not any thing made that was made" (John 1:3). Nothing has come into being except through the Word, the Son of God; by implication, the Son never came into being, but has always been. Paul joins with this exalted description of Jesus's creation power: "For by him all things were created, in heaven and on earth, visible and invisible, whether thrones or dominions or rulers or authorities—all things were created through him and for him" (Col 1:16). Elsewhere, Paul echoes the Shema (Deut 6:4) when he writes of Jesus's creation of the cosmos:

> For us there is one God, the Father,
> from whom are all things and for whom we exist,
> and one Lord, Jesus Christ,

---

37. It is common practice for theologians to refrain from calling the Son of God "Jesus" until his historical Incarnation in Mary's womb. Temporally speaking, before he took on human nature as Jesus of Nazareth, he was only the Son of God. Although Jude 5 does not follow this practice, it remains helpful for theological precision to call him "the Son" before the opening of the NT, and either "the Son" or "Jesus" thereafter.

through whom are all things and through whom we exist. (1 Cor 8:6)

The parallelism here is striking. The central prayer declaration of Judaism is expanded to understand Jesus as the Lord whom Israel worships and by whom the creation was made.[38] Nothing remains outside of Jesus's reach, for he is the Creator of all. In this way, the NT trains its readers to consider Jesus, the Son of God, as the answer for all that exists in the cosmos because he is fully divine.

Not only is Jesus the Creator of the cosmos, but he is also the one who is providentially responsible for its continued existence. Paul writes, "He is before all things, and in him all things hold together" (Col 1:17). Likewise, the author of Hebrews writes, "He upholds the universe by the word of his power" (Heb 1:3). Commenting on the Colossians passage, NT scholar Douglas Moo writes, "What holds the universe together is not an idea or a virtue, but a person: the resurrected Christ. Without him, electrons would not continue to circle nuclei, gravity would cease to work, the planets would not stay in their orbits."[39] According to the NT, God's providence is accomplished throughout the universe by the Son of God.

Divine names. Beyond these descriptions of Jesus's cosmic involvement, the NT affirms the deity of Jesus by applying divine names to him. Jesus's responsibility for creation and the sustenance of the cosmos illustrate how the NT portrays him as *Adonai Tzevaot* (יהוה צְבָאוֹת), the LORD Almighty, the LORD of heavenly hosts.[40] Additionally, throughout

---

38. One should not read "God" and "Lord" as referring to two deities or stating that only one of the words refers to the God of Israel. Both words refer to God (see below). As a commentary upon the Shema, 1 Cor 8:6 does not allow followers of Jesus to interpret the *echad* of Deut 6:4 as meaning "singularity" or "oneness without multiplicity." Paul's passage is compatible with seeing *echad* as a cardinal number, an ordinal number, a whole, a union of three, or some combination of these (cf. §2.2). See also Kinzer's handling of *echad* in contrast to Maimonides (Kinzer, "Judaism and Divine-Human Jesus"). For a discussion of the Christology of 1 Cor 8:6 and its relationship with the Shema, see Ciampa and Rosner, *First Letter to Corinthians*, 380–90.

39. Moo, *Letter to Colossians*, 125–26.

40. For the Hebrew Bible background of *tzevaot* and its relationship to the cosmos, see Neh 9:6; Isa 40:26; 45:12; and *TDOT* s.v. "צְבָאוֹת." The LXX translates *tzevaot* as *pantocrator* (παντοκράτωρ), meaning "all-powerful." The book of Revelation appears to reference Jesus as *pantocrator*: Rev 1:8; 19:6, 15; 21:22; cf. 19:16 and Matt 28:18. For early patristic usage of *pantocrator* to describe Jesus as the cosmic Almighty one, see Clement of Alexandria, *Paed.* 3.7; Tertullian, *Prax.* 17.

the NT, Jesus is called *theos* (θεός)[41] and *kurios* (κύριος).[42] In Koine Greek, *theos* has a range of meaning that includes non-divine connotations, but in Second Temple Judaism, the divine connotation is the most common. Only the monotheistic Jewish designation for God fits the NT's use of *theos* for Jesus.[43] *Kurios* is the Hellenistic Jewish translation of the Hebrew Tetragrammaton (יהוה), typically translated as "LORD," and used 6,814 times for the God of Israel in the LXX.[44] Moreover, the NT makes the equation between the Tetragrammaton and Jesus explicit when it refers to Hebrew verses containing יהוה and translates the word as *kurios* and refers it to Jesus. The table below presents a selection of verses with this phenomenon:

Table 16. New Testament Quotations of the Tetragrammaton Applied to Jesus

Hebrew Passage with Tetragrammaton (יהוה)	New Testament Quotation or Allusion	New Testament Referent
Ps 116:13	1 Cor 1:2	Jesus the *kurios*
Ps 118:26	Luke 13:35	Jesus, who comes in the name of the *kurios*
Isa 6:1–7	John 12:41	Jesus, the one Isaiah saw
Isa 28:16 (cf. LXX)	Rom 10:9–11	Jesus confessed as *kurios*
Isa 40:3	Mark 1:3	Jesus the *kurios* whose way is prepared by John
Isa 45:23 (יהוה is speaking from v. 19)	Phil 2:10–11	Jesus the *kurios* to whom all must bend their knee and confess as *kurios*
Joel 2:32	Acts 2:21; Rom 10:13	Jesus the *kurios* who saves those who call upon him

---

41. John 1:1, 18; 20:28; Phil 2:6; Col 1:15, 19; Heb 1:8–9; 2 Pet 1:1.

42. Grudem counts 441 uses of *kurios* for Jesus in the NT that include the attribution of deity (*Systematic Theology*, 680). On Jesus's divine titles, see Bowman and Komoszewski, *Putting Jesus in His Place*, 135–71; Wellum, *God the Son Incarnate*, 199–208; McFarland, *Word Made Flesh*, 106–10.

43. The standard BDAG lexicon lists three meanings of *theos* in Greek: (1) A transcendent being involved in human affairs; (2) The unique monotheistic God of the Hebrew and Christian tradition; (3) A nontranscendent being that is worthy of respect (BDAG 451). In light of the expansive cosmological roles applied to Jesus in the NT, only the first and second definitions are reasonable. Given the NT affirmation of only one *theos* (Jas 2:19; 1 Cor 8:6; Eph 4:4–6), only the second definition fits.

44. Grudem, *Systematic Theology*, 679.

The special use of divine names for Jesus extends to the scribal practices of those copying the NT manuscripts. Second-century scribes of the Greek NT adopted the Jewish practice of writing the names of God differently in Hebrew (*nomina sacra*). When they wrote the Greek names of Jesus (IHCOYC) or Christ (XPICTOC), they abbreviated the words in ways that marked his identity as divine (IH and XC, respectively).[45]

Jesus's divine actions. The NT describes Jesus as having attributes, functions, and abilities that only God has. As the Creator of the wind and the waves, he commands them to stop, and they obey (Matt 8:27). He takes his three closest disciples to a mountain, where he temporarily transfigures into brilliant white light (Matt 17).[46] Multiple passages speak of Jesus's omniscience (Matt 9:4; 12:25; John 21:17; Col 2:3). Jesus asserts his omnipresence (Matt 18:20; 28:20). He claims to have sovereign authority over all (Matt 11:27; 28:18), and people recognize the authority of his teaching (Matt 7:28–29). Jesus also accepts worship from his monotheistic Jewish followers (Matt 28:9; 28:17; Luke 24:52; John 20:28). In response to his teaching, some Jewish people who rejected Jesus recognized his divine claims, and they responded by trying to kill him (Matt 9:3; Mark 14:61–64; John 5:18; 10:33). Those who saw Jesus's actions and heard his teachings, including both friends and foes, recognized that he understood himself to be divine.[47]

10.5.2. The New Testament's Use of the Hebrew Scriptures to Justify a Divine Messiah

The NT writings not only make claims about Jesus in his first-century context, but also reach back into the Hebrew Scriptures and argue for his divinity based upon them. Jesus says, "If you believed Moses, you would believe me; for he wrote of me" (John 5:46). Such occurrences of Jesus in

---

45. Hurtado, *Earliest Christian Artifacts*, 97, 134.

46. The transfiguration is reminiscent of the Son's various divine embodiments in the Hebrew Scriptures, but it takes place after the Son has taken on a human nature in the Incarnation. It is both similar to and dissimilar from the theophanies in Israel's history, and it represents the culmination of the theophany tradition. Moses's face also shined when he spoke with God on Sinai (Exod 34:29), but two features of the transfiguration illustrate Jesus's preeminence: Jesus's entire body shined, not just his face, and Moses miraculously appears on the mountain in a subservient role to Jesus (Matt 17:2–3). In this way, the transfiguration presents Jesus as the greater Moses (cf. Deut 18:15–18; Heb 3:3).

47. On Jesus's self-understanding as divine, see Wellum, *God the Son Incarnate*, 147–69.

the Hebrew Scriptures can be classed in two types: first, his presence in historical events, and second, prophetic references to the divine Messiah.

The NT portrays Jesus as the God of Israel, specifically as the same God who interacted with the patriarchs and the children of Israel. In John 8:56, Jesus implies that he spoke with Abraham. His audience is confused, so in John 8:58, he declares, "Truly, truly, I say to you, before Abraham was, I am." By saying the grammatically ironic "I am," Jesus indicates that he existed before Abraham because he is the always-existing one. Moreover, "I am" in Greek is *ego eimi* (ἐγώ εἰμί), which is an allusion to Exod 3:14 LXX, where God told Moses that his name is *ego eimi ho on* (ἐγώ εἰμι ὁ ὤν). Thus, Jesus may have been alluding to the unique name of God revealed to Moses, a name that describes him as the necessary being who brings all other beings into existence (cf. John 1:3; Isa 48:12). Since necessary existence is a divine attribute,[48] in John 8:58 Jesus makes a clear claim to divinity by declaring to be the LORD who spoke with Abraham and Moses. His skeptical audience understands the meaning of this claim since they take up stones to punish Jesus for blasphemy (John 8:59).

The most quoted passage of the Hebrew Scriptures in the NT is Ps 110:1,[49] which says, "The LORD [יהוה] says to my Lord [לאדני, *ladoni*]: Sit at my right hand, until I make your enemies your footstool." In the Synoptic Gospels, Jesus quotes the verse and makes an argument based upon the different words translated as "Lord." The first subject, the Tetragrammaton, speaks to the second, whom David identifies as "my Lord." Who is David's Lord? Jesus appeals to contemporary Jewish interpretations that identified this second Lord as the Messiah.[50] In Matt 22:45, Jesus then asks the paradoxical question of how the Messiah could be the *Son* of David, if the Messiah was already David's Lord when he wrote the Psalm. The NT answers the paradox: David's Lord was the preexistent

---

48. Necessary existence and contingent existence are discussed in the philosophical discipline of modal logic. Necessary existence is that which must exist in all possible worlds. Contingent existence is that which may exist in some possible worlds but not others. In classical theology, only God is a necessary being; all other existing things are merely contingent, as they come into existence and go out of it (exception: human souls exist forever after conception).

49. Quotations are found in Matt 22:44, Mark 12:36, Luke 20:42–43, Acts 2:34–35, Heb 1:13. Many more NT allusions may be found when it speaks of Messiah "at the right hand" of the Father in heaven or describing Messiah's reign as having all things "under his feet."

50. 1 En. 45:3; 61:8; 62:1–5; T. Job 33:3; 11QMelch; cf. the later Gen. Rab. 85.9.

Son of God, whom David was aware would one day be born into David's line as Jesus of Nazareth.

Another repeatedly referenced passage is Dan 7:13–14, where an enigmatic "Son of Man" is envisioned in the heavenly throne room receiving dominion, glory, and a kingdom over all people on earth. Jesus's favorite self-designation is "Son of Man," and he explicitly cites Dan 7:13 in reference to himself during his trial for blasphemy (Mark 14:62; cf. Matt 24:30). Dan 7:13 accomplishes much in Jesus's favor, as it speaks of an exalted being with a unique relationship with God who is given authority over the entire earth.[51]

The Synoptic Gospels each cite Mal 3:1 in dual reference to Jesus and John the Baptist (Matt 11:10; Mark 1:2; Luke 7:27). In each case, Jesus uses the verse to say that John has prepared the way for Jesus to preach throughout Judea. Yet the verse says, "He will prepare the way before me. And the Lord [אָדוֹן, *Adon*] whom you seek will suddenly come to his temple; and the messenger of the covenant in whom you delight, behold, he is coming, says the LORD [יהוה] of hosts." The gospels state the "me" of the first clause is Jesus, who is also the one speaking in the passage ("LORD of hosts"). It is also prophesied that the Lord will come to "his temple"—meaning the Lord (אָדוֹן) in the passage is the Tetragrammaton (יהוה) who owns the Jerusalem temple, and he will physically visit the temple personally. Jesus, the Tetragrammaton made flesh, visits the temple frequently (Luke 2:27 being the first instance). Thus, under the gospels' exegesis, Mal 3:1 means, "John will prepare the way before me, Jesus the LORD."

The most controversial NT use of the Hebrew Bible, at least in contemporary Jewish circles, is Matt 1:22–23, which cites Isa 7:14 as being fulfilled in Jesus's birth.[52] Matthew writes, "All this took place to fulfill what the Lord had spoken by the prophet: 'Behold, the virgin shall conceive and bear a son, and they shall call his name Immanuel,' which

---

51. Boyarin, *Jewish Gospels*, 58–59; Bock, "Use of Daniel 7."

52. Isaiah 7:14 has figured prominently in Christian argumentation toward Jews ever since the second century (Justin Martyr, *Dial.* 67). Some Jewish opponents of Christianity are overly eager to discuss this verse, as they believe it is an easy example of Christian misreading and misappropriation that is reflective of other NT quotations of the Hebrew Bible. Deflecting this charge can be laborious, as it involves discussing Hebrew and Greek etymology, justifying the LXX, discussing the possibilities of simple literal prophecy, double-fulfillment prophecy, typological prophecy, *sensus plenior*, and a host of other complexities. Instead of confronting these complexities head-on, for strategic purposes I prefer making cases for Jesus's divinity without dependence upon Isa 7:14.

means, God with us." Key to the debate is Matthew's use of the Septuagint's *parthenos* (παρθένος), which means virgin. Discussions on the linguistic and prophetic complexities of the verse may be found elsewhere.[53] For our purposes, however, it is striking how Matthew portrays Jesus as "God with us." The baby son who is born is no mere human being; he has no human father but rather a heavenly one.

Many other passages in the Hebrew Scriptures could be cited as evidence for the deity of the Messiah, but not all are quoted or alluded to in the NT. Later followers of Jesus employed the patterns of interpretation laid out in the NT and identified other passages that argue for his divinity. Two of the most commonly cited passages that are not discussed in the NT are Isa 9:6 (MT v. 5) and the reference to "eternity" in Mic 5:2 (although see Matt 2:6).[54]

In sum, the NT presents a multifaceted case regarding Jesus's divinity as the God of Israel, including the use of divine names, divine attributes, historical encounters in the Hebrew Bible, and prophecies about a divine Messiah. He is not a created being, but truly God in the flesh.[55]

10.5.3. Jesus as a Jewish Human

Despite the emphasis on Jesus's deity in the NT, its authors never imply that his deity swallows or overtakes his humanity. Like all human beings after Adam, Jesus is born from a human mother and experiences childhood (Luke 2:7, 40). He grows in wisdom and maturity as he enters adulthood (Luke 2:52). Jesus himself claims to be a man (John 8:40). Likewise, the NT says Jesus was prophesied beforehand to be the son of David according to the flesh (Rom 1:3). He is a Jewish man who becomes hungry (Matt 21:18) and has limited strength (Luke 23:26; John 4:6).

His humanity is not limited to his physical features, but also includes a human intellectual and emotional life. Jesus has knowledge (John 13:1), perception (Luke 5:22), and reasoning (Mark 12:24). He claims to have

---

53. The amount of scholarly and lay attention given to this verse is staggering. Introductions may be found in Rydelnik and Blum, *Handbook of Messianic Prophecy*, 815–27; *AJOJ* 3:17–32; Beale and Carson, *New Testament Use*, 3–5.

54. For discussions on these Hebrew Bible passages and many others that support Jesus's divine identity, see Rydelnik and Blum, *Handbook of Messianic Prophecy*; Bateman et al., *Jesus the Messiah*. Many fruitful parallels in early Jewish thought may also be found in Lanier, *Corpus Christologicum*.

55. For a fuller treatment of the NT's presentation of Jesus as divine, see Wellum, *God the Son Incarnate*, 147–208; Bowman and Komoszewski, *Putting Jesus in His Place*. For a Messianic Jewish essay, see Klayman, "Jewish History."

a soul (Matt 26:38; John 12:27) that experiences sadness (John 11:33), anguish (Matt 26:38), and astonishment (Matt 8:10; Mark 6:6).

Thus, based on the verses above, the NT assigns the full human experience to Jesus. However, these verses could theoretically indicate that Jesus is merely *similar* to humans, experiencing many particularities about human experience but without being human himself. The author of Hebrews gives an explicit affirmation of Jesus's humanity, thus prohibiting the idea of mere similarity: "He had to be made like his brothers in every respect, so that he might become a merciful and faithful high priest in the service of God, to make propitiation for the sins of the people" (Heb 2:17). The entire concept of the Incarnation is embedded in the verb "made like" (ὁμοιωθῆναι, *homoiothenai*) in this verse. Everything humans have essentially, Jesus also has essentially. Humans have bodies, souls, minds, emotions, wills, and desires; Jesus has each as well.[56] Just as other human beings will be human for the remainder of eternity, so too Jesus will never relinquish his humanity; he remains human at the right hand of his Father today.

But there is good reason to say that Jesus's humanity goes even deeper in the NT's presentation. Jesus is not just a human like us, as if his humanity is derived from ours. Rather, our humanity is fully and perfectly exemplified and grounded in Jesus, the second Adam (1 Cor 15), the truest image of God (Col 1:15). Because in eternity past God had the idea to send his Son incarnate as a man,[57] the divine idea of humanity preexisted the creation of Adam. Thus, the first Adam was made in the image and likeness of the Son, and not the other way around.[58] Jesus's perfect exemplification of humanity is due to his sinlessness (Heb 4:15;

---

56. The key here is to recognize he took on *essential* human properties, not *accidental* ones. To be a sinner is an accidental property of humans after Adam's fall; so too, blonde hair, female gender, and ethnicity are accidental properties. By taking on a human nature with all essential human properties intact, Jesus represents each human being in all our accidental particularities. This distinction accounts for why salvation accomplished by Jesus does not only extend to male Jews like himself, but to all human beings who believe in him.

57. Eph 1:4; Titus 1:2–3; 1 Pet 1:20; Rev 13:8.

58. Wilkinson, *Crowned with Glory*, 85–96. Floyd writes, "The divine idea of the Incarnation not only contains the idea of the Imago Dei, which is intricately connected to the divine nature as a reflection of God, but also is the source of the Imago Dei: human nature itself. What I argue here is that the idea of the Incarnation serves as the blueprint for what human beings are to be like rather than human beings serving as the blueprint for what God Incarnate is to be like" (Floyd, "Deriving the *Imago Dei*," 7).

1 Pet 2:22; 1 John 3:5), an attribute that he shared with Adam and Eve, the first humans, before Adam sinned (Rom 5:12).

Finally, the crucial verse of Heb 2:17 should be connected with the phrase immediately preceding: "He helps *the offspring of Abraham*. Therefore he had to be made like his brothers in every respect" (Heb 2:16b–17a). Messiah came to help the offspring of Abraham, the chosen nation of the Jewish people, and it was into their humanity that he was made incarnate. "His brothers" is a direct reference to Jesus's fellow Jews, with whom he shares not only a human nature, but also a Jewish covenantal identity.[59] This reference to the Jewishness of Jesus's Incarnation does not rule out gentile participation in salvation, as Abraham was prophesied to be a blessing to all the families of the earth (Gen 12:3). All human beings are made in the image and likeness of God, having the same human nature as each other and Messiah himself (Gen 1:26; 5:1; Jas 3:9). Paul also clarifies that gentiles have Abraham as their spiritual father when they share in his faith (Rom 4:13–17). However, the author of Hebrews is not concerned with that in this instance; he wants to emphasize that it is fitting and proper for the Son of God to become incarnate as one of Abraham's literal sons, since it is Abraham's offspring that he helps.

10.5.4. The Need for Metaphysical Terminology

How could the divine Word who preexisted the world and made the world be "made like" human beings "in every respect" besides sin? He could have been made like human beings in every category only if he shared the same humanity as they: in other words, a human *nature*, unstained by Adam's sin. Is the use of the metaphysical word "nature" justified here?

The apostles accept the Greek metaphysical concept of *physis* (φύσις), affirming that existing things possess "natures" that distinguish different things. James speaks of birds, reptiles, and sea creatures having different natures (φύσις) than human beings (Jas 3:7). Paul speaks

---

59. Studies on the Incarnation that refer to Heb 2:17 rarely discuss the importance of Jesus becoming incarnate to help "the offspring of Abraham." When they discuss the idea, they tend to read Heb 2:16 with a supersessionist interpretation, saying that "the offspring of Abraham" are all who place their trust in Jesus, whether Jew or gentile (cf. Rom 4). But Hebrews is written to *Jewish* believers in Jesus, thus "offspring of Abraham" refers to Jews. Jesus says, "I was sent only to the lost sheep of the house of Israel" (Matt 15:24). This does not preclude subsequent gentile inclusion into Jesus's salvific purposes. For a commentary on the particularity of the reference to Abraham and its relation to the universality of the gospel message, see Ellingworth, *Epistle to the Hebrews*, 178–79.

of humans needing to act according to their nature (φύσις) (Rom 1:26), that is, the way humans were originally designed by God. He also speaks of God having a unique divine nature using the term *theiotes* (θειότης) (Rom 1:20; cf. Col 2:9). Likewise, Paul says that those who are not God do not have God's nature (φύσις) (Gal 4:8). The NT therefore teaches that humans are human by having a human nature (φύσις), and God is God because he alone possesses a divine nature (θειότης).

These are not the only Greek metaphysical terms the NT employs. Jesus cites the Septuagint's expansion of the Shema (Deut 6:5 LXX), which includes the metaphysical-spiritual term *dianoias* (διανοίας) (Mark 12:30)—signifying the abstract human mind or intellect—as a faculty that must be charged to love God.[60] Other NT metaphysical terms include *aorata* (ἀόρατα, invisible attributes) (Rom 1:20), *hypostaseos* (ὑποστάσεως, exact imprint [of God's nature]) (Heb 1:3), and Paul's unique use of *morphe Theou* (μορφή θεοῦ, form/nature of God) (Phil 2:6).

These Greek metaphysical concepts are essential for understanding the NT's portrayal of humanity and divinity, even though several have no Hebrew equivalents in the Hebrew Bible. Many other words of Greek origin have no equivalent in biblical Hebrew: theology, omniscience, infinity, ontology, metaphysics, physics, essence, substance, person, transcendence, immanence, providence, predestination, hermeneutics, teleology, exegesis, habit, and Bible. In line with the argument in §1.5, these words and concepts should *not* be discarded simply because of their non–Hebrew Bible origin. Instead, I believe these concepts support and complement a faithful understanding of the Hebrew Scriptures rather than compete with it. Similarly, the NT authors faithfully employ the metaphysical Greek terms previously mentioned in their quest to understand God, Scripture, and creation. While followers of Jesus need a discerning eye when considering Greek influence, they should not jettison *everything* coming from the Greek inheritance, for they would have to likewise discard the apostolic use of *physis*, *theiotes*, and other metaphysical words in the NT. As Steven Duby comments, "Apostolic Christianity does not shrink back from describing God with metaphysical language."[61]

---

60. The Hebrew Scriptures speak of people understanding, knowing, and thinking, but they typically place the seat of those actions in the heart (לֵב, לֵבָב). See *TDOT* 4:963–67. Jesus's use of the LXX of the Shema includes the heart (*kardia*) but also employs *dianoias*, an expanded intellectual nuance. Jesus thus uses a Greek metaphysical concept with a strong intellectual connotation to better explain what the Shema means. On Jesus's use of *dianoias* here, see France, *Gospel of Mark*, 479–80.

61. Duby, *Divine Simplicity*, 59.

In sum, it is incoherent to claim belief in the NT while criticizing all Greek metaphysics or philosophy in general.[62]

10.5.5. The Pre-Philosophical Belief in the Trinity and Incarnation

According to the NT presentation, Jesus possesses a human nature and a divine nature that are inseparably united in his one person. This indicates that NT Incarnation is different than any divine embodiment in the Hebrew Bible, where God merely appeared in physical form temporarily and never was "made like" human beings "in every respect" (Heb 2:17). Unlike previous theophanies, the NT insists that Jesus has a full human nature, which includes a human soul, mind, and body, as well as events such as birth, growth, temptation, and—for a Jewish man—the covenantal obligation of Israel's Torah. In this heightened species of divine embodiment, how could one person who is truly human also be truly divine?

The NT does not answer the ontological question regarding *how* Jesus could be both God and human. Instead, it focuses solely on asserting *that* Jesus is both God and human. The NT takes the same approach to the Trinity: it asserts *that* it is true without explaining *how* to understand the intricacies of God's tripersonal ontology. The NT provides the unrefined building blocks for the doctrines that would eventually be defined with the terms Incarnation and Trinity. Namely, six scattered teachings regarding the Trinity and the Incarnation can be seen throughout the NT:

---

62. A tendency among some in both gentile Christianity and the Messianic Jewish movement (and especially among "Hebrew roots" adherents) is to postulate a strict dichotomy between "Greek" and "Jewish" thought and terminology. Daniel Juster writes, "The Bible does not engage in abstract metaphysical definitions" and then cautions Messianic Jews against using Platonic and Aristotelian ideas ("Approaching God," 93, 103). Although a certain level of caution is warranted (see below), I believe Juster's conclusions and advice are exaggerated. Sometimes Paul's admonitions against "philosophy" are cited as evidence for this rejection of all Greek philosophy (Col 2:8). The Jewish apostles' use of Greek metaphysical concepts calls these attitudes into question, as does much of Second Temple Judaism. Colossians 2:8 is about the deceitfulness of false philosophy, not a rejection of philosophical thought in general.

Foundations of the Incarnation

Table 17. Six Basic New Testament Theological Teachings Relating to the Trinity and Incarnation

1.	There is only one God.	Mark 12:29; John 10:30; 1 Tim 2:5; 1 Cor 8:6; Jas 2:19
2.	The Father is God.	Matt 6:9; John 20:17; Rom 1:7; 1 Cor 8:6; Jas 1:27; 1 Pet 1:2
3.	The Son [Jesus] is God.	John 1:1; 20:28; Col 2:9; Phil 2:6; Heb 1:3
4.	The Holy Spirit is God.	Matt 28:19; John 14:16–17, 23; 15:26; 2 Cor 3:17–18; cf. Isa 63:10
5.	Jesus is human.	Rom 1:3; Heb 2:17; John 8:40; Luke 2:52
6.	Jesus is not the Father and not the Holy Spirit, nor is the Father the Spirit.	Matt 11:27; 26:39; Luke 3:21–22; John 15:1, 26

Believing these six statements individually, in isolation from the others, presents fewer problems than attempting to believe them all together with a unified theology. The NT asserts these claims about Jesus and the Trinity, but it would remain for later generations of theologians to articulate the concepts holistically, answering the question of *how*, to the extent that the human mind can understand. Later thinkers would find great assistance in the metaphysical tools provided to them by the Greek philosophical tradition. Still, their belief *that* Jesus is both God and human was not dependent upon the Greek metaphysics that would prove to be so valuable in answering the *how* question.

With respect to Christology, Christian orthodoxy's relationship with Greek philosophy is a posteriori: Greek philosophical concepts are used (and modified) *after the fact* to explain evidence already known through history and divine revelation. In other words, the Hebrew Scriptures, New Testament, and historical events have a higher epistemic priority than that of the Greek philosophical tradition. The early Jesus followers did not conclude that Jesus was divine through philosophical or metaphysical reflection but through the events they personally experienced. Chief among those events was the early believers' eyewitness claims that Jesus had risen from the dead after his crucifixion.[63] His resurrection provided them the motivation to travel to the ends of the known earth

---

63. For modern defenses of the historicity of the resurrection of Jesus, see Habermas, *Evidences*; Habermas and Licona, *Case for the Resurrection*; Licona, *Resurrection of Jesus*; Beck and Licona, *Raised on the Third Day*; Craig, *Son Rises*; N. Wright, *Resurrection of the Son*; Lapide, *Resurrection of Jesus*.

with the message of his divinity.[64] All of this was explainable from within a first-century Jewish context. Only later, in the second century, did the church fathers employ new philosophical tools to explain, defend, and define these already-believed truths. Theologian Craig Carter writes,

> So how did the [church] fathers do theology? They exegeted biblical texts, formulated doctrines based on these exegetical results, deduced metaphysical implications from those doctrines, and then used the metaphysical ideas as their philosophical framework for doing further exegesis. Along the way, the metaphysical implications of biblical doctrines led them to critique and correct ideas in their surrounding culture, thus making them suitable for use in Christian theology.[65]

Does a positive Christian affirmation of the Greek philosophical tradition undermine Christian theology in the same way Jewish affirmations undermine Maimonides and Kabbalah? At times, yes, when Christian theologians unscrupulously speculated under a broad acceptance of Greek paradigms that conflict with Scripture. Although this book is not focused on the errors of Platonizing church fathers who syncretized almost as much as Maimonides and Kabbalah, there were certainly some prime syncretizers in this respect: Origen, Clement of Alexandria, and Pseudo-Dionysius being chief among them.[66] Although these are lamentable exceptions to Carter's portrayal, by and large, the church fathers recognized that Greek philosophy had to be modified to serve biblical truth, rather than the other way around. The core beliefs of Jesus's divinity and the divinity of Father, Son, and Spirit were all in place before Christian thinkers started applying philosophical insights to those beliefs. The classic Christian theologians used the Greek tradition as a tool for solving intellectual problems,[67] rather than an a priori lens through which God, Scripture, and reality would be reinterpreted.

---

64. McDowell, *Fate of the Apostles*.

65. Carter, *Contemplating God*, 204.

66. For Origen, see McClymond, *Devil's Redemption*. Another example is the third-century CE Christian author Novatian. The significant similarity between Maimonides's *Guide* and Novatian's *On the Trinity* 1–8 (250 CE) illustrates how Neoplatonism, if placed epistemically prior to the Scriptures, makes belief in the Incarnation irrational even in a Christian context (Crawford, "Pathways," 117).

67. One might ask why the Greek tools were needed to solve problems. Why not do without Greek thought altogether? The short answer is that the Greeks founded entire intellectual disciplines that relate to Scriptural topics. Questions of unity and diversity, causality, modality, temporality and eternality, logic, and grammar are discussed at

10.5.6. The Evolutionary Argument against Jesus's Divinity

Up to this point, I have considered the writings of the NT as trustworthy records of events in the first century. Such acceptance involves a web of theological beliefs, including the existence of God, the possibility of miracles (such as resurrection), the unity of the apostles' beliefs, and ultimately Jesus's teachings about himself. However, belief in the NT's narrative at face value is difficult for some readers because they cannot imagine Jews coming to believe that a man is the Son of God. Such an idea, they assume, had to originate among pagan gentiles.

Since the nineteenth century, critical scholars have proposed a theory about Jesus's divinity being an evolutionary and innovative development that was not present in Jesus's self-consciousness or that of his earliest followers.[68] Usually, this argument is buttressed with the idea that belief in Jesus's divinity was a deviation from Judaism, developed under the influence of Greek mythology and philosophy. The advocates of this argument accept that the Gospel of John shows evidence of a high Christology (Jesus's divinity), but they attribute this to the lateness of the Fourth Gospel's composition. To these scholars, the Gospel of John reflects a later, more evolved Christology that turns Jesus into God, as opposed to the Synoptic Gospels, which do not. This theory accounts for why the belief in Jesus's divinity emerged in the church but attributes it to human ingenuity that is unconnected to the historical Jesus and divorced from Judaism itself. Ultimately, the evolutionary theory concerning Jesus's divinity concludes that it is inaccurate to follow historical Christian teaching that Jesus is the incarnate Son of God.

This skeptical evolutionary paradigm has lost scholarly momentum in recent decades due to new research sparked by Larry Hurtado's *One God, One Lord*, first published in 1988.[69] Hurtado investigates the early pattern of binitarian worship of Jesus, arguing that such worship

---

length in the Greek tradition—all of which relate to biblical theology and interpretation, yet are not discussed with similar depth in the Bible itself. Just as modern scientific studies of H2O can illuminate biblical passages about water (i.e., Jesus's miracle turning water into wine involved the creation of carbon atoms [John 2]), so too the Greek philosophical tradition can illuminate biblical subjects. On the value of philosophical studies for a NT worldview, see Moreland and Craig, *Philosophical Foundations*.

68. See §3.3 and Baur, *Christ Party*; Bousset, *Kyrios Christos*; Bauer, *Orthodoxy and Heresy*; Ehrman, *How Jesus Became God*.

69. For reflections on Hurtado's influence, see Fletcher-Louis, *Christological Origins*; Juncker, "Jesus and the Angel," 1–2.

was both partially continuous with existing Jewish tradition and an innovative "mutation" that occurred surprisingly early among Jesus's Jewish followers (i.e., the 30s CE). The earliness of these confessions of Jesus's deity erases the time span necessary for the evolutionary model to work and also restores the belief to a Jewish milieu. Hurtado's influential follow-up monograph, *Lord Jesus Christ* (2003), provides an analysis of christological material from the first and second centuries, further undermining theories of evolutionary development. He investigates all extant streams of Christ devotion from the era (Pauline, Petrine, Johannine, apocryphal, Valentinian, Marcionite, etc.) and concludes that all parties—both within and outside the theological mainstream—accepted Jesus's divinity in some sense.[70] Beyond this, Hurtado investigates early Christian worship practices, concluding that these practices, even outside any doxological or creedal context, imply the divinity of Jesus.[71] Hurtado writes, "In historical terms we may refer to a veritable 'big bang,' an explosively rapid and impressively substantial christological development in the earliest stage of the Christian movement."[72] Other scholars who have supported Hurtado's project include Martin Hengel, Richard Bauckham, Peter Schäfer, and the Jewish scholars listed in §3.3. These insights represent a sea change in contemporary scholarship. Consequently, old preconceptions about the non-Jewishness of the Incarnation must be revised.

10.6. Early Jewish-Christian Believers in Jesus's Divinity

The old paradigm may also be challenged by citing early Jewish-Christian authors' affirmations of Jesus's divinity. Among the earliest surviving Jewish-Christian works outside the NT are the Didache and the Odes of Solomon, dated by many scholars to the late first or early second century. Both illustrate belief in Jesus's divinity.[73]

---

70. Hurtado, *Lord Jesus Christ*, 560-61.

71. These practices include (1) prayer to Jesus; (2) invocation and confession of Jesus's name; (3) baptism in Jesus's name; (4) ritual celebration of "the Lord's Supper"; (5) hymns sung to Jesus; (6) prophecy in the name of Jesus; (7) the scribal practice of *nomina sacra* for Jesus's name (Hurtado, *Lord Jesus Christ*, 137-53, 625-27).

72. Hurtado, *Lord Jesus Christ*, 135.

73. Didache: ANF 7:369-83; Odes: OTP 2:725-34. Hurtado, "Christology," 181; Hurtado, *Lord Jesus Christ*, 609-18; Liderbach, *Christ in Early Christian*, 52; S. Wilhite, *Didache*.

The Didache says that believers must be baptized "in the name of the Lord"—who is identified as Jesus[74]—and then also says that believers must be baptized "in the name of the Father, and of the Son, and of the Holy Spirit," thus providing an early Trinitarian equation (Did. 7:1; 9:5).[75] Additionally, the Didache affirms Jesus's omnipresence (Did. 4:1). Likewise, the Odes of Solomon confesses, "For I believed in the Lord's Messiah, and considered that he is the Lord" (Odes Sol. 29:6). An early version of incarnational theology is included in the Odes:

> For there is a Helper for me, the Lord.
> He has generously shown himself to me in his simplicity,
> because his kindness has diminished his grandeur.
> He became like me, that I might receive him.
> In form he was considered like me, that I might put him on.
> And I trembled not when I saw him,
> because he was gracious to me.
> Like my nature he became, that I might understand him.
> And like my form, that I might not turn away from him.
> (Odes Sol. 7:3–6)[76]

More early Jewish evidence may be found in an epistle of Polycarp to the Philippians. According to a second-century letter,[77] Polycarp was Jewish and served as the bishop of Asia Minor, living until roughly 160 CE.[78] He was also one of the disciples of the apostle John. In the closing benediction of his letter, he calls Jesus both God and Lord:

> Now may God and the Father of our Lord Jesus Christ, and the eternal Priest himself, Jesus Christ, the Son of God, build you up in faith and truth, and in all gentleness, and without wrath, and in patience, and in longsuffering, and endurance, and purity, and may he give you a share and place with his saints, and to us with you, and to all under heaven who shall believe in our Lord and God Jesus Christ and in his Father who raised him from the dead. (Pol. Phil. 12.2)[79]

---

74. This identification is done through attributing the saying of Matt 7:6 to "the Lord" in Did. 9:5.

75. Brannan, *Apostolic Fathers in English*. In other words, Lord = יהוה = Jesus = Father, Son, and Spirit. This equation is made on the level of the divine nature, not equating the persons.

76. *OTP* 7:739–40.

77. Eusebius, *Hist. eccl.* 5.24.2–7; and 280n98 below.

78. Skarsaune and Hvalvik, *Early Centuries*, 516–24.

79. Brannan, *Apostolic Fathers in English*.

Part III: The Incarnation of the Son of God

Further early Jewish-Christian evidence of belief in Jesus's divinity is found in the Testaments of the Twelve Patriarchs. This set of documents is dated no later than the third century CE, but likely much earlier. Many scholars believe Jewish believers in Jesus took an earlier group of works penned by pre-NT Jews and then updated them to include teachings about Jesus as Messiah. Thus, the work's final form, which we have today, likely comes from the pens of Jewish Christians in the early centuries.[80]

In T. Sim. 7.2, there is a probable interpolation by an early Jewish Christian: "For the Lord will raise up from Levi someone as high priest and from Judah someone as king, God and man. He will save all the gentiles and the tribe of Israel."[81] The same theme is found in T. Naph. 8.3: "Through his kingly power God will appear dwelling among men on the earth, to save the race of Israel, and to assemble the righteous from among the nations."[82] In T. Ash. 7.3–4, the author speaks to Israel, saying,

> You will be scattered to the four corners of the earth; in the dispersion you shall be regarded as worthless, like useless water, until such time as the Most High visits the earth. He shall come as a man eating and drinking with human beings, crushing the dragon's head in the water. He will save Israel and all the nations, God speaking like a man. Tell these things, my children, to your children, so that they will not disobey him.[83]

These passages retain the original hope of the NT authors that Jew and gentile would be saved through a divine Messiah. After 70 CE, gentile Christian authors often obscure the Jewish hope and only speak of the nations (a form of supersessionism), but these Jewish Christian editors do not. For our purposes here, it is significant that these passages say Messiah would be both God and man.

Based on the evidence presented in this chapter, I conclude that belief in Jesus as the God of Israel emerged in Jewish circles soon after 30 CE, long before the Christian creeds or gentile involvement in the Jesus movement.[84] Belief in his divinity cannot be attributed to a gradual

---

80. *OTP* 1:771–828; Elgvin, "Jewish Christian Editing."
81. *OTP* 1:787. See also T. Sim. 6.5–7.
82. *OTP* 1:813.
83. *OTP* 1:818.
84. Some have claimed the adoptionist views of the Jewish Ebionites preserved an early and authentic Jewish-Christian Christology. See Hurtado, *Lord Jesus Christ*, 560–61. Hurtado concludes that the Ebionites of Epiphanius's fourth-century description (*Pan.* 30.16.5) leave no trace in first- or second-century christological debates and

evolution over the decades, brought about by Greek thought, culminating in the creeds. Instead, the earliest Jewish followers of Jesus believed in the six theological doctrines given above, and over time, Christians developed theological sophistication in explaining and defending the doctrines in response to external pressures.

10.7. The Theological Foundation: Christology Culminated in Chalcedon

The drive to articulate the historic faith of the NT with greater precision resulted from internal and external pressures to define the faith otherwise.[85] The early followers of Jesus found themselves in a three-front battle in which they needed to explain and defend their belief to skeptical Jews, Greeks, and schismatic heretics in their midst. Justin Martyr's *Dialogue with Trypho* (ca. 140 CE) contains the earliest sustained defense of Jesus's deity to Jewish audiences. Justin's strategic response to his Jewish audience is to highlight multiple lines of evidence in the Jewish Scriptures[86] that point to Israel's theophanic experiences with the preincarnate Messiah. Likewise, the rise of various gnostic groups in the second century CE prompted Christian apologists like Irenaeus to distinguish long-held theological belief from gnostic innovators.

Each heretical group promoted a theological system that accepted some, but not all, of the six NT theological doctrines. Below are a variety of heretical theologies and the NT doctrines they denied (see table 19):

1. *Adoptionism*: Jesus was adopted by God and became divine at his baptism. Denies (3), Jesus's divinity.

2. *Docetism*: Jesus only appeared to be human. Denies (5), Jesus's humanity.

---

are likely a later phenomenon.

85. D. Wilhite, *Gospel According to Heretics*. The topic of §10.7 is handled far more comprehensively in others' studies. For further reflection, consult Allison, *Historical Theology*; Behr, *Way to Nicaea*; Bray, *God Has Spoken*; Kelly, *Early Christian Creeds*; Sanders and Issler, *Jesus in Trinitarian Perspective*; Schaff, *Creeds of Christendom*; Skarsaune, "Making of the Creeds"; Erickson, *Word Became Flesh*; Svigel, "Power in Unity." For classic expositions of Trinitarian doctrine, see Athanasius, *Inc.*; Augustine, *Trin.*; John of Damascus, *De fide orth.*; Peter Lombard, *Sentences*; Aquinas, *ST*.

86. Since Justin argued from the LXX, it is not accurate to say that he reasoned from the Hebrew Scriptures.

3. *Modalism*: Father, Son, and Spirit are different modes of one person. Denies (6), the distinguishing of the Father, Son, and Spirit.
4. *Arianism*: The Son was the first and greatest creation of God. Denies (3), Jesus's divinity.
5. *Apollinarianism*: Jesus has a human body and a divine mind. Denies (5), Jesus's humanity.
6. *Nestorianism*: Jesus is a divine person plus a human person. This accounts for all six truths but not the singular "I" who speaks through Messiah in the NT. Jesus never talks to himself as if there are two persons in him.
7. *Monophysitism*: Jesus is a divine-human mixture. Denies (3), Jesus's divinity, and (5), Jesus's humanity.
8. *Contraction theology:* Jesus is a contraction, subset, or lower distillation of divinity (an early version of *tzimtzum*).[87] Denies (3), Jesus's full divinity.[88]

In response to each of these ideologies, the church fathers insisted that the *entire* witness of the NT be accepted as true, rather than denying one or more of its theological teachings. Anything less they labeled "heresy"—erroneous doctrine that put adherents outside salvation and the church. The disputes concerning the correct understanding of NT faith led to the development of proto-creeds among various church writers. The NT contains its own early creeds (1 Cor 8:6; 15:3–8; Phil 2:5–11), but the second-century rise of opposing groups necessitated the formulation of new summations of doctrine to combat denials of one or more of the NT's teachings about Messiah.

Perhaps the earliest post-apostolic creed was written by Ignatius (died ca. 115 CE), wherein Ignatius emphasized Jesus's humanity while combating docetism, the belief that Jesus is only divine and not truly human. Ignatius's formulation established a creedal pattern that subsequent creeds would follow.[89] Around 180 CE, Irenaeus responded to

---

87. The council at Sirmium (351 CE) defined this as heresy: "If any one affirms the essence of God to be dilated or contracted, let him be anathema. If any one says that the dilated essence of God makes the Son, or shall term the Son the dilatation of his essence, let him be anathema" (Socrates Scholasticus, *Hist. eccl.* 2.30).

88. For extended handlings of the christological heresies, see D. Wilhite, *Gospel According to Heretics*; Erickson, *Word Became Flesh*, 41–86; Macleod, *Person of Christ*, 121–203; Wellum, *God the Son Incarnate*, 255–311.

89. Ign. *Trall.* 9: "Jesus Christ, the one of the family of David, the one of Mary, he

the heresies of the gnostics by composing several creeds that included affirmations of the deity of the Father, Son, and Holy Spirit (*Haer.* 1.10.1; 3.4.2; 4.33.7). Other second- and third-century church fathers, such as Tertullian, Cyprian, and Origen, composed their own creeds with similar structure and content.[90] In his review of second-century church fathers' understanding of the Trinity, early church scholar Michael Svigel writes,

> The view of the earliest postapostolic fathers is best described as one in which Father, Son, and Holy Spirit are co-eternal and coequal with regard to deity and power, but in extra-Trinitarian actions the Father is the head, the Son is the mediator, and the Spirit is the pervasive active presence of God.[91]

Nevertheless, the church fathers during this period struggled to find consistent theological terminology to properly account for the six NT teachings. In the second century, Theophilus of Antioch coined the word Trinity (triunity) in Greek (*triados*) (*Autol.* 2.15), and Tertullian gave a Latin equivalent (*trinitas*) (*Prax.* 2). Other church fathers experimented with Greek and Latin forms of nature (*physis, natura*), substance (*ousia, substantia*), essence (*essentia*), person (*hypostasis, prosopon, persona*), and mutual indwelling (*perichoresis*).[92]

The Ecumenical Creeds of the fourth and fifth centuries CE were the culmination of this theological reflection. The first product of this era of articulation was the Nicene Creed of 325 CE, which was expanded in 381 CE by the Nicene-Constantinopolitan Creed. Although these fourth-century creeds mentioned Jesus's humanity, they focused primarily on articulating his full divinity (*homoousios*, the Son's "same essence" as the Father). The need for the Nicene Creed arose because of the claims of Arius, who asserted that Jesus is a created being who has only a *similar* essence to the Father. Contrary to the perceptions of some, the Nicene Creed does not represent a surrender to Greek thought but rather a rebellion against the Platonic metaphysics that Arius (and Origen before him) had brought

---

who truly was born, both ate and drank, truly was persecuted by Pontius Pilate, truly was crucified and died, being seen by those in heaven and on earth and under the earth, who also truly was raised from the dead, his Father having raised him. In the same way he also, his Father, will likewise raise up us who believe in him in Christ Jesus, without whom we do not have true life" (Brannan, *Apostolic Fathers in English*).

90. For a list of pre-Nicene creeds, see Schaff, *Creeds of Christendom*, 2:9–43.

91. Svigel, "Power in Unity," 39.

92. For the lexical background of these important theological terms, see Bray, *Doctrine of God*, 38–39, 127–28, 157–58, 167–69; Feinberg, *No One Like Him*, 477–92.

into the church. Neoplatonist scholar John Rist comments, "The Council of Nicaea forms a watershed in the relations between Christianity and Platonism. Before that, as in Origen, Platonic metaphysics could be used without radical reformulation in what was later to be called Trinitarian debate; after Nicaea that is no longer kosher."[93] Messianic Jewish theologian Mark Kinzer concurs: "In rejecting Arianism, the Nicene Creed took a stand *against* the common philosophical notions of the day, and *for* the biblical portrayal of the God of Israel."[94]

To continue the church's articulation of Jesus's identity, the Chalcedonian Definition of 451 CE clarified the Son's Incarnation: namely, the hypostatic (personal) union, the collective unity of one person who possesses both his divine and human natures without separation or mixing. The texts of the Nicene-Constantinopolitan Creed (usually just called the Nicene Creed) and the Chalcedonian Definition are given below:

Table 18. The Nicene Creed and Chalcedonian Definition[95]

The Nicene-Constantinopolitan Creed, 381 CE
I believe in one God, the Father Almighty, Maker of heaven and earth, and of all things visible and invisible.
And in one Lord Jesus Christ, the only-begotten Son of God, begotten of the Father before all worlds; God of God, Light of Light, very God of very God; begotten, not made, being of one substance [*homoousion*] with the Father, by whom all things were made.
Who, for us men for our salvation, came down from heaven, and was incarnate by the Holy Spirit of the virgin Mary, and was made man; and was crucified also for us under Pontius Pilate; He suffered and was buried; and the third day He rose again, according to the Scriptures; and ascended into heaven, and sits on the right hand of the Father; and He shall come again, with glory, to judge the quick and the dead; whose kingdom shall have no end.
And I believe in the Holy Ghost, the Lord and Giver of Life; who proceeds from the Father [and the Son]; who with the Father and the Son together is worshipped and glorified; who spoke by the prophets.
And I believe one holy catholic and apostolic Church. I acknowledge one baptism for the remission of sins; and I look for the resurrection of the dead, and the life of the world to come. Amen.

---

93. Rist, "Plotinus and Christian Philosophy," 404–5. See also Wellum, *God the Son Incarnate*, 258–59; Bray, *God Has Spoken*, 805–6; Anderson, *Paradox in Christian Theology*, 16–21.

94. Kinzer, "Significance of the Deity," 25.

95. Brannan, *Historic Creeds and Confessions*; emphasis in original.

Foundations of the Incarnation

> **The Chalcedonian Definition, 451 CE**
> We, then, following the holy Fathers, all with one consent, teach men to confess one and the same Son, our Lord Jesus Christ, the same perfect in Godhead and also perfect in manhood; truly God and truly man, of a reasonable [rational] soul and body; consubstantial [coessential] with us according to the manhood; in all things like unto us, without sin; begotten before all ages of the Father according to the Godhead, and in these latter days, for us and for our salvation, born of the Virgin Mary, the mother of God, according to the Manhood; one and the same Christ, Son, Lord, Only-begotten, to be acknowledged in two natures, *inconfusedly, unchangeably, indivisibly, inseparably*; the distinction of natures being by no means taken away by the union, but rather the property of each nature being preserved, and concurring in one person and one Subsistence, not parted or divided into two persons, but one and the same Son, and only begotten, God the Word, the Lord Jesus Christ, as the prophets from the beginning [have declared] concerning him, and the Lord Jesus Christ himself has taught us, and the Creed of the holy Fathers has handed down to us.

The Nicene Creed became necessary because of a growing movement of Arians who denied Jesus's divinity, and the Chalcedonian Definition became necessary because of multiple movements that diminished his full divinity, or his full humanity, or his distinction from the Father and the Spirit. In particular, Chalcedon's solution was to distinguish the *person* of the Son of God from the idea of a *nature* (or substance or essence). The person of the Son, roughly his center of consciousness, subsists in his divine nature and is united to his human nature in the Incarnation. In other words, one "I" or center of consciousness simultaneously animates and acts in and through his divine nature and his human nature. To illustrate this more clearly, the Chalcedonian Definition accounts for the fact that while Jesus the infant human was crying in the manger, the same Son of God was *also* holding together the atoms of the nebulas in a billion galaxies.[96] Chalcedon affirms that he truly was both God and man, mysteriously, at the same time, living and acting through two natures as one person.

These teachings were illustrated long before Chalcedon in 451 CE. For example, Ignatius of Antioch (ca. 35–107 CE) writes of the Messiah's dual natures as follows: "There is one physician, both fleshly and

---

96. Col 1:17, Heb 1:3. This theological doctrine has been called the *extra Calvinisticum*, since it was articulated in the Protestant era by John Calvin (*Institutes* 4.17.30), but it was first explained during the patristic era. See Athanasius, *Inc.* 17:1–2; Cyril of Alexandria *Epistle* 55.33; John of Damascus, *De fide orth.* 3.7; Peter Lombard, *Sentences* 3.3.4. See also Duby, *God in Himself*, 177–87; Ortlund, *Theological Retrieval for Evangelicals*, 99–108.

spiritual, born and unborn, God in man, true life in death, both of Mary and of God, first subject to suffering and then free of suffering, Jesus Christ our Lord" (Ign. *Eph.* 7.2).[97] Likewise, Melito of Sardis (late second century CE), a Jewish-Christian[98] bishop who served in Asia Minor, wrote a striking poem about the Messiah's dual natures. Melito says:

> He appeared as a sheep while remaining a shepherd,
> he was thought to be a slave, while not denying his sonship,
> he was born of Mary, while wearing the garment of his Father,
> walking on earth while filling the heavens,
> appearing as a child,
> while not falsifying the eternity of his nature,
> clothed in flesh
> whilst not constraining the simplicity of his divinity.
> Believed to be poor, but not deprived of his wealth,
> requiring nourishment, insofar as he was a needy human,
> not ceasing to nourish the world, as he was God.
> Putting on the likeness of a slave
> while not altering his likeness to the Father.
> In his unchangeable nature he was all things.
> He stood before Pilate and is seated with the Father,
> he was nailed on the tree and comprehended all things.[99]

Cyril of Alexandria (378–444 CE) writes likewise:

> If he became man, being God, in no way did he cease being God. If he became a part of creation, he also remained above creation. If, being legislator as God, he came to be "under the law," he was still legislator. If being master according to his divinity, he put on "the form of a slave," yet he still has the inseparable dignity of a master.[100]

---

97. Brannan, *Apostolic Fathers in English*.

98. Melito's Jewish background is inferred from Polycrates's letter where Polycrates calls seven bishops of Asia Minor, including Melito, John the Apostle, and Philip the Apostle, "my relatives" (Eusebius, *Hist. eccl.* 5.24). Since John and Philip were Jews, it is likely that Polycrates intended to convey that Melito was Jewish as well. The plausibility of Melito's Jewishness is increased by noting that he was a Quartodeciman (one who celebrated Easter/Passover on the fourteenth of Nisan on the Hebrew calendar) and who included themes in his *Peri Pascha* that parallel the Haggadah. Nevertheless, Melito is sometimes noted as being the first author who charged the Jewish people with the collective guilt of murdering God—deicide—an idea that would prove perilous to Jews in subsequent centuries. For more on Melito's Jewish identity, see Skarsaune and Hvalvik, *Early Centuries*, 516–28.

99. *Fragment* 14, in Melito of Sardis, *On Pascha*, 55:94–95.

100. *Epistle* 55.33, in Cyril of Alexandria, *Letters*, 31.

Foundations of the Incarnation

Thus, the teaching of one person with two natures was actively affirmed before 451 CE. The distinction between person and nature is central to the Chalcedonian Definition, as is the understanding that Messiah has two unmixed natures that are united in his one person (the hypostatic or personal union).

Table 19. Sub-Chalcedonian Heresies

Heresy	Summary	Jesus is:				Violates Chalcedon in:
		Truly God?	Truly Man?	One Person?	Not the Father or Spirit?	
Adoptionism	Jesus was adopted into the Godhead.	No	No	No	Yes	"truly God" "truly man" "one Person"
Docetism (Gnostics)	Jesus only appeared to be human.	Yes	No	Yes	Yes	"consubstantial with us"
Modalism (Sabellius)	Father, Son, and Spirit are different modes of one person.	Yes	Yes	Yes	No	"begotten before all ages of the Father"
Arianism	The Son was the first and greatest creation of God.	No	Yes	Yes	Yes	"truly God" "consubstantial with the Father" "begotten before all ages"
Apollinarianism	Jesus has a human body and a divine mind.	Yes	No	Yes	Yes	"truly man"
Nestorianism	Jesus is a divine person plus a human person.	Yes	Yes	No	Yes	"one person" "inseparably" "not divided into two persons"
Monophysitism (Eutyches)	Jesus is a divine/human mixture.	No	No	Yes	Yes	"inconfusedly"
Contraction theology	Jesus is a *tzimtzum* of God.	No	Yes	Yes	Yes	"truly God" "consubstantial with the Father"

10.8. The Importance of the Creeds for Gentile and Jewish Believers in Jesus

The creeds just discussed are not Scripture, and thus they are not invested with the inerrant authority of the New Testament itself. Nevertheless, the Christian church has never been able to come up with a better summary of doctrine that reasonably accounts for all six of the NT's teachings as given above. Rather, to deny the Nicene or Chalcedonian theological articulations is likely to deny one or more NT passages about the Father, Son, or Spirit. Thus, to deny the *homoousios* clause of Nicaea or the one person/two natures formulation of Chalcedon is to deny the teachings of the NT and to believe in another god or another Jesus than the one espoused in the NT.

On the one hand, these creeds are not controversial because they have become the bedrock of Christian orthodoxy across Catholic, Eastern Orthodox, and Protestant churches for millennia. On the other hand, these creeds *have* been highly controversial for a variety of factors. To the skeptic, the enforcement of these creeds by the Roman state-church appears to be an orthodoxy defined by the powerful. To the surviving Nestorian and Coptic churches of the East, Chalcedon should never have been accepted in the first place. To a minority of Protestants, to assert the truth of extra-biblical and man-made creeds is to deny the Bible's preeminent place.[101] And to some in the modern Messianic movement, any articulation of NT doctrine without the influence of Jewish believers, and *with* the influence of Greek thought,[102] appears suspect.[103]

These are complex objections to the creeds, not to be fully handled here. In my opinion, they are not strong enough to overturn the importance of the creeds' theological articulation of basic NT truths. Nevertheless, the grievances of Messianic Jews regarding Greek concepts have some merit. Both historical and contemporary Christian theologians

---

101. In response to this tendency, see Trueman, *Crisis of Confidence*.

102. Some Messianic Jews have a negative reaction to Greek metaphysical terms that did not originate in the Hebrew Scriptures or Jewish thought. For example, the metaphysical terms *hypostasis, ousia, substantia,* and *persona* each had their origin in Greek and Roman philosophical and legal discourse. See §10.5.4 and Bray, *Doctrine of God,* 38.

103. For Messianic discussions along these lines, see Juster, "Christological Dogma of Nicaea"; Skarsaune, "Christological Dogma of Nicaea." Messianic theologian Mark Kinzer discusses some of the skepticism in the Messianic movement and asks his audience to give the creeds the benefit of the doubt ("Finding Our Way"). See also Bock, "Response to Mark Kinzer."

Foundations of the Incarnation

have often shown a lack of awareness about the Platonic, not biblical, roots of many ideas and movements in the church. Allegorical and esoteric hermeneutics, elaborate divine hierarchies, mystical practices, the beatific vision, and intuitions about perichoresis, eternal generation, divine simplicity, and divine causality have had their discourse shaped by Platonic and Neoplatonic metaphysics that were subsequently imported into the church.

While the initial Platonic background of these ideas is not sufficient grounds for their rejection,[104] Platonic excesses and unbiblical notions may run unchecked when Christian theologians are unaware of an idea's Platonic background. This lack of awareness is dangerous because it can lead to the syncretized gospel of Platonism rather than the gospel of Christ. Lest Christian theologians make the same mistake as Maimonides and Kabbalah regarding a priori acceptance of Platonic concepts, any adoption of Greek philosophical categories and models must be held in check by Scripture and therefore modified from their pagan Greek forms.[105] At the same time, I have already illustrated how Jesus followers cannot reasonably jettison all Greek metaphysics from their theology (§10.5.4), as the NT integrates metaphysical concepts. As with Aristotle's Golden Mean and Goldilocks, followers of Jesus should accept aspects of Greek metaphysics, but not too little, and not too much.

The Messianic Jewish community also has concerns regarding the Nicene Creed's omissions and the anti-Jewish pronouncements made in the council's canons. Messianic Jewish theologian Mark Kinzer writes,

> The problem we see is not with what the Creed says, but with what it fails to say. . . . It summarizes the basic narrative of God's dealings with the world in a manner that ignores the central role played by the Jewish people. . . . Like all major Christian confessional statements before and after, the Nicene Creed omits any reference to the people of Israel and its crucial role in the story of God's dealings with the world.[106]

---

104. To reject ideas on the basis of their origin alone is the genetic fallacy. See §1.5.

105. For examples of Christian theologians who are aware that concepts originating in Greek metaphysics should be modified in Christian theology, see Bray, *God Has Spoken*, 115, 279, 805–6; Duby, *God in Himself*, 188–231; Wellum, *God the Son Incarnate*, 256–60; Poythress, *Mystery of the Trinity*, 438–40; Frame, *History of Western Philosophy*, 81.

106. Kinzer, "Finding Our Way," under "The Problem with the Creed." Kinzer ultimately accepts the truth of the Nicene Creed and identifies the divinity of Yeshua as a foundation stone of the Messianic movement. While partially agreeing with Kinzer's

Notably missing from the creeds is any mention of Jesus's Davidic or Jewish heritage, his life in Judea, his connection to Old Testament prophecy, his future return as Israel's king in Jerusalem, his status as the prophet like Moses, or his initiation of the new covenant. An outsider could read the creeds and come away without any conception of the relationship between Jesus, his Jewish people, and the Hebrew Scriptures. By omitting these important factors, the creeds appear to be more gentile in mindset than they should be for a church whose Messiah is Jewish, whose Scriptures are Jewish, and whose community is composed of Jew and gentile united as one (Eph 2).[107]

Despite these complex matters related to the historic creeds, there is good reason to retain the creeds as precious and helpful summations of accurate theology that are fully in concert with NT teaching and the teachings of the church fathers from the three centuries after Jesus. The anti-Judaic supersessionism of the later centuries was not part of the early church's continual tradition, but the teaching of Jesus's deity is a scarlet thread throughout the period, and the creeds accurately transmit that teaching. Without the creeds' theological precision as a limit against human ingenuity, believers in Jesus may unconsciously drift into heresy. Any creedal skeptics should engage the voluminous literature on the creeds as accurate biblical theology. For Messianic Jews especially, it would also be beneficial to consult the respectful tone taken by the Messianic Jewish contributors to the Borough Park Papers.[108] If segments of the Messianic Jewish movement hesitate to publicly adopt the creeds in their historical form, it may serve the movement well to produce a kosher version of the creeds, not by changing the substance of their content, but by reverently rearticulating and augmenting them to illuminate their compatibility with Jewish thought.[109]

---

critiques, Bock argues for a charitable attitude to the omissions of Nicaea ("Response to Mark Kinzer")

107. It is fair to note that the purpose of the councils was to combat false Christologies, and the Jewishness of Jesus and his connection with the Hebrew Scriptures was not up for debate. On these omissions, see P. Morris, "Creeds and Theology." R. Kendall Soulen calls omissions of this type "structural supersessionism" ("Standard Canonical Narrative).

108. Borough Park Symposium, *Symposium II.*

109. For previous attempts at producing Hebrew Christian and Messianic Jewish versions of the creeds, see Nerel, "Creeds Among Jewish Believers"; Nerel, "Christological Observations"; P. Morris, "Creeds and Theology."

Because of its theological and philosophical precision, I believe the Chalcedonian Definition is essential for articulating the Incarnation of the Son of God. Chalcedon delivers enduring positive descriptions of the Messiah, such as "truly God and truly man," "two natures," and "one person," but also negative descriptions that safeguard the affirmations. The one person of the incarnate Messiah possesses two natures, divine and human, that stand together in a hypostatic union without mixture or change. His two natures are unconfused, unchanged, undivided, and unseparated. In his Incarnation, the Son is the same as he was before, but different. As many church fathers summarize, "He remained what he was, and he became what he was not."[110] He retains his divine nature while adding a human nature. This is Christian orthodoxy, as well as Messianic Jewish orthodoxy. Now I turn to ask whether it makes any sense.

---

110. Various church fathers, but an early form is found in Origen, *Princ.*, preface.

11 Implications of the Incarnation
Rationality, Hermeneutics, and Explanatory Scope

But of all the marvellous and mighty acts related of Him, this altogether surpasses human admiration, and is beyond the power of mortal frailness to understand or feel, how that mighty power of divine majesty, that very Word of the Father, and that very wisdom of God, in which were created all things, visible and invisible, can be believed to have existed within the limits of that man who appeared in Judea. . . . The truth of both natures may be clearly shown to exist in one and the same Being. . . . To utter these things in human ears, and to explain them in words, far surpasses the powers either of our rank, or of our intellect and language. I think that it surpasses the power even of the holy apostles; nay, the explanation of that mystery may perhaps be beyond the grasp of the entire creation of celestial powers.

—Origen (third century CE)[1]

Using human logic, [they] are meddling with his ineffable union, inquiring into what is indescribable and asking "How?" And if they do not get an answer, they refuse to believe any longer.

—Mark the Monk (fifth century CE)[2]

---

1. Origen, *Princ.* 2.6.2 (*ANF* 4.282).
2. Mark the Monk, *Counsels*, 2:262.

Now that I have explained the Incarnation's basis in the NT and early Christian theology, this chapter will investigate various implications of the doctrine. First, I will discuss how a rational, thinking person can accept the doctrine of the Incarnation when it seems to have significant intellectual obstacles. The logical absurdity of the Incarnation is the heart of the Maimonidean objection to the idea. Because he sees the Incarnation as impossible, he concludes that the idea is idolatrous. After dealing with that objection, I will show how temporary divine embodiment provides the best answer for understanding God talk in the Hebrew Scriptures. Finally, I will examine how the mediating Son of God provides powerful solutions to a wide variety of theological topics that impact every human being and the cosmos at large, including creation, providence, prophecy, human nature, divine sympathy, salvation from sin, communion with God, and access to God's (metaphorical) listening ear.

11.1. The Rational Foundation of the Incarnation: Is the Doctrine Absurd?

Throughout this book, I have asked how it is possible that an infinite, incorporeal, omniscient, and necessary God could reside as a human being with a finite, corporeal, knowledge-limited, and contingent existence. When followers of Jesus confess belief in the Incarnation, as laid out by the Chalcedonian Definition, they are saying that the union of these two categorically different natures in Jesus *is* possible. Is such a position irrational nonsense? According to the opinions of mainstream rationalist Judaism (influenced by Maimonides) and others, the answer is yes: Christianity is based upon the absurd. In no way could God come into human flesh, any more than he can make one equal two, or make a circle equal a square. As contemporary Rabbi Meir Soloveichik writes:

> Jews believe that the Torah tells us that the Incarnation is incompatible with all that God has taught us about who he is. Christians embrace the concept of the Incarnation; but, from the Jewish perspective, a human God is the equivalent of a four-sided triangle.[3]

Soloveichik's Maimonidean statement is a significant intellectual challenge to the Incarnation, aligning with many Jewish people's thoughts at an intuitive, commonsense level: the illogicality of the Incarnation

3. Soloveichik, "No Friend in Jesus," 31.

appears so obvious that it is scandalous to suggest otherwise. However, there is good reason to be skeptical of these logical critiques. If the critiques fail, then so too does Maimonides's anti-incarnational rationalism, as represented here by Rabbi Soloveichik. I believe that the Incarnation, present within the NT, and best articulated by Chalcedon, withstands these objections and presents an accurate portrayal of God and his relationship with the world as given in the Hebrew Scriptures.[4]

11.1.1. The Relation of Divine Incomprehensibility to the Incarnation

One of the major problems with many rationalisms is their overly optimistic view of the human mind.[5] Although the Bible says people are made in the image and likeness of God (Gen 1:26), with rational capability endowed by God, humanity's ability to reason (noetic capability) is diminished from two directions. First, the ingrained propensity for humans to choose sin causes human beings to have darkened minds that reason poorly.[6] According to the NT, this may be partially remedied by new birth and the indwelling of the Spirit, but full redemption from the noetic effects of sin will come only with the resurrection of believers' bodies (Rom 8:18–25). However, there is a second vector through which human reason is dulled and can never be remedied: finite creatureliness. Even after living ten thousand years in a universe cleansed of sin (Rev 21), redeemed and resurrected humans will remain finite creatures who cannot grasp the unfathomable essence of God. Theologians call this second limit on human rationality *divine incomprehensibility*.

---

4. For other defenses of the logic of the Incarnation, see Anderson, *Paradox in Christian Theology*; Wellum, *God the Son Incarnate*, 445–65; T. Morris, *Logic of God Incarnate*; Erickson, *Word Became Flesh*, 531–76.

5. One of the church's early obstacles came from Eunomius, whom Venables calls "the Rationalist of the 4th century." Eunomius asserted that every doctrine must be shown to be consistent with human reason, or else should be rejected. This view was rejected by the orthodox party, illustrating how Christian orthodoxy is not a strictly logical system and needs room for mystery (Venables, "Eunomius (3)," 2:287).

6. Gen 3; Eph 4:17–18; Rom 1:21; John 3:19; Aquinas, *ST* II-II q.2 a.4 resp.; Calvin, *Institutes* 2.2.12; Geisler, *Baker Encyclopedia*, s.v. "Noetic Effects of Sin"; Plantinga, *Warranted Christian Belief*, 212–40. Christian theologian Albert Mohler lists fourteen noetic effects of the fall of man in Gen 3: ignorance, distractedness, forgetfulness, prejudice, faulty perspective, intellectual fatigue, inconsistencies, failure to draw the right conclusion, intellectual apathy, dogmatism and closed-mindedness, intellectual pride, vain imagination, miscommunication, and partial knowledge ("Way the World Thinks").

This doctrine is taught in various places throughout the Hebrew Scriptures and NT, classified in two forms. First, there is the operational form of divine incomprehensibility, whereby Scripture says that humans cannot fully understand the *thoughts* and *ways* of God. Isaiah gives a classic formulation of how humans cannot understand how God operates: "For my thoughts are not your thoughts, neither are your ways my ways, declares the Lord. For as the heavens are higher than the earth, so are my ways higher than your ways and my thoughts than your thoughts" (Isa 55:8–9; cf. Isa 29:14; Eccl 11:5; Job 36:26). Paul gives a succinct NT form: "Oh, the depth of the riches and wisdom and knowledge of God! How unsearchable are his judgments and how inscrutable his ways!" (Rom 11:33).

Second, the ontological form of divine incomprehensibility states that God's *essence* or *nature* is beyond human comprehension. Paul speaks of God as the one "who dwells in unapproachable light" (1 Tim 6:16). In Ps 139, David considers the omnipresence of God ("You hem me in, behind and before" [v. 5]; "Where can I go from your Spirit?" [v. 7]) and exclaims, "Such knowledge is too wonderful for me; it is high; I cannot attain it" (Ps 139:6). Job's friend Zophar, while questionable in other areas, concurs when he considers "the limit of the Almighty" and confesses, "It is higher than heaven—what can you do?" (Job 11:7–9). Statements like these articulate the biblical teaching of God's infinite nature; just as the mind cannot "reach" infinity, the Bible says humans are unable to grasp God's essence.[7]

The second form of divine incomprehensibility, the mystery of God's essence, is where the doctrine of the Incarnation finds its greatest foe, but also its greatest ally. The Platonic stream of thought asserts the incomprehensibility of the highest divinity (Plato, *Tim.* 28c) but closes the distance between God and man by pursuing ontological unification with the divine in mystical contemplation and eschatological destiny. Both Kabbalah and Maimonides absorb these Platonic themes, employing the unknowability of God's essence to make the Incarnation of Messiah either impossible or redundant. I have already addressed many reasons why Kabbalah's worldview should not be accepted (chs. 8–9), but Maimonides's position that divine embodiment is impossible has been only partially addressed (see §6.5). Ironically, the very doctrine that Maimonides wields to reject God in physical form—the incomprehensibility of the divine essence—may be

---

7. See 257n35 for my qualification for how I understand infinity to apply to God.

profitably employed to make Incarnation reasonable, possible, and the best fit for scriptural revelation. What if the incomprehensible God has the incomprehensible power to reveal aspects of his incomprehensible nature by taking upon himself a human nature as well?

11.1.2. Mystery, Paradox, and the Incarnation

Theologians have a venerable tradition of calling the Incarnation a great "mystery," a synonym for paradox.[8] A paradox is a statement or situation that appears to be contradictory or absurd, but upon closer examination, reveals a deeper and unexpected truth that is difficult to comprehend.[9] Alternatively stated, a paradox is a proposition that is inexplicably true despite being derived from apparently contradictory premises. Furthermore, a paradox is a mystery because humans do not have the intellectual capability to solve it or even to fully grasp it. These concepts accurately describe the status of the Incarnation in the human mind. While believers in Jesus may believe *that* the Incarnation occurred as described in the NT and may have some conceptual tools to partially understand *how* it occurred, there is a hard limit to how far humans can understand how Jesus can have both a human nature and a divine nature. It is ultimately a paradox: "No one knows the Son except the Father" (Matt 11:27).

However, paradox at the center of Christian theology leaves many feeling uncomfortable. Paradox is often believed to be the playground of superstition, magic, and mysticism—the antithesis of sound reason. Thus, some critics have charged the Chalcedonian Definition with absurdity. Many scholars attempt to escape this challenge while retaining some sort of belief in the Incarnation. In his book *Paradox in Christian Theology*, James Anderson assesses several of the proposed incarnational models that claim to eliminate paradox.[10] Some proposed models include dual psychology (Jesus possesses two ranges of consciousness with an asymmetrical accessing relation of his divine mind to his human

---

8. Church fathers: Hippolytus, *Contra Beronem* 2–4; Gregory of Nyssa, *Contra Eunomius* 5.5; Augustine, *Letter* 11.2; Basil, *On the Spirit*, 24.57; Gregory Nazianzen, *Oration* 39.13; Hilary, *Trinity* 12.51; Mark the Monk, *Counsels* 2.3.34. Modern writers: Anderson, *Paradox in Christian Theology*, 101–5; Wellum, *God the Son Incarnate*, 366, 440, 447; Feinberg, *No One Like Him*, 437; Macleod, *Person of Christ*, 100; Shedd, *Dogmatic Theology*, 248–49; Crisp, *Divinity and Humanity*, ch. 1.

9. For discussions on the paradoxes within Christian theology, see Anderson, *Paradox in Christian Theology*; Oliphint, *Majesty of Mystery*; Michel and Ramsey, *Surprised by Paradox*.

10. Anderson, *Paradox in Christian Theology*, 80–152.

mind),[11] kenoticism (the Son ceases having divine attributes during his Incarnation), anti-deductivism (nothing can be logically deduced about God), semantic minimalism (doctrines may state only what God is not, that is, *via negativa*), doctrinal revisionism (change doctrines to remove paradox), and anti-realism (doctrines are not tied to reality). Anderson's assessment concludes that these attempts to remove the paradox of the Incarnation either fall prey to sub-Chalcedonian heresy or fail to remove the paradox.

However, there may be no rational need to escape the paradox implied in the Incarnation. In his response to critics of the Incarnation, C. F. D. Moule writes, "It is a sacred duty for any thinking person to try to eliminate paradox. But if the data refuse to let us escape a paradox, it may be necessary to entertain it."[12] Samuel Lebens concurs:

> Whenever we're faced with a putative contradiction, there will always be a prima facie obligation to resolve it, since—on the basis of our faith in God's creative excellence—we trust that no contradiction will be true unless it's discovered to be glaring and necessary to fulfill God's narrative purposes.[13]

Indeed, one may be more rational to accept certain paradoxes than to reject them.

But are the contradictions implied within paradoxes *really* contradictions? That would seem to undermine a foundational principle of logic, the law of noncontradiction. But what if paradoxes include statements that *appear* to be contradictory but are not? Anderson writes, "The doctrine of divine incomprehensibility should lead us to *anticipate* paradox in some of our theological knowledge."[14] Instead of rejecting the Incarnation or sacrificing the law of noncontradiction, Anderson proposes an intellectually satisfying solution grounded in the doctrine of divine incomprehensibility. He calls it the "rational affirmation of paradoxical theology" and writes, "One can be rational in believing a paradoxical set of claims provided one has grounds for thinking that the contradiction is *merely* apparent."[15] Central to Anderson's argument is the distinction between *apparent* and *actual* contradictions, which shifts the conversation

---

11. T. Morris, *Logic of God Incarnate*, 102–7. See below.
12. Moule, "Three Points of Conflict," 140.
13. Lebens, *Principles of Judaism*, 104.
14. Anderson, *Paradox in Christian Theology*, 241; emphasis in original.
15. Anderson, *Paradox in Christian Theology*, 252; emphasis in original.

to epistemological concerns.[16] Because of the limitation of human noetic ability, there may be truths about God that human minds cannot penetrate, analyze, or confirm. The truths may *appear* to be contradictory, but they are not *actually* so, if only we could see from God's perspective. Thus, one is obligated to believe in the truth of the paradox about God if there is adequate warrant for it.

A delightful nineteenth-century parable illustrates the notion of paradoxical truths beyond human comprehension that are noncontradictory. In his novel *Flatland*, Edwin Abbott tells the story of a mind-bending thought experiment. The main character is a personified square who lives on a two-dimensional plane with a functioning shape society. One day, the square receives a visitor from the Third Dimension—a sphere—although the square has no noetic capability to conceive of the sphere as a sphere. The square knows only north, south, east, and west; the concepts of up, down, height, and depth are unintelligible to him. The square can perceive the sphere only where it intersects his two-dimensional plane, so the sphere appears to be a mere circle. However, the sphere insists that he is not merely a circle, but an infinite array of circles. Initially, the square cannot comprehend or accept this claim. Thus, the sphere conducts a series of actions to prove his claim. First, he moves up and down, intersecting the plane at different points, appearing to the square as if the sphere is changing size. Second, the sphere moves above the square's two-dimensional house and starts describing its contents and taking things out of it, despite its doors being shut. Since these kinds of actions are impossible in a two-dimensional world, the square is convinced that he has just experienced miracles. These proofs still do not enable the square to understand *what* the sphere is or *how* the sphere does his miracles, but they do lead him to believe that the sphere is real and only *apparently* absurd.

The point of the parable is to encourage reflection on the limits of human knowledge and understanding, including the possibility that there are truths about God beyond human comprehension, despite appearing to be absurd.[17] Simply because human minds cannot conceive of *how* Jesus's divinity and humanity coexist in the same person, it does not follow that they *cannot*. Similarly, the incomprehensibility of the tripersonal unity of the one God should not be conceived as evidence against

---

16. Anderson devotes many pages to base his theory upon Alvin Plantinga's epistemological work on warrant (*Paradox*, 155–216). See Plantinga, *Warrant*.

17. Swinburne, *Coherence of Theism*, 43–46.

its truth. As Hilary of Poitiers (300–368 CE) writes, "But human logic is fallacy in the presence of the counsels of God, and folly when it would cope with the wisdom of heaven; its thoughts are fettered by its limitations, its philosophy confined by the feebleness of natural reason."[18]

11.1.3. The Incarnation as an Unjustified "Mystery of the Gaps"?

Some might object that this is an irrational punting to mystery, a kind of "mystery of the gaps"[19] to make Christian orthodoxy work. That is incorrect for at least five reasons.

First, it must be recognized that the mystery being invoked is narrow in scope and not as wide ranging as critics suggest. The Incarnation does not entail a mixing of the divine and human natures such that it involves overt absurdities like saying "the infinite is finite" or "the omniscient is knowledge limited." The Incarnation does not result in the rejection of the principle of noncontradiction and the establishment of nonrational mysticism for all areas of inquiry. The surface area of the Incarnation's mystery, so to speak, is more modest, limited to the man Jesus.

For example, Meir Soloveichik claims the Incarnation requires belief in a "four-sided triangle."[20] This criticism is flawed. Christian theology does not appeal to mystery in order to justify belief analogous to a four-sided triangle. Rather, a better analogy would be to say that God is like a four-sided rectangle, and humans are like three-sided triangles, and in the Incarnation, the rectangle lived in and through the experience and nature of a triangle while also remaining a rectangle. In that case, we can ask ourselves in this analogy, "Is he four sided?" Yes, according to his rectangular nature. "Is he three sided?" Yes, according to his triangular nature. "Is he a four-sided triangle?" No, because that would mix the natures, which the NT (and Chalcedon) deny.[21] Therefore Meir Soloveichik is criticizing the heresy of Monophysitism, not orthodox Christian

---

18. Hilary of Poitiers, *On the Trinity* 5.1 (NPNF^2 9:85).

19. The phrase "God of the gaps" is commonly used to criticize premodern people who had the tendency to ascribe unknown natural phenomena to God's miraculous and inscrutable intervention. Examples include eclipses being omens from the gods, rainbows being good signs, and epidemics being divine punishments. If people think, "A divine being did it," then this answer can stifle curiosity and scientific investigation. The "mystery of the gaps" objection complains that attributing the Incarnation to mystery and paradox is a similar intellectual cop-out.

20. Soloveichik, "No Friend in Jesus," 31.

21. McFarland, *Word Made Flesh*, 79–80.

theology.²² Consequently, one must be precise about what, exactly, is the mystery that is being invoked. The mystery is the following: how one divine person (a living consciousness and agent) can truly possess two different natures, for human experience would lead us to believe that all things have only one nature.

Second, now that the character of the mystery is clear, the NT provides warrant to believe that the Incarnation is a *merely apparent* contradiction because of other comprehensible evidence that God has provided. The resurrection of Jesus from the dead (historical evidence),²³ eyewitness authenticity of the NT books (historical-textual evidence),²⁴ archaeological confirmations of the NT (historical evidence),²⁵ fulfillment of biblical prophecy (historical-textual evidence),²⁶ personal attraction to the character of Jesus (subjective experience), and personal rebirth by the Holy Spirit (subjective experience) provide tangible, rational, and intuitive evidence to encourage believers to trust Scripture in areas that their human minds cannot grasp.²⁷ In contrast, many non-biblical mystical, theosophical, magical, and speculative works (including Kabbalah)

---

22. Monophysites say the Incarnation entails the Son of God fusing or mixing his divine nature with his human nature, resulting in a new, single hybrid nature that is half and half of both. Orthodox Christian theologians charge this position with absurdity. What does it mean to be half transcendent beyond the universe? What does it mean to be half omnipresent? However, it is true God plays by different rules than us, so simply because an idea *sounds* absurd, it does not mean that it actually is. There are times where one should believe in paradoxes because there is good evidence in the paradox's favor. In the case of the Monophysite position, however, there is no such scriptural evidence. It is a creative philosophical theory that cannot be justified by the NT. It is an example of the bad philosophy Paul warned against in Col 2:8. Thus, Monophysitism is rejected not only as *apparent* absurdity, but as *actual* absurdity that is heresy as well.

23. Habermas, *Evidences*; Habermas and Licona, *Case for the Resurrection*; Licona, *Resurrection of Jesus*; Beck and Licona, *Raised on the Third Day*; Craig, *Son Rises*; N. Wright, *Resurrection of the Son*; Lapide, *Resurrection of Jesus*.

24. Keener, *Christobiography*; Bauckham, *Jesus and the Eyewitnesses*; Blomberg, *Historical Reliability of Gospels*; Blomberg, *Historical Reliability of John's Gospel*; Köstenberger and Kruger, *Heresy of Orthodoxy*.

25. Price with House, *Biblical Archaeology*.

26. Rydelnik and Blum, *Handbook of Messianic Prophecy*; Bateman et al., *Jesus the Messiah*.

27. It must be admitted that belief in Jesus's divinity requires subjective faith and experience, but it is not only that. Mysticism can so emphasize subjective experience that it becomes reductionistic, ignoring any rational, comprehensible critique or inquiry into the experiences themselves. In contrast, the Hebrew Bible and NT engage with the full range of the human person (Mark 12:30), including the life of the rational mind. On the need for both natural and supernatural knowledge of God, see Aquinas *ST* II-II q.2 a.3–4.

Implications of the Incarnation

make paradoxical claims about divine inner workings, yet they are not grounded in Israel's prophetic history or the eyewitness experience of Jesus and his teachings. An example in the Christian tradition is Pseudo-Dionysius's Neoplatonic claim that God is beyond being (or nonexistent), that he has no name, and cannot be known (negative theology).[28] Such supposed paradoxes should not be accorded similar rational warrant simply because of their intuitive beauty or profound coherence of thought.[29] When lacking exoteric and historical revelation from God himself through Israel's prophets or apostles, esoteric paradoxical claims about God that subvert or reframe biblical theology should be labelled false and speculative nonsense. For followers of Jesus, this judgment is reflective of the epistemological priority of the Hebrew Bible and NT, and how Israel's prophets and apostles alone may be cited as special revelation of God's inscrutable essence.

Third, an appeal to mystery in the Incarnation is coherent, given the nature of God. When it comes to the world of the senses and finite things, logic can and should hold. But when there exists a being whose essence is incomprehensible to finite beings, it should follow that there will be things about that being that will be mysterious. This point is analogous to the difference between mathematics in the finite realm, and the mathematics of infinity.[30] Simple operations of addition, subtraction, multiplication, and division work with logical regularity on finite numbers, but they do not function the same way (or at all) when considering infinite and transinfinite mathematics. Criticizing the Incarnation because it does not play by the rules of finite logic is like criticizing infinity mathematics for not following the rules of subtraction.

Fourth, belief in the Incarnation preserves scientific and rational investigation of the cosmos. While allowing for mystery in the ways and being of God, followers of Jesus are not supposed to see mystery in all other categories or concede mystery quickly when things do not make sense. In contrast to a magical worldview borne out of Platonic mysticisms, the *ex nihilo* standpoint of Scripture does not condone seeing mystery by default. Logic, evidence, and rationality hold in our world.

---

28. Psuedo-Dionysius, *Epistle* 1. Many of the arguments I have presented against Maimonides and Kabbalah may also be made against Pseudo-Dionysius's system.

29. For example, despite my rejection of Plotinus's Neoplatonic system, when reading *The Six Enneads* I can still be struck by the beauty of his phrasing and the interlocking symmetry of his thought. Beauty can be deceiving.

30. Cheng, *Beyond Infinity*.

The created order may have some contemporary mysteries, such as the essence of light, time, quantum mechanics, mathematical infinity, and what lies beyond the edge of the expanding universe. However, a biblical worldview indicates that contingent creation operates according to the order and rationality imposed upon it by God's regular laws (Jer 31:35; 33:25; Job 38:33; Gen 8:22), which humans themselves may comprehend (Job 38:36; cf. Eccl 1:5–10) because God's rationality is the source of man's rationality (Isa 28:23–29; Eccl 2:26). In principle, creation is potentially understandable by human minds, whereas God will always remain a mystery, even if he provides ways of knowing him partially.

Fifth, while the Incarnation may forever remain a mystery, the scope of the mystery may be reduced through further theological reflection and analogy. The field of Christology is anything but a morose, anti-intellectual, fideistic exercise in futile mystery. In recent years, multiple Christian theologians have proposed innovative and plausible models for decreasing the extent of the mystery of the Incarnation.[31]

Thomas Morris suggests that the Messiah has two ranges of consciousness that relate asymmetrically, such as when one client computer operating system operates within a host operating system.[32] Modern computer technology allows a client operating system (such as a more limited software like DOS from the 1980s) to operate within a complicated host operating system (such as Windows 11 from the 2020s). In this case, the host has access to everything the client does, but the client has access only to that which the host allows (such as keyboard and mouse input). This may be analogous to how the divine nature of Messiah has full access to his human nature, but his human nature does not have full access to his divine nature. This can explain, for example, why Jesus the man does not always have access to his omniscience, while the Son of God always remains omniscient in his divine nature—and can sometimes reveal his omniscience to Jesus's human mind (i.e., Luke 9:47).

Another theologian, Timothy Pawl, proposes a solution to the problem of incoherence by claiming that all predicates must be modified to consider natures that apply to them. For example, it might be seen as incoherent to claim that Messiah is both corporeal and incorporeal. A

---

31. Besides the authors referred to below, I also recommend the following: Crisp, *Divinity and Humanity*; Crisp, *Word Enfleshed*; Wellum, *God the Son Incarnate*; Poythress, *Mystery of the Trinity*; J. Clark and Johnson, *Incarnation of God*; Macleod, *Person of Christ*; Anderson, *Paradox in Christian Theology*.

32. T. Morris, *Logic of God Incarnate*.

traditional way of solving this has been to say that Messiah is corporeal according to (qua) his human nature, but incorporeal according to (qua) his divine nature. Pawl thinks such qua solutions are inadequate. Instead, he proposes that "visible" be understood as "has a nature that is able to be visually perceived" and "invisible" as "has a nature that is unable to be visually perceived."[33] With these definitions—which are hard to object to—the words "visible" and "invisible" may be applied to Messiah simultaneously without any logical contradiction, for he possesses both human (visible) and divine (invisible) natures.

The relationship between an author and his story has inspired hypothetical models for the Incarnation. Orthodox Jewish philosopher Samuel Lebens, while not accepting that God has entered his story as Jesus of Nazareth, plays around with the idea of authors writing themselves into their stories as characters.[34] When considering stories with multilevel complexity, Lebens approaches the logic of Chalcedon as he discusses the attributes of Superman and Clark Kent. Lebens holds that "Superman is strong and Clark Kent is not strong" is a rational belief under certain epistemological constraints, even though the two names refer to the same person. Similarly, Christian theologians Ian McFarland and Gavin Ortlund, in direct conversation with Chalcedon, also employ the author-fiction analogy.[35]

Another theologian, William Hasker, proposes an understandable model of the Incarnation through an analogy with the science-fictional movie *Avatar*, where a human being assumes full control of an alien being.[36] Hasker writes that innovative solutions like his *Avatar* model illustrate that "the Chalcedonian definition does not explain how the Incarnation took place; rather it established parameters within which an acceptable explanation must fall."[37] Thus, the theologian working under the constraints of Chalcedon is encouraged to seek out greater understanding of the Incarnation and thus lessen, but never eliminate, its intellectual mysteriousness.

---

33. Pawl, *Defense of Conciliar Christianity*, 173.

34. Lebens, *Principles of Judaism*, 121–25.

35. McFarland, *Word Made Flesh*, 80–84; Ortlund, *Theological Retrieval for Evangelicals*, 105.

36. Hasker develops a model that retains the mind and nature of the Na'vi alien of whom the human assumes control, thereby avoiding Apollinarianism.

37. Hasker, "Incarnation," 8:118.

Perhaps, one day, the mysteries of the finite created order will be comprehensible to human minds. However, God's thoughts and essence will forever remain outside of full human comprehension.[38] This biblical distinction—the knowability of creation and the mystery of the Creator—was a powerful motivator for the growth of science, and it deserves to remain intact.[39] Consequently, allowing for paradox in the essence and ways of God—including the Incarnation—does not force unfettered mystery to spill out into other areas of human inquiry. Neither is it an ad hoc appeal to make NT theology work; mystery is to be expected in the pursuit of knowing God.

11.1.4. Maimonides and the Impossibility of Declaring What Is Impossible for God

If one begins with strict logic and attempts to conform all theology to it, one will end up in unbelief or heretical divergence from the Scriptures. As theologian Craig Blaising writes of the Incarnation,

> Admittedly, this doctrine leaves many metaphysical questions unanswered. However, it should be noted that this doctrine was not produced as the fruit of philosophic speculation on the possible singular cosubsistence of the finite and the infinite. Rather it was offered as a precise description of the incarnation recorded in Scripture, drawn from the greatest extent of biblical data and making use of whatever language that might help in that descriptive task.[40]

Turning to Maimonides, this line of thought proves fatal to his belief in the impossibility for an incorporeal God to become embodied while retaining his incorporeality. What appears impossible for God to finite minds may not be impossible according to the reality of God's power.[41]

Thus, there is a limit to where a priori reasoning can take us. We should not exclusively reason a priori from a human perspective about what God can and cannot do. Instead, we should also consult the evidence that God provides, namely through Israel's prophets and apostles.

---

38. Paul writes in 1 Cor 13:12, "For now we see in a mirror dimly, but then face to face. Now I know in part; then I shall know fully." I do not understand "know fully" to mean exhaustive omniscience of the divine nature, but rather "as much knowledge of God as is creaturely possible."

39. Pearcey and Thaxton, *Soul of Science*, 80–81.

40. Blaising, "Hypostatic Union," 584.

41. Swinburne, *Coherence of Theism*, 43.

Readers should not conform Scripture to their philosophical preconceptions; rather, readers should conform their theology and philosophy to the a posteriori evidence of Scripture. If there are apparent contradictions in one's theology, the analysis that produced that theology could be mistaken because of faulty thinking, or else the theology could be correct due to unknown factors.[42] In the case of the Incarnation, faulty thinking does not apply, for high Christology was not developed through philosophical reasoning over time, but intuitively through the early believers' eyewitness experiences with the risen Messiah. Those tangible experiences provided grounds for paradox in Jerusalem in the 30s CE.

On the strength of that justification, as Athanasius (296–373 CE) writes, "It is better in perplexity to be silent and believe, than to disbelieve on account of the perplexity."[43] Elsewhere, Athanasius writes that in the Incarnation, God "demonstrates as possible what men mistake, thinking impossible."[44] Moreover, as Anselm of Canterbury (1033–1109) rightly claims, "For all necessity and impossibility is under his control. But his choice is subject to no necessity nor impossibility. For nothing is necessary or impossible save as he wishes it."[45] Humans are not capable of being the arbiters of the impossible for God. Augustine (354–430 CE) pastorally counsels, "If this is difficult to understand, then you must purify your mind with faith, by abstaining more and more from sin, and by doing good, and by praying with the sighs of holy desire that God will help you to make progress in understanding and loving."[46] Yet it must be emphasized that this attitude is legitimate only because of the comprehensible justification provided to the perplexed onlooker through Jesus's life, teachings, and resurrection.

The situation is not unlike a scientist using instruments to observe light, finding that some instruments indicate light is a wave and others indicate light is a particle. Despite the apparent contradiction of these observations, the scientist knows that light works in a noncontradictory way, *somehow*, and thus he allows the apparent contradiction of his observations to stand.[47] Similarly, based on evidence provided in Scripture,

---

42. Anderson, *Paradox in Christian Theology*, 294–97.
43. Athanasius, *Apol. Sec.* 2.36 (*NPNF*² 4:367).
44. Athanasius, *Inc.* 1 (*NPNF*² 4:36).
45. Anselm, *Cur Deus Homo* 2.18a (*Cur Deus Homo*, 273).
46. Augustine, *Trin.* 4.21 (*Trinity*, 221–22).
47. Physicist Glenn Stark explains how modern physicists have discovered that light has a surprising "wave-particle duality" that somehow works because of virtual

the apparent contradiction of the Incarnation must be allowed to stand as a warranted paradox about who God is and how he works, for Jesus's humanity and deity work together *somehow*.[48] Instead of scoffing at an idea considered impossible for God to do, like Sarah scoffs when told she would give birth at an old age (Gen 18:11–12), readers should listen to God's subtle rebuke of Sarah's disbelief: "Is anything too hard for the Lord?" (Gen 18:14). Accordingly, Mary remembers the Lord's rebuke of Sarah, and she accepts God's power to do the seemingly impossible (Luke 1:37–38).

Contemporary Jewish scholars note this weakness of Maimonides's objection to the Incarnation. In an essay entitled, "A Jewish Perspective on Incarnation," Orthodox Jewish scholar Michael Wyschogrod critiques common Jewish rejections of the notion, and Maimonides in specific. He claims Judaism should be ready to discard the holiness of Jerusalem if God cannot appear in physical form, since the Hebrew Scriptures say the locale is holy because of God's historical manifest presence in the location. Wyschogrod recognizes that most of his fellow Orthodox Jews would be unwilling to do so, highlighting an inconsistency in their incorporeal theology. However, in my view Wyschogrod's most insightful argument rests upon the notion of God's omnipotence. He believes it is arrogant for humans to determine what God can and cannot do based on philosophical presuppositions. He writes,

> It must be emphasized that the Jewish objection to an incarnational theology cannot be based on a priori grounds, as if something in the nature of the Jewish concept of God made his appearance in the form of humanity a rational impossibility. Very often, Jewish opposition to the incarnation is based on just such grounds without realization of the implications of such a posture. If we can determine a priori that God could not appear in the form of a man or . . . that there could not be a being who is both fully God and fully human, then we are substituting a philosophical scheme for the sovereignty of God. No Biblically oriented, responsible Jewish theology can accept such a substitution of an ontological structure for the God of Abraham, Isaac and Jacob whose actions humanity cannot predict and whose

---

photons that have been postulated to exist, despite their existence violating the conservation laws of energy and momentum ("Emission and Absorption Processes," under "Quantum Electrodynamics").

48. Swinburne develops a similar argument (*Coherence of Theism*, 43–46).

actions are not subject to an overreaching logical necessity to which they must conform.[49]

Wyschogrod is correct: human beings must not substitute a philosophical scheme for the sovereignty of God.[50] This is, of course, precisely what Maimonides does. In reviewing Wyschogrod's theological legacy, Jewish philosopher Shai Held comments,

> Michael Wyschogrod is Maimonides' worst nightmare.... [He] is this generation's most eloquent and emphatic critic of Maimonides; he is at his most compelling in insisting upon the irreducible tension between scriptural, covenantal monotheism, on the one hand, and abstract, philosophical monotheism, on the other. No amount of creative (i.e., destructive) Maimonidean exegesis, Wyschogrod insists, will ever be able to bridge the unbridgeable divide between philosophy's God and revelation's.[51]

Benjamin Sommer joins Wyschogrod's notable critique of Maimonides. He claims that Maimonides's insistence on the impossibility of divine embodiment approaches the creation of a "new religion." If consistent, Sommer claims, Maimonides would

> compel a rejection of most of the Written and Oral Torahs. It would entail, in other words, the creation of a new religion whose earliest sacred document would be found in the tenth-century C.E. philosophical writings of Maimonides' predecessor, Saadia Gaon.[52]

In conversation with Wyschogrod's work and in response to Maimonides, Esther Hamori writes, "Paradoxically, the assumption of what God can and cannot do limits God in our minds more than the incarnation does.... We have good reason not to limit our notions of what God is and is not free to do."[53] Likewise, the thirteenth-century Tosafist Moses Taku critiques those who allegorize corporealist passages: "They are issuing a decree to the Creator as to how He must be. By so doing they are degrading themselves."[54]

---

49. Wyschogrod, "Jewish Perspective on Incarnation," 204.
50. Recall also Blaise Pascal's quote at the beginning of ch. 4.
51. Held, "Promise and Peril," 316–17.
52. Sommer, *Bodies of God*, 136.
53. Hamori, "Divine Embodiment," 179.
54. *Ketav tamim* (ed. Kirchheim), 82, quoted in M. Shapiro, *Limits of Orthodox Theology*, 39.

Perhaps, these Jewish thinkers suggest, the real scandal is when a human being audaciously and presumptuously dictates to God what he cannot do. This turns the scandal of a divine Messiah on its head. When God is freed from the constraints placed upon him by human thought, Scripture may once again speak without Maimonides's esoteric rereading. When his exhaustive allegorical hermeneutic is questioned, Scripture may lead to the highly plausible and reasonable conclusion that God does, in fact, appear in physical form.

11.2. The Hermeneutical Foundation: How to Read Corporeal God Talk in the Hebrew Scriptures

If readers should allow the Scriptures to provide a posteriori evidence for building a theological worldview, how should they go about such a task? I have already illustrated how the NT leads to the result of the Incarnation as best articulated by Chalcedon. However, the unsolved mysteries of the Hebrew Scriptures remain to be addressed. This section proposes a hermeneutical model to account for the Older Testament's God talk (ch. 2).

On the topic of the possibility of divine embodiment, a central issue is the Hebrew Scriptures' use of corporeal concepts applied to God. When reading corporeal God talk in the Hebrew Scriptures, interpreters need to decide whether the corporeality is to be understood as metaphor or not. Interpreters may err by having a rigid yes or rigid no applied to all passages, but a NT Christophany hermeneutic provides a golden mean between extremes. This hermeneutic enables all three classic theological positions—*via positiva*, *via negativa*, and *via analogia*—to have their proper application in biblical interpretation.[55]

11.2.1. The NT Christophany Hermeneutic and *Via Positiva*

The NT instructs its readers how to interpret many instances of corporeal God talk in the Hebrew Bible: Whenever God appears visibly in Israel's history, it is the embodied (preincarnate) Son of God who appears. This enables believers in Jesus to read corporeal God talk as positive, real, and literal descriptions of God himself through a theological method called

---

55. For a fuller treatment of these three methods for interpreting God talk, see Geisler and Feinberg, *Introduction to Philosophy*, 304–19; Astley, *Exploring God-Talk*; Swinburne, *Coherence of Theism*.

via positiva. This dynamic is implied by several NT passages and made explicit in the Epistle of Jude.⁵⁶

In John 1:18, it is claimed that "no one has ever seen God." Likewise, Jesus teaches his Jewish audience, "[The Father's] voice you have never heard, his form you have never seen" (John 5:37; cf. 1 John 4:12). To this can be added God's warning in Exod 33:20: "Man shall not see me and live." This immediately raises the question: What about those passages in the Hebrew Scriptures where it says Israelites *have* seen God?⁵⁷ Earlier, I provided examples of passages that seem to imply God's physicality (§2.8). However, many of those passages are clear metaphors that should not be read as evidence of divine embodiment. God does not have eyes, a nose, or a body as part of his eternal divine essence. Rather, he is spirit (John 4:24) and invisible (Col 1:15; 1 Tim 1:17; Heb 11:27), essentially incorporeal.⁵⁸ But many other passages—commonly called theophany passages—do not allow for easy metaphorical readings.⁵⁹ These passages explicitly mention that humans saw God in human or otherwise physical form.

Is the Gospel of John contradicting these passages? Not at all. Immediately after saying, "No one has ever seen God," John 1:18 completes the thought: "The only God, who is at the Father's side, he has made him known." In other words, God the Father has never been seen, but God the Son, who is the only God, makes known the Father who has never been seen. Paul adds, "[Jesus] is the image of the invisible God" (Col 1:15), and Jesus himself explains, "Whoever has seen me has seen the Father" (John 14:9). According to these texts, the Son is the mediator who represents the LORD in physical form, making the invisible visible. Thus, the NT authors instruct their readers to conclude the following: if God truly appears physically in the Hebrew Scriptures, it is not the Father who is seen, but rather the Son cloaked temporarily in physicality, yet retaining the entire divine nature as the LORD.

The logic of the previous paragraphs is confirmed by Jude 4–5. In v. 4, Jude writes that "our only Master and Lord" is "Jesus Christ." Then in the following verse, an astonishing claim is made, linking Jesus to the God of the exodus: "*Jesus*, who saved a people out of the land of Egypt, afterward destroyed those who did not believe." Although many early

---

56. For a complementary study, see Westerman, "Presence and Involvement."

57. Gen 16:13; 32:30; Exod 24:10–11; 33:23; Num 12:8; Deut 5:24; Judg 6:11–24; 13:22; Isa 6:5; Ezek 1:26.

58. See 18n43.

59. E.g., Gen 32:30; Exod 3:1–6; 24:9–10; Isa 6:1–5; Ezek 1:26.

Greek manuscripts support the reading of "Jesus," others state that it was "the Lord" who saved a people.[60] For our purposes, the text-critical decision is inconsequential, because even if the reading of "Lord" is accepted, the idea holds, for "the Lord" is identified as Jesus in v. 4. Thus, Jude is telling his readers to attribute biblical passages about God's interaction with Israel during the exodus to the preincarnate divine embodiment of the Son of God.[61]

The implications are wide ranging and offer a veritable solution to the mysteries of the Hebrew Scriptures. For example, when God says that he will go before Israel in a visible cloud by day and a fire by night (Exod 13:21; 14:19), it is God the Son who accomplishes these things. When Moses and the elders of Israel "saw the God of Israel" (Exod 24:9–10), they saw God the Son. When God says he will send an angel before Israel with God's name "in him" (Exod 23:20), that messenger is God the Son.[62] While Jude limits himself to the exodus account, exegetes need not do the same. In my opinion, any time a truly physical experience of God is described in the Hebrew Scriptures, in order to escape scriptural contradiction, it is the Son of God who was seen, prior to his full Incarnation as Jesus.

Early church fathers grab hold of this Christophany hermeneutic with keen insight. Justin Martyr (ca. 160 CE) not only affirms that Jesus saved Israel from Egypt, but he extends the logic to the Son speaking to Moses in the bush and the Son filling the tabernacle with glory.[63] Like-

---

60. Metzger gives a long list of manuscript support for Ἰησοῦς (Jesus). The UBS committee had difficulty determining the text for this word, assigning it a low confidence level of D (Metzger, *Textual Commentary*, 657). The NET Bible commentary gives extra textual reasoning for accepting "Jesus" as the correct reading (*NET Bible*, Jude 5).

61. Fossum, "Kyrios Jesus"; Bartholomä, "Did Jesus Save." See 258n37.

62. Some may hesitate at this idea, given that Heb 1:4–5 distinguishes Messiah from angels. However, the word used for "angel" in Hebrew (*malakh*) and Greek (*angelos*) may refer to a species or a role. When speaking about a species, the words refer to a created heavenly being with a nature called an angel (Luke 1:11; John 20:12). When speaking about a role, the words refer to a messenger (of whatever nature) sent with a mission by someone else (Hag 1:13; Mal 2:7; Luke 7:24; 9:52; Jas 2:25). A key Johannine theme is that Messiah is *sent* by the Father (John 3:34; 6:57; 20:21; 1 John 4:9–14). Hebrews appears to be saying that Messiah is not the *species* of an angel, which is a finite created being. However, this does not rule out the possibility that Messiah could be the subject in passages where the "angel of the LORD" appears, since "angel" (*malakh*) in those passages could be referring to the *role* and not the species of the messenger (BDAG s.v. "ἄγγελος").

63. Justin Martyr, *Dial.* 120, 127–28; 1 *Apol.* 63.

wise, Tertullian (ca. 180 CE) writes, "It was the Son, therefore, who was always seen, and the Son who always conversed with men."[64] Theophilus of Antioch (ca. 170 CE) declares, "The Word, then, being God, and being naturally produced from God, whenever the Father of the universe wills, He sends Him to any place; and He, coming, is both heard and seen, being sent by Him, and is found in a place."[65] Many church fathers teach the same Christophany hermeneutic.[66] A formula adopted at Sirmium ca. 351 CE even makes the appearance of the Son to Abraham and Jacob a doctrine guarded by anathemas.[67]

Nevertheless, Augustine (354–430 CE) shifted exegesis of Old Testament passages away from Christophanies to appearances of mere angels or all the members of the Trinity.[68] As a result of Augustine's influence, the Christophany hermeneutic is not without its critics.[69] However, if it is accurate, the Christophany hermeneutic encourages interpreting some physical and anthropomorphic language in Scripture as literal (*via positiva*) descriptions of the Son interacting with the people of Israel. However, *via positiva* should not be applied in all cases, for that would result in corporealism and a contradiction with John 4:24 and related passages. The following sections will discuss other legitimate hermeneutical methods that should be considered depending upon the context.

11.2.2. Divine Incomprehensibility and *Via Negativa*

If there are contextual and canonical grounds to believe that a passage is describing the appearance of the Son of God in physical form, then a nonmetaphorical interpretation may be appropriate. However, when

---

64. Tertullian, *Prax.* 15 (*ANF* 3:611).

65. Theophilus of Antioch, *Autol.* 2.22 (*ANF* 2:103).

66. See Tertullian, *Praescr.* 13; Irenaeus, *Haer.* 4.10.1, 4.20.4–11; Clement of Alexandria, *Paed.* 1.7; Novatian, *On the Trinity* 17–18; Athanasius *Apol. Sec.* 1.38; *Syn.* 27 (anathemas 15–17); Cyprian, *Test.* 2.5; Hilary, *De synodis* 38; *On the Trinity* 5.17; Eusebius of Caesarea, *Dem. ev.* 1.5. Some sources are discussed in Butler, "Son of God Appeared"; Juncker, "Christ as Angel"; Oliphint, *Majesty of Mystery*, 73–74.

67. Athanasius, *Syn.* 27; Hilary, *De synodis* 38; Socrates Scholasticus, *Hist. eccl.* 2.30.

68. Schaff and Ware comment, "The Catholic doctrine is that the Son has condescended to become visible by means of material appearances. Augustine seems to have been the first who changed the mode of viewing the texts in question, and considered the divine appearance, not God the Son, but a created Angel" (*NPNF*[2] 4:465). The Platonic basis of Augustine's intuitions is apparent in *Trin.* 2.6–17. For a discussion on Augustine's views and an attempt to recover a pre-Augustinian Christophany hermeneutic, see Butler, "He Who Is." See also Cole, *God Who Became Human*, 116–20.

69. For a modern dissenting view, see López, "Identifying 'Angel of Lord.'"

there is no contextual clue that the embodied Son of God is in view, on the grounds of divine incomprehensibility, one should not assume that corporeal God talk is to be understood in a *via positiva* way.

Divine incomprehensibility states that human minds cannot completely understand God's knowledge, ways, and essence. He transcends human categories. Consequently, the doctrine urges caution when reading passages describing God's ways and attributes. The Hebrew Scriptures teach that God is "merciful and gracious, slow to anger, and abounding in steadfast love and faithfulness" (Exod 34:6). He is just (Deut 32:4), and holy (Lev 19:2), and great (Ps 145:3). The NT adds that God is love (1 John 4:8) and light (1 John 1:5). If God cannot be comprehended, then how should these descriptions of God be understood?

Maimonides, for example, takes an extreme position in calling such language metaphorical accommodation that must be interpreted to mean something other than it says. This is a generous framing of Maimonides's strategy; it could be more accurate to say that Maimonides describes Scripture as teaching falsehoods. I have already provided arguments for why Maimonides's use of *via negativa* ought to be rejected (§6.6), but I do not believe negative theology should be rejected completely.

If *via positiva* presents a thesis where human words can describe God accurately, *via negativa* presents an antithesis where human words cannot describe God accurately at all. *Via positiva* may be correct when describing the preincarnate and incarnate Son of God, and it needs no modification in those cases. Likewise, the true insight of negative theology is that God's nature is not human, and humans are not God; there is a categorical difference between our modes of being and thinking. However, this insight of negative theology, taken to its fullest extent, leads to zero human knowledge of God, which cannot be accurate.[70] Nevertheless, I believe it is wise for *via negativa* to chart a course away from using positive language for God when the divine nature is in view.

While negative theology guides us in the right direction in thinking about the divine nature, I cannot follow its path to the end. Theologian John Feinberg writes,

---

70. The fourth-century Syrian churches that produced the Apostolic Constitutions had little patience for those who employed Platonic *via negativa* to envision God: "Now all these [heresies] had one and the same design of atheism, to blaspheme Almighty God, to spread their doctrine that He is an unknown being, and not the Father of Christ, nor the Creator of the world; but one who cannot be spoken of, ineffable, not to be named, and begotten by Himself" (Apos. Con. 6.10 [*ANF* 7:453]).

> The element of truth is that we cannot know everything about God. There are undoubtedly mysteries about him which none of us understands. But we must recognize that this doesn't mean we know nothing about him whatsoever or that none of our claims, whether literal or figurative, are true.[71]

Instead, I see negative theology as a kind of palate cleanser or intermediate step that can illustrate the folly of using *via positiva* for the divine nature, but which prepares the interpreter for the better solution of *via analogia*, the way of analogy. When speaking of the divine nature, the thesis of *via positiva* is inappropriate, and so too is the antithesis of *via negativa*; the true synthesis is found in *via analogia*.

11.2.3. Accurate Revelation and *Via Analogia*

Negative theology, taken to its fullest Maimonidean extent, implies that Scripture teaches falsehoods whenever it speaks of God, turning him into an unknowable being. Jesus and the apostles object, encouraging people to increase in their knowledge of God.[72] Thus, knowledge about God is *possible*, not a fruitless endeavor under *via negativa* constraints. Instead of exclusively negative theology, a better solution is to affirm that the descriptions of God in Scripture do not match human conceptions, but that the descriptions are nevertheless accurate through analogy. Moreover, the Incarnation breaks the impasse regarding God talk in the Hebrew Scriptures and provides clear revelation concerning how to know God.[73]

It would be theologically dangerous to read "God is love" and think of all the ways that one has experienced love from parents, spouse, and children, only to conclude that God's love is the same as their love. This would be an inappropriate use of *via positiva*. Instead, "God is love" should be affirmed as a true statement, while noting that the "love" humans experience from created beings is not the same as God's love. Distinguishing between God's love and human love in this way is the intermediate step of *via negativa*. However, instead of saying, "God is not love" or "God is not holy," as Maimonides insists, an interpreter should say, "God *is* love and *is* holy, but he does not match *human* conceptions of love and holiness. The

---

71. Feinberg, *No One Like Him*, 76.

72. John 17:3; 1 Cor 15:34; 2 Cor 2:14; Phil 3:10; Col 1:10; 2 Pet 1:2–3; 3:18; 1 John 2:13; 5:20 (Grudem, *Systematic Theology*, 177–81). Grudem emphasizes that Scripture does not state that we can know only about God's actions and relations with us. Instead, Scripture says that we can know *him*.

73. McFarland, *Word Made Flesh*, 20–27.

perfection and extent of his love go far beyond our comprehension. His love is related to our love as source and effect, and his source is infinitely greater than the small effect of love we experience. However, our finite understanding of love still counts for something. *Our* love and *God's* love are still in the same *realm*." We can see this most clearly in the incomprehensible love exemplified by Messiah in his crucifixion on behalf of sinners, a love his followers are told to emulate (John 15:12).

Via analogia is the idea that God's attributes and man's attributes are infinitely distinguished from each other, yet they participate in the same realm with a relation between them. This method accounts for the Hebrew Scriptures' teaching that man is comparable to God due to being made in his image and likeness, but that God is also incomparable (see §2.5). This theological method is commonly attributed to Thomas Aquinas, who begins with negative theology as his initial method and works his way to meaningful theological knowledge through the principle of analogy.[74] Moreover, as I discussed with William Alston's functionalist model (§6.6), we can predicate similar functions between God and humans while still acknowledging that the means by which God and humans work are categorically different. While it may be true that God's love is not human love, *via analogia* states that God's love is *like* human love in some aspect. Human love may be imperfect, limited, and tainted by sin and competing concerns, but in some mysterious way, human finite love is analogous to God's perfect love. Additionally, our love may grow as we learn to emulate God's love.

The use of *via analogia* in theological reasoning and hermeneutics is widespread in Christian theology. Many modern expositions are available,[75] but the example of the Fourth Lateran Council (1215 CE) provides a simple formulation: "Between Creator and creature no similitude can be expressed without implying an even greater dissimilitude."[76] *Via analogia* allows for this simultaneous similarity and dissimilarity that is missing from the simple extremes of *via positiva* and *via negativa*. Theologian Jeff Astley helpfully comments,

> Employing theological language analogically is like walking a tightrope. You can fall over on one side if your God-talk

---

74. Aquinas, *SCG* 1.29–34; *ST* I q.13; Ashworth and D'Ettore, "Medieval Theories of Analogy."

75. Astley, *Exploring God-Talk*, 51–64; Geisler and Feinberg, *Introduction to Philosophy*, 304–19; Hart, "Concept of the Infinite," 265; Carter, *Contemplating God*, 69–70.

76. Interdicasterial Commission, *Catechism of the Catholic Church*, 17.

becomes too anthropomorphic—into the pit of univocity and anthropomorphism. Or you can fall off on the other side, falling into equivocity and agnosticism, by allowing your language to change its ordinary meaning so much when you apply it to God that it ceases to mean anything specific at all. The trick is to tread the tightrope between these two abysses.[77]

Striking this balance is not simple, but it is the ideal solution. *Via analogia* accounts for Scripture speaking about God wanting people to *know him*—that is, directly and personally—while also accounting for our inability to know him *exhaustively*. The distance between humanity and God is categorical and qualitative, but there is *some* similarity between human concepts and God. This complex relationship—that a concept is both like and not like God—defies strict logic, just as saying that Jesus is human and not merely human. It is not illogical to believe these things; rather, since these concepts involve God's limitness perfections, they go beyond the capability of human rationality.

The following example illustrates how this proposed hermeneutical solution may be carried out in practice when interpreting the God talk of Scripture. Consider "the arm of the LORD" in Isa 51:9–10. In this passage, there is no contextual clue that the embodied presence of the Son of God is in view, so a *via positiva* interpretation of the "arm" as God's physical limb is unwarranted. A *via negativa* interpretation would reply that "the arm of the LORD"—whatever the phrase refers to—is not the same thing as human arms. Rather, it is a metaphorical reference. However, we may complete the interpretive journey with *via analogia*, which illuminates the reason *why* the metaphor was employed. In the passage, the (metaphorical) strength of the LORD is in view, with his mighty power over the Red Sea during the exodus as a paradigmatic example. Thus, Isaiah uses the anthropomorphic concept of an "arm" to state that God has power to do mighty wonders. Human physical arms are *analogous* to God's metaphorical arm in that both are used to do actions by strength. However, beyond that relation by analogy, there is nothing else similar between the two kinds of arms, such as physicality or magnitude. God's strength is infinitely greater than man's strength (dissimilarity), but they still belong to the same conceptual realm (similarity).

This procedure can be profitably applied to any such metaphorical, poetic, or anthropomorphic language where the Son of God's historical

---

77. Astley, *Exploring God-Talk*, 58.

presence is not the intended referent. On the dual grounds of divine incomprehensibility and the truth of Scripture, the principle of analogy is the best hermeneutical method for language about God in the Hebrew Scriptures outside of instances where the Son of God is in view.

11.3. The Scope of the Son's Mediating Work

In 1 Tim 2:5, Paul alludes to the Shema and writes, "For there is one God, and there is one mediator between God and men, the man Christ Jesus." The idea of Jesus as mediator also appears in the book of Hebrews, where his mediating role is associated with saving sinners through the new covenant (Heb 8:6; 9:15; 12:24). However, his mediating role goes further than his accomplishment of human salvation. As the one appointed to bridge God's incomprehensible nature down to the realm of finite creation, the scope of the divine Son's mediation is wide ranging.

Both Maimonides and Kabbalah struggle with the idea of God's infinity reaching down into the finite world. Each proposes models to accommodate for this: Maimonides through a miraculous creation of the finite outermost heavenly sphere and human connection with the active intellect (§6.3.1), and Kabbalah through emanations that lessen in magnitude until finitude emerges (§§7.4; 8.4.3). I have critically examined both theories. Maimonides is self-contradictory when he denies that God does anything directly in the finite world, but then affirms that God reached down to create the finite outermost sphere and somehow moves the finite outermost sphere after its creation. If God is so transcendent that he cannot do things directly on finite Earth, then he likewise cannot do anything directly to the finite outermost sphere, including creating it. I criticized Kabbalah's model for not being able to account for how the transition from infinitude to finitude actually occurs, making the concept of finitude a mirage or a self-contradiction.

In NT theology, the Son of God is the one who is appointed by the Father to be the mediator between the infinite and the finite for all time. He can do this because of his omnipotent power to do the humanly unthinkable: the unification of the finite and the infinite in his two natures. When a gap needs to be bridged between God and man—or more broadly, God and finite creation—it is God the Son who accomplishes the miraculous bridge.[78] Under this understanding, the miraculous concep-

---

78. The Son's unique role is accomplished by the will of the Father with the power

tion of Jesus the Messiah in Mary's womb is the historical culmination of many instances where the Son of God has bridged the infinite down to the finite. He has bridged the infinite before and will continue to do so for eternity. The mystery of this position is acknowledged in Christian theology, but unlike Maimonides and Kabbalah, it has no self-contradictions or cosmological errors.

Few doctrines have the multifaceted depth and scope of the doctrine of the Son of God who has the incomprehensible power to "come down" (John 6:38; 3:13) from heaven. The doctrine of the Son coming down has implications for cosmology, anthropology, epistemology, soteriology, ecclesiology, ethics, eschatology, and more. It is like a scarlet thread woven throughout biblical theology. Below are but a few of the implications of the Son who bridges the gap between heaven and earth.

Creation. The Son of God bridged the gap between God's nature and finitude when he created finitude itself in the creation of the universe. "All things were made through him, and without him was not any thing made that was made" (John 1:3). The Son created directly, without needing any intermediaries such as angels or heavenly spheres to create. He is the Word (Logos) that was spoken with the power to create (Gen 1; John 1). The Earth does not emanate from a higher emanation, as with both Maimonides and Kabbalah, but was created directly by a divine person, and the creation was very good (Gen 1:31).[79]

Providence. Concerning the Son of God, Paul writes, "He is before all things, and in him all things hold together" (Col 1:17). The Son of God "upholds the universe by the word of his power" (Heb 1:3). The Son exercises providence over the creation directly, without being dependent upon angelic intermediaries or rolling spheres to enact his will. He can enact his sovereign will in the finite world through direct personal influence, using his angelic or other servants if he chooses to.[80]

The divine Word. As the divine Word (Logos), the Son of God is the expression of the divine mind with perfect power (John 1:1–4). Everything that the holy word יהוה (the Tetragrammaton) represents, and everything that יהוה is and can do, the Word of God is and can do. As taught in the Hebrew Scriptures, the Word of God creates, reveals,

---

of the Spirit. Thus, the entire Trinity is involved in the Son's mediation.

79. See §10.5.1.
80. See §10.5.1.

redeems, saves, delivers, and judges.[81] Jesus as the Son of God, the Word made flesh, does the same.

The words of Scripture. The mind of God is maximally perfect and incomprehensible, beyond the range of man's intellect. However, the Word (Son) of God is appointed to encapsulate the rationality, knowledge, and will of God into discrete, finite words given to Israel's prophets and apostles and spoken himself in Jesus (Heb 1:1–2). What would otherwise be incomprehensible is made understandable by the Son as he communicates the mind of God in discrete words. The Son does this work directly, not needing intermediary spheres to percolate his mind downward, or requiring man to reach upward through philosophical or mystical means. Israel's prophets speak by direct apprehension of the Word through his Holy Spirit. The Son chooses to reveal himself—that is, his Word—to whomever he wishes, personally (Matt 11:27), and in the Incarnation he speaks his words himself with no intermediary prophets (Heb 1:2). The Son makes grasping God's thoughts *possible* for human minds, but due to human sinfulness, human beings need the work of the Holy Spirit in their hearts to *actually* believe the words of the Son (John 3:3; 16:13; Titus 3:5).

The image of God. The Son in his Incarnation is "the image of the invisible God" (Col 1:15). As finite derivatives, humans are also created in the image and likeness of God (Gen 1:26–27). This crucial phrase likely refers to a set of communicable attributes[82] shared with God, including dominion, rationality, and goodness, such that humans are finite representatives of God.[83] For example, as God partakes in rationality perfectly and maximally, he creates humans as finite representatives of his rationality. The Son in his Incarnation is the image in which humanity has been made and to which it must be conformed (Rom 8:29; 2 Cor 3:18).[84]

---

81. Wellum, *God the Son Incarnate*, 202. For representative passages, see Ps 29:3–9; 33:6; 107:20; 119:25, 89; Isa 55:11; Jer 1:4.

82. Christian theology often distinguishes between the incommunicable and communicable attributes of God. Incommunicable attributes refer to those aspects of God's being that his creation does not participate in or share: aseity, immutability, eternity, omnipresence, and simplicity/unity. Communicable attributes refer to those attributes that God's creation—namely humans—participates in: rationality, knowledge, wisdom, goodness, love, mercy, justice, and many others.

83. For the exegetical possibilities about the meaning of "the image of God" in Christian thought, see Heiser, "Image of God." For the exegetical background of Gen 1:26, see Gentry and Wellum, *God's Kingdom*, 75–85.

84. Wilkinson, *Crowned with Glory*; Floyd, "Deriving the *Imago Dei*"; Crouzel, "Image," 2:320–22. Also see §10.5.3.

Thus, the image of God is another instance in which the divine Son has bridged the gap between heaven and earth, as he has created finite humanity in his likeness.

Divine sympathy. The Hebrew Bible portrays God as sympathizing with Israel's misfortunes and listening to her pleas. "In all their affliction he was afflicted. . . . In his love and in his pity he redeemed them" (Isa 63:9). Even in their exile to Babylon, God follows them there, so to speak, to be a sanctuary for them (Ezek 11:16). However, in the Incarnation, God reaches the apex of his sympathy for human beings, both Jew and gentile alike. He does not sympathize with humanity from some transcendent location, or even nearby, but rather *in* and *through* humanity itself. God knows what it means to be human not only because of propositional or third-person knowledge, but also through first-person *experience*.[85] The author of Hebrews, likening Jesus to Israel's high priest, says, "We do not have a high priest who is unable to sympathize with our weaknesses, but one who in every respect has been tempted as we are, yet without sin. Let us then with confidence draw near to the throne of grace, that we may receive mercy and find grace to help in time of need" (Heb 4:14–16). Thus, in the Incarnation, the Son of God crosses the divide on an emotional level, experiencing what we experience, feeling what we feel, suffering what we suffer, and strengthening us where we need to be strengthened. As Jesus is truly a man, and human beings live forever in the world to come, Jesus remains a man today and forevermore, even with his resurrection, ascension, and eventual return to earth. He will never relinquish his humanity, just as we will never relinquish our own. His sympathy with finite human beings will continue for eternity.

Salvation of sinners. Many classic works on the Incarnation—such as Athanasius's *On the Incarnation of the Word* and Anselm's *Why Did God Become a Man?*—concentrate on the atoning and salvific purpose of the Incarnation. This focus is fully justified, as Heb 2:17 states that Jesus "had to" be made human "to make propitiation for the sins of the people." In other words, the true, full atonement of human sin *requires* the Incarnation of the Son of God, including his propitiatory death on the cross to serve as a guilt offering for his people (cf. אָשָׁם, *asham*) (Isa 53:10).

---

85. For an insightful thought experiment about the difference between third-person propositional knowledge and first-person experiential knowledge, see Nagel, "What Is It Like." Jesus's experiential knowledge of human suffering is distinguished from the kabbalistic model, which Lebens portrays as the following: "Our suffering isn't real from God's transcendent perspective; it is no more real to God than the suffering of fictional characters is to their author" (*Principles of Judaism*, 80).

Why is this *necessary*, as Hebrews states? Post-temple Judaism, which rejects original sin, does not see the need. Orthodox Jewish atonement systems often involve the forgiveness of sin through God graciously responding to repentance and substitutions for animal sacrifices (prayers, study, ritual actions, charity), while also encouraging holiness through good habits.[86]

The atonement envisaged by the NT is more fundamental, on the level of human ontology. In Rom 5:12–21, Paul teaches that humanity has been fundamentally altered through sin; starting from Adam, human sin has corrupted human nature by introducing death and condemnation into the human condition. Despite the institution of the sacrificial system in the Torah to provide atonement, those sacrifices were never able to repair the root problem in the human heart (Heb 10:1). If humanity merely needed grace and forgiveness, and human ontology itself did not need repair, then the Orthodox Jewish methods of atonement could have some merit. However, the NT states that humans cannot cover over their failings through their performance but rather need to be reborn after the image of Jesus the Messiah and conformed to him, the sinless and resurrected one (Phil 3:21; Rom 8:29; 1 Cor 15:47–49; 2 Cor 3:18). In addition, humans need imputed divine righteousness bestowed upon them by the sinless, Torah-keeping Messiah (2 Cor 5:21; Matt 5:17; Gal 4:4–5), which results in justification and being born again by the Holy Spirit for the purpose of increasing sanctification (John 3; Rom 8:29–30). Not only do humans need a substitute to bear their sins (Isa 53:12) and declare them righteous in Messiah (Rom 3:26; 5:19; Phil 3:9), but they also need a righteous model to which they can be conformed at a fundamental level beyond human reach (Rom 8:29; 2 Cor 4:10). The crucified and risen Messiah, in partnership with the Father and the Spirit, accomplishes the necessary atonement, justification, and sanctification of sinners. Jesus, the perfect man, has the power as God to restore the tarnished image within humanity (Athanasius, *Inc.* 14). He restores humans by taking the penalty for sin—a *human* paying off humanity's sin—which he has the power to do because he is truly God. As Mark the Monk says in the fifth century, "Taking flesh, the Power of God redeemed human beings, not by arrogating power to himself, lest he abrogate justice, but by exchanging himself for us and acting with justice."[87] In order to exchange himself for

---

86. See Maimonides, *Eight Chapters*.
87. Mark the Monk, *Counsels*, 2:273.

humans, he became human and suffered as one, a vicarious atonement in which he suffered the judgment humanity deserved.

Human salvation falls apart if Jesus is not God in the flesh; he lacks the power to accomplish final human atonement if he is not divine. Thus, in the history of the Christian church, a denial of Jesus's deity has been associated with cutting oneself off from salvation and placing oneself outside the fellowship of the faithful. As Cyril of Jerusalem says in 380 CE, "For if the Incarnation was a phantom, salvation is a phantom also."[88]

Community and communion with God. After paying for sin through his death, Jesus then unites humans with him in his resurrection (Rom 6:3–5). He restores the human image by giving humans new life according to his resurrection life (1 Cor 15:49). Thus, the goal of salvation is ultimately conformity of human beings to the image of the Son of God (Rom 8:29; 1 John 3:2), which will culminate in the physical resurrection of their bodies (1 Cor 15) for eternal life in the world to come. Believers in Jesus are said to be "in him" and "united with him" by being conformed to his likeness (1 Cor 1:30; Col 2:10; Rom 12:5; John 15:5). This union is not impersonal or abstract, but rather a personal one in which God bestows divine love upon his redeemed and beloved people. The effect of this love is deep fellowship with God, transformed desires and actions, knowledge of one's purpose, and perseverance under trial. Given this goal of union with Messiah, the entire human nature needed to be assumed by Messiah in the Incarnation. Everything that human beings have, Jesus has as well, including a mind, soul, emotions, and limitations, except sin. Every human faculty is taken on by Messiah so he can conform each fallen human faculty to himself. Gregory Nazianzus (ca. 330–90) memorably writes, "The unassumed is the unhealed, but what is united with God is also being saved."[89] Thus, the mediating Son in the Incarnation bridges the gap down to humanity in order to atone for sin and enable humanity to be partakers of his holiness in union with him (Lev 11:44; Heb 12:10).[90]

---

88. Cyril of Jerusalem, *Catechetical Lectures* 4.9 (*NPNF*[2] 7:21).

89. Gregory Nazianzus, *Ep.* 101.5 (*On God and Christ*, 158; parallel translation in *NPNF*[2] 7:440).

90. The meaning of 2 Pet 1:4 and the associated idea of *theosis* is outside the scope of this book. However, I suggest extreme caution on this topic, as there are few ideas that have been overtaken by Neoplatonic metaphysics more than *theosis*. The Christian eschatological vision should not be swept away by the mystical speculations of Plotinus and Pseudo-Dionysius.

Part III: The Incarnation of the Son of God

Community and communion with others in Messiah. The Son's Incarnation not only provides mediation between God and humans, resulting in communion with God, but also provides mediation between people of all tribes, nations, and tongues, resulting in their communion with each other. All human beings are made in the image and likeness of God and thus share common dignity (Gen 1:26; 9:6; Jas 3:9). However, through their common faith in Jesus, people of all backgrounds are swept into an even more profound unity: the new covenant community of the redeemed, reconciled, justified, sanctified, adopted, and transformed sons and daughters of God. Paul writes, "For as many of you as were baptized into Christ have put on Christ. There is neither Jew nor Greek, there is neither slave nor free, there is no male and female, for you are all one in Christ Jesus" (Gal 3:27-28). With regard to salvation in Messiah in the new covenant (Jer 31:31-35; Heb 8), all distinctions between people are irrelevant; all are fellow brothers and sisters in Messiah (Rom 8:15; 2 Cor 13:11; 2 Thess 2:13).[91] The shed blood of Messiah "ransomed people for God from every tribe and language and people and nation" (Rev 5:9). Those who were previously separate from each other are now summoned to joyously meet in community, encouraging one another to grow in knowledge and holiness as they pursue conformity to Messiah together (Heb 10:24-25; Acts 2:42; Gal 6:1-2). Because of what Messiah has done, Jewish and gentile believers in Jesus may call each other brothers and worship the God of Israel together in unity (Eph 2), while still remaining distinct in their respective callings as Jews and gentiles.

The incarnate Messiah as the model for ethics. Followers of Jesus are called to imitate Jesus in his love of enemies and friends, believers and unbelievers. The foundation for ethics becomes he who says, "Just as I have loved you, you also are to love one another" (John 13:34; cf. Rom 5:8). As the perfect image of God, Jesus demonstrates what it means to live a human life that reflects God's character, marked by compassion, kindness, and selflessness (Col 3:12-17). In his teachings and actions, Jesus illustrates how to treat others with dignity and respect, even those

---

91. This equality in salvation does not rule out covenantal and promissory differences between Jews and gentiles. Just as men remain male after salvation, and women remain female, so too covenantal distinctions between Jews and gentiles remain in the Messiah's community. To say otherwise is to erase Jewishness as a meaningful category, something common in supersessionist theology but foreign to the NT (Acts 21:17-26; 22:3; 23:6; Rom 3:1-2; 9:1-5; 11:11-29). The Abrahamic covenant with ethnic Israel has not been abolished, and all yet-unfulfilled promises made to the Jewish people will be accomplished on their behalf at Messiah's return (Acts 3:21).

Implications of the Incarnation

who are different or have committed personal offense (Matt 5:44–48; Luke 10:25–37). He even asks for his Father to forgive those who want his death (Luke 23:34). Jesus's love for the marginalized, including the poor, the sick, and the outcasts, sets an example to prioritize others' needs and care for them (Matt 25:31–46). His humility and willingness to serve others, even to the point death, challenges his followers to adopt a similar posture of servanthood and humility (John 13:1–17; Phil 2:3–8). These ethical priorities have had incalculable impact on the world.[92]

Access to petition God in Jesus's name. The Hebrew Scriptures include many examples of God turning his face away from people due to the sin and rebellion in their hearts. God does not listen to petitions and prayers by default, as if the action of praying obligates God's attention. "Though they cry to me, I will not listen to them" (Jer 11:11). Micah writes, "But he will not answer them . . . because they have made their deeds evil" (Mic 3:4; cf. Isa 59:2). Furthermore, the sincerity, diligence, and repetition of the one praying do not persuade God to listen (Prov 1:28; Isa 1:15). Due to human sin, Israelites were always threatened with the possibility that God would hide his face from them.

However, God gives the following prophecy to Ezekiel: "I will not hide my face anymore from them, when I pour out my Spirit upon the house of Israel" (Ezek 39:29). Once God's Spirit is poured out on Israel, he will *always* listen. Although the complete fulfillment of this prophecy is awaiting the return of Messiah (Acts 3:21; Rom 11:25–26), the remnant of Israel has had the Spirit poured upon her ever since Pentecost in Acts 2.

Jewish believers in Jesus can banish any fears that God will turn his face away from them. Because of the atoning work of the Messiah to remove sin, and the indwelling Spirit to provide increasing sanctification, followers of Jesus can be assured that God is listening to all their prayers, not turning away in judgment (Rom 8:1). Jesus teaches, "Whatever you ask in my name, this I will do, that the Father may be glorified in the Son. If you ask me anything in my name, I will do it" (John 14:13–14). Because of what Messiah has done, "let us then with confidence draw near to the throne of grace, that we may receive mercy and find grace to help in time of need" (Heb 4:16). Followers of Jesus have this confidence not in themselves, but because of what Messiah has done on their behalf. Paul writes, "This was according to the eternal purpose that he has realized in Christ Jesus our Lord, in whom we have boldness and access with confidence through our

---

92. Holland, *Dominion*; R. Stark, *How the West Won*.

faith in him" (Eph 3:11–12). Through forgiveness of sin by the Son and the indwelling of the Spirit, the barrier to the Father has been removed.

The scope of these topics is immeasurably vast. The idea of the Incarnation is not restricted to the divinity of the man Jesus, but rather it has broad implications for what it means to be human, where humans have gone wrong, how humans can find peace with God, and how humans may be united with God and each other. The next and final chapter will discuss why it is more reasonable to accept this incarnational worldview over the principal alternatives considered in this book.

12 From Scandal to Shalom
A Defense of the Divine Messiah

[The Incarnation] is by far the most amazing miracle of the entire Bible—far more amazing than the resurrection and more amazing even than the creation of the universe. The fact that the infinite, omnipotent, eternal Son of God could become man and join himself to a human nature forever so that infinite God became one person with finite man—that will remain for eternity the most profound miracle and the most profound mystery in all the universe.

—Wayne Grudem[1]

Let each religion find their own axioms, and let us debate for the sake of heaven.

—Samuel Lebens[2]

Thus far in our theological journey, I have described multiple theoretical models of the relationship between God and creation. We have investigated quasi-divine mediators like the Logos and *Metatron*, rabbinic corporealism, and various Greek philosophical schools, and finally I have devoted extensive attention to the three models proposed by Maimonides, Kabbalah, and the NT.

These three models are the focus of this final chapter. Religious Jewish people accept either Maimonidean rationalism, kabbalistic mysticism, or some mixture of the two models. Christians and Messianic Jews

---

1. Grudem, *Systematic Theology*, 700.
2. Lebens, *Principles of Judaism*, 5.

accept the incarnational model. Which model has the greatest explanatory scope and plausibility, the least ad hoc (unevidenced and speculative) doctrines, and the least known falsehoods?[3] This chapter will present a variety of reasons why, despite the common Jewish objections, belief in the divinity of Jesus is more reasonable than rejecting him.

12.1. Comparing the Theological Models of the New Testament, Maimonides, and Kabbalah

My method up to this point has been to discuss Maimonides, Kabbalah, and the NT separately, only rarely putting them into direct conversation with each other. For this final chapter, I bring the three worldviews into simultaneous dialogue, juxtaposing their approaches to creation, providence, divine communication, and other themes, assessing them against each other. Most of the subjects discussed in this section have been mentioned previously, so section numbers are given for reference.

Cosmology and science: The Incarnation remains plausible under modern cosmology and science, whereas the cosmological-theological systems of Maimonides and Kabbalah are so outdated that they are now irrational (see §§5.5; 6.3; 7.4; 8.4; 9.2–9.3).

As a hypothetical thought experiment, imagine a NT gospel or epistle that teaches the following inaccurate science as theological fact about Jesus:

> Jesus is the incarnate Son of God, the divine microcosm who contains within himself the harmony of the macrocosm. As the Earth is the center of the cosmos, stationary and immovable, so too is Messiah the fixed center of our faith, around whom all our beliefs revolve. The Word became flesh when the Son traversed downward, through the celestial spheres of æther, to the terrestrial center of the cosmos, taking on more and more physicality as he defeated each of the seven archons. With a subtle contraction to imperceptible size, he descended into Mary's womb, passing through her blessed navel like a gentle breeze. From this sacred space, Jesus's body unfolded, manifesting the 248 members and 365 sinews that constitute the intricate

---

3. For these categories, see Craig, *Reasonable Faith*, 233; McCullagh, *Justifying Historical Descriptions*, 19.

harmony of every human form.[4] To demonstrate his dominion over matter and form, Jesus wrought a majestic display of transformation: drawing on the music of the spheres, he transmuted earth to air, air to water, and water to fire. Truly, truly, he illustrated his unfettered mastery over the four elemental forces that govern our sublunary sphere. As he united his soul with the One beyond the hebdomad, Jesus prophesied that those who follow him will ascend to the radiant sphere of the moon after death, from which place the New Jerusalem will descend in the world to come. Once the luminous city is united with Earth, Jesus will resurrect all his followers, like phoenixes from the ashes, bringing balance to their four humors. The active intellect, previously restricted to the moon, will then permeate every corner of our terrestrial sphere, transforming the masses into philosophers and prophets, as it is written, "For the earth shall be full of the knowledge of the LORD as waters cover the sea" (Isa 11:9). Amen and selah.[5]

What if this satirical and nonsensical paragraph was the central summary of NT doctrine about Jesus? What if its teachings filtered down into every theological work, every creed, every presentation of the message of Christianity? While the paragraph could have gone without criticism for centuries, eventually, it would have become an embarrassment with the rise of modern scientific discovery. Every sentence in that paragraph includes disproven concepts of cosmology, anatomy, geology, astronomy, or metaphysics. People who believed such false notions would have to dramatically modify their beliefs in light of new discoveries or else leave their faith altogether.

Returning to the real world, such a paragraph does not exist in the NT. None of the core doctrines of Trinitarian or incarnational theology are dependent upon now-disproven theories about the world. Rather, the

---

4. B. Mak. 23b: "Six hundred and thirteen commandments were given to Moses, three hundred and sixty-five negative ones, corresponding to the number of the days of the solar year, and two hundred forty-eight positive commandments, corresponding to the parts of man's body." The kabbalistic tradition transformed this into referring to 248 "limbs" and 365 "sinews" (Wolfson, "Bible in Mystical Tradition," 1986).

5. I never tired of composing and reediting this humorously absurd paragraph full of outdated scientific theories. This paragraph attempts to sound somewhat "orthodox" in its Christology and piety while presenting a corrupt cosmology, anthropology, epistemology, prophecy, and eschatology. Even so, this paragraph unfortunately sounds like many pious absurdities found in the Nag Hammadi Codices, Pseudo-Dionysius, Christian Kabbalists, alchemical manuals, and theosophical texts. This paragraph illustrates how easily syncretism can be cloaked in the garb of piety.

Part III: The Incarnation of the Son of God

key prerequisites to the Incarnation, such as creation *ex nihilo* and God's prior appearances in physical form, match scientific and scriptural evidence, respectively. Moving beyond these core doctrines, I believe there is no fundamental conflict between NT theology and science. Instead, science as we know it was developed by Christians who were explicitly dependent upon a Christian worldview.[6]

In contrast, the same logic that makes the satirical paragraph absurd also makes the worldviews of Maimonides and Kabbalah absurd. The two major schools that influence Orthodox Jewish theology throughout the centuries until today base their theological systems upon false cosmologies and scientific theories, leading to the collapse of their systems. Aristotle's spheres cosmology, to which Maimonides subscribes, has been universally rejected in the age of the telescope, Newtonian physics, and the Voyager probes. Unfortunately, Maimonides grounds his notions of divine providence, prophecy, and miracles upon the active influence of the now-discredited spheres.[7] This is how Maimonides accounts for God's (indirect) influence as attested in Scripture. Without the spheres, Maimonides's God has no way of doing anything on Earth—not even giving the Torah—a catastrophic deistic result. The loss of the spheres invalidates all the mechanics of Maimonides's system.

Similarly, Kabbalah's panentheistic and emanational *ex Deo* worldview is alien to Scripture and is rejected by pre-kabbalistic talmudic tradition, philosophical argument, and the findings of modern science. If there was a beginning of the universe, created out of nothing, then Kabbalah's elaborate theology-cosmology cannot even begin, and the kabbalistic concept of everything being divine sparks falls as well. Kabbalah's

---

6. For more on the relationship between Christianity and science, see Pearcey and Thaxton, *Soul of Science*; Copan et al., *Christianity and Science*; Carlson, *Science & Christianity*; Moreland, *Scientism and Secularism*; R. Stark, *How the West Won*.

7. A comparison between Maimonides and Aquinas is instructive. Both lived in a similar time with similar goals of integrating their religious system with the insights of Aristotle and Neoplatonism. Both accepted geocentricism and other outdated scientific theories. Both have modern adherents who, in light of modern scientific discoveries, must update, adapt, and correct their works for use in the modern world. As given in §6.3, Novak and Samuelson are modern Jewish thinkers who call for Maimonides's theology to be modified in this way. Similarly, neo-Thomists are modern philosophers who seek to update Aquinas's thought. However, since Aquinas held to an incarnational Trinitarianism where the Son of God provides creation, revelation, providence, and other biblical theological categories, he had less motivation to appeal to Aristotelianism or Neoplatonism to provide mechanisms in these areas. Thus, he escapes many of the predicaments I highlight in Maimonides's outdated science, and neo-Thomists have an easier job than Neo-Maimonideans.

deep acceptance of outdated superstitions and false scientific theories also leads to its falsification as a source of truth. In sum, modern science does not disqualify the NT's cosmological or theological teachings, but it undercuts the theology of both Maimonides and Kabbalah.

Epistemology: Scripture must have epistemological priority before Greek philosophies (see §§6.3–6.7; 7.8; 9.1–9.2; 10.5.5; 11.2).

The failure of the cosmologies above illustrates the folly of prioritizing esoteric and pagan Greek philosophical systems over the revelation of the Scriptures when building an epistemological hierarchy. In their theology, metaphysics, cosmology, and hermeneutics, Maimonides and the Kabbalists seek to be disciples of Neoplatonism, Neopythagoreanism, Aristotelianism, and Gnosticism first, and disciples of Moses second. This causes them to propose an ever-increasing ladder of esoteric knowledge with themselves at the top as the only sophisticated interpreters of the Judaism they inherit. As a result, they and the Judaism that followed refuse to read Scripture outside of predetermined philosophical frameworks. Unfortunately, these frameworks are ad hoc creations of human minds that fail the tests of Scripture and scientific observation. They should be moved out of the way so that the Scriptures regain their intended role as the primary revelation of God. While modified forms of Greek philosophical concepts were adapted by the church fathers in their defense of the Trinity and Incarnation, these central doctrines are not dependent upon Greek philosophy. The metaphysical language of Nicaea and the Chalcedonian Definition helps *articulate* Scripture's truth but does not *usurp* Scripture's truth. In this way, Nicaea and Chalcedon escape the epistemological criticism that undermines Maimonides and Kabbalah.

Encouragement toward scientific pursuits: The incarnational model affirms the goodness of creation and the suitability of the human mind to investigate and know its rational order, in contrast to Kabbalah's demotion of scientific investigation (see §§9.2.2; 9.3; 11.1).

The NT retains agreement with Genesis's declaration that the physical creation in its initial state[8] was "very good" (Gen 1:31), in contrast to

---

8. As with human nature, the current state of creation has been marred by Adam's sin (Rom 5). The universe as God initially created it had no decay, death, or corruption. Creation retains the fingerprint of God and his good design, but it yearns for

Kabbalah's rejection of physicality as evil and Maimonides's understanding of the physical world as the lowest and worst sphere of existence. The NT affirms that studying creation is worthwhile (Rom 1:20), providing evidence of God's goodness (Acts 14:17; Matt 5:45). These teachings are fully in accord with the Hebrew Scriptures' affirmation of the rational order God embeds in his good creation.[9] These affirmations encourage the Aristotelian model of investigation that informs modern science, which is preferable to the Platonic version of science that Kabbalah affirms. Moreover, by accepting the true humanity of Jesus, the NT encourages the study of every aspect of humanity and the human condition, since the humanity that has been marred by sin and death will one day be fully redeemed and restored according to Jesus's example.[10] The marred but still-present goodness of the human body encourages human inquiry into other physical beings and natural systems because they also reflect God's goodness and design. Kabbalah also encourages study of the human body and psyche, but it does so under the false cosmological paradigm of "as above, so below," thus invalidating its conclusions about the human body and psyche. Besides studying the human body and psyche, however, Kabbalah places little value upon scientific investigation, which does not align with the witness of Scripture.

Rejection of magical mechanisms: The incarnational model is free of cosmological correspondences that encourage astrology, incantations, and magic, in contrast to Kabbalah, which promotes a magical worldview and associated practice, and Maimonides, who accepted a magical worldview but disallowed its practice (see §§7.7; 9.2–9.3).

In the history of Western thought and practice, Platonic "science" and a magical worldview often coincide.[11] An increased acceptance of Platonic cosmological mechanisms, such as those of Pythagoras, Plotinus, and the Hermetic literature, correlates with an increase in incantations, warding off angels and demons, charms and amulets, astrology,

---

redemption (Rom 8). That restoration to the original "very good" will be accomplished by Messiah in the world to come.

9. Jer 31:35; 33:25; Job 38:33; Gen 8:22. For more on the NT's influence on scientific investigation, see Pearcey and Thaxton, *Soul of Science*.

10. For the importance of the Incarnation in knowing how to be human, see Wilkinson, *Crowned with Glory*; Floyd, "Deriving the *Imago Dei*."

11. Pearcey and Thaxton, *Soul of Science*.

and alchemy. In making this claim, I am not denying that Christians have fallen prey to such practices. They certainly have.[12] However, when Christians practiced such magic, they did so while under the influence of Platonic thought and in contradiction of biblical teaching. The NT rejects all such practice,[13] as do the Hebrew Scriptures.[14] Christian theologians throughout history have criticized popular superstitions and magical practices.[15] In contrast, Kabbalah encourages practices such as employing the divine name in incantations, the use of amulets and charms, warding off evil spirits through superstitious actions, listening to spirit guides (*maggidim*), the creation of golems, and the divinization of secret meanings in texts and correspondences and cosmological patterns.[16] The NT continues in the tradition of the Hebrew Scriptures on these matters, while Kabbalah gravely deviates from it. Maimonides is often known for his opposition to magic, amulets, and superstition, but he too gives up too much to the false magical worldview. Maimonides affirms the rabbinic notion, "There is no single herb below without its corresponding star above."[17] Thus, while rejecting the *practice* of magical arts, Maimonides continues to affirm a magical worldview of cosmic correspondences and signs.

Hermeneutics: Unmoderated via negativa *is a foreign contaminant in biblical interpretation (see §§6.4–6.7; 11.2.2).*

The Hebrew Scriptures contain no trace of the hermeneutical method called *via negativa*. Never do the Scriptures instruct the reader to interpret God talk in terms of negations. The same is true of the NT. Paul, the Jewish apostle, knew of the Greek tradition of worshiping an "unknown god" who is beyond all human grasp, and he responded, "What therefore you worship as unknown, this I proclaim to you" (Acts 17:23). The God of the NT and Hebrew Scriptures is knowable, albeit partially and finitely, but knowable by finite humans nonetheless. Negative theology did not enter Western discourse until Plato wrote various

---

12. Hamman, "Magic"; Versluis, *Magic and Mysticism*.
13. Acts 8:18–24; 13:6–12; 16:16–18; 19:17–20; Gal 5:19–20.
14. Exod 22:18; Lev 19:31; Deut 18:10–12; 2 Chr 33:6; Mal 3:5.
15. Did. 2.2; Hippolytus, *Haer.* 4.28–51; Lactantius, *Inst.* 2.17; Apos. Con. 2.62; Augustine, *Civ.* 8–10.
16. Avery-Peck, "Magic"; J. Jacobs, "Superstition."
17. *Guide* 2.10; cf. Gen. Rab. 10.6.

prototypical forms of the doctrine in the fourth century BCE, centuries *after* the completion of the Written Torah. It is highly implausible that God hid the meaning of innumerable Torah passages from Israel for a millennium until a gentile philosopher discovered the secret key to interpreting who God is. The doctrine did not have wide reach until Philo, the gnostics, and Plotinus successively integrated it into their teachings, with Plotinus having the most unrestrained application of the idea. None of these thinkers drew their idea of *via negativa* from the Hebrew Scriptures; rather, they inflicted the doctrine upon the Scriptures as a foreign contaminant. By integrating *via negativa* into the core intuitions of their theological systems, Maimonides and Kabbalah likewise corrupted their thought with pagan theology that had no right to overrule the revelations of Moses and the prophets. The NT is free of that contamination, and while later Christian theology (particularly of the Neoplatonism-infused mystical tradition) makes significant use of *via negativa*, it is by no means required for the understanding of the Trinity, Incarnation, or the meaning of God talk. The Protestant tradition, for example, tends to limit the use of negative theology and makes greater use of positive and analogical language for God.

Hermeneutics: Arcanization of prior Jewish texts is illegitimate, and the New Testament does not engage in such practice (see §§6.6; 7.6).

Arcanization, a term coined by Jewish mysticism scholar Moshe Idel, refers to the common Jewish phenomenon of developing new systems of interpretation for old texts, transforming the meaning of the texts into a new esoteric and mystical direction. Maimonides does this through his exhaustive lexicon of reinterpreting God talk (*Guide* pt. 1), and Kabbalah does this through its use of the *sod* interpretive method. While Maimonides's use of arcanization is narrower than Kabbalah's, both systems allow the newly appointed interpreters to make the texts mean whatever they come up with. The resulting interpretations are arbitrary, grounded in the interpreter's ingenuity, and result in removing the epistemological power of Scriptures' prophetic authors to convey their own message. Moreover, when Maimonides and the Kabbalists conform their interpretations to false cosmological and scientific notions, they expose their arcanization as artificial speculation with no origin in divine revelation or truth. In contrast, the NT never rejects the Hebrew Scriptures' exoteric meaning for esoteric or mystical reinterpretations.

The NT may provide additional information or clarity that helps readers understand better what was going on in the Hebrew Scriptures (i.e., Jude 4–5), or it may apply those texts to a NT context (*pesher*) or typologically, but it never cancels out the commonsense (*peshat*) meaning of a Scriptural passage.

Hermeneutics: The New Testament does not require the rejection or total reinterpretation of the Jewish theological thought that preceded it, whereas Maimonides and Kabbalah do (see §§3.3; 5.8; 7.6; 11.2).

The NT's theology is partially continuous with the Second Temple Judaism it was borne out of. As illustrated by many contemporary Jewish scholars, proto-Trinitarian and incarnational thought forms were discussed and affirmed by Jews in the first century and prior, before Jesus or the NT entered the historical scene. Although there are good reasons to avoid affirming *total* continuity with pre-Jesus Judaism (cf. Hurtado), there was significant continuity nonetheless. In contrast, Maimonides and Kabbalah take opposite and even adversarial theological paths compared to their forbears. Maimonides vehemently declared Jewish corporealists to be worse than idolators (*Guide* 1.36). Jewish scholar Benjamin Sommer says that Maimonides's theological positions "would entail the creation of a new religion whose earliest sacred document would be found in the tenth-century C.E. philosophical writings of Maimonides's predecessor, Saadia Gaon."[18] Likewise, Kabbalah reinterprets, diverts, redefines, and subtly rejects many aspects of premedieval Jewish theology under the guise of secret tradition. When viewed from a historical perspective, both Maimonides and Kabbalah represent decisive breaks away from the Judaism and Jewish theology they inherited. The NT does not accuse pre-NT Jews as being ignorant, unschooled, *am ha'aretz*, nonphilosophical, unenlightened, or stupid. Maimonides and Kabbalah, in contrast, employ such attacks against their forbears liberally—because they *must* in order to establish their new philosophical paradigms. The NT presents itself as fulfilling what came prior (Matt 5:17), whereas Maimonides and Kabbalah have an adversarial attitude toward the Jews who came before.

---

18. Sommer, *Bodies of God*, 136.

Part III: The Incarnation of the Son of God

Humble equality before God: The Incarnation ensures and encourages equal unity among all believers in Jesus, whereas Maimonides and Kabbalists promote the prideful elitism of philosophers and mystics, with themselves at the top of Israel (see §11.3).

For Maimonides, the sure route for personal union with God and ultimate salvation is found in one's philosophical attainments; humans must learn philosophy to be united with the active intellect in the sphere of the moon, thereby receiving wisdom, revelation, and union with God. What if an individual has not attained such philosophical heights? Maimonides calls such people ignorant, obstinate, and superficial, and he specifically mentions the young, women, and common people as incapable of such philosophical attainment (*Guide* 1.33). Thus, he establishes himself and his (male) followers as the only ones worthy of the highest union with God through the intellect. Kabbalah, too, promotes an anthropocentric salvation through its strong emphasis on esoteric truth known only to Kabbalists. Some Kabbalists, such as the contemporary Chabad movement, even promote an extra Jewish soul (*nefesh*) that will return to God by necessity. What, then, of gentiles? In contrast, the NT affirms, "For in Christ Jesus you are all sons of God, through faith. For as many of you as were baptized into Christ have put on Messiah. There is neither Jew nor Greek, there is neither slave nor free, there is no male and female, for you are all one in Christ Jesus" (Gal 3:26–28).[19] Because of the Incarnation and resurrection of Messiah, Jesus's followers are united with him such that their relationship with him is their primary identity, even more fundamental than their personal identities. With regard to eternal salvation, all are equal in the eyes of God because all are equally united with Messiah by faith in him. The NT has no place for prideful elitism, only humble equality and fellowship among Jesus followers from every tribe, language, people, and nation (Rev 5:9–10).

Theological justification: The fewer paradoxes needed to fit Scripture and reality, the better, and this favors the incarnational model (see §§5.6; 11.1).

The Hebrew Scriptures and the observed universe present questions that various schools of Jewish thought attempt to answer. Each model I have considered allows some amount of paradox. For example, I admit

19. See the important qualification of this statement in 316n91, which retains continued distinctions between Jews and gentiles in Messiah's community.

that one of the greatest objections against belief in the Trinity and the Incarnation is their apparently contradictory nature, which critics say is not *apparent* but *actually* absurd. However, the NT is not the only worldview I have considered that integrates paradox into core doctrines.

I propose a kind of Occam's razor[20] for paradoxes whereby answers with fewer paradoxes should be preferred over those with more. The various opinions in this book about the amount of paradox can be plotted as follows:

1. *No paradox allowed*, since all knowledge can be humanly comprehended in principle, and God is not infinite (exclusive *via positiva* and logical positivism)
2. *Limited paradox allowed*, due to limited divine incomprehensibility, limited divine infinity, the principle of analogy, and a strict Creator-creature distinction uniquely bridged in the Incarnation (*via analogia* as exemplified by Thomas Aquinas)
3. *Moderate paradox allowed*, due to absolute divine incomprehensibility, extensive divine infinity, and a strict Creator-creature distinction (theistic *via negativa* as exemplified by Maimonides)
4. *Extensive paradox allowed*, due to extensive divine incomprehensibility, absolute divine infinity, dual-tiered metaphysics, and minimized Creator-creature distinction (panentheistic *via negativa* as exemplified by Kabbalah and Plotinus)

In the course of this book, I have affirmed (2), the *limited paradox* view. I have only briefly considered and dismissed the first view when discussing divine corporealism, which I deny as unbiblical. I have devoted longer treatment to explain why Maimonides's *moderate paradox* and Kabbalah's *extensive paradox* models are incorrect.

Both Maimonides and Kabbalah unjustifiably employ more paradox than is needed to make sense of God and the world. Despite the claims of Scripture, Maimonides proposes a nonrational view of God that divests God of all essential predication. Kabbalah proposes a nonrational view of all reality, positing that all complex and finite entities are in fact

---

20. *Occam's razor* is a philosophical principle that states, "Entities should not be multiplied beyond necessity" or, more simply, "The simplest explanation is usually the best one." It advises observers to choose the hypothesis or theory that requires the fewest assumptions and postulates. This principle is named after William of Occam (also spelled "Ockham," 1285–1349).

simple and infinite. Unfortunately, these claims derive from questionable epistemic sources that are unsupported by Scripture. In contrast, the range of paradox in NT theology is limited to only certain aspects of God's thoughts, essence, actions, and the paradox that remains about God has corroborating non-paradoxical evidence. While the Chalcedonian Definition of the Incarnation may seem strange, it is only *apparently* so to finite minds, and one can trust that the difficulty is merely apparent because of other rational and existential evidence. These include the resurrection of Jesus from the dead, the fulfillment of biblical prophecy in history, and the internal rebirth by the Holy Spirit.[21]

In sum, my modified Occam's razor leads to the following conclusion: if the Hebrew Scriptures and known reality can be explained with a less paradoxical model, such as I have affirmed with the Incarnation, then the more paradoxical solutions ought to be suspect. Under this criterion, both Maimonides and Kabbalah are less preferable solutions than the model given in the NT.

Theology: Divine embodiment is impossible only under the a priori assumptions of Greek philosophy, not under the evidence of the Scriptures (see §§2.12; 5.6–5.8; 6.4–6.7; 10.5.5; 11.1).

It is a dangerous temptation for intelligent individuals to stand over God, so to speak, and determine by their human a priori reasoning what is possible and impossible for God to do. The Hebrew Scriptures say that God does not play by human intellectual rules or constraints, and they repeatedly show God doing things that were previously unknown and unthinkable to human beings. When a person trusts in logically constructed a priori reasoning too much, it can lead to ignoring the a posteriori evidence that challenges his resulting system. This is the mistake Maimonides makes when he accepts the logical intuitions of Neoplatonism and, on that basis, rejects all evidence of divine embodiment in Scripture.

Theology: Belief in the Incarnation is rational given the incomprehensibility of God's nature and power (see §11.1).

The God of the Hebrew Scriptures knows things beyond human rationality, including knowledge about himself. Claims about God

---

21. On these rational and existential evidences, see §11.1.3 and associated footnotes.

(including the Incarnation) should not be discounted simply because they do not make rational sense to human minds. While God's essence transcends humanity's finite understanding, he has shown his ability to bridge that infinite divide by creating the finite universe, interacting with his creation through miracles and providence, communicating understandable words, endowing rationality, and providing finite humans with likeness to his infinite self (Gen 1:26). Examples in Scripture illustrate how God can do what finite minds cannot conceive: bring the infinite down to the realm of the finite, such that the infinite participates in and with the finite. This is confessed in the Incarnation of Messiah, the most concrete way God has ever bridged the gap between himself and his creation. While it is not possible to understand *how* God does these actions, believers in the Hebrew Scriptures can trust *that* he does them.

Exaltation of God: Incarnational theology exalts God's role, power, and profundity in the salvation of humanity (see §11.3).

According to the NT, the Father initiates the salvation of sinners (Eph 1:4; John 6:44); the Son of God, who is fully divine, accomplishes salvation through his death and resurrection (Isa 53; Heb 2:17); and the Spirit sustains the salvation of the redeemed (2 Cor 1:22). Thus, the incarnational model begins and ends with the triune God as the primary actor in salvation. Individual human sinners are bit players who receive salvation by grace and not through any accomplishment or effort of their own. This aligns with the Hebrew Scriptures' declarations that God is the only savior and redeemer,[22] that God alone deserves praise and glory,[23] and that human beings should not attribute their blessings to their accomplishments.[24] In the Incarnation, God only is king, supporter, savior, and shield.[25] In contrast, Maimonides and Kabbalah promote human-centered pathways for improving the human condition. According to Maimonides, the ignorant need to learn philosophy to commune with God, effectively rescuing themselves. According to Kabbalah, the rescue

---

22. Isa 43:11; 44:6; 45:21; Hos 13:4.
23. Ps 62:7; 115:1; Isa 2:17; 48:11.
24. Deut 7:7–8; Ezek 36:22.
25. An allusion to the Shemoneh Esreh, Avot. King: John 1:49; 1 Tim 1:17; 6:15; Rev 1:5; 19:16. Supporter: Matt 11:28–30; John 15:1–5; 1 Pet 2:25. Savior: Luke 1:47; Acts 13:23; Titus 1:3–4; 2:13; 3:4–6; 2 Pet 1:1; Jude 25. Shield: Luke 12:11–12; 1 Pet 1:5; Jude 24.

of the entire universe is in Israel's hands. This is problematic, since God gives his glory to none other (Isa 42:8), and no one should take credit for their own forgiveness, salvation, or communion with God.

Epistemology: The incarnational model consistently holds to the single-tiered view of truth promoted by the Hebrew Scriptures (see §§4.1.4–4.1.5; 4.2.1; 8.1; 8.4.3; 10.5).

The incarnational model proposed by the NT maintains that truth is unequivocal, corresponding to reality and God's knowledge. While human understanding is limited in breadth and depth compared to God's, this does not make human knowledge untrue or partially true. Rather, if something is true, it is simply and fully true, reflecting an objective reality that can be known by both humans and God. The NT teaches that objectively true things happen in history and in the spiritual realm, and these things can be humanly known as true in the same way that God holds them as true. For example, Jesus was not just human according to *appearances* (docetism) but truly human. Jesus did not just *partially* fulfill messianic prophecies according to a *particular angle*, but truly *fulfilled* those he accomplished in his first coming. This understanding rejects the need for *via negativa* unlearning, instead acknowledging that human knowledge of God is partial and finite yet accurate. In this way, the NT's understanding of truth is consistent with the portrayal of truth in the Hebrew Scriptures. In contrast, the Platonic understanding of truth, which postdates the Hebrew Scriptures, bisects the idea of truth into the truth of mere appearances (the shadows on the cave wall) and the truer truth of the hidden reality underneath (the persons making the shadows, and ultimately, the world outside the cave). Kabbalah inherits this dual-tiered understanding of truth, thereby subverting the epistemology promoted in the Scriptures.

Theological knowledge: The New Testament portrays knowledge of God as fully true, as do the Hebrew Scriptures, not as pious falsehoods (Maimonides) or lower-level truths that must be transcended (Kabbalah) (see §§2.3; 2.14; 5.8; 7.5; 9.2; 11.2).

When Maimonides considers descriptions of God, such as "merciful and gracious, slow to anger, and abounding in steadfast love and faithfulness" (Exod 34:6), he trains his readers to reject such notions as child's talk. The mature Maimonidean philosopher knows that words cannot describe God. God is simply condescending to human knowledge by using nothing words to teach Israel pious falsehoods that are discarded by sophisticated Jewish philosophers. This Maimonidean logic turns the Hebrew Scriptures into a playground of falsehoods. Kabbalah takes a different route, employing the Platonic idea of two-tiered truth to have their cake and eat it too. According to the Kabbalists, the attributes of God in Exodus are true, but only in the lower realm of human experience and perception. Outside the human sphere, such descriptions are just as false as Maimonides holds. In Kabbalah, God knows that he is *not* "merciful and gracious"—because *Ein Sof* cannot be described at all—but he wants Israel to act *as if* he was. This, too, turns the Hebrew Scriptures into a playground of falsehoods, but this time under a veneer of lower-truth-value shadows. The NT rescues the reader of the Hebrew Scriptures from needing to ascribe any falsehood to God's Holy Scriptures. Under the principles of *via positiva* (when speaking about the embodied/pre-incarnate Son of God) and *via analogia* (in all other cases), the Hebrew Scriptures can be upheld as teaching accurate and unequivocal truth at all times. No falsehoods, no half-truths, and no misleading language is present.[26] In this way, the NT's handling of the Hebrew Scriptures is more faithful and respectful than the leading Jewish alternatives.

Existential yearning: The God of the New Testament is love, bestows love, and models love (see §11.3).

As three eternal persons united as one God, the Father, Son, and Spirit have always existed in a perfect and harmonious relationship. Compassion, care, deference, and love are not created virtues God chooses to exhibit after the creation of the cosmos. Rather, God has eternally exhibited those virtues because they are aspects of his eternal essence as manifested in the eternal relationships between the three persons of the triunity; as the NT declares, "God is love" (1 John 4:8) and "Love is from God" (1 John 4:7). God could not *be* love without there being an eternal subject-object relationship *within* God; love is not possible without two. Yet, God does not need to create finite beings in order to love. Since God

---

26. Some have been led to think that the shadow/form ideas present in Hebrews (see especially Heb 10:1) are evidence of Platonism in the NT canon. This assumption is likely incorrect, as argued by Hurst, *Epistle to the Hebrews*; Cockerill, *Epistle to the Hebrews*, 28–34.

is a triunity of persons, there have always been two, and three, loving each other for eternity. In this way, the triunity of God gives a satisfying solution to the philosophical problem of "the one and the many."[27] It also answers humanity's deepest questions about why love is inherently fulfilling: our finite human love is a clue that we need to reciprocate God's eternal and perfect Trinitarian love.

Turning to Maimonides, it is not possible to say that his deity "is love" or even directly bestows love on his creation. As a distant singularity without direct relationship with his creation, the Maimonidean deity has no one to love before creation. After creation, God is so transcendent that it is hard to conceive how he could love another. For Maimonides, love is primarily something creaturely that humans are commanded to do toward God and others; the theme of God's love is minor and undeveloped in the *Guide*.[28] This results in an emotional and relational void that makes love arbitrary, commandment based, and contingent, rather than existentially and eternally profound, reaching to the core of what it means to be humans created in the likeness of God. Some in the kabbalistic tradition say that it is true relative to our perception that God loves people, but it may not be true from God's perspective that he loves anyone.[29] Nothing of the sort is necessary with the God of the NT, who not only *is* love in a Trinitarian sense, but also *illustrates* love through the crucifixion of Messiah for sinners.

Misplaced objections: Common Jewish criticisms of the Incarnation are often straw-man arguments (see §§10.7; 11.1).

As a complex field of study with many wrong answers and only one accurate one, Christology is often misconstrued and misunderstood in

---

27. The one did not come first, nor did the many, but the one and the many (three persons) have existed as God in eternity past. On this subject, see Gunton, *One, Three, and Many*; McCormack, "One, Three and Many"; Pugliese, *One, Many, and Trinity*, 240–43. Also see 209n62.

28. In the *Guide*, the first mention of love with God as the subject is in *Guide* 2.29, which is a brief quotation of Isa 63:7. *Guide* 2.43 mentions God loving Israel based on Deut 26:17–18. *Guide* 3.53 is perhaps the most sustained discussion of God's love, but it amounts to a single paragraph. Maimonides states, "The very act of the creation is an act of God's loving-kindness." While this may be true, it still means that love is contingent upon God's choice to create, not innate to who and what God is. By my count in the Friedländer translation, nearly all of the seventy to eighty remaining references to "love" in the *Guide* pertain to human agents.

29. Lebens, *Principles of Judaism*, 99.

the Jewish world. Few Jesus followers have the Chalcedonian Definition of the Incarnation at the tip of their tongue when considering the deity of Jesus. How much less, then, would Jewish people have familiarity with the doctrine! Many Jews associate the Incarnation with Greek mythology, which is totally dissimilar to Chalcedon. Others believe the doctrine entails a man becoming God (adoptionism), or that Jesus followers affirm three gods (tritheism), or that the Incarnation entails believing in absurdities like four-sided triangles (Monophysitism). All these are false straw-man arguments against belief in Jesus, and a true understanding of the NT's theology withstands these objections.

Historical plausibility: Divine embodiment was once acceptable in Judaism (see ch. 3).

As shown by Jewish scholars such as Alan Segal, Daniel Boyarin, and Esther Hamori, it was once acceptable within Jewish circles to postulate an intermediary divine being who is uncreated, united with God, and capable of appearing in physical form. Other Jewish authorities, as shown by Marc Shapiro and Benjamin Sommer, once believed that God has a body eternally. These are now forgotten and minority opinions due to the success of Maimonides and Kabbalah within Jewish theology. However, many Jewish scholars considering these topics argue that the Christology of the NT is a descendant of ancient Jewish binitarianism and deserves to be called a legitimate Jewish option. If God's Son is considered the mediator between God and humanity—the one who has always been appointed to cross the infinite gulf—then many passages about God's physicality can reasonably be applied to God himself, via his Son. This is truer to the words of Scripture, providing a simpler and less anachronistic solution than Maimonides's and Kabbalah's Platonized systems.

Textual authenticity: The doctrine of the Incarnation derives from authentic first-century Jewish sources, not from pseudepigraphal mystical works as with Kabbalah, or mistaken sources like Maimonides's use of the Theology of Aristotle *(see §§5.5; 9.1).*

Both Maimonides and Kabbalah cite dubious works in the construction of their systems. Because Maimonides erroneously believed that Aristotle wrote the *Theology of Aristotle*, he assigned high epistemological authority to it, even though it was actually written by Plotinus. Kabbalists did not cite original Greek works, as they avoided providing sources for their ideas besides divine revelation to Israel. To cover up the fact that there are no Jewish sources teaching Greek mysticism before the Greeks, Jewish mystics falsely wrote mystical works in Hebrew and Aramaic that were attributed to long-dead patriarchs (*Sefer Yetzirah*, attributed to Abraham) and rabbinic sages (*Zohar*, attributed to Rashbi). Through the process of historical and textual analysis, scholars now know kabbalistic works originated in the medieval period, except for *Sefer Yetzirah*, which may date to the talmudic era.

In contrast, the principles of historical and textual analysis, when applied to the NT, show that they are first-century Jewish documents with a variety of evidence in favor of their traditional authorship, date, and place of origin—all of which place the authors of the NT in the category of eyewitnesses of Jesus.[30] This dramatically increases the stature of the NT's claims. As a result, the doctrine of the Incarnation is built upon confidently sourced Jewish primary documents with plausible evidence in favor of the events they record, including events and teachings that accord with Jesus's divinity.

Early high Christology: Incarnational theology has theological continuity dating to the first century (see §§3.3; 10.5–10.7).

Given the double evidence of pre-Christian Jewish theology and the earliest strata of NT Christology, it is no longer tenable to maintain that belief in Jesus's divinity evolved over time and was not present at the inception of the first-century Jesus movement. Hurtado writes that belief in his divinity was a "big bang" that emerged immediately in Judea in the 30s CE.[31] The NT and church fathers depict a historically continuous chain of belief, worship, and practice that ties the earliest followers of Jesus to Nicaea and Chalcedon. The Chalcedonian Definition was the culmination of four centuries of theological articulation concerning six pre-philosophical truths: (1) there is only one God; (2) the Father is God; (3) the Son, Jesus, is God; (4) the Holy Spirit is God; (5) Jesus is human; (6) Jesus is not the Father and not the Holy Spirit. These truths were held in tension long before the definition was articulated in 451 CE.

---

30. Keener, *Christobiography*; Bauckham, *Jesus and the Eyewitnesses*; Blomberg, *Historical Reliability of Gospels*; Blomberg, *Historical Reliability of John's Gospel*; Köstenberger and Kruger, *Heresy of Orthodoxy*.

31. Hurtado, *Lord Jesus Christ*, 135.

Historical epistemological warrant: As with the epistemological warrant of Sinai, incarnational theology is pre-philosophical, warranted by the apostles' historical experience with the risen Messiah (see §§10.5.5; 11.1.2–11.1.3).

The six beliefs listed above are present in the earliest strata of the NT and the practices of Jesus's earliest followers. Thus, the origin of the Incarnation doctrine cannot be attributed to man-made philosophical evolution, but rather to the lived experience of Jesus's Jewish eyewitness followers, who insisted upon his divinity based on what they had seen and heard. Chief among their claims was that they saw Jesus alive after his brutal death by crucifixion. They saw him, talked with him, ate with him, and touched him. The earliest creed of the church mentions five hundred who saw him alive after his resurrection (1 Cor 15:3–8).[32] Their eyewitness experiences provided them warrant to accept Jesus's teachings about his divine identity.

In Judaism since Judah Halevi's *Kuzari* (ca. 1140), religious Jewish people have been taught to prize public Israelite experiences of God's power as authenticating God's self-revelation. The Sinai event was God publicly declaring his authority to give a new covenant to Moses on the mountain, and the entire nation of Israel witnessed it. Although the entire nation did not witness Jesus's resurrection, it was witnessed by a wide variety of Jewish people who then fervently proclaimed what they saw to all Israel in Judea and the diaspora. Their experience of the resurrection deeply convinced them that Jesus was the divine Messiah who had come to bring Israel a new covenant that fulfills the covenant at Sinai.

12.2. Conclusion and Doxological Epilogue

This book has been about charting a course from scandal to shalom. A scandal is when word gets out that a person allegedly performed a forbidden action, bringing shame upon himself or herself and their community. Since the arrival of Jesus of Nazareth in the first century, the Jewish community has known the widespread allegation: "God became a man." Some accepted the allegation as true and became Yeshua's followers, but many did not. At first, this allegation was not as much forbidden in the

---

32. See especially the works of Gary Habermas on this early creed.

eyes of Yeshua's detractors as it was seen as simply false. Yet, other Jewish streams, such as the rabbinic corporealists, also alleged that God had a positive relationship with the physical world. Thus, the walls between the Jewish people and divine embodiment were initially porous and permeable. But as the centuries wore on, and conflict with the dominant and hostile Christian culture grew, the permeable walls were reinforced with brick, and what was previously plausible became forbidden. In the High Middle Ages and later, the Incarnation of the Son of God was not seen just as false, but as *shameful* for a Jewish person to even consider. Under the influence of Maimonides and the kabbalistic tradition, the idea of divine embodiment, and thus the related idea of an incarnate divine Messiah, became a scandal.

This scandal remains today, and in response I have sought new pathways for articulating the divinity of Jesus the Messiah in light of prevailing Jewish religious worldviews. It has been argued that the theological and philosophical positions of medieval Jewish philosophy and mysticism continue to serve as barriers that lessen or remove the plausibility of Jesus being the incarnate Son of God. These barriers, while formidable, can be credibly answered through patient theological and philosophical reflection upon the Scriptures, history, and creation itself. It is my contention that not only were the allegations about Jesus's divine identity *true*, but they were *designed and performed by the God of Israel*. Thus, what was a scandal should be no longer. The taboos have run their course.

In summary, throughout this book I have come to the following conclusions:

- The Incarnation is a profound mystery that rewards faithful study.
- A rational understanding of the Incarnation involves a wide variety of subdisciplines, encouraging the life of the mind and the love of God with the mind (Mark 12:30; 1 Pet 1:13).
- The Incarnation provides large-scale answers to the most significant questions of life.
- The Incarnation and divine embodiment find support in the Hebrew Scriptures, the NT, and the extra-biblical Jewish tradition.
- Too little Greek philosophy limits human capability to understand God and the world.
- Too much Greek philosophy twists, chokes, and overtakes biblical revelation.

- Historical Jewish attempts to fill the gap left vacated by an Incarnation-less theology have not been successful.
- The Jewish option presented in the Jewish-authored NT is the best fit for scriptural revelation, historical events, philosophical reflection, and scientific knowledge.

With these things in mind, I will allow myself to end this book with a more personal epilogue and doxology. Below is the final benefit of the Incarnation that I will mention, one that hits at an existential level:

Meta-epistemological shalom: Jesus as the incarnate LORD *provides the answers, fulfillment, and rest to which the Hebrew Scriptures point.*

As Jesus is the LORD of Israel and the nations, his followers have peace that is lacking without him. When asking questions about life purpose, meaning, morality, justice, marriage, the afterlife, and relationship with God, Jesus's followers have a simple pathway to find answers: "What was Jesus's opinion on the matter?" Although he did not handle every question human beings ask, Jesus's followers have a distinct advantage: if Jesus addressed the question, then the matter is beautifully *settled*. All other sources of knowledge are ordered, critiqued, and affirmed by his final word. That is what it means for him to be LORD. There is no need for endless searching, leaving the question open, or being stuck in an intellectual fog about the most important matters in life. There is no need to consider Jesus's opinion as but one rabbi's opinion among many. His opinion is the definitive one—completing one's searching, delivering the rest that comes with uncomplicated knowledge of the truth. While there is still much to question and pursue—the painful question *Why, God?* persists after following Jesus—nevertheless, many have found their most troubling questions settled as they listen to Jesus speak to them in the pages of the NT. As rabbi and LORD, Jesus asks all to *learn* from him to find rest: "Come to me, all who labor and are heavy laden, and I will give you rest. Take my yoke upon you, and learn from me, for I am gentle and lowly in heart, and you will find rest for your souls. For my yoke is easy, and my burden is light." (Matt 11:28–30). Learning from the incarnate Messiah is shalom for the soul.

Finally, I join Paul by marveling at the mystery of the Incarnation:

> Great indeed, we confess, is the mystery of godliness:
> He was manifested in the flesh,

Part III: The Incarnation of the Son of God

    vindicated by the Spirit,
    seen by angels,
    proclaimed among the nations,
    believed on in the world,
    taken up in glory. (1 Tim 3:16)

Beyond that, the incarnate LORD of Israel will return again, taking his seat on the throne of David as the King of Israel and Messiah of the nations. All that the prophets of Israel spoke concerning him will come to pass (Acts 3:21).

Maranatha!

Appendices

Appendix A
Glossary

A posteriori: Latin, "from the latter." Reasoning based on empirical evidence. Distinguished from a priori reasoning. See Epistemology.

A priori: Latin, "from the former." Reasoning based on self-evident or logical necessities and not dependent on observed evidence. Distinguished from a posteriori reasoning. See Epistemology.

Allegorization: The application of allegorical or deeper meanings to texts (biblical or otherwise) that were not previously understood as allegorical. See Allegory, PaRDeS.

Allegory: A literary genre where words have a literal, limited scope of meaning, as well as an expanded metaphorical meaning with correspondences determined by the author.

Anthropomorphism: Derives from Greek, "in the form of man." Metaphorically applying human characteristics, especially bodily, to non-human entities, such as God. See Corporealism, Divine Embodiment, Incorporealism, Theophany.

Arcanization: The process whereby a closed group of initiates interprets texts not previously understood as having secret meanings and associates secret meanings to which only the group has access. Coined by Moshe Idel (in *Absorbing Perfections*) in reference to Maimonides's and the Kabbalists' approach to biblical interpretation. See PaRDeS.

Appendix A

Aristotelianism: A school of philosophical reasoning derived principally from Aristotle (fourth century BCE) and his later followers. Often contrasted with Platonism.

Astrology: The practice of determining the positions and aspects of the stars and planets for the purpose of divining their influence on earthly affairs. Astrology is historically dependent upon a geocentric Aristotelian-Ptolemaic understanding of the universe.

Being: That which exists, or the state of existing. A key question in philosophical literature asks whether there is one being shared among all things, or whether all things constitute multiple beings. See Ontology.

Binitarianism: A modern term for a phenomenon in ancient Judaism whereby God is conceived as having some kind of duality within his unity, often regarded as a Father-Son relationship.

Chalcedonian Definition: The definitive post-NT formulation of orthodox Christian theology about the Son's Incarnation and deity, dated 451 CE. It involves the Son's embodiment plus a hypostatic union of his divine and human natures. See Incarnation.

Christology: The theology of the identity and work of the Messiah. Strictly speaking, Judaism has a Christology as well—by defining the future Messiah as merely human—but the term usually refers to the theology of Jesus-followers regarding the person and work of Jesus. See *Homoousios*, Incarnation, Trinity.

Church Fathers: The theologians, apologists, church authorities, and biblical interpreters of the first few centuries after the apostles, roughly from the early second century (Ignatius, Papias) through the fall of Rome in the late fifth century. They wrote primarily in Greek, Latin, and sometimes Syriac.

Copernican Revolution: The centuries-long sequence of events that led Western thinkers away from an Aristotelian-Ptolemaic geocentric model of the universe to the heliocentric solar system promoted by Nicholas Copernicus in the sixteenth century. Principal figures in the revolution included Brahe, Kepler, Galileo, Newton, and Foucault.

Corporealism: The belief that God in his eternal essence has a body. The Bible sometimes presents God in bodily ways, such as describing God's hands and ears and other divine body parts (e.g., Isa 59:1). Corporealism holds that these instances may be understood as concrete descriptions of God's being, thereby avoiding anthropomorphic (metaphorical) interpretations. See Incorporealism.

Cosmology: The origin, composition, and operation of the cosmos or universe. This book uses the wide sense of the term, which includes the subdiscipline of cosmogony, the origin of the cosmos. See Astrology, Copernican Revolution, Creation *ex Matria*, Creation *ex Nihilo*, Emanation *ex Deo*, Geocentrism.

Creation ex Matria: Latin, creation "from matter." The doctrine that God formed or fashioned the universe out of preexisting matter. See Cosmology.

Creation ex Nihilo: Latin, creation "from nothing." The doctrine that God created the universe out of nothing, entailing an ontological distinction between God and everything else. See Cosmology.

Demiurge: In Platonic philosophy, the divine "craftsman" responsible for fashioning primordial matter into the harmonious universe of form and function according to the pattern of immaterial Forms (or Ideas). See Creation *ex Matria*, Cosmology.

Divine Embodiment: An instance where God manifests his presence visibly and physically in a body. No union or assumption of natures is implied in mere divine embodiment. Divine embodiment is often associated with theophanies, such as with the physical manifestations of the burning bush (Exod 3), the back of God (Exod 33:23), and the cloud during the Sinai experience (Exod 34:5, 40:35). This book considers corporeal, incorporeal, and panentheist versions of divine embodiment. The corporealist version says God transforms his preexisting body into various forms. The incorporeal understanding states that God's incorporeal essence remains unchanged as he acts in and through a temporarily inhabited body. The panentheist understanding states that the entire cosmos is God's body.

Divine Incomprehensibility: The idea that God's nature cannot be known fully by any being except himself (cf. Isa 55:8–9).

Divine Nature: That which God is, including his attributes and being. Often synonymous with "divine essence" and "divine substance." The Pauline word for this is *theiotes* (θειότης [Rom 1:20, Col 2:9]). Perhaps the closest concept in the Hebrew Bible is the use of the Tetragrammaton.

Ein Sof: Hebrew, "That which has no end." The kabbalistic term for God in his highest, unknowable state.

Emanation: An overflow from the source of reality, often likened to a ray of sunshine or a flow of water. Each emanation is a distinct, yet interconnected, manifestation of the divine essence, which flows forth from its preceding level, resulting in a hierarchical structure where each subsequent emanation is a lesser reflection of the previous one, possessing fewer attributes of the divine and increasing levels of differentiation, fragmentation, and imperfection. See Neoplatonism, Kabbalah.

Emanation ex Deo: Latin, creation "from God." The cosmological idea that God emanates the universe by extending his own being. Thus, only one being exists. See Cosmology.

Epistemological Hierarchy: A ranking of sources of knowledge that are believed to be more or less authoritative than others. Sources higher in a hierarchy have controlling influence over those that are lower. Sources lower in a hierarchy may be accepted only when judged to be free of conflict with higher sources.

Epistemology: The branch of philosophy that studies the nature, grounds, and validity of knowledge. It investigates the question "How do we know the truth?"

Esoteric: A teaching that is obscure and designed to be limited to a closed circle of worthy initiates. It usually has the connotation of hidden mysticism. The opposite of exoteric.

Essence: The permanent and necessary aspects of a being's existence, also called its nature. To have no essence is to not exist. See Ontology.

Existence: That which is in objective reality. To exist is to be; to not exist is not to be.

Exoteric: A teaching that is understandable by the common person through the plain sense of a text without that person needing special or secret initiation. The opposite of esoteric.

Gematria: The practice of interpreting Hebrew letters, words, and phrases according to mathematical formulas.

Geocentrism: The belief that the earth is the center of the universe. This was the predominant cosmological view until the Copernican revolution.

Gilgul: The Hebrew term for reincarnation.

Gnosticism: A modern term given to a variety of religious schools of thought that were active in the second through fourth centuries and opposed by the church fathers. Key beliefs include the evil of the material world, the creation of the universe by an evil or ignorant deity, and emphasis on secret knowledge (gnosis).

God Talk: Words used to describe God's mode of being or actions.

Halakah: Hebrew, "to walk." Normative rabbinic law as practiced in Orthodox Judaism, developed over centuries. See Mishnah, Talmud.

Hebdomad: In Greek cosmology and philosophical speculation, the name of the seven mobile heavenly bodies visible to the naked eye. The Hebdomad became associated with the seven days of the week, astrological correlations, and magic. See Astrology.

Hellenistic: A culture or belief system that has adopted Greek modes of thought, ideals, or practice, usually referring to the Greco-Roman era (eighth century BCE through fifth century CE).

Hermeneutics: The methods and principles for interpreting a text, especially the Bible. See *Via Analogia*, *Via Negativa*, *Via Positiva*, PaRDeS.

Hermeticism: An ancient philosophical and spiritual tradition rooted in the teachings of Hermes Trismegistus in the Corpus Hermeticum (second–fifth centuries CE), emphasizing the unity of all existence (macrocosm/microcosm), divine potential within humans, and the pursuit of gnosis (spiritual insight) through alchemy, astrology, and mystical practices.

Homoousios: Greek, "same substance/essence/nature." This was the most important word in the Nicene Creed, as it firmly established that NT orthodoxy requires belief that Jesus's divinity is equivalent to the Father's divinity. See Christology, Incarnation, Trinity.

Human Nature: The essential set of properties of human beings, distinguishing them from nonhuman beings. Classically, the Christian theological tradition affirms human nature as consisting of the union of a body and a soul.

Hypostasis: Greek. In fourth-century theological discourse, this word describes the individuality and personhood of the Father, Son, and Spirit. Prior to the fourth century CE, this Greek word had other meanings. In Heb 1:3, the word refers to the divine nature. See Person, Trinity.

Hypostatic Union: The union of the divine and human natures of the Messiah in one person (hypostasis). See Chalcedonian Definition, Incarnation.

Idealism: The theory that the sensible world is not truly real; that is, having an external objective existence. True reality is spiritual or mental. Contrasted with realism.

Immanence: The idea of God inhabiting, indwelling, and being near to his creation. Related to God's omnipresence. Contrasted with transcendence.

Impossibility: That which cannot be done or cannot exist. See A Priori.

Incarnation: The eternal Son of God living as a Jewish human being for the purpose of rescuing humanity from sin. In Jesus of Nazareth, "all the fullness of God was pleased to dwell" (Col 1:19; 2:9). The Son of God is the eternal Word who became flesh (John 1:14). This involved the union of an incorporeal divine person to the human nature he created. This union is defined in the Chalcedonian Definition and known as the hypostatic union whereby the two natures are united but left unchanged. Consequently, the Son of God is able to live as one person in two natures, being fully God and fully human at the same time without mixing or separating the two natures. This personal union allows followers of Jesus to affirm his divinity (his divine nature) and his simultaneous humanity (his human nature), which includes an embodied presence and a human soul.

Incorporealism: The belief that God in his eternal essence does not have a body. God is essentially spiritual, with no positive eternal relationship to physicality. Under this understanding, biblical passages about God's body parts are generally interpreted as anthropomorphisms—that is, metaphorical language that ought not be interpreted as concrete descriptions of God's being. See Corporealism.

Infinite: That which is boundless, unlimited, endless, or qualitatively maximal in a particular context. An abstract property applicable to the domains of mathematics, philosophy, and theology. Different understandings of God's infinity lead to different theological narratives. This book argues against the Parmenidean and Kabbalistic notion of infinity, presenting an alternate understanding akin to Anselm's perfect being theology.

Intermediary: A being that mediates aspects of God's transcendent nature down to the finite realm. In various theological systems, this being may be fully divine and united with God, or a created thing.

Kabbalah: Hebrew, "to receive, tradition." The name attributed to Jewish mysticism since the eleventh and twelfth centuries. This book generally uses the term to refer to the Lurianic expression of Kabbalah, dating to the sixteenth century and popular in ultra-Orthodox Judaism. See *Ein Sof, Klippot*, Mysticism, *Sefirot, Tzimtzum*.

Klippot: Hebrew, "shells." In Kabbalah, the shards of the shattered vessels that encase the divine light, cause materiality to emerge, and constitute the lowest level of reality.

Metaphysics: A branch of philosophy focused on the study of the fundamental nature of reality, including categories of ontology, cosmology, aesthetics, and ethics. It often involves the study of abstract objects that are scientifically untestable.

Mishnah: A second and third century CE compilation of rabbinic law and traditions that were originally transmitted orally. The foundation of rabbinic halakah and the basis of later talmudic discussions.

Mystery: In the Hebrew Scriptures and NT, something beyond the grasp of human discovery and natural human intellectual efforts. Mysteries may be revealed by God and thus known by humans. See Epistemology, Paradox.

Mysticism: A type of piety based upon personal, subjective experience, especially in ecstatic experiences where the practitioner unites with a higher power by detaching from the external world. See Hermeticism, Kabbalah, Negative Theology, Neoplatonism, Theurgy.

Nature: See Essence.

Negative Theology: A method of approaching the knowledge of God by negating all positive statements about the divine. God cannot be known for what he is, but only for what he is not. Also known as apophatic theology and *via negativa*. See Mysticism, *Via Negativa*.

Neoplatonism: A Western mystical philosophical tradition originating with Plotinus (third century CE) that had significant influence on Judaism, Christianity, and Islam.

Neopythagoreanism: A first-century BCE to third-century CE Western mystical tradition based on the metaphysics of Pythagoras. The Neopythagorean tradition was absorbed into the Neoplatonic stream of thought.

Nicene Creed: The fourth-century CE summary of NT theology, namely the understanding of one God in three persons, including the full deity of the Son of God. See Christology, *Homoousios*, Trinity.

Noetic: Relating to intellectual capability and rational processes.

Ontology: The philosophical discipline of studying and describing that which exists. It is a branch of metaphysics.

Panentheism: The belief that the universe is contained within God and is God, and that God's existence goes beyond the universe.

Pantheism: A God-world relationship such that God is the universe, and the universe is God.

Paradox: A proposition that is true despite being derived from apparently contradictory premises. See Epistemology, Incarnation, Mystery.

PaRDeS: A Hebrew acronym for four types of biblical interpretation according to the *Zohar*: *peshat*, literal interpretation; *remez*, allegorical interpretation; *drash*, legal interpretation; *sod*, mystical and secret interpretation.

Person: A living consciousness with a rational nature that has capacity for choices and relationships. A person is an agent, an interacting self, and a possessor of a nature. Persons include human beings, angels, and the Father, Son, and Holy Spirit. See Hypostasis.

Philosophy: Derives from Greek, "love of wisdom." Philosophy involves the investigation of fundamental questions about reality, existence, knowledge, goodness, beauty, causality, purpose, and meaning.

Platonism: A school of philosophy deriving from Plato (fourth century BCE) and extended by his ideological successors. It is often contrasted with Aristotelianism.

Providence: The doctrine of God's guidance, sustenance, and care for creation as a whole and human beings in particular.

Rabbis: The successors of the Pharisees and the preservers and eventual leaders of Judaism, emerging from the destruction of the temple in 70 CE and continuing until today. Rabbis are experts in Jewish law, tradition, spiritual counsel, and Jewish community life. Jesus was called rabbi in a different pre–70 CE sense (John 1:38), where the word meant teacher. See Halakah, Talmud.

Realism: The belief that the human mind has access to external reality, which can be known and perceived accurately. Contrasted with idealism.

Reincarnation: The belief that people who die are given new bodies and new lives, repeatedly after each death, until some kind of moral perfection or goal is reached. See Platonism, *Gilgul*.

Sefirot: Hebrew, etymology contested. In the kabbalistic system, the ten principal emanations of the divine, named for potencies of God.

Sensible: That which is accessible to human senses.

Supersessionism: A theological concept that posits the Christian church as having inherited or fulfilled the spiritual promises and privileges originally given to Israel, effectively transferring God's covenantal blessings from the Jewish people to Christians. This often results in seeing the Jewish people as disinherited, cut off by God, and deserving condescension and worldly punishment.

Talmud: The vast compilation of rabbinic lore, argument, exegesis, and tradition that involves interpretation of the Mishnah and was written down between the fourth and sixth centuries CE. Two Talmuds exist: the earlier, the Yerushalmi or Jerusalem Talmud; and the later and more authoritative, the Bavli or Babylonian Talmud. Written in Hebrew and Aramaic. See Rabbis, Halakah.

Tetragrammaton: The Hebrew four-lettered divine name, יהוה. Out of reverence for God and a desire not to take his name in vain, this name is not pronounced in Judaism and is not transliterated in this book.

Theological Retrieval: The process of reexamining and reaffirming traditional doctrines, particularly those that have been neglected or marginalized over time.

Theology: Derived from Greek, "knowledge of God." Theology can involve anything that pertains to God's being or his actions.

Theophany: Greek, "an appearance of God." Different schools of thought debate on whether such appearances are historical, actual, physical, metaphorical, visionary, or something else. See Anthropomorphism, Corporealism, Divine Embodiment.

Theurgy: The use of practices and incantations to influence the divine sphere and produce the practitioner's desired results. See Hermeticism, Kabbalah, Mysticism.

Transcendence: That which is beyond, above, and wholly other than the world of human experience. Contrasted with immanence.

Trinity: The doctrine based in NT texts but formulated by the Nicene Creed, saying that God is one in essence (or nature) but three in personhood: the Father, the Son, and the Holy Spirit. See Hypostasis, Nicene Creed, Person.

Tzimtzum: Hebrew, "contraction." The Lurianic kabbalistic doctrine that *Ein Sof* contracts itself (metaphorically) to make "space" for finite immaterial and material objects to emanate within its infinitude.

Via Analogia: Latin, "the way of analogy." A theological method whereby truths about God may be adequately known through analogy to finite things and concepts.

Via Negativa: Latin, "the way of negative language." A theological method stating that truths about God can be described only by what he is not and thus may never be known. Also known as negative or apophatic theology.

Via Positiva: Latin, "the way of positive language." A theological method whereby truths about God may be known using regular language and categories. Also known as cataphatic theology and *via affirmativa*.

Worldview: A comprehensive and coherent framework of beliefs, values, and assumptions that shape an individual's or group's perception and understanding of reality, encompassing their views on the nature of God, existence, humanity, morality, and the universe. It serves as a cognitive lens through which one interprets experiences and makes sense of the world, and which also informs decisions, behaviors, and relationships.

Appendix B

The Philosophical Heritage of Medieval Jewish Theology

BELOW IS A SURVEY of the Islamic and Jewish philosophers who predate Maimonides and Kabbalah and held similar philosophical positions.[1]

Pre-Maimonidean Islamic Philosophers

The Mu'tazilites (ca. 750–900): A philosophical movement of Muslims who fused Hellenism with Islam. They stressed the absolute oneness of God, repudiated anthropomorphism, and promoted allegorization of the Qur'an when it engages in God talk.

Al-Farabi (ca. 870–950): Adapted the Aristotelian and Neoplatonic traditions preserved by Syrian Christian scribes and integrated them into Islam. Supported the absolute incorporeality of God, *via negativa*, and an Aristotelian cosmology. Posited ten separate intellects that overflow from the divine and are each linked with a celestial sphere. Each intellect generates the body of its celestial sphere. The active intellect provides rational forms to the sublunary sphere. Denied creation *ex nihilo*. Employed esoteric statements and style. Maimonides cited Al-Farabi in *Guide to the Perplexed* more than any other Islamic philosopher and recommended Al-Farabi's works in his letter to Samuel ibn Tibbon.

Avicenna (980–1037): Persian philosopher. Supported the absolute incorporeality of God, *via negativa*, and an Aristotelian cosmology. Posited ten separate intellects that overflow from the divine and are each

---

1. Key sources: Corresponding entries in *Encyclopaedia Judaica* and *Jewish Encyclopedia*; also see Pines, "Translator's Introduction"; Kraemer, "Islamic Context"; Pessin, "Influence of Islamic Thought."

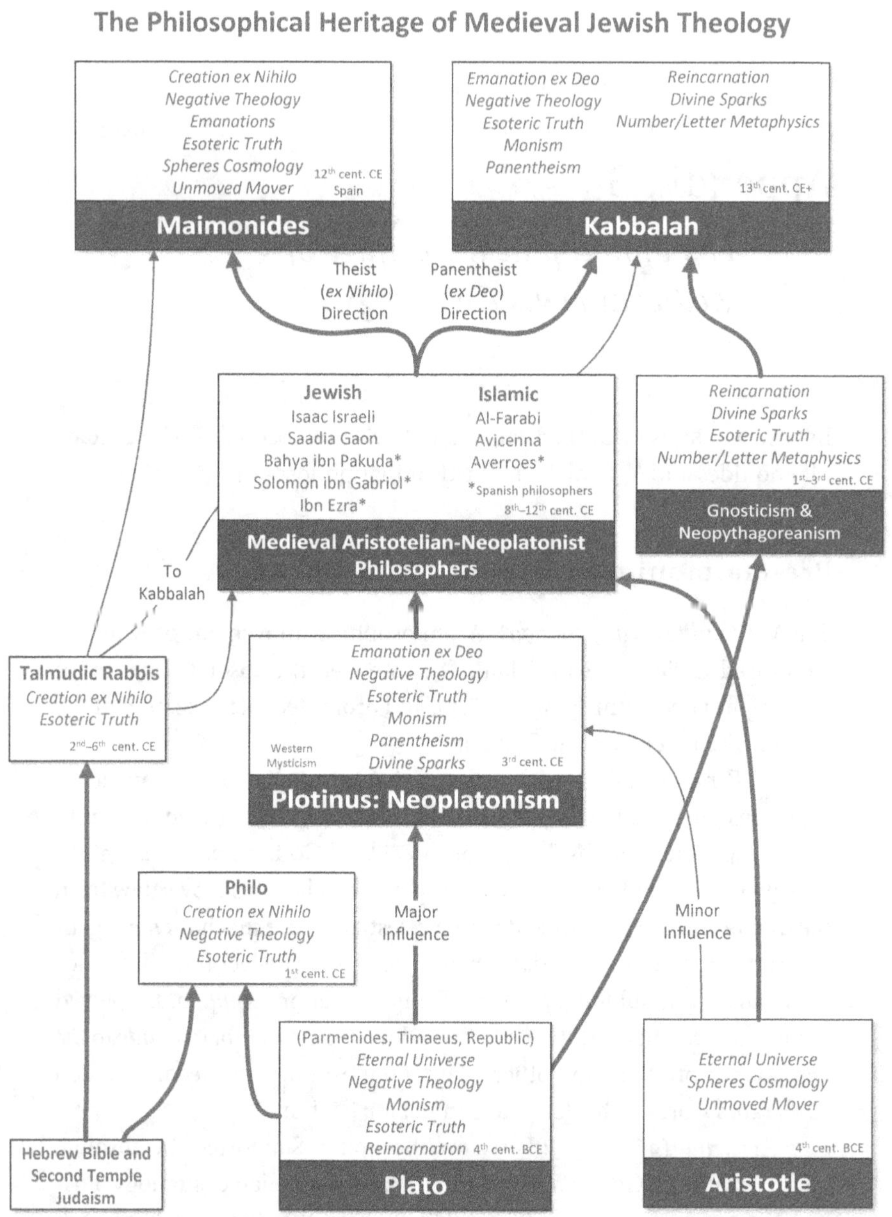

Appendix B

The Philosophical Heritage of Medieval Jewish Theology

Maimonides (12th cent. CE, Spain)
- Creation ex Nihilo
- Negative Theology
- Emanations
- Esoteric Truth
- Spheres Cosmology
- Unmoved Mover

Kabbalah (13th cent. CE+)
- Emanation ex Deo
- Negative Theology
- Esoteric Truth
- Monism
- Panentheism
- Reincarnation
- Divine Sparks
- Number/Letter Metaphysics

Theist (ex Nihilo) Direction → Maimonides
Panentheist (ex Deo) Direction → Kabbalah

Medieval Aristotelian-Neoplatonist Philosophers (8th–12th cent. CE)
- Jewish: Isaac Israeli, Saadia Gaon, Bahya ibn Pakuda*, Solomon ibn Gabriol*, Ibn Ezra*
- Islamic: Al-Farabi, Avicenna, Averroes*
- *Spanish philosophers

Gnosticism & Neopythagoreanism (1st–3rd cent. CE)
- Reincarnation
- Divine Sparks
- Esoteric Truth
- Number/Letter Metaphysics

Talmudic Rabbis (2nd–6th cent. CE)
- Creation ex Nihilo
- Esoteric Truth

To Kabbalah

Plotinus: Neoplatonism (3rd cent. CE)
- Emanation ex Deo
- Negative Theology
- Esoteric Truth
- Monism
- Panentheism
- Divine Sparks

Western Mysticism

Philo (1st cent. CE)
- Creation ex Nihilo
- Negative Theology
- Esoteric Truth

Major Influence → Plotinus
Minor Influence → Gnosticism

Plato (4th cent. BCE)
- (Parmenides, Timaeus, Republic)
- Eternal Universe
- Negative Theology
- Monism
- Esoteric Truth
- Reincarnation

Aristotle (4th cent. BCE)
- Eternal Universe
- Spheres Cosmology
- Unmoved Mover

Hebrew Bible and Second Temple Judaism

Figure 6. The Philosophical Heritage of Medieval Jewish Theology

linked with a celestial sphere. Each intellect generates the body of its celestial sphere. God is eternally involved in emanating existence. Souls and intellects may be eternal. Denied creation *ex nihilo*. His works were brought to Spain roughly a century after their publication, possibly in time for Maimonides to be exposed to them.

Averroes (1126–98): Spanish Arabian philosopher, contemporary with Maimonides. Supported the absolute incorporeality of God and an Aristotelian cosmology. Supported discarding literal interpretations of the Qur'an if in conflict with philosophy. Encouraged hiding esoteric truths from the masses. Rejected emanationism and *via negativa*. Denied creation *ex nihilo* and affirmed an eternal creation. Cited positively by Maimonides in his letter to Samuel ibn Tibbon, although Maimonides may not have known Averroes's works while writing the *Guide*.

Pre-Maimonidean Jewish Philosophers

Isaac ben Solomon Israeli (ca. 855–955): Egyptian Neoplatonist and physician. The father of Jewish Neoplatonism. Wrote on metaphysics, cosmology, and medicine in Arabic. Supported *via negativa*, creation *ex nihilo*, the unity of intellects, proposing that individual human intellects are connected to a universal Intellect. His works influenced later Jewish philosophers like Solomon ibn Gabirol and Abraham ibn Ezra.

Saadia Gaon (882–942): Egyptian-born and Arabic-speaking leader of the academy in Sura. Adapted Mu'tazilite theology for use in Judaism. Supported creation *ex nihilo*, the incorporeality of God, and *via negativa*. Believed biblical anthropomorphisms are metaphorical. Saadia was a contemporary of Isaac Israeli, and together they were the first Jewish philosophers of any stature after Philo of Alexandria (first century CE).

Solomon ibn Gabirol (ca. 1020–57): Spanish-born poet. Sometimes called the "Jewish Plato." Mediated Neoplatonism to the West. Supported absolute simplicity without form or attribute (*via negativa*). Supported divine emanations. Held to a metaphysical worldview that combined elements of Aristotle, Plotinus, and Proclus.

Bahya ben Joseph ibn Pakuda (late 1000s): Spanish-born Neoplatonist. Supported *via negativa*, the incorporeality of God, the divine origin of the human soul, and man as the microcosm of the universe.

Abraham ibn Ezra (1089–1164): Spanish-born Jewish Neoplatonist. Accepted the four elements of Empedocles, the intelligence of the heavenly spheres, the use of astrology, a sublunary world that had a combination of matter and form, and God as pure intellect. Supported creation *ex matria*. Prophecy occurs when the rational soul connects with the World Soul.

Abraham ibn Daub, Rabad I (ca. 1110–80): Spanish-born astronomer and philosopher who initiated the medieval project of integrating Judaism with Aristotelian thought. Contemporary with Maimonides. He believed in ten spiritual spheres, closely associated with "intellects," "souls," and the celestial planets. The outermost sphere is the Absolute One, which is beyond the visible world. The combinations of the lower spheres produce the four elements from which all visible creation is made. God created only one thing, which then emanated lower beings. Prophecy is the union of the human intellect with the active intellect. Although Ibn Daub was the first Jewish philosopher to deeply integrate Aristotelian thought with Judaism, Maimonides did not refer to him in his works.

Appendix C
Comparisons of Theological Models

Appendix C

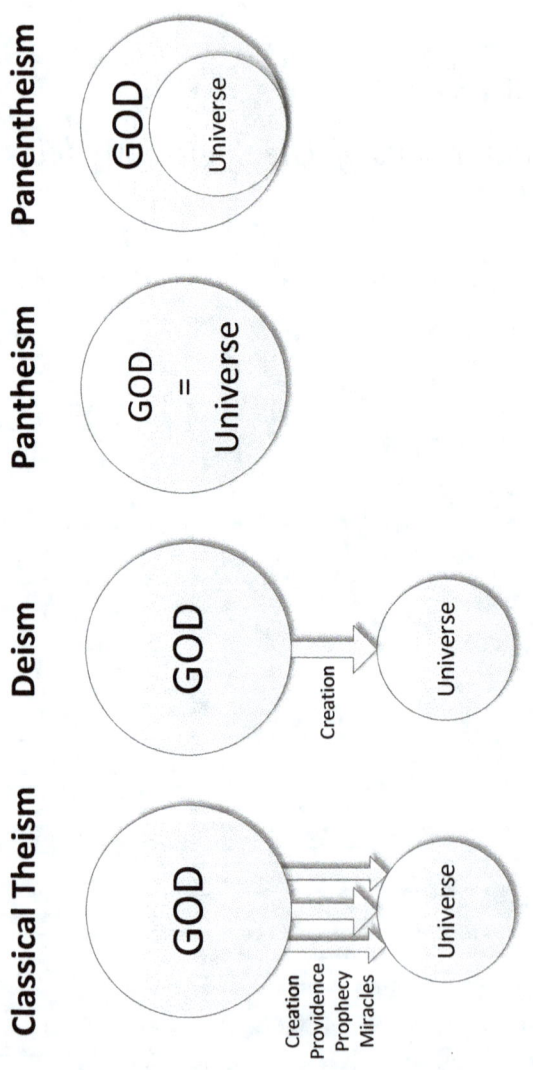

Figure 7. Generic Theological Cosmologies

Comparisons of Theological Models

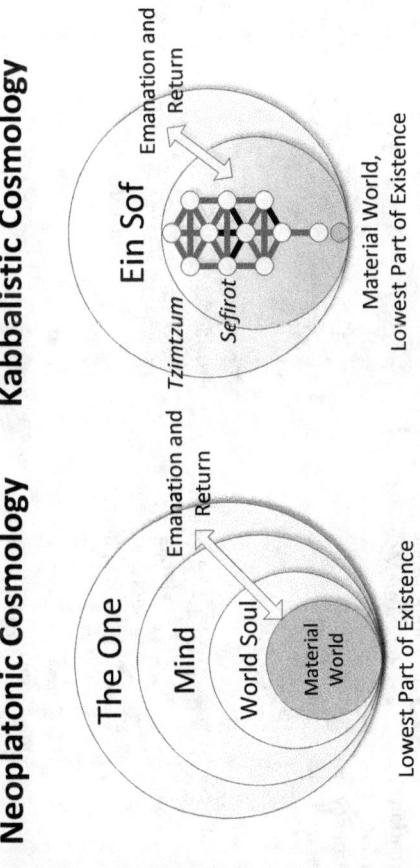

Figure 8. Neoplatonic and Kabbalistic Cosmologies

Appendix C

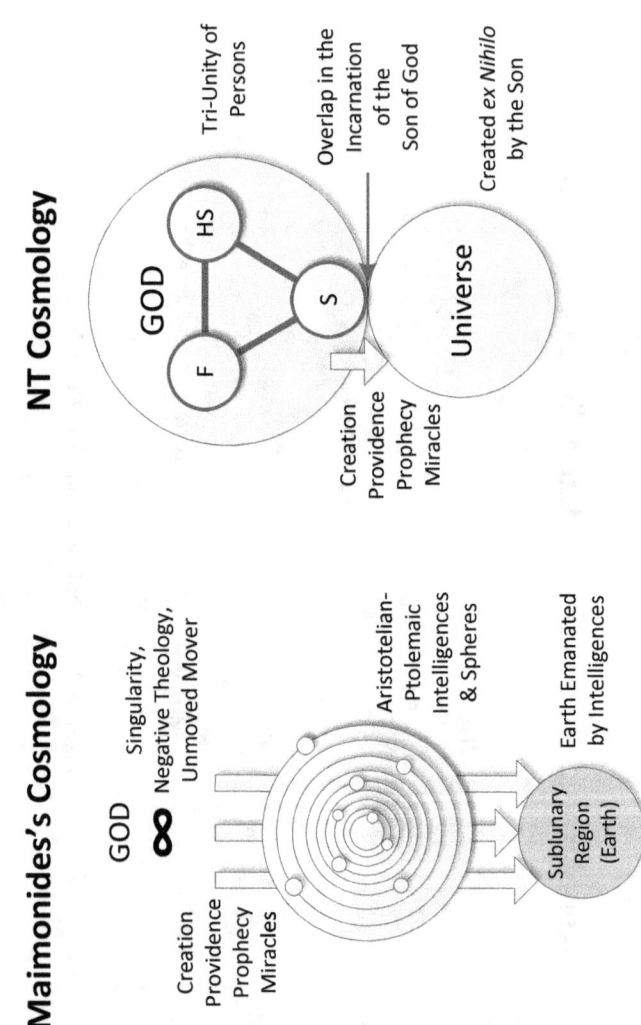

Figure 9. Maimonidean and New Testament Cosmologies

Comparisons of Theological Models

Table 20. Four Theological Worldviews Compared

	Neoplatonism	Kabbalah	Maimonides	New Testament Orthodoxy
Representative Thinker(s)	Plotinus, Iamblichus, Proclus	*The Zohar*, Luria, Chassidut	Maimonides	John, Paul, Athanasius, Augustine, Aquinas
God-World Relationship	Panentheism	Panentheism	Classical theism with modifications	Classical theism with modifications
Immanence/ Transcendence Emphasis	Major: Immanence Minor: Transcendence	Major: Immanence Minor: Transcendence	Transcendence	Major: Immanence in Jesus and the Holy Spirit Minor: Transcendence of the divine nature
Mode of Creation	*Ex Deo*	*Ex Deo*	*Ex Nihilo*	*Ex Nihilo*
Beginning of Universe?	No (eternal emanations)	No (eternal emanations)	Yes	Yes
God and Infinity	God's infinity extends to everything that exists.	God's infinity extends to everything that exists.	God's infinity extends to his own nature, distinct from his creation.	God's infinity extends to his own nature, distinct from his creation.
Can God Cross Infinity to the Finite?	Bad question: The finite is an illusion. Everything is infinite.	Bad question: The finite is an illusion. Everything is infinite.	No. He is absolutely transcendent.	Yes. He crosses physically through his Son and spiritually through his Spirit.
Can God Be Known Directly?	No	No	No	Yes, through his Son and his Spirit
Can God Be Known Indirectly?	Yes, through emanations	Yes, through emanations (*Sefirot*)	Yes, only through his indirect actions	Yes, by analogy, and directly in the incarnate Son of God and indwelling Spirit

Appendix C

	Neoplatonism	Kabbalah	Maimonides	New Testament Orthodoxy
Nature of Propositions about God	Not about God (the One): about emanations only	Not about God (*Ein Sof*): about emanations only	Meaningless: about actions only	Sufficiently true intellectually and ultimately true analogically
Nature of God's Oneness	Compound oneness with emanations	Compound oneness with emanations	Singularity	Compound: three persons in unity
Nature of God's Simplicity	Singularity (the One) and complex (emanations)	Singularity (*Ein Sof*) and complex (*Sefirot*)	Singularity (only)	Singularity (one divine essence) and complex (tri-unity of persons)
Is God a Person?	No (no propositions allowed)	*Ein Sof*: No (no propositions allowed) *Sefirot*: Yes	No (no propositions allowed)	Yes: tri-personal
Creator/Creation Distinction	Partially: panentheism	Partially: panentheism	Yes: strict separation	Yes: strict separation. Only in Jesus are the two united.
Divine Intermediaries?	Yes: Mind, World Soul, and everything	Yes: *Sefirot* and everything	Yes/No: heavenly spheres, but they are not divine	Yes: the Son of God and the indwelling Spirit

Appendix D

Ancient Jewish Sources of Greek Mystical Philosophies?

THROUGHOUT THIS BOOK, I draw a parallel between Maimonidean and kabbalistic theology and the philosophies of Plato, Aristotle, Pythagoras, Gnosticism, and Plotinus. As summarized in §§5.4 and 7.8, the parallels are striking and wide ranging. If we let M stand for the relevant Maimonidean doctrines, K for kabbalistic doctrines, and G for the corresponding Greek philosophical doctrines, a question arises: What is the relationship between M, K, and G?

Correlation does not equal causation, so it is not necessarily the case that G caused K, or K caused G. The temptation of parallelomania must be avoided.[1] Nor are later phenomena necessarily dependent upon earlier phenomena (the post hoc fallacy): just because K arose in the thirteenth century, and G came 1,000–1,500 years before, it does not mean that K was necessarily dependent upon G. So, then, how ought we account for the relationship between M, K, and G?

Given two hypothetical worldviews, A and B, a variety of relationships between them can be envisioned:

- *Direct causation:* Worldview B interacts with the preexisting ideas of Worldview A and indicates an acceptance of Worldview A's ideas through quotation or clear allusion to the people or works of Worldview A.

---

1. Sandmel, "Parallelomania." An example of parallelomania would be to note the agreement between two parties about the blueness of the sky on a sunny day, and conclude that Party B got that idea from Party A.

- *Plagiarism*: Worldview B interacts with the preexisting ideas of Worldview A but falsely portrays itself as the source of the ideas of Worldview A.

- *Indirect causation (stimulus diffusion)*: Worldview B interacts with the preexisting ideas of Worldview A without knowing that it is interacting with Worldview A, yet comes to accept the ideas of Worldview A, but never quotes or directly alludes to the people or works of Worldview A.

- *Mutual dependency*: Worldview A and Worldview B come to believe in the same ideas through mutual interaction and influence on each other, without one worldview holding to the belief before the other.

- *Independent traditions*: Worldview A and Worldview B come to believe in the same ideas, but without any interaction or causal relationship between them.

Which model fits the relationship between M, K, and G? Put in other terms: *Did the earlier Greek works influence the later Maimonidean and kabbalistic traditions, such that Maimonidean and kabbalistic schools are new Jewish versions of Greek philosophical schools?* Or, perhaps the influence should be understood in the opposite direction: *Did the Greeks steal their philosophy from Judaism?*[2] Or, *perhaps were they totally independent traditions without any causal dependency relationship between them at all?* Who influenced whom becomes a pressing question for determining not only the history of Jewish thought, but also its very integrity as a source of truth revealed by God.

The answer when considering aspects of Maimonidean thought (M) is straightforward, since Maimonides occasionally cites the sources of his ideas. At times, he gives credit to Aristotle, Aristotle as Plotinus, and the Islamic philosophers of his day. He does not claim that his ideas had been present in Judaism before Aristotle, or that Aristotle was dependent upon Judaism, but rather that Aristotle helped bring clarity of thought to Judaism. So, for Maimonidean thought, the earlier Greek philosophers were the cause or the basis of the correlations. Maimonides is an example of direct causation: *G caused M, and M is dependent upon G.*[3]

---

2. This has been called "the theft of the Greeks" (Löhr, "Theft of the Greeks"; Ciholas, "Plato: The Attic Moses?"; Whittaker, "Moses Atticizing"; Edwards, "Atticizing Moses?").

3. Ivry, "Maimonides' Philosophical Sources."

Ancient Jewish Sources of Greek Mystical Philosophies?

What about Kabbalah (K)? There are two general positions on this issue, as exemplified by two of the greatest scholars of Kabbalah in the past century, Gershom Scholem (1897–1982) and Moshe Idel (1947–).

Gershom Scholem is widely acknowledged as the scholar who elevated the academic study of Kabbalah to a place of honor and acclaim. Instead of studying Kabbalah through contemporary texts and Hasidic masters, Scholem embarked on a quest to find and study the oldest kabbalistic texts and to trace the development of Jewish mysticism over the centuries. Scholem maintained that both pre-kabbalistic Merkavah mysticism and medieval Kabbalah were derived from Gnosticism.[4] He attributed many medieval elements of kabbalistic theosophy to newly-popular Neoplatonic ideas.[5] He credited the numerical-mystical speculation of Kabbalah to Neopythagorean sources, whereas "the idea of 'letters of which heaven and earth were created' may well come from within Judaism itself."[6] Thus, while the Kabbalists may have taken already-existing ideas from their pagan sources, they augmented them with unique innovations. Additionally, since the Kabbalists did not give credit to their sources, it is unclear to which historical works they had access and how the Kabbalists obtained them.

Thus, Gershom Scholem provides us with the first answer to our question: *The Kabbalists adapted ideas from already-existing Greek mystery philosophies and morphed them into a unique Jewish mystical blend. G caused K. Moreover, since the Kabbalists did not cite the source of their ideas, and rather promoted anachronistic dates for their texts, they fall under the category of plagiarism from Greek sources.*

Although the correlations between Greek philosophy and kabbalistic thought are not well known in the Orthodox Jewish world, some have responded as follows: "Similarities with Greek thought are no problem. Whatever similarities they have with us, they stole from Judaism." This attitude is often combined with the belief that God gave Kabbalah to Israel at Sinai, or even provided it to humanity through Adam. This combination—Kabbalah's divine origin and the dependence of Greek sources on Judaism—encourages belief that Kabbalah is true and dismisses any correlations with non-Jewish sources. In this view, the Greeks are the ones guilty of plagiarism.

---

4. Scholem, *Origins of the Kabbalah*, ch. 1.3, locs. 530–620.
5. Scholem, *Origins of the Kabbalah*, ch. 3.8, locs. 6304–7580.
6. Scholem, *Origins of the Kabbalah*, ch. 1.4, loc. 690.

Appendix D

Coming to prominence shortly after Scholem's death, Moshe Idel's 1988 *Kabbalah: New Perspectives* seeks to build upon Scholem's legacy while critiquing Scholem's methodology in multiple areas. Idel surveys Scholem's handling of the relationship between Gnosticism and Kabbalah and proposes the opposite answer:

> I would propose another explanation: ancient Jewish motifs that penetrated Gnostic texts remained at the same time the patrimony of Jewish thought and continued to be transmitted in Jewish circles, ultimately providing the conceptual framework of Kabbalah. This theory postulates a long series of links that cannot be proven by extant Jewish texts; however, this difficulty also holds if we accept Scholem's theory that the earliest Kabbalistic documents derived from ancient Gnostic traditions.[7]

Idel maintains that ancient Judaism provided distinctive doctrines to the gnostics, and those doctrines survived independently within Jewish circles for centuries before emerging in the twelfth century as kabbalistic doctrines—doctrines that appeared to be gnostic but were actually recovered from ancient Judaism.[8] Thus, Idel provides the second answer to our question: *While there are correlations between ancient Gnosticism and medieval Kabbalah, ancient Judaism was the source that predated and influenced both. K caused G. The Greeks stole their philosophy from the Jews.*

Which answer is more plausible? The historical relationship between Greek philosophy and Judaism has received thorough treatment from scholars.[9] Throughout the course of the book, I side with Scholem's position: the kabbalistic schools inherited much of their theology and philosophy from preexisting doctrines in the Greek philosophical traditions. These doctrines had not originally been part of Judaism, or explicitly or implicitly present within the Hebrew Scriptures.

Below are several reasons why I believe it is more reasonable to believe that the Jewish mystical tradition took its doctrines from the Greeks, rather than the other way around.

---

7. Idel, *Kabbalah*, 31. See also Idel, *Ben*, 66.

8. Idel's theory is similar to that of Philo scholar Edwin Goodenough, who discusses the commonalities and differences between Philo and the kabbalistic theosophy (*By Light, Light*, 369).

9. Whittaker, "Moses Atticizing"; Ciholas, "Plato: The Attic Moses?"; Edwards, "Atticizing Moses?"; Löhr, "Theft of the Greeks"; Lemche, "How Does One Date"; Grabbe, *Did Moses Speak Attic?*; Sterling, "Theft of Philosophy"; Veltri, "Theft." The pre–Nag Hammadi (and thus obsolete) *Jewish Encyclopedia* was enthusiastic in affirming (with much speculation) the Jewish origin of Gnosticism (Blau, "Gnosticism").

Ancient Jewish Sources of Greek Mystical Philosophies?

There are no Jewish texts teaching kabbalistic doctrines that predate Pythagoras and Plato. Pythagoras (sixth century BCE) and Plato (fourth century BCE) are among the earliest and most influential proponents of doctrines with correlations to the Jewish mystical tradition. If there were Jewish texts that included such doctrines before Pythagoras and Plato, none have survived. The Torah's exoteric, explicit teachings do not promote Pythagorean or Platonic metaphysics. Only later groups would contend that the esoteric, implicit meaning of the Torah teaches such doctrines. However, the exoteric/esoteric dichotomy is itself an import from Pythagoras and Plato. Thus, it is circular logic to claim that the Torah contains the mystical doctrines.

There is no evidence of a pre-sixth-century-BCE Jewish oral tradition that teaches the kabbalistic doctrines. Just as there are no written texts on these subjects, there are no hints of an unwritten kabbalistic tradition that predate the Greek philosophical period. While it is possible that such an oral tradition existed, perhaps deriving from Sinai, there is no positive evidence in its favor, and thus this position is speculative and unlikely.

The Greek philosophers and schools, only Gnosticism excepted, did not cite Judaism for the source of their ideas. Pythagoras, Socrates, Plato, Aristotle, and Plotinus never claimed that they had derived their philosophical ideas from Judaism, the Jewish people, Jewish scholars, or Jewish texts. These authors were willing to discuss and quote the sources of ideas in their writings, so they were not opposed to providing intellectual credit. To hold to Greek dependence upon Judaism, it must be suggested that the Greek philosophers were unaware of their dependence upon Moses, or that they covered up such dependence. This appears highly unlikely. Gnosticism does show signs of Jewish influence in the second and third centuries CE. While the gnostics cited Jewish texts, sometimes positively, they often cited them subversively and critically.

The earliest claim of Greek theft from Judaism is from Aristobulus (second century BCE) and it is highly implausible. Aristobulus writes, "It is evident that Plato imitated our legislation and that he had investigated thoroughly each of the elements in it.... For he was very learned, as was Pythagoras, who transferred many of our doctrines and integrated them into his own system of beliefs."[10] Aristobulus provided no evidence for this position; evidently, in his mind, unarticulated correlation is sufficient for causation. Somehow, Aristobulus believed that exposure to

---

10. Fragment 3 (*OTP* 2:839); cf. Eusebius, *Praep. ev.* 13.12.

the Torah alone was sufficient to account for Greek philosophy, but this strains the imagination, as the Greeks discuss much about which the Torah is silent. Recognizing that the Torah was translated into Greek (the LXX) *after* Plato and Pythagoras, Aristobulus maintained that the Torah had been translated into Greek *before* Alexander's conquests so that Plato and Pythagoras could read it. While such a prior translation is possible but unlikely,[11] it is highly improbable that such a translation made it to Greece and formed the basis of Greek philosophy. Note that Pythagoras lived in the sixth century BCE, requiring an extremely early translation of the Torah into Greek—of which there is no evidence.[12]

Josephus, like Aristobulus, claimed Greek dependence on Moses but did not cite anything but similarity of ideas. In Josephus's apologetic work *Against Apion*, he makes several claims that the Greek philosophers were followers of Moses (*Ag. Ap.* 2.168, 2.257, 2.281). For example, he states Plato followed Moses in that Plato required citizens to study Greek laws and to prevent foreigners from mixing with them (2.257). As with Aristobulus's claims, this is mere correlation without any proven dependency or historical causation.

Philo of Alexandria, the early and seminal Platonic Jewish philosopher, did not claim the Greeks stole Jewish thought. Philo cited the ideas of Pythagoras, Plato, and Pythagoreans throughout his writings, but he never claimed that their ideas had been derived from Judaism. He made several dubious claims about Zeno and Heraclitus being influenced by Jewish law, but theologian Winrich Löhr writes, "On the whole Philo is not very interested in the theme."[13] A chief goal of Philo's writings was to show the compatibility of Greek and Jewish thought; had he believed that the Greeks had stolen Jewish wisdom, it is highly likely that he would have said so, as it would have bolstered his case. Instead, Philo depicted Hebrew wisdom as shut off from the world for centuries until Ptolemy Philadelphus commissioned a translation of the Torah (*Moses* 2.25–27).

The Letter of Aristeas was written under the premise that the Greek world lacked access to Jewish philosophy before the LXX in the third century BCE. The Letter of Aristeas (third century BCE–first century CE) is an extended account of how the Hebrew manuscripts of the Torah were translated into Greek and placed into the famed Library of Alexandria

---

11. Let. Aris. 30 (*OTP* 2:14–15). However, see the footnote on the verb translated as "transcribed."

12. Sterling, "Theft of Philosophy," 78–79.

13. Löhr, "Theft of the Greeks," 405–6.

by Ptolemy Philadelphus. Although the historicity of the account is questioned, nevertheless it is the earliest and only story on record about how the Torah was translated into Greek.[14] Letter of Aristeas 30 says that the books of the Torah were missing from the library, which would be odd if they had been widely influencing Greeks for hundreds of years. Letter of Aristeas 31 gives the reason why the books were needed in the library as follows: "This legislation, as could be expected from its divine nature, is very philosophical and genuine."[15] If the greatest library in the ancient world had lacked access to the Hebrews' philosophy and remedied the omission by commissioning a translation, then it is highly unlikely that the Hebrews' philosophy was widespread throughout the Greek world beforehand.

Numenius made a memorable but unevidenced claim of Greek dependence upon Moses. The pagan Platonist Numenius (third century CE) made a famous claim: "For what is Plato, but Moses speaking in Attic Greek?"[16] Our surviving fragments of Numenius do not give his reasons for this equation.[17]

The claims of the Platonist Clement of Alexandria are implausible and biased. The most ardent early proponent of the "theft of the Greeks" from Judaism was the Platonist church father Clement of Alexandria (third century CE).[18] Clement quoted Numenius's maxim and sought to elaborate reasons why Numenius was right.[19] Unfortunately, Clement cited mere similarities of ideas as evidence of causal influence, providing an early example of parallelomania.[20] Clement was weak in employ-

---

14. *OTP* 2:10. Josephus, Philo, and various church fathers accepted the Letter of Aristeas as accurate and added their own legendary details (Caragounis, "Epistle of Aristeas," 116).

15. *OTP* 2:15.

16. Quoted in Clement of Alexandria, *Strom.* 1.22 (*ANF* 2:334–35). Also cited in Eusebius, *Praep. ev.* 9.6.

17. Boys-Stones, "Fragments of Numenius"; Sterling, "Theft of Philosophy."

18. See also Justin, *1 Apol.* 60: "It is not, then, that we hold the same opinions as others, but that all speak in imitation of ours" (*ANF* 1:183).

19. The quotation of Numenius is in *Strom.* 1.22, but Clement's defense of the concept is in *Strom.* 5.14. Also see *Strom.* 2.1: "For we shall not only show that they have imitated and copied the marvels recorded in our books; but we shall prove, besides, that they have plagiarized and falsified (our writings being, as we have shown, older) the chief dogmas they hold" (*ANF* 2:347).

20. Clement of Alexandria, *Strom.* 5.14 (*ANF* 2:465–76). Examples of Clementine parallelomania: Callimachus refers to people as "clay," so he must have read Gen 2:7. The Greeks call the seventh day of the week sacred, so they must have read the Torah.

ing tangible lexical or grammatical evidence, nor did he attempt to explain historically and geographically how so many Greeks had access to the Hebrew Scriptures. Clement had motive to ignore these factors (confirmation bias) since he was a proponent of syncretizing Platonic thought with Christianity.

However, his project of syncretism posed a problem. The Greeks were not at the top of a Christian's epistemological hierarchy: Scripture was. Thus, to retain a Christian epistemology, Clement was incentivized to make all Greek knowledge subservient and derivative of the Hebrew Scriptures. This made apologetic sense in his context since the Jews were widely held to be one of the oldest people groups in the world. The combination of the Jews' antiquity and the tenuous claims of intellectual influence on the Greeks made Clement's case. Other Christian Platonists like Origen (third century CE) agree with the argument (*Cels.* 7.30). Eusebius of Caesarea (fourth century CE) quotes Clement's argumentation at length (*Praep. ev.* 11; 13.12). However, Eusebius is more judicious, merely claiming similarity of thought, rather than causal dependence: "Whence these ideas came to Plato, I cannot explain: but what I can truly say is that thousands of years before Plato was born this doctrine also had been acknowledged by the Hebrews" (*Praep. ev.* 11.26).[21]

There is evidence of Jewish influence on Gnosticism, but the extent of the influence is inconclusive. The various second- and third-century CE gnostic groups, as found in Nag Hammadi and Irenaeus, displayed clear evidence of interaction with Judaism, the Hebrew language, and Jewish culture. However, the gnostics attempted to ingest, corrupt, and syncretize a wide variety of worldviews, including Platonism and early Christianity. It is speculative to state that there was a distinct, intact version of "Jewish gnosis" or proto-Kabbalah from which the gnostic groups drew. Gnosticism scholar Markshies writes, "There is no text in extant ancient Jewish literature which contains the various motifs which according to our model characterize the ancient movement of 'knowledge' as completely and clearly as, say, the texts from Nag Hammadi or Medinet Madi." He continues, "Therefore it probably makes more sense

---

Menander paraphrases Jer 23:23–24 when he says, "God ever present sees." Orpheus's teachings about Zeus's power in heaven "are plainly derived" from Isaiah and Jeremiah—although Clement's selections from the prophets have no lexical overlap with Orpheus. The poet Pindar writes, "It is hard for mortal mind the counsels of the gods to scan," of which Clement claims dependence upon Isa 40:13.

21. Eusebius, *Preparation for Gospel*, 594.

to speak of Jewish roots of 'gnosis' rather than of a fully developed 'Jewish gnosis.'"[22] The interaction between the gnostics and Jewish thought deserves further investigation, such as Wolfson's study of proto-Kabbalist doctrines within Jewish-Christian texts like the Clementine Homilies.[23] However, it goes beyond the evidence to say that Gnosticism was a direct import from preexisting Jewish mystical thought.

Claims of Greek dependence on Judaism were revived in the Middle Ages, but for anachronistic reasons. After the popular rise of Kabbalah in the Middle Ages, Christians began reading kabbalistic works. What they read seemed strikingly familiar to the Platonic works that were well known in Christian circles. These Christians accepted the Kabbalists' claims to antiquity uncritically, proclaiming that the Kabbalist works were portals into a long-hidden secret wisdom of the Jews that derived from Sinai. Since Sinai predated Plato, it was only natural to view Plato and the Greek philosophical tradition as an uncircumcised adaptation of Moses. This book provides many reasons to reject this sequence of events as ahistorical fantasy.

Holding to Greek dependence on Judaism undermines Judaism's claim to have infallible divine revelation (as well as Christianity's claim). This book illustrates many aspects of Greek philosophical thought that were once held to be true but have been decisively disproven in the modern scientific era. Examples include Aristotelian-Ptolemaic geocentric cosmology, the seven heavens, "as above, so below," and the theory of the four elements. These beliefs were influential in Jewish, Christian, and Islamic thought throughout the premodern era. During this time, these beliefs were viewed as complementary to Scripture and helpful for understanding the universe. Hypothetically, in that premodern context, if someone claimed that such beliefs originated within Judaism before Christ, it would not have offended many: both Jews and Christians in the premodern era placed the Hebrew Scriptures and pre-Jesus Judaism at the top of their epistemological hierarchy. A claim of Greek dependence on Judaism would have fit Westerners' plausibility structures, retaining ancient Judaism as the vehicle for divine revelation. However, we now know that beliefs like geocentrism are false. If those beliefs originated from pre-Jesus Judaism, then this would undermine pre-Jesus Judaism as the preeminent source of truth in contemporary Judaism and

---

22. Markschies, *Gnosis*, 70.
23. Wolfson, "Tree That Is All."

Christianity. It would entail that Judaism before Jesus was ignorant and misleading about fundamental facts about the universe, with the result that Jewish claims of divine revelation were false. Thus, religious Jews and Christians should have no incentive to promote speculative Jewish origins for Greek philosophical doctrines that have been proven false. Instead, they should point out the speculative, anachronistic, and un-evidenced nature of claims of the Jewish origins for Greek thought, as indeed I have done throughout this book.

Appendix E
Kabbalah in the New Testament?

THE ARGUMENTS IN THIS book undermine the philosophical doctrines of Kabbalah while also tying their origin to pagan, anti-biblical mystical philosophies such as Neopythagoreanism, Gnosticism, and Neoplatonism. However, it might be objected that this argument is fallacious and anachronistic since there are kabbalistic concepts in the NT itself.[1] If the NT includes kabbalistic thought, then followers of Jesus should not avoid it. Let us briefly consider some of the evidence brought in favor of this understanding of the NT:

The number 666 as gematria in Rev 13:18. In a book full of symbols, the number 666 may be Revelation's most enigmatic. The verse reads, "Let the one who has understanding calculate the number of the beast, for it is the number of a man, and his number is 666." Indeed, many have seen gematria as the key to unlock the secret meaning of the number. However, this is not the only method available for interpreting the number.

Gregory Beale's commentary on Revelation includes a long section on historical gematria attempts to interpret 666.[2] The most common solution is that the number refers to Caesar Nero with Hebrew spelling. However, Beale points out that this solution relies on a defective Hebrew spelling of Caesar that does not show up in the Dead Sea Scrolls or the Talmud. Additionally, it is a poor assumption that the intended name should be in Hebrew; given the writing of Revelation in Greek and the widespread use of first-century *geometrikos* in the Greek language,

---

1. An overlapping question is whether there was a pre-Christian Gnosticism that influenced the NT. Answering with a negative, see Yamauchi, "Pre-Christian Gnosticism."

2. Beale, *Book of Revelation*, 718–28.

it would be more reasonable to assume a Greek referent.[3] The earliest church fathers were not aware of the Nero solution (or a Hebrew gematria solution),[4] and one can find innumerable other world leaders whose names can be made to fit with 666 as well. Beale writes, "None of the many proposed solutions using *gematria* is ultimately satisfactory because there are so many names, ancient and modern, that come to 666. There are so many proposals because it is easy to turn a name into a number but hard to deduce the right name from a number."[5]

Thus, some commentators conjecture that the 666 is a symbolic reference to the incompleteness and evil of Revelation's anti-trinity of the beast, false prophet, and Satan, since the "perfect biblical number" is seven.[6] Consequently, the assumption that 666 must be interpreted by gematria of the Greek or Hebrew variety has significant problems, and the interpreter is not bound to accept the assumption, as there are other options.

Even so, assuming for the sake of argument that the verse expects a solution by gematria, there is still no justification for the use of gematria as a hermeneutical tool for the interpretation of other biblical words or passages. Gematria as practiced in Jewish mysticism is infused with metaphysical and cosmological baggage derived from its Pythagorean roots, and this method of interpretation is nowhere permitted in Scripture. As a general hermeneutic, gematria is foreign to the Scriptures and should not be admitted into the tools of the biblical exegete.

Fourteen as gematria in Matt 1:17. This verse, given after the genealogy of Jesus, says that there were fourteen generations between Abraham and David, fourteen generations from David to the Babylonian exile, and fourteen generations from the exile to the coming of Jesus. D. A. Carson and Craig Blomberg approve of a solution that ties the fourteen to the numerical value of "David" in Hebrew (דוד).[7] While this is possible, it is weakened by the fact that Matthew was written in Greek, and that there is no explicit indication of a deeper meaning of the number in the text. It could have simply been an expression of historical symmetry. Craig

---

3. Deissmann and Strachan, *Light from the Ancient East*, 275–77.
4. Weinrich, *Revelation*, 210–13.
5. Beale, *Book of Revelation*, 720–21.
6. Trail, *Exegetical Summary of Revelation 12–22*, 55.
7. Longman and Garland, *Matthew-Mark*, 93–94; Beale and Carson, *New Testament Use*, 3.

Keener acknowledges the scholars who accept the "David" gematria but proposes solutions that are not dependent upon gematria.[8]

For the sake of the argument, if fourteen is a gematria reference to David, there is still no justification for the use of gematria as a hermeneutical tool for the interpretation of other biblical words or passages. At best, gematria may be useful for interpreting Rev 13:18 and Matt 1:17, but not elsewhere.

Second Corinthians 12:1–10 as Paul's participation in Merkavah mysticism. In this passage, Paul recounts being "caught up to the third heaven" where "he heard things that cannot be told, which man may not utter." Paul does not know whether this experience took place in the body or out of the body. He describes "the surpassing greatness of the revelations" and afterward how he was given "a messenger of Satan to harass me," perhaps as a means to humble him after his visions. Some have seen this as an example of first-century Jewish mysticism that would one day be called Merkavah mysticism.

While the later Merkavah mysticism undoubtedly has similarities with Paul's ascent, they are distinguished from each other in their mechanics, content, and purpose. In his article on the NT and mysticism, Jon Laansma writes, "The attempt to correlate details of Paul's account in 2 Corinthians 12 with the Merkabah traditions are strained but possible."[9] The following are some of the details that make the comparison strained. Second Temple Judaism introduced the Hellenistic idea that there are seven heavens (associated with the seven planets) and the eighth realm beyond, where God lives. Merkavah mysticism inherited this Hellenistic and geocentric cosmology, but Paul rejected it, instead retaining the understanding of the Hebrew Scriptures.[10] Paul's reference to "the third heaven" refers to the realm beyond the atmosphere (first heaven) and the sun, moon, and stars (second heaven); thus, the third heaven is the highest heaven where God dwells. Paul's experience also differs from Merkavah mysticism with its lack of grounding in Ezekiel, its lack of warnings of danger for secret knowledge, its lack of practices for inducing an ecstatic or trance state, its lack of encouragement for others to seek experiences like Paul's, its lack of intellectual or mystical combat with the archons of the spheres, its lack of secret words or pass phrases to continue ascent, and Paul's refusal to put to words what he saw. In

---

8. Keener, *Gospel of Matthew*, 74.
9. Laansma, "Mysticism," 733.
10. Mare, "New Testament Concept."

my opinion it would be incorrect to posit Paul's experience as an early example of Merkavah.

Are some expressions of Christianity more compatible with Kabbalah than others? Yes. The Christian (and Messianic Jewish) theology promoted in this book seeks to be grounded in the primacy of Scripture and skeptical toward outside ideologies that obscure biblical teaching. Other faith traditions are less skeptical toward outside influences. In general, one's acceptance of kabbalistic thought into Christianity or Messianic Judaism will be a function of how much one implicitly accepts Neoplatonic, gnostic, and Pythagorean influences on one's faith. The NT can be syncretized with Kabbalah to promote a Christianized version of Kabbalah, but kabbalistic concepts cannot be (and historically *were* not) derived from the NT by itself. I see such syncretism as detrimental to Jewish and gentile followers of Jesus.

Bibliography

Abbott, Edwin A. *Flatland: A Romance Of Many Dimensions*. 2nd ed. Oxford: Basil Blackwell, 1884.
Abelson, J. "Maimonides on the Jewish Creed." *JQR* 19 (1906) 24–58.
Abrams, Daniel. "The Boundaries of Divine Ontology: The Inclusion and Exclusion of Meṭaṭron in the Godhead." *HTR* 87 (1994) 291–321.
Adler, Mortimer J., ed. *The Syntopicon: An Index to the Great Ideas*. 2nd ed. Vols. 1–2 of *Great Books of the Western World*. Chicago: Encyclopedia Britannica, 1990.
Aeschylus, et al. *Aeschylus; Sophocles; Euripides; Aristophanes*. Edited by Mortimer J. Adler and Philip W. Goetz. 2nd ed. Vol. 4 of *Great Books of the Western World*. Chicago: Encyclopedia Britannica, 1990.
Alexander, Philip. "Mysticism." In *The Oxford Handbook of Jewish Studies*, edited by Martin Goodman, 705–32. Oxford Handbooks. New York: Oxford University Press, 2002.
Alfonsi, Petrus. *Dialogue Against the Jews*. Translated by Irven M. Resnick. Fathers of the Church, Medieval Continuation 8. Washington, DC: Catholic University of America Press, 2006.
Allison, Gregg R. *Historical Theology: An Introduction to Christian Doctrine*. Grand Rapids: Zondervan, 2011.
Alper, Becka A., et al. *Jewish Americans in 2020*. Washington, DC: Pew Research, 2021. https://www.pewresearch.org/religion/2021/05/11/jewish-americans-in-2020/.
Alston, William P. *Divine Nature and Human Language: Essays in Philosophical Theology*. Eugene, OR: Wipf and Stock, 2020.
———. "Religious Language." In *The Oxford Handbook of Philosophy of Religion*, edited by William J. Wainwright, 220–44. Oxford Handbooks. Oxford: Oxford University Press, 2007.
Altmann, Alexander. "Astrology." In *Encyclopedia Judaica*, edited by Fred Skolnik and Michael Berenbaum, 2:616–20. Detroit: Macmillan Reference and Keter, 2007.
———. "Maimonides on the Intellect and the Scope of Metaphysics." In *Studien zur Judischen Geistesgeschichte*, 60–129. Texts and Studies in Medieval and Early Modern Judaism 2. Tübingen, Germ.: Mohr Siebeck, 1987.
Anderson, James. *Paradox in Christian Theology: An Analysis of Its Presence, Character, and Epistemic Status*. Paternoster Theological Monographs. Waynesboro, GA: Paternoster, 2007.

Bibliography

Anselm of Canterbury. *Proslogium; Monologium; An Appendix, In Behalf of the Fool, by Gaunilon; and Cur Deus Homo*. Translated by Sidney Norton Deane. Chicago: Open Court, 1939.

Ariel, David S. *Kabbalah: The Mystic Quest in Judaism*. Lanham, MD: Rowman & Littlefield, 2006.

Ariel, Yaakov S. *Evangelizing the Chosen People: Missions to the Jews in America, 1880–2000*. Chapel Hill, NC: University of North Carolina Press, 2000.

Aristotle. *Select Fragments*. Edited by David Ross. The Works of Aristotle 12. Oxford: Clarendon, 1952.

———. *The Works of Aristotle, Volume I*. Edited by Mortimer J. Adler and Philip W. Goetz. Translated by W. D. Ross. 2nd ed. Vol. 7 of *Great Books of the Western World*. Chicago: Encyclopedia Britannica, 1990.

Artson, Bradley Shavit. "Holy, Holy, Holy! Jewish Affirmations of Panentheism." In *Panentheism Across the World's Traditions*, edited by Loriliai Biernacki and Philip Clayton, 18–36. New York: Oxford University Press, 2013.

Arzy, Shahar, and Moshe Idel. *Kabbalah: A Neurocognitive Approach to Mystical Experiences*. New Haven, CT: Yale University Press, 2015.

Ashworth, E. Jennifer, and Domenic D'Ettore. "Medieval Theories of Analogy." *Stanford Encyclopedia of Philosophy* Archive, Nov. 29, 1999; last revised Dec. 1, 2021. Edited by Edward N. Zalta. https://plato.stanford.edu/archives/win2021/entries/analogy-medieval/.

Association for the Philosophy of Judaism. "Symposium on Samuel Lebens's *The Principles of Judaism*." APJ, 2022. https://www.theapj.com/event/symposium-on-samuel-lebenss-the-principles-of-judaism/.

Astley, Jeff. *Exploring God-Talk: Using Language in Religion*. Exploring Faith: Theology for Life. London: Darton, Longman, and Todd, 2004.

Athanassiadi, Polymnia, and Michael Frede. *Pagan Monotheism in Late Antiquity*. Oxford: Oxford University Press, 1999.

Augustine. *The Trinity, De Trinitate*. Edited by John E. Rotelle. Translated by Edmund Hill. 2nd ed. Vol. 5 of *The Works of Saint Augustine: A Translation for the 21st Century*. Hyde Park, NY: New City, 2015.

Avery-Peck, Alan J. "Magic, Magic Bowls, Astrology in Judaism." In *The Encyclopaedia of Judaism*, edited by Jacob Neusner et al., 2:832–44. Leiden: Brill, 2000.

Barrett, Matthew, ed. *On Classical Trinitarianism: Retrieving the Nicene Doctrine of the Triune God*. Downers Grove, IL: IVP Academic, 2024.

Barron, James. "A Closer Look at *The Times*'s Report on Hasidic Schools." *New York Times*, Sept. 15, 2022. https://www.nytimes.com/2022/09/15/nyregion/a-closer-look-at-the-times-report-on-hasidic-schools.html.

Barry, Kieren. *The Greek Qabalah: Alphabetical Mysticism and Numerology in the Ancient World*. Illustrated ed. York Beach, ME: Weiser, 1999.

Bartholomä, Philipp F. "Did Jesus Save the People Out of Egypt? A Re-Examination of a Textual Problem in Jude 5." *NovT* 50 (2008) 143–58.

Bartholomew, Craig G. *The God Who Acts in History: The Significance of Sinai*. Grand Rapids: Eerdmans, 2020.

Bartholomew, Craig G., and Michael W. Goheen. *Christian Philosophy: A Systematic and Narrative Introduction*. Grand Rapids: Baker Academic, 2013.

Bateman, Herbert W., IV, et al. *Jesus the Messiah: Tracing the Promises, Expectations, and Coming of Israel's King*. Grand Rapids: Kregel Academic, 2012.

Bibliography

Bauckham, Richard. *Jesus and the Eyewitnesses: The Gospels as Eyewitness Testimony.* 2nd ed. Grand Rapids: Eerdmans, 2017.

———. "Sabbath and Sunday in the Post-Apostolic Church." In *From Sabbath to Lord's Day: A Biblical, Historical, and Theological Investigation,* edited by D. A. Carson, 251–98. Eugene, OR: Wipf & Stock, 1999.

———. *"Son of Man": Early Jewish Literature.* Grand Rapids: Eerdmans, 2023.

Bauer, Walter. *Orthodoxy and Heresy in Earliest Christianity.* Philadelphia: Fortress Press, 1971.

Baur, Ferdinand Christian. *The Christ Party in the Corinthian Community.* Edited by David Lincicum. Translated by Wayne Coppins et al. ECL 29. Atlanta: SBL, 2021.

Beale, G. K. *The Book of Revelation: A Commentary on the Greek Text.* Grand Rapids: Eerdmans, 1999.

Beale, G. K., and D. A. Carson, eds. *Commentary on the New Testament Use of the Old Testament.* Grand Rapids: Baker Academic, 2007.

Beck, W. David, and Michael R. Licona, eds. *Raised on the Third Day: Defending the Historicity of the Resurrection of Jesus.* Bellingham, WA: Lexham, 2020.

Behr, John. *The Way to Nicaea.* Vol. 1 of *The Formation of Christian Theology.* Crestwood, NY: St. Vladimir's Seminary Press, 2001.

Ben-Sasson, Haim Hillel, et al. "Maimonidean Controversy." In *Encyclopaedia Judaica,* edited by Fred Skolnik and Michael Berenbaum, 13:371–81. 2nd ed. Detroit: Macmillan Reference and Keter, 2007.

Berger, David. "Christians, Gentiles, and the Talmud: A Fourteenth-Century Jewish Response to the Attack on Rabbinic Judaism." In *Persecution, Polemic, and Dialogue: Essays in Jewish-Christian Relations,* 158–76. Judaism and Jewish Life. Academic Studies: Boston: 2010.

Berlin, Adele, et al., eds. *The Jewish Study Bible.* New York: Oxford University Press, 2004.

Biale, David. *Gershom Scholem: Kabbalah and Counter-History.* Cambridge, MA: Harvard University Press, 1982.

Blaising, Craig A. "Hypostatic Union." In *Evangelical Dictionary of Theology,* edited by Walter A. Elwell, 583–84. 2nd ed. Grand Rapids: Baker Academic, 2001.

Blau, Ludwig. "Gnosticism." In *The Jewish Encyclopedia,* edited by Isidore Singer, 5:681–86. New York: Funk & Wagnalls, 1901–6.

Block, Daniel Isaac. "How Many Is God? An Investigation into the Meaning of Deuteronomy 6:4–5." *JETS* 47 (2004) 183–212.

Blomberg, Craig L. *The Historical Reliability of John's Gospel.* Leicester, UK: InterVarsity, 2001.

———. *The Historical Reliability of the Gospels.* 2nd ed. Downers Grove, IL: IVP Academic, 2007.

Bock, Darrell L. "Is It Kosher to Substitute Jesus into God's Place? A Look at Key Teaching from the Early Jesus Community." *Mishkan* 59 (2009) 41–50.

———. "Response to Mark Kinzer's *Finding Our Way Through Nicaea.*" Hashivenu Forum, *Encountering the God of Israel in the Messiah of Israel,* Los Angeles, 2010.

———. "The Use of Daniel 7 in Jesus' Trial, with Implications for His Self-Understanding." In *"Who Is This Son of Man?": The Latest Scholarship on a Puzzling Expression of the Historical Jesus,* edited by Larry W. Hurtado and Paul L. Owen, 78–100. LNTS. New York: T&T Clark, 2011.

Bibliography

Boethius. "*The Theological Tractates*" and "*The Consolation of Philosophy*." Translated by H. F. Stewart and E. K. Rand. Cambridge, MA: Harvard University Press, 1918.

Bohak, Gideon. "Gematria." In *The Eerdmans Dictionary of Early Judaism*, edited by John J. Collins and Daniel C. Harlow, 661. Grand Rapids: Eerdmans, 2010.

Borough Park Symposium, ed. *Symposium II: The Deity of Messiah and the Mystery of God, April 12–14, 2010*. Borough Park Papers. Clarksville, MD: Messianic Jewish, 2012.

Boskey, Avner. "The Messianic Use of Rabbinic Literature." *Mishkan* 71 (2013) 4–40.

Bousset, Johann Franz Wilhelm. *Kyrios Christos: Geschichte des Christusglaubens von den Anfängen des Christentums bis Iranuaus*. Göttingen: Vandenhoeck & Ruprecht, 1913.

Boustan, Ra'anan S. "Hekhalot Literature." In *The Eerdmans Dictionary of Early Judaism*, edited by John J. Collins and Daniel C. Harlow, 719–21. Grand Rapids: Eerdmans, 2010.

Bowman, Robert M., and J. Ed Komoszewski. *Putting Jesus in His Place: The Case for the Deity of Christ*. Grand Rapids: Kregel, 2007.

Boyarin, Daniel. "Beyond Judaisms: Metatron and the Divine Polymorphy of Ancient Judaism." *JSJ* 41 (2010) 323–65.

———. *Border Lines: The Partition of Judaeo-Christianity*. Divinations. Philadelphia: University of Pennsylvania Press, 2004.

———. "Enoch, Ezra, and the Jewishness of 'High Christology.'" In *Fourth Ezra and Second Baruch*, edited by Matthias Henze and Gabriele Boccaccini, 337–61. JSJSup 164. Leiden: Brill, 2013.

———. *The Jewish Gospels: The Story of the Jewish Christ*. New York: New Press, 2012.

———. *Judaism: The Genealogy of a Modern Notion*. Key Words in Jewish Studies. New Brunswick, NJ: Rutgers University Press, 2018.

———. "Two Powers in Heaven: Or, the Making of a Heresy." In *The Idea of Biblical Interpretation: Essays in Honor of James L. Kugel*, edited by Hindy Najman and Judith Newman, 331–70. JSJSup 83. Leiden: Brill, 2004.

Boys-Stones, George. "The Fragments of Numenius of Apamea." Academia, 2014. https://www.academia.edu/6410739/The_fragments_of_Numenius_of_Apamea.

Brannan, Rick. *Historic Creeds and Confessions*. Oak Harbor, WA: Lexham, 2001. Logos Bible Software e-book.

———, trans. *The Apostolic Fathers in English*. Bellingham, WA: Lexham, 2012. Logos Bible Software e-book.

Brannan, Rick, et al., eds. *The Lexham English Septuagint*. Bellingham, WA: Lexham, 2012. Logos Bible Software e-book.

Brashear, William. "Word Magic." In *The Eerdmans Encyclopedia of Early Christian Art and Archaeology*, edited by Paul Corby Finney, 2:718–21. Grand Rapids: Eerdmans, 2017.

Bray, Gerald L. *The Doctrine of God*. Contours of Christian Theology. Downers Grove, IL: InterVarsity, 1993.

———. *God Has Spoken: A History of Christian Theology*. Wheaton, IL: Crossway, 2014.

Brill, Alan. "A Jewish View of Contemporary Ideas of the Trinity." *Modern Theology* 39 (2023) 307–26.

Brookhaven National Laboratory. "Collisions of Light Produce Matter/Antimatter from Pure Energy." Brookhaven National Laboratory, 2021. https://www.bnl.gov/newsroom/news.php?a=119023.

Bibliography

Brown, Benjamin. "'But Me No Buts': The Theological Debate Between the Hasidim and the Mitnagdim in Light of the Discourse-Markers Theory (English)." *Numen*, 61 (2014) 525–51.

Brown, Jeremy. *New Heavens and a New Earth: The Jewish Reception of Copernican Thought*. Oxford: Oxford University Press, 2013.

Brown, Michael L. *Our Hands Are Stained with Blood: The Tragic Story of the Church and the Jewish People*. Rev. ed. Shippensburg, PA: Destiny Image, 2019.

Broydé, Isaac. "The Ten Sefirot." In *The Jewish Encyclopedia*, edited by Cyrus Adler and Isidore Singer, 11:154–55. New York: Funk & Wagnalls, 1901–6.

Brueggemann, Walter. "'Impossibility' and Epistemology in the Faith Tradition of Abraham and Sarah (Gen 18:1–15)." *ZAW* 94 (1982) 615–34.

Brumbach, Joshua. "Review of *Border Lines*, by Daniel Boyarin." Hashivenu Forum, *Encountering the God of Israel in the Messiah of Israel*, Los Angeles, 2010.

Burnett, Stephen G. "Distorted Mirrors: Antonius Margaritha, Johann Buxtorf and Christian Ethnographies of the Jews." *Sixteenth Century Journal* 25 (1994) 275–87.

———. "Luther's Chief Witness: Antonius Margaritha's *Der Gants Judisch Glaub* (1530/1531)." In *Revealing the Secrets of the Jews: Johannes Pfefferkorn and Christian Writings About Jewish Life and Literature in Early Modern Europe*, edited by Jonathan Adams and Cordelia Heß, 183–200. Berlin: De Gruyter, 2017.

Butler, Rex D. "'He Who Is and the Angel of Him Who Is': Nicene and Post-Nicene Views of Christophanies." *Journal for Baptist Theology & Ministry* 19 (2022).

———. "'The Son of God Appeared to Prophets and Patriarchs': Ante-Nicene Views of Christophanies." *Journal for Baptist Theology and Ministry* 18 (2021) 63–83.

Buxtorf, Johann. *The Jewish Synagogue, or, An Historical Narration of the State of the Jewes at This Day Dispersed over the Face of the Whole Earth*. Translated by A. B. London: Roycroft, 1663.

Cantor, Ron. "Reconciling the Antisemitism of the Church Fathers with Their Devotion to Messiah." *Kesher*, Apr. 30, 2023. https://www.kesherjournal.com/article/reconciling-the-antisemitism-of-the-church-fathers-with-their-devotion-to-messiah/.

Carabine, Deirdre. *The Unknown God: Negative Theology in the Platonic Tradition: Plato to Eriugena*. Louvain Theological & Pastoral Monographs 19. Grand Rapids: Eerdmans, 1995.

Caragounis, Chrys C. "Epistle of Aristeas." In *Dictionary of New Testament Background*, edited by Craig A. Evans and Stanley E. Porter Jr., 114–18. IVP Bible Dictionary. Downers Grove, IL: IVP Academic, 2000.

Carasik, Michael, ed. *Deuteronomy*. Commentators' Bible. Philadelphia: Jewish Publication Society, 2015.

———, ed. *Exodus*. Commentators' Bible. Philadelphia: Jewish Publication Society, 2005.

Carlson, Richard F., ed. *Science & Christianity: Four Views*. Downers Grove, IL: IVP Academic, 2000.

Carroll, James. *Constantine's Sword: The Church and the Jews*. Boston: Houghton Mifflin, 2001.

Carter, Craig A. *Contemplating God with the Great Tradition: Recovering Trinitarian Classical Theism*. Grand Rapids: Baker Academic, 2021.

Cathcart, Kevin, et al., eds. *Targum Neofiti 1: Exodus and Targum Pseudo-Jonathan: Exodus*. Vol. 2 of *The Aramaic Bible*. Collegeville, MN: Liturgical, 1994.

Bibliography

———. *The Targum Onqelos to Genesis*. Vol. 6 of *The Aramaic Bible*. Collegeville, MN: Liturgical, 1990.

Chajes, J. H. "Spheres, Sefirot, and the Imaginal Astronomical Discourse of Classical Kabbalah." *HTR* 113 (2020) 230–62.

Chazan, Robert. *Barcelona and Beyond: The Disputation of 1263 and Its Aftermath*. Berkeley: University of California Press, 1992.

Cheng, Eugenia. *Beyond Infinity: An Expedition to the Outer Limits of Mathematics*. New York: Basic Books, 2017.

Chosen People Ministries. "Doctrinal Statement." Chosen People Ministries, n.d. https://www.chosenpeople.com/our-mission/doctrinal-statement/.

Ciampa, Roy E., and Brian S. Rosner. *The First Letter to the Corinthians*. Grand Rapids: Eerdmans, 2010.

Ciholas, Paul. "Plato: The Attic Moses? Some Patristic Reactions to Platonic Philosophy." *Classical World* 72 (1978) 217–25.

Ciucu, Cristina. "Kabbalistic Pan(En)Theism: Neoplatonic Philosophy and Mystical Practice." In *Oxford Handbook of Jewish Philosophy*. Oxford Handbooks. Oxford: Oxford University Press, forthcoming. https://www.academia.edu/59263523.

Clark, David A., and Norman L. Geisler. *Apologetics in the New Age: A Christian Critique of Pantheism*. Eugene, OR: Wipf & Stock, 2004.

Clark, John C., and Marcus Peter Johnson. *The Incarnation of God: The Mystery of the Gospel as the Foundation of Evangelical Theology*. Wheaton, IL: Crossway, 2015.

Cockerill, Gareth Lee. *The Epistle to the Hebrews*. NICNT. Grand Rapids: Eerdmans, 2012.

Cole, Graham A. *The God Who Became Human: A Biblical Theology of Incarnation*. Edited by D. A. Carson. New Studies in Biblical Theology 30. Downers Grove, IL: InterVarsity, 2013.

Coleridge, Samuel Taylor. *Specimens of the Table Talk of Samuel Taylor Coleridge*. 2nd ed. London: Murray, 1836.

Commission for Religious Relations with the Jews. "The Gifts and the Calling of God Are Irrevocable (Rom 11:29): A Reflection on Theological Questions Pertaining to Catholic-Jewish Relations on the Occasion of the 50th Anniversary of *Nostra Aetate* (No. 4)." Vatican, Dec. 10, 2015. https://ccjr.us/dialogika-resources/documents-and-statements/roman-catholic/vatican-curia/crrj-2015dec10.

Cooper, John W. *Panentheism—the Other God of the Philosophers: From Plato to the Present*. Grand Rapids: Baker Academic, 2006.

Cooperman, Alan, and Gregory A. Smith. "Eight Facts About Orthodox Jews from the Pew Research Survey." Pew Research Center, Oct. 17, 2013. https://www.pewresearch.org/fact-tank/2013/10/17/eight-facts-about-orthodox-jews-from-the-pew-research-survey/.

Cooperman, Alan, et al. "A Portrait of American Orthodox Jews: A Further Analysis of the 2013 Survey of U.S. Jews." Pew Research Center, Aug. 26, 2015. https://www.pewresearch.org/religion/2015/08/26/a-portrait-of-american-orthodox-jews/.

Copan, Paul, and William Lane Craig. *Creation Out of Nothing: A Biblical, Philosophical, and Scientific Exploration*. Grand Rapids: Baker Academic, 2004.

Copan, Paul, et al., eds. *Dictionary of Christianity and Science: The Definitive Reference for the Intersection of Christian Faith and Contemporary Science*. Grand Rapids: Zondervan, 2017.

Bibliography

Costa, José. "The Body of God in Ancient Rabbinic Judaism: Problems of Interpretation." Translated by Cadenza Academic Translations. *RHR* 227 (2010) 283–316 (cited as i–xxxiii). https://doi.org/10.4000/rhr.7617.

Craig, William Lane. *The Cosmological Argument from Plato to Leibniz*. Eugene, OR: Wipf and Stock, 2001.

———. *The Kalām Cosmological Argument*. Edited by John Hick and H. G. Wood. Library of Philosophy and Religion. Eugene, OR: Wipf and Stock, 2000.

———. *Reasonable Faith: Christian Truth and Apologetics*. 3rd ed. Wheaton, IL: Crossway, 2008.

———. *The Son Rises: The Historical Evidence for the Resurrection of Jesus*. Eugene, OR: Wipf and Stock, 2000.

———. *Time and Eternity: Exploring God's Relationship to Time*. Wheaton, IL: Crossway, 2001.

Crawford, Brian J. "Christian Antisemitism's Potent Recipe: Theological, Ethical, Ecclesiastical, and Political Ingredients in Historical Context." *Mishkan* 85 (2022) 56–83.

———. "Forgotten Cohanim: Contrasting the Rabbinic Origin Story with the High Priesthood of Yeshua." Chosen People Answers, 2023. https://www.chosenpeopleanswers.com/articles/11.

———. "Pathways for Addressing Jewish Theological and Philosophical Objections to the Incarnation." DMin thesis, Biola University, 2021. http://www.proquest.com/pqdtglobal/docview/2610388914/.

Crescas, Hasdai. *The Refutation of the Christian Principles*. Edited by Kenneth Seeskin. Translated by Daniel J. Lasker. Albany, NY: SUNY Press, 1992.

Crisp, Oliver D. *Divinity and Humanity: The Incarnation Reconsidered*. Current Issues in Theology. New York: Cambridge University Press, 2007.

———. *Retrieving Doctrine: Essays in Reformed Theology*. Special ed. Downers Grove, IL: IVP Academic, 2011.

———. *The Word Enfleshed: Exploring the Person and Work of Christ*. Grand Rapids: Baker Academic, 2016.

Crouzel, H. "Image." In *Encyclopedia of Ancient Christianity*, edited by Angelo Di Berardino et al., 2:320–24. Downers Grove, IL: IVP Academic, 2014.

Crowe, Michael J. *Theories of the World from Antiquity to the Copernican Revolution*. 2nd ed. Mineola, NY: Dover, 2001.

Cyril of Alexandria. *Letters, 51–11*. Edited by Thomas P. Halton. Vol. 77 of *Fathers of the Church*. Washington, DC: Catholic University of America Press, 1987.

Dahl, Nils A. "The Arrogant Archon and the Lewd Sophia: Jewish Traditions in Gnostic Revolt." In *The Rediscovery of Gnosticism: Sethian Gnosticism: Proceedings of the International Conference on Gnosticism at Yale, New Haven, Connecticut, March 28–31, 1978*, edited by Bentley Layton, 2:689–712. SHR. Leiden: Brill, 1981.

Dalfin, Chaim. *Demystifying the Mystical: Understanding the Language and Concepts of Chasidism and Jewish Mysticism*. Northvale, NJ: Aronson, 1995.

Dan, Joseph, ed. *The Early Kabbalah*. Translated by Ronald C. Kiener. Classics of Western Spirituality. New York: Paulist, 1986.

———. "Imago Dei." In *20th Century Jewish Religious Thought*, edited by Arthur A. Cohen and Paul Mendes-Flohr, 473–79. Philadelphia: Jewish Publication Society, 2009.

———. "Jewish Gnosticism?" *JSQ* 2 (1995) 309–28.

Bibliography

———. *Jewish Mysticism*. 4 vols. Northvale, NJ: Aronson, 1999.

D'Ancona, Cristina. "The Theology Attributed to Aristotle: Sources, Structure, Influence." In *The Oxford Handbook of Islamic Philosophy*, edited by Khaled El-Rouayheb and Sabine Schmidtke, 8–29. Oxford Handbooks. Oxford: Oxford University Press, 2016.

Dauben, Joseph W. "Georg Cantor and Pope Leo XIII: Mathematics, Theology, and the Infinite." *Journal of the History of Ideas* 38 (1977) 85–108.

David, Marian. "The Correspondence Theory of Truth." *Stanford Encyclopedia of Philosophy*, May 10, 2022; last revised May 28, 2015. Edited by Edward N. Zalta. https://plato.stanford.edu/entries/truth-correspondence/.

Davidson, Herbert A. "Maimonides on Metaphysical Knowledge." In *Maimonidean Studies*, edited by Arthur Hyman, 3:49–103. New York: Scharf Publication Trust of Yeshiva University Press, 1995.

Davies, Daniel. *Method and Metaphysics in Maimonides' "Guide for the Perplexed."* AAR Reflection and Theory in the Study of Religion. Oxford: Oxford University Press, 2011.

Davis, Menachem, ed. *Siddur for Weekdays with an Interlinear Translation*. Schottenstein ed. Brooklyn, NY: Mesorah, 2002.

Deissmann, Adolf, and Lionel Richard Mortimer Strachan. *Light from the Ancient East: The New Testament Illustrated by Recently Discovered Texts of the Graeco-Roman World*. London: Hodder & Stoughton, 1910.

Dennis, Geoffrey W. "Astrology." In *The Encyclopedia of Jewish Myth, Magic & Mysticism*, 45–46. 2nd ed. Woodbury, MN: Llewellyn, 2016.

———. *The Encyclopedia of Jewish Myth, Magic & Mysticism*. 2nd ed. Woodbury, MN: Llewellyn, 2016.

Derovan, David. "Gematria." In *Encyclopaedia Judaica*, edited by Fred Skolnik and Michael Berenbaum, 7:424–25. Detroit: Macmillan Reference and Keter, 2007.

DeWeese, Garrett J., and J. P. Moreland. *Philosophy Made Slightly Less Difficult: A Beginner's Guide to Life's Big Questions*. 2nd ed. Downers Grove, IL: IVP Academic, 2021.

Downey, Amy Karen. *Maimonides's Yahweh: Rabbinic Judaism's Attempt to Answer the Incarnational Question*. Eugene, OR: Wipf and Stock, 2019.

———. "What Hath Maimonides Wrought?" *Mishkan* 82 (2020) 31–37.

Driver, S. R., and Adolf Neubauer, trans. *The Fifty-Third Chapter of Isaiah According to the Jewish Interpreters*. 2 vols. Oxford: Parker and Co., 1877.

Dubov, Nissan Dovid. "Adam." Chabad, 2006. https://www.chabad.org/library/article_cdo/aid/361873/jewish/Adam.htm.

———. *Discovering Jewish Mysticism*. Vol. 1 of *The Key to Kabbalah*. New York: Dwelling Place, 2006. https://www.chabad.org/article.asp?aid=361868.

———. "Key FAQs." Chabad, 2006. https://www.chabad.org/library/article_cdo/aid/361872/jewish/Key-FAQS.htm.

———. "Tzimtzum." Chabad, 2006. https://www.chabad.org/library/article_cdo/aid/361884/jewish/Tzimtzum.htm.

Duby, Steven J. *Divine Simplicity: A Dogmatic Account*. T&T Clark Studies in Systematic Theology. London: Bloomsbury, 2016.

———. *God in Himself: Scripture, Metaphysics, and the Task of Christian Theology*. Downers Grove, IL: IVP Academic, 2019.

Bibliography

Dunn, James D. G., ed. *Jews and Christians: The Parting of the Ways, A.D. 70 to 135: The Second Durham-Tübingen Research Symposium on Earliest Christianity and Judaism.* Grand Rapids: Eerdmans, 1999.

Dutmer, Evan. "The Miracle of Mosaic Prophecy in *The Guide of the Perplexed*." *Journal of Religious & Theological Information* 22 (2023) 85–103.

Dweck, Yaacob. *The Scandal of Kabbalah. Jews, Christians, and Muslims from the Ancient to the Modern World.* Princeton, NJ: Princeton University Press, 2011.

Easwaran, Kenny, et al. "Infinity." *Stanford Encyclopedia of Philosophy* Archive, Apr. 29, 2021. Edited by Edward N. Zalta. https://plato.stanford.edu/archives/win2021/entries/infinity/.

Edwards, Mark Julian. "Atticizing Moses? Numenius, the Fathers and the Jews." *Vigiliae Christianae* 44 (1990) 64–75.

Ehrman, Bart D. *How Jesus Became God: The Exaltation of a Jewish Preacher from Galilee.* New York: HarperOne, 2014.

Eisenmenger, Johann Andreas. *Entdecktes Judentum.* Repr., Dresden: Brandner, 1893.

Elgvin, Torleif. "Jewish Christian Editing of the Old Testament Pseudepigrapha." In *Jewish Believers in Jesus: The Early Centuries*, edited by Oskar Skarsaune and Reidar Hvalvik, 278–304. Peabody, MA: Hendrickson, 2007.

Eliezrie, David. "US Jewry Is Shifting Profoundly and Chabad Is on Rise—Pew Research." *Jerusalem Post*, May 30, 2021. https://www.jpost.com/opinion/pew-us-jewry-is-shifting-profoundly-chabad-is-on-rise-669549.

Elior, Rachel. *Jewish Mysticism: The Infinite Expression of Freedom.* Littman Library of Jewish Civilization. Oxford: Littman Library of Jewish Civilization, 2010.

Elior, Rachel, and Jeffrey M. Green. *The Paradoxical Ascent to God: The Kabbalistic Theosophy of Habad Hasidism.* Albany: State University of New York Press, 1992.

Elior, Rachel, and David Louvish. *The Three Temples: On the Emergence of Jewish Mysticism.* Littman Library of Jewish Civilization. Portland, OR: Littman Library of Jewish Civilization, 2004.

Ellingworth, Paul. *The Epistle to the Hebrews: A Commentary on the Greek Text.* NIGTC. Grand Rapids: Eerdmans, 1993.

Ephrem the Syrian. *Ephrem the Syrian: Hymns.* Edited by Bernard McGinn. Translated by Kathleen E. McVey. Classics of Western Spirituality. Mahwah, NJ: Paulist, 1989.

Erickson, Millard J. *The Word Became Flesh.* Grand Rapids: Baker, 1991.

Fagenblat, Michael. "Introduction: Delineations: Negative Theology as Jewish Modernity." In *Negative Theology as Jewish Modernity*, edited by Michael Fagenblat, 1–29. New Jewish Philosophy and Thought. Bloomington: Indiana University Press, 2017.

Faivre, Antoine. *Western Esotericism: A Concise History.* SUNY Series in Western Esoteric Traditions. Albany: State University of New York Press, 2010.

Feinberg, John S., ed. *Continuity and Discontinuity: Perspectives on the Relationship Between the Old and New Testaments; Essays in Honor of S. Lewis Johnson, Jr.* Westchester, IL: Crossway, 1988.

———. *No One Like Him: The Doctrine of God.* Foundations of Evangelical Theology. Wheaton, IL: Crossway, 2001.

Feldman, Seymour. "Philosophy and Theology of Medieval Judaism." In *The Encyclopaedia of Judaism*, edited by Jacob Neusner et al., 2:711–35. Boston: Brill, 2000.

Bibliography

Ferguson, Everett. "Numerology." In *The Eerdmans Encyclopedia of Early Christian Art and Archaeology*, edited by Paul Corby Finney, 2:233–35. Grand Rapids: Eerdmans, 2017.

Finney, Paul Corby. "Hand of God." In *The Eerdmans Encyclopedia of Early Christian Art and Archaeology*, edited by Paul Corby Finney, 1:630–31. Grand Rapids: Eerdmans, 2017.

Fischer, John. "The Rabbinic View of God: A Contrast to Maimonides." Academia, 2001. https://www.academia.edu/74817279/THE_RABBINIC_VIEW_OF_GOD_A_CONTRAST_TO_MAIMONIDES_by.

Fishbane, Michael. "Biblical Interpretation." In *The Oxford Handbook of Jewish Studies*, edited by Martin Goodman, 680–704. Oxford Handbooks. New York: Oxford University Press, 2002.

Fletcher-Louis, Crispin. *Christological Origins: The Emerging Consensus and Beyond*. Vol. 1 of *Jesus Monotheism*. Eugene, OR: Whymanity, 2019.

Floyd, Graham. "Deriving the *Imago Dei* from the Incarnation." Evangelical Philosophical Society, 2019. https://www.epsociety.org/articles/deriving-the-imago-dei-from-the-incarnation/.

Fossum, Jarl. "Kyrios Jesus as the Angel of the Lord in Jude 5–7." *NTS* 33 (1987) 226–43.

Frame, John M. *A History of Western Philosophy and Theology*. Phillipsburg, NJ: P&R, 2015.

———. *Systematic Theology: An Introduction to Christian Belief*. Phillipsburg, NJ: P&R, 2013.

France, R. T. *The Gospel of Mark: A Commentary on the Greek Text*. NIGTC. Grand Rapids: Eerdmans, 2002.

Frank, Daniel H. "Maimonides and Medieval Jewish Aristotelianism." In *The Cambridge Companion to Medieval Jewish Philosophy*, edited by Daniel H. Frank and Oliver Leaman, ch. 7. Cambridge Companions to Philosophy. New York: Cambridge University Press, 2003. Kindle.

Frank, Daniel, and Aaron Segal, eds. *Maimonides' "Guide of the Perplexed": A Critical Guide*. Cambridge: Cambridge University Press, 2021.

Frede, Dorothea, and Marije Martijn. "Alexander of Aphrodisias." *Stanford Encyclopedia of Philosophy* Archive, Oct. 13, 2003; last revised Apr. 23, 2024. Edited by Edward N. Zalta and Uri Nodelman. https://plato.stanford.edu/archives/sum2024/entries/alexander-aphrodisias/.

Fredriksen, Paula. *Augustine and the Jews: A Christian Defense of Jews and Judaism*. New Haven, CT: Yale University Press, 2010.

Frey, Joseph Samuel Christian Frederick. *Joseph and Benjamin: Letters on the Controversy Between Jews and Christians*. 2 vols. New York: Hill, 1837.

Friedman, Theodore, et al. "Kedushah." In *Encyclopaedia Judaica*, edited by Fred Skolnik and Michael Berenbaum, 12:50–56. Detroit: Macmillan Reference and Keter, 2007.

Fruchtenbaum, Arnold G. *Messiah Yeshua, Divine Redeemer: Christology from a Messianic Jewish Perspective*. Edited by Christiane Jurik. Come and See 3. San Antonio: Ariel Ministries, 2015.

———. *What We Know About God: Theology Proper*. Edited by Christiane K. Jurik. 2nd ed. Come and See 2. San Antonio: Ariel Ministries, 2019.

Gatti, Maria Luisa. "Plotinus: The Platonic Tradition and the Foundation of Neoplatonism." In *The Cambridge Companion to Plotinus*, edited by Lloyd P.

Gerson, 10–37. Cambridge Companions to Philosophy. Cambridge: Cambridge University Press, 1996.

Geisler, Norman L. *Baker Encyclopedia of Christian Apologetics*. Baker Reference Library. Grand Rapids: Baker Academic, 1998.

———. "First Principles." In *Baker Encyclopedia of Christian Apologetics*, 250–53. Baker Reference Library. Grand Rapids: Baker Academic, 1998.

———. *Thomas Aquinas: An Evangelical Appraisal*. Eugene, OR: Wipf and Stock, 2003.

Geisler, Norman L., and Paul D. Feinberg. *Introduction to Philosophy: A Christian Perspective*. Grand Rapids: Baker, 1980.

Gentry, Peter J., and Stephen J. Wellum. *God's Kingdom Through God's Covenants: A Concise Biblical Theology*. Wheaton, IL: Crossway, 2015.

Gericke, Jaco. *The Hebrew Bible and Philosophy of Religion*. RBS. Atlanta: Society of Biblical Literature, 2012.

Gerson, Lloyd P., ed. *The Cambridge Companion to Plotinus*. Cambridge Companions to Philosophy. Cambridge: Cambridge University Press, 1996.

Ginsburg, Christian D. *The Kabbalah: Its Doctrines, Development, and Literature*. Routledge Revivals. London: Routledge, 2016.

Ginzberg, Louis. "Adam Kadmon." In *The Jewish Encyclopedia*, edited by Isidore Singer, 1:181–83. New York: Funk & Wagnalls, 1901–6.

———. "Allegorical Interpretation." In *The Jewish Encyclopedia*, edited by Isidore Singer, 1:403–11. New York: Funk & Wagnalls, 1901–6.

———. "Sefer Yezirah." In *The Jewish Encyclopedia*, edited by Isidore Singer, 12:602–6. New York: Funk & Wagnalls, 1901–6.

Glaser, Mitch. "Messianic Jewish National Organizations." In *Introduction to Messianic Judaism: Its Ecclesial Context and Biblical Foundations*, edited by David Rudolph and Joel Willitts, 116–25. Grand Rapids: Zondervan, 2013.

Glaser, Mitchell Leslie. "A Survey of Missions to the Jews in Continental Europe, 1900–1950." PhD diss., Fuller Theological Seminary, 1999.

Goldberg, Louis. *God, Torah, Messiah*. Edited by Richard A. Robinson. San Francisco: Purple Pomegranate, 2009.

Goodenough, Erwin R. *By Light, Light: The Mystic Gospel of Hellenistic Judaism*. Amsterdam: Philo, 1969.

———. *An Introduction to Philo Judæus*. New Haven, CT: Yale University Press, 1940.

Goodman, Lenn E. "Depopulating the Heavens: Translating the Guide & What Rambam Would Say Today." Interview by Judaism Demystified. YouTube, Mar. 3, 2024. https://www.youtube.com/watch?v=I9ab875Dnhw.

———, ed. *Neoplatonism and Jewish Thought*. Studies in Neoplatonism 7. Albany: State University of New York Press, 1992.

———. "The Object of the *Guide*." In *The Guide to the Perplexed: A New Translation*, by Moses Maimonides, locs. 96–301. Translated by Lenn E. Goodman and Phillip I. Lieberman. Stanford, CA: Stanford University Press, 2024. Kindle.

———. "What Is Positive in Negative Theology?" In *Negative Theology as Jewish Modernity*, edited by Michael Fagenblat, 104–39. New Jewish Philosophy and Thought. Bloomington: Indiana University Press, 2017.

Goodman, Micah. *Maimonides and the Book That Changed Judaism: Secrets of "The Guide for the Perplexed."* Translated by Yedidya Sinclair. Philadelphia: Jewish Publication Society, 2015.

Bibliography

Gordon, Bruce L. "Idealism." In *Dictionary of Christianity and Science: The Definitive Reference for the Intersection of Christian Faith and Contemporary Science*, edited by Paul Copan et al., 372–73. Grand Rapids: Zondervan, 2017.

Goshen-Gottstein, Alon. "The Body as Image of God in Rabbinic Literature." *HTR* 87 (1994) 171–95.

Grabbe, Lester L., ed. *Did Moses Speak Attic? Jewish Historiography and Scripture in the Hellenistic Period*. European Seminar in Historical Methodology. Sheffield, UK: Sheffield Academic, 2001.

Gregory of Nazianzus. *On God and Christ: The Five Theological Orations and Two Letters to Cledonius*. Edited by John Behr. Crestwood, NY: St. Vladimir's Seminary Press, 2002.

Grudem, Wayne. *Systematic Theology: An Introduction to Biblical Doctrine*. 2nd ed. Grand Rapids: Zondervan Academic, 2020.

Gunton, Colin E. *The One, the Three, and the Many: God, Creation, and the Culture of Modernity*. New York: Cambridge University Press, 1993.

Gurary, Noson. *The Thirteen Principles of Faith: A Chasidic Viewpoint*. Rev. ed. Brooklyn, NY: Menachem Education Foundation, 2017.

Guyer, Paul, and Rolf-Peter Horstmann. "Idealism." *Stanford Encyclopedia of Philosophy Archive*, Aug. 30, 2015; last revised Feb. 5, 2021. Edited by Edward N. Zalta and Uri Nodelman. https://plato.stanford.edu/archives/spr2023/entries/idealism/.

Habermas, Gary. *Evidences*. Vol. 1 of *On the Resurrection*. Nashville: B&H, 2024.

Habermas, Gary R., and Michael Licona. *The Case for the Resurrection of Jesus*. Grand Rapids: Kregel, 2004.

Hachlili, Rachel. *Ancient Synagogues—Archaeology and Art: New Discoveries and Current Research*. HdO 105. Boston: Brill, 2013.

Halbertal, Moshe. *Concealment and Revelation: Esotericism in Jewish Thought and Its Philosophical Implications*. Translated by Jackie Feldman. Princeton, NJ: Princeton University Press, 2007.

———. *Maimonides: Life and Thought*. Princeton, NJ: Princeton University Press, 2013.

Hamman, Adelbert. "Magic." In *Encyclopedia of Ancient Christianity*, edited by Angelo Di Berardino et al., 2:654–55. Downers Grove, IL: IVP Academic, 2014.

Hamori, Esther J. "Divine Embodiment in the Hebrew Bible And Some Implications For Jewish and Christian Incarnational Theologies." In *Bodies, Embodiment, and Theology of the Hebrew Bible*, edited by S. Tamar Kamionkowski, 161–83. LHBOTS 465. New York: T&T Clark, 2010.

Hankey, Wayne J. *Aquinas's Neoplatonism in the "Summa Theologiae" on God: A Short Introduction*. South Bend, IN: St. Augustine's, 2019.

Harari, Yuval, et al. "Magic." In *Encyclopedia Judaica*, edited by Fred Skolnik and Michael Berenbaum, 13:342–52. Detroit: Macmillan Reference and Keter, 2007.

Harrington, Daniel J. "Wisdom Christology in the Light of Early Jewish and Qumran Texts." *Mishkan* 44 (2005) 36–42.

Hart, David Bentley. "Notes on the Concept of the Infinite in the History of Western Metaphysics." In *Infinity: New Research Frontiers*, edited by Michael Heller and W. Hugh Woodin, 255–74. Cambridge: Cambridge University Press, 2011.

Harvey, Richard S. *Mapping Messianic Jewish Theology: A Constructive Approach*. Studies in Messianic Jewish Theology. Colorado Springs, CO: Paternoster, 2009.

Bibliography

———. "Raymundus Martini and the Pugio Fidei: A Survey of the Life and Works of a Medieval Controversialist." MA thesis, University College London, 1991.

———. "Worship and Witness to the Deity of Yeshua." In *Symposium II: The Deity of Messiah and the Mystery of God, April 12–14, 2010*, edited by Borough Park Symposium, 123–57. Borough Park Papers. Clarksville, MD: Messianic Jewish, 2012.

Harvey, Warren Zev. "A Third Approach to Maimonides' Cosmogony-Prophetology Puzzle." *HTR* 74 (1981) 287–301.

Hasker, William. "Incarnation: The Avatar Model." In *Oxford Studies in Philosophy of Religion*, edited by Jonathan L. Kvanvig, 8:118–41. Oxford: Oxford University Press, 2017.

Hasselhoff, Görge K., and Alexander Fidora, eds. *Ramon Martí's "Pugio Fidei": Studies and Texts*. Exemplaria Scholastica. Santa Coloma de Queralt, Spain: Obrador Edendum, 2017.

Heiser, Michael S. "Image of God." In *The Lexham Bible Dictionary*, edited by John D. Barry. Bellingham, WA: Lexham, 2016.

Held, Shai. "The Promise and Peril of Jewish Barthianism: The Theology of Michael Wyschogrod." *Modern Judaism* 25 (2005) 316–26.

Helsinki Consultation. "Helsinki Consultation Statement on Jewish and Christian Tradition." Helsinki Consultation, 2014. https://static1.1.sqspcdn.com/static/f/1106451/25126838/1404043387950/NetherlandsFINAL.pdf?token=CG1tQSEbfIP4CSYRFZcNbiKmNQE%3D.

Hendrie, Shifra. "The Kabbalah of Speech." Chabad, 2005. https://www.chabad.org/library/article_cdo/aid/327516/jewish/The-Kabbalah-of-Speech.htm.

Hengel, Martin. *Studies in Early Christology*. Translated by Rollin Kearns. New York: T&T Clark, 2004.

Henry, Carl F. H. *God, Revelation, and Authority*. 6 vols. Wheaton, IL: Crossway, 1999.

Herrera, Robert A. "An Episode in Medieval Aristotelianism: Maimonides and St. Thomas on the Active Intellect." *Thomist* 47 (1983) 317–38.

Herschell, Ridley Haim, ed. *The Voice of Israel*. 2 vols. London: Unwin, 1845.

Hippolytus of Rome. *Philosophumena or the Refutation of All Heresies*. Edited by W. J. Sparrow-Simpson and W. K. Lowther Clarke. 2 vols. London: Macmillan, 1921.

Hirsch, Ammiel, and Reinman Yosef. *One People, Two Worlds: A Reform Rabbi and an Orthodox Rabbi Explore the Issues That Divide Them*. New York: Schocken, 2002.

Holland, Tom. *Dominion: How the Christian Revolution Remade the World*. New York: Basic Books, 2021.

Horwitz, Daniel M. *A Kabbalah and Jewish Mysticism Reader*. JPS Anthologies of Jewish Thought. Philadelphia: Jewish Publication Society, 2016.

Huffman, Carl. "Pythagoreanism." *Stanford Encyclopedia of Philosophy* Archives, Mar. 29, 2006; last revised July 31, 2019. Edited by Edward N. Zalta. https://plato.stanford.edu/archives/fall2019/entries/pythagoreanism/.

Hurst, L. D. *The Epistle to the Hebrews: Its Background of Thought*. Society for New Testament Studies Monograph Series 65. Cambridge: Cambridge University Press, 1990.

Hurtado, Larry W. "Christology." In *Dictionary of the Later New Testament & Its Developments*, edited by Ralph P. Martin and Peter H. Davids, 170–84. Downers Grove, IL: IVP Academic, 1997.

Bibliography

———. *The Earliest Christian Artifacts: Manuscripts and Christian Origins*. Grand Rapids: Eerdmans, 2006.

———. *Lord Jesus Christ: Devotion to Jesus in Earliest Christianity*. Grand Rapids: Eerdmans, 2003.

———. *One God, One Lord: Early Christian Devotion and Ancient Jewish Monotheism*. 3rd ed. T&T Clark Cornerstones. New York: Bloomsbury T&T Clark, 2015.

Huss, Boaz. *The Zohar: Reception and Impact*. Translated by Yudith Nave. London: Littman Library of Jewish Civilization, 2016.

Idel, Moshe. *Absorbing Perfections: Kabbalah and Interpretation*. New Haven, CT: Yale University Press, 2002.

———. *Ben: Sonship and Jewish Mysticism*. New York: Continuum, 2008.

———. "Kabbalah." In *Encyclopedia Judaica*, edited by Fred Skolnik and Michael Berenbaum, 11:681–92. Detroit: Macmillan Reference and Keter, 2007.

———. *Kabbalah: New Perspectives*. New Haven, CT: Yale University Press, 1988.

———. *Middot: On the Emergence of Kabbalistic Theosophies*. Brooklyn, NY: KTAV, 2021.

———. "Mysticism." In *20th Century Jewish Religious Thought*, edited by Arthur A. Cohen and Paul Mendes-Flohr, 643–55. Philadelphia: Jewish Publication Society, 2009.

———. *Primeval Evil in Kabbalah: Totality, Perfection, Perfectibility*. Brooklyn, NY: KTAV, 2020.

Interdicasterial Commission. *Catechism of the Catholic Church*. Translated by the US Conference of Catholic Bishops. 2nd ed. Washington, DC: United States Catholic Conference, 2000.

Irenaeus of Lyons. *Against the Heresies*. Edited by John J. Dillon. Translated by Dominic J. Unger. 4 vols. Ancient Christian Writers 55, 64–65, 72. Mahwah, NJ: Newman, 1992–2024.

Ivry, Alfred L. "The *Guide* and Maimonides' Philosophical Sources." In *The Cambridge Companion to Maimonides*, edited by Kenneth Seeskin, locs. 1656–2270. Cambridge Companions to Philosophy. Cambridge: Cambridge University Press, 2005. Kindle.

———. "Maimonides and Neoplatonism: Challenge and Response." In *Neoplatonism and Jewish Thought*, edited by Lenn Evan Goodman, 137–56. Studies in Neoplatonism 7. Albany: State University of New York Press, 1992.

———. "Maimonides on Creation." In *Creation and the End of Days: Judaism and Scientific Cosmology*, edited by David Novak and Norbert M. Samuelson, 185–213. Studies in Judaism. New York: University Press of America, 1986.

Jacobs, Joseph. "Superstition." In *The Jewish Encyclopedia*, edited by Isidore Singer, 11:597–601. New York: Funk & Wagnalls, 1901–6.

Jacobs, Joseph, and J. D. Eisenstein. "Golem." In *The Jewish Encyclopedia*, edited by Isidore Singer, 6:37. New York: Funk & Wagnalls, 1901–6.

Jacobs, Louis. "God." In *20th Century Jewish Religious Thought*, edited by Arthur A. Cohen and Paul Mendes-Flohr, 291–98. Philadelphia: Jewish Publication Society, 2009.

Janicki, Toby, et al. *Love and the Messianic Age: Study Guide and Commentary*. 4th ed. Messianic Luminaries. Marshfield, MO: Vine of David, 2012.

Jews for Jesus. "Statement of Faith." Jews for Jesus, n.d. https://jewsforjesus.org/about/statement-of-faith/.

Bibliography

J. J. Kimche. "J. J. Kimche: Assessing the Gush Tanakh Method (Yeshivat Har Etzion) An Overview and Two Critiques." Interview by Judaism Demystified. YouTube, Feb. 22, 2024. https://www.youtube.com/watch?v=PvQrg4kQQTw.

Jocz, Jakób. "The Invisibility of God and the Incarnation." *Canadian Journal of Theology* 4 (1958) 179–86.

———. *The Jewish People and Jesus Christ: A Study in the Controversy Between Church and Synagogue*. Wycliffe College, 2019. Digital ed. https://www.wycliffecollege.ca/sites/default/files/The-Jewish-People-Jesus-Christ.pdf.

Jones, Richard, and Jerome Gellman. "Mysticism." *Stanford Encyclopedia of Philosophy*, Nov. 11, 2022; last revised June 29, 2022. Edited by Edward N. Zalta and Uri Nodelman. https://plato.stanford.edu/archives/fall2022/entries/mysticism/.

Juncker, Gunther H. "Christ as Angel: The Reclamation of a Primitive Title." *TJ* 15 (1994) 220–50.

———. "Jesus and the Angel of the Lord: An Old Testament Paradigm for New Testament Christology." PhD diss., Trinity Evangelical Divinity School, 2001.

Junik, Dovid. "Can God Become Man? A Study on Corporealism in Biblical and Rabbinic Literature." Jewish Belief Reimagined, Oct. 29, 2019. https://jewishbelief.com/can-god-become-man-a-study-on-corporealism-in-biblical-and-rabbinic-literature/.

Juster, Daniel C. "Approaching God: The Essence of Messianic Jewish Theology." In *Messianic Jewish Orthodoxy: The Essence of Our Faith, History and Best Practices*, edited by Jeffrey Seif, 59–103. Clarksville, MD: Lederer, 2019.

———. "Response: The Christological Dogma of Nicaea—Greek or Jewish?" *Mishkan* (1984) 51–52.

Kamesar, Adam, ed. *The Cambridge Companion to Philo*. Cambridge Companions to Philosophy. Cambridge: Cambridge University Press, 2009.

Kärkkäinen, Veli-Matti. *Doing the Work of Comparative Theology*. Grand Rapids: Eerdmans, 2020.

Kasher, Hannah. "Biblical Miracles and the Universality of Natural Laws Maimonides' Three Methods of Harmonization." *Journal of Jewish Thought and Philosophy* 8 (1999) 25–52.

Kaufman, Stephen A. *Targum Neofiti to the Pentateuch*. Comprehensive Aramaic Lexicon. Cincinnati: Hebrew Union College Press, 2005.

———, ed. *Targum Onqelos to the Pentateuch*. Comprehensive Aramaic Lexicon. Cincinnati: Hebrew Union College Press, 2005.

Kavka, Martin. "The Politics of Negative Theology." In *Negative Theology as Jewish Modernity*, edited by Michael Fagenblat, 530–61. New Jewish Philosophy and Thought. Bloomington: Indiana University Press, 2017.

Keener, Craig S. *Christobiography: Memory, History, and the Reliability of the Gospels*. Grand Rapids: Eerdmans, 2019.

———. *The Gospel of Matthew: A Socio-Rhetorical Commentary*. Rev. ed. Grand Rapids: Eerdmans, 2009.

Kellner, Menachem. *Maimonides' Confrontation with Mysticism*. London: Littman Library of Jewish Civilization, 2006.

———. *Must a Jew Believe Anything?* 2nd ed. Littman Library of Jewish Civilization. Liverpool: Littman Library of Jewish Civilization in association with Liverpool University Press, 2006.

Bibliography

———. "On the Status of the Astronomy and Physics in Maimonides' *Mishneh Torah* and *Guide of the Perplexed*: A Chapter in the History of Science." *British Journal for the History of Science* 24 (1991) 453–63.

———. *Science in the Bet Midrash: Studies in Maimonides*. Emunot: Jewish Philosophy and Kabbalah. Brighton, MA: Academic Studies, 2009.

———. *We Are Not Alone: A Maimonidean Theology of the Other*. Emunot: Jewish Philosophy and Kabbalah. Boston: Academic Studies, 2021.

Kelly, J. N. D. *Early Christian Creeds*. 3rd ed. New York: Continuum, 2006.

Kenny, Anthony. *An Illustrated Brief History of Western Philosophy*. 3rd ed. Hoboken, NJ: Wiley-Blackwell, 2018.

Kinbar, Carl. "'I Will Dwell Among Them': The Shekhinah and the People of God in Midrash." *Kesher*, Jan. 19, 2020. https://www.kesherjournal.com/article/i-will-dwell-among-them-the-shekhinah-and-the-people-of-god-in-midrash/.

Kinzer, Mark S. "Finding Our Way Through Nicaea: The Deity of Yeshua, Bilateral Ecclesiology, and Redemptive Encounter with the Living God." *Kesher*, July 3, 2010. https://www.kesherjournal.com/article/finding-our-way-through-nicaea-the-deity-of-yeshua-bilateral-ecclesiology-and-redemptive-encounter-with-the-living-god/.

———. "Is Jesus of Nazareth Still King of the Jews? New Testament Christology and the Jewish People." *Kesher*, Aug. 11, 2021. https://www.kesherjournal.com/article/is-jesus-of-nazareth-still-king-of-the-jews-new-testament-christology-and-the-jewish-people/.

———. "Judaism and the Divine-Human Jesus." In *Stones the Builders Rejected: The Jewish Jesus, His Jewish Disciples, and the Culmination of History*, edited by Jennifer M. Rosner, 40–48. Eugene, OR: Cascade, 2024.

———. "The Significance of the Deity of Yeshua." In *Symposium II: The Deity of Messiah and the Mystery of God, April 12–14, 2010*, edited by Borough Park Symposium, 23–30. Borough Park Papers. Clarksville, MD: Messianic Jewish, 2012.

———. *Stones the Builders Rejected: The Jewish Jesus, His Jewish Disciples, and the Culmination of History*. Edited by Jennifer M. Rosner. Eugene, OR: Cascade, 2024.

Klayman, Elliot. "Jewish History and the Deity of Yeshua." In *Symposium II: The Deity of Messiah and the Mystery of God, April 12–14, 2010*, edited by Borough Park Symposium, 41–75. Borough Park Papers. Clarksville, MD: Messianic Jewish, 2012.

Klein-Braslavy, Sara. "Maimonides' Exoteric and Esoteric Biblical Interpretations in the *Guide of the Perplexed*." In *Study and Knowledge in Jewish Thought*, edited by Howard Kreisel, 137–64. Tel Aviv: Ben-Gurion University of the Negev Press, 2006.

Koellner, Peter. "The Continuum Hypothesis." *Stanford Encyclopedia of Philosophy Archives*, May 22, 2013. Edited by Edward N. Zalta. https://plato.stanford.edu/archives/spr2019/entries/continuum-hypothesis/.

Kohler, Kaufmann. "Cosmogony." In *The Jewish Encyclopedia*, edited by Isidore Singer, 4:280–83. New York: Funk & Wagnalls, 1901–6.

Köstenberger, Andreas J., and Michael J. Kruger. *The Heresy of Orthodoxy: How Contemporary Culture's Fascination with Diversity Has Reshaped Our Understanding of Early Christianity*. Wheaton, IL: Crossway, 2010.

Bibliography

Kraemer, Joel L. "Farabi, Abu Nasr Muhammad Al-." In *Encyclopaedia Judaica*, edited by Fred Skolnik and Michael Berenbaum, 6:709–11. Detroit: Macmillan Reference and Keter, 2007.

———. "The Islamic Context of Medieval Jewish Philosophy." In *The Cambridge Companion to Medieval Jewish Philosophy*, edited by Daniel H. Frank and Oliver Leaman, ch. 3. Cambridge Companions to Philosophy. New York: Cambridge University Press, 2003. Kindle.

Kreisel, Howard T. "*Imitatio Dei* in Maimonides' *Guide of the Perplexed*." *AJS Review* 19 (1994) 169–211.

Kroeber, A. L. "Stimulus Diffusion." *American Anthropologist* 42 (1940) 1–20.

Kuhn, Thomas S. *The Structure of Scientific Revolutions*. 50th anniv. ed. Chicago: University of Chicago Press, 2012.

Laansma, Jon C. "Mysticism." In *Dictionary of New Testament Background*, edited by Craig A. Evans and Stanley E. Porter Jr., 725–37. IVP Bible Dictionary. Downers Grove, IL: IVP Academic, 2000.

Langermann, Y. Tzvi. "Maimonides and Miracles: The Growth of a (Dis)Belief: Jewish History." *Jewish History* 18 (2004) 147–72.

Lanier, Gregory R. *Corpus Christologicum: Texts and Translations for the Study of Jewish Messianism and Early Christology*. Peabody, MA: Hendrickson Academic, 2021.

Lapide, Pinchas. *The Resurrection of Jesus: A Jewish Perspective*. Translated by Wilhelm C. Linss. Eugene, OR: Wipf and Stock, 2002.

Lasker, Daniel J. *Jewish Philosophical Polemics Against Christianity in the Middle Ages*. Portland, OR: Littman Library of Jewish Civilization, 2007.

Lebens, Samuel. "Creation and Modality: A Response to Ryan Mullins." *Philosophia Christi* 25 (2023) 45–59.

———. *The Principles of Judaism*. Oxford Studies in Analytic Theology. Oxford: Oxford University Press, 2020.

Lemche, Niels Peter. "How Does One Date an Expression of Mental History? The Old Testament and Hellenism." In *Did Moses Speak Attic? Jewish Historiography and Scripture in the Hellenistic Period*, edited by Lester L. Grabbe, 220–24. European Seminar in Historical Methodology. LHBOTS 317. Sheffield, UK: Sheffield Academic, 2001.

Lennox, John C. *Seven Days That Divide the World: The Beginning According to Genesis and Science*. Grand Rapids: Zondervan, 2011.

Levertoff, Paul Philip. *Love and the Messianic Age*. 2nd ed. Marshfield, MO: Vine of David, 2009.

Levine, Amy-Jill. "Bearing False Witness: Common Errors Made About Early Judaism." In *The Jewish Annotated New Testament*, edited by Amy-Jill Levine and Marc Zvi Brettler, 759–63. 2nd ed. New York: Oxford University Press, 2017.

Levine, Amy-Jill, and Marc Zvi Brettler, eds. *The Jewish Annotated New Testament*. 2nd ed. Oxford: Oxford University Press, 2017.

Levine, Lee I. "Jewish Art: Invention and Innovation in Late Antiquity." In *The Eerdmans Encyclopedia of Early Christian Art and Archaeology*, edited by Paul Corby Finney, 1:749–50. Grand Rapids: Eerdmans, 2017.

———. *The Ancient Synagogue: The First Thousand Years*. 2nd ed. New Haven, CT: Yale University Press, 2005.

Licona, Michael R. *The Resurrection of Jesus: A New Historiographical Approach*. Downers Grove, IL: IVP Academic, 2010.

Liderbach, Daniel. *Christ in the Early Christian Hymns*. New York: Paulist, 1998.

Bibliography

Lilla, Salvatore. "Neoplatonism." In *Encyclopedia of Ancient Christianity*, edited by Angelo Di Berardino et al., 2:890–905. Downers Grove, IL: IVP Academic, 2014.

———. "Plotinus." In *Encyclopedia of Ancient Christianity*, edited by Angelo Di Berardino et al., 3:230–31. Downers Grove, IL: IVP Academic, 2014.

Löhr, Winrich Alfried. "The Theft of the Greeks: Christian Self Definition in the Age of the Schools." *RHE* 95 (2000) 403–26.

Longman, Tremper, III, and David E. Garland, eds. *Matthew-Mark*. Rev. ed. Expositor's Bible Commentary 9. Grand Rapids: Zondervan, 2010.

López, René A. "Identifying the 'Angel of the Lord' in the Book of Judges: A Model for Reconsidering the Referent in Other Old Testament Loci." *BBR* 20 (2010) 1–18.

Lorberbaum, Yair. *In God's Image: Myth, Theology, and Law in Classical Judaism*. New York: Cambridge University Press, 2014.

Lowenthal, David. "Fabricating Heritage." *History and Memory* 10 (1998) 5–24.

Lucretius, Epictetus, Marcus Aurelius, and Plotinus. *The Way Things Are; The Discourses Of; The Meditations Of; The Six Enneads*. Edited by Mortimer J. Adler et al. Translated by Stephen MacKenna and B. S. Page. 2nd ed. Vol. 11 of *Great Books of the Western World*. Chicago: Encyclopedia Britannica, 1990.

Lugo, Luis, et al. *A Portrait of Jewish Americans: Findings from a Pew Research Center Survey of U.S. Jews*. Washington, DC: Pew Research, 2013. https://www.pewresearch.org/wp-content/uploads/sites/20/2013/10/jewish-american-full-report-for-web.pdf.

Macleod, Donald. *The Person of Christ*. Edited by Gerald Bray. Contours of Christian Theology. Downers Grove, IL: InterVarsity, 1998.

Magid, Shaul. *From Metaphysics to Midrash: Myth, History, and the Interpretation of Scripture in Lurianic Kabbala*. Biblical Literature. Bloomington: Indiana University Press, 2008.

———. *Hasidism Incarnate: Hasidism, Christianity, and the Construction of Modern Judaism*. Encountering Traditions. Stanford, CA: Stanford University Press, 2014.

———. *Piety and Rebellion: Essays in Hasidism*. New Perspectives in Post-Rabbinic Judaism. Boston: Academic Studies, 2019.

Maimonides, Moses. *The Eight Chapters of Maimonides on Ethics (Shemonah Perakim): A Psychological and Ethical Treatise*. Edited and translated by Joseph I. Gorfinkle. Columbia University Oriental Studies 7. New York: Columbia University Press, 1912.

———. *The Guide of the Perplexed*. Translated by Shlomo Pines. 2 vols. Chicago: University of Chicago Press, 1963. Kindle.

———. *The Guide to the Perplexed: A New Translation*. Translated by Lenn E. Goodman and Phillip I. Lieberman. Stanford, CA: Stanford University Press, 2024.

———. "Letter on Astrology." In *Medieval Political Philosophy: A Sourcebook*, edited by Ralph Lerner and Muhsin Mahdi, translated by Ralph Lerner, 227–36. Ithaca, NY: Cornell University Press, 1972.

———. *Maimonides—Essential Teachings on Jewish Faith & Ethics: The Book of Knowledge & the Thirteen Principles of Faith—Annotated & Explained*. Edited by Marc D. Angel. Woodstock, VT: SkyLight Paths, 2011.

———. *A Maimonides Reader*. Edited by Isadore Twersky. Library of Jewish Studies. New York: Behrman, 1972. Kindle.

Manekin, Charles H. "Belief, Certainty, and Divine Attributes in *The Guide of the Perplexed*." In *Maimonidean Studies 1*, edited by Arthur Hyman, 117–41. New York: Scharf Publication Trust of Yeshiva University Press, 1990.

Bibliography

Mare, W. Harold. "The New Testament Concept Regarding the Regions of Heaven with Emphasis on 2 Corinthians 12:1–4." *Grace Journal* 11 (1970) 1–10.

Margulies, Ezra A. "What Do We Mean by 'Orthodox' Judaism?" *Modern Judaism—A Journal of Jewish Ideas and Experience* 42 (2022) 1–26.

Markos, Louis. *From Plato to Christ: How Platonic Thought Shaped the Christian Faith.* Downers Grove, IL: IVP Academic, 2021.

Markschies, Christoph. *Gnosis: An Introduction.* New York: T&T Clark, 2003.

Mark the Monk. *Counsels on the Spiritual Life.* Edited by John Behr. Translated by Tim Vivian and Augustine Casiday. 2 vols. Popular Patristics Series. Crestwood, NY: St. Vladimir's Seminary Press, 2009.

Marmorstein, Arthur. *The Old Rabbinic Doctrine of God.* 2 vols. London: Oxford University Press, 1927–37.

Mason, Steve. "Jews, Judaeans, Judaizing, Judaism: Problems of Categorization in Ancient History." *JSJ* 38 (2007) 457–512.

Matt, Daniel C. "Ayin: The Concept of Nothingness in Jewish Mysticism." *Tikkun* 3 (1988) 43–47.

———, ed. *Zohar: Annotated & Explained.* Woodstock, VT: Jewish Lights & SkyLight Paths, 2012.

Matz, Robert J., and A. Chadwick Thornhill, eds. *Divine Impassibility: Four Views of God's Emotions and Suffering.* Downers Grove, IL: IVP Academic, 2019.

McCaul, Alexander. *Lectures on the Prophecies, Proving the Divine Origin of Christianity.* London: John W. Parker, 1846.

———. *The Old Paths; or, A Comparison of the Principles and Doctrines of Modern Judaism with the Religion of Moses and the Prophets.* London: London Society's Office, 1837.

McClymond, Michael J. *The Devil's Redemption: A New History and Interpretation of Christian Universalism.* 2 vols. Grand Rapids: Baker Academic, 2018.

McCormack, Bruce L. "The One, the Three and the Many: In Memory of Colin Gunton." *Cultural Encounters* 1 (2005) 7–17.

McCullagh, C. Behan. *Justifying Historical Descriptions.* Cambridge Studies in Philosophy. Cambridge: Cambridge University Press, 1984.

McDowell, Sean. *The Fate of the Apostles: Examining the Martyrdom Accounts of the Closest Followers of Jesus.* New York: Routledge, 2016.

McFarland, Ian A. *The Word Made Flesh: A Theology of the Incarnation.* Louisville: Westminster John Knox, 2019.

McKirahan, Richard. "Philolaus on Number." In *On Pythagoreanism*, edited by Gabriele Cornelli et al., 179–201. Studia Praesocratica 5. Berlin: De Gruyter, 2013.

Melito of Sardis. *On Pascha: With the Fragments of Melito and Other Material Related to the Quartodecimans.* Edited by John Behr. 2nd ed. Popular Patristics 55. Yonkers, NY: St. Vladimir's Seminary Press, 2016.

Messianic Jewish Alliance of America. "Statement of Faith." MJAA, Apr. 25, 2023. https://mjaa.org/statement-of-faith-2/.

Messianic Jewish Theological Institute. "Core Values." Messianic Jewish Theological Institute, n.d. https://www.mjti.org/about/core-values/.

Metzger, Bruce M. *A Textual Commentary on the Greek New Testament.* 4th ed. New York: United Bible Societies, 1994.

Michel, Jen Pollock, and Russ Ramsey. *Surprised by Paradox: The Promise of "And" in an Either-Or World.* Westmont, IL: IVP, 2019.

Bibliography

Michelson, Jay. "Bible Codes: A Lie That Won't Die." *Forward*, May 31, 2012. https://forward.com/culture/157033/bible-codes-a-lie-that-won-t-die/.

Midgley, Ben, et al. *Be Mature in Understanding: A Handbook of Theology for Jewish Believers in Messiah*. Eugene, OR: Wipf & Stock, 2021.

Miller, Alexander. "Realism." *Stanford Encyclopedia of Philosophy* Archives, July 8, 2002; last revised Dec. 13, 2019. Edited by Edward N. Zalta and Uri Nodelman. https://plato.stanford.edu/archives/sum2024/entries/realism/.

Mohler, Albert. "The Way the World Thinks: Meeting the Natural Mind in the Mirror and in the Marketplace." Desiring God, Oct. 2, 2010. https://www.desiringgod.org/messages/the-way-the-world-thinks-meeting-the-natural-mind-in-the-mirror-and-in-the-marketplace.

Moo, Douglas J. *The Letters to the Colossians and to Philemon*. PNTC. Grand Rapids: Eerdmans, 2008.

Moore, A. W. *The Infinite*. 3rd ed. New York: Routledge, 2018.

Moore, George Foot. "Intermediaries in Jewish Theology: Memra, Shekinah, Metatron." *HTR* 15 (1922) 41–85.

Moore, Kathleen. "Ultra-Orthodox Rabbis Decide to Sue New York over Having to Teach in English, Science." *Times Union*, Sept. 14, 2023. https://www.timesunion.com/education/article/ultra-orthodox-rabbis-say-sue-n-y-teaching-18364224.php.

Moreland, J. P. *Scaling the Secular City: A Defense of Christianity*. Grand Rapids: Baker Academic, 1987.

———. *Scientism and Secularism: Learning to Respond to a Dangerous Ideology*. Wheaton, IL: Crossway, 2018.

Moreland, J. P., and William Lane Craig. *Philosophical Foundations for a Christian Worldview*. 2nd ed. Downers Grove, IL: IVP Academic, 2017.

Morris, Paul. "Creeds and Theology: Expressing the Jewish Context." *Mishkan* 72 (2014) 36–43.

Morris, Thomas V. *The Logic of God Incarnate*. Repr., Eugene, OR: Wipf and Stock, 2001.

Moule, Charles. "Three Points of Conflict in the Christological Debate." In *Incarnation and Myth: The Debate Continued*, edited by Michael D. Goulder, 131–41. Grand Rapids: Eerdmans, 1979.

Mullins, R. T. *The End of the Timeless God*. Oxford Studies in Analytic Theology. New York: Oxford University Press, 2016.

———. "Theism Does Not Give Birth to Idealism." *Philosophia Christi* 25 (2023) 27–44.

Nagel, Thomas. "What Is It Like to Be a Bat?" *Philosophical Review* 83 (1974) 435–50.

Nash, Ronald H. "The Notion of Mediator in Alexandrian Judaism and the Epistle to the Hebrews." *WTJ* 40 (1977) 89–115.

Navon, Chaim. "Negative Attributes." Yeshivat Har Etzion, 2015. Translated by Kaeren Fish. https://etzion.org.il/en/philosophy/great-thinkers/rambam/negative-attributes.

Nerel, Gershon. "Christological Observations Within Yeshua Judaism." *Mishkan* 59 (2009) 51–62.

———. "Creeds Among Jewish Believers in Yeshua Between the World Wars." *Mishkan* 34 (2001) 63–81.

NET Bible First Edition Notes, The. Spokane, WA: Biblical Studies, 2006.

Bibliography

Neusner, Jacob, ed. *The Babylonian Talmud: A Translation and Commentary*. Translated by Jacob Neusner et al. 22 vols. Peabody, MA: Hendrickson, 2011.

———. *Introduction to American Judaism: What the Books Say, What the People Do*. Eugene, OR: Wipf & Stock, 2004.

———. *The Mishnah: A New Translation*. New Haven, CT: Yale University Press, 1988.

———. *Torah Through the Ages: A Short History of Judaism*. Eugene, OR: Wipf & Stock, 2004.

Neusner, Jacob, and Bruce D. Chilton. *God in the World*. Eugene, OR: Wipf & Stock, 2004.

Nishma Research. *The Nishma Research 2023 Jewish Community Profile*. West Hartford, CT: Nishma Research West Hartford, 2023.

Novak, David. *Athens and Jerusalem: God, Humans, and Nature*. Toronto: University of Toronto, 2019.

———. "Can We Be Maimonideans Today?" In *Maimonides and His Heritage*, edited by Idit Dobbs-Weinstein et al, 193–210. SUNY Series in Jewish Philosophy. Albany, NY: SUNY Press, 2009.

———. "Maimonides's View of Christianity." In *Jewish-Christian Dialogue: A Jewish Justification*, edited by David Novak, 57–72. Oxford: Oxford University Press, 1992.

———. "The Mind of Maimonides." *First Things* 90 (1999) 27–33.

———. "Self-Contraction of the Godhead in Kabbalistic Theology." In *Neoplatonism and Jewish Thought*, edited by Lenn E. Goodman, 297–316. Albany: State University of New York Press, 1992.

Oegema, Gerbern S. "Creation." In *The Eerdmans Dictionary of Early Judaism*, edited by John J. Collins and Daniel C. Harlow, 496–500. Grand Rapids: Eerdmans, 2010.

Oliphint, K. Scott. *The Majesty of Mystery: Celebrating the Glory of an Incomprehensible God*. Bellingham, WA: Lexham, 2016.

Olitzky, Kerry M., and Ronald H. Isaacs. *I Believe: The Thirteen Principles of Faith: A Confirmation Textbook*. Hoboken, NJ: KTAV, 1999.

O'Meara, Dominic. "The Hierarchical Ordering of Reality in Plotinus." In *The Cambridge Companion to Plotinus*, edited by Lloyd P. Gerson, 66–81. Cambridge Companions to Philosophy. Reprint with corrections. New York: Cambridge University Press, 1999.

One for Israel. "Statement of Faith." One for Israel, n.d. https://www.oneforisrael.org/statement-of-faith/.

Orfali, Moisés. "Anthropomorphism in the Christian Reproach of the Jews in Spain (12th–15th Cent)." *Immanuel* 19 (1984) 60–73.

Origen. *Origenis Hexaplorum Quae Supersunt Sive, Veterum Interpretum Graecorum in Totum Vetus Testamentum Fragmenta*. Edited by Frederick Field. 2 vols. Oxford: Clarendon, 1875.

———. *The Philocalia of Origen: A Compilation of Selected Passages from Origen's Works Made by St. Gregory of Nazianzus and St. Basil of Caesarea*. Translated by George Lewis. Edinburgh: T&T Clark, 1911.

Orlov, Andrei A. *The Glory of the Invisible God: Two Powers in Heaven Traditions and Early Christology*. Jewish and Christian Texts in Contexts and Related Studies 31. London: T&T Clark, 2019.

———. "Metatron." In *The Eerdmans Dictionary of Early Judaism*, edited by John J. Collins and Daniel C. Harlow, 942–43. Grand Rapids: Eerdmans, 2010.

Bibliography

Ortlund, Gavin. *Theological Retrieval for Evangelicals: Why We Need Our Past to Have a Future*. Wheaton, IL: Crossway, 2019.

Oxlee, John. *The Christian Doctrines of the Trinity, and Incarnation Considered and Maintained on the Principles of Judaism*. 3 vols. London: Wertheimer & Co., 1815–50.

Pascal, Blaise. "Memorial." Christian Classics Ethereal Library, 1654. https://www.ccel.org/ccel/pascal/memorial.i.html.

Patterson, Charles H. "The Philosophy of the Old Testament." *Journal of the National Association of Biblical Instructors* 2 (1934) 60–66.

Pauli, Christian William Henry. *The Great Mystery; or, How Can Three Be One?* London: Macintosh, 1863.

Pawl, Timothy. *In Defense of Conciliar Christology: A Philosophical Essay*. Oxford Studies in Analytic Theology. Oxford: Oxford University Press, 2016.

Pearcey, Nancy, and Charles B. Thaxton. *The Soul of Science: Christian Faith and Natural Philosophy*. Wheaton, IL: Crossway, 1994.

Pearson, Brook W. R. "Hermeticism." In *Dictionary of New Testament Background*, edited by Craig A. Evans and Stanley E. Porter Jr., 482–85. IVP Bible Dictionary. Downers Grove, IL: IVP Academic, 2000.

Pessin, Sarah. "The Influence of Islamic Thought on Maimonides." *Stanford Encyclopedia of Philosophy* Archives, June 30, 2005; last revised May 28, 2014. Edited by Edward N. Zalta. https://plato.stanford.edu/archives/spr2016/entries/maimonides-islamic/.

Peter the Venerable. *Against the Inveterate Obduracy of the Jews*. Translated by Irven Michael Resnick. Fathers of the Church, Medieval Continuation 14. Washington, DC: Catholic University of America Press, 2013.

Philo. *Philo*. Translated by F. H. Colson and G. H. Whitaker. 11 vols. LCL. Cambridge, MA: Harvard University Press, 1929.

Philo of Alexandria. *The Works of Philo: Complete and Unabridged*. Translated by Charles Duke Yonge. Repr., Peabody, MA: Hendrickson, 1995.

Pick, Bernhard. *The Cabala: Its Influence on Judaism and Christianity*. Chicago: Open Court, 1913.

Pines, Shlomo. "Judaism, Jewish Tradition, Jewish Philosophy." In *Encyclopedia Britannica*. Chicago: Encyclopedia Britannica, 2016. Logos Bible Software e-book.

———. "Translator's Introduction: The Philosophic Sources of *The Guide of the Perplexed*." In *The Guide of the Perplexed*, by Moses Maimonides, translated by Shlomo Pines, locs. 1126–2714. Chicago: University of Chicago Press, 1963. Kindle.

Plantinga, Alvin. *Warranted Christian Belief*. New York: Oxford University Press, 2000.

———. *Warrant: The Current Debate*. Gifford Lectures in Natural Theology. New York: Oxford University Press, 1993.

Plato. *The Dialogues of Plato; The Seventh Letter*. Edited by Mortimer J. Adler and Philip W. Goetz. 2nd ed. Vol. 6 of *Great Books of the Western World*. Chicago: Encyclopedia Britannica, 1990.

———. *The Republic*. Edited by T. E. Page et al. Translated by Paul Shorey. 2 vols. LCL. Cambridge, MA: Harvard University Press, 1942.

Postell, Seth. "Messiah as Wisdom: The Delight of God and Men." *Mishkan* 64 (2010) 35–42.

Poythress, Vern S. *The Mystery of the Trinity: A Trinitarian Approach to the Attributes of God*. Phillipsburg, NJ: P&R, 2020.

Bibliography

Price, Randall, with H. Wayne House. *Zondervan Handbook of Biblical Archaeology: A Book by Book Guide to Archaeological Discoveries Related to the Bible.* Grand Rapids: Zondervan, 2017.

Proclus. *The Elements of Theology: A Revised Text with Translation, Introduction, and Commentary.* Edited by E. R. Dodds. 2nd ed. New York: Clarendon, 1992.

Pruss, Alexander R. *Infinity, Causation, and Paradox.* Oxford: Oxford University Press, 2018.

Pseudo-Dionysius. *Pseudo-Dionysius: The Complete Works.* Edited by John Farina. Translated by Colm Luibheid. Mahwah, NJ: Paulist, 1987.

Psillos, Stathis. "Realism and Theory Change in Science." *Stanford Encyclopedia of Philosophy* Archive, May 3, 2018; last revised July 11, 2022. Edited by Edward N. Zalta and Uri Nodelman. https://plato.stanford.edu/archives/fall2022/entries/realism-theory-change/.

Ptolemy, et al. *The Almagest; On the Revolutions of the Heavenly Spheres; Epitome of Copernican Astronomy: IV–V; The Harmonies of the World: V.* Edited by Mortimer J. Adler and Philip W. Goetz. 2nd ed. Vol. 15 of *Great Books of the Western World.* Chicago: Encyclopedia Britannica, 1990.

Pugliese, Marc A. *The One, the Many, and the Trinity: Joseph A. Bracken and the Challenge of Process Metaphysics.* Washington, DC: Catholic University of America Press, 2011.

Quispel, Gilles. "Judaism and Gnosis." In *Gnostica, Judaica, Catholica: Collected Essays of Gilles Quispel*, edited by Johannes van Oort, 539–65. Nag Hammadi and Manichaean Studies 55. Leiden: Brill, 2008.

Rabinowicz, Tzvi, ed. *The Encyclopedia of Hasidism.* Northvale, NJ: Aronson, 1996.

Ramelli, Ilaria. "Gnosis-Gnosticism." In *Encyclopedia of Ancient Christianity*, edited by Angelo Di Berardino et al., translated by Joseph T. Papa et al., 2:140–47. Downers Grove, IL: IVP Academic, 2014.

———. "Pleroma." In *Encyclopedia of Ancient Christianity*, edited by Angelo Di Berardino et al., translated by Joseph T. Papa et al., 3:226–29. Downers Grove, IL: IVP Academic, 2014.

———. "Psychici." In *Encyclopedia of Ancient Christianity*, edited by Angelo Di Berardino et al., translated by Joseph T. Papa et al., 3:347–49. Downers Grove, IL: IVP Academic, 2014.

Rashi. *Pentateuch with Targum Onkelos, Haphtaroth and Prayers for Sabbath and Rashi's Commentary.* Translated by M. Rosenbaum and A. M. Silbermann. London: Shapiro, Vallentine & Co., 1929–34. https://www.sefaria.org/Rashi_on_Leviticus.

Ravitzky, Aviezer. "Maimonides' Esotericism and Educational Philosophy." In *The Cambridge Companion to Maimonides*, edited by Kenneth Seeskin, ch. 11. Cambridge Companions to Philosophy. Cambridge: Cambridge University Press, 2005. Kindle.

Reason, Gabriela. "Competing Trends in Messianic Judaism: The Debate over Evangelicalism." *Kesher*, Jan. 2, 2005. https://www.kesherjournal.com/article/competing-trends-in-messianic-judaism-the-debate-over-evangelicalism/.

Reines, Alvin Jay. "Maimonides' Concept of Miracles." *HUCA* 45 (1974) 243–85.

Reinhartz, Adele. "What's in a Label? 'Jews,' 'Judaism,' and 'Jewish' in the Study of Antiquity." In *Within Judaism? Interpretive Trajectories in Judaism, Christianity, and Islam from the First to the Twenty-First Century*, edited by Karin Zetterholm and Anders Runesson, 35–48. Lanham, MD: Lexington, 2024.

Bibliography

Remes, Pauliina. *Neoplatonism*. Ancient Philosophies. Stocksfield, UK: Routledge, 2008.

Rist, John. "Plotinus and Christian Philosophy." In *The Cambridge Companion to Plotinus*, edited by Lloyd P. Gerson, 386–413. Cambridge Companions to Philosophy. Cambridge: Cambridge University Press, 2005.

Robinson, Rich. "The Jewish Nature of the Doctrine of the Trinity." Academia, 2014. https://www.academia.edu/6983399/The_Jewish_Nature_of_the_Doctrine_of_the_Trinity.

Rogers, Katherin A. "An Anselmian Defense of the Incarnation." In *Debating Christian Theism*, by J. P. Moreland et al., 393–403. Oxford: Oxford University Press, 2013.

Ross, Tamar. "The Doctrine of *Tzimtzum Shelo Kepshuto* and Its Power." Torah, 2014. https://www.thetorah.com/article/the-doctrine-of-tzimtzum-shelo-kepshuto-and-its-power.

———. "Traditional Concepts of God and Kabbalistic Interpretation: An Overview." Torah, 2014. https://www.thetorah.com/article/traditional-concepts-of-god-and-kabbalistic-interpretation-an-overview.

Rowland, Christopher. "Apocalypticism." In *The Eerdmans Dictionary of Early Judaism*, edited by John J. Collins and Daniel C. Harlow, 345–48. Grand Rapids: Eerdmans, 2010.

Ruderman, David B. *Missionaries, Converts, and Rabbis: The Evangelical Alexander McCaul and Jewish-Christian Debate in the Nineteenth Century*. Jewish Culture and Contexts. Philadelphia: University of Pennsylvania Press, 2020.

Rudolph, David. "Messianic Judaism in Antiquity and in the Modern Era." In *Introduction to Messianic Judaism: Its Ecclesial Context and Biblical Foundations*, edited by David Rudolph and Joel Willitts, 21–36. Grand Rapids: Zondervan, 2013.

Rudolph, David, and Joel Willitts, eds. *Introduction to Messianic Judaism: Its Ecclesial Context and Biblical Foundations*. Grand Rapids: Zondervan, 2013.

Runia, David T. "Philo and the Early Christian Fathers." In *The Cambridge Companion to Philo*, edited by Adam Kamesar, 210–30. Cambridge Companions to Philosophy. Cambridge: Cambridge University Press, 2009.

Rydelnik, Michael, and Edwin Blum, eds. *The Moody Handbook of Messianic Prophecy: Studies and Expositions of the Messiah in the Old Testament*. Chicago: Moody, 2019.

Rynhold, Daniel. *An Introduction to Medieval Jewish Philosophy*. International Library of Historical Studies 57. New York: Tauris, 2009.

Saadia Gaon. *The Book of Beliefs and Opinions*. Translated by Samuel Rosenblatt. Yale Judaica Series. New Haven, CT: Yale University Press, 1989.

Sadik, Shalom. "When Maimonideans and Kabbalists Convert to Christianity." *JSQ* 24 (2017) 145–67.

Salmon, George. "Hebdomas." In *A Dictionary of Christian Biography, Literature, Sects and Doctrines*, edited by William Smith and Henry Wace, 2:849–51. London: Murray, 1877–87.

Samuelson, Norbert M. "The Challenges of the Modern Sciences for Jewish Faith." In *Norbert M. Samuelson: Reasoned Faith*, edited by Hava Tirosh-Samuelson and Aaron W. Hughes, 81–95. Library of Contemporary Jewish Philosophers. Leiden: Brill, 2015.

Bibliography

———. *Jewish Faith and Modern Science: On the Death and Rebirth of Jewish Philosophy.* Lanham, MD: Rowman & Littlefield, 2009.

———. "Maimonides' Doctrine of Creation." *HTR* 84 (1991) 249-71.

Sanders, Fred, and Klaus Issler. *Jesus in Trinitarian Perspective: An Introductory Christology.* Nashville: B&H, 2007.

Sanders, Fred, and Scott R. Swain, eds. *Retrieving Eternal Generation.* Grand Rapids: Zondervan, 2017.

Sandmel, Samuel. "Parallelomania." *JBL* 81 (1962) 1-13.

Schäfer, Peter. *Two Gods in Heaven: Jewish Concepts of God in Antiquity.* Translated by Allison Brown. Princeton, NJ: Princeton University Press, 2020.

Schaff, Philip. *The Creeds of Christendom, with a History and Critical Notes.* 3 vols. New York: Harper & Brothers, 1878-90.

Scherman, Nosson. *The Chumash: The Torah: Haftaros and Five Megillos with a Commentary Anthologized from the Rabbinic Writings.* Edited by Hersh Goldwurm et al. 11th ed. Brooklyn, NY: Mesorah, 2013.

Schochet, Jacob Immanuel. "Mystical Concepts in Chasidism." In *Tanya—Likutei Amarim,* a35-116. Brooklyn, NY: Kehot, 2014.

Scholem, Gershom. "Gematria." In *Encyclopaedia Judaica,* edited by Fred Skolnik and Michael Berenbaum, 7:425-27. Detroit: Macmillan Reference and Keter, 2007.

———. "Gilgul." In *Encyclopedia Judaica,* edited by Fred Skolnik and Michael Berenbaum, 7:602-4. Detroit: Macmillan Reference and Keter, 2007.

———. "Kabbalah." In *Encyclopedia Judaica,* edited by Fred Skolnik and Michael Berenbaum, 11:585-677. Detroit: Macmillan Reference and Keter, 2007.

———. *Major Trends in Jewish Mysticism.* 2nd ed. New York: Schocken, 1995.

———. "Merkabah Mysticism." In *Encyclopedia Judaica,* edited by Fred Skolnik and Michael Berenbaum, 14:66-67. Detroit: Macmillan Reference and Keter, 2007.

———. *Origins of the Kabbalah.* Edited by R. J. Zwi Werblowsky. Translated by Allan Arkush. Princeton, NJ: Princeton University Press, 2018. Kindle.

———. "Sefirot." In *Encyclopedia Judaica,* edited by Fred Skolnik and Michael Berenbaum, 18:244. Detroit: Macmillan Reference and Keter, 2007.

———. "Shabbetai Zevi." In *Encyclopedia Judaica,* edited by Fred Skolnik and Michael Berenbaum, 18:340-59. Detroit: Macmillan Reference and Keter, 2007.

———. "Zohar." In *Encyclopedia Judaica,* edited by Fred Skolnik and Michael Berenbaum, 21:647-61. Detroit: Macmillan Reference and Keter, 2007.

Scholem, Gershom, and Moshe Idel. "Isaac Ben Solomon Luria." In *Encyclopedia Judaica,* edited by Fred Skolnik and Michael Berenbaum, 13:262-67. Detroit: Macmillan Reference and Keter, 2007.

Schonfield, Hugh. *The History of Jewish Christianity: From the First to the Twentieth Century.* London: Duckworth, 1936.

Seeskin, Kenneth, ed. *The Cambridge Companion to Maimonides.* Cambridge Companions to Philosophy. Cambridge: Cambridge University Press, 2005.

———. "Maimonides on Creation." In *Jewish Philosophy: Perspectives and Retrospectives,* edited by Raphael Jospe and Dov Schwartz, 185-99. Emunot: Jewish Philosophy and Kabbalah. Boston: Academic Studies, 2012.

———. "No One Can See My Face and Live." In *Negative Theology as Jewish Modernity,* edited by Michael Fagenblat, 83-103. New Jewish Philosophy and Thought. Bloomington: Indiana University Press, 2017.

Segal, Aaron. "His Existence Is Essentiality: Maimonides as Metaphysician." In *Maimonides' "Guide of the Perplexed": A Critical Guide*, edited by Daniel Frank and Aaron Segal, 102–24. Cambridge: Cambridge University Press, 2021.

———. "Immortality: Two Models." In *Jewish Philosophy Past and Present: Contemporary Responses to Classical Sources*, edited by Daniel Frank and Aaron Segal, 151–60. Current Controversies in Philosophy. New York: Routledge, 2017.

Segal, Alan F. "Mysticism." In *The Eerdmans Dictionary of Early Judaism*, edited by John J. Collins and Daniel C. Harlow, 982–86. Grand Rapids: Eerdmans, 2010.

———. *Two Powers in Heaven: Early Rabbinic Reports About Christianity and Gnosticism*. Repr., Waco: Baylor University Press, 2012.

Sela, Shlomo. "Astrology in Medieval Jewish Thought (Twelfth–Fourteenth Centuries)." In *Science in Medieval Jewish Cultures*, edited by Gad Freudenthal, 292–300. New York: Cambridge University Press, 2012.

Seuren, P. A. M. "Aristotle and Linguistics." In *Concise Encyclopedia of Philosophy of Language and Linguistics*, 25–27. Concise Encyclopedias of Language and Linguistics. Oxford: Elsevier Science, 2010.

Shanks, Hershel, ed. *Partings: How Judaism and Christianity Became Two*. Washington, DC: Biblical Archaeology Society, 2013.

Shapira, Itzhak. *Return of the Kosher Pig*. Clarksville, MD: Lederer Messianic, 2013.

Shapiro, David S. "Possible *Deus Homo*?" *Judaism* 32 (1983) 358–65.

Shapiro, Marc B. *Changing the Immutable: How Orthodox Judaism Rewrites Its History*. Oxford: Littman Library of Jewish Civilization, 2015.

———. *Studies in Maimonides and His Interpreters*. Scranton, PA: University of Scranton Press, 2008.

———. *The Limits of Orthodox Theology: Maimonides' Thirteen Principles Reappraised*. Portland, OR: Littman Library of Jewish Civilization, 2004.

Shapiro, Rami, trans. *Tanya, the Masterpiece of Hasidic Wisdom: Selections Annotated & Explained*. Woodstock, VT: Jewish Lights & Skylight Paths, 2014.

Shatz, David. "The Biblical and Rabbinic Background to Medieval Jewish Philosophy." In *The Cambridge Companion to Medieval Jewish Philosophy*, edited by Daniel H. Frank and Oliver Leaman, ch. 2, locs. 487–944. Cambridge Companions to Philosophy. New York: Cambridge University Press, 2003. Kindle.

Shedd, William Greenough Thayer. *Dogmatic Theology*. Edited by Alan W. Gomes. 3rd ed. Phillipsburg, NJ: P&R, 2003.

Shermer, Michael. "Michael Shermer: *The Ben Shapiro Show* Sunday Special Ep. 6." Interview by Ben Shapiro. YouTube, June 17, 2018. https://www.youtube.com/watch?v=ZaxUG3n1KMA.

Shyfrin, Eduard. *From Infinity to Man: The Fundamental Ideas of Kabbalah Within the Framework of Information Theory and Quantum Physics*. N.p.: White Raven, 2019. Kindle.

Sigal, Phillip. "Further Reflections on the 'Begotten' Messiah." *HAR* 7 (1983) 221–33.

Silverman, Howard. Review of *Incarnation: Myth or Fact*, by Oscar Skarsaune. Hashivenu Forum, *Encountering the God of Israel in the Messiah of Israel*, Los Angeles, 2010.

Silverstein, Shraga, trans. *Sifra*. Sefaria, 2014. https://www.sefaria.org/Sifra?tab=contents.

Simon, Maurice, et al., trans. *The Soncino Zohar*. Judaica Classics. Brooklyn, NY: Judaica, 1984. DVD-ROM.

Bibliography

Singer, Tovia. *Let's Get Biblical.* Expanded ed. 2 vols. Forest Hills, NY: Outreach Judaism, 2014.

Skarsaune, Oscar. "The Christological Dogma of Nicaea—Greek or Jewish?" *Mishkan* (1984) 41–50.

———. "The Making of the Creeds." *Mishkan* 34 (2001) 21–37.

———. *Spain 300–1300 C.E.* Vol. 2 of *Jewish Believers in Jesus.* Jerusalem: Caspari Center, 2022.

Skarsaune, Oskar, and Reidar Hvalvik, eds. *The Early Centuries.* Vol. 1 of *Jewish Believers in Jesus.* Peabody, MA: Hendrickson, 2007.

Skeb, Matthias. "'Pharisees' and Early Christian Heresiology." In *The Pharisees*, edited by Joseph Sievers and Amy-Jill Levine, 257–77. Grand Rapids: Eerdmans, 2021.

Slifkin, Natan. "Rashi's Stance on Corporealism: A Response to Rabbi Zucker." *Hakirah: The Flatbush Journal of Jewish Law and Thought* (2010) 45–79.

———. "Was Rashi a Corporealist?" *Hakirah: The Flatbush Journal of Jewish Law and Thought* (2009) 81–105.

Sobel, Jason. *Mysteries of the Messiah: Unveiling Divine Connections from Genesis to Today.* Nashville: W Publishing, 2021.

Solomon, Norman. "Judaism and Natural Science." In *The Encyclopaedia of Judaism*, edited by Jacob Neusner et al., 2:960–75. Leiden: Brill, 2000.

Soloveichik, Meir. "No Friend in Jesus." *First Things* 179 (2008) 29–32.

Sommer, Benjamin D. *The Bodies of God and the World of Ancient Israel.* Cambridge: Cambridge University Press, 2009.

Soulen, R. Kendall. *The God of Israel and Christian Theology.* Minneapolis: Fortress, 1996.

———. "The Standard Canonical Narrative and the Problem of Supersessionism." In *Introduction to Messianic Judaism: Its Ecclesial Context and Biblical Foundations*, edited by David Rudolph and Joel Willitts, 282–91. Grand Rapids: Zondervan, 2013.

Sperling, Harry, et al., eds. *The Zohar: An English Translation.* 2nd ed. Judaica Classics. Brooklyn, NY: Judaica, 1984. DVD-ROM.

Staetsky, L. Daniel. *Haredi Jews Around the World: Population Trends and Estimates.* Institute for Jewish Policy Research, 2022. https://www.jpr.org.uk/reports/haredi-jews-around-world-population-trends-and-estimates.

Stark, Glenn. "Emission and Absorption Processes." *Encyclopedia Britannica*, July 26, 1999; last revised Oct. 21, 2024. https://www.britannica.com/science/light/Emission-and-absorption-processes.

Stark, Rodney. *How the West Won: The Neglected Story of the Triumph of Modernity.* Wilmington, DE: ISI, 2015.

Stein, Ludwig. "Arabic-Jewish Philosophy." In *The Jewish Encyclopedia*, edited by Isidore Singer, 2:45–49. New York: Funk & Wagnalls, 1901–6.

Sterling, Gregory E. "The Theft of Philosophy." In *Studies in Hellenistic Judaism*, edited by David T. Runia et al, 71–85. SPhiloA 27. Atlanta: SBL, 2015.

Stern, Josef, et al., eds. *Maimonides' "Guide of the Perplexed" in Translation: A History from the Thirteenth Century to the Twentieth.* Chicago: University of Chicago Press, 2019.

Stroumsa, Gedaliahu G. "Gnosis." In *20th Century Jewish Religious Thought*, edited by Arthur A. Cohen and Paul Mendes-Flohr, 285–90. Philadelphia: Jewish Publication Society, 2009.

Bibliography

Sutter, James. "Is the James Webb Space Telescope Really 'Breaking' Cosmology?" Space, July 15, 2024. https://www.space.com/is-jwst-breaking-cosmology.

Svigel, Michael J. "Power in Unity, Diversity in Rank: Subordination and the Trinity in the Fathers of the Early Church." ETS conference, San Antonio, Nov. 18, 2004. https://www.retrochristianity.org/wp-content/uploads/2016/06/Power-in-Unity-Diversity-in-Rank-Paper-ETS-National-Version-2.pdf.

Sweeney, Marvin A. *Jewish Mysticism: From Ancient Times Through Today*. Grand Rapids: Eerdmans, 2020.

Swinburne, Richard. *The Coherence of Theism*. 2nd ed. Clarendon Library of Logic and Philosophy. New York: Oxford University Press, 2016.

Szpiech, Ryan. "From *Testimonia* to Testimony: Thirteenth-Century Anti-Jewish Polemic and the Mostrador de Justicia of Abner of Burgos/Alfonso of Valladolid." PhD diss., Yale University, 2006.

Tal, Abraham, ed. *Genesis: Critical Apparatus and Notes*. 5th ed. Stuttgart: Deutsche Bibelgesellschaft, 2015.

Tapp, Christian. "Infinity in Mathematics and Theology." *Theology & Science* 9 (2011) 91–100.

Thesleff, Holger. "Pythagoreanism." In *Encyclopedia Britannica*. Chicago: Encyclopedia Britannica, 2016. Logos Bible Software e-book.

Thompson, A. E. *A Century of Jewish Missions*. Chicago: Revell, 1902.

Tigay, Jeffrey H. *Deuteronomy*. JPS Torah Commentary. Philadelphia: Jewish Publication Society, 1996.

Tirosh-Samuelson, Hava. "Kabbalah and Science in the Middle Ages: Preliminary Remarks." In *Science in Medieval Jewish Cultures*, edited by Gad Freudenthal, 476–510. New York: Cambridge University Press, 2012.

———. "Philosophy and Kabbalah: 1200–1600." In *The Cambridge Companion to Medieval Jewish Philosophy*, edited by Daniel H. Frank and Oliver Leaman, ch. 11, locs. 4765–5640. Cambridge Companions to Philosophy. New York: Cambridge University Press, 2003. Kindle.

Tobin, Thomas H. "Logos." In *The Anchor Yale Bible Dictionary*, edited by David Noel Freedman, 4:348–56. New York: Doubleday, 1992.

Tov, Emanuel. *Textual Criticism of the Hebrew Bible*. 3rd ed. Minneapolis: Fortress, 2012.

Trail, Ronald L. *An Exegetical Summary of Revelation 12–22*. 2nd ed. Dallas: SIL International, 2008.

Tripolitis, Antonía. *Religions of the Hellenistic-Roman Age*. Grand Rapids: Eerdmans, 2002.

Troki, Isaac ben Abraham. *[Hizuk Emunah] or Faith Strengthened*. New York: KTAV, 1970.

Trueman, Carl R. *Crisis of Confidence: Reclaiming the Historic Faith in a Culture Consumed with Individualism and Identity*. Wheaton, IL: Crossway, 2024.

Two Messianic Jews. "Did Jesus Claim to Be God? Traditional and Messianic Jewish Scholars Discuss." YouTube, Apr. 15, 2021. https://www.youtube.com/watch?v=iOl_EBMzdJg.

Union of Messianic Jewish Congregations. "Statement of Faith." UMJC, July 19, 2012. https://www.umjc.org/statement-of-faith.

Utterback, Kristine T., and Merrall Llewelyn Price, eds. *Jews in Medieval Christendom: Slay Them Not*. Études sur le Judaïsme médiéval. Leiden: Brill, 2013.

Bibliography

Valabregue, Sandra. "The Limits of Negative Theology in Medieval Kabbalah and Jewish Philosophy." In *Negative Theology as Jewish Modernity*, edited by Michael Fagenblat, 55–80. New Jewish Philosophy and Thought. Bloomington: Indiana University Press, 2017.

Valabregue-Perry, Sandra. "Philosophy, Heresy, and Kabbalah's Counter-Theology." *HTR* 109 (2016) 233–56.

Van der Heide, A. "Pardes: Methodological Reflections on the Theory of the Four Senses." Edited by Géza Vermes. *JJS* 35 (1983) 147–59.

Van Nuffelen, Peter, and Stephen Mitchell. *One God: Pagan Monotheism in the Roman Empire*. Cambridge: Cambridge University Press, 2010.

Varner, William. "The Christian Use of Jewish Numerology." *Master's Seminary Journal* 8 (1997) 47–59.

Veltri, Giuseppe. "The 'Theft' of Written and Oral Wisdom." In *Alienated Wisdom*, 21–34. Studies and Texts in Scepticism 3. Berlin: De Gruyter, 2018.

Venables, Edmund. "Eunomius (3)." In *A Dictionary of Christian Biography, Literature, Sects and Doctrines*, edited by William Smith and Henry Wace, 2:286–90. London: Murray, 1877–87.

Versluis, Arthur. *Magic and Mysticism: An Introduction to Western Esoteric Traditions*. Lanham, MD: Rowman & Littlefield, 2007. Logos Bible Software e-book.

Walton, Michael T. *Anthonius Margaritha and the Jewish Faith: Jewish Life and Conversion in Sixteenth-Century Germany*. Detroit: Wayne State University Press, 2012.

Weinberg, Yaakov, and Mordechai Blumenfeld. *Fundamentals and Faith: Insights into the Rambam's 13 Principles*. Spring Valley, NY: Targum, 1991.

Weinrich, William C. *Revelation*. ACCS NT 12. Downers Grove, IL: InterVarsity, 2005.

Weiss, Dov. "The Rabbinic God and Medieval Judaism." *CurBR* 15 (2017) 369–90.

Wellum, Stephen J. *God the Son Incarnate: The Doctrine of Christ*. Edited by John S. Feinberg. Wheaton, IL: Crossway, 2016.

Werblowsky, R. J. Zwi. "Dualism." In *Encyclopedia Judaica*, edited by Fred Skolnik and Michael Berenbaum, 6:29–31. Detroit: Macmillan Reference and Keter, 2007.

Westerman, Edjan. "Presence and Involvement: The Pre-Incarnate Messiah in the History of Israel." *Kesher*, Aug. 15, 2022. https://www.kesherjournal.com/article/presence-and-involvement-the-pre-incarnate-messiah-in-the-history-of-israel/.

Whitehead, Alfred North. *Process and Reality: An Essay in Cosmology*. Gifford Lectures. New York: Macmillan, 1929.

Whittaker, John. "Moses Atticizing." *Phoenix* 21 (1967) 196–201.

Wiersma, Syds. "Pearls in a Dunghill: The Anti-Jewish Writings of Raymond Martin O.P. (ca. 1220–ca. 1285)." PhD diss., Tilburg University, 2015.

Wilhite, David E. *The Gospel According to Heretics: Discovering Orthodoxy Through Early Christological Conflicts*. Grand Rapids: Baker Academic, 2015.

Wilhite, Shawn J. *The Didache: A Commentary*. Cambridge: Clarke & Co., 2020.

Wilkinson, Michael A. *Crowned with Glory and Honor: A Chalcedonian Anthropology*. Studies in Historical and Systematic Theology. Bellingham, WA: Lexham Academic, 2024.

Williams, A. Lukyn. *Adversus Judaeos: A Bird's-Eye View of Christian Apologiae Until the Renaissance*. Cambridge Library Collection. Repr., Cambridge: Cambridge University Press, 2012.

———. *A Manual of Christian Evidences for Jewish People*. 2 vols. London: Society for Promoting Christian Knowledge, 1919.

Wilshire, Bruce Withington. "Metaphysics." In *Encyclopedia Britannica*. Chicago: Encyclopedia Britannica, 2016. Logos Bible Software e-book.

Wilson, Brittany E. *The Embodied God: Seeing the Divine in Luke-Acts and the Early Church*. New York: Oxford University Press, 2021.

Wolfson, Elliot R. "The Bible in the Jewish Mystical Tradition." In *The Jewish Study Bible*, edited by Adele Berlin et al., 1976–90. New York: Oxford University Press, 2004.

———. "Jewish Mysticism: A Philosophical Overview." In *History of Jewish Philosophy*, edited by Daniel H. Frank and Oliver Leaman, 450–98. Routledge History of World Philosophies 2. New York: Routledge, 1997.

———. "Judaism and Incarnation: The Imaginal Body of God." In *Christianity in Jewish Terms*, edited by Tikva Frymer-Kensky et al., 239–54. Boulder, CO: Westview, 2000.

———. "Judaism and Mysticism." In *The Encyclopaedia of Judaism*, edited by Jacob Neusner et al., 2:926–36. Leiden: Brill, 2000.

———. "Metatron and Shi'ur Qomah in the Writings of Haside Ashkenaz." In *Mysticism, Magic and Kabbalah in Ashkenazi Judaism*, edited by Karl Erich Grözinger and Joseph Dan, 60–92. SJ 13. Boston: De Gruyter, 1995.

———. "Paul Philip Levertoff and the Popularization of Kabbalah as a Missionizing Tactic." *Kabbalah: Journal for the Study of Jewish Mystical Texts* 27 (2012) 269–320.

———. *Through a Speculum That Shines: Vision and Imagination in Medieval Jewish Mysticism*. Princeton, NJ: Princeton University Press, 1994.

———. "The Tree That Is All: Jewish-Christian Roots of a Kabbalistic Symbol in Sefer Ha-Bahir." *Journal of Jewish Thought and Philosophy* 3 (1993) 31–76.

———. "*Via Negativa* and the Imaginal Configuring of God." In *Giving Beyond the Gift*, 14–33. Apophasis and Overcoming Theomania. Fordham University, 2014.

———. "*Via Negativa* in Maimonides and Its Impact on Thirteenth-Century Kabbalah." In *Maimonidean Studies 5*, edited by Arthur Hyman and Alfred Ivry, 393–442. New York: Scharf Publication Trust of Yeshiva University Press, 2008.

Wright, N. T. *The Resurrection of the Son of God*. Vol. 3 of *Christian Origins and the Question of God*. London: Society for Promoting Christian Knowledge, 2003.

Wright, William M., IV, and Francis Martin. *Encountering the Living God in Scripture: Theological and Philosophical Principles for Interpretation*. Grand Rapids: Baker Academic, 2019.

Wyschogrod, Michael. *Abraham's Promise: Judaism and Jewish-Christian Relations*. Edited by R. Kendall Soulen. Radical Traditions. Grand Rapids: Eerdmans, 2004.

———. *The Body of Faith: God in the People Israel*. 2nd ed. Northvale, NJ: Aronson, 1996.

———. "A Jewish Perspective on Incarnation." *Modern Theology* 12 (1996) 195–209.

Xiuyuan, Dong. "Maimonides' Cosmogony-Prophetology Puzzle: Revisiting the Traditionalist Approach." *Aleph: Historical Studies in Science & Judaism* 22 (2022) 101–23.

Yamauchi, Edwin. "Pre-Christian Gnosticism, the New Testament and Nag Hammadi in Recent Debate." *Them* 10 (1984) 22–25.

Bibliography

Young, James O. "The Coherence Theory of Truth." *Stanford Encyclopedia of Philosophy*, Sept. 3, 1996; last revised June 26, 2018. Edited by Edward N. Zalta. https://plato.stanford.edu/entries/truth-coherence/.

Yuter, Josh. "Biblical Criticism for the Shomer Torah." Yutopia, July 24, 2013. https://joshyuter.com/2013/07/24/random-acts-of-scholarship/biblical-criticism-for-the-shomer-torah/.

Zalman of Liadi, Schneur. *Tanya: Likutei Amarim*. Translated by Nissan Mindel. Rev. bilingual ed. Brooklyn, NY: Kehot, 2014.

Zetterholm, Karin, and Anders Runesson, eds. *Within Judaism? Interpretive Trajectories in Judaism, Christianity, and Islam from the First to the Twenty-First Century*. Lanham, MD: Lexington, 2024.

Zetterholm, Karin, et al., eds. *Negotiating Identities: Conflict, Conversion, and Consolidation in Early Judaism and Christianity (200 BCE–600 CE)*. ConB. New York: Fortress Academic, 2022.

Zucker, Saul. "No, Rashi Was Not a Corporealist." *Hakirah: The Flatbush Journal of Jewish Law and Thought* (2010) 15–43.

Ancient Document Index

HEBREW BIBLE

Genesis

1	168, 311
1–2	81, 237
1–4	114
1:1	40, 200–201
1:3	43, 200
1:3–26	179
1:5	36
1:6	43
1:14	141
1:26	39, 43, 154, 231, 255, 266, 288, 312, 316, 331
1:27	55, 312
1:31	134, 209, 227, 311, 323
2:7	369
2:8	47
2:21–22	228
2:24	36
3	191, 209, 227, 237
3:8	5, 47, 62, 128, 255, 288
5:1	39, 255, 266
5:3	39
6:5–6	209, 227
6:6–7	43
8:21	47, 128
8:22	134, 296, 324
9:6	316
11:5–7	41
12:1–3	227
12:3	231, 266
12:7	45–46
14:18	37
16:7–13	61
16:13	46, 303
17:1	45
17:6	25
17:17	3
17:22	41
18	3–4, 16, 131
18:1	45, 131
18:3	4, 131
18:10	3
18:11–12	300
18:14	4, 149, 300
18:16	4
18:21	41, 131
18:22–23	4, 41
18:23	131, 255
18:33	4
22:11–18	61
26:2	45
26:24	46
28:13	41, 47
31	55
31:11–13	61
31:13	55
32	16
32:30	46, 303
35:9	46
35:13	41
48:3	46

Ancient Document Index

Exodus

3	16, 345
3:1–6	303
3:2	61
3:2–3	46
3:4	42
3:5	41
3:6	46
3:14	262
3:16	46
4:1	46
4:5	46
4:14	43
4:21	231
6:3	121
9:15–16	42
12:40	43
13:21	304
14:19	304
15:3	59
15:7	43
15:11	37–38
15:13	43
16:10	46
17:6	41
19:2–3	42
19:3	41, 255
19:18–20	41
19:20	255
20:3	35, 206
20:5	43
20:7	61
20:21	41
20:4–6	207
22:18	229, 325
23	62
23:20	16, 304
23:20–21	42, 61
24:1	41–42
24:1–2	41
24:3	36
24:9–10	303–4
24:10	47
24:10–11	46
25:22	41
28:30	26
29:45	5
31:1–5	193
33:19–20	45
33:20	46–47, 255, 303
33:20–23	45
33:21	41–42, 255
33:23	46, 303, 345
34:29	261
34:5	345
34:6	36, 43, 49, 62, 255, 306, 332
34:6–7	170
36:13	36
40:35	60, 345

Leviticus

9:4	46
9:23	46
9:6	46
11:44	315
14:10	36
19:2	37, 306
19:31	325
23	7
24:16	61
26:11–12	3
26:12	5–6
26:31	47

Numbers

11:1	43, 47
11:10	43
11:24–30	193
12:6–8	121, 142, 160
12:8	45–46, 145, 255, 303
12:9	47
14:10	46
14:14	5, 46
16:9	41
16:19	46
17:7	46
20:6	46
22:21–35	61
23:19	40
24:7	25

Deuteronomy

2:30	231

4:15	45
4:24	43
4:35	174
4:39	41
5:24	47, 303
5:31	41
6:4	35, 111, 193, 258–59
6:5	267
6:15	43
7:7	43
7:7–8	331
17:14	25
17:15	25
18:10–12	229, 325
18:15–18	261
18:22	61
23:14–15	5
26:17–18	334
29:29	32, 43
31:15	46
32:3	61
32:4	37, 255, 306
33:16	46

Joshua

11:20	231
24:19	43

Judges

2:1–4	61
5:23	61
6:11–16	61
6:11–24	303
8:23	25
13:3	61
13:13–22	61
13:22	303

1 Samuel

2:3	44
8:5–7	25
8:7	26
8:21	47
14:41	26
15:11	43
15:29	40
15:35	43
20:14	43
23:9–13	44
28:8	224
28:15	224

2 Samuel

7	26
22:10	41, 47
22:11	46
22:26	49
24:1	43
24:16	43, 61

1 Kings

3:5	46
4:22	36
8:27	37, 255
8:39	44
8:60	231
9:2	46
11:9	46
19:5–7	61
19:12	47
22:19	41–42, 47

2 Kings

1:3	61
1:15	61
19:35	61

1 Chronicles

21:12–18	61
28:18	168
29:11	226

2 Chronicles

1:7	46
7:12	46
16:9	47
18:18	41
32:8	201
32:21	61
33:6	229, 325

Ancient Document Index

Nehemiah
9:2	43
9:6	259

Job
1:6–12	226
11:7–9	37, 289
23:9	41
36:5	37
36:26	289
37:16	44
38:33	296, 324
38:36	296
40:9	38

Psalms
2:4	47
7:17	61
8	201, 227
9:7	47
19	145
20:7	61
29:3–9	312
33:6	200, 312
33:6–9	201
33:13–15	44
34:7–8	61
34:15	47, 255
35:5–6	61
47:8	47
47:8–9	231
62:7	331
65:1	148
68:32	231
71:19	38, 255
72:18	201
78:41	205
86:10	201
86:11	43
90:2	40
96:1–9	231
98:2–3	231
102:7	38
102:15	61, 231
102:17	46
102:22	231
102:25–28	201
102:26–27	40
102:27	226
103:19	226
106:1	205
107:1	205
107:20	312
110:1	262
113:2	61
115:1	331
116:4	61
116:13	260
117:1	231
118:1	205
118:10–11	61
118:26	260
119:25	312
119:89	312
124:8	61
136:1	180
139	289
139:6	289
139:7–10	41
139:8	41
144:4	38
145:14	47
145:3	37, 306
148:5	61
148:13	61

Proverbs
1:26	47
1:28	317
6:16	43
8	57
8:22–31	201
15:3	41, 47
18:10	61

Ecclesiastes
1:5–10	296
2:17	331
2:26	296
5:2	201
11:5	289

Isaiah

1:4	205
1:9	38
1:15	317
6:1	47
6:1–5	303
6:1–7	260
6:3–5	205
6:5	46, 303
6:9–10	231
7:14	20, 263
9:6	20, 264
11	237
11:9	321
12:4–5	231
14:1	231
25:6	231
28:16	260
28:23–29	296
29:14	289
31:3	201
37:16	201
37:36	61
40:13	370
40:17	208
40:25	38, 255
40:26	259
40:28	37, 39
40:3	260
41:10	47
42:8	35, 42, 332
43:11	201, 331
44:6	331
46:5	38, 255
45:7	180, 206
46:9	35
45:12	259
45:21	201, 331
45:23	260
48:11	331
48:12	262
51:5	231
51:9–10	309
52:10	231
53	20, 25, 331
53:10	313
53:12	314
55:8–9	44, 289, 345
55:9	37
55:11	43, 312
56:6–8	231
59:1	47, 344
59:2	317
60:2	46
60:3	231
61:8	43
62:5	43
63:1–6	47
63:7	334
63:9	313
63:10	269
63:15	41
63:17	231
65:17	227

Jeremiah

1:4	312
1:5	44
10:12	201
11:11	317
18:11	206
23:23–24	41, 370
23:24	255
23:29	43
30:21	41
31:3	46
31:31–35	316
31:35	227, 296, 324
31:36	134
32:41	43
33:20	134
33:25	296, 324
38:17–18	44
51:5	205

Ezekiel

1	168
1:26	39, 255, 303
1:26–27	48
3:6	231
3:12	41–42
11:16	313
11:23	41, 47

Ezekiel (cont.)

24:14	40
25:14	43
36:22	331
37	224
38:18	43
39:29	317
44:13	41

Daniel

2:22	43
4:35	208
7	48
7:9	47–48
7:9–10	59
7:13	263
7:13–14	263
8:26	231
12:2	224
12:4–10	231

Hosea

13:4	331

Joel

2:32	260

Amos

3:6	206
5:21	43
7:7	47
9:1	47
9:2	41

Micah

1:12	206
3:4	317
5:2	264

Nahum

1:2	43

Zephaniah

3:9–10	231
3:12	43
3:17	43

Zechariah

1:10–13	61
2:11	231
3:1–6	61
4:10	47
9:7	231
9:14	46
12:8	61
14:4	47
14:9	36
14:16–19	231

Malachi

1:11	231
2:7	304
3:1	263
3:5	41, 325
3:6	40, 226

APOCRYPHA

2 Maccabees

7:28	201

3 Maccabees

2:3	201

Judith

16:14	201

Sirach

16:26–29	227
24:3–4	57
24:5	57
24:9	57
49:8	168

PSEUDEPIGRAPHA

1 Enoch
2:1—5:3	227
45:3	262
61:8	262
62:1–5	262
69:20–21	227

2 Baruch
14:17	201
48:9	227

3 Enoch
10	62
11	62
12:5	62
48C:7	62
48C:8	62

4 Ezra
3:20–22	25
6:38	201

Jubilees
12:4	201

Letter of Aristeas
30	368–69
31	369

Odes of Solomon
7:3–6	273
16:13–19	227
16:18—19	202
29:6	273

Psalms of Solomon
18:11–14	227

Sibylline Oracles
1.7–21	201

Testament of Asher
7.3–4	274

Testament of Job
33:3	262

Testament of Naphtali
8.3	274

Testament of Simeon
6.5–7	274
7.2	274

Wisdom of Solomon
7:25–28	57
9:1	201
11:17	201
13:3–9	145

NEW TESTAMENT

Matthew
1:17	374, 375
1:22–23	263
2:6	264
5:17	314, 327
5:44–48	317
5:45	324
6:9	269
7:6	231, 273
7:28–29	261
8:10	265
8:27	261
9:3	261
9:4	261
11:10	263
11:27	261, 269, 290, 312
11:28–30	331, 339
12:25	261
15:24	266
16:26	194
17	261
17:2–3	261
18:20	261
21:18	264

Matthew (cont.)

22:44	262
22:45	262
24:30	263
25:31–46	317
26:38	265
26:39	269
28:9	261
28:17	261
28:18	259, 261
28:19	269
28:20	261

Mark

1:2	263
1:3	260
6:6	265
12:24	264
12:29	269
12:30	267, 294, 338
12:36	262
14:61–64	261
14:62	263

Luke

1:11	304
1:35	4, 16
1:36	4
1:37	3, 4
1:37–38	300
1:47	331
2:7	264
2:27	263
2:32	xxi
2:40	264
2:52	264, 269
3:21–22	269
5:22	264
7:24	304
7:27	263
9:47	296
9:52	304
10:25–37	317
12:11–12	331
13:35	260
16:19–31	224
20:42–43	262
23:26	264
23:34	317
24:52	261

John

1	56, 311
1:1	258, 260, 269
1:1–4	311
1:3	201, 258, 262, 311
1:14	56, 348
1:18	18, 111, 256, 260, 303
1:38	351
1:49	331
2	271
3	193, 314
3:3	312
3:7	194
3:13	311
3:19	288
3:34	304
4:6	264
4:24	111, 134, 256, 303, 305
5:18	261
5:37	303
5:46	261
6:38	311
6:44	331
6:57	304
8:40	264, 269
8:56	262
8:58	262
8:59	262
10:30	269
10:33	261
11:33	265
12:27	265
12:41	260
13:1	264
13:1–17	317
13:34	316
14:9	303
14:13–14	317
14:16–17	269
14:23	269
15:1	269
15:1–5	331

15:5	315
15:12	308
15:26	269
16:13	312
17:3	307
20:12	304
20:17	269
20:21	304
20:28	190, 260, 261, 269
21:17	261

Acts

2	317
2:21	260
2:34–35	262
2:42	316
3:21	316, 317, 340
8:18–24	325
13:6–12	325
13:23	331
13:43	23
14:17	324
16:16–18	325
17:23	102, 325
19:17–20	325
21:17–26	316
22:3	316
23:6	316

Romans

1:3	264, 269
1:7	269
1:16	xvi, 12
1:20	134, 145, 267, 324, 345
1:21	288
1:26	267
3:1–2	316
3:26	314
4	266
4:9–12	231
4:13–17	266
4:17	201
5	50, 237, 323
5:8	316
5:12	266
5:12–21	314
5:19	314
6:3–5	315
8	324
8:1	317
8:15	316
8:18–25	288
8:20–23	194
8:29	312, 314
8:29–30	314, 315
9:1–5	316
10:1	xii, 11
10:9	190
10:9–11	260
10:9–12	11
10:13	260
10:14–17	12
11	xvi
11:5	xvi, 246
11:11–29	316
11:25–26	317
11:33	289
11:36	201
12:5	315

1 Corinthians

1:2	260
1:30	315
8:6	201, 259, 260, 269, 276
13:12	298
15	224, 265, 315
15:3–8	276, 337
15:34	307
15:47	50
15:47–49	314
15:49	315

2 Corinthians

1:22	193, 331
2:14	307
3:17–18	269
3:18	312, 314
4:10	314
5:8	224
5:21	314
6:16	5
12:1–6	224

2 Corinthians (cont.)

12:1–10	375
12:2–4	225
13:11	316

Galatians

1:13–14	23
3:26–28	328
3:27–28	316
4:4–5	314
4:8	267
5:19–20	325
6:1–2	316

Ephesians

1:4	265, 331
1:20–23	62
2	253, 284, 316
3:11–12	318
4:4–6	260
4:17–18	288

Philippians

1:23	224
2:3–8	317
2:5–11	62, 190, 276
2:6	260, 267, 269
2:10–11	260
3:10	307
3:9	314
3:21	314

Colossians

1:10	307
1:15	18, 50, 260, 265, 303, 312
1:15–17	56
1:15–20	62
1:16	201, 258
1:17	259, 279, 311
1:19	260, 348
2:3	261
2:8	268, 294
2:9	7, 267, 269, 345, 348

2:10	315
3:12–17	316

1 Timothy

1:17	18, 111, 256, 303, 331
2:5	269, 310
3:16	xxi, 340
6:15	331
6:16	289

Titus

1:2–3	265
1:3–4	331
2:13	331
3:4–6	331
3:5	312

Hebrews

1:1–2	142, 312
1:2	312
1:3	7, 15, 71, 259, 267, 269, 279, 311, 347
1:4–5	304
1:8–9	260
1:13	262
2:16	266
2:16–17	xii, 245, 266
2:17	71, 265, 266, 268, 269, 313, 331
3:2–6	142
3:3	142, 261
4:14–16	313
4:15	265
4:16	317
8	316
8:6	310
9:15	310
9:27	224
10:1	314, 333
10:24–25	316
11:3	201
11:27	18, 303
12:10	315
12:24	310

James

1:27	269
2:19	260, 269
2:25	304
3:7	266
3:9	266, 316

1 Peter

1:2	269
1:5	331
1:13	338
1:20	265
2:22	265–66
2:25	331
3:15	252

2 Peter

1:1	260, 331
1:2–3	307
1:4	315
3:18	307

1 John

1:5	306
2:13	307
3:2	315
3:5	266
4:7	333
4:8	306, 333
4:9–14	304
4:12	18, 303
5:20	307

Jude

4–5	56, 303, 304, 327
5	258, 304
24	331
25	331

Revelation

1:4–8	62
1:5	331
1:8	259
5:9	316
5:9–10	328
6:9	224
13:8	265
13:18	373–75
19:6	259
19:15	259
19:16	259, 331
19:20	224
21	288
21–22	194
21:22	259
22	237

DEAD SEA SCROLLS

11QMelch	262
1QS 3.15	201

GRECO-ROMAN WRITINGS

Aeschylus
Agamemnon 103

Alexander of Aphrodisias
commentary on *Metaphysics* 91–92

Aristotle
Categories

4	91–92
5	84

De Anima

2.4	85
3.5	121

Metaphysics

1.5	90–92
1.6	85
4.3	85
5.8	84
7.1–3	84
7.6	85
12.7	86, 88
12.8	86–87

Nicomachean Ethics

10.8	88

Ancient Document Index

Aristotle (cont.)

On Interpretation
14	85

On the Heavens
1.1	91
1.2–3	86
2.1	88
2.2	222
2.9	90
2.12	86
2.13	92, 222

Posterior Analytics
1.4	84

Diogenes Laertius

Lives of Eminent Philosophers
8.25–26	91
8.25–27	89

Plato

Parmenides
141	80
142	80
143	80
166	80

Phaedo
79	79
81–82	79

Republic
377–92	129
378d–e	83
507b–c	81
509b	81
514–20	82
515b–c	82
517c–d	82, 235
617	90

Symposium
203a	79

Theaetetus
174	82, 235
176	79

Timaeus
28c	80, 102, 289

32c	81
34a–b	81
36d–e	81
37c–d	81

Plotinus

The Six Enneads
1.7.1	101, 239
1.7.6	239
2.3.9	106
2.9	105
3.2	100, 102, 120, 125
3.2.7	100, 125
4—6	117
5.1.2	100, 105, 125
5.1.3	101
5.1.8	102
5.1.10	100, 125
5.2	102
5.2.1	101
5.3.13	103, 112, 125
5.3.13–14	99
5.3.14	104
5.4.1	99–100, 124
5.4.2	101
5.5.6	104, 147
5.5.11	174
5.6.3	99, 124
6.4.4	100, 125
6.5.4	104
6.6.13	99–100, 124
6.7.29	158
6.7.38	99, 125
6.9	99, 124
6.9.6	102

Ptolemy

Almagest
3.4–9	118

Tacitus

Histories
5.5	60

Ancient Document Index

EARLY JEWISH WRITINGS

Aristobulus
Fragment 2	83
Fragment 3	367

Josephus
Against Apion
2.168	368
2.257	368
2.281	368

Jewish War
2.160–66	23

Philo
Allegorical Interpretation
1.65	57

On Dreams
1.34	94
1.234–31.235	83, 103
1.238–39	55
2.45	55
2.249	55

On Flight and Finding
91–92	55
101	54

On Planting
50	201

On the Confusion of Tongues
62–63	54
146	54

On the Contemplative Life 23

On the Creation of the World
16	55
24–25	55

On the Life of Moses
2.25–27	368

On the Posterity of Cain
15	103

On the Sacrifices of Cain and Abel
101	103

On the Special Laws
1.32	80

Questions and Answers on Genesis
2.62	54
3.34	55

Who is the Heir?
69–74	55
205–6	54
231	55

EARLY CHRISTIAN WRITINGS

Apostolic Constitutions
2.62	325
6.10	306

Aristedes
Apology
2	202

Arnobius
Against the Gentiles
3.12	59

Athanasius
Against the Arians
1.38	305
2.33	239
2.36	299

On the Councils of Ariminum and Seleucia
27	305

On the Incarnation
1	299
14	314
17:1–2	279

Augustine
The City of God
8–10	325
Letter 11.2	290

On the Trinity
2.6–17	305
4.21	299
6.7	147

Basil of Caesarea
On the Spirit
24.57	290

Ancient Document Index

Boethius
Contra Eutychen
3 — 15

Cassian, John
Conferences
1.6.6 — 206

Chalcedonian Definition
279

Chrysostom, John
Of Demons
1.5 — 206

Clement of Alexandria
Christ the Educator
1.7 — 305
3.7 — 259
Miscellanies
1.22 — 369
2.1 — 369
5.14 — 369

Council of Nicaea
Canon 52 — 247
Nicene Creed — 278

Cyprian
To Quirinius
2.5 — 305

Cyril of Alexandria
Epistle 55
33 — 279–80

Cyril of Jerusalem
Catechetical Lectures
4.9 — 315

Didache
2:2 — 325
4:1 — 273
7:1 — 273
9:5 — 273

Ephrem the Syrian
Hymns on the Nativity
27 — 90

Epistle of Diognetus
7.2 — 202

Eusebius of Caesarea
Demonstration of the Gospel
1.5 — 305
Ecclesiastical History
4.22.6 — 23
5.24 — 273, 280
Preparation for the Gospel
8.9–10 — 129
8.10 — 83
9.6 — 369
11 — 370
11.26 — 370
13.12 — 370
14.17 — 238
15.8 — 34
15.23–58 — 86

Gregory Nazianzen
Epistle 101.5 — 315
Oration 39.13 — 290

Gregory of Nyssa
Contra Eunomius
5.5 — 290

Hilary of Poitiers
On the Synods
38 — 305
On the Trinity
5.1 — 293
5.17 — 305
12.51 — 290

Hippolytus

Contra Beronem
2–4   290

Refutation of All Heresies
1.2   91
4.28–51   325
4.51   91
6.18–23   91
6.24   96

Ignatius

To the Ephesians
7.2   279–80

To the Trallians
9   276–77

Irenaeus

Against Heresies
1.1–2   96
1.10.1   277
1.11.1   228
1.14   220
1.17.2   97
1.18   220, 225
1.21.3   228
1.24.2   230
1.30   92
2.4.2   204
2.8.2   204
2.14   232
2.14.2   232
2.14.3   232
2.34.2   202
3.4.2   277
3.8.3   202
4.10.1   305
4.20.4–11   305
4.33.7   277

John of Damascus

On the Orthodox Faith
3.7   279
4.19   206

Justin Martyr

1 Apology
60   369
63   304

Dialogue with Trypho
5   202
67   263
68   19
80   23
114   59
120   304
123   247
127–28   304
135   247

Lactantius

The Divine Institutes
2.17   325

Mark the Monk

Counsels
2.3.34   290
2:262   286
2:273   314

Melito of Sardis

Fragment 14   280

Novatian

On the Trinity
1–8   117, 270
17–18   305
18.4–5   239

Origen

Against Celsus
6.31–32   92
7.30   370

On First Principles
preface   285
1.2.7   239
2.6.2   286

Philocalia
2.3   32

Polycarp

To the Philippians

12.2   273

Pseudo-Clementine Homilies

3.33   228
17.9   90, 169

Pseudo-Dionysius

Epistle 1   295

Shepherd of Hermas

Mandate 1.1   202

Socrates Scholasticus

Church History

2.30   276, 305

Tertullian

Against Marcion 2.13   206
Against Praxeas
2   277
13   239
15   305
17   259
Prescription against Heretics 13   305

Theodoret of Cyr

Commentary on Isaiah 14.45.7   206

Theophilus of Antioch

To Autolycus

2.15   141, 277
2.22   305

RABBINIC WRITINGS

Babylonian Talmud

Avodah Zarah 3b   59
Baba Metzia 59b   26
Berakhot
6a   59
7a   59
Betzah 16a   189
Hagigah
13a   168
14b   168
Ketubbot 19b   221
Makkot 23b   321
Megillah 13b   201
Pesahim 112a   215, 221
Sanhedrin
19a   201
38b   59, 62
65b   168, 186
111a   59
Shabbat 145b–146a   25

Genesis Rabbah

8:10   59
9.5   221
10.6   237, 325
13:13   171
68.9   173
85.9   262

Jerusalem Talmud

Moed Qatan 3:1   26
Taanit 4:2   221

Mishnah

Hagigah 2:1   10, 168, 182, 192
Pirke Avot 1   23
Sanhedrin 10:1   109, 113

Pesiqta of Rab Kahana

12.24   59
suppl. 7   59

Sifra Behuqqotai

3   5

Targum Neofiti

on Exod 34:6   62

Targum Onqelos

on Gen 3:8   62

Tosefta
Avodah Zarah 5:2   60

NAG HAMMADI WRITINGS

Discourse of Seth
62:27   96

Exegesis of the Soul
133:4–9   228

Gospel of Philip
67:31–34   96
68:22–26   228
70:9–22   228

Gospel of Thomas
22   228

Pistis Sophia
1   97

Secret Book of James
27:1–10   97

Secret Book of John
2:33—3:30   96
9:25—11:22   96
11:4–35   96
15:13—19:15   97
19:10   97
22:3—23:4   228
22:3–28   96

Tripartite Tractate
1.2   96
1.4   96
132:16–28   98

MEDIEVAL JEWISH WRITINGS

Crescas, Hasdai
Or Hashem 1:3:3   145, 157
Refutation of Christian Principles   9

Gersonides
Wars of the Lord 3.3   145, 159

Ibn Ezra
commentary on Exodus 3:6   46

Maimonides
Commentary on
   Kings and Wars 11   112
Commentary on
   Mishnah Avodah Zarah   111
Eight Chapters   117, 122, 314
Guide to the Perplexed
   outline   114
   Introduction   129
   1.1   154–55
   1.1–48   130
   1.4   131
   1.10   131
   1.17   130
   1.18   131
   1.32–1.35   130
   1.33   129, 328
   1.33–1.35   130
   1.35   158
   1.36   129, 327
   1.46   129
   1.50   112, 125–26, 146
   1.52–53   124
   1.53   129
   1.54   129
   1.56   125
   1.57   157
   1.59   125, 148, 158
   1.60   156
   1.61   131
   1.68   154, 157
   1.70   120, 129
   1.71   124, 126, 139

Maimonides (cont.)

1.72	119, 124, 140–41, 154, 158
1.75	127
1.76	126
Introduction to Part 2	140, 150
2.2	146
2.4	119, 122
2.6	119
2.10	118–20, 237–38, 325
2.11	119, 121
2.12	118, 120–21
2.13	120, 127–28, 151–52
2.16	120
2.17	151
2.17–2.22	152
2.19	150
2.22	89
2.24	118–19
2.25	121
2.29	120, 122–23, 334
2.32	121, 142
2.35	123
2.36	121
2.36–2.37	121
2.41	160
2.42	131
2.43	334
2.45	121
2.46	123
2.48	158
3.8	128
3.13	134
3.14	120, 139
3.15	127, 149, 151
3.17	120
3.17–18	120
3.50	120, 123
3.51	122, 142, 154
3.53	334
Letter Concerning Astrology	118, 120
Letter to Yemen	112

Moses Taku

Ketav tamim	301

Rashi

commentary on Leviticus 26:12	5

Saadia Gaon

Book of Beliefs and Opinions

1.1	9
2.1	147
2.2	228
2.4	147
2.5	147
6.8	225
7.2	217
7.4	217

Zohar, the

1.11b	208
1:19b–20a	181
1:29b	170
2:20a	180
2:23b	238
3.202a	184

MEDIEVAL CHRISTIAN WRITINGS

Anselm of Canterbury

Cur Deus Homo 2.18a	299

Aquinas, Thomas

Summa Contra Gentiles

1.14	148
1.29–34	148, 308
2.16	202

Summa Theologica

I q.3 a.1	18
I q.3 a.3 ad 1	147
I q.13	308
I q.29 a.1	15
I q.45 a.1	202
I q.49 a.2	206
II-II q.2 a.3–4	294
II-II q.2 a.4 resp.	288

Peter Lombard

Sentences 3.3.4	279

EARLY MODERN WRITINGS

Calvin, John
Institutes of the Christian Religion
2.2.12	288
4.17.30	279

Pascal, Blaise
Memorial	77

Spinoza, Baruch
Theologico-Political Treatise 7	145

Tanya, the
1.1	238
1.6	238
1.8	236
2.6	208

General Index

Abraham, 3–4, 77, 120, 131, 133, 152, 214, 231, 245, 262, 266, 300, 305, 336, 374
   God's covenant with, 40, 231
active intellect (*see under* intellect)
Adam Kadmon, 178, 181
allegory, 53, 82–83, 94, 149
Alston, William, 155–56
Amidah, 37, 331 (*see also* prayer in Judaism)
Anaximander, 204
Anderson, James, xx, 149, 251, 278, 288, 290–92, 296, 299
Angel of the LORD, the, 56, 60–62, 304
   Jesus as, 304–5
   Logos as, 55–56
   Metatron as, 62
   (*see also* binitarianism; theophany)
angels
   as heavenly spheres, 119, 140, 311
   as intermediaries to perform divine acts, 140–43
Ani Ma'amin, 107, 109–10, 127 (*see also* Thirteen Principles of Faith)
Anselm of Canterbury, 194, 257, 299, 313
anthropomorphisms, 51, 55, 60, 67, 112, 135, 161, 255, 305, 309 (*see also under* attributes of God)
apologetics, xvi, xix, 19–20, 68, 198, 249
   Christian, to Jews, 19–22, 252
   Jewish, to Christians, 6–9, 20, 111–13

Messianic Jewish, to Jews, 20–21, 249–51, 252–53
apophatic theology (*see via negativa*; negative theology)
Aquinas, Thomas, 15, 18, 117, 147–48, 155, 202, 206, 247, 275, 288, 294, 308, 322, 329, 361
Aristarchus of Samos, 118
Aristobulus, 83, 129, 146, 367–68
Aristotle, 14, 18, 21, 34–35, 78, 84–92, 98, 116–21, 134, 137–38, 145, 151–52, 189, 195, 197, 214, 218, 222, 234–36, 322, 335, 355, 363–64, 367
   cosmology of, 86–88
   metaphysics of, 84–86
   relation to Maimonides, 84, 116–24, 134, 138, 140, 151–52
   science of, 84–85, 234–36
   theology of, 88–89
astrology, 28, 87, 169, 180, 229, 234, 236–37, 324–25 (*see also* magic)
astronomy, 84, 88, 117–19, 321 (*see also* Copernican Revolution; cosmology; geocentrism)
Athanasius, 247, 299, 361
attributes of God, 32–51, 110, 114, 125, 127, 131, 145, 147, 157, 169–70, 181, 188, 193, 217, 226, 255–57, 261, 264, 267, 291, 306, 308, 312, 333
   anthropomorphic, 47–48
   denial of, 110, 112, 125, 131, 157–58

General Index

attributes of God (cont.)
    echad (*see echad*, meaning of)
    emotive, 42–44
    eternality, 39–40
    immanence, 41, 49–51, 57, 63, 193, 255, 267, 361
    immutability, 39–40, 312
    incomparablility, 38–39
    incomprehensibility, 37–39
    infinity, 37–38, 204–5, 257
    likeness with humanity, 38–39, 48, 50, 154–55, 255, 265–66, 280, 288, 308, 312–13, 315–16, 331, 334
    localizable, 41–42
    omnipresence, 41–42, 44, 49–50, 57, 100, 125, 257, 261, 273, 289, 294, 312
    omniscience, 44, 114, 147, 209, 261, 267, 287, 293, 296, 298
    options for dealing with the, 48–51, 302–10
    personhood (*see* person)
    rational (intelligent), 42–43, 120, 156
    seen, 45–47
    transcendent, 7, 37–39, 44, 49–51, 54, 57, 63, 66, 80, 99–100, 120, 124–25, 127, 141–42, 144, 162, 200, 205, 231, 255–56, 267, 294, 310, 313, 334, 361
    unseen, 44–45
Augustine of Hippo, 99, 102, 147, 194, 247, 299, 305, 361

Baal Shem Tov, 11, 166, 172
Bahya ben Asher, 226
Baruch she'amar prayer, 201
Beit Alfa synagogue, 59
Bible codes, 221 (*see also* gematria)
biblical interpretation
    allegorical, 83–84, 128–31, 134, 160–61, 182–85, 217, 283, 302
    in the *Guide*, 124–31, 145–61
    in Kabbalah, 180–87, 219–21, 325–27, 329, 332–33
    in the NT, 259–64, 302–5
    peshat, 33, 160, 184–85, 217, 327

    using *gematria*, 182–87
    via analogia, 49–50, 110, 135, 148, 153–55, 302, 307–10, 329, 333
    via negativa, 28, 49, 54, 80, 96, 99, 102–4, 124–31, 145–50, 153–61, 188, 233, 291, 302, 305–10, 325–26, 329, 332, 353–55
    via positiva, 6, 49, 110, 153, 302–9, 329, 333
    (*see also* God talk)
binitarianism, 53, 57, 60, 65, 70–71, 131, 162, 271–72, 335
    definition of, 53, 71
    Jewish scholars on, 64–69
    in Second Temple Judaism, 54–57
    in the Talmudic era, 60–64
Boethius, 15, 98–99
Boyarin, Daniel, 23, 29, 52–53, 65, 67–68, 71, 263, 335
Brown, Jeremy, 137, 236
Brown, Michael, xx, 21, 249, 253–54

Chabad, 137, 162, 166–67, 172, 174–75, 186, 189, 195, 206, 231, 328
    (*see also* Hasidic Judaism)
Chalcedonian Definition, 8, 15, 190, 278–79, 281–82, 285, 287, 290–91, 297, 323, 330, 335–36
Christianity
    anti-Judaism in, 19–22
    evidences for, 269–70, 294, 299, 330
    historical separation from Judaism (*see* parting of the ways)
    relation to Judaism, 14, 22–25, 64–69, 246, 261–64, 272–75
    relation to Messianic Judaism, xvi, 7–8, 246–54
    sects of
        Catholicism, 8, 77, 117, 137, 282
        Eastern Orthodox, 8, 282
        Protestantism, 8, 20, 26–28, 33, 247–49, 279, 282, 326
    skeptical origins of, 64–65, 271–72
    theology of (*see* Chalcedonian Definition; Incarnation, the; Nicene Creed, the; Trinity, the)

General Index

Christian kabbalists, , 194, 241, 321, 371, 376
Christological heresies, 127, 275–79, 281–82, 293–94, 335 (*see also* Christology; Jesus; Trinity, the)
Christology, 64–71, 248–50, 258–64, 269–72, 275–81, 296, 299, 321, 334–36
    early high, 64–71, 258–64, 269–75 (*see also* Chalcedonian Definition; Incarnation, the; Jesus; Nicene Creed, the)
church fathers, helpful contributions of, 252–54, 266–85, 290–318 (*see also* philosophy, dangers of)
Clement of Alexandria, 56, 99, 146, 270, 369–70
coherence theory of truth, 196, 213
comparative theology, 67, 194
contradiction, 42, 118, 128, 155, 157–58, 195, 197, 216–17, 291, 297, 299–300, 304–5, 310–11, 325
    accusations against Incarnation, 6–9, 111–13, 287–88, 293
    apparent, 195, 291–94, 299–300 (*see also* paradox)
    relation to impossibility (*see* impossibility)
    (*see also* mystery; noncontradiction, principle of)
Copernican Revolution, 88, 136–38, 141–44, 236 (*see also* cosmology)
Cordovero, Moses, 171
correspondences, spurious, 180–82, 220, 222, 229, 240, 324–25
correspondence theory of truth, 196, 198
cosmology, 13, 34, 72, 78–79, 84, 86–94, 114, 117–24, 135–45, 150, 161–62, 173–80, 199, 201–3, 210, 220, 222–23, 225, 240–41, 258–59, 311, 320–23, 353–55, 371, 375
    Aristotelian-Ptolemaic, 86–88
    Kabbalistic, 173–80, 223, 236
    Maimonidean, 117–24
    in the NT, 258–59, 311, 320–23

Platonic, 81
    (*see also* Copernican Revolution; *ex Deo*, emanation; *ex matria*, creation; *ex nihilo*, creation)
Counter-Earth, 92, 222
Craig, William Lane, 40, 73, 115, 144, 195, 200, 202, 237, 246, 269, 271, 294, 320
Crescas, Hasdai, 8, 20, 145, 157
Cyril of Alexandria, 280
Cyril of Jerusalem, 315

demiurge, 81, 96, 198, 227
DeWeese, Garrett J., xi–xiv, xvi, xx, 13, 70, 78
Didache, the, 272–73
divine embodiment (*see* God, models of)
divine intermediaries, 54–64, 141, 312, 335, 362 (*see also* Angel of the Lord, the; *Kavod*, the; *Logos*, the; *Memra*, the; *Metatron*; *Shekhinah*, the; *Sophia*)
divine nature (*see* God, nature of)
divine sparks, 94–95, 97, 103, 105, 163, 179, 186, 189–90, 223, 225, 230–31, 233, 271, 322
divine warrant, 26, 29, 31, 292, 294–95, 300, 337 (*see also* epistemology)

echad, meaning of, 35–36, 111, 221, 259
Ein Sof, 102, 163, 169–70, 173–80, 190, 193, 195–97, 203–10, 214, 226–27, 233, 235, 239, 241, 333, 362
emanation, 56–57, 100, 103, 120–25, 140–41, 150, 169–70, 173, 175, 186, 188, 195, 200, 202, 206–7, 211, 214, 225, 227, 230, 233, 239, 256–57, 310–11, 355 (*see also ex Deo*, emanation)
Empedocles, 86, 169, 189, 232, 355
enlightenment, mystical, 165, 182 (*see also* esoteric and exoteric)
Enlightenment, the, 10, 137, 230
epistemological hierarchy, 70, 146, 323, 370–71

General Index

epistemology, xi, 13–14, 19, 29–31, 56, 70, 72, 90, 117, 134, 146, 151, 158, 195–98, 208–9, 237–38, 292, 295, 297, 311, 321, 323, 326, 332, 335, 337, 339, 370–71
    value of extra-biblical ideas, 27–29, 266–68, 283
eschatology, 5, 12, 171, 179, 248, 289, 311, 315, 321
esoteric and exoteric, 10, 55, 66–67, 79, 83–84, 95, 97, 99, 128–30, 146, 150, 152, 158–61, 165, 182–90, 218, 225, 230, 236, 283, 295, 302, 323, 326, 328, 353, 355, 367
essence (*see* nature)
eternity, eternal, 18, 39–40, 53, 56–58, 60, 81, 86, 88, 95, 100, 114, 119–20, 125, 127, 134, 151–52, 200, 203, 237, 239, 257, 264–65, 277, 280, 283, 303, 311–13, 315, 317, 319, 328, 333–35, 355, 361
ethics, 12, 72, 84, 108, 117, 311, 316–17
evangelism, Jewish, xv, 11–12, 68, 191, 251
evil, 9, 25, 41, 80, 96–97, 114, 174, 179–80, 188, 190, 197–98, 205–7, 209, 226–28, 235, 238, 317, 324–25, 374
    Kabbalah's view of, 179–80, 188, 190, 197–98, 205–7, 226–27, 235, 238, 324–25
ex Deo, emanation, 100, 200, 202, 256–57, 322, 361
existence (*see* ontology)
ex matria, creation, 200–202, 256–57, 356
ex nihilo, creation, 43, 89, 100, 119–20, 125, 134, 140–41, 143, 151–53, 173, 190, 199–203, 210, 229, 231, 233, 236–37, 256–58, 295, 322, 353–55, 361
exodus, the, 303–4, 309

Feinberg, John, 40, 257, 277, 290, 306–7

finite, 9, 40, 45, 100–101, 119, 127, 134, 140–41, 144, 151, 153, 155, 157, 163–64, 169–70, 174–75, 190, 200–202, 204–5, 207–8, 210, 221, 237, 239–40, 256–57, 287–88, 293, 295, 298, 304, 308, 310–13, 319, 325, 329–34, 361 (*see also* infinity, the infinite)
first principles, 22, 150
four elements (*see* Empedocles)

Gaon, Saadia, 9, 108, 126, 147, 201, 217, 225, 228, 237, 301, 327, 355
gematria, 94, 184, 186–88, 219–21, 373–75 (*see also geometrikos arithmos*)
genetic fallacy, 27, 218, 283
geocentrism, 28, 30, 86–88, 90, 118–19, 136–38, 189, 219, 222–24, 236, 322, 371, 375 (*see also* Copernican Revolution; cosmology)
geometrikos arithmos, 93–94, 97, 219–20, 373 (*see also gematria*)
Gersonides, 147, 159, 201–2, 237
gilgul, 171, 214, 224–25 (*see also* reincarnation)
Glaser, Mitch, xix, 246–48, 250 (*see also* omnicompetence)
Gnosticism
    influence from Judaism, 96, 181, 216, 225–32, 363–72
    relation to Kabbalah, 77–78, 98, 168–69, 181, 187–89, 211, 218, 224–32, 323, 363–72
    teachings of, 93–98, 206, 220, 277, 281, 326
God
    attributes of (*see* attributes of God)
    God of Abraham vs. of the philosophers, 77–78, 145
    models of
        absolute incorporealism, 17–18 (*see also under* Maimonides)
        corporealism, 5, 17, 50–51, 53, 55, 58–60, 63, 110, 116, 126–

General Index

29, 135, 146, 154, 256, 305, 327, 329, 338
Incarnation (*see* Incarnation, the)
incorporealism, 6–7, 14, 17–19, 50–51, 53–56, 58, 60–64, 111, 113–14, 116, 126–30, 133, 151–52, 156, 162, 201, 256, 287, 297–98, 300, 303, 353–56
panentheism (*see* panentheism)
pantheism, 18, 49, 204, 257
Trinity, the (*see* Trinity, the)
nature of, 7–8, 10, 15–19, 33–34, 39–40, 45, 49, 51, 53, 60–61, 71, 78, 113, 124, 126–27, 134, 180, 200–201, 229–30, 256–57, 265–68, 273, 277, 279–80, 285, 289–90, 293–98, 303, 306–7, 310–11, 330, 361
(*see also* salvation; theology; theophany; Trinity, the)
God talk, 4, 10, 47–48, 58, 83, 128–31, 136, 148, 160–62, 185–86, 256, 287, 302–10, 325–26, 353
Greek philosophy (*see* Aristotle; Gnosticism; Neoplatonism; Neopythagoreanism; Plato; Plotinus; Pythagoras; philosophy)
Guide to the Perplexed
background, xii, 14, 108–9, 113–16
critique, 135–62, 319–40
exposition, 118–32
outline, 114
(*see also* Maimonides)

halakah, 11–12, 24, 26, 108, 215, 217
Haredi Judaism, xiv, 10, 12, 24, 172, 213, 251–52
Hasidic Judaism, 10–11, 53, 66, 166–67, 172, 175, 182–83, 193, 208, 236, 365 (*see also* Chabad; Haredi Judaism)
Hebrew Bible
interpretation of (*see* biblical interpretation)
relation to philosophy, 33–35
religious authority of, 27, 32

theological ambiguities in, 48–51, 255–56
theological doctrines of, 35–48
Hebrew Christianity, 20, 247, 250, 284 (*see also* Jewish believers in Jesus; Messianic Judaism, Messianic Jews)
Held, Shai, 301
Hellenistic Judaism, 54–58, 63, 69, 260, 375
hermeneutics (*see* biblical interpretation)
Hermeticism, 95–96, 98, 187–89, 229, 324
historical evidence
for early high Christology (*see under* Christology)
for the New Testament, 24, 294, 336
for the origin of the *Zohar*, 215–16
for the resurrection of Jesus, 269–70, 294, 337
for the Sinai event, 337
historical-textual approach, the, 31, 52–73, 249
limitations of, 69–71
historical critique of Kabbalah, 212–18
history
in Haredi Judaism, 213
inclusion in the Hebrew Bible, 15–16, 45, 212, 337
vs. heritage, 212–13
Holocaust, the, 21–22, 250
Holy Spirit, the, 4, 6, 15, 121, 193, 269, 273, 277–78, 294, 312, 314, 330, 336, 361
homoousios, 71, 277–78, 282 (*see also* Nicene Creed, the)
human nature, 43, 135, 256–57, 266–67, 287, 314–15, 323
of Jesus, xi, 8, 15–16, 18, 40, 71, 126, 162, 258, 261, 265–66, 268, 279, 285, 290, 294, 296–97, 315, 319
NT metaphysical language for, 266–68
Hurtado, Larry, 31, 53, 65, 71, 261, 271–72, 274, 327, 336
hyponoia (*see* allegory)

General Index

hypostasis (*see* person)
hypostatic union, 15, 126, 162, 207, 278, 281, 285 (*see also* Chalcedonian Definition; Incarnation, the)

idealism, 173, 195–98
Idel, Moshe, 35, 54, 57, 61–62, 65–66, 68, 125, 130, 134, 166–67, 169, 172–73, 180–86, 206, 326, 365–66
Iggulim, 178, 223
image of God, 54–55, 59, 265, 312–13, 316
immanence (*see under* attributes of God)
impossibility
  asserted of divine embodiment, xi, 6–9, 111–13, 135–36, 144, 149, 252, 287–88, 293
  different kinds of, 71, 150–51, 153, 158, 292
  Maimonidean view of, 111, 126–28, 135–36, 144, 149–52, 252, 289, 298–302
  in relation to God's actions, 3–4, 8, 111, 126–28, 150–52, 298–302, 330
  (*see also* contradiction)
Incarnation, the
  definition of, 15–19, 275–81
  incompatibility with Kabbalah, 190–91, 198–203, 240–42
  incompatibility with Maimonides (*see under* impossibility)
  as a mystery or paradox, 290–93, 298–300, 328–30
  NT evidence for, 258–72
  patristic discussions of, 272–81, 290–302
  precedents in Judaism, 52–71, 271–72
  relation to rationality, 287–302
  the worldview scope of, 310–18
infinity, the infinite
  Greek views on, 80–81, 100–101, 104, 204
  impossibility of an actual, 202
  Kabbalistic view of, 163–65, 169, 173–80, 186, 190, 193, 202, 204–5, 207–8, 239–40, 310, 329–30, 361
  Maimonidean view on, 120, 127, 140–41, 153–55, 310, 329, 361
  in mathematics, 204, 207, 295–96 (*see also* set theory, Cantor's)
  relation to biblical theology, 37–38, 204–5, 257, 289, 293, 295, 298, 308–11, 319, 329, 331, 334–35, 361
  (*see also* finite; *see also under* attributes of God)
intellect
  active, 121, 142, 157, 310, 321, 328, 353, 356
  angelic, 119, 140, 142
  divine, 42–44, 118, 122, 142, 154–56
  heavenly spheres as, 119, 140, 353
  human, 55, 142, 154–55, 267, 312, 328
  in Neoplatonism, 100, 102, 125, 362
  in Platonism, 81, 85
intellectual assimilation, 22, 28–29, 241
  (*see also* syncretism)
Irenaeus of Lyons, 95, 187, 225, 232, 275–76, 370
Israeli, Isaac ben Solomon, 9, 355

Jesus
  deity of (*see* Chalcedonian Definition; Incarnation, the; Nicene Creed, the)
  eschatological role of, 284, 313, 316–17, 340
  eyewitness evidence for, 269, 294–95, 299, 337
  humanity of, 264–66, 279, 313
  as a Jewish man, 264, 266, 268
  worship of, 71, 190, 261, 271–72
Jewish believers in Jesus, 246–47, 249–51, 253, 266, 274, 282–84, 317
  (*see also* Messianic Judaism, Messianic Jews; parting of the ways)

General Index

Judaism
- compatibility of Incarnation and Trinity with, 5–6, 52–71, 271–72, 319–40
- definitions of, 22–31
- historical change in, 22–31, 107–32, 163–91, 326–27, 335
- incompatibility of Incarnation and Trinity with, 6–12, 131–32, 190–91
- NT relation to, 24–25, 64–71
- Orthodox, xiv–xv, xvii, 6, 9–12, 23–24, 29, 31–33, 58, 69–70, 72, 109–10, 116, 137–38, 149, 158, 162, 167, 172, 197, 212–13, 218, 224, 236, 249–52, 297, 300, 314, 322, 365 (see also Haredi Judaism; Hasidic Judaism; Modern Orthodox)
- sects of, non-Orthodox, 10, 30, 70, 230

Justin Martyr, 19, 146, 247, 275, 304

Kabbalah
- compared to NT, 9–12, 190–91, 319–40, 361–62
- cosmology of (see cosmology, Kabbalistic)
- hermeneutics of (see PaRDeS; see under biblical interpretation)
- history of, 167–72
- Lurianic, 171–72, 178, 198, 240
- relation to Gnosticism, 187–90, 225–32, 363–72
- relation to Neoplatonism, 187–90, 203–10, 233
- relation to Neopythagoreanism, 187–90, 219–25
- relation to science (see science, Kabbalah and)
- sexualized theology in, 170–71, 182, 189, 225, 227–29 (see also Gnosticism)
- (see also Baal Shem Tov; divine sparks; *Ein Sof*; *ex Deo*, emanation; Hasidic Judaism; infinity, the infinite; León, Moses de; Luria, Isaac; magic; Mitnagdim; panentheism; *Sefirot*; sin, in Kabbalah; salvation, Kabbalah's view of; *Tanya*, the; theurgy; *tikkun olam*; *tzimtzum*; Tzvi, Shabbatai; *Zohar*, the)

Kavod, the, 60, 63, 169

Kellner, Menachem, 29, 36, 58, 107, 109, 115, 119, 126–28, 135–36, 139, 143, 161–62, 169, 185, 193

Kinzer, Mark, 21, 69, 249–50, 253, 259, 278, 282–84

Klippot, 177, 179, 190–91, 197, 204, 214, 226–27

Lebens, Samuel, 116, 122, 158–59, 167, 173–75, 195–98, 202, 208, 224, 291, 297, 313, 319, 334

León, Moses de, 170, 215–16

Letter of Aristeas, 368–69

Levine, Amy-Jill, 24, 246

Logos, the
- in the NT, 146, 258, 311
- in Philo, 54–57, 71, 319

Luria, Isaac, 167, 171, 361 (see also Kabbalah)

McCaul, Alexander, 20–22, 130, 250, 256

McClymond, Michael, xx, 97–99, 102, 153, 165, 167, 174, 180, 203, 241–42, 251, 253, 270

magic
- in the Greek tradition, 94–96, 98, 187, 189, 220, 229, 294–95 (see also Hermeticism)
- in Kabbalah, 167, 189, 220, 229–30, 236, 294, 323–25
- Maimonides's view of, 135, 325
- NT's view of, 230, 295–96, 323–25
- in Platonic science, 234, 324 (see also astrology; theurgy)

Maimonidean Controversy, 113

Maimonideanism, contemporary, 10–11, 107–16

Maimonides
- influence of, 9–12, 107–16
- life of, 108
- major works of, 108, 113

General Index

Maimonides (cont.)
  on Christianity, 7, 111–13, 126, 146
  on cosmology, 118–24
    argument against, 136–45
  on divine embodiment, 110–15, 118–32
    argument against, 135–62
  on divine impossibility, 111, 120, 126–28, 131, 135, 144, 149, 151
    argument against, 148–53, 298–302
  on *echad*, 111, 259
  on God talk, 128–31
    argument against, 145–48, 160–61, 307–10
  on lesser kinds of people, 130, 142, 328
  on miracles, 122–24
    argument against, 143
  on prophecy, 120–22
    argument against, 141–42
  on providence, 88–89, 120
    argument against, 141
  on *via negativa*, 124–26, 128–31
    argument against, 145–48, 153–61
  philosophical influences upon, 116–26, 128–29
  scholars of, 115
  (*see also* biblical interpretation; contradiction; *Guide to the Perplexed*; impossibility; intellect; Neo-Maimonideans; science, Maimonides and; Thirteen Principles of Faith)
Melito of Sardis, 280
Memra, the, 60, 62–63, 71, 170
Merkavah mysticism, 114, 168, 225, 365, 375–76
Messiah
  Christian views on, xiv, xvi, 7–8, 11–12, 207, 246–340
  Jewish views on, xiii, 6, 8, 11, 20, 25, 52, 59, 65–66, 112, 171
Messianic Judaism, Messianic Jews, xvi, 8, 11, 14, 20–21, 36, 52, 68, 115, 247–54, 264, 268, 278, 282–85, 319, 376

messianic prophecy, xiii, xvi, 6, 20, 26, 121, 212, 261–64, 294, 332
metaphysics, xvii, 13, 15, 33–34, 56, 63, 66, 71–72, 78–85, 90–93, 95–96, 98, 108, 114, 117, 130, 134, 136, 138–39, 146, 148, 150–53, 161, 166, 173, 175, 178–81, 183, 188, 192, 196, 198–99, 203–10, 218–25, 228–34, 236, 238–41, 266–69, 277–78, 282–83, 298, 315, 321, 323, 329, 355, 367, 374 (*see also* Aristotle; attributes of God; cosmology; God, models of; intellect; nature; ontology; Plato; Plotinus; Pythagoras)
Metatron, 60, 62, 65, 319
middot, 33, 170
miracles
  as evidence for Jesus, 261 (*see also* resurrection, of Jesus)
  in Maimonides's system (*see under* Maimonides)
  seeming impossibility of, 3–4, 149–53, 299–300
Mishnah, 21–22, 108, 111, 168, 182, 185, 214
Mitnagdim, 10, 167, 172, 175
modal logic, 262
Modern Orthodox, Judaism, 6, 10, 167, 197, 212, 252 (*see also* Judaism, Orthodox)
Moreland, J. P., xiv, xvi, xix–xx, 13, 70, 78, 144, 195, 202, 271, 322
Morris, Thomas, 288, 291, 296
mysticism
  definition of, 163–65
  Neoplatonic influence upon, 99, 102–3, 165
  Western vs. Eastern, 99
  (*see also* Kabbalah; Neoplatonism; Neopythagoreanism)

name of the Lord, 33, 42, 45, 54, 61–63, 107, 110, 170, 260, 262, 273, 304 (*see also* Tetragrammaton, the)

General Index

nature
  divine (*see* God, nature of)
  human, xi, 8, 15–16, 18, 40, 43, 71, 126, 135, 162, 258, 261, 265–68, 279, 285, 287, 290, 294, 296–97, 314–15, 319, 323
negative theology (*see via negativa*)
Neo-Maimonideans, 322
Neoplatonism
  arguments against, 199–210, 233
  influence of, 98–99, 106
  key persons in, 98–99, 187, 233
  key teachings of, 98–106
  (*see also* divine sparks; emanations; mysticism; One, the; panentheism; Plotinus; syncretism; world soul)
Neopythagoreanism, 78, 89–95, 98, 187–88, 211, 218–25, 323, 365, 373
  critique of, 219–25
  theological system of, 89–95
Nestorianism, 276, 281–82
Neusner, Jacob, 23, 58, 77, 182, 201
New Age, 99, 165
noetic effects of the Fall, 288, 292
noncontradiction, principle of, 9, 85, 197, 291, 293
Novak, David, 7, 10, 29, 101, 111–12, 115, 126, 138–40, 143, 210–11, 322
Numenius, 94, 98, 369
numerology
  critique of, 219–21
  in Kabbalistic thought, 182–87
  in Pythagorean thought, 90–94

Occam's razor, 329–30
Ogdoad, 93
omnipresence (*see under* attributes of God)
omniscience (*see under* attributes of God)
One, the, 46, 97, 99–105, 124–25, 174, 233, 321, 362 (*see also* Ein Sof; Neoplatonism)
ontology, 13, 51, 63, 72, 188–89, 195, 231, 257–58, 267–68, 314

(*see also* God, nature of; metaphysics; nature)
Origen, 32, 102, 146, 148, 254, 270, 277–78, 286, 370
Orthodox Judaism (*see under* Judaism)

panentheism, 18, 50, 79, 98, 100, 102, 125, 173–75, 180, 188, 190, 193, 198–99, 204–5, 207, 230–31, 233, 240–42, 256–57, 322, 329, 354, 361–62
pantheism, 18, 49, 204, 257, 358
paradox, 9, 13, 47, 51, 81, 124, 262, 290–93, 298–300, 328–30 (*see also* mystery)
PaRDeS, 170, 184, 189, 214, 217 (*see also* biblical interpretation)
Parmenides, 80–81, 85, 100, 102–4, 111, 173, 188, 204, 241, 256–57
parody, 147, 159, 320–21
parting of the ways, 68 (*see also* binitarianism; Christianity, anti-Judaism in; Jewish believers in Jesus; Quartodeciman controversy; supersessionism)
Paul, the apostle, xiii, xvi, 7, 11–12, 214, 225, 231, 246, 258–59, 266–67, 289, 294, 298, 303, 310–11, 314, 316–17, 325, 339, 361, 375
Pawl, Timothy, 296–97
Pearcey, Nancy, xx, 234, 251, 298, 322, 324
person
  definition of, 15
  relation to the Trinity, 15, 56, 66, 71, 111, 126, 162, 193, 259, 267–68, 273, 276–79, 281–82, 285, 292, 294, 311, 319, 333–34, 362
Philo of Alexandria, 9, 23–24, 54–57, 70, 80, 83, 94, 103, 108, 146, 181, 189, 211, 216, 245, 326, 355, 366, 368–69

General Index

philosophy
  dangers of, 34, 99, 137, 146, 268, 270, 282–83, 320–24, 338, 369–70
  need for, 33–34, 269–70, 277–79, 282–83, 338
  (*see also* Aristotle; cosmology; epistemology; evil; Gnosticism; God, models of; idealism; infinity; metaphysics; Neoplatonism; ontology; Plato; Platonism; Plotinus; Pythagoras; realism)
Plato
  influence of, 79–80, 99
  key teachings of, 79–84
  life of, 79
Platonism, 13, 34, 77, 80, 99, 101, 117, 146, 189, 197, 215, 254, 278, 283, 333, 369–70 (*see also* Neoplatonism)
Plotinus
  key teachings of, 98–106
  life of, 98, 106
  (*see also* mysticism; Neoplatonism; One, the; panentheism; *via negativa*)
prayer
  in Judaism, 35, 37, 109–10, 172, 201, 259, 314
  in the NT, xii, 11, 317–18
Proclus, 98, 150, 187–88, 233, 355, 361
  (*see also* Neoplatonism)
prophecy, xiii, xvi, 5–6, 20–21, 25–26, 61, 109, 114, 119–23, 135, 140–43, 212, 229, 263–64, 272, 284, 287, 294, 317, 321–22, 330, 332, 356
  mechanisms to explain, 119–21, 123, 141–42, 311–12
  (*see also* messianic prophecy, eschatology)
Protestantism (*see under* Christianity)
providence, divine, 88–89, 109, 114, 119–20, 122–24, 135, 140–41, 143, 193, 200, 257, 259, 267, 287, 311, 320, 322

Ptolemy, Ptolemaic, 28, 30, 86–88, 117–18, 136, 138, 150, 169, 189, 233, 236, 368–69, 371
Pythagoras, 72, 89–90, 187, 189, 211, 218–19, 324, 363, 367–68

Quartodeciman controversy, 247, 280

rabbinic Judaism, 23, 34, 60, 67, 70, 116, 221 (*see also* Mishnah, Talmud)
Rashi, 5–7, 9, 36, 60, 206
realism, 67, 82, 85, 195–98
redemptive analogy, 194, 241
reincarnation, 28, 90, 94–95, 171, 189, 219, 223–25 (*see also* gilgul)
Reinhartz, Adele, 23–24
resurrection, general, 224, 271, 278, 288, 315
resurrection, of Jesus, 137, 269–70, 294, 299, 313, 315, 319, 328, 330–31, 337
revelation, divine, xxi, 26–27, 46, 54, 77, 84, 89, 145–49, 152, 159, 171, 212, 232, 245, 269, 290, 295, 307, 322–23, 326, 328, 336–39, 371–72
Rynhold, Daniel, 125, 145, 148, 157–59

salvation
  the Incarnation's relation to, 40, 311, 313–16, 331–32
  Kabbalah's view of, 10, 179–80, 190–91, 209–10, 231, 233, 331–32
  Maimonides's view of, 142, 328, 331 (*see also* sin)
Samuelson, Norbert, 29, 114–15, 120, 139–40, 322
Sandmel, Samuel, 56, 363
Schochet, Immanuel, 166, 174–78, 180, 207–8, 239
Scholem, Gershom, 77, 164, 166–74, 186–87, 212, 216, 218, 223–25, 365
science
  Aristotelian and Platonic, 82, 84–85, 233–40

438

General Index

Christianity and, 320–24
cosmology (*see* cosmology)
Kabbalah and, 199–203, 233–40
Maimonides and, 118–24, 136–45
obsolete theories of, 143–44 (*see also* Copernican Revolution)
Second Temple Judaism, xi, 5, 21, 23–24, 30, 49, 53–54, 58, 64–65, 69–70, 131, 162, 167, 225, 246, 250, 260, 268, 327, 375
Seeskin, Kenneth, 115, 120, 125
Sefer Bahir, 167, 171, 214, 232
Sefer Yetzirah, 168–69, 186, 214, 217, 220, 223, 232, 336
Sefirot, 44, 169–70, 178–81, 183, 188, 193, 195–96, 208–9, 214, 216–17, 222–23, 226–27, 229, 235, 237–38, 241, 361–62
Segal, Aaron, 115, 126, 169, 224
Segal, Alan, 31, 53, 60, 63, 65, 335
set theory, Cantor's, 204, 207, 295 (*see also* infinity)
sexualized theology in Kabbalah (*see under* Kabbalah)
Shapiro, Ben, 6–8
Shapiro, David S., 8, 128
Shapiro, Marc B., 25, 29, 53, 58–59, 110, 115, 212–13, 221, 251, 301, 335
Shapiro, Rami, 9, 163
Shekhinah, the, 60, 62–63, 127
Shema, the, 35–36, 111, 193, 258–59, 267, 310
Shemoneh Esreh (*see* Amidah)
siddur, 37, 107, 109–10, 112 (*see also* prayer in Judaism)
Sigal, Philip, 66
sin
  in biblical theology, 25, 194, 226–27, 240, 266, 279, 287–88, 299, 308, 313–15, 317–18, 323–24
  in Kabbalah, 179–80, 190–91, 198, 209
  in Orthodox Judaism, 25, 314
Sinai, 23, 25, 41, 45, 57, 59, 212, 216–17, 232, 255, 261, 337, 365, 367, 371 (*see also* epistemological hierarchy; epistemology)

Socrates, 79, 235, 367
Sod (*see* PaRDeS)
Soloveichik, Meir, 287–88, 293
Sommer, Benjamin, 5–6, 53, 58, 65–66, 127, 145, 301, 327, 335
Son of God
  in Judaism, 57, 61–62, 66, 68
  in NT theology, xii, xv, 4, 7, 13, 15, 18–19, 40, 50–51, 61, 69, 71, 114–15, 142, 161, 191, 199, 240, 245, 256–59, 263, 266, 271, 273, 278–79, 285, 287, 294, 296, 302, 304–6, 309–13, 315, 319–20, 322, 331, 333, 338, 361–62
Sophia, 54, 57, 97
sphaira, 222–23
stimulus diffusion, 26, 28, 364
supersessionism, 21–22, 248, 254, 274, 284
Swinburne, Richard, 151, 158, 239, 292, 298, 300, 302
syncretism, 21, 27–29, 34, 70, 90, 194, 204, 225, 232, 241, 321, 370, 376

Talmud, the, 59, 69, 160, 183, 185–86, 215, 221, 225, 230, 250, 373
Tanya, the, 9, 163, 165, 172, 189, 208, 236, 238 (*see also* Chabad)
Tapp, Christian, 205
Targums, 5, 62–63
Tetragrammaton, the, 4, 33, 62, 260, 262–63, 311 (*see also* name of the Lord)
theological-philosophical approach, the, 31, 72–73, 253
theological retrieval, xi, xvi, 22, 252–53
theology (*see* Angel of the Lord, the; God; Incarnation, the; Judaism; Kabbalah; Maimonides; Messianic Judaism; Thirteen Principles of Faith; Trinity, the; attributes of God; rabbinic Judaism; theophany; *see under* Christianity)

General Index

theophany, 16–18, 45–46, 52, 55, 70, 131, 146, 256, 261, 268, 303 (*see also* God, models of)
theurgy, 186, 189, 225, 229–30 (*see also* magic)
Thirteen Principles of Faith, 10–11, 25, 108–12, 116
    Ninth Principle, 112
    Second Principle, 110–11, 113, 133, 161–62
    Third Principle, 107, 110–14, 116, 127, 133, 135, 153–55, 160–62
    (*see also* Maimonides, *Yigdal, Ani Ma'amin*)
tikkun olam, 171–72, 179, 227
Tirosh-Samuelson, Hava, 82, 85, 169, 234–36
Torah, the, 59, 69, 83, 111–12, 121, 129, 138, 145, 149, 160, 183, 185, 204, 212, 221, 227, 230–32, 247–48, 268, 287, 314, 322, 326, 367–69
transcendence (*see under* attributes of God)
Trinity, the
    articulated in church creeds (*see* Chalcedonian Definition; Nicene Creed)
    NT evidences for, 258–85
    precedents in Judaism (*see* binitarianism)
    rejected by Maimonides (*see* Maimonides on Christianity)
    relation to Kabbalah, 240–42
    views in Messianic Judaism, 246–54
    (*see also* Angel of the LORD; Christianity; Christology; Incarnation, the; Son of God)
truth (*see* coherence model of truth; correspondence theory of truth; epistemology)

tzimtzum, 171, 174–75, 178–79, 190, 199, 203–4, 207–10, 214, 226, 276, 281
Tzvi, Shabbatai, 10, 171–72

via analogia (*see under* biblical interpretation)
via negativa (*see under* biblical interpretation)
via positiva (*see under* biblical interpretation)

Wellum, Stephen, 39, 260–61, 264, 276, 278, 283, 288, 290, 296, 312
Wolfson, Elliot, 45, 47, 53, 65–66, 90, 115, 117, 147, 158, 161, 164–67, 169, 171, 181–82, 185, 194, 229, 321, 371
world soul, 81, 85, 100, 102, 125, 356, 362 (*see also* intellect in Neoplatonism; intellect in Platonism)
worldview, xii, 11, 13–14, 22, 27–28, 31, 72, 90, 96, 106, 124, 131–33, 135, 137, 143–45, 150–52, 160, 173, 183, 191, 193, 195, 197–99, 202, 212–13, 217, 220, 226, 229, 232–33, 236, 240–41, 246, 249, 271, 289, 295–96, 302, 318, 322, 324–25, 329, 355, 363–64 (*see also* philosophy)
Wyschogrod, Michael, 29, 36, 53, 145, 150, 158, 300–301

Yigdal, 109

Zalman of Liadi, 163, 208, 236
Zohar, the, 163, 165, 167, 170–71, 180–81, 184, 187, 208, 214–17, 223, 229, 232, 238, 336, 361
    historical origin of (*see under* historical evidence)

ADDITIONAL RESOURCES

Chosen People Ministries

Over 130 years ago—in Brooklyn, New York—Rabbi Leopold Cohn founded the mission to share the knowledge of Yeshua (Jesus) the Messiah with God's chosen people. Today, Chosen People Ministries serves in 20 countries, including Israel and many cities in the United States.

Go to chosenpeople.com for articles, videos, books, Bible studies, newsletters, and opportunities to participate in the fulfillment of Romans 11.

CHOSENPEOPLE.COM

Also by Brian J. Crawford:
*Rethinking the Jewish Messiah:
How Scripture Points in Only One Direction*
Available now at Ratio Christi Press

Stay Connected with Brian J. Crawford
Receive Brian's monthly prayer letter or donate at:
chosenpeople.com/pray4brian

www.ingramcontent.com/pod-product-compliance
Lightning Source LLC
Chambersburg PA
CBHW071233300426
44116CB00008B/1017